HUXFORD'S

COLLECTIBLE

Advertising

AN ILLUSTRATED VALUE GUIDE

FOURTH EDITION

COLLECTOR BOOKS
A Division of Schroeder Publishing Co., Inc.

The current values in this book should be used only as a guide. They are not intended to set prices, which vary from one section of the country to another. Auction prices as well as dealer prices vary greatly and are affected by condition and demand. Neither the Authors nor the Publisher assumes responsibility for any losses which might be incurred as a result of consulting this guide.

Searching For A Publisher?

We are always looking for knowledgeable people considered experts within their fields. If you feel that there is a real need for a book on your collectible subject and have a large comprehensive collection, contact Collector Books.

On the Cover:

Front:
Hoosier Bay Coffee tin, 1-lb, paper label, NM, D6, $425.00. (Photo courtesy David Hirsch)
Canada Dry Pale Ginger Ale sign, die-cut tin bottle, 40", NM, A12, $750.00. (Photo courtesy David Hirsch auction)
Plow Boy Tobacco store bin, tin, EX, A18, $1,132.00. (Photo courtesy Sandy Rosnick Auctions)
Oilzum Motor Oils display sign, tin, 24", D11, $1,000.00. (Photo courtesy Darryl Fritsche.)

Back:
Cinco Cigars, display case, D6, $450.00.
Thaddius Davids Co sign, embossed, self-framed, tin, 18"x26", EX+, D6, $1,000.00.
Mother's Crushed Oats box, 3"x8½", VG+, D6, $100.00.
Fairbanks' Gold Dust Washing Powder display box, 2-sided, 9¼"x19", NM, D6, $1,000.00.
(All back photos courtesy David Hirsch.)

Editorial staff:
Editors:
Sharon and Bob Huxford

Research and Editorial Assistant:
Donna Newnum

Cover Design:
Beth Summers

Book Design:
Holly C. Long

Printed in the U.S.A. by Image Graphics Inc., Paducah KY

Collector Books
P.O. Box 3009
Paducah, KY 42002-3009

Copyright © 1999 by Bob & Sharon Huxford

Introduction

The field of collectible advertising is vast and varied. Offering an almost infinite diversity of items, it has the obvious potential to appeal to nearly anyone, with any interest, within any budget. With this in mind, we have attempted to compile a guide that would be beneficial to all collectors of advertising memorabilia. This book includes over ten thousand descriptive listings and hundreds of photos. The format has been kept as simple as possible by using an alphabetical sequence starting with product or company name.

Items are sorted primarily by alphabetizing the product name as worded on each specific sign, tray, tin, etc. For instance, you'll find listings for Pabst Blue Ribbon Beer, others under Pabst Brewing Co., still another under Pabst Malt Extract. Each variation indicates the primary, most obvious visual impact of the advertising message. There are some exceptions. Even though many examples of Coca-Cola advertising are simply worded 'Coke,' all have been listed under the title 'Coca-Cola.' The advertising message as it actually appears is given in the description. There are several other instances where this applies — Cracker Jack and Pepsi-Cola, for example. When they seemed appropriate, cross references were added.

After the product (or company) name, the form of the item is given, i.e. sign, tin, mug, ashtray, etc. Following phrases describe materials, graphics, colors, and sizes. When only one dimension is given, it is height; and height is noted first when two or more are noted. The date is given when that information was available.

Condition is indicated by standard abbreviations: NOS for new old stock, M for mint, NM for near mint, EX for excellent, VG for very good, and G for good. Plus and minus signs were used to indicate levels in between. See the section 'Condition and Its Effect on Value' for more information.

We have given actual sizes when that information was available to us, otherwise sizes are approximate.

Because our listings have been compiled from many sources, we have coded each line to indicate that the suggested value is (A), an auction result or a price actually realized by another type of sale, or (D), a dealer's 'asking' price. As everyone is aware, auction prices are sometimes higher than dealers' prices, but they are just as apt to be lower. At any rate, they are legitimate prices for which merchandise actually changed hands and have always been used by dealers as a basis for their evaluations. This edition contains listings with codes identifying the dealer, collector, or auction house who provided us with that information. Feel free to contact these people if you are interested in buying, selling, or need information about specific items. Many dealers tend to specialize in specific areas of advertising, and even if they no longer have the item in question, they may be able to locate it for you. We'll tell you how to decipher the codes in the following pages. Please remember, as you should regard any price guide, this one is offered as only a tool to be used in addition to your own personal observations of market dealings, show sales, and tradepaper ads.

Acknowledgments

We are indebted to the following dealers, collectors, and auction galleries who have contributed photographs that help make this guide a success:

Autopia Advertising Auctions	Darryl Fritsche	Gary Metz
Noel Barrett Antiques and Auctions Ltd.	Lynn Geyer's Advertising Auctions	Mike's General Store
Bill Bertoia Auctions	Henry Hain III	Wm Morford
Buffalo Bay Auction Co.	Roy and Linda Hartman	Judy Posner
Collector's Auction Service	David Hirsch	Postcards International
Dunbar's Gallery	James D. Julia Inc.	Sandy Rosnick Auctions
Fink's Off the Wall Auctions	Allan Licht	David Zimmerman
Donald Friedman	Robert and Louise Marshall	

Identification of Coded Auctions and Dealers

Our listings contain two-character codes indicating the dealer, collector, or auction house who provided us with the description and value. These codes are located at the very end of the line. These codes give the reader an invaluable network of dealers, collectors, and auction houses from which to buy, sell, trade, or inquire about specific advertising collectibles.

As all collectors know, lapse time between data entry and the actual release date of a price guide can involve several months. During that time these dealers may buy and sell identical or very similar pieces of merchandise several times, and since they must sometimes pay more to restock, their prices will fluctuate, so don't regard the prices they sent us as though they were etched in stone! Over the months that elapse, market values may appreciate, and if you're an advertising collector, you should hope that this is the case. An active market is healthy for both dealers as well as collectors. But even if the item you want to purchase is no longer in stock, as I'm sure you're aware, there is a nationwide network of dealer connections, and the contact you make may be able to steer you to someone else that will be able to help you.

Please, if you make an inquiry by mail, send the dealer or auction gallery a self-addressed, stamped envelope. This is common courtesy. In the long run it not only makes the transaction more convenient for the dealer, but it assures you that his response will make its way back to the proper address. Handwritten addresses are often difficult to make out. If you call and get his answering machine, when you leave your message and your number, tell him by all means to call you collect with his response.

If you're a dealer who regularly or even occasionally puts out a 'for sale' listing of merchandise and would like to be involved in our next edition, please contact us at Huxford Enterprises, 1202 7th Street, Covington, Indiana 47932.

Auction Directory

(A1)
Autopia Advertising Auctions
15209 NE. 90th St.
Redmond, WA 98052
(425) 883-7653; fax (206) 867-5568
Automobilia and general advertising

(A2)
Bill Bertoia Auctions
2413 Madison Ave.
Vineland, NJ 08360
(609) 692-1882; fax (609) 692-8697
General advertising

(A3)
Buffalo Bay Auction Co.
Lawrence Manos
5244 Quam Circle
Rogers, MN 55374
(612) 428-8480; fax (612) 428-8879
General advertising

(A4)
Marc Cardelli
25 Phillips St.
Weymouth, MA 02188
(781) 337-3314
Coca-Cola, Pepsi-Cola, and other soft drinks

(A5)
Cerebro
P.O. Box 327
East Prospect, PA 17317-0327
(800) 695-2235; fax (717) 252-3685
Cigar labels

(A6)
Collector's Auction Service
RR#2 Box 431; Oakwood Rd.
Oil City, PA 16301
(814) 677-6070; fax (814) 677-6166
Automobile, gasoline, and general advertising

(A7)
Frank's Antiques
P.O. Box 516
Hillard, FL 32046
(904) 845-2870; fax (904) 845-4888
General advertising

(A8)
Lynn Geyer's Advertising Auctions
300 Trail Ridge
Silver City, New Mexico 88061
(505) 538-2341; fax (505) 388-9000
Breweriana and general advertising

(A9)
James D. Julia Inc.
P.O. Box 830
Fairfield, ME 04937
(207) 453-7125; fax (207) 453-2502
General advertising

(A10)
Bob Kay
P.O. Box 1805
Batavia, IL 60510-1805
(630) 879-6214
Beer labels

(A11)
Kurt R. Krueger
P.O. Box 275
Iola, WI 54945-0275
Pin-back buttons and pocket mirrors

(A12)
David Hirsch
6601 Maple St.
Morton Grove, IL 60053
(845) 965-1132
Tobacco tins, coffee tins,and signs

(A13)
Gary Metz's Muddy River Trading Company
263 Key Lakewood Dr.
Moneta, VA 24121
(540) 721-2091; fax (540) 721-1782
Coca-Cola, Pepsi-Cola, and other soft drinks

(A14)
Mike's General Store
52 St. Anne's Rd.
Winnipeg, Manitoba, Canada R2M-2Y3
(204) 255-3463
e-mail: Mikesgen@ilos.net
General advertising

(A15)
Wm Morford
RD #2
Cazenovia, NY 13035
(315) 662-7625; fax (315) 662-3570
General advertising

(A16)
Nostalgia Publications
Allan J. Petretti
21 South Lake Dr.
Hackensack, NJ 07601
(201) 488-4536 (evenings)
Coca-Cola and other soft drinks

(A17)
Postcards International
Martin J. Shapiro
P.O. Box 5398
Hamden, CT 06518515
(203) 248-6621; fax (203) 248-6628
e-mail: postcrdint@aol.com
website: www.csmonline.com/poscardsint/
Vintage picture postcards

(A18)
Sandy Rosnick Auctions
3 Big Rock Rd.
Manchester, MA 01944
(508) 526-1093; fax (508) 741-1132
Tins and bins, country store, spool cabinets

(A19)
Fink's Off the Wall Auctions
108 East 7th St.
Lansdale, PA 19446
(217) 855-9732; fax (217) 855-6325
Breweriana

(A20)
Dave Beck
P.O. Box 435
Mediapolis, IA 52637
(319) 394-3943
Signs, fobs, pin-backs, and mirrors

(A24)
Dunbar's Gallery
Howard and Leila Dunbar
76 Haven St.
Milford, MA 01757
(508) 634-8697; fax (508) 634-8698
Signs and general advertising

Dealer Directory

(D1)
Flake World
Scott Bruce
PO Box 481
Cambridge, MA 02140
(617) 492-5004
Cereal boxes, premiums (1950s – 1980s)

(D2)
Dave Beck
P.O. Box 435
Mediapolis, IA 52637
(319) 394-3943
Signs, fobs, pin-backs, mirrors

(D3)
Cairn's Antiques
P.O. Box 44026
Lemon Cove, CA 93244
(209) 597-2242
Crate labels

(D4)
Marc Cardelli
25 Phillips St.
Weymouth, MA 02188
(781) 337-3314
Soft drink and automotive collectibles

(D5)
Cerebro
P.O. Box 327
New Prospect, PA 17317-0327
(800) 695-2235; fax (717) 252-3685
Cigar box labels

(D6)
David Hirsch
6601 Maple St.
Morton Grove, IL 60053
(845) 965-1132
Tobacco tins, coffee tins, and signs

(D8)
Dunbar's Gallery
Howard and Leila Dunbar
76 Haven St.
Milford, MA 01757
(508) 634-8697; fax (508) 634-8698
Signs and general advertising

(D9)
Frank's Antiques
Box 516
Hillard, FL 32046
(904) 845-2870 or (904) 845-4888
fax (904) 845-4000
General advertising

(D10)
Donald Friedman
660 W. Grand Ave.
Chicago, IL 60610
(708) 656-3700 (day); (312) 226-4741
(evenings and weekends)
fax (708) 656-6292
Advertising puzzles

(D11)
Darryl's Old Advertising Signs
Darryl Fritsche
1525 Aviation Blvd.
Redondo Beach, CA 90278
(310) 376-3858
Signs

(D12)
Gaylord's Mercantile
Bill Gaylord
1015 Second St.
Sacramento, CA 95814
(919) 444-5738
e-mail: gaylord@ns.net
website: www.pageweavers.com/
gaylords.html
Crate labels

(D13)
Ed Janey
1756 65th St.
Garrison, IA 52229
(319) 477-8888
Advertising, monster items, space toys

(D14)
Henry Hain III Antiques and
   Collectibles
2623 Second St
Harrisburg, PA 17110
(717) 238-0534; fax (717) 238-0338
e-mail: antcolbks@ezonline.com
*General advertising, small antiques
and collectibles*

(D15)
Roy R. and Linda M. Hartman
13139 Country Ridge Dr.
Germantown, MD 20874
De Laval and Crawford Cooking Ranges

(D16)
Jan and Linda Henry
135 S, 23rd St.
LaCrosse, WI 54601
(608) 784-5443
Root beer and soda fountain collectibles

(D17)
Hesson Collectibles
Judy Hesson
1261 S. Lloyd
Lombard, IL 60148
(630) 627-3298
Mail-order catalogs

(D18)
Charles E. Kirtley
P.O. Box 2273
Elizabeth City, NC 27906
(919) 335-1262
*Pin-backs, pocket mirrors, and general
advertising*

(D20)
That Toy Guy Collectibles
Michael Paquine
502 E Baltimore Pike
Lansdowne, PA 19050
(610) 394-8697
*Advertising characters and character
collectibles*

(D21)
Mike's General Store
52 St. Anne's Rd.
Winnipeg, Manitoba, Canada R2M-2Y3
(204) 255-3463; fax (204) 253-5123
e-mail: mikesgen@ilos.net
website: www.mikesgeneralstore.com
General advertising

(D22)
Wm. Morford
RD#2
Cazenovia, NY 13035
(315) 662-7625; fax (315) 662-3570
e-mail: morf2bid@aol.com
General advertising

(D23)
Bill and Pat Poe
220 Dominica Circle E.
Niceville, FL 32578-4085
(850) 897-4163; fax (850) 897-2606
e-mail: McPoes@aol.com
Fast-food memorabilia

(D24)
American Pie Collectibles
John and Sheri Pavone
29 Sullivan Rd.
Peru, NY 12972
(518) 643-0993; fax (518) 643-8152
e-mail: apc1@worldnet.att.net
website: www.serftech.com/apc
General advertising

(D25)
Judy Posner Collectibles
June – September
RD #1 Box 273
Effort, PA 18330
(717) 629-6583 fax (717) 629-0521
e-mail: judyandjef@aol.com
October – May
P.O. Box 2194
Englewood, FL 34295
(941) 475-1725; fax (941)-475-2645
e-mail: judyandjef@aol.com
Black Americana

(D26)
Postcards International
Martin J. Shapiro
P.O. Box 2930
New Haven, CT 06515
(203) 865-0814
Vintage postcards

(D27)
Jim Rash
135 Alder Ave.
Pleasantville, NJ 08232
(609) 646-4125
e-mail: rasharoo@msn.com
Cereal premiums, figures, and Dr. Seuss

(D28)
Bill Retskin
P.O. Box 18481
Ashville, NC 28814-0481
(704) 254-4487; fax (704) 254-1006
e-mail: bill@matchcovers.com
website: www.matchcovers.com
Matchbooks and related ephemera

(D29)
The Soup Collector Club
David and Micki Young
714 Country Ln. Ct.
Wauconda, IL 60084
(847) 487-4917; fax (847) 487-4917
e-mail: soupclub@aol.com
Soup advertising

(D30)
Signs of Age
Robert and Louise Marshall
115-117 Pine St.
Catasaugua, PA 18032
(215) 264-8986; fax (610) 264-9200
Soft drink advertising

(D31)
Steve Sourapas
1212 9th Ave. West Unit 2
Seattle, WA 98119
(206) 282-9922
Hires Root Beer

(D32)
Craig and Donna Stifter
P.O. Box 6514
Naperville, IL 60540
(630) 789-5780
website: www.cocacola@enteract.com
Soft-drink collectibles

(D33)
Nate Stoller
960 Reynolds Ave.
Ripon, CA 95366
(209) 599-5933; fax (209) 529-1246
e-mail: multimotor@aol.com
website: www.geocities.com/
Heartland/Plains/6385
Pre-WWII Maytag collectibles

(D34)
The Sign Sez
Larry and Nancy Werner
P.O. Box 188
Winfield, IL 60190
(630) 690-2960
Tin and porcelain signs

(D37)
David Zimmerman
6834 Newtonsville Rd.
Pleasant Plain, OH 45162
(513) 625-5188
Small and sample tins

Condition and Its Effect on Value

Condition, more than any other consideration, is very important when assessing the value of advertising collectibles. On today's market, items in good to very good condition are slow to sell unless they are extremely rare. Mint or near mint examples are high.

The following criteria are generally used by most dealers and auction galleries when describing condition (corresponding numbers are sometimes used instead of letter codes; these are also given).

Mint (M) (10) —	Unused, absolutely no wear, like new.
Near Mint (NM) (9) —	Appears new, but on closer examination minor wear, a few very light scratches, or slight dullness can be seen.
Excellent (EX) (8) —	General appearance is very pleasing with only a few very minor dents, scratches, and loss of paint to distract.
Very Good (VG) (7) —	Still attractive to display, but with more defects than one in excellent condition; has some rust, pitting, and fading.
Good (G) (6) —	Used, faded; has paint wear, dents, scratches, and rust. Generally not collectible unless the item is especially hard to find.
Good- (G-) (5) —	Has serious problems.

To help you arrive at values for items in conditions other than those specifically given, we suggest the following guidelines. These are only in general, and there are of course exceptions to the rule.

Using excellent as a basis, equate the same item in mint condition at 2X; NM at 1½X; VG at -½X; and G at -¾X. For instance, an item in EX condition worth $100 used as a basis makes the same in M condition $200; NM, $150; VG, $50 (or less).

A Bauder, calendar, 1905, cardboard, die-cut, young boy/girl on wagon framed by roses, 14x11", complete, EX+, A3 ....**$175.00**

A Kostka Grocers, calendar, 1917, cardboard, die-cut, young Gypsy girl/puppies framed by apples/blossoms, 20x12", complete, NM, A3 ....**$165.00**

A Parker & Co's Nerve Cigars, cigar box label, inner lid, nautical image, VG, A5 ....**$340.00**

A Sur-Shot Bot & Worm Remover, tin, rectangular, Indian/horse/pig scene, red on yellow, Canadian, 3x4x2½", EX, A15 ....**$100.00**

A Zaphirio & Co Cigarettes, tin, flat, holds 100, Egyptian graphics, EX+, A3 ....**$40.00**

A&P, see also Sunnyfield Quick Rolled Oats

A&P Coffee, jigsaw puzzle, A&P Coffee Experts At The Plantation In South America..., ca 1932, 8½x10", EX, D10 ..**$60.00**

A&P, sign, porcelain, Welcome To A&P!/Free Parking/Please! One Hour Only!..., auto shoppers, white/red/black, 24x36", EX, A24 ....**$300.00**

A&P Tea Co, trade card, Intruder, Would You Mind Sharing Your Nightcap With Me?..., man walks in on startled lady, 8½x6½", EX+, A3 ....**$55.00**

A-Corn Salve, tin, round, Removes Corns, lettering around acorn graphic, ½x1¼", EX, D37 ....**$15.00**

A-Corn Salve, tin, round, That Will Do The Work, lettering around acorn graphic, ¼x1¼", EX, D37 ....**$20.00**

A-Treat Beverages, calendar, 1959, complete, EX, A16.**$85.00**

A-Treat Beverages, menu board, tin, red/white/blue with blackboard, 20x13", NM+, D30 ....**$40.00**

A-Treat Beverages, sign, cardboard, die-cut Santa in sleigh above houses, 22x28", EX, D30 ....**$75.00**

A-Treat Beverages, sign, porcelain, Take Home..., red/blue on speckled blue/white, blue line border, 10x20", EX+, D30 ....**$100.00**

AAA, license plate frame, brass, beaver atop AAA oval logo, 1940s, 9x13", NM, A1 ....**$135.00**

AAA Approved, sign, porcelain, oval, red/white/blue, 2-sided, 23x30", VG, A6..........................**$80.00**

AAA Official Gas Station, sign, porcelain, oval, white lettering on blue band around blue AAA on white, red trim, 2-sided, 17x23", EX+, A1 ....**$350.00**

Abbey Brand Peaches, can label, ruins of church, VG, D5 ....**$20.00**

Abbott's Bitters, thermometer, wood, man pouring bitters, lettering below on white, arched top, 1908-15, 21", EX+, A13 ....**$170.00**

Abbotts Ice Cream, sign, tin, Once You Try It You'll Always Buy It, Quaker lady with tray, red/white/gray, wood frame, 35x26", VG, A7 ....**$450.00**

ABC Bohemian Brewing Co, sign, tin, Watching A Good Thing, oval image of bulldog staring at bottle, rectangular self-frame, 21x24", G, A7 ....**$100.00**

ABC Bohemian Brewing Co, sign, tin, Watching A Good Thing, oval image of bulldog staring at bottle, doghouse-shaped self-frame, 28x30", NM, A1 ....**$1,000.00**

ABC Export Beer, label, oval, Consumers Albany Brewing Co/Albany NY, pre-1920, M, A10 ....**$77.00**

ABC Old Ale, label, 11-oz, Aztec Brewing Co/San Diego CA, IRTP or WF statement, 1933-50, M, A10 ....**$40.00**

ABC Old Stout, label, 11-oz, Aztec Brewing Co/San Diego CA, IRTP or WF statement, 1933-50, M, A10 ....**$28.00**

Abion, crate label, California orange, bouquet of roses, 1920, M, D5 ....**$30.00**

Absaraka, cigar box label, inner lid, shows Indian chief/arrows/peace pipe, 6x9", M, D5 ....**$65.00**

Abts Monopole, sign, tin, smiling lady with glass/bottle, name on bottom band, 14x10", NM+, D30..........**$75.00**

AC Service, sign, flange, tin, round AC panel atop rectangular Service panel, 3 chained product panels, dated 9/47, NM+ (NOS), A1..**$300.00**

AC Spark Plugs, display floor case, oak & glass, gold lettering on marque atop 3-tiered stand with slant front, footed, 40", EX, A2..**$440.00**

AC Spark Plugs, pull toy, slush cast, Sparky the Horse in bathtub with rubber wheels, Spark Plugs Need Cleaning Too..., 5", VG, A1..**$110.00**

AC Spark Plugs, sign, tin, Change...Every 10,000 Miles/For Better Engine Performance, blue ground, embossed, 1929, 14x10", EX+ (NOS), A1 ....$275.00

AC Spark Plugs, sign, tin, Dirty Or Worn Plugs Waste Gas/Replace Every 10,000 Miles, logo in center, embossed, 34x10", EX+, D11 ....$250.00

AC Spark Plugs, sign, tin, graphic of spark plug above round red logo, blue ground, white self-border, dated 11-41, 9x18", NM+ (NOS), A1 ....$180.00

AC Spark Plugs, thermometer, metal, Spark Plugs Need Cleaning Too!, horse showering in tub, blue, arched top/square bottom, 21x8", G, A6 ....$150.00

Ace Quality Combs, display case, wood with glass top, 10x12x20", EX, A3 ....$75.00

Acme Ale, sign, crystal plaque, cowboy on horse with rope, bottle and name below, Maynard Dixon artwork, 1926, 12x9", EX, A8 ....$150.00

Acme Beer, mug, ceramic, black on white, silver trim, 5", NM, A8...$115.00

Acme Beer, sign, cardboard, Acme beer stein in front of western still life with broken wagon wheel, framed, 21x28", EX+, A3 ....$225.00

Acme Beer, sign, tin, Ask For...In Cans/More Convenient!, tilted can at left of lettering, 17x24", VG, A8........$40.00

Acme Beer, sign, tin/cardboard, octagonal, pilsner glass/bottle/ pipe with dead game birds, beveled wood-grain border, 15", VG+, A8 ....$260.00

Acme Boots, sign, cardboard trifold, mountain hunting party on horseback with large elk in sight, artist J Clymer, 23x37", EX, A9 ....$150.00

Acme Coffee, can, 1-lb, key-wind lid, yellow/black/red, NM+, A3...$25.00

Acme Coffee, can, 1-lb, pry lid, white dots on blue lower half, NM, A3 ....$35.00

Acme Quality Motor Car Finish, sign, tin, embossed, ...For Refinishing Old Or Shabby Automobiles, man working on early Ford at left, 7x20", EX, A2 ....$900.00

Acme Quality Paints, sign, flange, porcelain, image of large paint can, red/yellow/black/white, 20x15", EX+, A1 ....$250.00

Ada Olive Oil, sign, tin, The Best Brand/Imported From Italy..., lettering/product can over olive branch on red, 13x19", VG, A7...$300.00

Adam Scheidt Brwg Co's Standard & Lotos Beer, sign, reverse glass, round logo with hops in center, gold on black, 1890s, brass frame, vertical, NM, A19...**$2,080.00**

Adams Chicklets Chewing Gum, display, tin, rectangular with vertical compartments which hold various flavors, 5x9", G, A9 ....$100.00

Adams Chicklets Chewing Gum, display box, cardboard with glass insert, leaf design, Five Cents The Ounce on gold seal, EX, A16...$40.00

Adams Chicklets Chewing Gum, display box, tin with glass top, Exchange Your Pennys For.../1¢, G+, A16....$35.00

Adams Chicklets Chewing Gum, magazine ad, cameo image of lady in profile above 2 gum packs/text, black/white, early, 7x5", M, A16...........................$20.00

Adams Chicklets Chewing Gum, trade card, Wood Pewee, bird series, vertical, VG+, A16 ....$25.00

Adams Chicklets Chewing Gum, trolley sign, You Should Never Be Without.../Really Delightful, black/white image of woman on green, 11x21", VG+, A3...............$120.00

Adams Pepsin Chewing Gum, jar, round, straight-sided, original marked metal lid, VG, A13....................$250.00

Adams Pepsin Tutti-Frutti Chewing Gum, display box, This Box Contains 36 Bars/180 Pieces, girl on glass panel, orange ground, 4x10", EX, A2.................$100.00

Adams Pepsin Tutti-Frutti Chewing Gum, display case, paper-covered shadow box, lady with moving arm that originally held package of gum, 22x13", Fair, A9.$450.00

Adams Pepsin Tutti-Frutti Chewing Gum, tin, box shape, 6x7x5", VG, A6..$450.00

Adams Pepsin Tutti-Frutti Chewing Gum, vendor, wood with porcelain panels, 2 columns, Railway Automated Sales Co, 29", VG, A9...........................**$2,500.00**

Adams Pure Chewing Gum, jar, clear glass with etched logo, thumbnail-type lid, ca 1915, NM+, A13..$110.00

Adams' Red Rose Chewing Gum, box, cardboard with hinged lid, white lettering on blue around 7 ladies in colorful dresses on lid, 1x6x13", EX+, A15...$575.00

Adams Silver Roll, display, tin, round canister on pedestal, 7", VG, A18...$75.00

Adams Yucatan Chewing Gum, single stick, M, A16 .$20.00

Adams' Joy Buzzer (Hand Shaker & Ticker), display, cardboard die-cut stand-up, World Of Fun, 2 cartoon fellas using buzzer, with 12 buzzers, 13x15", NM (NOS), A1....$170.00

Adkin's Empire Nut Brown Tobacco, sign, porcelain, Adkin's in script above product name, For That Nutty Flavour in script below, 12x18", Fair, A9..............$50.00

Adkin's Nut Brown Tobacco, store bin, tin box, In Packets Only, red, VG, A3...$100.00

Admiral Cigarettes, sign, paper, scantly clad lady lookout standing on net of sailing ship pointing to land, 23x16", EX+, A3...$150.00

Admiral Coffee, pot scraper, tin, red/blue on white, 3",
EX+, A15 ....$700.00

Admiral Hopkins, cigar box label, inner lid, American Rev-
olution/man/ship, 1933, 6x9", M, D5 ....$45.00

Admiral Rough Cut Tobacco, tin, round, knob lid, gold
trim, EX, A18..$140.00

Admiration, cigar box label, inner lid, woman looking into
hand mirror, 6x9", M, D5 ....$10.00

Adolphus Busch, cigar box label, inner lid, oval image, Geo
L Schlegel litho, 1913, EX, A5..............................$185.00

Adolphus Busch, pocketknife, red/black enamel inlay with gold
lettering/trim, Schrade Walden, 1950s, VG, A3 ....$100.00

Adorn's Colombia, Mara & Mocha Coffee, can, 1-lb, key-
wind lid, red/white lettering, black band around middle,
EX, A3...$20.00

Adorn's Colombia Java & Mocha Coffee, can, 1-lb,
key-wind lid, white on red/black, gold trim, NM
(full), A18 ....$40.00

Adriance Farm Machinery, sign, paper, 3 children on horse
with circular inset lower left, c 1902, framed, image:
27x20", VG, A9 ....$1,100.00

ADS Croup Ointment/American Druggist Syndicate, tin,
round, 1x2¼", EX, D37...$15.00

ADS Gastro Tonic Tablets, tin, rectangular, rounded corners, ½x1x1½", EX, D37 ....$30.00

Advance Thresher Co, catalog, 1911, 42 pgs, image
of early steam tractor against yellow sky, NM+,
A3..$100.00

Advona Kidney Beans, can label, 2 bowls of kidney beans,
Deco style, EX, D5...$15.00

Aero, cigar box label, outer, image of a zeppelin over Paris,
Geo Schlegel litho, VG, A5 ....$165.00

Aero, see also Jenney Aero

Aero Eastern Motor Oil, can, 1-qt, oval image of white
twin-engine plane, red/white/black, EX, A15 ....$230.00

Aeroplane, cigar box label, outer, airplane with body of
cigar, 4½x4½", M, D5 ....$35.00

Aeroshell Oil, see Shell

Aetna Auto Ass'n of the USA, sign, porcelain, die-cut
shield, row of stars above US map, white/red on
blue, 2-sided, 1920s, 14x20", NM, A24 ....$500.00

After Dinner, cigar box label, outer, men playing card game,
4½x4½", M, D5..$35.00

After Dinner Salted Peanuts, tin, 10-lb, round, pry lid,
blue/yellow with red lettering, VG, A2...............$100.00

After Glow Coffee, pail, 4-lb, straight-sided, slip lid, bail
handle, metallic gold on red, EX+, A18..............$120.00

Air Float Baby Talc, tin, blue or tan top, EX-EX+, A18, from
$165 to...$190.00

Air Float Lily of the Valley Talcum, tin, vertical square, 8",
EX, A3...$35.00

Air Race Motor Oil, see Deep Rock

Aircraft Allspice, container, cardboard, EX, A3 ....$25.00

Aircraft Ginger Ale, menu board, tin, embossed, ...Properly
Aged/Special To-Day, 20x14", NM, A3.................$60.00

Aircraft Pure Rolled White Oats, container, 3-lb, cardboard, red/white/blue, bird carrying letter & circling aircraft, EX+, A3 ....$200.00

Aircraft Radio Corporation, sign, porcelain, Authorized
Sales & Service For..., red/black on white, 15x24", EX,
A6...$325.00

Airdale, cigar box label, inner lid, head of dog, 6x9", M,
D5 ....$20.00

Airedale 5¢ Cigar/East Prospect Cigar Co, sign, cardboard, die-cut, round, name/dog on red band around
open center, company name on bottom tab, 12x9", NM+,
A3...$40.00

Airline, crate label, California orange, globe/wings/stars on
blue, Fillmore, EX, D3 ....$3.00

Airport Coffee, can, 1-lb, key-wind lid, yellow/black, EX+,
A3...$210.00

Airship, crate label, apple, old transport ship above apples,
Zupan & Lucich, 1920, M, D5.............................$250.00

Airship, crate label, California orange, 4-prop plane on blue
ground, red logo, Fillmore, EX, D3......................$15.00

AJ Robinson & Son Milk/Cream, sign, porcelain, round, From Tubercelin Tested Herds/Roslindale, name around Milk/Cream, red/yellow/black, 30", EX, A2........**$385.00**

Ajax Cleanser, tin, round, sample, lady holding up sign reading New Type Foaming Cleanser/Polishes As It Cleans, 2½x1¾", EX, D37 ....**$25.00**

AL Foss Pork Rind Minnow, tin, rectangular, square corners, red with white lettering/image of minnow on lid, VG+, A18...**$30.00**

Al-U-Pa, cigar box label, inner lid, map of Alaska/1909 AYP Expo, 6x9", M, D5....................................**$35.00**

Alabama Brewing Co/Ideal Bottled Beer, tray, round, **The Two Ideals, gold lettering/trim on green rim around image of lady/bottle, EX+, A8 ....$1,155.00**

Aladdin Gas, gas globe, 3-pc, blue metal body, glass lenses, blue name/pyramid on white, 15", VG, A6........**$325.00**

Aladdin Security Oil/Standard Oil Co, pin-back button, celluloid, round, lamp logo, multicolor on yellow, red border, late 1800s, 1¼" dia, NM, A1 ....**$450.00**

Alaska Chewing Gum, box, cardboard, paper label with **image of mountain, Cleansing Of Teeth & Sweetening Of Breath, 1x2x1", EX+, A15 ....$210.00**

Albers Carnation Quick Oats, container, 1-lb 4-oz, no lid o/w EX, A3..**$10.00**

Aldolphus Busch, pocketknife, red/black enamel inlay with gold lettering/trim, Schrade Walden, 1950s, NM, A8...**$290.00**

Alexander Kielland, crate label, Washington apple, 2 red apples on green background/yellow logo, Cashmere, M, D12 ....**$12.00**

Alexander's Celebrated Panhard Oil, sign, porcelain, The Oil That Lubricates.../Exclusive Right To Above Name..., white on blue, 15x18", G, A2 ....**$300.00**

Alexander's Complexion Gum, sign, cardboard hanger, Cleanses the System, Beautifies the Complexion, lady in blue dress, 11x7", VG, A9.............................**$1,400.00**

Alfred Anderson's Best Choice Wines & Liquors, tray, oval, A Lady Of Quality, plain rim, advertising on back, Meek litho, c 1904, 17x14", VG, A9 ....**$200.00**

Alice Foote MacDougall Coffee, can, 1-lb, key-wind lid, short, EX+, A3 ....**$60.00**

Alice Foote MacDougall Coffee, can, 1-lb, slip lid, tall, EX+, A3...**$55.00**

Alka-Seltzer, bank, Speedy figure, vinyl, 5½", EX, D25 .**$85.00**

Alka-Seltzer, dispenser, tin cylinder on chrome base with 2-prong foot, 'Be Wise Alkalize,' 15", NM, A3.......**$385.00**

Alka-Seltzer, dispenser, tin cylinder on chrome base with 2-prong foot, 'Be Wise Alkalize,' 15", VG, A3 ....**$120.00**

Alka-Seltzer, doll, Speedy, painted rubber, Canadian, 5", EX, A14 ....$215.00

Alka-Seltzer, doll, Speedy, squeeze vinyl, 1960, 8", EX, D27...**$600.00**

Alka-Seltzer, sign, cardboard, die-cut, Speedy atop stairway made of product boxes, 1960s, 12x8", EX+, A4.**$225.00**

Alka-Seltzer, sign, celluloid, All-Over Relief.../There's Nothing Like It, Speedy pointing to glass, blue/gold, 1950s, 6x9", M, A4..**$310.00**

Alka-Seltzer, sign, neon on reverse glass case, blue, 7x27x6", EX+, A1..**$400.00**

Alka-Seltzer, tape dispenser/product display, painted tin, white with red graphics, 12x11x7", EX, A1 .....$50.00

All American Cigars, tin, round, red, oval images of Lincoln, Washington & Ben Franklin, EX+, A3........**$530.00**

All Detergent, radio, shaped like product box, G, D13 ..**$30.00**

All Jacks Cigarettes, sign, tin, Hard To Beat..., image of tilted open pack in center on gold/cream/black, 14x10", NM+, A3 .**$80.00**

All-Jersey Milk, license plate attachment, aluminum, Drink.../Elsie-type cow on yellow die-cut emblem, 6x10", NM+ (NOS), A1....................**$120.00**

All Nations Tobacco/J Wright Co tin, rectangular, rounded corners, EX+, A18..............................**$130.00**

All Right, cigar box label, salesman's sample, jester doing handstand, Geo S Harris & Son litho #871, VG, A5.......**$225.00**

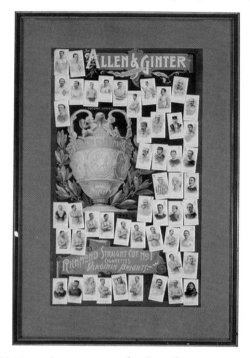

Allen & Ginter, sign, paper, depicts fancy urn-type trophey with 50 card-type images of world champion sportsmen, 28x16", rare, VG+, A9............$15,000.00

Allen & Ginter's Dixie Chop Cut Plug Smoking Tobacco, tin, rectangular, square corners, yellow, EX+, A18..**$30.00**

Allen & Ginter's Granulated Imperial Smoking Mixture, tin, rectangular, square corners, aqua, EX+, A3 ...**$70.00**

Allen & Ginter's Imperial Cube Cut Smoking Mixture, tin, round, snap lid, blue, NM, A3........................**$75.00**

Allen & Ginter's Pet Cigarettes, sign, cardboard die-cut stand-up, ...Are The Best, girl seated on tree branch, embossed, 1905, no size given, EX+, A3............**$150.00**

Allen & Ginter's Pet Cigarettes, sign, cardboard hanger, Pet Cigarettes Are The Best... above picture of girl at well, sepia tones, 10x4", EX+, A3 ....**$75.00**

Allen-A Hosiery, sign, cardboard stand-up, blond pin-up girl posing in black gown on blue satin pillow, 1930s, 12x8", unused, M, A24 ....**$90.00**

Allen-A Hosiery, sign, cardboard stand-up, brunette pin-up girl seated in red gown, legs exposed, black ground, 1930s, 12x8", EX+ A24..**$65.00**

Allied Mills Inc, sign, porcelain, die-cut feed bag, black silhouette of horseman on red/white striped IQ bag, 32x25", NM, A1 ....**$300.00**

Allied Van Lines, toy truck, Buddy L, tractor-trailer with pull handle, pressed steel, orange, advertising on side of trailer, 30", VG, A1 ....**$275.00**

Alligator Steel Belt Lacing, sign, tin/cardboard, beveled, black/yellow lettering & yellow product box on green, 9x13", NM, A7 ....**$75.00**

Allis-Chalmers, watch fob, metal, square, embossed image of earth mover, name above, EX, A20 ....**$100.00**

Allis-Chalmers Tractors/Machinery, clock, octagonal, red neon, black numbers around red letters on white, green/white frame, 22x21", NM, A6 ....**$850.00**

Allstate Hi-Plus Premium Gasoline, pump sign, porcelain, round, red/white/blue on white, 10" dia, NM+, A1 ..**$950.00**

Allwin Folding Go-Cart, postcard, Baby's Health & Mother's Comfort Are Not Complete Without An..., shows baby in cart, used 1908, VG+, A17.......$80.00

ALO Paints/Buffalo Aged Linseed Oil Paints, sign, flange, 2-sided with positive/negative blue & white images, ...Sold Here, product can above, 24x8", EX, A1.**$550.00**

Alone Mild Mellow Cigars, tin, vertical oval, holds 50, yellow, Back To 5¢, EX, A18 ....**$45.00**

Alpena Motor Cars/Providence RI Agency, pocket mirror, oval, lettering on blue band around black/white image of early auto, 3x2", EX, A2 ....**$990.00**

Alpine Coffee/Nestle, can, 1-lb, key-wind lid, tall, VG+, A3 ....**$35.00**

Alta Coffee, jar/kerosene lamp, promotional, when jar is empty of coffee it is used as lamp, with glass globe, NM (unused), A3 ....**$220.00**

Alta Crest Farm/Ayrshire Cattle, sign, porcelain, steer head/red lettering on yellow circle with black outline, red square border, 12x12", EX, A1 ....**$250.00**

Alta Crest Farms, thermometer, celluloid over cardboard, stork logo above gauge, rounded top/bottom, 6", NM, A1..**$85.00**

Atlantic Tea Co, sign, cardboard, early depiction of boy in blue overalls/girl in yellow dress, text on back, 2-sided, 21x16", EX, A3 ....**$80.00**

Altes Beer, display, hand-held bottle, plaster, It's Brisk...It's Clear...It's Altes Beer on black cuff, EX, A8........**$150.00**

Altes Sportsman Ale, sign, reverse on glass, name in fancy filigree lettering framed buy band, red/silver/gold, Becco, 1950s, 9x11", VG+, A8 ....**$100.00**

Altex Air Tested Prophylactics, tin, rectangular, rounded corners, 3 for 50¢ on white dot, white lettering on orange, 2", EX+, A15 ....**$600.00**

Altpeter's Beverages, bottle topper, cardboard, Keep Cool With..., baseball players confronting umpire, NM, D30............**$18.00**

Altpeter's Beverages, bottle topper, cardboard, Step Right Up For..., baseball player at bat, NM, D30 ....**$18.00**

Alumni, tin, horizontal rectangular box, concave bottom, white, gold trim, EX, A3......................................**$100.00**

Alumni Tobacco, pocket tin, flat, concave, white, EX, A18..**$60.00**

Alvarez Lopez y Ca Perfections 50, tin, round, slip lid, tropical scene with 2 classical women, EX+, A3..**$75.00**

Amalie Motor Oil, clock, octagonal, neon light-up, orange advertising oval on white surrounded by black letters, 18x18", EX, A15........................$600.00

Amalie Motor Oil, clock, round, light-up, glass, metal frame, numbers (oil cans at 12-3-6-9) around red oval logo, 1950s, 18", NM, A24 ....**$500.00**

Amalie Motor Oil, thermometer, round dial type, NM, D34...**$200.00**

Amalie Motor Oil, thermometer, round dial type, VG+, D30 ....**$100.00**

Amami Bouquet Talcum, tin, sample, girl looking up, 2¼", EX, D37 ....**$100.00**

America's Cup Radiant Roasted Coffee, can, 1-lb, key-wind lid, EX+, A18....................................**$35.00**

America's Delight, crate label, apple, red apple/ orchard/snowy mountains, EX, D3.........................**$5.00**

American, gas globe, 3-pc, white glass body, glass lenses, red/white/blue, 12", EX, A6................................**$200.00**

American Ace Coffee, can, 1-lb, key-wind lid, blue lettering on white, red bottom band, VG+, A3 ....**$40.00**

American Ace Coffee, can, 1-lb, key-wind lid, red lettering on blue, EX+, A18 ....**$125.00**

American Automobile & Supply, catalog, 1920, 100 pgs, EX, D17...**$75.00**

American Beauty Fine Mixture, pocket tin, flat, large, EX, A18...**$75.00**

American Bosch Authorized Sales & Service, sign, porcelain, red/white daredevil logo on blue ground, 1-sided, 24x15", G+, A2...**$230.00**

American Bosch Car-Radio Service/Authorized Sales & Service, sign, porcelain, red/white daredevil logo on blue ground, bolted-on Car-Radio Service panel, 2-sided, 24x16", EX, A1 ....**$550.00**

American Bosch Official Sales & Service, sign, flange, steel, Official Bosch Sales & Service/American Bosch Magneto Corp/logo, red/black on yellow, 12x16", G, A2...**$500.00**

American Brewing Co, sign, tin, The Two Kings, lion/whiskey bottle on cliff overlooking valley, Meek & Beach litho, 29x49", VG, A7 ....**$800.00**

American Brewing Co, tray, round, Good Morning, lady at open window, American Art Works, 1913, 13", EX, A8...**$160.00**

American Can Co/1904 St Louis World's Fair, calling card, tin, 2-sided, given to visitors at the 1904 St Louis World's Fair, 3x5", VG, A9 ....**$100.00**

American Candy Co/Fair Art, sign/calendar, 1902, die-cut painter's palette embossed with 3-D pop-up of 3 ladies at easel, 22x12", NM, D6......................$750.00

American Cherry Phosphate/American Soda Fountain Co, tip tray, round, lettered rim around shamrock logo & lettering, gold, 6" dia, EX, A7 ....**$450.00**

American Conquest, cigar box label, inner lid, Spanish American War Peace Commission, 1898, 6x9", M, D5 ......**$75.00**

American De-Luxe Art Calendars, calendar, 1948, Anticipation, boy/dog wait for dad's flapjacks at campsite, JF Kernan art, 44x22", complete, EX, A9 ....**$10.00**

American Deluxe Coffee/National Tea Co, can, 1-lb, key-wind lid, red/white/blue, EX, A3 ....**$20.00**

American Eagle Chewing Tobacco, pocket tin, flat, sample, white on blue, EX, A3 ....**$200.00**

American Eagle Chewing Tobacco, tin, rectangular, concave sides, slip lid, Ginna, VG+, A18....................**$85.00**

American Eagle Chewing Tobacco, tin, rectangular, rounded corners, EX, A3...**$300.00**

American Eagle Toy Savings Bank/J&E Stevens, trade card, full color with advertising around image in center, horizontal, VG, A2...**$150.00**

American Express Co Agency, sign, porcelain, patriotic shield in center, red/white/blue, 3-line border, 17x19", EX+, A15 ....**$1,550.00**

American Express Money Orders, sign, flange, Money Orders arched over American Express logo, For Sale Here below, white on blue, 13x20", G, A2....................**$300.00**

American Family Soap, sign, cardboard, A Soap-Certificate, I Used Your Soap Two Years Ago & Have Not Used ... writes hobo, 28x20", VG, A9 ....**$500.00**

American Home Brand Fresh Roasted Coffee, container, 1-lb, cardboard, round, tin top/bottom, NM+, A3...........**$230.00**

American Lady Shoe, sign, tin, The HB Idea 'Keep the Quality Up,' lettering flanked by shoe & oval logo, C Shonk litho, 9x20", EX, A9...................................**$65.00**

American Line/Red Star Line, letter folder, metal, die-cut, ship at sea with advertising, 3x12", EX, A6....$230.00

American Maid High Grade Bottled Beer, tray, round, lettering on gray rim around lady seated on table with vase of flowers, 13" dia, VG, A8..................$125.00

American Mills Blend Coffee, tin, horizontal box, rounded corners, red, boy on lion, EX+, A3 ....$80.00

American Nut Co Salted Pecans, can, 8-lb, pry lid, red/blue on white, 11x8" dia, EX, A24.................................$65.00

American Oil Co/Daley's Service Station, calendar, 1946, paper, pin-up girl in playful pose with dog on dk blue ground, 34x16", complete, NM, A3 ....$100.00

American Oil Corporation, game, Put Or Take, round pocket type, celluloid back with advertising, celluloid/cardboard face on game side, 2", EX, A1..............$65.00

American Pilsner Exquisite, drinking glass, stemmed, clear, etched, A-&-eagle logo (tucked wings), VG+, A8.$110.00

American Red Cross, display sign, cardboard die-cut stand-up, nurse holding globe with red cross, Join... below, 1930s-40s, 22x14", NM, A13.................................$200.00

American Royal Coffee, can, 1-lb, key-wind lid, red on white, EX, A3 ....$50.00

American Rubbers, sign, die-cut cardboard, young lady on swing, American litho, c 1900, 25x12", G, A9 .$600.00

American Seal Paint, calendar, 1899, Uncle Sam & eagle acknowledging Spanish-American War heroes, 21x13", NM, A3...$335.00

American Seal Paints, thermometer, wood, When You Paint Use..., shows Uncle Sam, orange/black on white, arched top/square bottom, 21", EX, A15........................$200.00

American Steel Farm Fences, match holder, tin, green/white, 1920s-30s, VG+, A13 ....$40.00

American Telephone & Telegraph Co/Southern Bell, sign, porcelain, Public above & Telephone below circle Bell System logo on white, black band below, 23x18", EX, A13...$625.00

American Telephone & Telegraph Co & Associated Companies, sign, porcelain, Long Distance Telephone/Bell System, bell logo on square ground, blue/white, 2-sided, 18x18", EX+, A3 ....$145.00

American Tobacco Co, catalog, 1910-12 Catalogue Of Presents For Tobacco Tags/Coupons, 45 pgs, 10x7", EX, D22 ....$25.00

American Traveler, cigar box label, inner lid, embellished lettering above image of buffalo, photo mechanical, VG, A5...$75.00

American Wine Co, sign, tin, oval, dapper man seated in front of plate of oysters sipping from glass, 1905, self-framed, 28x22", EX, A7 ....$3,200.00

Amicus, cigar box label, inner lid, woman behind store counter, 1899, 6x9", 1899, VG, D5 ....$125.00

Amocat Brand Mace, tin, red, gold top, oval mountain scene, EX, A3...$80.00

Amoco, lamp, plastic/metal, electric, Amoco emblems repeated on white panels around Tiffiny-type shade, 18x9" dia, M, A6 ....$135.00

Amoco, service hat, green cloth with vinyl bill, red/white/blue oval logo, top snaps to bottom, EX, A6.....$200.00

Amoco Specialties/American Oil Co, rack, metal, 2-tiered with 3 signs each side, For Auto-Home/Office & Factory, red/black/white, 41x22x16", EX, A6...................$140.00

Amoco 586 Special Piston & Valve Stem Oil, bank, can shape, 3x2" dia, NM+, A3.....................................$25.00

Anacapa, crate label, California lemon, gull flying over ocean/islands, Saticoy, EX, D3...............................$3.00

Anaco, crate label, California orange, Kangaroo faces ostrich at sundown, San Francisco, M, D12......................$20.00

Anchor Line Twin Screw Steamships, sign, tin, image of passenger liner, lettering on scalloped self-frame, gold trim, 25x38", NM, A7 ....$1,250.00

Anderson's Washing Powder, container, 3-oz, cardboard, red/white/black on yellow, VG+, A3 ....$20.00

Andullo Tiger Brand 'Tigre' Tobacco/Galban & Co Inc, label, paper, image of tiger in jungle ready to pounce, geometric border, 10x10", EX, A5 ....$110.00

Andy Gump, cigar box label, outer, octagonal, Tops 'Em All, cartoon image of Andy smoking cigar, M, A5......$75.00

Angeles Beer, sign, tin, curled corners, Griselda, circular image of pretty long-haired girl, Meek Co litho, c 1907, 15x15", VG, A9...$150.00

Angeles Brewing & Malting Co, tip tray, round, Seattle 1909, lettering on rim around bottle against flag, EX+, A8...$315.00

Angelica Jacket Company, watch fob, metal oval with enameled center showing black chef, Compliments Of.../The Mail Order..., 1900s, EX, D25..............$250.00

Angelus Marshmallows, pocket mirror, oval, 2 cherubs leaning on product box, NM+, A3.....................$100.00

Angelus White Shoe Dressing, sign, cardboard die-cut hanger, Be Sure You Say..., lady in suit flanked by tennis player/nurse, 12x19", EX+, A3.............$65.00

Angler Beer, label, 12-oz, Mound City Brewing Co/New Athens IL, IRTP or WF statement, 1933-50, EX, A10..............$18.00

Angora, cigar box labels, set of 2, cat holding sign, Schumacher & Ettliner litho #6259/6260, EX, A5.......$135.00

Anheuser-Busch, ashtray, brass emblem with red enameled A-&-eagle logo in relief, VG+, A8.........................$60.00

Anheuser-Busch, beer pail, porcelain, straight-sided, bail handle, white with A-&-Eagle logo decal, 1930s (?), 4", VG+, A8...$220.00

Anheuser-Busch, corkscrew, metal with engraved brass plate, beer bottle shape, A-&-eagle logo (tucked wings), EX, A8...$35.00

Anheuser-Busch, dispenser, stoneware, A-&-eagle logo flanked by name above/5¢ on sides/St Louis Mo USA below, Pat 1919, 10", EX, A8..............................$330.00

Anheuser-Busch, display figure, waiter, chalkware, white shirt, black pants, yellow apron, medal around neck, square base, 20", EX, A6..........................$190.00

Anheuser-Busch, drinking glass, stemmed, clear, gold etched, A-&-eagle logo, 6", EX, A8.....................$30.00

Anheuser-Busch, knife/corkscrew, embossed, EX, A8 ..$75.00

Anheuser-Busch, light globe, milk glass, round, flat-sided, Anheuser Busch On Draught around A-&-eagle logo decal, 8" dia, VG+, A8...$230.00

Anheuser-Busch, match safe, rectangular with rounded corners, A-&-eagle logo in center with embellished corners, EX, A8...$185.00

Anheuser-Busch, match safe, rectangular with spring-loaded top, 2-sided, A-& eagle logo/Pullman car & Adolphus Busch, EX, A8..$240.00

Anheuser-Busch, match safe, rectangular with spring-loaded top, 2-sided, A-&-eagle logo/locomotive & coal tender, 1880s, VG, A6 ....$175.00

Anheuser-Busch, matchbook, horse-drawn wagon on front, colorful, 40 strike, front striker, M, D28........$8.00

Anheuser-Busch, plate, metal, Cheers, by Norman Rockwell, 10" dia, EX+, A8...$70.00

Anheuser-Busch, print, A Fight For The Overland Mail, framed, EX, A8...$200.00

Anheuser-Busch, print, Attack On An Emigrant Train, framed, EX, A8...$200.00

Anheuser-Busch, print, The Father Of Waters, framed, EX, A8...$200.00

Anheuser-Busch, print, The Relief Train, framed, EX, A8 ....$200.00

Anheuser-Busch, print, Westward Ho, framed, EX, A8 ....$200.00

Anheuser-Busch, sign, flange, oval, On Draught, A-&-eagle logo above cream lettering on red, green border, 14x18", NM, A19...$530.00

Anheuser-Busch, sign, plaster, brown 3-D oval image of brewery & St Louis with horse-drawn traffic, rectangular border, 42x54", VG, A2 ....$1,200.00

Associated Gasoline, sign, porcelain, round, Use... around More Miles To The Gallon on pitcher, red/white/blue, 2-sided, 28" dia, NM, A2 ....**$3,850.00**

Astor, cigar box label, inner lid, busy street scene/guilded building, 6x9", M, D5 ....**$35.00**

Astor Coffee, can, 1-lb, key-wind lid, dk blue/red, EX+, A3 ....**$30.00**

Astor Coffee, can, 1-lb, key-wind lid, white/red, NM, A3 ....**$35.00**

Astor House Brand Coffee, can, 1-lb, screw lid, product lettering around image of hotel with street scene, EX, D2 ....**$100.00**

Astoria Salmon, crate label, aerial view of Fort Astoria in 1813, M, D5 ....**$35.00**

Ath-Lo-Pho-Ros Searless Remedy For Rheumatism/ Neuralgia, display, cardboard trifold, 2 men discussing product at sign on city street, 19x29", EX, A6 .....**$85.00**

Athleta Hose Supporters 15¢, display case, tin, simulated wood-grain finish, slant front with graphics/ advertising, 18x10", VG, A2 ....**$330.00**

Athlete, crate label, California lemon, 3 runners at finish line, Claremont, M, D3/D12, from $5 to.........................**$7.00**

Athlete, crate label, California orange, 3 runners at finish line, Claremont, M, D3/D12, from $5 to **$8.00**

Athletic Smoking Mixture, tin, rectangular, rounded corners, shows product name next to boxer in landscape, EX, A18...**$175.00**

Atlantic & Pacific Tea Co, see Condor Coffee

Atlantic Ale & Beer, sign, cardboard, America's Finest!.../ Outsells Them All In South Carolina, Pan-Am Clipper in sky, 1942, 22x27", VG+, A13..............................**$250.00**

Atlantic Ale & Beer, sign, neon, black waiter flanked by neon Atlantic Ale/Beer on yellow, Full Of Good Cheer below, framed, 17x30", EX, A6.........................**$3,250.00**

Atlantic Ale & Beer/Steinerbru Ale & Beer, contest poster, paper, Packard Six Sedan offered to the one with the highest winning football game tickets, 1938, VG, A3 ....**$45.00**

Atlantic Gasoline, gauge stick, wood, Atlantic Gasoline Puts Pep In Your World, Atwater Kent Gasoline Gauge Pat Mat 18 1907, 17", VG+, D14.................................**$45.00**

Atlantic Gasoline/Motor Oil, pocket calendar, 1931, Quality Service, red/white/blue, EX, A1 ....**$5.00**

Atlantic Imperial, gas globe, 3-pc, Gill, name on metallic gold shield, white body, EX+, A1/A6.................**$350.00**

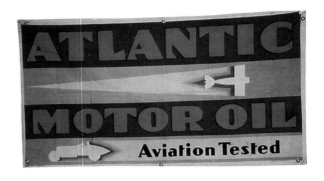

Atlantic Motor Oil, banner, cloth, Aviation Tested, red lettering on gray bands between plane & racer, Sweeny Litho Co, 29x54", NM, A6.................**$500.00**

Atlantic Motor Oil, sign, paper, Let's Get Ready For Spring! says serviceman to boy on go-cart, yellow, white border, 44x28", VG+, A6 ....**$130.00**

Atlantic Motor Oil/Aviation High Film Strength, can, 1-qt, ribbed, twin-engine plane logo, red/white/blue on white, EX+, A1...**$40.00**

Atlantic Outboard Motor Oil, can, 1-qt, SAE 20W-40, red/white/blue, boat/buoy in water, VG+, A6 .....**$65.00**

Atlantic Refining Co, flag, cloth, round red/white/black logo on black, 54x87", EX, A6..............................**$70.00**

Atlantic Refining Co, pump sign, porcelain, curved square, crossed arrow logo, red/white/blue, 13x13", VG, A1..**$150.00**

Atlantic Refining Co, pump sign, porcelain, irregular circle, crossed arrow logo, red/white/blue, 9" dia, EX+, A1.**$375.00**

Atlantic Refining Co Gasoline/Polarine Oil & Greases, sign, porcelain, ...For Sale Here, white lettering/white border with scrolled corner decoration, 20x28", EX+, A1 ....**$650.00**

Atlantic White Flash, pump sign, porcelain, Atlantic above White Flash lettered in circle, white/black on red, white trim, vertical, EX, D34 ....**$185.00**

Atlantic White Flash Plus, sign, cardboard, black/red lettering above 3 cartoon gents with top hats marked White/Flash/Plus, 29x26", VG+, A6 ....**$35.00**

Atlas, crate label, California orange, Atlas with globe on back, 1930, M, D5...**$35.00**

Atlas Certificate Brew/Coca-Cola Bottling Co, sign, tin, lettering with tilted bottle on yellow, 1910s-20s, Fair, A13...**$160.00**

Atlas Kiln Dried Oats, container, 3-lb 7-oz, cardboard, yellow, Kansas City, EX+, A3 ....**$390.00**

Atlas Runabouts & Touring Cars/Havens Motor Car Co, pin-back button, round, image of blue auto, black type on white, 1" dia, EX, A2..................$580.00

Atwater Kent Ignition/Official Repair Station, sign, flange, steel, round, lettering on double bands around image of product, black/white/cream/orange, 18"dia, EX, A2 ....$2,750.00

Atwood's Coffee, can, 1-lb, key-wind lid, white/yellow on red, NM, A19 ....$50.00

Auburn Beauty Six/Harvey G Wilson Distributor, note case/calendar, 1921, swivels open, early auto/distributor's name on front, 2x4", EX, A2 ....$275.00

Aug Wolf & Co's Works, sign, paper, nighttime aerial factory scene, Friedenwald litho, wooden frame, image: 22x31", EX, A9 ....$400.00

August Kern Barber Supply Co, sign, tin, Compliments Of..., nypmh/cherub in landscape, self-framed, 29x22", EX, A7 ....$2,700.00

Aultman Co, see C Aultman Co

Aunt Fanny's Restaurant, drinking glass, image of mammy on frosted ground, 7", M, D25..................$28.00

Aunt Hannah's Bread, jigsaw puzzle, images of animals hidden in picture with fishing boy/girl eyeing loaf of bread, 1932, 7½x8½", EX, D10..................$45.00

Aunt Jemima, booklet, Life Of Aunt Jemima, 1895, NM, A3 ....$100.00

Aunt Jemima, brochure, Aunt Jemima's Kitchen/As You Travel..., lists locations of 28 restaurants/planned locations, 1950s, EX, D25..................$45.00

Aunt Jemima, canister, features various Aunt Jemima products in colorful nostalgic background, dated 1983, 6x5¼" dia, EX, D25..................$42.00

Aunt Jemima, doll, Breakfast Bear, blue plush, wearing chef's hat/apron/bandana, 13", M, D25..................$175.00

Aunt Jemima, Junior Chef Pancake Set, Argo Industries, 1949, EX, D25 ....$150.00

Aunt Jemima, pancake shaker, yellow plastic, Perfect Pancakes In 10 Shakes...Aunt Jemima embossed on lid, 1940s-50s, 9", EX, D25..................$90.00

Aunt Jemima, place mat, The Story Of Aunt Jemima.../Aunt Jemima At Disneyland, drawings based on NC Wyeth art, 1955, 10x14", EX, D25 ....$35.00

Aunt Jemima, promotional poster book, Mr Grocer Here's Your Year-Round Promotional Parade!, ad layouts, etc, spiral, 1940s, EX, D25 ....$550.00

Aunt Jemima, recipe booklet, Pancakes Unlimited, full color, 31 pgs, 1958, 6x4½", EX, D25..................$75.00

Aunt Jemima, recipe cards, complete set of 16, I Know You Will Enjoy These...As Much As I Enjoy Sending Them..., M, D25..................$250.00

Aunt Jemima, restaurant table card, die-cut relief, ...Time For AJ Pancakes, trademark image/breakfast, 1953, 3x4¾", M, D25..................$45.00

Aunt Jemima, salt & pepper shakers, plastic, embossed Aunt Jemima/Uncle Mose, F&F Mold Die Works, 5¼", EX, D14, pair..................$75.00

Aunt Jemima, sign, cardboard stand-up, Aunt Jemima Says: Here's The Place To Get The Eatin'est Hot Cakes In Town!, 15x21", EX, A2..................$100.00

Aunt Jemima, spatula, metal with Plastic handle reading Hooray! It's Aunt Jemima Day, 1940s, EX, D25 .$125.00

Aunt Jemima Buckwheat Corn & Wheat Flour/Quaker Oats Co, product box, heavy cardboard, 2-sided stamped images of Aunt Jemima, contained 24 packages, 1911, 14x9", EX, A3 ....$100.00

Aunt Jemima Butter Lite Syrup, clipboard, masonite with metal clip, advertising on clip & board, post-1968 image, 15½x9", EX, D25..................$145.00

Aunt Jemima Flour, sign, porcelain, curved, Excels For All Baking Purposes, lettering above/below head image, 22x18", VG, A9 ....$4,000.00

Aunt Jemima Ready-Mix Buckwheat Corn & Wheat Flour, poster, Delicious! Let's Have Aunt Jemima's Often!..., cartoon image of family at breakfast, 20x13", EX, D25 ....$165.00

Aunt Jemima White Corn Meal, product bag, paper, 1950s, M (unused), D25..................$55.00

Aunt Jemima's Magic Pantry, sign, paper, You Can't Beat Your Aunt Jemima, Aunt Jemima holding plate of pancakes, framed, 21x17", Fair, A9..................$75.00

Aunty, crate label, Florida Citrus, smiling Southern black woman, M, D5 ....$30.00

Aurora Brewing Co, sign, tin, Greetings..., oval image of girl in pink dress/plumed hat, wood-grain beveled border, 1904, 19x13", VG, A7..................$350.00

Aurora Brewing Co, tray, square, Bertha, waist-length image, lettered rim, Meek Co litho, c 1905, 13x13", VG, A9..................$200.00

Austin Bantam, pin-back button, celluloid, round, I Want To Win.../Buy The Pittsburgh Sun-Telegram around man by car, 2" dia, EX, A2................................$470.00

Austin Bantam, sign, tin, The Austin Bantam...A Car To Run Around In, red/white/black, wood frame, 47x90", EX, A6 ....**$1,300.00**

Austin Powder Co, sign, paper, 3 dogs' heads, Edm H Osthaus, 1891, framed, 31x28", EX, A7 ....**$2,450.00**

Austin Service, sign, porcelain, Austin in fancy script above Service, red on white, black border, 2-sided, 17x36", G, A2..$250.00

Auto License Lock, sign, cardboard, Foil The Auto Thief With... above busy street scene, text below, wood frame, 26x18", VG, A2..$385.00

Auto-Lite Authorized Electric Service, sign, porcelain, white/red/blue on yellow, 2-sided, 25x36", EX, A2...**$550.00**

Autobacco, pocket tin, vertical, red, gold top, 4x3½x1½", EX+, A18...$150.00

Autobacco, tin, rectangular, red, round image of driver, short, G+, A18..$75.00

Autobacco, tin, rectangular, red, round image of driver, tall, EX+, A18..$220.00

Autocar Parts-Service, sign, porcelain, Autocar on emblem above Parts-Service on ribbon banner, black on white, 2-sided, 28x36", EX, A2 ....$715.00

Autocrat Coffee, can, ½-lb, key-wind lid, red bird & steaming cup on yellow, NM, A3..................................$75.00

Autocrat Coffee, can, 3-lb, pry lid, steaming cup on label, EX, A18...$125.00

Autocrat Sauerkraut, can label, formal dinner party, VG, D5 ....$25.00

Automatic Electric Washer Co, paperweight, celluloid over marble (?), round, Compliments Of..., bust image of pretty girl in profile, EX, A3 ....$55.00

Avalon Cigarettes, sign, cardboard stand-up, You'd Never Guess — They Cost You Less, seductive girl in hat/product pack, 30x20", VG, A8................................$35.00

Avio/Ace High Oils, sample display set, 6 corked vials on beveled blue/white base, 15x3x7" (with bottles), EX+, A1 ....$450.00

Avon, catalog, 1957, dealer book, gifts/Christmas, 46 pgs, D17 ....$75.00

Avon Skin So Soft, radio, bottle shape, NMIB, D13 .**$30.00**

Ayer's Cathartic Pills, sign, cardboard, die-cut, The Country Doctor, black doctor with baby on knee, brother watches, c 1883, 13x7", EX+, A9 ....$550.00

Ayer's Hair Vigor, sign, paper, Restores Gray Hair With Natural Vitality & Color, bust image of lady with thick dark hair, 13x10", VG, A9 ....$400.00

~~~ **B** ~~~

B&B Baby Talc, tin, sample, 2", VG+, A3 ....$55.00

B&B Liqeur, ashtray, amber glass bottle with white fired-on graphics, EX, D25 ....$35.00

B-B Dairy/Poultry Feeds, sign, tin, Feed The B-B Way/Maritime Milling Co Buffalo NY, black/red on yellow, black border, 12x24", EX, A3......................................$40.00

B-1 Lemon-Lime Soda, bottle display/ bottle, cardboard, More Zip In Every Sip!, white/red dot on blue/white sign, EX, D30..$65.00

B-1 Lemon-Lime Soda, bottle topper/bottle, cardboard, Don't Forget Your Carton Of..., lady shopper, EX, D30 ....$55.00

B-1 Lemon-Lime Soda, display, cardboard, automated, More Zip In Every Sip!, star lights flash behind screen, 1960, 16x13x4", EX, A23 ....$100.00

B-1 Lemon-Lime Soda, sign, tin, embossed, Drink upper left of red dot, Plus Vita in B1, black ground, 17x23", NM+, D30 ....$125.00

B-1 Lemon-Lime Soda, thermometer, tin, More Zip In Every Sip!, exclamation mark gauge on blue/white striped ground, embossed, 17x5", NM, A3......................$65.00

Babbit's Soap Powder, see BT Babbit's

Babcock & Teague Registered Druggists, calendar, 1900, cardboard, die-cut, girl in pink behind sign with violets, string-attached pad below, 12x8", NM+, A3 ....**$125.00**

Baby Dear Nursery Toilet Powder, tin, vertical rectangle, white on lt blue, EX+, A18 ....$180.00

Baby Stewart Breakfast Cocoa, tin, square, pry lid, orange, oval portrait, 6x3½x2½", EX+, A3......................$125.00

Baby Stewart Butter Scotch Patties, tin, 1-lb, oval portrait in center, EX, A3...$55.00

Baby's Own Powder, can, round, cardboard, image of baby on white, pink/blue ribbon trim top/bottom, 4", full, NM, A3..$60.00

Bachelor Cigars, display case, tin with framed glass lid on slant front, Canada's National Smoke on marque, 11x12", G, A2 ....$230.00

Bachrach Collar Buttons, display case, brass with glass dome front that pivots back to show buttons, Sampson Backrach, Pat 1910, 10x14", EX, A9 ....$1,800.00

Backwith Co, sign, paper/cardboard, Doe-Wah-Jack, profile image above company label on grained background, embossed, 14x10", EX+, A3 ....$150.00

Bacon & Stickney Eagle Brand Coffee, can, 1-lb, key-wind lid, blue eagle, blue/white, NM, A3 ....$65.00

Bacon & Stickney Eagle Brand Coffee, can, 1-lb, key-wind lid, eagle logo, blue/white, VG+, A18...............$30.00

Bacon & Stickney Sage, tin, blue/white, EX, A3 ......$25.00

Badger Refining Co's Badger Lubricant/Wadhams, can, 10-lb, round, slip lid, black on red, NM, A1.........$225.00

Bagdad Coffee, pail, 5-lb, EX+, A3 ....$200.00

Bagdad Short Cut, pocket tin, vertical, short, EX, A18..$115.00

Bagdad Short Cut, pocket tin, vertical, tall, VG+, A18 ..$125.00

Bagdad Tobacco, jar, ceramic, trademark image, blue, NM, A18 ....$165.00

Bagley's, see also Game Fine Cut

Bagley's Burley Boy Pipe & Cigarette Tobacco, pocket tin, vertical, EX+, A18 ....$950.00

Bagley's Burley Boy Pipe & Cigarette Tobacco, pocket tin, vertical, VG+, A3...............................$600.00

Bagley's Compass Cut Plug Tobacco, tin, round, pry lid, red/white on blue, lid missing o/w EX, A3.........$65.00

Bagley's Compass Cut Plug Tobacco, tin, round, slip lid, silver, paper label, 6x5" dia, EX, A18....................$65.00

Bagley's Fast Mail Chewing Tobacco, pail, tapered, slip lid, bail handle, red, VG+, A18 ....$385.00

Bagley's Fast Mail Chewing Tobacco, pocket tin, flat, VG, A18...$250.00

Bagley's Fast Mail Chewing Tobacco, shipping box, wood, paper labels, original leather strap, 15x10", EX+, A3...$515.00

Bagley's Lime Kiln Club Smoking Tobacco, tin, rectangular, rounded corners, 4x6", EX, A18......................$75.00

Bagley's Old Colony Tobacco, pocket tin, vertical, silver, EX, A18...$140.00

Bagley's Old Colony Tobacco, pocket tin, vertical, white, EX+, A18...$175.00

Bagley's Old Colony Tobacco, tin, rectangular, slip lid, 4x3x3", scarce, NM, A18...............................$110.00

Bagley's Old Colony Tobacco, tin, round, ashtray lid, silver, 6", EX+, A18...$120.00

Bagley's Red Belt Pipe or Cigarette Tobacco, pocket tin, vertical, red on white, short, EX+, A18..............$115.00

Bagley's Sun Cured, sign, papier-mache, round hanger, Union Made, molded face of sun framed by white lettering on black, 25" dia, VG, A7................$700.00

Bagley's Sweet Tips, display box, cardboard, name/tilted pocket tin on front, white on red, held 12 tins, 10x6x3", EX+, A15...$100.00

Bagley's Sweet Tips, pocket tin, vertical, gold with black label, oval, VG+, A3 ....$65.00

Bagley's Sweet Tips, pocket tin, vertical, gold with black label, regular, EX+, A3....................................$140.00

Bagley's Wild Fruit Flake Cut Tobacco, lunch box, VG+, A18...$85.00

Bagley's Yoc-O-May Hash Cut, pocket tin, flat, red on yellow, EX+, A18...$50.00

Bailarina Beer, label, 11-oz, Vernon Brewing Co/CA, IRTP or WF statement, 1933-50, M (traces of paper or scrapes on back), A10...$35.00

Bailey's Supreme Coffee, can, 1-lb, key-wind lid, EX+, A3...$85.00

Baker's Chocolate, jar, Caracas Chocolate Tablets, glass, square, thumbprint lid, embossed advertising, 5¢ A Bundle, 11x4½", EX, A15...$400.00

Baker's Chocolate, poster, image of Chocolate Girl with tray, matted & framed, 36x26", NM, D8.............$300.00

Baker's Chocolate, sign, tin, Pure/Delicious/Nutritious/Cost Less Than One Cent A Cup, Chocolate Girl with tray, framed, 23x17", VG, A7....................................$700.00

Baker's Chocolate, tin, Breakfast Cocoa, round, sample, EX, D37 ....$145.00

Baker's Chocolate, tin, Century Vanilla Chocolate, round, sample, EX, D37 ....$50.00

Baker's Chocolate, tin, Cocoa, square, sample, EX, D37 ....$120.00

Baker's Chocolate, tin, Cocoa, square, 10-lb, G, A2 ...**$200.00**

Baker's Chocolate, tray, oval, 4 product packages on plain background, decorative rim, 1900-10, 17", rare, EX, A13 ....**$150.00**

Baker's Friend Peaches, can label, shows baker trimming pie, M, D5 ....**$35.00**

Bald Eagle, cigar box label, inner lid, eagle perched on rock, 6x9", M, D5 ....**$30.00**

Ball Blue Washing Crystal, sign, paper, lady/children in landscape, wood frame, image: 19x26", G, A9 ..**$900.00**

Ballantine & Co's Export Beer, sign, reverse on glass, black lettering/trademark on gold leaf, orante gold frame, 29x42", VG+, A8 ....**$500.00**

Ballantine Ale, sign, neon, spells out name/3 intertwined yellow circles, 1950s, 3-color, 13x23", EX+, A19 ....**$180.00**

Ballantine Ale, toy train boxcar, HO scale, yellow, 1960s, NM+, A19 ....**$25.00**

Ballard Pancake Flour, sign, cardboard, Fresh.../Good & Healthy, boy ready to take a bite & product box on table, 7x13", VG, A3 ....**$60.00**

Balsam-Wool Blanket, sign, tin, It Tucks In!, lettering over silhouette image of snow-covered house on hillside with trees, 23x35", EX, A9 ....**$70.00**

Baltimore American Beer/American Brewery Inc, matchbook, 20 strike, front striker, M, D28 ....**$10.00**

Baltimore Enamel & Novelty Co, catalog, Signs — How To Use & What Kind To Use, 1926, full-color illustrations, 8x11", EX, A2 ....**$415.00**

Bambino Smoking Tobacco, pocket tin, vertical, EX+, A18............**$1,600.00**

Banania Beverage, cup/plate/canister, china cup & plate, tin canister marked Scure Poudre (Powdered Sugar), Creation Thalassa, EX, D25, set............**$225.00**

Bang-O Pop Corn, container, round, cardboard with tin top/bottom, EX (full), A3 ....**$35.00**

Bang-O Pop Corn, container, round, tin, Yellow Hybrid, NM (full), A18 ....**$85.00**

Bank Note, cigar tin, vertical square, rounded corners, slip lid, Five Cents, NM, A18/A3, from $40 to............**$60.00**

Bank Roll Tobacco, tin, round, slip lid, NM, D6 ..$200.00

Banker's Bond, tin, round, slip lid, Hand Made/5¢, VG+, A18............**$20.00**

Banner Baking Powder, sign, paper, Great American Powder For Great American People, Uncle Sam on balcony, crowd, eagle above, 20x30", G, A9............**$300.00**

Banner Fine Cut, match holder, heavy cast-metal banner with large flower, nickel-plated, green lettering, 7x5", EX, A6............**$220.00**

Banner Rolled Oats/Quaker Oats Co, container, 3-lb, cardboard, blue/yellow/white, EX, A3............**$55.00**

Banquet Club Coffee, can, 1-lb, key-wind lid, blue/white on silver, EX+, A3............**$65.00**

Banquet Club Coffee, can, 1-lb, key-wind lid, white with white name on blue center band, red trim, NM, A3............**$20.00**

Banquet Roasted Moca Java Coffee/OV Tracy & Co can, 2-lb, vertical box, white on red, Bouquet Coffee trademark image of steaming cup, EX, A18............**$150.00**

Banquet Tea, teapot dispenser, ceramic, black with embossed white lettering, no stand, 11", VG, A9..**$50.00**

Banquet Tea, teapot dispenser, ceramic, black with embossed white lettering, black metal stand, 11", EX+, A2 ....$450.00

Bantam, cigar box label, inner lid, cock fight, 6x9", EX, D5 ....**$45.00**

Bantam '60,' postcard, For Business/For Pleasure/Up To 60 Miles Per Gallon/America's Only Economy Car, shows roadster/van, NM, A17 ....**$250.00**

Bar-None Syrup, can, ½-gal, vertical rectangle, small round screw lid, lady on rearing horse/wagon train graphics, EX, A3............**$100.00**

Bar-None Syrup, can, 5-lb, vertical rectangle, small round screw lid, bucking bronc/wagon train graphics, EX, A3............**$70.00**

Barbarossa Premium Beer, sign, composition hanger, rounded corners, round image on lt wood-tone, gold decor/lettering, embossed, 14x11", NM, A3............**$50.00**

Barber Shop, pole, stained glass striped panels with ornate brass work, lighted globe atop, 82", EX, A2..**$2,200.00**

Barber Shop, pole, wood with wire hanger, hand-painted, gold ball atop red/white/blue pole, 35", VG, A6..**$500.00**

Barber Shop, sign, flange, porcelain, red/white/blue diagonal stripes around white block letters on blue, blue trim, 12x24", EX, A3 ....**$75.00**

Barber Shop, sign, porcelain, curved, white lettering on blue with red/white/blue diagonally striped border, 24x15", VG+, A6............**$100.00**

Barbour's Acadia Baking Powder, tin, round, screw lid, red/yellow/red, image of Evangeline's Well-Grand Pre, NM, A3............**$30.00**

Barker's Nerve & Bone Liniment, sign, paper, ...For Men & Beast..., vast forest scene with animals/bridge spanning mountain river, 25x32", EX, A6............**$800.00**

Barney & Berry, display, cardboard, die-cut image of ice skate blade with lettering/decoration on blade, 8x34", EX, A6..$260.00

Barq's, sign, cardboard, Drink.../It's Good, red/white lettering at left of bottle on red dot, blue ground, 11x28", NM, D30 ....$75.00

Barq's, sign, flange, metal, oval, Drink.../It's Good, with bottle, orange/white/brown on black, 14x22", EX, A6........$90.00

Barq's, sign, tin, Drink.../It's Good Ice Cold on blue center, black Gas/Oil price panels above/below, 1930s, 35x12", EX, A13..$550.00

Barrington Hall Coffee, can, 1-lb, key-wind lid, white on red, EX+, A3..$50.00

Barrister, cigar box label, inner lid, shows attorney/courthouse/court scene, 6x9", M, D5..$25.00

Bartel Perfection Work & Play Clothes, sign, cardboard stand-up, Stands The Wear & Tear, man/4 boys in various activities in landscape, 1920, 17x24", VG+, A3..$140.00

Bartels, scoreboard, The Professor Says.../There Is None Better at top of baseball scoreboard, horizontal, EX, D30..$300.00

Bartels Brewing Co, tray, round, lancer looking up at frothy stein, ca 1900, 12" dia, NM+, A3..$150.00

Bartels Malt Extract, sign, tin/cardboard, An Ideal Tonic..., bottle left of lettering, beveled, 6x13", EX, A1.....$70.00

Bartholomay Beers, Ales & Porter, tip tray, round, deep rim, girl on winged wheel, C Shonk litho, 4" dia, EX+, A8..$115.00

Bartholomay Brewery Rienzi Beer, tip tray, round, cavalier on horse, EX, A8..$210.00

Bartholomy Brewing Co, sign, cardboard, girl on winged wheel in clouds, Hyneman & Schmidt litho, framed, 41x30", EX, A7..$2,250.00

Bartles Gasoline, sign, porcelain, round, Bartles Gasoline around arrow over 'B' logo, yellow/black/blue, orange arrow, 42" dia, EX, A2..$1,650.00

Basketball, crate label, lemon, women playing basketball, 1920, EX, D5..$50.00

Baskin Robbins, toy figures, vinyl, set of 3, 2 ice-cream clown heads with cone hats/ice-cream man with paper-cup body, EX, D20..$45.00

Bassett's Licorice All Sorts, tin, oblong octagon, green/yellow, heads of boy & girl with open product box, 4x6x9", EX, A3..$25.00

Bata Super Bullets Sneakers, display sneaker, plaster, 3-D, white 'Chuck Taylor' type, 24", VG, A9 ....$250.00

Baterland/Schultz & Co's Family Soaps, sign, paper, Dutch girl holding oversized bar of Baterland Soap, Courier litho, 44x25", VG, A9..$75.00

Battington Hall Coffee, can, 1-lb, key-wind lid, NM, A18..$40.00

Bauer & Black Baby Talc, tin, sample, EX+, A3.......$85.00

Baum's Polish, sign, cardboard die-cut stand-up, Shines Like Magic..., pictures front end of car with girl driver, 13x9", EX+, D22..$75.00

Bausch & Lomb, catalog, 1929, Microscopes & Scientific Instruments, 318 pgs, EX, D17..$90.00

Bavarian Lager Beer, label, 12-oz, Wyandotte Brewing Co/MI, IRTP or WF statement, 1933-50, M, A10..$35.00

Baver & Black Elastic Supports, display figures, composition, man & woman on beveled base wearing various supports, 30", VG, A6..$250.00

Baxter's Drum 5¢ Cigar, sign, tin, Baxter's above lettered drum, red/black on white, embossed, 28x22", VG, A6..$400.00

Bay, gas globe, 3-pc, white plastic body with glass lenses, red/black/white Bay shield on white, 13½", NM, A6..$200.00

Bay State Lawn Mower, trade card, The Old Homestead, colorful farm scene with child using Bay State Lawn Mower, 3x6", EX, A6..$65.00

Bay State Paints & Varnishes, sign, flange, porcelain, black lettering above/below round pilgrim logo on green band, orange ground, 19x12", NM, A24..$300.00

Bay State Standard Screw Fastened Boots & Shoes, sign, paper, One Pair Of These Boots Or Shoes Will Outwear Two Pairs Nailed Or Pegged, girl with roses, 28x13", G, A9..$250.00

Bay State Standard Screw Fastened Boots & Shoes, sign, paper, oval image of gent giving lady shoes, badminton game beyond, 15x20", EX+, A9..$2,600.00

Bayuk Mapacuba Cigars, humidor display case, simulated wood-grain tin with slanted glass front/marque, 17x22", VG, A9..$250.00

Bayuk Philadelphia Cigar, display stand, glass/metal, Three Likeable Sizes, sign in center, red/black/white/gold, gold trim, 81x11x8", EX, A6..$150.00

Beachwood Roaster Fresh Coffee, can, 1-lb, key-wind lid, metallic purple with white/black lettering & trim, NM+, A3..$35.00

Beacon Blankets, sign, cardboard, die-cut stand-up, B-r-r-r-r! says man in bed pulling up blanket, 41x40", EX (unused), A24..$130.00

Beacon Blankets (Traveling Rugs & Motor Robes), sign, cardboard, Beacon Blankets Make Warm Friends, pictorial inset of lady entering car upper right, 27x21", VG+, A6..$180.00

Beacon Coal, sign, tin, round, Nature Made It Good/Modern Methods Make It Better!, name on beam of light from lighthouse, 14", NM, A3..$125.00

Beacon Oil, sign, porcelain, round, black/white lettering around center of 'spinning' white/green field, 2-sided, 30", NM, A1..$1,150.00

Beacon Shoes, mirror/sign, Union Made, name radiates from light of lighthouse above mirror, wood-tone shaped frame, 27x19", G, A7..$150.00

Bear, sign, tin, die-cut, happy bear on white above white name on red, beveled, 24x20", EX, A6 ....**$160.00**

Bear Authorized Wheel Aligning/Axle & Frame Service, sign, neon/porcelain, neon around bear shape holding sign, 56x45", NM+, A6 ....**$3,000.00**

Bear Creek, crate label, Oregon pear, name in white above snarling bear on black background, Medford, M, D12..**$65.00**

Bear Springs Distributors, sign, porcelain, ...London, Ont/Guaranteed..., 2 bears, red/white/black, curved top corners, 2-sided, 1940s-50s, NM, A13..................**$525.00**

Bear Wheel-Steering Service, sign, tin, die-cut bear holding sign, red/black on yellow, 2-sided, 40x29", EX+, A6 ....**$325.00**

Bear-Ring Motor Oil/Coleman Oil Co, can, 1-qt, bear holding piston ring, red/white, EX, A1 ....**$925.00**

Bear's Jack Frost For Head Colds, tin, round, Free Sample, trademark bear, EX, D37 ....**$35.00**

Bears Brothers Paint, change tray, copper plating over plastic, 2 figural bears holding oval sign atop recessed tray, VG, A2 ....**$100.00**

Bears' Honeydew Cigarettes/London, sign, porcelain, black/red lettering & image of elephant on yellow, red/black border, 18x13", EX, A6 ....**$450.00**

Beatles, see With the Beatles Talc

Beats All, cigar box label, inner lid, filigreed image of boy's head with sports crowd beyond, Schmidt & Co, 1899, EX, A5...**$220.00**

Becker's Fisherman's Grain, sign, paper, fisherman reeling in large boot, Milwaukee litho, framed, image: 20x27", VG+, A9...**$850.00**

Beech-Nut Baby Food, sign, cardboard stand-up, It's Beech-Nut above 4 children at table, embossed, dated 1905, 10x12", EX+, A15 ....**$300.00**

Beech-Nut Black Cough Drops, sign, trolley, Keep A Package Between You & A Cold, open pack between man & cold, 1920s-30s, 11x21", NM, A13........................**$200.00**

Beech-Nut Chewing Tobacco, sign, porcelain, Chewing lettered on arrow pointing to unopened pack, red/white/blue, 11x22", EX+, A1 ....**$325.00**

Beech-Nut Chewing Tobacco, store bin, tin, slant lid, blue, We Keep It Fresh/Quality Made It Famous, EX+, A18 ...**$730.00**

Beech-Nut Chewing Tobacco, store bin, tin, slant lid, yellow, It's Dust Proof/Quality Made It Famous, VG+, A18 ....**$175.00**

Beech-Nut Coffee/Foods Of Finest Flavor, display sign, cardboard trifold with coffee can on stage, Grown In The High Tropics, mountain scene, 28x48", EX, A2 ....**$650.00**

Beech-Nut Gum, display box, Mint Flavored/5¢, shows young girl, no gum packs, G, A16 ....**$150.00**

Beech-Nut Gum, display box, Wintergreen Flavored/5¢, shows young girl, complete with original gum packs, rare, G+, A16...**$475.00**

Beech-Nut Gum, display case, tin, 2-tiered with curved sides, lt wood-tone, front panel shows various flavors, 10x6x20", EX+, A1 ....**$100.00**

Beech-Nut Gum, display case, tin, 4-tiered slanted shelves with marque, 15x6x7", VG+, A15 ....**$850.00**

Beech-Nut Gum, sign, cardboard die-cut stand-up, lady in red dress offering a piece of gum from labeled drum, 39x14", VG+, A1..**$80.00**

Beech-Nut Gum, trolley sign, cardboard, Famous For Fine Flavor/Wonderful In Chewyness, girl/large pack on white, 11x21", NM, A15..**$550.00**

Beech-Nut Preserves/Peanut Butter, stamps, red or blue images of children & product, set of 6, 2x1½", NM+, A3 ....**$35.00**

Beech-Nut Products, display sign, cardboard trifold, The Mohawk Valley.../Entrance To.../Gateway To Flavor/The Home Of..., 36x60", VG, A6...................................**$50.00**

Beech-Nut Tomato Catsup, trolley sign, cardboard, Excuse Me For Reaching, elderly gent reaching for catsup bottle, white ground, 12x21", VG, A6............................**$100.00**

Beech-Nut Whole Bean Coffee, can, 1-lb, slip lid, red paper label, white steaming cup, EX, A3 ....**$40.00**

Beehive Overalls, pocket mirror, oval, bare-shouldered girl in overalls, NM, A3...**$300.00**

Beeman's Gum, see also Dentyne/Clove/Beeman's/ Chicklets Gum

Beeman's Pepsin Gum, display box, Good For Digestion, round portrait/banner, VG, A16.............................$60.00

Beeman's Pepsin Gum, display case, wood with glass sides/top, decal on front, 12x21x21", EX, A6.....$200.00

Beeman's Pepsin Gum, watch fob, celluloid with leather strap, lettering around head image on Mr Beeman, multicolored, EX, A6..$80.00

Bel Bon Talcum Powder For Babies, tin, gold trim, EX+, A18..$125.00

Bel-Cap-Sic Plaster, calendar, 1903, cardboard die-cut trifold, months flank girl/dog in oval center, filigree/floral trim, 10x13", EX+, A3 ....$50.00

Belden Auto Garage, calendar, 1919, cardboard, die-cut, steamship bursting with pink roses, small pad, 11x17", incomplete, VG+, A3 ....$75.00

Belfast Old Fashioned Mug Root Beer, thermometer, round dial with mug in center, 1950, NM, A1 ....$275.00

Bell (The) Magnolia Mills Roasted Coffee, can, 2-lb, smaller round slip lid, red, gold stenciling, bell logo, ca 1880, EX+, A3...$240.00

Bell Ethyl, gas globe, 3-pc, white glass body, metal base, glass lenses, name above Ethyl on bell logo, 13½" dia, EX, A6 ....$750.00

Bell Ethyl, gas globe, 3-pc, white plastic Capolite body, BELL in blue & white above blue bell with Ethyl logo on orange, NM, A1 ....$300.00

Bell Oil Co's Lubricants, sign, porcelain, white bell logo & lettering on red, 4x27", EX+, A15 ....$700.00

Bell System, globe, milk glass, Local & Long Distance Telephone lettered on blue-painted bell, 10", NM+, A13 ....$450.00

Bell System, sign, flange, Illinois Bell Telephone Co/American Telephone & Telegraph Co surrounds Bell System bell, 12x11", EX+, A13 ....$140.00

Bell System, sign, porcelain, Local Long Distance Telephone lettered on bell against white dot, blue square border, 17x17", EX+, A13 ....$225.00

Bell System, sign, porcelain, Public Telephone in white right of New England/Bell System bell logo, blue ground, 6x19", VG+, A13 ....$130.00

Bell System, sign, porcelain, Telephone Payments, blue die-cut emblem with lettering above/below round bell logo, 24x18", EX+, A13 ....$400.00

Bell's Imperial Coffee, pocket mirror, EX, A6 ....$50.00

Bell's Mocha & Java Coffee, pocket mirror, NM, A3 ..$55.00
Belle of Buffalo Fine Cut, see Buffalo Tobacco Works

Bellmore Whiskey, sign, tin hanger, curled corners, Bernard Fisher/product name lettered around man with bottle/glass, 14x14", EX, A1 ....$350.00

Belmont Beer, tray, round, deep rim, Don't Say Beer Say Belmont, logo with name/bell/hops, red/white/blue, 14" dia, EX, A19 ....$165.00

Belt, crate label, California orange, encircled by a tooled belt, E Highlands, EX, D3 ....$5.00

Belvedere, cigar box label, outer, men & women dining, 4½x4½", EX, D5...$40.00

Ben Bey Cigars, tin, rectangular, square corners, Egyptians on horses in desert, decorative border, EX+, A3.$90.00

Ben Franklin Fire Insurance Co, sign, tin, bust image on emblem with company name above/below, framed, HD Beach litho, c 1905, VG, A9..............................$475.00

Ben-Hur Coffee, can, 1-lb, key-wind lid, red, EX, A18/A3, from $30 to..$50.00

Ben-Hur Pure Allspice, tin, 2-oz, red, NM+ (unopened), A3 ....$22.00

Ben-Hur 5¢ Cigars, sign, tin, fancy oval image of rider on chariot on simulated wood backdround, C Shonk litho, beveled, 19x27", EX, A9 ....$650.00

Bendix Home Laundry, sign, neon, glass/metal Deco housing, Washes/Rinses/Damp Dries...Automatically, lights red, 10x33", EX, A6...$275.00

Bengal Brand Coffee, can, cardboard with tin top/bottom, paper label, VG, A3..$100.00

Bengal Ranges, clock, octagonal, light-up, red border and numbers around red trademark center, 18x18", NOS, A6 ....$475.00

Benson & Hedges Cigarettes, pen, ball point, gold-tone, 1970s, NM, D24.................................**$6.00**

Benton Mixture Smoking Tobacco, tin, horizontal box, square corners, yellow, 2x4½x3", EX, A18..........**$70.00**

Berger, sign, tin, die-cut image of majorette holding large bottle, multicolored, 19x6", EX, A6......................**$180.00**

Bergoff Beer, poster/calendar, 1939, image of baseball game flanked by vertical rows of prominent players, calendar below, VG+, A3.................................**$55.00**

Berina Malted Milk Food, sign, porcelain, For Energy & Strength, Scotsman with hand on hip peering over lake, large product box, 24x60", EX+, A13...$675.00

Berkhardt Special, display sign, bottle on lighted arched panel atop round gold/red stepped base, 1930s-40s, 14x7", EX+, A13.................................**$350.00**

Berma Choice Mountain Grown Coffee, can, 1-lb, screw lid, brown/metallic gold, EX, A18......................**$30.00**

Berma Coffee, can, 1-lb, screw lid, red, NM, A18.....**$65.00**

Bermarine Quinine Pomade, tin, rectangular, slip lid, 1½x2½x3", EX, D37.................................**$45.00**

Bermarine Quinine Pomade, tin, round, Free Sample, ¼x1½" dia, EX, D37.................................**$30.00**

Bernice Fine Flavor Coffee, can, 1-lb, key-wind lid, NM (unused), A18.................................**$85.00**

Berrella Beverage, label, 12-oz, Oertel Co/Louisville KY, L-type permit #, 1920-28, EX, A10......................**$42.00**

Best Strike, crate label, apple, baseball player, 1920, M, D5/D12.................................**$45.00**

Best Value, cigar box label, inner lid, gold scales, 6x9", M, D5.................................**$30.00**

Best Value Coffee, can, 1-lb, key-wind lid, blue, EX+, A3..**$45.00**

Bestoval Crushed Plug, see Schermerhorn's

Bestyet Coffee, can, 1-lb, key-wind lid, EX+, A18....**$80.00**

Betsy Ross 5¢ Cigar, cigar cutter, cast-iron base holds nickel-plated placard with paper image, 9", VG, A2.........**$300.00**

Betty Zane Ohio Super Yellow Popcorn, can, yellow, M (full), A3.................................$165.00

Betty Zane Popcorn, can, silver, NM (full), A18.$120.00

Betty Zane White Popcorn, can, white, EX+ (full), A18..$110.00

Beverly Homogenized Peanut Butter, can, 48-oz, red with multicolored lettering, boy & girl graphics, Canadian, EX+, A3.**$100.00**

Beverwyck Famous Lager, tip tray, round, lettering on rim around exterior factory scene with horse-&-buggy traffic, VG+, A8.................................**$100.00**

Beverwyck Irish Cream Ale, sign, cardboard, dog looking at Irishman holding glass & bottle behind Dutch door, wooden frame, 18x15", EX+, A8.................................**$60.00**

Beverwyck Irish Cream Ale, sign, cardboard, dog looking at Irishman holding glass & 2 puppies while seated on bench, wooden frame, 18x15", EX, A8.................................**$50.00**

Bevo, label, 12-oz, Anheuser-Busch/St Louis, Pro (no L-type Perit #), 1920-28, EX+ (traces of paper or scrapes on back), A10.................................**$85.00**

Bevo, magazine ad, A-&-eagle logo on horseshoe-shaped border around text above image of factory & traffic, 14x10", VG, A8.................................**$40.00**

Bevo, sign, cardboard hanger, The All-Year-Round Soft Drink, emblem flanked by bottle & mascot, 8x13", VG+, A8.................................**$135.00**

Bevo, sign, paper, nymph holding up glass of Bevo while resting on rocky cliff with A-&-eagle logo, 24", EX, A2.......**$750.00**

Bevo, tip tray, rectangular, The All-Year-Round Soft Drink, horse-drawn wagon, 6½", EX+, A8.................................**$300.00**

Bevo, tray, rectangular, 6 horses pulling wagon with product & fox, lettered rim, 11x13", G, A9......................**$125.00**

BF Goodrich, sign, paper, Aida, artist Seppard Muhltz (?), Gray Co litho, c 1901, 34x28", VG, A9.................................**$125.00**

BF Goodrich, sign, paper, Goodrich Tires around head of girl looking down, company name below, Gies & Co, c 1897, 30x25", EX, A9.................................**$300.00**

BF Goodrich, sign, paper, Kate, artist A Asti, c 1900, 34x28", VG+, A9.................................**$150.00**

BF Goodrich, sign, paper, The Goodrich Rubber Man's Vacation/Moonlight On Rubber Island, bears at campsite, c 1899, 25x32", EX, A9.................................**$275.00**

BF Gravely's Best Flue Cured Plug Cut, tin, horizontal box square corners, Ginna, pre-1901, EX, A18..............**$75.00**

Bickmore Easy-Shave Cream, display sign, cardboard die-cut stand-up, 35¢, round image of man loading shaving brush with cream, 31x21", EX, A6..$135.00

Bickmore Fly Salve, tin, round, 'Keeps-'Em-Away' From Farmers-Woodsmen-Sportsmen & Campers..., ¼x1¼", EX, D37.**$18.00**

Bickmore's Gall Cure, sign, cardboard die-cut trifold, delivery wagon/man with horse/farmer & cows, 34x50", VG, A6.................................**$250.00**

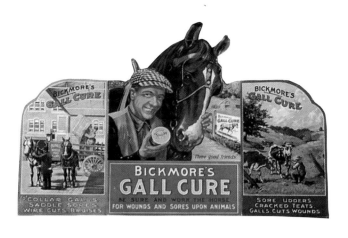

Bickmore's Gall Cure, sign, cardboard die-cut trifold, delivery wagon/man with horse/farmer with cows, 34x50", NM, D30 ....**$450.00**

Bidu, sign, tin, We Serve Ice Cold.../The New South American Drink, caballero logo, embossed, curved corners, 16x16", EX, A1 ....**$125.00**

Bidwell Thresher Works, thermometer, wood, arched top/square bottom, pictures various machines on white, 15x6", EX+, A15 ....**$200.00**

Bieres du Coq Hardi, sign, flange, porcelain, oval, name above crowing rooster standing on barrel, sun-striped background, 25x19", EX, A6 ....**$650.00**

Big 'C' Brand Baltimore Oysters, pail, 1-gal, straight-sided, bail handle, bull's-eye logo on black/white diamond background, EX, A3.......................................**$80.00**

Big Bear Cigar, cigar box label, inner lid, brown bear next to large cigar, 1903, 6x9", M, D5 ....**$30.00**

Big Bear Cigar, cigar box label, outer, bear holding cigar, 1903, 4½x4½", M, D5 ....**$12.00**

Big Bear Ice Cream, sign, tin, Finest Quality, pictures sundae on red/white divided ground, curved corners, 20x20", NM (NOS), A1 ....**$375.00**

Big Ben Chewing Tobacco, tin, round, key-wind lid, clock, EX+, A18...**$30.00**

Big Ben Tobacco, pocket tin, vertical, clock, EX, A18..**$950.00**

Big Ben Tobacco, pocket tin, vertical, horse, EX, A18 ...**$40.00**

Big Ben Tobacco, pocket tin, vertical, horse, marked Specimen, EX+, A3 ....**$50.00**

Big Ben Tobacco, sign, paper, product name above image of pocket tin left of Beau Peavine (champion stallion) & rider, 14x20", NM, D22 ....**$45.00**

Big Ben Tobacco, tin, round, pry lid, horse, EX+, A18.**$50.00**

Big Boy, ashtray, glass, round, red logo in center, 3¾" dia, EX, D25...**$28.00**

Big Boy, figurine, Big Boy with hamburger, pewter, limited edition, M, D25 ....**$100.00**

Big Boy, night light, plastic, 1974, 7", EX, D27...........**$75.00**

Big Boy, salt & pepper shakers, ceramic, Big Boy figures, vintage, EX, D25 ....**$350.00**

Big Boy, sign, tin, A Real Drink..., boy's head sipping on bottle, yellow-orange background, red/black border, 35x11", EX, D30 ....**$275.00**

Big Boy (Bob's), comics, Adventures of Big Boy, 6 issues, VG+, A3 ....**$25.00**

Big Boy (Bob's), matchbook, image of Big Boy serving hamburger/Bob's Seasoning Salt on back, EX (unused), D25...**$32.00**

Big Boy (Bob's), matchbook, lists California locations, red/tan/white on brown, lettering on each match, EX, D25 ....**$35.00**

Big Boy (Elias), plate, china, oval, Elias trademark on rim with decorative flowers/stems/leaves, 9½", EX, D25 .....**$125.00**

Big Boy (Frisch's), ashtray, glass, square with round bowl, Frisch's logo/American's Favorite Hamburger in center, 3½x3½", EX, D25...**$28.00**

Big Boy (Frisch's), matchbook, die-cut, Big Boy with hamburger on front/back, 20 strike, front striker, Lion Match Co, M, D28 ....**$8.00**

Big Boy (Kip's), matchbook cover, Merry Christmas, Big Boy dressed as Santa next to wreath on white, EX, D25.**$30.00**

Big Boy Beverages, bottle topper, cardboard, Drink Big Boy/For Growing Boys & Everyone/All Flavors, 4 boys playing marbles, 15x10", NM, A3 ....**$110.00**

Big Boy Beverages, sign, washable stock paper, Drink Big Boy Beverages lettered next to boy sipping from bottle on yellow, 18x35", EX+, A3 ....**$110.00**

Big Boy Pale Dry, sign, tin, ...In Green Bottles Only flanked by bottle/5¢ symbol, blue/white, 10x19", NM (NOS), D30...**$125.00**

Big Boy Soda, sign, tin, A Real Drink, image of boy's head sipping from straw on yellow, self-framed, 1940s, 35x11", EX+, A13...**$275.00**

Big Chief, crate label, Canadian apple, Indian in full headdress, Vernon BC, M, D12...........................**$10.00**

Big Chief Malt Syrup, can label, man in uniform smoking cigar, 1929, EX, D5 ....**$30.00**

Big Giant Cola, sign, tin, 16 oz (on bottle cap)/Bigger 'N Better..., with bottle, red/white/blue, 12x30", NM+, D30 ....**$100.00**

Big Giant Cola, sign, tin, 16 oz/For A Real Lift!/More For Your Money!, weight lifter bottle, red/white/blue, blue trim, 24x12", EX, D30 ....**$100.00**

Big Hit Coffee, can, 1-lb, key-wind lid, red, white/black lettering, NM, A3 ....**$40.00**

Big Horn Coffee, can, 1-lb, key-wind lid, white, image of ram in center, rare, G+, A3 ....**$160.00**

Big Jo Flour, sign, tin, The Secret Of Better Baking on brown strip below product bag/name on yellow, brown border, 8x12", NM, A3 ....**$25.00**

Big Jo Flour, tip tray, round, lettering on rim around Big Jo in block letters with back light, 4" dia, EX+, A8 ..**$60.00**

Blackhawk Beer, tray, round, deep rim, round logo in center, 13" dia, VG+, A8......................$80.00

Blackwell's (WT) Durham, trade card, Which Is The Best Looking Tobacco?/Lift Up The Cover & Find Out, man's head in pipe, 5x3", VG, A5........................$75.00

Blackwell's Durham Smoking Tobacco, sign, tin, exterior factory scene, Tuchfarber litho, wood frame, 31x24", EX, A7.........................$4,000.00

Blair's Snow White Hair Beautifier, tin, round, image of couple's heads with lettering, decorative border, 1x3½", EX, D37.........................$25.00

Blake's Milk & Cream, light cover, milk-bottle shape, milk glass, We Sell...Better Milk For Particular People, 20x8" dia, VG, A6......................$1,000.00

Blanke's Mojav Coffee, can, 2-lb, square, smaller round slip lid, girl on horse, early, VG+, A3........................$60.00

Blatz Beer, display, bottle/pilsner glass on base with sign, plastic, glass bubbles, 13", VG+, A8........................$130.00

Blatz Beer, display figure, bottle man holding tray with mug, VG+, A8........................$75.00

Blatz Beer, display figure, keg man holding mug while standing next to sign, EX, A8........................$100.00

Blatz Beer, display figures, baseball players (barrel man as ump/bottle man as catcher/can man as runner), VG+, A8.....**$175.00**

Blatz Beer, match safe, brass-colored, engraved, EX, A8....**$100.00**

Blatz Beer/Val Blatz Brg Co, sign, canvas, red car parked next to lake & partons on porch of inn, mountains in distance, gold frame, 27x35", EX, A7....................**$1,300.00**

Blatz Brewing Co, sign, tin, bottles/glasses on table reflected against mirror/drape, HD Beach litho, self-framed, 22x28", EX, A9........................$500.00

Blatz Old Heidelberg Beer, sign, plaster relief, barmaid dancing atop barrel, name below, multicolored, 1933, 36x22", VG, A3........................$120.00

Blatz Old Heidelberg Beer, sign, plaster relief, patrons enjoying brew under tree with river/castle beyond, multicolored, 1933, 25x43", EX+, A7........................$225.00

Blatz Old Heidelberg Beer, toy train boxcar, HO scale, yellow, 1950s, NM, A19........................$100.00

Blatz Old Heidelberg Beer, tray, rectangular, 4 men at table under tree, river valley beyond, brown rim, 1930s, 11x13", NM+, A19........................$185.00

Blend 150 Regular Grind Coffee, can, 1-lb, key-wind lid, gold/blue, VG+, A3........................$30.00

Bleriot, cigar box label, inner lid, man/airplane, 1909, 6x9", EX, D5........................$60.00

Bleser Better Beer/Manitowoc WI, tap knob, ball shape, black with red/gold/brown/mustard metal insert, VG+, A8........................$100.00

Blevins Bee Hive Hybrid Popcorn, can, 10-lb, white, no lid o/w EX+, A3........................$25.00

Blony Gum, display, cardboard truck with wooden wheels, lithoed advertising, Biggest Piece Of Gum In The World..., 8x14", EX, A6........................$350.00

Bludwine, sign, flange, Ice Cold Bludwine For Your Health's Sake 5¢, blue/red/green panel, bottle on white, 1915, 10x13", EX, A13........................$475.00

Blue & Scarlett Plug Cut, tin, rectangular, slip lid, paper label, red/white/blue, gold trim, 1902 stamp, 4x6", EX, A18........................$150.00

Blue Belle Cigar, cigar box labels, 2-pc set, embellished round bust image of lady, Schmidt & Co #1042/1043, VG+, A5........................$120.00

Blue Bird Cigars, cigar box label, inner lid, bird perched on fence, 6x9", VG, D5........................$60.00

Blue Bird Coffee, pail, 3-lb, straight-sided, slip lid, bail handle, yellow/red, EX+, A3........................$400.00

Blue Bird Marsh-Mallows, tin, round, pry lid, yellow, EX+, A3........................$80.00

Blue Boar, tin, round, smaller round slip lid, embossed town scene on bare metal, flared bottom, EX, A18.....**$100.00**

Blue Boar Cut Plug Tobacco, tin, round, smaller round slip lid, paper label, EX, A18........................$25.00

Blue Boar Nut Brown Ale, display, cardboard foldout, For The Cooler Days, 2 bottles flank snowy inn scene with coach, 1940s, 24x31", VG+, A19........................$80.00

Blue Boar Rough Cut, tin, triangular with rounded corners, blue image/yellow lettering on purple ground, 2x3", VG+, A3 ....$40.00

Blue Boar Rough Cut Tobacco, tin, 14-oz, round, snap lid, EX+, A18..$20.00

Blue Bonnet Margarine, doll, 9", MIB (unused), A14 .**$15.00**

Blue Eagle Guaranteed Motor Oil, can, 2-gal, rectangular, eagle logo, white/blue on blue, tall, VG+, A6 .....**$80.00**

Blue Goose Prophylactics, tin, rectangular, flat, rounded corners, 3/No 80, red/white/blue with Blue Goose logo, EX+, A15 ....**$1,950.00**

Blue Grass Rye/The Froeb Co, sign, tin, Daniel Boone Discovering The Kentucky River AD 1769, self-framed, 1907, 20x16", EX, A7 ....**$3,000.00**

Blue Hill Coffee, milk can, 5-lb, bail handle, black/white on blue, EX+, A3...**$240.00**

Blue Jay Tobacco, lunch box, slip lid, double swing handles, EX, A18 ....**$70.00**

Blue Knot Coffee, can, 1-lb, key-wind lid, blue/yellow, NM, A3..**$85.00**

Blue Label, label, Meyer Brewing Co/Bloomington IL, pre-1920, VG (attached to paper), A10......................**$50.00**

Blue Larkspur, crate label, apple, bay racehorse with blue winner's neck wreath, EX, D3 ....**$5.00**

Blue Moon Little Cigars, product box, cardboard, embossed, holds 10, EX+, A18..........................**$60.00**

Blue Plate Coffee & Chicory, can, 1-lb, key-wind lid, blue, EX+, A3...**$30.00**

Blue Plate Coffee & Chicory, can, 1-lb, key-wind lid, yellow, NM, A3..**$30.00**

Blue Poll, cigar box label, inner lid, image of young woman, 6x9", M, D5 ....**$35.00**

Blue Ribbon Baking Powder, can, 3-lb, red, NM, A3.**$50.00**

Blue Ribbon Bourbon, sign, canvas, distillery scene, ornate gold frame, 36x46", EX, A7 ....**$350.00**

Blue Ribbon Bourbon, sign, plaster relief, The Colonel's Favorite, distillery scene, ornate gold self-frame, 33x42", G, A7 ....**$300.00**

Blue Ribbon Cayenne, tin, 1½-oz, rectangular, blue bow in center/red lettering on white, EX+, A3 ....**$22.00**

Blue Ribbon Coffee, can, 1-lb, key-wind lid, red, round ribbon with 2 tails, VG+, A3 ....**$40.00**

Blue Ribbon Coffee, can, 5-lb, pry lid, red, no ribbon logo, VG+, A3...**$80.00**

Blue Ribbon Coffee, sign, cardboard, You Get The Real Mocha & Java Flavor In..., native's loading ship & product can, 1930s, 19x26", EX+, A3 ....**$125.00**

Blue Ribbon Cream of Tartar, tin, 1¾-oz, rectangular, red/white/blue, VG+, A3......................................**$22.00**

Blue Ribbon Pennsylvania Motor Oil, can, 1-qt, orange/blue, twin-engine plane flying over early car in landscape, G+, A6 ....**$230.00**

Blue Ribbon Savory, tin, 1½-oz, red, NM, A3 ....**$25.00**

Blue Ridge Coffee, can, 1-lb, key-wind lid, yellow/red, EX+, A3..**$35.00**

Blue Seal Grain Products/HK Webster Co, Lawrence MA, sign, porcelain, round red/white/blue seal with scalloped border on white square ground, blue trim, 20x20", EX, A2 ....**$250.00**

Blue Sunoco, see Sunoco (Blue)

Blue Valley Butter, thermometer, metal, Blue Valley Butter Is Good/That's Why Millions Use It, yellow/blue trim, curved ends, 39x8", VG, A6..............................**$235.00**

Bluebird Bus Tickets, sign, porcelain, blue on white, blue line border, 8x16", NM+, A1 ....**$200.00**

Bluebird Smoking Mixture, tin, horizontal rectangle, rounded corners, white, EX+, A18 ....**$35.00**

Bluhill Coffee, can, 1-lb, key-wind, white/blue, EX+, A18.**$60.00**

Bluhill Coffee, pail, 5-lb, straight-sided, slip lid, blue, tall, EX+, A3...**$85.00**

Blushing, crate label, vegetable, '40s pinup girl trying to cover up as breeze takes her wrap away, Firebaugh CA, M, D12 ....**$8.00**

BMW, sign, porcelain, round, BMW arched at top of band around circle with 2-color design, white/2-tone blue, 24", EX, A2 ....**$440.00**

Bo-Ka Coffee, can, 1-lb, key-wind lid, red, EX+, A3.**$70.00**

Bo-Lo, sign, tin, Drink Bo-Lo Healthful & Refreshing/5¢ At The Soda Fountain, lady tipping glass, 1890s, 28x20", G, A13 ....**$400.00**

Boardman's Putman Coffee, can, 1-lb, key-wind lid, EX, A3..**$440.00**

Bob White Pumpkin, can label, bird on fence/pumpkin, Vienna MD, M, D12 ....**$6.00**

Bob White Tobacco, pocket tin, vertical, short, VG, A18 ......**$120.00**

Bobby Lou Lithiated-Lemon, sign, cardboard, Serve..., The Best Mixer In Town/A Stratford Product, girl in red shawl, H Coffin art, 20x15", EX+, D30...............**$200.00**

Bocan's Knight Caps, tin, rectangular, rounded corners, A Good Laxative..., graphic of knight, American Can Co, ½x1½x2¾", EX, D37 ....**$35.00**

Bock Beer, label, ½-gal, McHenry Brewing Co/IL, IRTP or WF statement, 1933-50, M, A10 ....**$45.00**

Bock Beer, label, 12-oz, Southern Brewing Co/Tampa FL, M, A10 ....**$27.00**

Bock Beer, sign, paper, king & goat leaning on keg while peasant boy dispenses beer to crowd, 1890-1900 (?), framed, 24x31", EX, A8 ....$100.00

Bodes Gum, vendor, tin cylinder with cast-iron front panel reading One Cent Bodes Gum, VG, A2...........$2,860.00

Bohemian, label, 12-oz, Thieme & Wagner Brewing Co/Lafayette IN, pre-1920, VG (traces of paper or scrapes on back), A10...$35.00

Bohemian Export Bottled Beer/Union Brewing Co, tip tray, round, large bottle, VG+, A8 ....$70.00

Bohemian Girl Special Brew, label, Neef Bros Brewing Co/Denver CO, pre-1920, EX (traces of paper or scrapes on back), A10..$50.00

Bohemian Mixture No 1, tin, horizontal box, holds 100, gold on green, 2x3x6", EX+, A18 ....$60.00

Bohemian's Bread, sign, paper, Take..., image of pilgrim walking to fort with turkey over musket, text below, metal strips, 35x12", NM, A3 ....$40.00

Boker Coffee, can, trial size, screw lid, VG, A3 ....$22.00

Bomb-Buster Giant Golden Pop Corn, can, 16-oz, cardboard canister with tin lid, lettering over graphics of popcorn exploding around bomb, NM+, A3...............$75.00

Bon Jour Coffee, can, 1-lb, key-wind lid, red/white, black lettering, VG+, A3 ....$20.00

Bon-Air Smoking Mixture, pocket tin, vertical, white, EX, A18...$70.00

Bonanza Mixed Fruit, can label, white (Old English) logo on blue band/mixed fruit, San Francisco, M, D12 ....$6.00

Bonanza Sirloin Pit, matchbook, Ben Cartwright, Hoss or Little Joe, 20 strike, front striker, M, D28, each $15.00

Bond Bread, blotter, The Lone Ranger Says...Always Be Careful!, image of Lone Ranger on Silver, VG+, A16......$15.00

Bond Bread, sign, linen, rabbit in overalls with basket of Easter eggs walking towards open loaf of bread, 33x12", G, A9 ....$100.00

Bond Bread, sign, paper, Easter Greetings above girl watering pot of Easter lilys, loaf/Bond below, 1930s, 38x13", NM, A13..$160.00

Bond Bread, sign, porcelain, Bond The Vitamin-D Bread, green/red lettering on yellow with white, horizontal rectangle, G, A2..$50.00

Bond of Union Smoking Mixture, tin, horizontal box, rounded corners, EX+, A3...................................$80.00

Bond Street Pipe Tobacco, pocket tin, vertical, sample, NM, A18 ....$125.00

Bonita Coffee, can, 1-lb, pry lid, white on red, gold trim, EX+, A18...$60.00

Bonner Brand Peaches, can label, packing house/peach, EX, D5 ....$25.00

Booberry Cereal, see General Mills Booberry Cereal

Boot Jack Chewing Tobacco, sign, paper on glass, Above All.../Costliest Because Best, gold lettering on browns/black, 12x8", VG, A6................................$85.00

Boot Jack Plug, boot jack, cast iron, embossed with advertising, 10x4", EX+, A3..$120.00

Boot Jack Plug Tobacco, box, wood, oval label, 13x4", EX+, A18...$35.00

Booth's Compound Derma-Talcum, container, round, cardboard, paper label, blue, embellished image of cherubs, EX+, A3 ....$200.00

Booth's Hyomei Dry-Air, sign, paper, Hymoei Cures Catarrh/Coughs/Colds/Bronchitis/Etc, Breathe It, classical lady running with can, 49x25", Poor, A9......$150.00

Borden's, activity book, Elsie's Funbook/Cut Out Toys & Games, full color, 1940s, 10x7", EX, D25..............$65.00

Borden's, board game, board shows barn with names & head images of Elsie/Elmer/Beulah on daisy ground, complete, EX (no box), D25................................$70.00

Borden's, bottle topper, Season's Greetings From Borden's And... (space for name) Your Milkman, Elmer in wreath, EX, D25...$35.00

Borden's, cookie cutter, round yellow plastic with embossed head image of Beulah, 2¼" dia, EX, D25 ....$48.00

Borden's, doll, Elsie sitting, plush with vinyl head, brown with yellow hands/feet, yellow bow with plastic charm, 16", M, D25 ....$135.00

Borden's, lamp base, ceramic, figural Elsie sitting on chair holding baby Beauegard, 7½", EX, D14 ....$215.00

Borden's, letter opener, red plastic with round image of Elsie flashing to Borden's Milk 23 Ways Guarded, EX, D23 ....$70.00

Borden's, mug, china, trademark image of Elsie on white Coke-glass shape with handle, EX, D25 ....$60.00

Borden's, needle book, black/white trademark image of Elsie above phrase on red, 1940s, 5¼", EX, D25 ....$55.00

Borden's, paper hat, 1857/daisy logo/1957 on receding pennant-type graphic, c Borden Co, blue on white, 5x11", M, D25 ....$50.00

Borden's, place mat, paper, Elsie Says 'For Over 125 Years Folks Have Known...,' 5 color scenes/geometric border, 11x17", M, D25...$25.00

Borden's, plate, porcelain, daisy logo in center with embossed design on scalloped rim, gold trim, 6½" dia, M, D25 ....$125.00

Borden's, recipe book, Elsie's Cook Book/By Elsie The Cow/Tested Recipes Of Every Variety, 1st ed, 1952, 374 pgs, 8x5", EX, D25...$32.00

Borden's, recipe book, Elsie's Hostess Recipe Book/...Sour Cream/Cottage Cheese/Lite-Line Yogurt, Elsie in apron, 1970s, M, D24 ....$24.00

Borden's, recipe leaflet, Try These Nine Such Recipes! says Elsie, 1949, M, D25 ....$29.00

Borden's, salt & pepper shakers, Beulah (flowers on head) & Beauregard (wearing green shorts), Japan, 3½", EX, D25 ....$85.00

Borden's, sweater, V-neck with embroidered daisy logo, 1960s, M, D25...$40.00

Borden's, tablecloth, cotton, printed scene with Elsie/family at outdoor barbecue, 1940s, 36x56", EX, D25..........$145.00

Borden's, tie clasp, gold-tone metal bar with encircled image of Elsie hanging from double chain, EX, D25......$55.00

Borden's, toy train kit, Elsie's Good Food Line Train, 1940s, unpunched, M (original envelope/instructions), D25 ....**$200.00**

Borden's, tumbler, clear glass with applied graphics of Elmer in tiny car/Beulah with checkered flag, 1930s, 4¾", M, D25 ....**$55.00**

Borden's Evaporated Milk, can, sample, Silver Cow, 2¼x1¼", EX, D37 ....**$25.00**

Borden's Ice Cream, sign, porcelain, If It's Borden's It's Got To Be Good, oval in center, red/white/black, 2-sided, 36x48", EX, A6 ....**$375.00**

Borden's Ice Cream, sign, tin button, white/blue lettering & Elsie's head on red/white contour background, embossed, c TBC, 36" dia, VG, A6 ...**$525.00**

Borden's Ice Cream, thermometer, tin, ...Very Big on Flavor, daisy logo, lt blue ground, rounded corners, 1960s, 25", NM, A4 ....**$500.00**

Borden's Instant Coffee, can, 2-oz, round, pry lid, sample, bold lettering on front, EX, D37 ....**$30.00**

Borden's Malted Milk, container, aluminum, EX, A13 ....**$140.00**

Borden's Malted Milk, container, stainless steel, rare, EX, A13 ....**$120.00**

Borden's Malted Milk, sign, paper, Drink Our 'Elsie Special'.../Smooth! Rich!/Delicious..., Elsie with glass/ad/price oval, 9x27", EX, A6 ....**$125.00**

Borden's Milk, sign, tin, Elsie logo on blue/white ground, red/blue lettering, 28x20", NM, A1 ....**$300.00**

Borden's Milk & Cream, sign, flange, enameled steel, Elsie says If It's Borden's, white/blue on brown/white contour ground, 12x20", NM, A24 ....**$475.00**

Borden's Sun State Dairy, sign, tin, diagonal, Elsie on sunflower logo above red lettering on white, yellow-lined border, 1950s, 12x12", NM, A24 ....**$180.00**

Born Steel Ranges, match holder, tin, black/white image of early stove & red lettering on white, 5x3", EX, A15 ....**$400.00**

Boschee's German Syrup/Green's August Flower, sign, tin, oval image of lady with names above/below, framed, 36x28", G, A7 ....**$750.00**

Boscul Coffee, can, 1-lb, key-wind lid, blue/white/gold on red, waiter saying 'Here You Are Sir' on either side, 1930s, EX, D14 ....**$50.00**

Boscul Coffee, can, 1-lb, key-wind lid, red/white/blue, metallic gold trim, EX+, A3 ....**$25.00**

Boss, crate label, Florida Citrus, white-bearded southern colonel, Winter Garden, M, D12 ....**$10.00**

Boss Steam Car, pin-back button, round, dealer listed above image of early auto, name below, sepia, 1¼" dia, EX, A2 ....**$1,075.00**

Bossy Brand Bottled Milk, pocket calendar, 1921, celluloid, I'm The Boss Of Bossy Brand, cow behind fence, EX, A20 ....**$45.00**

Boston & Maine Bus Depot, sign, porcelain, Tickets Here To All Points/Countryside Connections, 2-sided, 10x20", EX+, A2 ....**$525.00**

Boston Cigar, change tray, embossed cast-iron oval dish, VG, A2 ....**$135.00**

Boston Herald Newspaper, tip tray, On Sale Everywhere..., boy hawking papers, red/yellow, 3½" dia, EX, A7 ..**$175.00**

Boston Herald Newspaper, watch fob, metal, oval, embossed lettering around image of boy hawking papers, 5½", VG, A6 ....**$75.00**

Boston Montreal Coachline, sign, porcelain, Motor Coach Stop/Ticket Agency above/below company name on diamond, white ground, 11x17", EX+, A2 ....**$690.00**

Boston Store, calendar, 1898, cardboard, die-cut, embossed, mother & daughter, multicolored, 12x8", incomplete, EX+, A3 ....**$160.00**

Botl'O Orange, sign, tin, Call For A.../And Other Flavors, with tilted bottle, green/orange/white, 12x24", NM+, A1 ....**$110.00**

Boucher's Special Cigars, tin, round, slip lid, embossed, 2 For 5¢, VG+, A3 ....**$60.00**

Bounty Blended Turkish & Domestic Tobacco, pocket tin, vertical, Cigarette Case/Roll Your Own, 3", EX+, A18 ....**$130.00**

Bouquet Ramee Talcum, tin, embossed paper label, floral decor, EX+, A18 ....**$50.00**

Bouquet Roasted Coffee, can, 1-lb, round, screw lid, white on red, EX+, A18 ....**$200.00**

Bouquet Roasted Coffee, can, 1-lb, vertical box, white on red, EX+, A18 ....**$150.00**

Bouquet Roasted Moca Java Coffee, see also Banquet

Bow Knot Salmon, can label, large red bow, M, D5 ..**$15.00**

Bowey's Hot Chocolate Powder/Liquor Chocolate, tin, 10-lb, square, round screw lid, blue on tan, EX+, A18 ....**$100.00**

Bowl of Roses Pipe Mixture, pocket tin, vertical, short, EX, A3 ....**$135.00**

Bowl of Roses Pipe Mixture, pocket tin, vertical, tall, NM, A18...$280.00

Bowl of Roses Pipe Mixture, tin, round, screw lid, EX+, A18...$85.00

Bowler Bros Brewers, match safe, metal, celluloid, multi-colored, VG+, A8......................................$100.00

Bowler Bros Tadcaster Ale/Lager Beer, match safe, metal, 2-sided engraved logo, VG, A8.............................$75.00

Bowling Club, cigar box label, inner lid, interior bowling scene, Schmidt & Co litho #1374, 1902, EX, A5.$400.00

Bowser Filtered Gasoline, letter opener, bronze, gas pump on embossed oval at top, 9", EX, A6.................$150.00

Boyce Motometer, sign, tin/cardboard, We Install... 'Free,' man pointing to motometer on red hood, white ground, beveled, 27x19", VG+, A2 ...$1,870.00

Boye Needle Co Crochet Hooks, box, cardboard, shows woman examining hook, orange/black on white, ad on back, 1920s, 5½", G, D14...$8.00

Boye Needles, dispenser, metal disk, red/white/blue, some needles included, 16" dia, VG, A6......................$120.00

Boyle's Brand Fresh String Beans/Erie Preserving Co, can, paper label, Packed At Buffalo Erie Co, girl in garden with dove, Calvert Litho Co, pre-1880s (?), 5", VG, A3...$165.00

Bradley & Metcalf Co, sign, tin, The Bradley Shoe For Men & Women, lettered triangle in center, white/red/silver, embossed, 7x20", EX, A3 ....$80.00

Bradley & Vrooman Guaranteed Varnishes, display shelves, die-cut tin half-image of lady with arm attached to sign atop black shelving unit, 66x41x9", EX+, A1.................$1,850.00

Brandy Wine, sign, cardboard, Let's Drink... above girl in red dress on the back of soaring eagle, 22" dia, NM+, D19 ....$550.00

Braniff International Coffee, can, 1-lb, key-wind lid, pink/orange, unopened, VG+, A3.........................$55.00

Brasso, sign, porcelain, Brasso/Beautifies Brass, red oval on blue/white receding stripes, yellow banner, 14x30", NM, A13...$350.00

Brater's Powder For Spasms of Asthma, tin, rectangular, rounded corners, man's portrait in center, 1x1¾x3", EX, D37 ....$40.00

Brazilla, dispenser, ceramic barrel shape, replaced pump, 15", VG+, A9.......................................$1,250.00

Breakfast Call Coffee, can, 3-lb, smaller round slip lid, red, 'Sugar' on reverse, EX, A18.................$140.00

Breakfast Cheer Coffee, can, 1-lb, pry lid, lady on front/couple on back, white on red, very rare, NM+, A15...$2,300.00

Breakfast Cheer Coffee, can, 1-lb, pry lid, lady on front/couple on back, white on red, very rare, G, A3........$230.00

Breakfast Cup Coffee, can, 1-lb, key-wind lid, red, EX+, A3, from $15 to...$25.00

Breakfast Delight Coffee, can, 1-lb, key-wind lid, red, VG+, A3...$20.00

Breidt's Ale, tap knob, ball shape, chrome, white-on-green enamel insert, EX, A8......................................$120.00

Breyers Ice Cream, sign, porcelain sidewalk, Eat Breyers (on green leaf)/All-Ways/Ice Cream on white oval on green, 28x20", NM, A13......................................$275.00

Briar Gold Beer, label, 12-oz, Best Brewing Co/Chicago IL, IRTP or WF statement, 1933-50, M, A10 ....$10.00

Briar Tobacco, sign, paper, die-cut image of black child holding up 2 packages of Briar Tobacco, framed, image: 10x5", EX, A9 ....$50.00

Briardale Coffee, can, 1-lb, key-wind lid, blue/silver, EX, A3...$70.00

Bridal Veil, crate label, California lemon, Bridal Veil Falls at Yosemite with lemon, Santa Paula, VG, D3............$6.00

Bridges Motorcar & Rubber Co, pin-back button, round, lettering around image of car on bridge, blue on white, 1" dia, EX, A2...$750.00

Briggs & Stratton 4-Cycle Engines, clock/sign, rectangular, light-up, Authorized Service-Parts/Ask About Easy-Spin Starting, clock at left, 10x38", EX, A1.................$275.00

Briggs Pipe Mixture, pocket tin, vertical, Complimentary, full size, EX+, A18 ....$115.00

Briggs Smoking Tobacco, humidor, cedar barrel with lettering, 7x5", EX, A5 ....$150.00

Bright's Kidney Beans, tin, rectangular, rounded corners, ...For Pain In The Back..., Statue of Liberty, Norton Bros, ½x1½x2½", EX, D37 ....$150.00

Brimfull Pure Cocoa, container, 2-lb, cardboard, vertical square, yellow, EX, A3......................................$25.00

Brite-Mawnin Vacuum Packed Coffee, can, 1-lb, screw lid, white/red/green, VG+, A3......................................$75.00

British Navy Chewing Tobacco/McAlpin Tobacco Co, sign, cardboard, ...Leads The World/Strictly Union Made, men swimming after dog on raft, 17x9", VG+, A3..........$65.00

British Oak Shag/Lambert Butler, London, sign, cardboard, In Packets Only, old sea captain in red jacket sitting enjoying pipe, framed, 25x21", EX, A7........$400.00

Broadway Brewing Co Pure Beers, tip tray, round, hand-held lance, lettered rim, EX, A8.........................$85.00

Broadway Brewing Co Standard Beer, drinking glass, shell, etched, 4", NM, A8.....................................**$100.00**

Broadway Saloon, trade card, die-cut bust image of young girl in hat behind sign with filigree/floral border, 1890s, 7x10", EX, A3 ....**$85.00**

Brockway Motor Trucks Sales & Service, sign, porcelain, white lettering on blue, white boder, 20x30", VG, A2.........**$300.00**

Broggs Pipe Mixture, pocket container, cardboard, vertical, Victory Package, EX+, A18.....................**$40.00**

Bromo-Seltzer, dispenser, original bottle with newer glass, part of knob missing o/w EX, A3 ....$60.00

Bromo-Seltzer, drinking glass, cobalt blue with white fired-on advertising, M, D25 ....**$18.00**

Bromo-Seltzer, matchbook, bottle, red top, 20 strike, front strike, Diamond Quality, M, D28...........................**$7.00**

Brookside Beans, can label, pile of beans/country brook, 1924, M, D5 ....**$9.00**

Brookside Carnation Talcum, tin, sample, 2", EX, D37..**$125.00**

Brookside Grapefruit, can label, grapefruit/country brook, 1924, EX, D5...**$7.00**

Brother Jonathan Tobacco, store bin, tin, round, square lid, G-, A7..**$350.00**

Brotherhood Tobacco, lunch box, bail handle with grip, G, A18..**$20.00**

Brotherhood Tobacco, tin, horizontal box, EX, A3..**$50.00**

Brotherhood Tobacco, tin, round, smaller round slip lid, scarce, VG+, A18 ....**$300.00**

Brown, Forman Co, sign, tin, Pleasant Reminder, salesman gives bartender sample, C Shonk litho, wood & plaster frame, image: 19x27", G, A9......................**$1,750.00**

Brown Bear Blend, pocket tin, vertical, paper label, cut-down, VG, A18 ....**$50.00**

Brown Berry Coffee, can, 1-lb, key-wind lid, EX, A3 ..**$50.00**

Brown Betty Coffee, can, 1-lb, key-wind lid, lady's profile, EX+ (unopened), A3.........................**$200.00**

Brown Self Sealing Oil Can, 5-gal, with original paper label depicting young girl filling lamp, ca 1895, VG+, A3..**$135.00**

Brown Shoe Co's Star-Five-Star $2.50 & $3.50 Shoes, sign, tin, For Men & Women/Sold By..., hands displaying sole of shoe, black on orange, 14x20", EX, A6..**$130.00**

Brown's Boot Shop, sign, tin, mare & colt in stall looking down on 3 dogs, self-framed, 1908, 14x14", NM, A7...**$1,050.00**

Brown's Camphorated Saponaceous Dentifrice, sign, cardboard, 3 Victorian women admiring product on pedestal, 14x11", EX+, A15 ....**$775.00**

Brown's Iron Edge Dustpan/Wilshire Hardware Co, postcard, A Dustpan Free..., images of lady sweeping the Old Way/New Way, coupon below, used 1909, VG, D26 ....**$40.00**

Brown's Jumbo Bread, sign, tin, die-cut elephant with advertising on red back blanket, 13x15", NM+, A1........**$450.00**

Brownie Brand Salted Peanuts, can, 10-lb, blue, EX+, A18..**$190.00**

Brownie Chocolate Soda, sign, cardboard, die-cut, ...And Always Remember...If You Like..., teacher/2 Brownie students, 1927, 12x7", G, A16................................**$70.00**

Brownie Chocolate Soda, sign, cardboard, If You Like Chocolate Soda above Brownie holding bottle, Drink Brownie below, 88x19", EX, A9 ....**$400.00**

BrownieKar/Omar Motor Co, pin-back button, round, name above full-color image of goggled boy in auto, Mfg By..., red/black type, 1¼", EX, A2.......$1,200.00

Brownies, crate label, California orange, brownies preparing orange juice/yellow sun, blue ground, Lemon Cove, EX, D3..**$5.00**

Bruinoil/Bruin Gasoline, sign, painted metal, Buy...The Bear Of Them All above ferocious-looking bear, multicolored, 48x60", EX, A6 ....**$1,600.00**

Brundage Star Maid Coffee, can, 1-lb, key-wind lid, white/blue, tall, VG+, A3 ....**$210.00**

Brundage Star Maid Salted Peanuts, tin, 10-lb, round, blue/gold on white, no lid, VG, A3 ....**$55.00**

Brunswick Coffee, can, ½-lb, screw lid, steaming cup on center oval, red, gold top, EX+, A15...................**$110.00**

Brunswick-Balke-Collender Co, sign, cardboard, Billiard Experts Of The World, wood frame, 32x42", VG, A7..**$1,750.00**

BSA Genuine Oil, can, 1-qt, It Pays To Use Only..., BSA triangular logo with text above/below, red, white/blue on green, EX+, A1..**$100.00**

BT Babbitt's Best Soap, jigsaw puzzle, girl holding kitten while standing on soap box, ca 1900, 7x5", EX, D10............**$50.00**

BT Babbitt's Cleanser (Babbitt's), can, waxed cardboard, tin top/bottom, At Your Service, oval image of trademark boy standing at attention, 5", EX, A6 ....**$30.00**

BT Babbitt's Cleanser, trolley sign, cardboard, Saves Half The Time, split image of lady cleaning by day/out for the evening, 11x22", VG, A3 ....**$70.00**

Buffalo Brewing Co, sign, tin, 4 bottles/tankard on red table by window, gold self-frame, 28x22", NM, A7 ....**$1,350.00**

Buffalo Brewing Co, tray, rectangular, Buffo, Dutch girl on wood-grain ground, 13", VG, A8 ....**$90.00**

Buffalo Brewing Co, tray, rectangular, Happy Days, lady in white coat/hat ready to sip from glass on blue ground, 13", NM, A8 ....**$290.00**

Buffalo Brewing Co Bohemian, charger, tin, That Delicious Beer, pretty lady, lettering on rim, 24" dia, EX, A7 ....**$2,900.00**

Buffalo Brewing Co Bohemian, tray, round, majestic buck, VG+, A8 ....**$135.00**

Buffalo Club Rye Whiskey, sign, tin tray shape, round, open bottles/glasses, decorative rim, C Shonk litho, 12" dia, VG, A9 ....**$100.00**

Buffalo Co-Operative Brewing Co Beer/Ale/Porter, tray, round, deep rim, 2 bottles on draped ground, gold trim, EX+, A8 ....**$100.00**

Buffalo Courier Daily & Sunday, sign, flange, painted metal, horizontal keyhole shape, ...Sold Here, cream on blue, 14x18", EX, A6 ....**$150.00**

Buffalo Distilling Co, sign, tin, buffalo flanked by 4 kegs of various products, embossed, wood frame, 19x26", EX, A7 ....**$1,250.00**

Buffalo Tobacco Works/Clingstone Fine Cut, label, oval image of lady peering from behind tree/trademark emblem, geometric border, 10x12", EX, A5 ....**$250.00**

Buffalo Tobacco Works/Nelle Of Buffalo Fine Cut, label, portrait image/trademark emblem, geometric border, 10x12", EX, A5 ....**$250.00**

Buffalo Tobacco Works/Queen City Fine Cut, label, portrait of lady in floral hat/trademark emblem, geometric border, 10x12", VG+, A5 ....**$180.00**

Buffum's Soda Water, fan, cardboard, wood handle, young man helping young woman with shoe in country scene, 13x7", EX, A6 ....**$55.00**

Bugler Cigarette Tobacco, sign, heavy paper, Roll 20 Or More Cigarettes 5¢, name on blue circle above cigarette roller, 15x17", NM, A3 ....**$40.00**

Buick, blotter, open touring car in landscape/logo, 1924, 4x9", NM, A14 ....**$28.00**

Buick, clock, round face in center of cloisonne radiator shape, award, Whitehead & Hoag on reverse, 6x4", nonworking, EX, A1 ....**$350.00**

Buick, display, wooden cabinet with color combinations available for the 1960 Buick, drawer holds fabric, 16x21", G+, A2 ....**$200.00**

Buick, lighter, pressed-tin car, silver tone, white rubber wheels, Occupied Japan, late 1940s, 5", EX, A1 ....**$220.00**

Buick, photograph, Prosperity Train, tinted, 190 Buicks on train crossing bridge, 1915, matted & framed, 14x24", EX, A2 ....**$700.00**

Buick, sign, neon/porcelain, round Valve In Head logo above name on Deco housing, 39x82x8", NM+, A6 ....**$2,750.00**

Buick Authorized Service, sign, porcelain, round, Valve-In-Head Buick Motor Cars, blue/white, 1-sided, 42" dia, Fair, A2 ....**$275.00**

Buick Authorized Service, sign, porcelain, round, Valve In Head, red/white/blue, 2-sided, 42" dia, NM, A2 ..**$935.00**

Buick Fireball Eight, bank, globe, Best Buick Yet, white on red, 5", EX+, A2 ....**$110.00**

Buick Lubricare, sign, neon/porcelain, die-cut top, white tubing on red lettering on white, 18½x68", NM+, A6........**$1,600.00**

Buick Motor Cars, thermometer, porcelain, rounded top/bottom, white on blue, white border, Pat Mar-16-15, 27x7", EX+, A1 ....**$700.00**

Buick Motor Cars, thermometer, porcelain, rounded top/bottom, white on blue, white border, Pat Mar-16-15, 27x7", G+, A2 ....**$220.00**

Buick Quick Service, sign, porcelain, white/black/white lettering on red/white/blue bands, 2-sided, 16x26", NM, A24 ....**$550.00**

Buick Valve-In-Head Motor Cars, catalog, 1915, 32 pgs, EX (with original mailing envelope), EX, A2 ....**$110.00**

Buick Valve-In-Head Motor Cars, sign, tin, reflective, white/blue on white square on blue field, white courtesy band below, wood frame, 48x48", EX+, A1 ....**$450.00**

Bull Dog Cut Plug, sign, tin, ...Mild & Sweet/Won't Bite, bulldog in center, red/white on black, framed, 12x9", EX+, A15 ....$600.00

Bull Dog Cut Plug DeLuxe, pocket tin, vertical, regular, NM (full), A18..$675.00

Bull Dog Smoking DeLuxe, pocket tin, vertical, oval, EX, A18 ....$425.00

Bull Durham, postcards, set of 33, each shows a different nation with symbolism & poem about tobacco, NM, A16 ....$4,200.00

Bull Durham, sign, cardboard, My! It Shure Am Sweet, black couple sitting on fence kissing behind torn umbrella, 30x21", EX, A7 ....$1,500.00

Bull Durham, sign, paper, Teaching Time, metal strips, 1895-1905, 28x21", NM+, A13 ....$600.00

Bull Durham, sign, tin, Prize Winners, original frame, 36x36", G-, A2 ....$700.00

Bull Durham, sign, tin, Prize Winners, original frame, 36x36", NM, A7 ....$7,500.00

Bull Durham, sign, tin, Tie Up With Bull.../5¢, black/white image of couple & horse on red/white ground, 10x15", VG, A6 ....$200.00

Bull Durham, watch fob, die-cast metal bull, gold-tone, 1", VG, A6 ....$75.00

Bull Frog Brand, tray, rectangular, 2 Dutch girls seated on bench, lettering on decorative rim, blue, 13", EX, A8 ....$125.00

Bullard Improved Hay Tedder/Belcher & Taylor Agl. Tool Co, trade card, image of farmer on horse-drawn hay tedder, 4x6", EX, A6 ....$95.00

Bulova, clock, square, gold cast-metal dial with faux wood inlay/appliques at 12-3-6-9, 15x15", NM, A1 ......$135.00

Bulova, display, automated, Bulova Watch Month Trade-In Sale, magician in top hat nods, ca 1920, 30x23x10", EX, A23..$550.00

Bulwark Cut Plug, tin, rectangular, rounded corners, slip lid, multicolored graphics on yellow, 4x6x4", VG+, A18 .$60.00

Bunker Hill Breweries, see PB Ale

Bunker Hill Coffee, can, 1-lb, pry lid, red, tall, EX+, A3/A2, from $175 to..$225.00

Bunnies Salted Peanuts, store bin, 10-lb, round, red, VG+, A18 ....$250.00

Bunny Bread, sign, tin, die-cut loaf, 1950s-60s, 28x52", EX+, A13 ....$300.00

Bunte, jar, clear glass, 10-sided canister with round fluted lid, Bunte embossed on sides, 12", VG, A9 ....$50.00

Bunte Chocolates/Candies, signs, cardboard die-cut standups, rabbit couple, he ready to present her with box of Bunte, 23", NM (NOS), A1, pair $300.00

Bunte Marshmallows, tin, 5-lb, round, pry lid, 10x13" dia, EX+, A6 ....$450.00

Bunte Marshmallows, tin, 4-oz, round, pry lid, blue/white with red/black lettering, graphics of child opening can, ca 1914, VG, A2..$100.00

Burch's Best Jumbo Pop Corn, tin, 9-oz, elephant against background of popped corn, red/white/blue, EX, A18.....$135.00

Burger Ale, sign, tin hanger, Cincinnati's Famous Ale, riverfront view of city above name, green/gold, self-framed, 8x14", VG+, A8 ....$265.00

Cadet (Havana), cigar tin, round, slip lid, blue, Liberty Can, EX, A18 ....$75.00

Cadets, cigar box label, outer, Indian boy lighting white boy's cigar, 1901, 4½x4½", M, D5 ....$30.00

Cadetship, cigar box labels, 2-pc set, embellished round image of cadet, Geo L Schlegel litho, G/EX, A5 ..$115.00

Cadillac, clock, desk type, light-up, square, numbers around Cadillac emblem, ca 1960, 9x10", working, NM, A24 ....$200.00

Cadillac, license plate, porcelain, Cadillac 1914, diagonal script left of date, white on red, EX, A2 ....$1,100.00

 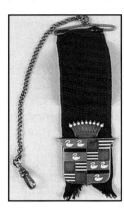

Cadillac, watch fob, emblem, black ducks, sterling silver with red/black/white cloisonne, black fabric strap, NM, A1 ....$200.00

Cadillac, watch fob, emblem, white swans, gold tone with red/black/white cloisonne, black fabric strap, EX+, A1 ....$100.00

Cadillac Authorized Service, sign, porcelain, round, crown shield in center with white lettering on blue, 2-sided, 42" dia, VG, A2 ....$1,025.00

Cadillac Authorized Service, sign, porcelain, round, crown shield in center with white lettering on blue, 1-sided, 42" dia, EX, A6 ....$1,500.00

Cadillac Official Service, sign, porcelain, lettering centered with crown shields in lower corners, white on brown, 2-sided, 30x40", Fair, A2.............................$525.00

Cadillac Sales, clock, octagonal, glass front, metal frame, numbers on band around lettering/emblem, 18x18", VG, A6..$600.00

Cadillac V8.V12.V16/La Salle V8, sign, porcelain, 2 car emblems left of white lettering on blue, double white stripes top/bottom, 2-sided, 24x30", EX, A2...$4,070.00

Cadillac 30, pin-back button, round, 1911...$1700 above image of auto, dealer name below, black/yellow on white, 1½" dia, EX, A2.........................$690.00

Cafe Blue Mountain, can, 1-lb, key-wind lid, red/yellow lettering, blue mountains around bottom, EX+, A3 .$45.00

Cafe Bustelo, can, 1-lb, key-wind lid, black/yellow triangular image of woman on yellow, red bottom band, EX+, A3..$75.00

Cafe de Luxe Coffee, can, 1-lb, pry lid, America's Finest Family..., EX+, A18 ....$50.00

Cafe Savoy Coffee, can, rectangular, slip lid, sample, crest in center, EX, D37 ....$160.00

Caffe Pastene Italian Roast Coffee, can, 1-lb, key-wind lid, yellow, EX+, A3 ....$70.00

Caffe Vivo Coffee, can, 1-lb, key-wind lid, red, EX+, A3.....$25.00

Cain's Regular Grind Hotel & Restaurant Blend Coffee, can, 1-lb, key-wind lid, 5¢ Off, EX+, A3...............$18.00

Caisse General Fire Co, ledger marker, image of Statue of Liberty, 12x3", EX+, A15.....................................$275.00

Cali-Orange, dispenser, frosted globe on reverse-painted base with decals front/back, chrome spigot/lid, EX, A3...$290.00

California Co Petroleum Products, pin-back button, celluloid, white/blue logo on white oval, green trim, 2x3", NM+, A1...$275.00

California Dream, crate label, California orange, 2 peacocks, Placentia, EX/NM, D3/D12, from $18 to ...$25.00

California Gold Label Beer, wagon light, The Flavor Of The West, lettered cloth top over wooden wagon, 1950s, 12x23", complete, EX, A19.................................$130.00

California Perfume Co, product gift set, Baby Set, includes soap box/toilet water bottle/talcum tin, EX (in box), A15...$525.00

Calotabs, sign, tin, Tongue Coated? You Need.../We Sell Them-10¢ & 35¢, man looking in mirror/large pack, 1930s, 14x20", EX, A13.....................................$575.00

Calso Gasoline, pump sign, porcelain, round, white lettering on red, white border, black trim, 11" dia, EX+, A1 ....$160.00

Calso Gasoline, pump sign, porcelain, round with bottom 3-chevron emblem, red/white/blue, 14x11", NM, A1..$450.00

Caltex, key chain, enameled star/lettering on round metal emblem, St Christopher medal on reverse, red/black/white, 3", EX, A6 ....$75.00

Caltex Kerosene, sign, porcelain, red star logo upper left of red key on white, 'flaming' white letters on black below, 24x36", VG, A6...$300.00

Calumet Baking Powder, clock, regulator, wood case, glass front, Time To Buy.../Best By Test, numbers 1-31 around Roman numerals, 38", EX, A7.............................**$750.00**

Calvert, clock, round, light-up, glass/metal, Switch To Calvert/Milder...Smoother..., red letters as numbers, 14", EX, A6...**$125.00**

Camay Toilet Soap, sign, tin, square corners, Fragrant As Flowers After Rain/We Have It, wrapped bar above, deep rose ground, 27x6", EX, A3............................**$500.00**

Camel Brand 5¢ Cigar, tin, vertical box, canted corners, EX+, A3...**$100.00**

Camel Brand 5¢ Cigars, tin, vertical box, rounded corners, EX+, A18...**$90.00**

Camel Cigarettes, salt & pepper shakers, Joe Camel as the Blues Brothers, plastic, 4", NM, pair $55.00

Camel Cigarettes, sign, cardboard, die-cut football with player/open pack, Always In Prime Condition/Smoke A Fresh..., 47x34", EX+, A15.................................**$750.00**

Camel Cigarettes, sign, cardboard die-cut stand-up, Camels Never Get On Your Nerves Say Hugo & Mario Zacchini..., 35x30", EX+, A1...**$100.00**

Camel Cigarettes, tin, round, pry lid, 100's, EX, A18 .**$45.00**

Camellia, crate label, California orange, spray of 6 camellias on white satin background, Redlands, M, D12 ....**$20.00**

Cameron & Cameron Co Finest Grade Smoking Tobacco, tin, rectangular, rounded corners, decorative dome lid with latch closure, white with trademark graphics, VG+, A18...**$75.00**

Cameron's Gold Medal Cut Plug, pocket tin, flat, large, scarce, EX+, A18...**$135.00**

Cameron's Gold Medal Cut Plug, tin, rectangular, rounded corners, yellow, G+, A3..**$45.00**

Cameron's Gold Medal Cut Plug, tin, rectangular, square corners, 1x5x3", EX+, A18..................................**$185.00**

Cameron's Private Stock, tin, rectangular, square corners, G+, A18...**$25.00**

Campbell Brand Blend Coffee, pail, 4-lb, yellow, EX, A3/A18...**$75.00**

Campbell's Horse Foot Remedy, sign, paper, Axtell At Home, black stable boy watches as family tends to horse, ads on wall, framed, 23x18", EX, A2..................**$650.00**

Campbell's Soups, bank, Campbell Boy & Girl, cast iron molded into 1 pc, AC Williams, 1910, 3½x4", M, D29...**$210.00**

Campbell's Soups, bank, Campbell Kid in chef's garb, ceramic, Oriental lettering/Campbell's lettered on hat, 1970s (?), 8", EX, D25...**$65.00**

Campbell's Soups, bank, pail with lid, metal, plastic handle, 6 different Campbell Kids graphics, Shackman, 1980, 2½", M, D29..**$15.00**

Campbell's Soups, bank, 1905 Ford truck replica with Pork & Beans advertising, die-cast, Ertl, 1987, 5", M, D29 ..**$40.00**

Campbell's Soups, bell, porcelain, Christmas Cheer, plays Joy To The World, Fenton Art, 1983, 6", M, D29 .**$40.00**

Campbell's Soups, calendar, 1974, linen hanger, M'm! M'm! Good!, Campbell Kid as chef, Norcross, 27x16", M, D29..**$12.00**

Campbell's Soups, calendar, 1990, image of Campbell Kids, M, D29...**$5.00**

Campbell's Soups, canister set, ceramic, Campbell Kids graphics, Westwood, 1991, 4-pc set, MIB, D29 ....**$65.00**

Campbell's Soups, Christmas ornament, Warm & Hearty Wishes, Kid atop soup can, plaster, Enesco, 1993, MIB, D29 ....**$20.00**

Campbell's Soups, clock, round, Tomato Soup can on face, black frame, 1996, 9", M, D29 ....**$16.00**

Campbell's Soups, comic book, Captain America & The Campbell Kids, promotional, Marvel, 1980, M, D29..**$8.00**

Campbell's Soups, cookbook, Campbell Soup International, 1980, blue cover, M, D29 ....**$9.00**

Campbell's Soups, cookie jar, ceramic, white with Campbell Kids graphics, Westwood, 1991, MIB, D29..........**$35.00**

Campbell's Soups, cup, ceramic, Campbell Kids graphics, Westwood, M, D29...**$5.00**

Campbell's Soups, cup, ceramic, M'm! M'm! Good!, M, D29...**$3.00**

Campbell's Soups, cup, ceramic, Salute America, Campbell Kids as Uncle Sam/Liberty, 1986, M, D29.............**$15.00**

Campbell's Soups, cup, ceramic, soup labels, Heritage, 1996, set of 4, M, D29 ....**$12.00**

Campbell's Soups, cup, plastic, figural Campbell Kid head, yellow hair, numbered 1-6, 1976, set of 6, NM, A3 ....$25.00

Campbell's Soups, cup, plastic, with lid, M'm! M'm! Good!, Campbell Kids graphics, microwavable, 1992, M, D29 ....**$3.00**

Campbell's Soups, decal, Boy chef with spoon raised in front of barbecue, Meyercord, 1954, 5x6x5", M, D29........**$8.00**

Campbell's Soups, dinnerware, child's set, stoneware, plate/bowl/cup/saucer, Campbell Kids graphics, 1992, MIB, D29 ....**$12.00**

Campbell's Soups, dinnerware, tumbler/bowl/spoon, Campbell Kids graphics, Zak Designs, 1995, MIP, D29 ....**$20.00**

Campbell's Soups, display sign, cardboard, die-cut, Campbell Kids as pilgrims, 1980, 18", EX, D29..............**$8.00**

Capitol Club Beverages, sign, cardboard, die-cut, The Toast Of The Nation Drink... on white arrow wrapped around bottle neck, 22x10", EX+, A1 .... **$30.00**

Capitol Coffee, can, 5-lb, pry lid, blue, oval image of the Capitol Building, VG, A2 .... **$150.00**

Capt Chester, cigar box, image of Captain of the USS Cincinnati, VG+, A5 .... **$160.00**

Capt Jack, cigar box labels, set of 2, rabbits/birds at bucket, Witsch & Schmidt litho #996/997, VG+, A5 .... **$365.00**

Captain Corker, cigar box label, inner lid, army general smoking cigar, 6x9", M, D5 .... **$75.00**

Captain D's Seafood, bank, Captain D figure with arm up, vinyl, 1970s, NM, D20 .... **$200.00**

Captain's Fancy Brown Coffee, can, 1-lb, key-wind lid, brown, NM+, A3 .... **$135.00**

Carborundum, sign, cardboard, die-cut, name on band around profile image of Indian chief, product display below, 30x39", Fair, A9 .... **$300.00**

Carborundum & Aloxite Brand Grinding Wheels, sign, canvas litho, man holding chisel in triangular field with round Indian logo on red, 30x28", NM (NOS), A1 .... **$135.00**

Carborundum Brand Sharpening Stones, sign, canvas litho, 3 men sharpening stones in triangular field with round Indian logo on red, 40x28", NM (NOS), A1 .... **$135.00**

Cardinal, crate label, California orange, religious leader dressed in red, 1920, M, D5 .... **$50.00**

Cardinal Beer, tray, round, porcelain, Drink Cardinal Beer, Costs 25% More To Brew But Worth More, 12" dia, G+, A9 . **$50.00**

Cardinal Cherry, dispenser, ceramic, ball shape, flared base, green, red/green embossed cherry decor, 1920, 15", original pump, NM+, A9 .... **$5,700.00**

Cardinal Cherry, dispenser, ceramic, ball shape, flared base, green, red/green embossed cherry decor, 1920, 15", no pump o/w NM, A13 .... **$2,600.00**

Cardinal Cut Plug, pocket tin, vertical, EX+, A3 . **$2,200.00**

Cardinal Gum, vendor, vertical box with white porcelain front panel, 1¢ in red above black Cardinal Gum, red image of bird, VG, A13 .... **$300.00**

Carey Salt Co, bill hook, celluloid, round, red/white/blue, EX, A15 .... **$100.00**

Cariboo Brand Lobster, can label, Cariboo in mountains, Canadian, early, M, D5 .... **$35.00**

Carling's Ale, sign, tin/cardboard, Nine Pints Of The Law, 9 English bobbies enjoying ale, artist Lawson Wood, beveled, 13x20", VG, A9 .... **$25.00**

Carlton Club Mixture, pocket tin, vertical, EX+, A18 .. **$220.00**

Carnation Butter Churn, butter churn, name lettered on 2-color crock with multicolored stripes, metal stand, 21", restored, A2 .... **$400.00**

Carnation Evaporated Milk, sign, tin, shows large can on blue ground, 1950s, 18x12", NM+ (NOS), A13 ... **$200.00**

Carnation Fresh Milk, badge (hat), die-cut emblem, white/red/green, with milk bottle, 2x2", NM+, A1 .... **$400.00**

Carnation Fresh Milk, sign, painted metal, die-cut emblem, lettering/bottle on red/white ground, white/green border, 24x24", EX, A1 .... **$275.00**

Carnation Fresh Milk, sign, porcelain, die-cut emblem, lettering/bottle on red/white ground, white/green border, 1950s, 23x22", NM+, A13 .... **$425.00**

Carnation Ice Cream, badge, painted metal emblem, name/sundae on red/white ground, green border, 2x2", NM+, A1 .... **$775.00**

Carnation Ice Cream, sign, aluminum, die-cut emblem, name/sundae on red/white ground, white/yellow/white border, 24x24", NM, A1 .... **$300.00**

Carnation Malted Milk, container, aluminum, EX, A13 .. **$200.00**

Carnation Malted Milk, container, milk glass, metal lid, red/green lettering, EX, A13 .... **$170.00**

Carnation Malted Milk, container, porcelain, metal lid, red/white, 6", EX+, A1 .... **$625.00**

Carnation Malted Milk, dispenser, glass cylinder with metal lid, tall footed porcelain base, 18", EX, A6 .... **$425.00**

Carnation Milk, bookmark, cardboard, die-cut carnation at top, Souvenir Of Panama-Pacific Exposition/San Francisco 1915, 7", NM, A1 .... **$65.00**

Carnation Milk, sign, cardboard, Here It Is Muvvie!, toddler with bare bottom reaching for a can, large can at right, 22x36", EX+, A1 .... **$375.00**

Carnation Mixture, tin, rectangular, square corners, black on red, gold trim, EX, A18 .... **$100.00**

Carnation's His/Her Majesty's Formula, signs, card-board, die-cut babies dressed as king/queen, slots in bibs hold directions for formula, 16x9", NM+, A1, pair $375.00

Carolina Gem Long Cut/Brown Bros Co, tin, rectangular, square corners, small, EX+, A18..........................$100.00

Carom, cigar box label, sample, 2 men playing pool, Geo S Harris & Sons woodcut #791, 1874, EX, A5 ....$1,020.00

Carriage Trade Coffee, can, 1-lb, key-wind, gold, NM (full) A18..$350.00

Carson Pirie Scott & Co, catalog, 1940, notions/store supplies/stationary/leather goods/etc, 146 pgs, EX, D17...$75.00

Carson Pirie Scott & Co, catalog, 1942, Jewelry Yearbook, 382 pgs, EX, D17 ....$90.00

Carta Blanca, tip tray, round, lettering on rim around pretty girl in pigtails in center, 4½" dia, EX, A8..............$60.00

Carter White Lead All Weather Paint, thermometer, porcelain, name above gauge, bucket below, Pat March 16, 1915, 28x7", EX, A6 ....$200.00

Carter's Ideal Ribbons & Carbons, sign, tin, Portia's Choice, self-framed, 19x13", VG, A7 ....$500.00

Carter's Infants Underwear, sign, cardboard die-cut stand-up, toddler seated atop sign looking up, 14x16", VG+, A3 ....$220.00

Carter's Infants Underwear, sign, cardboard die-cut stand-up, toddler seated on pillow holding up climbing monkey toy, 19x15", EX+, A3 ....$400.00

Carter's Ink, ink holder, ceramic, 'Ma Carter,' head pulls out to fill reservoir, German, ca 1914, 4x2", NM+, A3 ....$40.00

Carter's Ink, sign, tin, oval image of man writing, square frame, Kaufmann & Strauss litho, self-framed, 1900, 25x19", VG, A9...$400.00

Carter's Inky Racer, tin, rectangular, rounded corners, slip lid, black boy running, red, 2x3x2", EX, A15.....$300.00

Carter's Knit Underwear, display, papier-maché, armless male figure with Carter's printed on forehead standing on lettered box, 33½", EX, A12.............................$725.00

Carter's Overalls, sign, cardboard stand-up, Guaranteed A New Pair..., mason laying bricks/backside of carpenter on blue, 20x14", EX+, D22.................................$85.00

Carter's Overalls, sign, porcelain, Union Made, speeding train in center surrounded by lettering, red/white/blue, 6x15", EX+, A1.................$1,350.00

Carter's Union Suits for Girls, sign, cardboard die-cut stand-up, girl standing on stool writing Carter's on chalkboard, ca 1910, 15x14", NM, A3 ....$645.00

Carter's Wash & Wear Overalls, sign, cardboard stand-up, Guaranteed-A New Pair If You Are Not Satisfied, 2 workers on 2-tone blue, 20x14", EX+, D22...................$85.00

Carus, cigar box label, inner lid, ancient Olympic games/athlete, 6x9", M, D5...$35.00

Casablanca Fan Co, sign, flange, porcelain, Authorized Dealer For above round logo, World's Finest Ceiling Fans on blue, 20x16", NM, A24 ....$500.00

Cascade Club Coffee, sign, tin, Now!.../At Your Grocer's, black/blue/white lettering on yellow, white border, 14x30", VG+, A3...$50.00

Cascarets, pocket mirror, round, All Going Out — Nothing Coming In/Cascarets Did It, image of child on chamber pot, EX+, A18...$60.00

Cascarets, sign, screened, Do It Now To-Night, woman resting on tail of C in Cascarets, 10¢ 25¢ 50¢ Sold Here, 11x21", G, A2...$385.00

Cascarets Candy Cathartic, sign, cardboard flange with cloud-shaped edge, They Work While You Sleep, lady sleeping on tail of C, 20x26", VG, A6 ....$50.00

Case, sign, neon/porcelain, eagle on globe next to block lettering on red Deco-style housing, 2-sided, 40x72x12", NM, A6 ....$2,200.00

Cashmere Bouquet, see Colgate's Cashmere Bouquet

Castellano's Havana Cigars/AJ Mitchell Cigar Co, cigar box opener/hammer, metal, engraved lettering, VG, A5.$75.00

Castle Hall, sign, cardboard hanger, The New Arrivals/Twin Cigars, stork/pack/castle by water, embellished border, 10x12", NM, A3 ....$60.00

Castrol Authorized Dealer, sign, tin, round, black/white on red-orange, embossed, 18" dia, EX, A6.................$80.00

Castrol/Wakefield Motor Oil, sign, porcelain, British Owned, black/white/yellow on red, 12x15", EX, A6...........$300.00

Caswell Blend Coffee, can, 3-lb, brown/white, key-wind lid, flower logo, EX+, A18...................................$35.00

Champion Dependable Spark Plugs, thermometer, wood, die-cut spark plug at top, black/gray on white, 21x5", EX+, A15..$550.00

Champion Harvesting Machines, calendar, 1912, old farmer guiding young boy on white work horse down path, 20x13", incomplete, EX+, A3.....................$170.00

Champion Hay Binders, magazine ad, centerfold, 1890s, 1 side depicts field scene, other side shows mother carrying boy on back, 10x15", NM, A3 ....$45.00

Champion Spark Plugs, radio, plastic spark plug on base, EX, D25 ....$225.00

Champion Spark Plugs, sign, reverse glass, Dependable.../America's Favorite, sign post/spark plug/boat/car, framed, image: 13x10", EX, A1 ....$220.00

Champion Spark Plugs, sign, tin, Champion...Cost Less/More Power, white arrow pointing to spark plug, red/white/blue, embossed, 6x15", NM, A1.........$400.00

Champion Spark Plugs, sign, tin, Champion on arrow pointing to spark plug, Cost Less/More Power, red/white/blue, embossed, 6x15", NM, A1.........$500.00

Champions, sign, tin, We Clean & Check Spark Plugs/And Recommend..., red diamond/blue & white text on yellow/blue, 14x30", EX, A1 ....$250.00

Champlin Presto Gasoline, gas globe, 2-pc, white glass body, glass lens, red/blue on white, 13½", NM, A6 ....$275.00

Channel, crate label, California lemon, gulls flying around vignette of Santa Barbara Channel, M, D12............$4.00

Chappel Star Brand Pup-E-Crumbles/Ken-L-Ration, tin, square, shows 3 puppies/4 terriers/factory, gold trim, 7x4x4", EX+, A15 ....$500.00

Chappel's Pup-E-Crumbles, sample box, cardboard with bright graphics, 4x4", EX, A15 ....$200.00

Charles Denby Cigars, cigar cutter, reverse-glass top mounted on fancy-footed nickel-plated base, G, A2......$150.00

Charles Denby Cigars, tin, vertical square, slip lid, paper label, oval portrait, EX+, A18................................$35.00

Charles Thomson 5¢ Cigar, tin, vertical square, portrait image, yellow, 5", EX+, A18 ....$110.00

Charm of the West, pocket tin, flat, EX, A18..........$300.00

Chartres Indian Head Typewriter Ribbon, tin, square, rounded corners, 1x2½x2½", EX, D37, minimum value $50.00

Chas Ehlermann Hop & Malt Co, sign, tin, Souvenir/40th Year/1860-1900, oval portrait/factory, gold tray-like rim, 26x18", VG-EX, A18/A7, from $300 to $600.00

Chas H Dorsey, calendar, 1912, die-cut embossed cardboard, image of girl with lamb holding sign against flowers/trees, 17x10", EX, A3 ....$300.00

Chas O Whitnell Wagons, Buggies, Carriages..., calendar, 1902, cardboard, winter barn scene with boy pushing wheelbarrow framed by acorns & birds, 14x11", EX, A3 ...$40.00

Chas S Higgins' German Laundry Soap, display sign, cardboard, die-cut, black woman washing clothes in wooden tub, 12x7", EX, A6..............................$200.00

Chase & Sanborn Coffee, can, sample, slip lid, High Grade, NM, A3...$38.00

Chase & Sanborn Coffee, can, ½-lb, key-wind lid, Seal Brand/Drip Grind, Montreal Canada, EX, A3 ....$40.00

Chase & Sanborn Coffee, can, 1-lb, key-wind lid, Regular Grind, NM, A3...$15.00

Chase & Sanborn Coffee, can, 1-lb, key-wind lid, Regular Grind/4¢ Off, NM (unopened), A18.......................$25.00

Chase & Sanborn Coffee, can, 1-lb, key-wind lid, Seal Brand/Drip Grind, EX+ (unopened), A18.............$45.00

Chase & Sanborn Coffee, can, 1-lb, key-wind lid, Seal Brand/Drip Grind, NM, A3..................................$25.00

Chase & Sanborn Coffee, can, 1-lb, key-wind lid, Vacuumed Packed/Regular Grind, black/white/red on silver, Canada, EX+, A3 ....$18.00

Chase & Sanborn Coffee, can, 2-lb, paper label, The Coffee Served At The World's Fair, VG, A3 ....$85.00

Chase & Sanborn Coffee, game, Charlie McCarthy's Radio Party, 1938, NM (original envelope), A3..............$40.00

Chase & Sanborn's Coffees, jigsaw puzzle, Old Fashioned New England Country Store, 1910, 6x8", EX, D10 ....$50.00

Chase & Sanborn's Coffees, sign, cardboard, Choicest Private Growths, image of various product packs, original wood frame, 29x20", EX, A18............................**$300.00**

Chase & Sanborn's Royal Gem Package Teas, sign, cloth-backed, We Sell above diagonal shadowed lettering, diamond logo, metal strips top/bottom, 35x25", EX, A2...**$100.00**

Chase & Sanborn's Tea, jigsaw puzzle, dark-skinned woman picking tea leaves, large product tin lower left, framed, 9x6", EX (original box), A3......$120.00

Chaser, sign, tin, Drink.../Drinks Swell/Mixes Well, bottle, red/white/green, embossed, 12x24", VG-EX+, A6/D11, from $70 to..**$150.00**

Chautauqua Brew/Jamestown Brewing Co, tray, round, deep rim, eagle with bottle on green, white lettering, 12" dia, VG+, A8...**$80.00**

Chautauqua Java-Mocha, can, 1-lb, slip lid, paper label, blue, EX, A18...**$165.00**

Checker Cab, hat, cloth, blue with metal badge, EX, A2...**$200.00**

Checker Strawberry Jam, can, round, pry lid, 2 elves at table on front/strawberries on back, red/white/blue, gold top/bottom, EX, A15...............................**$110.00**

Checkers, cigar box label, inner lid, men playing game of checkers, 6x9", M, D5......................................**$35.00**

Checkers Popcorn, whistle, tin, Checkers stamped across mouthpiece, 2 barrels, 2", EX, D14 ....**$16.00**

Checkers Tobacco, humidor, tin, round, slip lid with knob, gold on red/black checkered ground, EX+, A18 .**$250.00**

Checkers Tobacco, pocket tin, vertical, NM, A18..**$670.00**
Checkers Tobacco, pocket tin, vertical, VG, A18 ...**$135.00**

Cheer Up, sign, tin, Cheer Up/A Delightful Beverage, owl whistling tune, blue ground, green border, 19x19", NM+, A13...**$550.00**

Cheer Up, sign, tin, Cheer Up/A Delightful Beverage, owl whistling tune, with bottle, blue ground, 18x54", EX, D30...**$250.00**

Cheer Up, sign, tin, Drink... (round logo) lower left of bottle pouring into glass on wood-tone ground, 11x10", EX+, D30...**$220.00**

Chekola, crate label, Washington pear, vista of the 'wide hollow in the Yakima Valley,' early, Yakima, M, D12..**$12.00**

Chero-Cola, change purse, leather/metal, embossed horse race scene, G, A16...**$215.00**

Chero-Cola, clock, 1 hand, round dial on pedestal foot, One Hand Clock Co, 11x9" dia, VG, A9 ....**$350.00**

Chero-Cola, notebook/calendar, 1920, EX+, A16 ......**$50.00**

Chero-Cola, pocket mirror/pin holder, celluloid, round, EX+, A16...**$35.00**

Chero-Cola, sign, tin, Drink.../There's None So Good, lettering on oval with octagonal border on rectangle, multi, 14x20", EX, D30...**$175.00**

Cherry Blossom Shoe Polish, sign, tin, There's Always Time For A Daily Shine!, 3 kittens in 3 different shoes, green, white border, 28x18", NM, A1...$175.00

Cherry Blossoms, bottle topper, cardboard, die-cut, Drink.../5¢, girl's head framed by cherry blossom, EX, D30...**$30.00**

Cherry Blush, sign, tin, Drink.../Cherries Only Rival, lettering over image of cherry branch on black, beveled, 7x9", EX+, A3...**$390.00**

Cherry Cheer, sign, cardboard, Cheer Up/Drink..½¢/It's Good, girl framed with Art Nouveau design of cherries/bottle, 14x10", EX, A6 ....**$260.00**

Cherry Cheer, sign, paper litho, Drink.../Believe Me Kid It's Some Drink!, cherry branch above lady at table, 1910-20, 11x7", NM, A24 ....**$375.00**

Cherry Chic, syrup dispenser, ball shape, flared base, green, embossed cherry decor, J Hungerford Smith Co, 10", no pump o/w VG+, A9 ....**$6,000.00**

Cherry Smash, bottle topper, cardboard, colonial boy with bottle, EX, D30...**$50.00**

Cherry Smash, bottle topper, cardboard, colonial boy with full glass, NM, A16.......................................**$75.00**

Cherry Smash, dispenser, glass bowl with white lettering, red/white marque, metal base clamp, 1930s, EX+, A13 ....$475.00

Cherry Smash, dispenser, glass jug inverted on pyramid-shaped milk glass base, NM, A16........................$650.00

Cherry Smash, dispenser, glass jug with round paper label inverted on porcelain base with advertising, EX, A2...$1,265.00

Cherry Smash, drinking glass, flare top, applied decal with 5 people drinking from straws, EX, A16.............$165.00

Cherry Smash, pencil, image of George Washington, EX+ (unused), A16...$30.00

Cherry Smash, pin-back button, round, image of George Washington, Whitehead & Hoag, NM+, A16 ......$140.00

Cherry Smash, postcard, Cherry Smash lettered on George Washington's Mt Vernon lawn with black man serving him & Martha, G, A16 ....$20.00

Cherry Smash, sign, paper, die-cut circle with Fowler's Cherry 5¢ Smash lettered over glass, yellow ground, 1920s, 12" dia, NM, A13...................................$230.00

Cherry Smash, sign/menu, tin, Drink CS/A True Fruit Blend on disk with menu panel hanging from chain, 9", G+, A16...$225.00

Cherry Smash, syrup bottle, clear glass, label under glass at shoulder, 5¢ zigger cap, 1905-10, VG+, A13..........$210.00

Cherry Smash, syrup jug, 1-gal, clear glass, embossed, early, NM, A16 ....$180.00

Cherry Smash, syrup jug, 1-gal, clear glass, paper label, screw cap, EX, A16..$85.00

Cherry Smash, watch fob, ornate metal border around cloisonne center with cherries, EX, A16 ....$800.00

Cherry Smash Sundae, sign, cardboard, die-cut hanger, cherry sundae against yellow circle with cherry logo at stem of dish, 13x12", EX+, A13.........$110.00

Cherry Sparkle, sign, cardboard, Drink Exquisite..., with sprig of cheeries, 7x16", EX, D30 ....$75.00

Cherry Sparkle, sign, cardboard, Exquisite.../The Taste Tells The Tale, emblem right of Alfred E Neuman with bottle, 6x14", EX, A6 ....$425.00

Chester Ale, tray, round, deep rim, The Beer That Makes Friends, image of bottle/pilsner glass on tray, red rim, 1940s, 12", EX+, A19 ....$150.00

Chesterfield, pocket tin, vertical, paper label, oval portrait, EX+, A18...$100.00

Chesterfield Cigarettes, door plate, porcelain, ...They Satisfy/And The Blend Can't Be Copied, pack in center, white on blue, 9x4", NM+, A13....................................$325.00

Chesterfield Cigarettes, postcard, It's A Chesterfield, head image of doughboy with cigarette, Lyendecker, EX, D26...$35.00

Chesterfield Cigarettes, sign, cardboard, actress Maureen O'Hara lighting fighter pilot's cigarette on airfield, with ad text, 23x22", NM, A1 ....$170.00

Chesterfield Cigarettes, sign, cardboard, bust image of lady taking a cigarette from package, framed, 30x24", VG+, A8 ....$100.00

Chesterfield Cigarettes, sign, cardboard, I Always Say Yes To A Chesterfield, blond girl against white feathers/red ground, 17x14", EX, A3 ....$45.00

Chesterfield Cigarettes, sign, cardboard stand-up, Buy Your Christmas Gifts Here..., Bing Crosby on hand-held Christmas carton, 18x13", EX+, A3 ....$30.00

Chesterfield Cigarettes, sign, flange, die-cut unopened pack on red panel, Buy Chesterfield Here!, yellow/white on red, 12x15", EX, A1 ....$50.00

Chesterfield Cigarettes, sign, tin, ...Best For You on blue left of 2 unopened packs, red ground, white border, embossed, 12x30", NM, D11 ....$85.00

Chesterfield/L&M Cigarettes, sign, tin, die-cut, Buy...Here, shows pack of cigarettes, 2-sided, 15x12", VG, A9 ..$25.00

Chesty Potato Chips, doll, Chesty Boy, squeeze vinyl, 1958, M (in original mailer), D27 ....$325.00

Chesty Potato Chips, tin, 1-lb, round, slip lid, white/yellow/ blue with image of the Chesty Boy, EX, A18 ....$50.00

Chevrolet, bank, tin globe, The Symbol Of Savings For 27 Years, Chein, 5", EX+, A2 ....$60.00

Chevrolet, clock, round, dealer name above, bow-tie logo at bottom on white, 1-12, yellow/black border, EX, D30 ....$600.00

Chevrolet, lamp shade, plastic stained-glass look, multicolored, 15" dia, VG, A6 ....$250.00

Chevrolet, matchbook, Dealers (1953-1967), 20 strike, front striker, M, D28, each..$11.00

Chevrolet, pocketknife, blue bow-tie logo on cream plastic casing, 3½", EX, A6 ....$20.00

Chevrolet, sign, light-up, molded plastic, Chevrolet/Over The Years/America's 1st Choice, red/white/blue emblem, 24x28", VG, A6...$130.00

Chevrolet, sign, masonite, bow-tie logo atop V-shaped emblem, red/white, ca 1956-57, 10x21", EX, A1 ..$220.00

Chevrolet, sign, neon/porcelain, bow-tie logo, 40x120x8", EX+, A6 ....$5,550.00

Chevrolet, sign, neon/porcelain, name in block lettering above 3 lines of tubing on Deco-style housing, 34x84x12", NM, A6 ....$3,700.00

Chevrolet, sign, porcelain, die-cut bow tie, white lettering on blue, white border, 7x20", EX+, A6 ....$350.00

Chevrolet, thermometer, round dial type, metal frame with glass front, white porcelain face with logo, red/blue, 19", EX, A2 ....$1,375.00

Chevrolet, trolley sign, cardboard, For Economical Transportation/bow-tie logo/Fastest Selling.../dealer, 1920s, 11x21", NM, A14 ....$150.00

Chevrolet, see also OK

Chevrolet Corvette, pin, metal, round, Chevrolet Corvette Owner, crossed-flag logo in center, 1955-56, NM, A6 ....$260.00

Chevrolet Covair/OK, thermometer, tin, gauge at right, red/white/black on white, vertical, rounded corners, beveled, EX, D34...$225.00

Chevrolet Motor Company, calendar attachment, desk-top type, heavy metal 3-D sedan atop beveled base with embossed logos/lettering, 2x5", EX, A6 ....$275.00

Chevrolet Sales & Service, sign, porcelain, For Economical Transportation/logo/Sales & Service, rectangular, white on blue, 28x40", EX, A2 ....$880.00

Chevrolet Sales & Service, sign, porcelain, For Economical Transportation/logo/Sales & Service, trapezoid emblem, blue/white, 28x48", EX, A2 ....$1,320.00

Chevrolet School Bus, lighter, gold metal with image of school bus on porcelain inlay, 1½x2", EX, A6 .....$55.00

Chevrolet Super Service, sign, porcelain, round with extended bow-tie logo, yellow/white/blue, 2-sided, 42x49" dia, NM, A2..$2,200.00

Chevrolet Task-Force Trucks, banner, cloth, New 1956...On Display!, close-up image of front of truck left of lettering, white/yellow, 33x91", VG, A6 ....$70.00

Chevron Gasoline, pump sign, painted tin, round with 3-chevron emblem at bottom, winged 'V' in Chevron, red/white/blue, 14x12", NM+, A1.......................$400.00

Chevron Supreme Gasoline, pump sign, painted tin, round with 3-chevron emblem at bottom, winged 'V' in Chevron, red/white/blue, 14x11", NM+, A1 ....$475.00

Chi-Namel Paints, light globe (gas pump type), metal body with glass inserts, name around boy on dot, 2-sided, early, 21x19x7", EX, A15 ....$400.00

Chi-Namel Wood Finishes, sign, paper, die-cut Chinese lantern with image of Chinese man using product, multicolored, EX+, A15..$70.00

Chicago Cable Havana Filled Five Cent Cigar, cigar box, Chicago scene, late 1800s, VG, A5.....................$350.00

Chicago Kahn Bros Made To Measure Clothes, display bin, tin, orange 2-compartment tray with open front, All Wool All One Price/$25 on marque, 10x13x12", NM+, A3...**$150.00**

Chicago Rock Island & Pacific RY, poster, black/white images around bold lettering on blue, red/white/black decorative border, late 1800s, 27x16", NM, A1...**$400.00**

Chicken Delight, bank, chicken figure, rubber, yellow with red accents/base, 5½", NM+, A14...........................**$75.00**

Chicken Dinner Candy, sign, cardboard die-cut stand-up, Get Your..½¢ Here!/Delicious Candy, chicken on yellow dot, NM+, A3...**$260.00**

Chicken In The Rough/Oklahoma City, pail, tin, give-away promoting ½ fried chicken, white ground, EX+, A3...**$20.00**

Chicklets Gum, see Adams Chicklets Chewing Gum

Chicklets Gum, see Dentyne/Clove/Beemans/Chicklets Gum

Chief Cook, cigar box labels, 2-pc set, round image of chef holding up tray, Witsch & Schmitt #515/516, VG+, A5...**$340.00**

Chief Joseph, crate label, apple, pictures chief on blue ground, EX, D3...**$4.00**

Chief Paints, sign, tin, yellow name next to colorful Indian head in full headdress, 2-sided, 12x28", VG, A6..**$125.00**

Chippewa's Pride Beer, tray, round, deep rim, Indian maiden in profile on yellow, red rim, American Art Works, 14" dia, NM, A19.......................................**$85.00**

Chips Ahoy, doll, girl in blue dress wearing cookie hat, vinyl, 4½", NM+, A14...**$10.00**

Chlorodont Toothpaste, trade card, mechanical, swing tab moves eyes/hand-held toothbrush on black girl's face, orange/purple/green, EX+, A17..$125.00

Chock Full of Nuts Coffee, can, 1-lb, key-wind lid, The Heavenly..., blue/yellow background, VG, A3.....**$20.00**

Chocolat Revillon, clock, painted tin, wind-up, scalloped frame with name around Roman numerals on round face, 23x18", EX, A6...**$475.00**

Chocolate Cream Coffee, can, 1-lb, key-wind lid, brown on yellow, NM, A3...**$60.00**

Chocolate Cream Steel Cut Brand Coffee, can, 2½-oz, pry lid, 2x3", EX, D37...**$115.00**

Chocolate Crush, sign, cardboard, Drink..., tilted bottle over soda glass on blue emblem, yellow ground, 11x9", EX, D30...**$130.00**

Chocolate Crush, sign, tin, Drink.../A Rich Creamy Chocolate Soda In A Bottle, white/black on gold, 1930s, 14x20", EX+, A14...**$150.00**

Chocolate Soldier, sign, tin, Drink Sterilized...In Bottles on bottle cap next to tin soldier, embossed, 19x27", EX+, A16...**$120.00**

Chocolate-Menier, sign, cardboard, backview of girl writing Drink Chocolate Menier, product in basket, American version, 23x16", VG, A9.......................................**$150.00**

Choice Family Tea, pail, straight-sided, dome lid, bail handle, yellow, Ginna, pre-1901, NM, A18..............**$150.00**

Choisa Coffee, can, 1-lb, key-wind lid, NM (unopened), A3..**$110.00**

Christian Diehl Brewing Co, tray, round, deep rim, A New Diehl, nymph holding up arms to large bottle in mountains, 12" dia, EX, A8........................$100.00

Christian Diehl Brewing Co, tray, round, deep rim, without phrase, nymph holding up arms to large bottle in mountains, 12" dia, NM, A8................................**$125.00**

Christian Feigenspan Breweries, tip tray, round, lettering on bottom rim around girl in profile, 1910-11, VG+, A8........**$150.00**

Christian Feigenspan Brewing Co, see PON

Christian Moerlein Brewing Co, sign, paper, National Export & Barbarossa Bottled Beer, embellished image with bottles/kegs/symbols, 15x11", EX, A8........**$185.00**

Christian Moerlein National Export & Barbarossa Beer, sign, paper, elderly couple at table enjoying brew, logo upper left, pre-1920s, framed, 27x23", NM+, A19..**$250.00**

Christo Cola, bottle, Drink Christo Cola 5¢ in script lettering, with original pour spout, Richmond VA, NM, A13..**$425.00**

Christo Cola, compact, celluloid, round, ...She Also Drinks..., G, A16..**$45.00**

Christo Cola, paperweight, cast-metal turtle with celluloid top, EX, A16...**$150.00**

Christy Girl Whalebone Corsets, sign, paper, woman golfer/couple flank bust portrait of Christy Girl, ca 1920, 9x12", NM, A3...**$140.00**

Christy's Choice Quality Oysters, tin, 1-gal, round, pry lid, 7", EX+, A18...**$65.00**

Chrysler, bank, Mr Fleet, vinyl, 1970s, NM, D20.....**$350.00**

Chrysler, license plate attachment, tin, It Pays To Buy A Fine Car/Chrysler, black top hat/gloves/cane on red oval, 6x9", VG+, A1...**$275.00**

Chrysler, sign, neon, tube-formed logo, original transformer, 24x25", EX, A6..**$1,100.00**

Chrysler, sign, porcelain, die-cut emblem, blue name on white center band, blue ground, blue/white border, 2-sided, 24x36", EX, A6..**$425.00**

Chrysler, see also MoPar

Chrysler Approved Service, sign, porcelain, round, red/white/blue, 2-sided, 30" dia, EX, A6 ....$325.00

Chrysler Sales/Service, globe sign, white glass body, 2 glass lenses, seal-type logo in center on red, black reproduction scounce, 13½", EX, A6 ....$375.00

Chrysler/Plymouth Approved Service, sign, porcelain, round with extended center band, yellow/red/black, 2-sided, 42x44" dia, VG, A6.....................$700.00

Chrysler/Plymouth Sales & Service, sign, porcelain, white lettering/graphics on black, white outline, 2-sided, 18x35", VG+, A2 ....$715.00

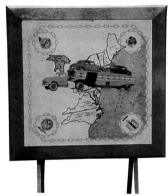

Chrysler/Plymouth/Dodge/DeSoto, table, wood, fold-down top inlayed with advertising showing car carrier over map of eastern seaboard, 24x26x26", VG, A6 ....$330.00

CHYP Intercollegiate Mixture, tin, rectangular, square corners, VG+, A18...$175.00

Ciba/Geigy Corp, pen stand with figure, smiling Ritalin Man lifting hat from head, 1970s, 7", NM, D20 ....$125.00

Cigars, sign, light-up, metal, cream lettering with red/orange lights on brown background, 6x15", VG, A6 .....$385.00

Cincinnati Burger Brau, sign, tin hanger, oval, Vas You Efer In Zinzinnati, German gent with mug on pine swag above, embossed, 10x14", NM, A3.....................$100.00

Cincinnati Cream Beer, tray, round, deep rim, Handsome Waiter holding up tray with bottle, American Art Works litho, 13" dia, VG, A9 ....$120.00

Cinco Cigars, display case, metal/glass, slant top with folding marque, 12x10x15", EX+, D6.....................$450.00

Circus Club Marshmallow, tins, complete set of 6, Elephant/Dog/Cat/Monkey/Bear/Pig, G+ to EX+, A3..$935.00

Cities Service, pocket mirror, round, celluloid, cartoon image of serviceman/lettering on green ground, 2" dia, EX, A5 ....$90.00

Cities Service, winterfront, cardboard, white/black logo above white Cities Service on black band, green ground, framed, 13x21", EX, A1..$50.00

Cities Service Oils, sign, porcelain, ...Once-Always, cover-leaf logo in center, black/white, 2-sided, 42" dia, G, A2.$300.00

Cities Services/Gasoline/And Motor Oils, sign, porcelain, logo & blue/white/blue lettering on white/blue/white field, blue border, 2-sided, 36x60", EX+, A2.......$470.00

Citizen's Club, cigar box, image of chess & pool game, VG+, A5..$350.00

City Club Crushed Cubes, pocket tin, vertical, short, VG+, A18...$175.00

City Club Crushed Cubes, pocket tin, vertical, tall, VG+, A18...$200.00

City Club/Jacob Schmidt Brewing Co, matchbook, 20 strike, front strike, Diamond Quality, M, D28 ......$10.00

CL Centlivre Brewing Co, sign, paper, aerial factory scene with river/horse-drawn traffic, pre-prohibition, 25x38", NM, A8..$400.00

Clabber Girl Baking Powder, banner, cloth, Guaranteed Pure/Clabber Girl Baking Powder/Makes Delicious Biscuits, yellow/blue/yellow, 18x36", EX+, A3..........$50.00

Clabber Girl Baking Powder, sign, tin, Clabber Girl The Double-Acting Baking Powder in red/black on cream, 2-sided, 1950s-60s, 12x34", EX, A13....................$60.00

Clark B&B, thermometer, wood, arched top, beveled edge, Clark Bar O'Clock above gauge, lettering below, yellow, vertical, VG+, A3...$50.00

Clark Horton Store, sign, painted wood, 6 Miles To The Horse Clothier & Furnisher.../Afton NY, bust image of Yellow Kid, 47x12", EX, A15 ....$1,600.00

Clark's Mile-End Spool Thread, cabinet, oak, 2-drawer, lettering on glass inserts, 7x15x23", NM, A3..........$110.00

Clark's Peanut Butter, pail, 1-lb, EX-NM, A3/A15, from $320 to $500.00

Clark's Spool Cotton, see also John J Clark's Spool Cotton

Clark's Spool Cotton, sign, paper, My Mama Wants A Spool Of..., country store scene with girl at counter/clerk/customers, 25x21", VG, A6 ....$650.00

Clark's Teaberry Gum, display case, wood frame with glass sides/top/2 shelves, beveled base, paper label on front, 16x15x10", EX, A6 ....$300.00

Clark's Teaberry Gum, display stand, vaseline glass, square dish on pedestal base, 3x5x7", NM+, A3 ....$55.00

Clark's Teaberry Gum, sign, tin, A Happy Thought/That Mountain Tea Flavor, lettering/large pack on yellow, red border, 9x12", EX, A13 ....$180.00

Clarke's Pure Rye, sign, canvas, elderly gent with bottle/jigger, no advertising, wood frame, 44x34", VG, A7 ....$300.00

Clarke's Pure Rye, sign, cardboard, elderly gent with bottle/jigger, Clarke's Pure Rye/Bottle In Bond, ornate gold frame, 46x36", EX, A7...$700.00

Coca-Cola, bank, dispenser, red, Drink C-C/Refresh Yourself/ Ice Cold, single glass, 1950s, EX+, A13 ....$375.00

Coca-Cola, banner, canvas, Drink C-C From The Bottle Through A Straw, bottle at left, red/black on white, 1910, 16x70", VG+, A13 ....$4,000.00

Coca-Cola, baseball counter, perpetual, keeps runs, hits & errors of both teams, 1907, VG, A16..................$100.00

Coca-Cola, bicycle, boys, full-size, red on white, 1950s, NM+ (NOS), A13 ....$425.00

Coca-Cola, blotter, Dells C-C Bottling Co/Dells Wisconsin, 6-pack/bottle in upper corners, EX+, A16 ....$485.00

Coca-Cola, blotter, Drink C-C in Bottles/How C-C Is Bottled/C-C Bottling Co, shows bottle in center, rare, NM, A16..$265.00

Coca-Cola, blotter, 1913, Pure & Healthful.../5¢ Everywhere, bottles flank oval, G, A16.......................................$15.00

Coca-Cola, blotter, 1920, Drink C-C/D&R, on oval flanked by hand pouring Coke into fountain glass from tap, NM, A3...$25.00

Coca-Cola, blotter, 1929, One Little Minute For A Big Rest, man with bottle, EX, A16.....................................$425.00

Coca-Cola, blotter, 1929, The Pause That Refreshes, couple toasting with bottles, red on white, VG+, A14 .....$35.00

Coca-Cola, blotter, 1935, A Home Run With Three On, boy on bicycle, NM+, A16...$200.00

Coca-Cola, blotter, 1935, Delicious/Wholesome/Refreshing, bottle & receding logo on ruler/protractor, Canadian, NM+, A13 ....$325.00

Coca-Cola, blotter, 1936, 50th Anniversary/1886-1936, EX+, A14..$25.00

Coca-Cola, blotter, 1937, Cold Refreshment, tilted bottle, NM, A16..$35.00

Coca-Cola, blotter, 1940, The Greatest Pause On Earth, clown with bottle, EX+, A16 ....$45.00

Coca-Cola, blotter, 1942, Wherever Thirst Goes, girl with bottle in boat, smaller size, EX+, A16 ....$18.00

Coca-Cola, blotter, 1944, How About A Coke, 3 girls with bottles, M, A16 ....$15.00

Coca-Cola, blotter, 1947, Have A Coke, couple with bottles/ receding logo, NM, A14 ....$19.00

Coca-Cola, blotter, 1948, Hospitality, 2 girls sitting on sofa entertaining young man, Canadian, NM, A14.......$14.00

Coca-Cola, blotter, 1951, Drink C-C/D&R, arrow pointing to Sprite Boy behind bottle, NM+, A16 ....$20.00

Coca-Cola, blotter, 1951, Play Refreshed, bottle/button logo with sporting equipment, fish & fowl, Canadian, EX+, A14...$17.00

Coca-Cola, blotter, 1953, Good!, Sprite Boy with bottle in snow mound, Canadian, NM, A14......................$12.00

Coca-Cola, blotter, 1955, party crowd in front of fireplace, Canadian, NM+, A14...$24.00

Coca-Cola, blotter, 1956, Friendliest Drink On Earth, hand-held bottle over image of Earth, NM+, A16..........$15.00

Coca-Cola, bookends, brass bottle shape on bases, 1963, 8", NM, A13, pair..$325.00

Coca-Cola, booklet, The Coca-Cola News, April 15 1896/Vol 1/No 3 edition, 8x6", NM+ (unopened), A13 .....$125.00

Coca-Cola, bookmark, 1898, heart shape, celluloid, NM, A13...$725.00

Coca-Cola, bookmark, 1900, heart shape, celluloid, NM, A15...$750.00

Coca-Cola, bookmark, 1905, Lillian Nordica, EX+ (unused), A16...$850.00

Coca-Cola, bookmark, 1906, owl, EX+, A16 ....$650.00

Coca-Cola, bottle, blue, Canada, pre-1915, EX, A14..$40.00

Coca-Cola, bottle, clear, straight-sided, C-C Bottling Works, Rochester, 1910s, 4-oz, NM+, A13 ....$325.00

Coca-Cola, bottle, clear, straight-sided, Rochester NY, 1910s, regular size, NM+, A13 ....$75.00

Coca-Cola, bottle, green, straight-sided, Birmingham Bottling Co in white lettering, G, A13...........................$1,300.00

Coca-Cola, bottle, olive green, Canada, pre-1915, rare, EX+, A14...$70.00

Coca-Cola, bottle caddy for shopping cart, Enjoy C-C While You Shop/Place Bottle Here, white on red, EX, A1.........$65.00

Coca-Cola, bottle caddy for shopping cart, Place Bottles Here/C-C/Take Some Home Today, yellow/white on red, 1950s, 5x6", NM, A13 ....$250.00

Coca-Cola, bottle carrier, aluminum, wire handle, Delicious/ Refreshing, with 6 bottles, 1950s, VG+, A2 ....$230.00

Coca-Cola, bottle carrier, cardboard, 6 For 25¢, white on red, 1939, EX, A13......................$50.00

Coca-Cola, bottle carrier, cardboard box, Six Bottles C-C/Serve Ice Cold, white on red, 6 original full bottles, 1930s, EX+, A13.......................$200.00

Coca-Cola, bottle carrier, wood, rounded corners, double-rope handle, 6 holes for bottles, EX+, A16........$840.00

Coca-Cola, bottle carrier, wood, wing logos on natural, wire handle with wood grip, no dividers, 1930s-40s, NM, A13.....................$100.00

Coca-Cola, bottle carrier, wood, wing logos on natural, wire handle with wood grip, 6 original 6½-oz bottles, 1930s-40s, VG, A9......................$250.00

Coca-Cola, bottle carrier, wood, wing logos on yellow, cut-out handle, 1930s-40s, VG+, A13......................$100.00

Coca-Cola, bottle carrier, wooden box, dovetailed corners, rope handle, holds 6 bottles, Refresh Yourself..., EX+, A16......................$330.00

Coca-Cola, bottle case, wood, bent at corners, yellow/red, 1940, G, A16......................$150.00

Coca-Cola, bottle opener, metal, bottle shape, flat, 1950s, EX+, A14......................$22.00

Coca-Cola, bottle opener, metal, die-cut flat bottle with octagonal opener, engraved lettering on bottle, 1950s, EX+, A14......................$10.00

Coca-Cola, bottle opener, plastic handle (white), Serves Hospitality In The Home, M, A16......................$30.00

Coca-Cola, bottle opener/spoon, C-C In Bottles (block lettering), early, EX, A16......................$250.00

Coca-Cola, bottle topper, cardboard, bathing beauty on arrowhead-shaped emblem, receding logo, 1929, 9x7", VG+, A13......................$1,500.00

Coca-Cola, bottle topper, cardboard, Chick 'n Que/You'll Want Plenty Of Coke, barbecue couple, EX, D30............$30.00

Coca-Cola, bottle topper, cardboard, Refresh Yourself, ice skating couple on bench, receding logo, Canada, 1926, 13x13", EX+, A13 ....$3,600.00

Coca-Cola, bottle topper, plastic, We Let You See The Bottle on base, button sign flanked by gold bottles, **1950s, 7", NM, A13.......................$750.00**

Coca-Cola, bottle topper/bottle, cardboard, die-cut, Ice Cold/C-C (on oval logo)/King Size, resembles hot air balloon, EX, D30......................$32.00

Coca-Cola, bottle topper/bottle, cardboard, Have A Party From Your Pantry/Check Your Needs Now, sign atop plate, EX, D30......................$30.00

Coca-Cola, bowl, ceramic, green, embossed logos around fluted rim, 1936, M, D32......................$475.00

Coca-Cola, calendar, 1901, no pad, G, A13...........$1,850.00
Coca-Cola, calendar, 1904, incomplete, VG+, A13.$2,300.00
Coca-Cola, calendar, 1905, incomplete, EX+, A13 ..$7,500.00
Coca-Cola, calendar, 1907, complete, EX+, A13...$17,000.00
Coca-Cola, calendar, 1908, incomplete, G+, A13....$1,100.00
Coca-Cola, calendar, 1913, incomplete, G, A13......$4,000.00
Coca-Cola, calendar, 1914, no bottle, top only, EX+, A13......................$1,000.00

Coca-Cola, calendar, 1914, with bottle, complete, rare, NM+, A13......................$16,000.00
Coca-Cola, calendar, 1914, with bottle, incomplete, rare, EX, A13......................$5,000.00
Coca-Cola, calendar, 1915, complete, VG, A13.....$1,800.00
Coca-Cola, calendar, 1916, complete, EX+, A13...$2,100.00
Coca-Cola, calendar, 1917, with glass, complete, EX+, A13......................$2,300.00
Coca-Cola, calendar, 1918, beach scene, complete, rare, EX+, A13......................$10,500.00

Coca-Cola, clock, square, fishtail (Drink C-C), green numbers/dots, glass front, metal frame, 1960s, 15", EX-NM, A1 from $175 to $285.00

Coca-Cola, clock, square, red dot (Drink C-C In Bottles), black numbers, wood frame with rounded corners, 1939, 16", EX+, A13...$400.00
Coca-Cola, clock, square, Things Go Better With Coke/Drink C-C button, green numbers, plastic, 1960s, EX, A13/D30...$100.00
Coca-Cola, clock, vertical, reverse glass square face with red numbers, Drink C-C light-up panel below, 1960s, 12x11", VG, A6 ....$200.00

Coca-Cola, clock, wing panel, white button, red dots as numbers, 1948, 36", EX, A13/D32, from $425 to $475.00
Coca-Cola, cooler, airline, red, Drink C-C, grip handle on hinged lid, insulated, opener, 1950s, restored, NM, A13 ....$375.00

Coca-Cola, cooler, airline, red, Drink C-C, grip handle on hinged lid, insulated, opener, 1950s, VG+, A24.$235.00
Coca-Cola, cooler, floor, chest-type, red, Drink C-C/Ice Cold on sides, 34x18x26", 1930s, NM, A13..................$775.00
Coca-Cola, cooler, floor, Glascock Jr (single), green with red side panels, oval Drink C-C logos, with opener, 1929, restored, A13...$550.00
Coca-Cola, cooler, floor, wood, 4-legged, open slant top, zinc lined, red on yellow, 1910s-20s, 35x38x25", VG, A13...$950.00

Coca-Cola, cooler, floor, wood, 4-legged, tin sides, Serve Yourself/Drink C-C/Please Pay The Clerk, 29x32x21", no top o/w EX, A6 ....$1,700.00
Coca-Cola, cooler, picnic, metal, red, Drink C-C, carrying handle only, horizontal, 12x18x9", EX, A6 ....$200.00
Coca-Cola, cooler, picnic, metal, red, Drink C-C, grip handle on lid/carrying handle, 1940s, vertical, VG, A16..$165.00
Coca-Cola, cooler, picnic, metal, unpainted, Drink C-C In Bottles, grip handle on lid/carrying handle, food tray, 19x17x12", NM, A1 ....$525.00
Coca-Cola, cooler, picnic, 6-pack, metal, red, Drink C-C, grip handle/carrying handle, opener 1950s, NM, A13.$475.00
Coca-Cola, cooler, picnic, 6-pack, metal, unpainted, Drink C-C, grip handle on lid/carrying handle, opener, 1950s, EX+, A13..$425.00
Coca-Cola, coupon, Free Drink, 1934 Chicago Century Of Progress, NM, A16 ....$38.00
Coca-Cola, coupon/postcard, Enjoy These 6 Bottles... (coupon)/So Easy To Take Home The Six-Bottle Carton (postcard), NM, D26 ....$35.00
Coca-Cola, cutout for children, Circus (1927 version), 3-pc, incomplete, VG, A13 ....$65.00
Coca-Cola, cutout for children, Circus (1930s version), 7-pc, complete, NM, A6...$140.00
Coca-Cola, cutout for children, Toonerville Town, 1930s, 10x15", EX, A6 ....$160.00

Coca-Cola, decal, Drink C-C In Bottles, red horizontal rectangle with rounded corners, 1950s, 9x15", NM+, A13 ....$45.00
Coca-Cola, decal, King Size/Ice Cold, bottle on yellow background, 1950s, 17x8", NM, A13 ....$35.00
Coca-Cola, decal, script logo, 1950s, 10x28", NM, A13..$20.00
Coca-Cola, desk set, mini cooler on plastic base flanked by 2 pen holders, EX+, A16 ....$100.00
Coca-Cola, dispenser, 1896, bowl on pedestal base, ceramic, white with fancy gold trim, complete, G-VG, A13, from $3,000 to...$4,600.00

Coca-Cola, dispenser, 1896 (1950s repro), hard rubber, VG, A13...$325.00

Coca-Cola, dispenser, 1920s-30s, frosted glass container with lid on red porcelain base marked Drink C-C, complete, 17", NM, A13 ....$6,200.00

Coca-Cola, dispenser, 1930s, arched top, red, Drink C-C on sides, NM+, A4...$1,500.00

Coca-Cola, dispenser, 1940s, streamline, red, Drink C-C Ice Cold, Have A Coke lettered on tap, EX, A13 .....$375.00

Coca-Cola, dispenser, 1950s, barrel, wood, 15-gal, red, chrome bands, footed, 2 spigots, 28", NM, A1 ....$750.00

Coca-Cola, dispenser, 1950s, barrel, wood, 15-gallon, red, chrome bands, footed, 2 spigots, 28", VG+, A1 ....$375.00

Coca-Cola, dispenser, 1950s, tombstone style with 4 spigots (different flavors), button logo, red/white, 14x11x8", VG+, A14...$565.00

Coca-Cola, dispenser, 1960s, Dole, Drink C-C/Ice Cold/Sign Of Good Taste, red/white lettering on red/white box, NM, A13 ....$2,100.00

Coca-Cola, display, cardboard, clown balancing upside down on Coke bottle & holding carton, 2-sided, 1950s, 60x48", NM, A13..............................$3,300.00

Coca-Cola, display, cardboard, Friends For Life, Norman Rockwell's fishing boy & dog sitting on bank, with pond, 1935, 36", VG, A13 ....$2,500.00

Coca-Cola, display bottle, 1930s, green glass, Pat'd Dec 25, 1923, 20", NM (VG cap), A13 ....$325.00

Coca-Cola, display bottle, 1930s, green glass, Pat'd Dec 25, 1923, 20", no cap o/w NM, A13 ....$225.00

Coca-Cola, display bottle, 1960s, green glass, with cap, 20", NM+, A14...$80.00

Coca-Cola, display bottle, 1980s, green glass, 20", no cap o/w NM+, A14...$45.00

Coca-Cola, display building, cardboard, replica of the Coke Bottling Co building in San Diego, red/black on white, 7x14", EX, A13 ....$50.00

Coca-Cola, doll, Buddy Lee, composition, in uniform, with hat, 1950s, EX+, A13...$875.00

Coca-Cola, doll, Frozen C-C mascot, stuffed striped cloth, 1960s, NM+, A16...$145.00

Coca-Cola, door knobs, brass, round, embossed with C-C script logo, EX+, A16, pair..............................$3,000.00

Coca-Cola, door plate, Come In! Have A C-C, yellow/white on red, porcelain, curved ends, 1930s-40s, 12", NM, A13/A14, from $300 to $415.00

Coca-Cola, door plate, Drink above ½ litre bottle, white on red, Canadian, 1970s, 10x4", NM+, A14 ....$70.00

Coca-Cola, door plate, Drink C-C, bottle on white ground, red/yellow/green border, embossed tin, 1930s, 13x5", EX, A13....................................$425.00

Coca-Cola, door plate, Prenez Un C-C, yellow/white on red, porcelain, curved ends, 1930s, horizontal, 7", NM, A13...$120.00

Coca-Cola, door plate, Pull/Refresh Yourself!, white/green with red disk logo, porcelain, 1940s-1950s, 8x4", NM, A13, from $425 to $525.00

Coca-Cola, door plate, Thanks Call Again For A C-C, yellow/white on red, curved ends, 1930s, 12x4", NM, A13 ....$450.00

Coca-Cola, door pull, aluminum, die-cut bottle with Drink C-C disk logo above, EX+, A16...............................$380.00

Coca-Cola, door pull, plastic figural bottle on metal bracket, Have A Coke!, 1950s, 8x2", NM (original box), A13 ....$425.00

Coca-Cola, door push bar, Buvez C-C Glace, yellow/white on red, porcelain, Canada, 1950s, 32", NM+, A13 .....$130.00

Coca-Cola, door push bar, Coke Adds Life..., contour logo at left, black ground, tin, 1970s, 3x32", EX+, A14 ....$35.00

Coca-Cola, match striker, porcelain, Drink C-C/Strike Matches Here, Canada, 1938, NM, A13/A14, from $425 to ..**$575.00**

Coca-Cola, matchbook, Refresh Yourself, small bottle on back, green/red/white, 20 strike front strike, Diamond Quality, M, D28................**$14.00**

Coca-Cola, matchbook, 50th Anniversary, 1936, 20 strike, front striker, M, D28................**$6.00**

Coca-Cola, matchbook cover, C-C/D&R on top fold, shows upright bottle, EX+, D30 ....**$6.00**

Coca-Cola, matchbook cover, Drink C-C, shows full glass, horizontal pinstripe ground/diagonal logo, EX, D30.......**$4.00**

Coca-Cola, matchbook cover, Drink C-C D&R (receding billboard logo)/Refresh Yourself (tilted bottle), EX, D30 ..**$5.00**

Coca-Cola, matchbook cover, Drink C-C/Have A Coke, shows hand-held bottle, EX, D30 ....**$5.00**

Coca-Cola, matchbook cover, Season's Greetings/Drink C-C on button logo/Santa with bottle, NM, A16..........**$35.00**

Coca-Cola, mechanical pencil, mother-of-pearl finish with advertising, EX+, A16 ....**$90.00**

Coca-Cola, mechanical pencil/fountain pen, stamped advertising, NM, A16 ....**$140.00**

Coca-Cola, menu, Soda Menu, Hilda Clark, 1903, EX, A16 ....**$850.00**

Coca-Cola, menu board, C-C/Sign Of Good Taste, bottles lower corners, wood-tone border, cardboard, 1959, 28x19", EX+, A13 ....**$200.00**

Coca-Cola, menu board, C-C/Sign Of Good Taste, fishtail on white arched panel, green lines/trim, tin, 1959, NM, A13 ....**$425.00**

Coca-Cola, menu board, Drink C-C, fishtail logo (no clock) above Delicious With Food flanked by menu slots, 1960s, 16x57", NM, A13 ....$575.00

Coca-Cola, menu board, Drink C-C, fishtail logo clock above Delicious With Food flanked by menu slots, 1960s, 16x57", NM, A13 ....$1,000.00

Coca-Cola, menu board, Drink C-C, molded floral decor atop sign above slots/embossed bottle, wood, Kay Displays, 1930s, EX+, A4 ....**$500.00**

Coca-Cola, menu board, Drink C-C, red panel atop board, 11 menu slots, curved bottom corners, plywood, 1930s-40s, 24x14", EX+, A13 ....**$325.00**

Coca-Cola, menu board, Drink C-C, silhouette logo, red panel above green board, tin, 1941, 28x20", EX, A13.....**$425.00**

Coca-Cola, menu board, Drink C-C In Bottles, metal button at top of leather-look board, 10 menu slots, 29x17", EX, A13................**$525.00**

Coca-Cola, menu board, Drink C-C/Be Really Refreshed, fishtail logo, glass panel with menu slots, metal frame, 20x30", VG, A13................**$450.00**

Coca-Cola, menu board, Drink C-C/Specials To-Day, blackboard with red oval logo, red/yellow/green trim, tin, vertical, G, A2 ....$165.00

Coca-Cola, menu board, Drink C-C/Specials To-Day, blackboard with red/green/yellow striped trim, tin, 1930s, 24x17", NM, A13................$650.00

Coca-Cola, menu board, Drink C-C/Specials To-Day, blackboard with red/green/yellow striped trim, tin, 1930s, 27x19", G+, A1................$125.00

Coca-Cola, menu board, Enjoy C-C, panel with red stars above 7-sloted panel, light-up, plastic/metal, gold frame, 22x22", EX, A6 ....**$150.00**

Coca-Cola, menu board, Enjoy C-C/Things Go Better With Coke, red dot on white above green board, white border, tin, 28x20", EX, A1 ....**$85.00**

Coca-Cola, menu board, Enjoy Frozen C-C, white panel with design, plastic, curved corners, board below, 14x13", NOS, A6................**$70.00**

Coca-Cola, menu board, Good With Food, fishtail logo flanked by menu slots, light-up, plastic, 19x49", EX, D30 ....**$200.00**

Coca-Cola, mileage meter, plastic, red with white lettering, 1950s, EX, A13................**$1,550.00**

Coca-Cola, miniature case with bottles, plastic, EX, A16 .....**$25.00**

Coca-Cola, miniature crate, wood, stenciled logo, EX+, A16 ....**$42.00**

Coca-Cola, miniature 6-pack, paper, wire handle, 6 bottles, NM, A16................**$300.00**

Coca-Cola, music box, shaped like floor cooler with doll on revolving disk, red, 1950s, EX+, D32................**$2,700.00**

Coca-Cola, napkin holder, red metal floor cooler-type with bottle opener, napkins dispense from top, Mexican, 1930s-40s, VG, A13................**$950.00**

Coca-Cola, needle case, 1924, EX+, A16 ....**$65.00**

Coca-Cola, needle case, 1925, NM, A16 ....**$90.00**

Coca-Cola, note pad, 1902, 5x2½", NM, D32.......$950.00

Coca-Cola, note pad, 1903, 5x2½", EX+, A16 ....$875.00

Coca-Cola, notebook, leather, Compliments Of The C-C Co stamped in gold, lists of dispensers & gallons used for 1903, EX, A16...$400.00

Coca-Cola, patch, Drink C-C in bottles red disk logo, 1950s, 7" dia, VG+, A13 ....$20.00

Coca-Cola, pencil holder, 1896 dispenser, ceramic, 1960s, 7", EX, A1...$150.00

Coca-Cola, periodical, The C-C News, Vol 1 issue, NM, A16..$2,200.00

Coca-Cola, photo album, 1940 C-C Golden Gate International Expo, gold-stamped cover, with 8x10" glossy photos, NM, A16...$340.00

Coca-Cola, pillow, race-car shape, stuffed print cloth with other advertising, #16, 'Goodyear' tires, 1970s, 15", NM, A16..$100.00

Coca-Cola, pin-back button, Member Hi-Fi Club, multicolored, 1950s, EX, A16 ....$20.00

Coca-Cola, plate, Drink C-C/D&R (on red panels)/Refresh Yourself on rim, bottle/glass in center, Knowles, 1930s, 8", rare, EX, A13 ....$750.00

Coca-Cola, plate, Drink C-C/Refresh Yourself on rim, bottle & glass in center, Knowles, 1930s, 7", EX+, A13.....$375.00

Coca-Cola, playing cards, Sprite Boy/bottle, Canadian Playing Card Co/Tougas & Nicholson Coca-Cola Ltd, complete, NM (EX box), A16 ....$1,000.00

Coca-Cola, playing cards, 1915, M (sealed box), D32 .$3,500.00

Coca-Cola, playing cards, 1928, Refresh Yourself!, girl sipping from straw, complete, NM (no box), A13..$2,500.00

Coca-Cola, playing cards, 1951, cowgirl with bottle, complete, NM (VG+ box), A16................................$110.00

Coca-Cola, playing cards, 1958, Welcome Friend, 'Old Man Winter' with bottle, complete, M (VG box), A16.$100.00

Coca-Cola, playing cards, 1960, Be Really Refreshed, masquerade party, NMIB, A16 ....$165.00

Coca-Cola, playing cards, 1961, Coke Refreshes You Best!, bowling girl, complete, EX+, A16.......................$60.00

Coca-Cola, playing cards, 1963, Zing! Refreshing New Feeling, complete, EXIB, A16 ....$70.00

Coca-Cola, playing cards, 1976, C-C Adds Life To...Everything Nice, MIB (sealed), A16............................$30.00

Coca-Cola, pocket lighter, flip top, fishtail logo, 1960, EX+, A16...$120.00

Coca-Cola, pocket mirror, 1910, EX+, A13..........$250.00

Coca-Cola, pocket mirror, 1911, VG+, A13..........$150.00

Coca-Cola, pocket mirror, 1916, EX, A13............$200.00

Coca-Cola, pocket mirror, 1936, C-C/Memos/Delicious & Refreshing, VG+ (original envelope), A16.........$140.00

Coca-Cola, pocket mirror, 1936, C-C/Memos/50th Anniversary, EX+, A16...$120.00

Coca-Cola, pocketknife, brass, 2-blade, with cork screw, C-C Bottling Co, Kaster & Co, 1905-15, EX, A16 ...$385.00

Coca-Cola, pocketknife, Drink C-C In Bottles 5¢ in red lettering on white pearlized inlay, EX, A6 ....$135.00

Coca-Cola, pocketknife, with corkscrew, embossed metal, leaf-vine design with bottle/logo, 3½", EX, A6 ..$70.00

Coca-Cola, pocketknife, with opener, C-C script logo, Lancaster Bottling Works, VG+, A16 ....$55.00

Coca-Cola, postcard, Coca-Cola Girl, 1910, NM+, A13...$775.00

Coca-Cola, poster, cardboard, Dancing Lady/Joan Crawford Clark Gable Refresh With C-C, 1930s, EX, A13 ..$1,900.00

Coca-Cola, pretzel bowl, aluminum, round with 3 cast bottles, 8" dia, EX+, A1...$185.00

Coca-Cola, printer's proof, cardboard hanger sign, boy's head sipping from bottle against burst of light rays, 1920s, 9x4", G, A16 ....$500.00

Coca-Cola, puzzle, jigsaw, 2000 pieces, NMIB, A13 .$25.00

Coca-Cola, radio, airline cooler-type, mirrored lid opens to controls, Refreshes You Best logo, red/white, 1950s, VG+, A13...$3,800.00

Coca-Cola, radio, bottle form, all original, 1933, 24", NM+, A13 ....$8,000.00

Coca-Cola, radio, bottle form, all original, 1933, 24", non-working o/w EX+, A13 ....$5,300.00

Coca-Cola, radio, cooler form, plastic, red, Drink C-C Ice Cold, 1950s, VG+, A13 ....$450.00

Coca-Cola, radio, cooler form, wood, red, Drink C-C Ice Cold, black knobs, transistor, 1940s-50s, 5x7x4", EX+, A13...$725.00

Coca-Cola, sign, cardboard, Drink C-C, ballpark lady in red with bottle & fur stole draped over her arm, 1940, 50x30", EX+, A13 ....**$825.00**

Coca-Cola, sign, cardboard, Drink C-C, bathing beauty in yellow suit with bottle on red blanket, 1937, 50x30", VG+, A13 ....**$2,100.00**

Coca-Cola, sign, cardboard, Drink C-C, bathing beauty leaning against rock, ocean beyond, Sundblum art, 1938, 50x30", EX+, A13 ....**$4,000.00**

Coca-Cola, sign, cardboard, Drink C-C, beach couple, he wrapping her in red blanket, 1930s, vertical, G+, A13 ....**$225.00**

Coca-Cola, sign, cardboard, Drink C-C, girl with bottle standing beside horse against billowy sky, 1938, large vertical, VG+, A13 ....**$1,000.00**

Coca-Cola, sign, cardboard, Drink C-C In Bottles, couple at buffet table serving from Lazy Susan, vertical, EX, D30 ....**$200.00**

Coca-Cola, sign, cardboard, Drink C-C In Bottles/Sign Of Good Taste, 2 bottles/saddle/fence/button, 1956, framed, 24x37", EX+, A19 ....**$275.00**

Coca-Cola, sign, cardboard, Drink C-C/D&R, bathing beauty seated on diving board with bottle, 1939, 50x30", NM+, D32 ....**$850.00**

Coca-Cola, sign, cardboard, Drink C-C/D&R, beach girl in blue swimsuit holding Coke bottle, 1940, 50x29", EX+, D32 ....**$1,400.00**

Coca-Cola, sign, cardboard, Drink C-C/D&R, Betty, 1914, 41x26", VG, A7....................................**$650.00**

Coca-Cola, sign, cardboard, Drink C-C/D&R, bottles on white flank phrase on red, green trim, 1920s, tin frame, 21x60", NM, A13 ....**$1,450.00**

Coca-Cola, sign, cardboard, Drink C-C/D&R, couple strolling by couple in touring car & couple on horseback, 1924, 18x33", VG+, A13..**$800.00**

Coca-Cola, sign, cardboard, Drink C-C/D&R, cowboy wiping brow, 1941, gold frame, 27x16", VG+-NM+, A13, from $1,600 to..**$2,600.00**

Coca-Cola, sign, cardboard, Drink C-C/D&R, girl cyclist with Coke bottle leaning against stone wall, 1939, 30x14", EX+, D32 ....**$750.00**

Coca-Cola, sign, cardboard, Enjoy That Refreshing New Feeling, bongo couple with bottles, 1960s, aluminum frame, 39x22", VG, A16..**$50.00**

Coca-Cola, sign, cardboard, Entertain Your Thirst, girl with bottle standing at microphone, 1941, 20x36", EX+, A13 ....**$500.00**

Coca-Cola, sign, cardboard, Entertain Your Thirst, 2 ballerinas with bottles, 1942, 27x16", G, A13 ....**$125.00**

Coca-Cola, sign, cardboard, Extra Bright Refreshment/ Refreshment Through 70 Years, lady with umbrella, 1957, 20x36", G-, A16..**$110.00**

Coca-Cola, sign, cardboard, Friendly Pause, 3 girls with bottles, 1948, 27x16", NM+, A13 ....**$1,550.00**

Coca-Cola, sign, cardboard, Good Taste For All, button/ hand-held bottle/rain viewed through cut-out bottle, 1955, 27x16", NM, A13 ....**$225.00**

Coca-Cola, sign, cardboard, Got Enough Coke On Ice?, 3 girls on sofa planning a party, Canada, 1945, VG+, A13 ....**$725.00**

Coca-Cola, sign, cardboard, Have A Coke, cheerleader with megaphone/bottle, 1946, 20x36", EX+, A16 ....**$300.00**

Coca-Cola, sign, cardboard, Have A Coke, girl in purple dress with 2 bottles by cooler, 1943, 27x16", EX-NM, A13, from $525 to..**$675.00**

Coca-Cola, sign, cardboard, Have A Coke, tilted bottle on iceberg, white border, 1944, 20x36", NM, A13 ...**$300.00**

Coca-Cola, sign, cardboard, Have A Coke/C-C/The Global High-Sign, lady in purple dress with 2 bottles, 1943, 50x30", NM, A13 ....**$650.00**

Coca-Cola, sign, cardboard, Hello Refreshment, girl leaving pool to enjoy a bottle of Coke, 1942, 20x36", EX, A13 ....**$425.00**

Coca-Cola, sign, cardboard, Hello Refreshment, girl leaving pool to enjoy a bottle of Coke, 1942, 50x29", EX+, A13 ....**$600.00**

Coca-Cola, sign, cardboard, Here's Something Good!, couple at masquerade party, 1951, gold frame, 27x16", VG (EX+ frame), A13...**$350.00**

Coca-Cola, sign, cardboard, Here's To Our GI Joes, 2 girls with bottles & globe, 1944, horizontal, EX+, A13..........**$700.00**

Coca-Cola, sign, cardboard, Hospitality, gardening mother/daughter in bonnets with bottle, 1950, 20x36", VG+, A16...**$175.00**

Coca-Cola, sign, cardboard, Hospitality, 2 couples at open fridge, 1948, gold frame, 27x16", EX, A16..........**$370.00**

Coca-Cola, sign, cardboard, Hospitality In Your Hands, lady with tray of bottles, 1949, gold frame, 16x27", EX+, A13...**$425.00**

Coca-Cola, sign, cardboard, How About A Coke, 3 girls with bottles, 1944, 30x50", EX+, A13 ....$575.00

Coca-Cola, sign, cardboard, I'm Heading For A C-C, flight attendant departing plane, 1942, veritcal, VG+, A13 ....$525.00

Coca-Cola, sign, cardboard, Inviting You To Refreshment, girl at table, 1940, cardboard frame, horizontal, VG+, A13...$450.00

Coca-Cola, sign, cardboard, It's Twice Time/Twice The Convenience, couple on scooter, 1960s, 32x67", NM+, A13...**$200.00**

Coca-Cola, sign, cardboard, Join The Friendly Circle, party around picnic cooler, gold frame, 1954, horizontal, EX, A13...**$400.00**

Coca-Cola, sign, cardboard, La Pause Qui Rafraichit, girl in white with bottle, ocean beyond, Canada, 1939, 26x52", VG, A13..**$1,000.00**

Coca-Cola, sign, cardboard, Let's Watch For 'Em/Slow School Zone/Drink C-C, policeman/schoolgirl on red, 1956, framed, EX, A13 ....$1,800.00

Coca-Cola, sign, cardboard, Me Too!, boy gawking at oversized bottle, yellow ground, 27x56", EX+, D30..**$400.00**

Coca-Cola, sign, cardboard, Mind Reader, sunbather in lounge chair reaching for hand-held bottle, 1944, 30x50", EX, A13...**$625.00**

Coca-Cola, sign, cardboard, Mom Knows Her Groceries, girl getting Cokes from fridge, 1946, vertical, VG+, A13 .....**$400.00**

Coca-Cola, sign, cardboard, Nothing Refreshes Like A Coke, serviceman/girl on bicycles with Coke bottles, 1943, 50x29", EX+, D32..................................**$1,100.00**

Coca-Cola, sign, cardboard, Now Family Size Too!/Same Sparkling Refreshment..., Sprite Boy, yellow, framed, 1955, 20x36", NM, A13 ....**$500.00**

Coca-Cola, sign, cardboard, Now! Family Size Too!/Take Home Coke..., Sprite Boy/bottles, yellow, 1955, 27x16", EX, A13...**$250.00**

Coca-Cola, sign, cardboard, Now! For Coke, trapeze artist reaching for bottle of Coke, gold frame, 1959, 20x36", VG, A1 ....**$300.00**

Coca-Cola, sign, cardboard, Pause!, clown & ice skater, 1950s, 27x16", NM+, A13 ....**$2,800.00**

Coca-Cola, sign, cardboard, Play Refreshed, cowgirl, 1951, gold frame, 20x36", EX+, A13...........................**$700.00**

Coca-Cola, sign, cardboard, Play Refreshed, cowgirl, 1951, no frame, 20x36", G+, A13.............................**$375.00**

Coca-Cola, sign, cardboard, Play Refreshed, tennis girl seated atop cooler, 1949, gold frame, 28x20", EX, A1 .....**$625.00**

Coca-Cola, sign, cardboard, Quality In Cups/C-C..., Sprite Boy behind red/white paper cup, white ground, 1940s, 12x15", G, A13 ....**$350.00**

Coca-Cola, sign, cardboard, Refresh, girl seated on docked boat with dog watching, signed Elvgren, gold frame, 50x29", EX, D32.........................$475.00

Coca-Cola, sign, cardboard, Refresh Yourself!, cheerleader with bottle by cooler, 1944, 27x16", NM, A13.**$1,150.00**

Coca-Cola, sign, cardboard, Refreshing, girl holding sunglasses & bottle, 1947, 20x36", NM+, A13 ....**$1,350.00**

Coca-Cola, sign, cardboard, Refreshing C-C, teen party, signed Bill Gregg, 1952, 27x56", scarce, G+, A13 ....**$300.00**

Coca-Cola, sign, cardboard cutout, Drink C-C, bathing beauty with bottle on blue diamond, 1940, 27x23", VG+, A13 ....**$675.00**

Coca-Cola, sign, cardboard cutout, Drink C-C, cowgirl with glass, fancy scrolled border, stand-up/hanger, 17x15", EX+, A16..**$385.00**

Coca-Cola, sign, cardboard cutout, Drink C-C Anywhere/ Anytime, hand-held bottle bursts through center of clock, 1958, 21", VG, A13 ....**$300.00**

Coca-Cola, sign, cardboard cutout, Drink C-C/D&R, woman riding aquaplane, trifold, 1922, EX, D32 ....$6,000.00

Coca-Cola, sign, cardboard cutout, Drink C-C/The Pause That Refreshes, woman with bottle on oval, 2-sided, 1936, 13x21", VG, A1 ....**$1,700.00**

Coca-Cola, sign, cardboard cutout, Eddie Fisher On Radio..., head images/button logo, 1954, 20x12", EX, A13................**$130.00**

Coca-Cola, sign, cardboard cutout, For That Refreshing New Feeling, state trees on diamond with glass/Drink diamond, 16x18", EX, A1 ....**$50.00**

Coca-Cola, sign, cardboard cutout, Have A Large Coke, waitress in shadow of full glass with sandwich, 1960s, 18x14", NM, A13..**$50.00**

Coca-Cola, sign, cardboard cutout, Ice Cold C-C/Serve Yourself on red disk with red arrow, gold border, 1944, 20x14", VG, A13..**$150.00**

Coca-Cola, sign, cardboard cutout, Lionel Hampton with bottle on drum, fancy scrolled border, stand-up, 1953, 15x12", NM, A13..............................$975.00

Coca-Cola, sign, cardboard cutout, Partner In Good Work In Hollywood & Everywhere, Jackie Cooper/Wallace Berry, 1930s, EX+, A4..**$1,800.00**

Coca-Cola, sign, cardboard cutout, Refreshing!/Have A Large Coke At Our Fountain!, lady being offered glass, 1956, 19x18", VG+, D32 ....**$225.00**

Coca-Cola, sign, cardboard cutout, Serve Cold, Old Man Winter with large bottle/6-pack, 1953, 21x16", NM, A13 ....**$225.00**

Coca-Cola, sign, cardboard cutout, So Refreshing!, girl in white swimsuit/red cap, green umbrella, 1930, 38x21", G-, A13..**$525.00**

Coca-Cola, sign, cardboard cutout, Stop For A Pause/Go Refreshed, traffic cop with bottle behind signal, 1937, 32x42", G+, A13..**$1,050.00**

Coca-Cola, sign, cardboard cutout, Take Enough Home, elves pulling along 3 large bottles in snowy landscape, 1953, 20x12", EX, A13 ....**$180.00**

Coca-Cola, sign, cardboard cutout, Take Home, sailor girl with signal flags/red Drink C-C button logo, 1952, 7x11", NM, A13..**$350.00**

Coca-Cola, sign, cardboard cutout, The Pause That Refreshes, girl at cooler with bottle looking over shoulder, 1940, 41x32", G, A16 ....**$240.00**

Coca-Cola, sign, cardboard cutout, Uncle Remus & The Happy Animals, Uncle Remus/boy by fireplace, stand-up, 7x6", EX, A6 ....**$450.00**

Coca-Cola, sign, cardboard cutout, Votre Soif S'eavole, aviator tips bottle, stand-up, Canadian, 1941, 17x13", NM, A13 ....**$1,550.00**

Coca-Cola, sign, cardboard cutout, Welcome Friend/Have A 'Coke,' Sprite Boy/bottle, wood-grain, curved ends, 1944, 14x30", EX, A1 ....**$650.00**

Coca-Cola, sign, cardboard cutout, 3-D mechanical, lady with fan on red circle with Drink C-C sign, 1953, very rare, NM+, A4..**$50.00**

Coca-Cola, sign, cardboard hanger, airplane, Avenger, 1943, 13x15", EX+, A14 ....**$55.00**

Coca-Cola, sign, cardboard hanger, airplane, B26 Marauder, 1943, 13x15", EX+, A14 ....**$55.00**

Coca-Cola, sign, cardboard hanger, airplane, King Fisher Sea Plane, 1943, 13x15", EX+, A14..**$55.00**

Coca-Cola, sign, cardboard hanger, airplane, P-40 Warhawk, 1943, 13x15", EX+, A14 ....**$55.00**

Coca-Cola, sign, cardboard hanger, Buvez C-C, encircled girl drinking from bottle, gold trim, Canada, 1939, 22x15", EX, A13..**$1,600.00**

Coca-Cola, sign, cardboard hanger, Cold Refreshment, Drink C-C sign above bottle/text on dark blue, diagonal, 1937, 24x24", NM, D32 ....$1,500.00

Coca-Cola, sign, cardboard hanger, Cooling Refreshment/ Drink C-C, hand pulling bottle from ice, 2-sided, 1935, horizontal, G, A13..**$160.00**

Coca-Cola, sign, cardboard hanger, Drink C-C, bathing beauty with bottle on blue diamond, 1940, 23x24", NM+, A13 ....**$1,550.00**

Coca-Cola, sign, cardboard hanger, Drink C-C/Be Refreshed on red disk with Sprite Boy, 2-sided, Canada, 1950, 11", NM, A13 ....**$2,200.00**

Coca-Cola, sign, cardboard hanger, Drink/C-C/5¢, orange/white on red, round, 2-sided, 1940s-50s, 6½" dia, EX+, A14 ....**$60.00**

Coca-Cola, sign, cardboard hanger, Welcome Friend/Have A Coke, Sprite Boy/bottle, wood-grain panel, cutout, 1944, 30", NM, A13 ....**$900.00**

Coca-Cola, sign, cardboard hanger/stand-up, Have A Coke above glass, Refreshing on yellow ribbon with flower, 1949, 12", EX+, A13 ....**$120.00**

Coca-Cola, sign, cardboard hanger/stand-up, Have A Coke/Ice Cold/12 Ounce King Size, Sprite Boy/bottle, yellow, 1957, 18", EX, A13.................................**$175.00**

Coca-Cola, sign, cardboard menu, Burger & Coke, 1960s, 7x24", EX+, A14.....................................**$25.00**

Coca-Cola, sign, cardboard menu, Carry Out Orders, 1960s, 7x24", EX, A14......................................**$20.00**

Coca-Cola, sign, cardboard menu, Corned Beef With Coke, 1960s, 7x24", EX+, A14 ....**$25.00**

Coca-Cola, sign, cardboard menu, Delicious With Coke, 1960s, 7x24", NM, A14.................................**$39.00**

Coca-Cola, sign, cardboard menu, Egg Salad With Coke, 1960s, 7x24", NM, A14.................................**$39.00**

Coca-Cola, sign, cardboard menu, French Fries & Coke, 1960s, 7x24", EX, A14....................................**$17.00**

Coca-Cola, sign, cardboard menu, Grilled Cheese & Coke, 1960s, 7x24", EX+, A14 ....**$28.00**

Coca-Cola, sign, cardboard menu, Ham & Cheese & Coke, 1960s, 7x24", EX+, A14 ....**$20.00**

Coca-Cola, sign, cardboard menu, Hot Pizza With Coke, 1960s, 7x24", NM+, A14..............................**$50.00**

Coca-Cola, sign, cardboard menu, Large Size, 1960s, 7x24", EX, A14 ....**$20.00**

Coca-Cola, sign, cardboard menu, Pie A La Mode & Coke, 1960s, 7x24", EX+, A14 ....**$22.00**

Coca-Cola, sign, cardboard stand-up, Coke Convenient on banner, family above, 6-pack below, yellow, Canadian, 1948, 24x18", NM, A13 ....**$200.00**

Coca-Cola, sign, cardboard stand-up, Kit Carson Kerchief, 1950s, 24x16", EX, A13.................................**$200.00**

Coca-Cola, sign, cardboard stand-up, On Your Break/Be Really Refreshed/Get..., girl/bottle, 3-D, self-frame, 1960s, 14x18", NM, A13.......................................**$175.00**

Coca-Cola, sign, cardboard stand-up, Take Enough Home, elves pulling 6-pack on wagon in snowy landscape, 1953, 27x16", EX, A13 ....**$175.00**

Coca-Cola, sign, cardboard stand-up, Thirst Asks Nothing More/Drink C-C, hand-held bottle on red, 1939, 16x12", NM, A13 ....**$1,800.00**

Coca-Cola, sign, cardboard stand-up, Zing For Your Supper With Ice Cold Coke/Refreshing New Feeling! with space kid, 1960s, NM, A13 ....**$160.00**

Coca-Cola, sign, cardboard standee, Wayne Gretsky in hockey gear with Coke bottle, life-size, NM+, A14......**$75.00**

Coca-Cola, sign, celluloid, C-C (lettered) over bottle on red, gold border, 1950s, 9", M (original envelope), A16........**$300.00**

Coca-Cola, sign, celluloid, C-C lettered over bottle on red, gold border, 1950s, 9", NM (original envelope), A13 .....**$250.00**

Coca-Cola, sign, celluloid, C-C/D&R, silver/white lettering on red disk, silver border, 1940s-50s, 9" dia, EX+, A13........**$300.00**

Coca-Cola, sign, celluloid, Drink C-C Highballs (The Morning After), gold on black, beveled, chain hanger, 1921, 6x11", EX, A13 ....**$6,200.00**

Coca-Cola, sign, celluloid, Drink C-C/'Coke'/Ask For It Either Way, red, gold border, 1940s, 9" dia, NM, A13 ..**$575.00**

Coca-Cola, sign, celluloid, Pause/Go Refreshed, full glass in center, gold border, round, 9" dia, Fair, A16......**$110.00**

Coca-Cola, sign, celluloid/tin, Refresh Yourself (script)/Drink C-C, yellow/white on red, green trim, beveled, 1927, 6x12", G+-EX, A13, from $525 to....................**$1,800.00**

Coca-Cola, sign, fiberboard, round, molded, Pause/Go Refreshed/C-C, hand-held bottle/wings, white/gold/red, 1940s, 10", NM (NOS), A6......................................**$850.00**

Coca-Cola, sign, fishtail, tin, C-C, white on red, 12x26", NM (NOS), A6......................................**$250.00**

Coca-Cola, sign, fishtail, tin, Drink C-C, white on red, 6x12", NM+, A13...**$160.00**

Coca-Cola, sign, flange, Buvez C-C Glace, porcelain, vertical rectangle, yellow/white on red, Canada, 1950, 19x18", NM+, A13...**$200.00**

Coca-Cola, sign, flange, C-C Iced Here, porcelain, yellow/white lettering on red oval on yellow vertical panel, 20x18", EX, A6...**$700.00**

Coca-Cola, sign, flange, Drink C-C, tin, bottle on yellow dot, die-cut, 1940s, 20x24", EX+, A13......................**$550.00**

Coca-Cola, sign, flange, Drink C-C, tin, emblem with filigree top, curved bottom, cutout corners, white/red, 1936, 13x20", EX, A13...**$700.00**

Coca-Cola, sign, flange, Drink C-C (flat red disk)/Ice Cold & bottle on arrow, tin, 1951, 22x18", VG-EX+, A11/A13, from $375 to......................................**$575.00**

Coca-Cola, sign, flange, Drink C-C Here, porcelain shield, white/yellow on red, yellow trim, 1940, 20x17", EX-NM, A14, from $600 to......................................**$950.00**

Coca-Cola, sign, flange, Drink C-C Ice Cold, back-to-back buttons with die-cut arrow featuring glass/Ice Cold, tin, 1952, EX+, A13..............................**$1,350.00**

Coca-Cola, sign, flange, Drink C-C Ice Cold, pictures bottle & button logo, NM, D32..............................**$450.00**

Coca-Cola, sign, flange, Enjoy C-C In Bottles, tin, bottle/phrase on red disk, 1950s, 18" dia, rare, VG+-NM, A13, from $475 to **$770.00**

Coca-Cola, sign, flange, Enjoy That Refreshing New Feeling, fishtail on white with green stripes/trim, 1960s, 15x18", EX, A13...**$350.00**

Coca-Cola, sign, flange, Have A C-C, porcelain, vertical rectangle, yellow/white on red, yellow trim, 1951, 19x17", EX, A13...**$400.00**

Coca-Cola, sign, flange, Ice Cold C-C Sold Here, tin, white on green/red/green, 1930s, 12x16", EX-EX+, A1/D32, from $750 to......................................$950.00

Coca-Cola, sign, flange, Iced C-C Here, porcelain, yellow/white on red oval on yellow square ground, Canada, 1952, 20x18", NM, A13..........................**$575.00**

Coca-Cola, sign, flange, Refresh Yourself!/C-C/Sold Here/Ice Cold, porcelain shield, yellow/white on red, 1930s, 20x17", G-EX+, A13/A14, from $475 to **$800.00**

Coca-Cola, sign, flange, Sign Of Good Taste, tin, fishtail on white with green stripes/trim, 1959, 15x18", NM, A1/A13, from $350 to......................................**$450.00**

Coca-Cola, sign, glass, Buy Checks From Cashier/Drink C-C/Thank You, round, 1920s, 11" dia, EX, A13.$1,600.00

Coca-Cola, sign, glass, Drink C-C, oval, red, chain hanger, 1932, VG+, A13......................................$3,500.00

Coca-Cola, sign, glass, Drink C-C, rectangular panel, red, chrome trim top/bottom, Burnoff, 1930s, NM+, A4.............**$3,500.00**

Coca-Cola, sign, glass, Drink C-C/Please Pay Cashier, oval, white on red, chrome frame, 1932, 12x20", VG+, A13......**$1,400.00**

Coca-Cola, sign, glass, Drink/D&R, silver ribbon around C-C in script on black, mother-of-pearl C's, wood frame, horizonal, EX, A8...**$415.00**

Coca-Cola, sign, glass, Refresh Yourself (script)/Drink C-C, yellow/white on red, bordered, 1927, 6x12", VG+, A13...**$325.00**

Coca-Cola, sign, Kay Displays, Battleship lettered on winged sign/battleship/red C-C logo on blue, wood, 1940s, 8½x25", VG+, A13 ....$625.00

Coca-Cola, sign, Kay Displays, Drink C-C, bowling theme on wooden disk with wire frame, ribbon logo, 1940s, 16" dia, EX+, A13...**$350.00**

Coca-Cola, sign, Kay Displays, Drink C-C, button on white rounded panel, 2 Sprite Boys, wood, gold trim, 1940s-50s, 36", EX, A13...**$1,150.00**

Coca-Cola, sign, Kay Displays, Drink C-C, red button with gold-tone bars on white panel with rounded ends, gold trim, 36", EX+, A13...**$700.00**

Coca-Cola, sign, Kay Displays, Drink C-C, red disk with ribbed silver-tone footed frame, tin/cardboard stand-up, 10x9", EX+, A13...**$650.00**

Coca-Cola, sign, Kay Displays, Drink C-C, red triangle with gold bottle, gold leaf decor atop, gold trim, 1923, 24x23", VG+, A1...**$825.00**

Coca-Cola, sign, Kay Displays, Drink C-C, 2 12x9" emblems with concave corners, 37" panel with emblem, wood, 1930s, 3-pc, NM, A13...**$2,800.00**

Coca-Cola, sign, Kay Displays, Drink C-C Ice Cold, disk (red) with silver-tone bottle/arrow, plywood/metal, 17" dia, VG+, A13...**$400.00**

Coca-Cola, sign, Kay Displays, Drink C-C Ice Cold, triangle (green)/white arrow pointing down, wood, 2-sided, 1930s, 28", VG-EX+, A13, from $500 to **$750.00**

Coca-Cola, sign, Kay Displays, Ice Cold C-C, silhouette girl on yellow dot on red masonite disk, 1939, 17" dia, G+, A13..**$150.00**

Coca-Cola, sign, Kay Displays, Lunch With Us, round compo hanger, disk logo with glass atop beaded border, 1920s, 13" dia, EX, A16..**$1,935.00**

Coca-Cola, sign, Kay Displays, Pause Here/Drink C-C, phrase on panel above emblem, wood, metal trim, 1930s, 10x37", VG, A13..**$1,550.00**

Coca-Cola, sign, Kay Displays, Stop For A Pause/Drink C-C/Go Refreshed, policeman directing traffic, die-cut wood, 1940s, EX, A4............................$3,500.00

Coca-Cola, sign, Kay Displays, Thirst Asks Nothing More, natural wood panel, red Drink C-C emblem below, 10x38", VG, A13..**$775.00**

Coca-Cola, sign, light-up, 1930s, reverse glass, Brunoff, Coke glass on yellow dot on red disk, leaf trim, base, 14x12", EX+, A16..............................$3,570.00

Coca-Cola, sign, light-up, 1940s-50s, cash register topper, framed, see-through base, 8x18", EX+, A13 ....**$950.00**

Coca-Cola, sign, light-up, 1940s-50s, cash register topper, framed, see-through base, 8x18", VG, A16.........**$400.00**

Coca-Cola, sign, light-up, 1948, Edgebrite counter-top, trapezoid with Coke glass ornament atop, 9x20", EX-NM, A16, from $700 to **$1,200.00**

Coca-Cola, sign, light-up, 1948, Edgebrite hanger, trapezoid with bottom ornament, 12x20", EX+, D32 ....**$1,750.00**

Coca-Cola, sign, light-up, 1950s, counter-top, clock (round), 9x20", EX+, A16 ....**$635.00**

Coca-Cola, sign, light-up, 1950s, counter-top, clock (square), 9x20, EX, D32 ....**$475.00**

Coca-Cola, sign, light-up, 1950s, counter-top, motion (Pause), 9x20", VG, D32 ....$750.00

Coca-Cola, sign, light-up, 1950s, counter-top, motion (waterfall), 9x20", EX, A1 ....**$1,300.00**

Coca-Cola, sign, light-up, 1950s, disk on rotating base, plastic, Shop Refreshed/Drink C-C in bottles, NM, D32 ....$950.00

Coca-Cola, sign, light-up, 1950s, plastic hanger, illusional courtesy panel/Drink C-C panel(red)/Fountain panel, 24x28", EX, A13 ....**$425.00**

Coca-Cola, sign, light-up, 1950s, Work Safely on light-up panel with cup/Work Safety-Wise, box frame, 16x16", VG, A13 ....**$725.00**

Coca-Cola, sign, light-up, 1950s, Work Safely on light-up panel with cup/Safety Is A Job/Work At It, box frame, 16x16", VG+, A13..**$775.00**

Coca-Cola, sign, light-up, 1950s-60s, cup shape, plastic, Delicious/Ice Cold Drinks/Drink C-C/Serve Yourself, red/white, EX, A13...**$1,300.00**

Coca-Cola, sign, light-up, 1960s, bottle (gold)/starburst on dark squared ground, applied Drink C-C fishtail panel, 16x14", VG, A13..**$500.00**

Coca-Cola, sign, light-up, 1960s, diamond design on end panels, Drink C-C on red center panel, plastic, horizontal, EX, A16 ....**$140.00**

Coca-Cola, sign, light-up, 1960s, round front/green illusion around red center dot, metal footed frame, EX, A16/A13, from $650 to..**$775.00**

Coca-Cola, sign, light-up, 1960s, Drink C-C in Bottles, round, 1-sided, light-up border, plastic/metal, 16", NM, A1..**$750.00**

Coca-Cola, sign, light-up, 1960s, Drink C-C in Bottles, round, 2-sided, light-up border, plastic/metal, 16", NM+, A13 ....**$1,050.00**

Coca-Cola, sign, light-up, 1990s, counter-top, 20-oz bottle on red panel with white-lined contour logo on base, 13x12", NMIB, A13.....................................**$120.00**

Coca-Cola, sign, masonite, Beverage Department, red button on white panel flanked by Sprite Boys, gold trim, 1950s, 12x78", EX, A13 ....**$850.00**

Coca-Cola, sign, masonite, Drink C-C, girl tipping bottle on red, yellow/green border, 1940s, 20x28", NM, A13..........**$900.00**

Coca-Cola, sign, masonite, Drink C-C, girl tipping bottle on red, yellow/green border, 1940s, 12x34", EX+, A13.........**$250.00**

Coca-Cola, sign, masonite, Drink C-C, phrase (yellow/white) above bottle on yellow dot on red, 1946, diagonal, 42x42", NM+, A13..**$950.00**

Coca-Cola, sign, masonite, Have A Coke, teen couples against die-cut records, 1950s, 12" dia, EX, A13, pair...**$2,200.00**

Coca-Cola, sign, neon, Coca-Cola Classic/The Official Soft Drink Of Summer, palm tree in center, 3-color, 1980s, 28" dia, NM+, A13.....................................**$1,700.00**

Coca-Cola, sign, neon, Drink C-C, plastic/metal, round, neon border, red/white, 1950s, NM, D32.........................**$450.00**

Coca-Cola, sign, neon, Drink in block letters above C-C in script, red, 1930s-40s, 12x27", EX+, A13..........**$1,200.00**

Coca-Cola, sign, neon, Drug Store/C-C/Fountain Service, red center C-C panel with top/bottom lettered appendages, 58x86x8", EX, A6..**$3,500.00**

Coca-Cola, sign, paper, Chinese girl seated with glass, logo in Chinese, 1936, framed, 22x14", NM+, A13 ....**$1,600.00**

Coca-Cola, sign, paper, Drink C-C/Cold, bottle on iceberg with red disk logo, COLD in 'icy' floating letters, 1942, 18x57", EX, A13 ....**$130.00**

Coca-Cola, sign, paper, Drink C-C/D&R, flapper girl looking at bottle with straw, 1920s, 20x12", VG+, A13 ...**$400.00**

Coca-Cola, sign, paper, Drink C-C/Refresh, bottle nestled in snow bank with blue water, red lettering, 1940s-50s, 18x57", EX, A13 ....**$275.00**

Coca-Cola, sign, paper, Pause A Minute/Refresh Yourself, girl in profile with bottle, yellow/green border, 1920s, 20x12", EX+, A13 ....**$700.00**

Coca-Cola, sign, paper, That Taste-Good Feeling/Drink C-C/D&R, boy with hot dog/bottle of Coke, 1920s, 20x12", VG+, D30...**$350.00**

Coca-Cola, sign, paper, The Pause That Refreshes, lady in red dress seated holding bottle/glass, 1940s, 20x18", EX, D30 ....**$135.00**

Coca-Cola, sign, paper, Treat Yourself Right/Drink C-C/D&R, man opening bottle, 1920s, 20x12", EX, A13......**$550.00**

Coca-Cola, sign, paper, 5¢ Drink C-C 5¢, white on red, white border, 1930s, 6x24", EX+, A16...........................**$70.00**

Coca-Cola, sign, paper cutout, hand-held bottle, M, A16 ....**$75.00**

Coca-Cola, sign, paper cutout, Home Refreshment in green arched above 25¢ 6-pack on yellow, 1941, 16x22", NM, A13..**$45.00**

Coca-Cola, sign, Plexiglas oval on wood base, Drink C-C, yellow/white on red, white line border, Canadian, 1940s-50s, EX+, A13 ....**$185.00**

Coca-Cola, sign, porcelain, Buvez C-C, Sprite Boy behind bottle on yellow dot, yellow/white on red, 1940s-50s, 18x58", EX, A13 ....**$750.00**

Coca-Cola, sign, porcelain, C-C, emblem with silhouette carhop/car on white, panel below, die-cut hanger, 1940s, 52", NM, A24 ....**$1,200.00**

Coca-Cola, sign, porcelain, C-C, logo in die-cut script, white with black outline, 1930s, 6x18", NM, A13.........**$950.00**

Coca-Cola, sign, porcelain, C-C Sign of Good Taste, fishtail on white ground with green stripes, wrapped edges, 1960s, VG+, A13 ....**$230.00**

Coca-Cola, sign, porcelain, C-C Sold Here, white C-C on red above red Sold-Here on white, 1910s-20s, rectangular, G+, A13 ....**$850.00**

Coca-Cola, sign, porcelain, C-C Sold Here Ice Cold, white/yellow on red, yellow border, curved corners, 1955, 12x29", EX, A13 ....**$200.00**

Coca-Cola, sign, porcelain, C-C Vendu Ici Glace, white/yellow on red, yellow/green border, Canada, 1939, 12x29", NM, A13..**$200.00**

Coca-Cola, sign, porcelain, Candy/Films/Drink C-C, disk logo on green ground, white border, 1950s, 30x18", EX+, A13 . **$700.00**

Coca-Cola, sign, porcelain, Come In! Have A C-C, diagonal script, yellow/white on red, curved ends, 1940s, 54x18", EX **$575.00**

Coca-Cola, sign, porcelain, Delicatessen/Drink C-C/D&R, gold/white on green/red, gold trim, 2-sided, 42x60", VG+, A2..**$900.00**

Coca-Cola, sign, porcelain, Delicious/Refreshing, green lettering around bottle on white, 1950s, 24x24", EX, A13 ....**$300.00**

Coca-Cola, sign, porcelain, Drink C-C, die-cut script, 6x18", M, A13 ....**$775.00**

Coca-Cola, sign, porcelain, Drink C-C, dispenser, hand on spigot, yellow ground, curved corners, 2-sided, 1940s, 26x25", NM, A13 ....**$25.00**

Coca-Cola, sign, porcelain, Drink C-C, emblem, curved bottom, cutout corners, yellow/white on red, 1942, 24x36", VG, A13 ....**$225.00**

Coca-Cola, sign, porcelain, Drink C-C, emblem, yellow/white on red, white trim, 2-sided, 1940, 38x60", EX+, A1..**$380.00**

Coca-Cola, sign, porcelain, Drink C-C, fishtail on white with green-striped ground, green rolled edge, 1960s, 16x44", VG, A6 ....**$180.00**

Coca-Cola, sign, porcelain, Drink C-C, oval sign (red) on yellow rectangle, curved corners, Canada, 1955, 12x29", EX, A13..**$250.00**

Coca-Cola, sign, porcelain, Drink C-C, oval with top courtesy panel, yellow/white on red, yellow trim, 2-sided, 1949, 28x58", EX, A6 ....**$450.00**

Coca-Cola, sign, porcelain, Drink C-C, white lettering on red, white line border, 1910s, 18x45", EX+, A13 ....**$1,000.00**

Coca-Cola, sign, porcelain, Drink C-C, white lettering on red, yellow/green border, 1920s, 10x30", NM, A13 ...**$925.00**

Coca-Cola, sign, porcelain, Drink C-C, white lettering on red, yellow/green border, 1920s, 10x30", VG, A1......**$315.00**

Coca-Cola, sign, porcelain, Drink C-C, yellow/white on red, yellow stripe top/bottom, Canada, 12x29", EX+, A1 .....**$300.00**

Coca-Cola, sign, porcelain, Drink C-C Ice Cold, dispenser/Coke glass, curved corners, banded edge, 2-sided, 1950s, 28x27", VG+, A13..**$900.00**

Coca-Cola, sign, porcelain, Drink C-C Ice Cold, dispenser/Coke glass, curved corners, banded edge, 2-sided, 1950s, 28x27", NM+, A6.....................................**$1,900.00**

Coca-Cola, sign, porcelain, Drink C-C Ice Cold, triangle hanger, filigree top, bottle, red/green, 2-sided, 1930s, 25", VG+-NM+, A13, from $4,200 to **$9,700.00**

Coca-Cola, sign, porcelain, Drink C-C Ice Cold, yellow/white lettering on red, yellow border, curved corners, 1951, 20x28", EX, A6 ....**$450.00**

Coca-Cola, sign, porcelain, Drink C-C In Bottles, white lettering on red, curved ends, 1950s, 16x44", EX, A13 ..**$90.00**

Coca-Cola, sign, porcelain, Drink C-C With Soda 5 CTS/C-C For Wheelmen/C-C With Soda For Headache 5 Cents, white/blue, 24x8", EX, A7.............................**$12,000.00**

Coca-Cola, sign, porcelain, Drink C-C/Sold Here Ice Cold, white/yellow on red, yellow/green border, 1930s, 12x31", VG+, A13...**$425.00**

Coca-Cola, sign, porcelain, Drug Store/Drink C-C/D&R, hanger, white on green/red, yellow trim, 2-sided, 1933, 42x60", EX, A13 ....$1,100.00

Coca-Cola, sign, porcelain, Drugs/Soda, Drink C-C disk logo in center, lt green ground, 1950s, 30x18", NM, A13 ...**$950.00**

Coca-Cola, sign, porcelain, Entrez Et Buvez Un C-C, yellow/white on red, curved ends, Canada, 1930s, 54x18", VG, A13...**$400.00**

Coca-Cola, sign, porcelain, Fountain Service/C-C, white/red/white panels, die-cut, 2-sided, 1950s, 55x60", VG+, A13..**$1,300.00**

Coca-Cola, sign, porcelain, Fountain Service/Drink C-C, button on red pin-striped center band, white ground, 1950s, 12x30", EX, A3 ....**$175.00**

Coca-Cola, sign, porcelain, Fountain Service/Drink C-C, emblem, curved bottom/cutout corners, red/green, 1930s, 14x27", EX-NM+, A13, from $1,000 to **$1,800.00**

Coca-Cola, sign, porcelain, Fountain Service/Drink C-C, emblem, red/green diagonal ground, 2-sided, 1930s, 26x22", VG+, A13.....................................**$800.00**

Coca-Cola, sign, porcelain, Fountain Service/Drink C-C, emblem with fountain taps flanking lettering, 1930s, 14x27", G+-VG+, A1/A9, from $925 to **$1,500.00**

Coca-Cola, sign, porcelain, Fountain Service/Drink C-C, green/red ground with red pointing to green, 1950s, 12x28", EX, A13 ....**$800.00**

Coca-Cola, sign, porcelain, Fountain Service/Drink C-C, green/white on green/red, 3 white wavy lines, white trim, 12x28", EX+, A1 ....**$400.00**

Coca-Cola, sign, porcelain, Fountain Service/Drink C-C, slanted sign/ribbon banner, yellow, 1950s, 12x28", EX, A6/A13, from $500 to **$625.00**

Coca-Cola, sign, porcelain, Fountain Service/Drink C-C, yellow on green/white on red, yellow/green trim, 1937, 48x96", NM, A13...**$1,800.00**

Coca-Cola, sign, porcelain, Lunch/Drink C-C/Pause Refresh, slanted sign/ribbon banner, yellow, 2-sided, 1950s, 26x28", NM, A13...**$1,300.00**

Coca-Cola, sign, porcelain, Luncheon/Drink C-C, hanger, round flanked by fountain taps, sign below, 2-sided, 1930s, 58x64", G+, A13...............................$2,300.00

Coca-Cola, sign, porcelain, 1923 bottle, round, white scroll design, EX+, 18" dia, EX+, A13 ....**$225.00**

Coca-Cola, sign, rack, C-C/Take Home A Carton 25¢, round with arrow pointing down, white/yellow on red, 1940s, 18x10", VG+, A14..**$220.00**

Coca-Cola, sign, rack, Enjoy C-C At Home/Take Home A Carton 36¢, round with tab, yellow/white on red, 1940s, 16x11", VG, A14..**$200.00**

Coca-Cola, sign, rack, Have A Coke/Take Some Home, Sprite Boy behind bottle, white/yellow on red, tin, 1949, 23x16", EX, A13 ....**$300.00**

Coca-Cola, sign, rack, King Size Here/Regular Here, lettering flanks C-C button, black/red on white, 1960s, 7x12", EX+, A14 ....**$50.00**

Coca-Cola, sign, rack, Serve C-C/Sign Of Good Taste, yellow/red/white/green geometric ground, 2-sided, 1960s, 10x17", VG+, A13..**$100.00**

Coca-Cola, sign, rack, Take Home A Carton/C-C/6 Bottles Plus Deposit, round, yellow/white on red, 2-sided, 1930s, 13", EX, A13..**$200.00**

Coca-Cola, sign, resin, Pause.../Go Refreshed/C-C, round, text above winged hand-held bottle, white/gold/red, 1940s, 8½", NM, A13 ....**$3,700.00**

Coca-Cola, sign, school, policeman, die-cut metal, 2-sided, 1950s, VG-NM+, A2/A13, from $1,870 to......$4,700.00

Coca-Cola, sign, school, schoolgirl, wood, metal base, 2-sided, 1950s-60s, EX+, A13..........................$425.00

Coca-Cola, sign, sidewalk, Stop Here/Drink C-C, yellow/white on green/red, green porcelain frame, Canadian, 1941, 46x27", G, A13..................................**$225.00**

Coca-Cola, sign, tin, Betty, 1914, self-framed, 41x36", EX, A7 ....**$10,000.00**

Coca-Cola, sign, tin, Billiards/Drink C-C, emblem with courtesy panel atop, red/green, die-cut, 1934, 49x63", VG, A13 ....**$1,300.00**

Coca-Cola, sign, tin, bottle on white ground, gray raised border, curved corners, 1953, 33x18", NM, A13 ......**$450.00**

Coca-Cola, sign, tin, C-C, fishtail (vertical) above bottle/can on white, green stripes, green raised rim, 1960s, 54x18", NM, A13 ....**$1,150.00**

Coca-Cola, sign, tin, C-C, fishtail (horizontal) flanked by bottle/can on white ground with green stripes, green raised rim, 18x54", VG, A13 ....**$300.00**

Coca-Cola, sign, tin, C-C, oval, woman offering bottle & logo on red, gold raised rim, 1926, 7½x10½", VG+, A13 ....**$4,700.00**

Coca-Cola, sign, tin, C-C, round, script logo over bottle on red, green/yellow border, 1937, 46", NM, A13..**$1,000.00**

Coca-Cola, sign, tin, C-C, round, script logo over bottle on red, metallic gold rim, 9" dia, NM, A19...$125.00

Coca-Cola, sign, tin, C-C, round, Sprite Boy/bottle/button logo on gold, white rim, 1950s, 12" dia, M, A4..........$2,100.00

Coca-Cola, sign, tin, C-C/Sign Of Good Taste/Ice Cold, fishtail/bottle/Ice Cold on white, green rim, 1960s, 18x54", NM, A13 ....**$300.00**

Coca-Cola, sign, tin, Delicious/Refreshing, Lillian Nordica with 5¢ bottle & glass, self-framed, 1905, 33x23", VG, A9 ....**$18,500.00**

Coca-Cola, sign, tin, Drink C-C, bottle (tilted) on yellow dot lower right, yellow/white on red, silver trim, 1940, 11x34", EX, A13 ....**$175.00**

Coca-Cola, sign, tin, Drink C-C, bottle (tilted) on yellow dot lower right, yellow/white on red, silver trim, 1940, 20x28", NM, A13 ....**$375.00**

Coca-Cola, sign, tin, Drink C-C, bottle (1915) in center, white ground, beveled edge, cardboard back, 1920s, 13x6", VG, A13 ....**$1,400.00**

Coca-Cola, sign, tin, Drink C-C, bottle on white in center, yellow/red/green trim, 1931, 6x13", G+, A16.....**$365.00**

Coca-Cola, sign, tin, Drink C-C, bottle on white left of phrase on red, embossed, 1931, 12x34", VG+, A13 ....**$250.00**

Coca-Cola, sign, tin, Drink C-C, bottle outlined in yellow, yellow/white on red, yellow trim, 1948, vertical, 53x17", NM, A13..**$875.00**

Coca-Cola, sign, tin, Drink C-C, bottle outlined in yellow, yellow/white on red, yellow trim, 1951, horizontal, 18x54", EX+, A13 ....**$550.00**

Coca-Cola, sign, tin, Drink C-C, bottles on white flank phrase on red, yellow/green trim, 1936, 19x54", G, A13...**$375.00**

Coca-Cola, sign, tin, Drink C-C, couple with bottle, white on red, black wood frame, 1942, 32x68", EX+, A13..**$800.00**

Coca-Cola, sign, tin, Drink C-C, couple with bottle, yellow/white on red, green trim, 1942, 32x56", EX, A13 ....$525.00

Coca-Cola, sign, tin, Drink C-C, couple with bottle far right, yellow/white on red, green trim, 1942, 12x34", NM+, A13 ....**$700.00**

Coca-Cola, sign, tin, Drink C-C, girl tipping bottle, yellow/white on red, yellow/green trim, 1942, 20x28", VG-EX, A13, from $225 to **$475.00**

Coca-Cola, sign, tin, Drink C-C, girl tipping bottle, yellow/white on red, yellow/green trim, 1942, 32x56", VG-EX+, A13, from $300 to **$725.00**

Coca-Cola, sign, tin, Drink C-C, girl with glass leaning on hand & looking over shoulder, self-framed, 1916, 30x20", VG+, A13 ....**$3,100.00**

Coca-Cola, sign, tin, Drink C-C, phrase on red, green raised rolled rim, 1920s, 14x42", EX-NM, A13/A4, from $750 to **$800.00**

Coca-Cola, sign, tin, Drink C-C, phrase on red oval, green rectangular border, gold beveled rim, hanger, 1931, 8x11", G, A13 ....**$200.00**

Coca-Cola, sign, tin, Drink C-C, white on red, yellow/green beveled rim, embossed, Dasco, 1930s, 6x18", VG-NM, A6/A13, from $170 to **$350.00**

Coca-Cola, sign, tin, Drink C-C, white on red field pointing to bottle on white, 1950s, 12x32", VG+, D30 .....**$100.00**

Coca-Cola, sign, tin, Drink C-C, white on red oval, green border with arrow-shaped corners, gold trim, 1920s, 15x20", VG, A1..**$650.00**

Coca-Cola, sign, tin, Drink C-C, white on red oval, green rectangular border, gold beveled rim, 1926, 8x11", EX+, A13 ....$1,800.00

Coca-Cola, sign, tin, Drink C-C, yellow/white on red oval, green top courtesy panel, yellow trim, 2-sided, 1949, 28x58", NM, A13 ....$1,200.00

Coca-Cola, sign, tin, Drink C-C, 3 bottles with shadow on 2-tone green at left of script logo on red, 1930s, 19x54", EX, D32 ....$450.00

Coca-Cola, sign, tin, Drink C-C Ice Cold, bottle (1923) on lt green left of red/dk green fields, metal rim, 1937, 20x28", EX+, A13..**$525.00**

Coca-Cola, sign, tin, Drink C-C Ice Cold, bottle on partial yellow dot, yellow/white on red, green border, 1938, 36x60", VG+, A13..**$400.00**

Coca-Cola, sign, tin, Drink C-C Ice Cold, bottle/lettering on red/2-tone green ground, embossed, 1937, 19x27", NM, A1..**$725.00**

Coca-Cola, sign, tin, Drink C-C Ice Cold, triangle hanger with filigree top, shows bottle, red/white, 2-sided, 1930s, 23", G+-NM, A13, from $675 to **$1,750.00**

Coca-Cola, sign, tin, Drink C-C Ice Cold, white on red field pointing to bottle white, 1950s, 20x28", NM, D32.$275.00

Coca-Cola, sign, tin, Drink C-C Ice-Cold/D&R, disk (red) with bars above yellow lettering, green ground, 1940, 28x20", VG+, A13..**$350.00**

Coca-Cola, sign, tin, Drink C-C In Bottles 5¢, bottle (1916-curved) on green left of phrase on red, white trim, 12x36", G+, A16..**$400.00**

Coca-Cola, sign, tin, Drink C-C In Bottles 5¢, bottles (straight-sided) on green flank phrase on red center, 1908, 12x36", NM, A13................................**$4,200.00**

Coca-Cola, sign, tin, Drink C-C In Bottles/D&R, bottle on white left of yellow/white phrase on red, green trim, 10x28", VG+-NM+, D32/A13, from $675 to..$1,600.00

Coca-Cola, sign, tin, Drink C-C 5¢ In Bottles, white on red, 1922, 6x23", EX+, A13 ....**$400.00**

Coca-Cola, sign, tin, Drink C-C/D&R, bottle (straight) in center, white ground, beveled edge, cardboard back, 1908, 13x6", G-, A13..**$650.00**

Coca-Cola, sign, tin, Drink C-C/D&R, bottle (1916) on green left of white phrase on red, yellow/green trim, 1926, 11x35", EX, A13 ....**$950.00**

Coca-Cola, sign, tin, Drink C-C/D&R, bottle (1923) on white left of white phrase on red, yellow/green trim, 1929, 11x35", VG, A13..**$525.00**

Coca-Cola, sign, tin, Drink C-C/D&R, bottle (1923) on white left of white phrase on red, yellow/green trim, 1933, 11x35", EX, A13 ....**$900.00**

Coca-Cola, sign, tin, Drink C-C/D&R, couple with bottle lower right on red, yellow/green border, 1942, 20x28", EX+, A13..**$550.00**

Coca-Cola, sign, tin, Drink C-C/D&R, girl tipping bottle in center, yellow/white on red, yellow/green trim, 1940s, 54x18", EX, A1 ....**$575.00**

Coca-Cola, sign, tin, Drink C-C/Refresh, bottle on red/white ground, Robertson 5-52, silver-tone self-frame, 54x18", VG+, A6 ....**$250.00**

Coca-Cola, sign, tin, Drink C-C/Sign Of Good Taste, fishtail (vertical) above bottle on white, green stripes, 1959, 54x17", NM+, A3 ....**$350.00**

Coca-Cola, sign, tin, Drink C-C/Sold Here Ice Cold, bottle (tilted) on yellow center dot, green border, 1939, 54x18", EX, A13 ....**$675.00**

Coca-Cola, sign, tin, Drink C-C/6 Bottle Carton 27¢, 6-pack (cardboard box) on red, yellow/green border, 1930s, 60x36", VG+, A4 ....**$1,000.00**

Coca-Cola, sign, tin, Drink/C-C/Trade Mark Reg, white on red, white border, curved corners, 1970s, 12x24", NM+, A14 ....**$25.00**

Coca-Cola, sign, tin, Enjoy Big King Size/C-C/Ice Cold Here, fishtail next to bottle on white, green stripes, 1960s, 20x28", EX, A6 ....**$160.00**

Coca-Cola, sign, tin, Enjoy That Refreshing New Feeling, fishtail (vertical) above bottle, green border, 1963, 54x18", EX+, A14 ....**$250.00**

Coca-Cola, sign, tin, Enjoy That Refreshing New Feeling Ice Cold, fishtail/phrase left of bottle, 1963, 20x28", NM+, A14 ....**$250.00**

Coca-Cola, sign, tin, Gas To-Day/Drink C-C Ice Cold/Drink C-C Sold Here, black price dot on square green center, 1931, 54", VG, A13 ....**$1,300.00**

Coca-Cola, sign, tin, Gas To-Day/Drink C-C Ice Cold/Drink C-C Sold Here, black price dot on round green center, 1936, 54", EX, A13 ....**$1,700.00**

Coca-Cola, sign, tin, Gas Today/Drink C-C While You Wait, black price dot/hand-held bottle on red/green, 1926, 15x24", VG+, A13 ....**$775.00**

Coca-Cola, sign, tin, Gas Today/Drink C-C While You Wait, black price triangle on red/green, 1929, 20x28", VG, A13 ....**$650.00**

Coca-Cola, sign, tin, Ice Cold, phrase (black) on white sign above bottle with shadow on red, bare metal frame, 54x18", EX, A13 ....**$600.00**

Coca-Cola, sign, tin, Ice Cold, phrase (white) left of paper cup with fishtail logo on blue, 1960s, 20x28", NM, A13.**$675.00**

Coca-Cola, sign, tin, Ice Cold C-C Sold Here, round, yellow/white on red, yellow/green rim, 1932, 20", NM+, A13 ....**$1,250.00**

Coca-Cola, sign, tin, Ice Cold C-C Sold Here, round, yellow/white on red, yellow/white/green rim, 1933, 20", EX+, A13 ....**$800.00**

Coca-Cola, sign, tin, Ice Cold C-C Sold Here, yellow/white on red, green border, 1934, 28x19", NM, D32....**$550.00**

Coca-Cola, sign, tin, Ice Cold C-C/Enjoy That Refreshing New Feeling, fishtail/bottle on white, green stripes/trim, 20x28", VG, A1..**$175.00**

Coca-Cola, sign, tin, Ice Cold/C-C/Sold Here, bottle (straight) on white next to green/red/green field, 1914, 20x28", EX, A13..**$1,700.00**

Coca-Cola, sign, tin, Ice Cold/C-C/Sold Here, bottle (straight) on white next to green/red/green field, 1914, 20x28", NM, A4 ....**$2,400.00**

Coca-Cola, sign, tin, Ice Cold/C-C/Sold Here, receding sign with large bottle on green, embossed, 1932, 19x27", G, A13..**$375.00**

Coca-Cola, sign, tin, Ice Cold/C-C/Sold Here, yellow/white/yellow on red field (curved corners), green border, vertical, EX, A13 ....**$350.00**

Coca-Cola, sign, tin, In Bottles/Drink C-C/5¢, white on red, yellow line border, embossed, 1920s, 6x23", VG-EX+, A13, from $140 to..**$275.00**

Coca-Cola, sign, tin, Now Enjoy C-C At Home/Handy Home Carton Sold Here, hand-held carton in center, Canada, 1930s, 54x18", G+, A13 ....**$1,050.00**

Coca-Cola, sign, tin, Pause/Drink C-C, tilted bottle on yellow dot in center, red ground, silver self-frame, 1940, 54x18", NM+, A13 ....**$1,200.00**

Coca-Cola, sign, tin, Pick Up 6 For Home Refreshment, 6-pack in center on white, raised rim, 1964, 50x16", EX, A13..**$450.00**

Coca-Cola, sign, tin, Refresh Yourself!/Drink C-C/Sold Here Ice Cold, bottle in center on white, Canada, 1920s-30s, 54x18", G+, A13 ....**$600.00**

Coca-Cola, sign, tin, Refresh Yourself!/Drink C-C/Sold Here Ice Cold, bottle on white next to phrase on red, 1927, 20x28", VG, A14..**$285.00**

Coca-Cola, sign, tin, Refresh Yourself!/Drink C-C/Sold Here Ice Cold, phrase on red, yellow/green trim, 28x29", VG+, D30 ....**$350.00**

Coca-Cola, sign, tin, Ring A Bottle/One Ring/Over Gold Bottle/Wins Doll Or Radio/5 Rings..25¢..., bottle on white, 18x22", EX, A24 ....**$180.00**

Coca-Cola, sign, tin, Serve C-C At Home, 6-pack on yellow dot in center on red, yellow trim, 1951, 53x17", NM, A1 ....**$1,000.00**

Coca-Cola, sign, tin, Serve Yourself/Drink C-C/Please Pay The Clerk, cooler insert, yellow/white on red, 1931, 11x31", VG, A13...**$140.00**

Coca-Cola, sign, tin, Sign Of Good Taste, die-cut yellow ribbon banner with phrase in red, 10x42", EX, A24 ....**$75.00**

Coca-Cola, sign, tin, Take A Case Home Today/$1.00 Plus Deposit/C-C/D&R, red, yellow trim, 1-sided, 1949, 28x20", NM, A13 ....**$275.00**

Coca-Cola, sign, tin, Take A Case Home Today/$1.00 Plus Deposit/C-C/D&R, red, yellow trim, 2-sided, 1949, 28x20", VG, A13...............................**$300.00**

Coca-Cola, sign, tin, Take A Case Home Today/Quality Refreshment, case on red triangle/yellow dot/white, 1952, 28x20", NM+, A13 ....**$350.00**

Coca-Cola, sign, tin, Take A Case Home Today/Quality Refreshment, case on red carpet leading to house, 28x19", NM+, D32........................**$350.00**

Coca-Cola, sign, tin, Take Home A C-C In Cartons, yellow/red lettering on red dot on square white field, 16x14", EX+, A3 ....**$200.00**

Coca-Cola, sign, tin, Take Home A Carton, fishtail (C-C/SOGT) logo above 6-pack on white, green trim, 1958, 28x20", EX+, A13 ....**$550.00**

Coca-Cola, sign, tin, Take Home A Carton, 6-pack on white above yellow lettering on green, metal rim, 1954, 28x20", NM, A13.........................**$600.00**

Coca-Cola, sign, tin, Take Home A Carton, 6-pack on yellow above phrase on red, curved corners, Canada, 1951, 54x36", EX, A13 ....$475.00

Coca-Cola, sign, tin, Take Home A Carton, 6-pack on yellow center dot on red, yellow trim, curved corners, 1940, 60x36", G, A13 ....$200.00

Coca-Cola, sign, tin, Take Home A Carton, 6-pack on yellow center dot on red, yellow trim, curved corners, 1939 – 42, 54x18", VG-EX, D32/A13, from $375 to..............**$500.00**

Coca-Cola, sign, tin, Take Home A Carton, 6-pack on yellow dot with bars on green, yellow lettering, 1941, 28x20", EX, A13.................................**$550.00**

Coca-Cola, sign, tin, Things Go Better With Coke, phrase/Drink C-C disk logo/bottle on white, raised rim, 1960s, 54x18", VG-NM, A13/A14, from $200 to.....................**$400.00**

Coca-Cola, sign, tin, Things Go Better With Coke/Ice Cold/Prepared By C-C, white cup on white/green, 1960s, 20x28", NM, A13.....................................**$600.00**

Coca-Cola, sign, tin, Tomese C-C/En Botellitas 6¢ Plata, bottles (straight) on green ends, white on red, 1908, 12x36", EX, A13...**$2,300.00**

Coca-Cola, sign, trolley, Around The Corner From Anywhere, lady in hat & gloves/receding logo, 1927, 11x21", EX+, A13 ....$2,600.00

Coca-Cola, sign, trolley, Drink C-C/D&R, white phrase on red, white/green border, 11x21", EX+, A13 ...$675.00

Coca-Cola, sign, trolley, Drink C-C/D&R/5¢ At Fountains/ In Bottles 5¢, fancy red emblem on green, 1907, 10x20", G+, A13 ....$3,400.00

Coca-Cola, sign, trolley, Drink C-C/Relieves Fatigue/ Sold Everywhere 5¢, man with glass, white on black, 1907, 10x21", G+, A13 ....$3,400.00

Coca-Cola, sign, trolley, Fall/Winter/Spring/Summer, Drink C-C/Delicious All Year 'Round, 1923, 10x20", NM, A13 ....$4,000.00

Coca-Cola, sign, trolley, Tired? C-C Relieves Fatigue, soda jerk, red/green, 1907, 10x20", VG, A13 ......$2,300.00

Coca-Cola, sign, trolley, Yes, sunbather in white 2-pc suit eyeing hand-held bottle/disk logo on white, 1946, 11x28", VG, A13.................................**$325.00**

Coca-Cola, sign, trolley, Yes, sunbather in white 2-pc suit eyeing hand-held bottle/disk logo on white, 1946, 11x28", EX+, A13 ....**$750.00**

Coca-Cola, sign, truck, Every Bottle Coca-Cola Sterilized, wood, white on red, 1910s-20s, 12x120", VG+, A13 ....**$425.00**

Coca-Cola, sign, truck cab, porcelain, curved, Drink C-C Ice Cold, yellow/white red, yellow border, 1940s-50s, 10x50", VG, A13...**$130.00**

Coca-Cola, sign, truck cab, porcelain, curved, Drink C-C In Bottles, red on white, 1940s-50s, 10x51", EX+, A1........**$375.00**

Coca-Cola, stamp holder with calendar, celluloid, resembles addressed envelope, 1900, 1½x2½", EX+, A13 .**$1,200.00**

Coca-Cola, string holder, Take Home C-C In Cartons, back-to-back curved tin panels, white, 1930s, VG+, A4 ....**$700.00**

Coca-Cola, string holder, Take Home In Cartons, 2 back-to-back curved tin panels, red, 1930s, NM, A13..**$1,000.00**

Coca-Cola, swimsuit, young child's, red with allover white script logo, NM, A16.............................**$40.00**

Coca-Cola, syrup barrel, 10-gal, wood, round paper end label, ca 1917, 30x21" dia, EX+, A3 ....**$330.00**

Coca-Cola, syrup barrel, 10-gal, wood, round paper end label, 21x15" dia, VG, A2.............................**$265.00**

Coca-Cola, syrup bottle, clear glass, etched wreath logo (gold), gold-tone metal jigger cap, 1910, NM, A13.............**$700.00**

Coca-Cola, syrup bottle, clear glass, etched wreath logo (white), metal jigger cap, 1910, EX, A13 ....**$375.00**

Coca-Cola, syrup can, 1-gal, paper label, white on red, C-C on white circle with red/white striped band, EX+, A1.**$120.00**

Coca-Cola, syrup jug, paper label, Coke glass on red rectangular logo, 1950s, EX, D30..................................**$20.00**

Coca-Cola, syrup jug, paper label, Coke glass on red round logo, 1950s, EX, D30 ....**$20.00**

Coca-Cola, syrup jug, paper label, paper cup/Coke glass, 1960s, EX, D30 ....**$20.00**

Coca-Cola, syrup jug, paper label, white round logo on red, 1940s, EX+, D30 ....**$55.00**

Coca-Cola, syrup jug, stoneware, cone top, round paper label, VG+, A16 ....**$1,600.00**

Coca-Cola, syrup jug, stoneware, paper label, early 1900s, rare, NM, A16.....................................**$2,750.00**

Coca-Cola, thermometer, dial, Drink C-C, bottle, 1948, 12" dia, NM+, A13 ....$600.00

Coca-Cola, thermometer, dial, Drink C-C In Bottles, red, 1950s, 12" dia, EX+, A13 ....**$170.00**

Coca-Cola, thermometer, dial, Drink C-C/Sign Of Good Taste, red, 1950s, 12" dia, EX, A16/A13, from $120 to..**$160.00**

Coca-Cola, thermometer, dial, Enjoy C-C In Bottles, red, 1950s, 12" dia, VG, A13......................................**$130.00**

Coca-Cola, thermometer, dial, Things Go Better With Coke, white, 1964, 12" dia, EX+, A13 ....**$300.00**

Coca-Cola, thermometer, masonite, Thirst Knows No Season, bottle/slanted gauge, 1944, 17", VG-EX, A16/A13/A14, from $300 to.......................................**$500.00**

Coca-Cola, thermometer, mirror with inserted gauge, Drink C-C In Bottles/silhouette girl on red bottom panel, 1939, 14x10", G+, A13 ....**$325.00**

Coca-Cola, thermometer, plastic, Drink C-C, orange/white, 1960s, 18", EX, A13...............................**$30.00**

Coca-Cola, thermometer, plastic, gauge atop cube base with contour logo, 1980s, EX, D30 ....**$25.00**

Coca-Cola, thermometer, porcelain, Drink C-C/Coke Refreshes, 1950s, 36", EX+, A2 ....**$1,320.00**

Coca-Cola, thermometer, porcelain, Drink C-C/La Soif N'a Pas De Saison, silhouette girl, red, Canadian, 1942, 18", G, A13..**$185.00**

Coca-Cola, thermometer, porcelain, Drink C-C/Thirst Knows No Season, silhouette girl, Canadian, 1939, 18", VG-NM, A13, from $400 to...**$1,050.00**

Coca-Cola, thermometer, tin, bottle (gold) on red panel, 1936, 16", EX-NM, A13/A16, from $275 to.........**$400.00**

Coca-Cola, thermometer, tin, bottle shape, gold, 1956, 8", EX, A13..**$40.00**

Coca-Cola, thermometer, tin, bottle shape, 1923 Christmas bottle, 1931, 17", G, A2 ....**$150.00**

Coca-Cola, thermometer, tin, bottle shape, 1950s, 17", VG+, A13...**$100.00**

Coca-Cola, thermometer, tin, bottle shape, 1950s, 17", NMIB, A16..**$150.00**

Coca-Cola, thermometer, tin, bottle shape, 1958, 17", NM+, A13...**$160.00**

Coca-Cola, thermometer, tin, bottle shape, 1958, 17", VG, A14/D30, from $75 to.....................................**$85.00**

Coca-Cola, thermometer, tin, bottle shape, 1958, 30", EX, A9...**$100.00**

Coca-Cola, thermometer, tin, Drink C-C, double bottles, 1941, 16", VG-EX+, A1/A13, from $350 to.........**$450.00**

Coca-Cola, thermometer, tin, Drink C-C/D&R, silhouette girl, 1939, 16", EX, A13 ....**$300.00**

Coca-Cola, thermometer, tin, Drink C-C/Sign Of Good Taste/Refresh Yourself, cigar shape, red/white, 1950s, 30", NM, A13.......................................**$525.00**

Coca-Cola, thermometer, tin, Drink C-C/Sign Of Good Taste/Refresh Yourself, cigar shape, red/white, 1950s, 30", VG, A6 ....**$200.00**

Coca-Cola, thermometer, wood, Drink C-C 5¢/D&R, 1905, 21", VG-VG+, A13/D32, from $400 to ..$475.00

Coca-Cola, tie, men's, silk-screened image of the Sprite Boy with bottle, 1940s (?), 5" wide at bottom, NM (appears unused), D22............................**$225.00**

Coca-Cola, tie clip, gold/enameled bar, 5-Year, NM, A16 ..**$75.00**

Coca-Cola, tip tray, 1903, VG, A13 ....**$900.00**
Coca-Cola, tip tray, 1906, EX+, A13 ....**$725.00**
Coca-Cola, tip tray, 1907, EX, A16 ....**$725.00**
Coca-Cola, tip tray, 1909, EX+, A13......................**$875.00**

Coca-Cola, tip tray, 1910, NM+, A16 ....**$1,540.00**
Coca-Cola, tip tray, 1913, G, A16............................**$200.00**
Coca-Cola, tip tray, 1913, NM+, A16 ....**$1,000.00**
Coca-Cola, tip tray, 1914, NM+, A3.........................**$330.00**
Coca-Cola, tip tray, 1916, EX+, A13 ....**$275.00**
Coca-Cola, tip tray, 1920, EX+, A16 ....**$260.00**
Coca-Cola, toy, Robin Hood Bo-Arro (Boys & Girls), 1920s-30s, NM (unassembled/unused, with original promotional card), A13...........................**$175.00**
Coca-Cola, toy airplane, 1973-74 Albatros, red/white, black markings, EX+, A13 ....**$100.00**

Coca-Cola, toy bus, Ashi Toys (ATC)/Japan, tin litho/plastic windows, friction, 14½", NM, A14 ..$1,300.00
Coca-Cola, toy bus, ATC/Japan, 1950s-60s, Gray-Line/New York's First Air Conditioned Sightseeing Coach, metal, 4x14", VG, A13................................**$300.00**
Coca-Cola, toy dispenser, #16, with 4 plastic flared glasses, NMIB, A1 ....**$135.00**

Coca-Cola, toy truck, Buddy L, 1962-64, #5426, delivery, pressed steel, 2-tiered divided bay, whitewalls, 15", VG+, A14........................**$155.00**
Coca-Cola, toy truck, Buddy L, 1970s, #5117, delivery, red/white, contour logo, chrome hubs, 9", VG+, A14.................**$40.00**
Coca-Cola, toy truck, Buddy L, 1980s, #5270J, tractor-trailer, steel, red/white, clear plastic cab top, 14", complete, EX-NM+, A14/A16, from $25 to **$40.00**
Coca-Cola, toy truck, Budgie, 1950s, C-C Van, die-cast, 5", EX+, A14........................**$120.00**
Coca-Cola, toy truck, Budgie, 1950s, delivery, die-cast, divided open bay, orange, orange hubs, 5", EX+, A14......**$120.00**
Coca-Cola, toy truck, Budgie, 1980s, VW truck, die-cast, red cab/bed, white bed cover, NMIB, A13.................**$70.00**
Coca-Cola, toy truck, Lincoln Toys, 1950s, #809/Canada, flatbed, pressed steel, red, 15½", restored, A14.**$275.00**
Coca-Cola, toy truck, Linemar, 1950s, squash cab, tin, friction, lithoed, yellow, red trim, 1 from set of 6, 3", EX+, A14........................**$140.00**
Coca-Cola, toy truck, Marusan (SAN), 1956-57, #3441, tin, friction, open bay, yellow/blue, red trim, 8", no bottles, EX, A16........................**$275.00**

Coca-Cola, toy truck, Marusan (SAN) 1956-1957, #3431, tin, friction, yellow/blue, red trim, 8", complete, NM+, D32 ....**$750.00**
Coca-Cola, toy truck, Marx, 1940s-50s, #991, stake bed, pressed steel, yellow cab/bed, Sprite Boy logo, 20¼", G-, A16........................**$150.00**
Coca-Cola, toy truck, Marx, 1950-54, Chevy delivery, plastic, red/yellow, enclosed bed, top ad panel, 11", complete, EX, A16........................**$800.00**
Coca-Cola, toy truck, Marx, 1954-56, #21, delivery, tin, yellow, red wheel covers, 12½", NM (EX box), A13 ....**$650.00**
Coca-Cola, toy truck, Marx, 1954-56, #21, delivery, tin, yellow, red wheel covers, 12½", complete, EX, A1/A13, from $180 to........................**$230.00**
Coca-Cola, toy truck, Marx, 1956, #1088, stake bed, tin, Sprite Boy logo, yellow, red/blue trim, 18¾", NM+ (VG box), A13 ....**$1,150.00**
Coca-Cola, toy truck, Marx, 1956, #1088, stake bed, tin, Sprite Boy logo, yellow, red/blue trim, 18¾", G+, A14 ....**$180.00**
Coca-Cola, toy truck, Marx, 1956, delivery, plastic, 6 plastic cases with lithoed cardboard inserts, EX+ (EX box), A13........................**$475.00**
Coca-Cola, toy truck, Marx, 1956-57, #1090, delivery, tin, yellow/red trim, open bay with center ad panel, 7 cases, 17½", VG+, A16........................**$500.00**

Coca-Cola, toy truck, Marx/Canada, 1950-54, Chevy style, plastic, red, wood wheels, 2-tiered, with bottles, 11", EX+ (G box), A13..........................$1,300.00
Coca-Cola, toy truck, Matchbox, 1950s-60s, #37, even load, die-cast, yellow, red trim, 2¼", NMIB, A14 ....$115.00

Coca-Cola, toy truck, Matchbox, 1950s-60s, #37A, uneven load, die-cast yellow, red trim, 2¼", M (G box), A14 ....$250.00
Coca-Cola, toy truck, Matchbox, 1950s-60s, #37B, even load, die-cast, yellow, red trim, 2¼", NM+ (NM box), A14 ....$175.00
Coca-Cola, toy truck, Metalcraft, 1932, #171, A-Frame, pressed steel, red/yellow, 10 bottles, 11", VG-EX+, A13, from $600 to...$800.00
Coca-Cola, toy truck, Sanyo, 1960s, Route Truck For C-C, tin, yellow/white, red trim, 12½", EXIB, A16............$450.00
Coca-Cola, toy truck, TT (Japan), 1970s, tin/plastic, friction, yellow, image of 2 bottles/red disk logo on van, 3¾", NM, A16...$40.00

Coca-Cola, trade card, folding, Drink C-C/High Ball, shows waitress serving 2 gents, waitress in bathtub on back, 1907, VG+, A13 ....$1,250.00
Coca-Cola, tray, 1906, 13x11", VG+, A13.................$750.00

Coca-Cola, tray, 1907, 13x11", G, A16 ....$300.00
Coca-Cola, tray, 1909, 17x14", VG+, A13 ....$1,250.00
Coca-Cola, tray, 1910, 13x11", VG, A16...................$580.00
Coca-Cola, tray, 1913, 15x13", oval, EX, A16 ....$650.00
Coca-Cola, tray, 1914, 13x11", EX+, A16 ....$775.00
Coca-Cola, tray, 1914, 15x13", oval, G-, A16...........$225.00

Coca-Cola, tray, 1916, 19x9", EX, A16 ....$500.00
Coca-Cola, tray, 1920, 13x11", EX, A13 ....$725.00
Coca-Cola, tray, 1921, 13x11", EX+, A16 ....$880.00
Coca-Cola, tray, 1922, 13x11", EX+, A16 ....$750.00
Coca-Cola, tray, 1924, 13x11", G, A16 ....$275.00

Coca-Cola, tray, 1925, 13x11", EX, A16.....................$375.00
Coca-Cola, tray, 1927, 13x11", EX+, A16 ....$600.00
Coca-Cola, tray, 1928, 13x11", NM, A16......................$650.00
Coca-Cola, tray, 1929, 13x11", Coke glass, EX+, A13.........$325.00
Coca-Cola, tray, 1930, 13x11", bathing beauty, EX, A13...$425.00

Coca-Cola, tray, 1930, 13x11", phone girl, VG, A13..$225.00
Coca-Cola, tray, 1931, 13x11", NM, A16 ....$1,230.00
Coca-Cola, tray, 1934, 11x13", VG, A7......................$550.00
Coca-Cola, tray, 1935, 13x11", EX+, A16 ....$330.00
Coca-Cola, tray, 1936, 13x11", EX, A16 ....$290.00
Coca-Cola, tray, 1937, 13x11", EX, A1 ....$275.00
Coca-Cola, tray, 1938, 13x11", EX, A16 ....$250.00
Coca-Cola, tray, 1939, 13x11", NM, A16 ....$350.00

Coca-Cola, tray, 1940, 11x13", NM, A9 ....$325.00
Coca-Cola, tray, 1941, 13x11", NM, A16.........$325.00
Coca-Cola, tray, 1942, 13x11", EX+, A1/A13 ....$325.00
Coca-Cola, tray, 1947, 13x11", VG, A13....................$200.00
Coca-Cola, tray, 1948, 13x11", G+, A8 ....$80.00
Coca-Cola, tray, 1950-52, 13x11", EX+, A16 ....$90.00
Coca-Cola, tray, 1953-60, 13x11", NM+, A16 ....$85.00
Coca-Cola, tray, 1957, 13x11", NM, A14 ....$75.00
Coca-Cola, tray, 1961, 11x13", EX, A16, ...$50.00
Coca-Cola, truck grille plate, aluminum, Drink C-C In Bottles
in die-cut lettering, 7x17", NM+, A13.................$250.00
Coca-Cola, truck grille plate, aluminum, Drink C-C in die-cut
lettering, 1920s, 5x17", NM+, A13........................$150.00
Coca-Cola, umbrella, white with stenciled red/black lettering
& gold bottles, 1930s, 60", VG, A13 ....$900.00
Coca-Cola, vendor, stadium, metal, red, embossed lettering,
1930s, strap missing, G-, A13.............................$350.00
Coca-Cola, vendor, stadium, metal, red, white Drink C-C,
side opener/straps, 1940s, VG, A6 ....$325.00
Coca-Cola, vendor, stadium, wood, red, white Drink C-C,
with strap, 1950s, NM (NOS), A13 ....$325.00

Coca-Cola, Vienna art plate, topless girl seated, gold
frame, EX+, A13 ....$1,100.00
Coca-Cola, Vienna art plates, with frame, VG-EX, A13, from
$400 to...$575.00
Coca-Cola, watch, 100th Anniversary, round gold-tone face
with black leather strap, NM, A13.......................$120.00
Coca-Cola, watch fob, Duster Girl, rectangular, painted
image, raised silver border, black leather strap, 1911,
EX+, A13..$800.00
Coca-Cola, watch fob, Relieves Fatigue/Drink C-C In Bottles
5¢, sterling silver, embossed, 1907, EX+, A16 ......$90.00
Coca-Cola, water bottle, clear glass, embossed with horses,
flat-sided, screw cap, NM+, A16..........................$625.00
Coca-Cola, see also My Coca or Sun-Rise Flavors
Coca-Cola Chewing Gum, blotter, 1916, Made To
Chew/Best Sanitary/Franklin-Caro Co, shows 2 packs of
gum, red/black on white, M, rare, A4 ....$975.00

Coca-Cola Chewing Gum, jar, 1903-05, embossed lettering, beaded lid, beveled corners, VG+-NM, A13 from
$475 to $700.00
Coca-Cola Chewing Gum, jar, 1905-11, embossed lettering,
Franklin Caro lid, beveled corners, NM, A13 .....$700.00
Coca-Cola Chewing Gum, jar, 1905-11, embossed lettering,
scalloped lid, beveled borners, EX-NM, A13, from $660
to...$900.00
Coca-Cola Chewing Gum, jar, 1905-11, embossed lettering,
scalloped lid, square corners, EX, A13 ....$775.00
Coca-Cola Gum, fan, cardboard, heart shape with head
images of young ladies, Chew Coca-Cola Gum on
reverse, wood handle, VG, A9 ....$4,500.00
Coca-Cola Peppermint Pepsin Gum/Franklin Caro Co,
gum wrapper, matted/framed, rare, EX+, A16 ..$1,480.00

Coca-Cola Pepsin Gum, jar, 1912-14, paper label,
Franklin Caro lid, square corners, NM (VG label),
A13 ....$1,200.00
Coca-Cola Pepsin Gum, magazine ad, Everybody's Maga-
zine, 1906, black/white, 1x3" ad on full page with Stan-
dard Typewriter Exchange ad, NM, A16............$135.00
Cocktail Cigars, sign, paper, Take A Cocktail 5¢/And Look
Pleasant 5¢ flank oval image, Schumacher & Ettlinger
litho, 6x18", VG, A9...$275.00
Coffee House Coffee, can, 1-lb, key-wind lid, hearth scene,
EX+, A15...$400.00
Coiner Hand Made Cigar, tin, vertical square, embossed,
EX, A18..$165.00
Coke Dandruff Cure & Hair Tonic, sign, cardboard, diago-
nal hanger, ...10 Cents Extra, image of bottle in center,
blue lettering on white, 8x8", VG+, A3..............$110.00
Coke Distilleries Co Ltd, sign, tin, Pure Pot Still, bottle next
to box of corks, self-framed, 13x16", VG+, A3...$100.00
Colchester Rubber Co, fan, paper on wood cigar with fan
on top, 7", EX+, A3...$40.00
Cold Spring Brewery, tray, oval, girl hugging horse's nose,
decorative rim, 16", VG+, A8 ....$400.00
Cold Spring Red Star Tonic, label, 12-oz, Cold Spring
Brewing Co/MN, IRTP/U-type permit #, 1933-36, M
(creased or folded), A10.......................................$37.00
Cole's Penetrating Liniment, sign, porcelain, Safe &
Sure.../Removes All Aches & Pains/All Druggists Sell It...,
white on blue, 6x16", EX, A1 ....$525.00

Conoco, sign, porcelain, triangle, red/white, 2-sided, 30x26", NM (NOS), A6 ....**$425.00**

Conoco, sign, tin, Conoco Bronze Gasoline/Conoco Chek-Chart Greasing, black/white graphics on red/black white, 2-sided, EX, D34 ....**$1,100.00**

Conoco Gasoline, sign, porcelain, round, blue/red name & minuteman logo on yellow, blue/white border, 2-sided, 25" dia, EX, A6 ....**$2,950.00**

Conoco Harvestor Oil, can, ½-gal, yellow/white, minuteman logo on can/cap, EX, A1 ....**$675.00**

Conoco Household Lubricant, can, 8-oz, round, with oiler spout, lettering above/below Continental soldier, 1920s, 5", EX, A6 ....**$650.00**

Conoco Super Motor Oil, bank, oil can shape, EX, D25 ...**$38.00**

Conoco Travel Bureau Branch, sign, metal, Free Travel Information, logo upper left, speeding car below, red/green/white, 18x24", NM, A6 ....**$1,200.00**

Conoco/Amalie/Continental Oil Co, lubester sign, porcelain, round, blue lettering on gold band around blue/white emblem on red dot, 2-sided, 11", EX, A1 ....**$850.00**

Conquest Coffee, can, 1-lb, key-wind lid, blue with red diagonal red stripe, profile of soldier on emblem, EX+, A3 ....**$300.00**

Conquest Strictly Pure Mustard Seed, tin, image of helmeted soldier in profile, EX+, A3 ....**$90.00**

Conrad Seipp Brewing Co/Malt Sinew, tray, rectangular, For Health & Strength, decorative rim around girl in pigtails holding up glass, VG, A8 ....**$90.00**

Consolidated Biscuit Co, toy house biscuit box, cardboard, 2-story with lithoed detail, red roof, dated 1932, 9x9x5", EX+, A3 ....**$85.00**

Consumer's Beer/Consumer's Brewery Co Inc, sign, tin hanger, round, lettering on band around portrait inset above ...Ask Father, orange, 1930s, 14" dia, NM, A19 ....**$100.00**

Consumers Ale/Consumers Brewing Co, matchbook, drawing of plant on back, 20 strike, front strike, M, D28 ....**$5.00**

Continental Cubes, pocket tin, vertical, concave, G-EX, A3/A9/A18, from $250 to **$500.00**

Continental Fire Insurace Co/New York, sign, porcelain, Continental soldier with musket standing next to blue lettering on white, 12x16", EX, A6 ....**$650.00**

Continental Radial Tires, key chain, figural man with name on hat, painted rubber, 2", EX, D14 ....**$28.00**

Continental Trailways, sign, porcelain, Bus Depot, winged logo above, red/white/blue, rounded corners, 18x36", NM, A1 ....**$250.00**

Convention Hall Coffee, can, 1-lb, smaller screw lid, orange, EX, A3 ....**$675.00**

Cook's Beer, sign, cardboard, His Master's Choice, dog at master's knee, original wood frame with brass plaque, 19x15", EX-EX+, A6/A9, from $175 to **$250.00**

Cook's Beer, sign, tin hanger, Call For on blue banner over top of bottle, Bottled Air Free on green band below, 20x7", NM+, A13 ....**$700.00**

Cook's Beer, sign, tin/cardboard, De Boss Sho' Likes His Cook's, black servant rushes by surprised mammy, beveled, 13x21", VG+, A3 ....**$140.00**

Cook's Beer, sign, tin/cardboard, early busy traffic scene with dog barking at frightened horses, American Art Works, 13x21", VG, A8 ....**$100.00**

Cook's Goldblume, ashtray, metal, round with 3 rests, lettering on rim/logo in center, 5" dia, EX, A8 ....**$40.00**

Cook's Goldblume Beer, sign, tin, A Quality Cargo In 1853, busy levee scene, artist Frederic Mizen, framed, image: 22x28", Fair, A9 ....**$125.00**

Cook's Goldblume Beer, sign, tin, lady in red dress & hat enjoys glass of Goldblume, artist I Patten, 1938, framed, image: 26x20", VG, A9 ....**$300.00**

Cook's Imperial Extra Dry, postcard, 1904 St Louis World's Fair exhibit building by the American Wine Co, NM, D26 ....**$85.00**

Cook's Paprika, tin, 3-oz, round C logo, orange/black on white, 5", EX+, A3 ....**$22.00**

Cool Roasted Full Flavor Coffee, can, 1-lb, key-wind lid, EX+, A3 ....**$35.00**

Coon Brand Collars & Cuffs, sign, porcelain, round, white name on blue band around Coon & Co/trademark racoon on white center, 8½" dia, EX, D11 ....**$175.00**

Coon Chicken Inn, matchbook, black boy on front/3 addresses with chicken on back, 20 strike, front striker, Diamond Match Co, M, D28 .... $17.00

Coon Chicken Inn, plate, ceramic, white, winking black man, decorative border, 6", NM, A1 .... $150.00

Coon Chicken Inn, plate, ceramic, white, winking black man, floral border, 6", NM, A1/D25, from $160 to $200.00

Coon Chicken Inn, plate, ceramic, white, winking black man, floral border, 8", NM, A1 .... $230.00

Coon Chicken Inn, postcard, shows Seattle restaurant with 3 insets of the outlets, linen, Curt Teich, EX+, D26 ... $250.00

Cooper's Old Bohemian Beer, tap knob, ball shape, black, gold-on-blue metal insert, NM, A8 .... $110.00

Cooper's Yorktown Golden Cream Ale, tap knob, ball shape, black, gold-on-red metal insert, EX, A8 .... $55.00

Coors (Adolph), tray, round, mountain (C logo) in center, 13" dia, rare, EX, A6 .... $220.00

Coors (Adolph), tray, round, mountain (no logo) in center, 13" dia, rare, EX, A6 .... $220.00

Coors Beer, ashtray, porcelain, white with logo, 6" dia, EX, D24 .... $4.00

Coors Beer, radio, can shape, EX, D13 .... $25.00

Coors Beer, sign, neon, Coors in red script neon/mountain design in white neon, white Beer on black bottom panel, NM, A13 .... $100.00

Coors Beer, toy train boxcar, HO scale, 1950s, EX, A19 .... $25.00

Coors Golden Malted Milk/Adolph Coors Co, tin, 25-lb, square, small wire grip handle, G+, A8 .... $80.00

Coors Old Style Beer, matchbook, cavalier/long-neck bottle with glass, 20 strike, front strike, full, M, D28 .... $6.00

Copenhagen, sign, porcelain, Made From High Grade Tobacco/Best Chew Ever Made above/below vertical name, 14x4", NM, A1 .... $150.00

Copenhagen, sign, tin, ...Chews Better, white lettering on black, 1940s, 3x18", NM, A3 .... $110.00

Copenhagen High Grade Tobacco, door push, porcelain, Best Chew Ever Made, Deco styling, white/black/yellow/red, 13x4", EX, A24 .... $275.00

Copley Coffee, can, 1-lb, key-wind, 5¢ Off, NM (unopened), A3 .... $62.00

Coppertone, sign, cardboard stand-up, yellow ad panel over famous image of girl/dog on beach, 1960s, 32x22", EX, A13 .... $180.00

Copy Right Ribbon, tin, square, rounded corners, red, Indian top/bottom, NM, A18 .... $80.00

Cordove Cigar Co's Class Cigars, tin, horizontal box, pry lid, green, EX+, A18 .... $12.00

Cork Distilleries Co Ltd Whisky, sign, tin, Pure Pot Still, bottle/box, self-framed, 15x19", VG-EX, A6/A17, from $130 to $200.00

Corn Products, sign, cardboard, ...Ask For Corn Products Cook Book, pages of baked goods flank Corn Maid, ca 1920, 22x21", EX, A3 .... $150.00

Cornelius & Baker, sign, paper, factory scene with horse-drawn traffic, WH Rease litho, 20x27", VG, A9 .. $200.00

Cornona Wool Fat, cabinet, wood, glass front, white stenciled lettering on yellow wood, 24x13x8", EX, A3 .... $150.00

Corona Blend Coffee, store can, 15-lb, key-wind lid, green, EX+, A3 .... $175.00

Corona Larks, humidor, tin, hinged glass lid, reverse-glass marque, copper colored, 8½x8x9½", EX+, A18 ...... $75.00

Coronation Cigarettes, tin, rectangular, flat, holds 100, gold on red, EX+, A18 .... $175.00

Coronet Coffee, can, 1-lb, key-wind lid, red, white lettering, EX+, A3 .... $20.00

Coronet Flake, tin, horizontal box, rounded corners, Somers Bros litho, EX+, A18 .... $35.00

Corylopsis of Japan Talc Powder, tin, oval, small round top, Japanese graphics on emblem, 5", EX+, D22 .... $150.00

Cosden Liquid Gas Special, sign, porcelain, Horsepower+ Plus, lettering on green dot encircled by blue/red horse heads, 2-sided, 42" dia, EX, A2 .... $7,700.00

Cott, sign, cardboard, ZaZa Gabor at table, 22x32", NM+, D30 .... $125.00

Cott, sign, enameled steel, It's Cott To Be Good, red cloud-like emblem next to bottle on white, 1950s, 31x56", NM (unused), A24 .... $125.00

Cott, sign, tin, It's Cott To Be Good, white-on-red oval with radiating rings of white/yellow, raised border, 12x18", NM+, D30 .... $65.00

Cuestra-Rey Cigars, sign, tin/cardboard with celluloid cover, beveled, row of 15 cigars shown actual size, 10x17", EX, A8 ....**$50.00**

Culticura Talcum Powder, tin, sample, EX+, A18 ....**$90.00**

Culture Crush Cut Smoking Tobacco, pocket tin, vertical, EX-NM+, A3/A18, from $100 to **$270.00**

Culture Crush Cut Smoking Tobacco, pocket tin, vertical, 10¢ label, VG+, A18 ....**$75.00**

Culture Crush Cut Smoking Tobacco, tin, round canister, knob lid, EX+, A18 ....**$175.00**

Culture Smoking Tobacco, product pack, cardboard, sample, 1909 tax stamp, VG+ (full), A18 ....**$35.00**

Cunningham's Ice Cream, tray, oval, The Factory Behind The Product, exterior view of building, lettered rim, gold trim, 15x19", EX+, A3 ....**$110.00**

Cunrad Line, sign, tin, Maurentania, scalloped rope self-frame, 28x39", EX, A7 ....**$1,300.00**

Cunrad Lines/RMS Aquitania, tip tray, rectangle, image of 4-stack steamship, VG+, A3 ....**$60.00**

Cunrad Steamers, sign, tin, steamship with 2 red stacks, scalloped wood-tone self-frame, 1905, 28x39", EX, A7 ....**$2,400.00**

Cupid, crate label, California orange, Cupid's face, 1920, EX, D5 ....**$50.00**

Cupid Bouquet Little Cigars, tin, square, flat, EX, A18...**$75.00**

Cupid Sliced Plug, pocket tin, flat, rounded corners, 5¢, cherubs, Canadian, VG+, A18 ....**$50.00**

Curad Bandages, bank, Taped Crusader, vinyl, premium, 1975, 7", NM, D20...**$100.00**

Curlee Clothes/Koritsky's Your Clothier, thermometer, tin, red/white on green, rounded top/bottom, 39", EX+, A1 ....**$90.00**

Curtice Brothers Tomato Ketchup, bottle, clear glass, screw cap, paper label, EX, D24 ....**$45.00**

Curtis' Pepsin Gum, sign, cardboard, die-cut, young girl atop ledge, Chew.../Flavor Delicious & Permanent, 1890s, 9x7", EX, A15 ....$850.00

Curtiss Baby Ruth Peppermint Gum, box, cardboard, The Flavor Sticks 5¢, red/white, dated 1928, 1x4x6", EX+, A15...**$200.00**

Curtiss Candies 5¢, display case, tin, 3-tiered with fold-down marque, each shelf lettered Baby Ruth/Butterfinger/East Aces, 20x21", G, A2 ....**$100.00**

Curtiss Golden Giant Pop Corn, can, white with red/white striped bands top/bottom, EX+, A3......................**$80.00**

Custon House Club Perfectos, tin, round, slip lid, image of building on white, Liberty Can, VG+, A18 ....**$100.00**

Cuticura Soap, sign, cardboard, ...Medical & Toilet/Price 25 Cents, tortoise shell frame, 16x10", EX+, A3 .....**$60.00**

Cuticura Talcum Powder, tin, sample, EX, A3 ....**$50.00**

Cuticura Talcum Powder, tin, 4-oz, NM+, A3...........**$60.00**

Cutting, pin-back button, oval, black/white image of early auto with driver, 1", EX, A2 ....**$200.00**

Cycle Brand Salomon, can label, Victorian woman on bike, M, D5 ....**$35.00**

Cyclo Ethyl, gas globe lenses, No-Knock/More Power in red on white band around red name on green center, 14" dia, NM, A1, pair..**$650.00**

Cyclo Ethyl, magazine ad, Canadian Homes & Gardens, 1933, black/white image of Indian chief with peace pipe, framed, 20x16", EX, A6...**$30.00**

Cyclone Twister Cigar Five Cents, sign, cardboard hanger, red/black lettering above/below trademark image on yellow, 16x12", NM (unused), A24.........................**$130.00**

Cycol, pin-back button, The Navy Uses Cycol, white lettering on red dot, white/green border, 2" dia, NM, A1...**$185.00**

Cycol Motor Oil/Flying 'A' Gasoline, badge, painted metal convex pin-back, white on red/green, 2" dia, faded o/w VG, A1 ....**$160.00**

∽ D ∼

D Crawford's & Co, sign, cardboard die-cut stand-up, New Store/Easter Greeting, boy pushing girl on sleigh, 1899, 8x7", EX+, A3 ....**$40.00**

D&LE Morische Lafayette Lager Beer, mug, clear glass, embossed lettering in circle, 4½", rare, NM, A8.**$215.00**

D-X, license plate attachment, saleman's sample, tin, yellow lettering on red diamond reflector, with pouch, 4x6", NM, A1...**$70.00**

D-X Credit Cards, sign, porcelain, diamond logo above Credit Cards Honored Here, red/white/blue, curved corners, 2-sided, 12x18", VG, A1 ....**$65.00**

Dad's Old Fashioned Draft Root Beer, sign, tin, Enjoy Your Day/Drink!.../Gallons Quarts & 12 Oz Bottles, diagonal bands/lettering, 11x14", EX+, D30.....................**$135.00**

Dad's Old Fashioned Root Beer, sign, tin, Have A.../...It's Delicious, yellow diagonal band in center on blue, red border, embossed, 19x27", EX+, A1 ....**$300.00**

Dad's Root Beer, clock, square, light-up, Tastes Like Root Beer Should, cap logo, black numbers on gold/white striped frame, 16", EX, A1 ....**$200.00**

Dad's Root Beer, sign, tin, bottle (straight-sided) on blue tray, yellow ground, red border, 1940s-50s, 29x13", EX+, A13...**$280.00**

Dad's Root Beer, sign, tin, die-cut, Deliciously Yours..., blank panel with raised rim atop bottle cap, 28x20", NM (NOS), A9...**$100.00**

Daddy's Choice, can, 1-lb, screw lid, tall, VG, A3 ..**$120.00**

Daggett's Orangeade, dispenser, textured-glass globe atop green-painted glass base with lettering, original spigot, 15", G, A9...**$350.00**

Dahlia, crate label, California orange, photo of 3 pink dahlias with script logo, Redlands, M, D12 ....**$6.00**

Daily Habit Cigars, tin, round, slip lid, The Cigar Of Merit, parrot against tobacco field, VG+, A3.................**$235.00**

Dainty Maid, crate label, apple, smiling girl holding apple, 1930, M, D5...**$12.00**

Dairy Queen, salt & pepper shakers, Dairy Queen Girls, ceramic, 1960s, 4", EX, D25, pair **$225.00**

Dairy Queen, sign, tin, 2 vertical rows of goodies with Coca-Cola cup upper right on white, DQ oval at top, 1950s, 28x22", NM, A13 ....**$250.00**

Dairylea Ice Cream, fan, round, image of cow jumping over moon, ice cream cone handle, NM, A3 ....$155.00

Dairylea Milk, pin-back button, tin litho, round, Miss Dairylea/Safety & Dairylea Milk Go Hand In Hand, baby's head, 1¼", EX, D14......................................**$6.00**

Daisy Fresh Coffee, can, 1-lb, key-wind lid, large white daisy logo, NM, A3 ....**$50.00**

Daisy Quianine Tonic, sign, tin, A Daisy Tonic For Your Hair/Look Your Best/It Pays lettered above/below graphics, 10x9", VG, A6...**$160.00**

Dallas Brewery Home Beer, tip tray, round, Keep A Case In Your Home/Prompt Delivery, bottle in center, lettered/decorative rim, 4" dia, EX, A6....................**$125.00**

Damascus Milk, sign, porcelain, 2 die-cut milk bottles wrapped in red banner, 29x18", EX+, A1........**$1,650.00**

Dan Patch Cut Plug, tin, rectangular, curved corners, black/red on yellow, EX-NM, A3/A7, from $125 to **$185.00**

Dan Patch Perfectos, cigar box, wood, trademark image on inside lid label, EX, D22 ....**$165.00**

Dandro Solvant, sign, tin/cardboard, You Too Can Have.../Insist On.../For Dandruff..., hand-held bottle on black, beveled, 9x13", NM, A3...........................**$175.00**

Dandy, cigar box label, sample, man in top hat sitting with leg up, Heppenheimer & Maurer litho #1689, 1879, EX, A5...**$275.00**

Dandy Joe, cigar box label, sample, man standing by garden steps, Witsch & Schmitt litho #725, EX, A5 ....**$80.00**

Dandy Smoke, cigar box label, sample, dog in hat smoking pipe, Geo S Harris & Sons litho #4499, NM, A5 ..**$155.00**

Dandy-Line Brand Typewriter Ribbon/David L Morrow, tin, square, curved corners, ¾x2½x2x5", EX, D37...........**$50.00**

Daniel Boone Mix, sign, Glo-Glass, Try...Ice Cold/A Mixer A Blender..., bottle on white at right, blue ground, 1930s, 10x12", NM, A13 ....**$400.00**

Dante, cigar box label, inner lid, images from poem Divine Comedy, 6x9", M, D5 ....**$125.00**

Dante, cigar box label, outer, red devil/stern-faced man, 4½x4½", M, D5 ....**$30.00**

Dargai Cigar/Geo Kelly & Co, sign, tin, oval image of Scotsman flanked by flags/insets offering premiums, patterned border, 2-sided, 7x10", EX+, A3...........................**$150.00**

Darkie Toothpaste/Hawley & Hazel Chemical Co Ltd, product tube & box, image of black man in top hat, black/white, 7", EX (unused), A6 ....**$75.00**

Dauntless Coffee, can, 1-lb, paper label, red, EX, A18..**$85.00**

Davenport Malting Co's Unexcelled Bottle Beer, tip tray, round, lady sipping on glass, lettered rim, VG, A8.**$100.00**

David's Prize Soap, sign, paper, Dar's Money In It!, comical black family scene, framed, image: 26x36", VG+, A9..........**$250.00**

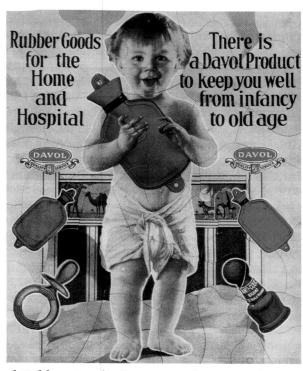

Davol Rubber Goods, jigsaw puzzle, ...For The Home & Hospital..., baby holding hot-water bottle while standing on bed, 1932, 10x8", EX, D10 ....$60.00

Dawson's Ale & Beer, tray, round, deep rim, Naturally Better, couple at table, pink ground, 12" dia, VG+, A8.....**$50.00**

Dawson's Ale & Lager, tray, round, deep rim, The Royal Beer You'll Be Loyal To, couple at table, gold ground, 12" dia, EX, A8...**$70.00**

Del Monte Food Products, sign, porcelain, Distributors Of... on white band above logo on green, 20x24", EX-EX+, A2/D32, from $580 to $750.00

De Luxe Brand Coffee, can, 3-lb, blue/white stripes, GSD octagonal logo, EX, A3...$65.00

Demotcar, pocket mirror, oval, Isn't This What You're Looking For? image of early auto, dealer below, blue on white, 2x3", VG+, A2...$990.00

Denman Tires, sign, porcelain, Unconditionally Guaranteed, orange/white on blue, 2-sided, 14x20", NM, A2 ..$550.00

Dennison's Coffee, pennant, felt, Ask For.../Pure And/Delicious (lettered vertically), white on red, 25", NM, A3 ....$80.00

Dentogen Tooth Powder, tin, round, smaller round top, NM, A18..$45.00

Dentyne Chewing Gum, display case, plastic/metal, New Sanitary Package, square marque atop curved shelves, 4½", EX, A6 ....$110.00

Dentyne Chewing Gum, toothbrush holder, figural boy, 1930s, rare, NM+, A4 ....$275.00

Dentyne/Clove/Beemans/Chicklets Gum, display rack, wire, colorful signs in shape of gum packs, folds down, 14x8x8", EX+, A1 ....$135.00

Deodo Powder, sign, cardboard die-cut stand-up, Ideal For Under Arm, nude lady next to large image of tin, 1920s, 25x21", VG+, A15...........................$130.00

Dependon Coffee, can, 1-lb, key-wind lid, red, EX+, A3 ..$100.00

Derby Cream Ale, label, 12-oz, Haberle Congress Brewing Co/Syracuse NY, IRTP/U-type permit #, 1933-36, M, A10..$10.00

Derby Diesel, gas globe, 3-pc, white Gill body, glass lenses, red/white/blue, 13½", NM, A6.............................$400.00

Derby Gasoline/Derby, gas globe, 3-pc, white Gill body, glass lenses, red/white/blue, 13½", NM, A6.......$425.00

Derby King Beer, tray, round, deep rim, lettered banner over racing scenes, 13" dia, VG, A8....................$100.00

Derby Pale A, label, 32-oz, oval, Haberle Congress Brewing Co/Syracuse, IRTP or WF statement, 1933-50, M, A10..$15.00

Derby Peter Pan Peanut Butter, see Peter Pan

Desert Bloom, crate label, California grapefruit, yucca plants blooming in high desert landscape, Redlands, NM-M, D3/D12, from $5 to $6.00

DeSoto Authorized Dealer, sign, metal emblem, Top Value, 2-color ground, red/yellow/blue/white, 16x36", VG, A6..$235.00

DeSoto High Grade Coffee, can, 1-lb, pry lid, yellow/black, tall, EX+, A18 ....$100.00

DeSoto/Plymouth Approved Service, sign, porcelain, round with extended center banner, yellow/blue/red, 2-sided, 42x44", G-EX, A2/A6, from $300 to $650.00

Detroit Brewing Co, art plate, decorative gold/green border around bare-breasted brunette in profile, VG+, A8...$80.00

Detroit Brewing Co's Bottled Beer, sign, tin, lady with flowers sipping from glass, beveled, 1911, 19x13", VG, A7 ....$500.00

Detroit Electric, pin-back button, round, 1910 Detroit Electric lettered around image of early auto, 1¼", EX, A2..$690.00

Deutsch Tailoring Co, tape measure, celluloid/metal, round, If You Take The Measure Of Your Tailor..., black man in center, 1½" dia, EX, A6 ....$80.00

Devilish Good Cigar, sign, tin, None Better/5 Cents, open cigar box showing 3 boys on lid, embossed, 10x14", G, A9..$225.00

Devilish Good Cigar, sign, tin, None Better/5 Cents, open cigar box showing 3 boys on lid, embossed, 10x14", EX-EX+, A3/A7, from $375 to...........$500.00

DeVoe's Makings, pocket tin, vertical, VG, A18......$300.00

DeVoe's Sweet Smoke, pocket tin, vertical, VG+-NM, A18, from $350 to...$500.00

DeWitt's Compound Cadoul Tonic Pills, sign, cardboard die-cut stand-up, old fisherman standing behind sign catching fish using product as bait, 13x21", VG, A3 ....$235.00

Diadem (The) of Old Virginia/TC Williams Co, caddy label, vertical, woman with spear/diadem (crown), Hoen litho, approx: 14x7", NM, A3 ....**$25.00**

Diadem Fine Cut/JG Flint Jr, pocket tin, flat, yellow, VG+, A18...**$65.00**

Dial Smoking Tobacco, sign, cardboard, 1¾-oz Tin 10¢, tin/lettering on yellow, framed, 18x14", EX, A3 ...**$60.00**

Dial Smoking Tobacco For Pipes & Cigarettes, pocket tin, vertical, red, EX+, A18.......................................**$55.00**

Dial 100% Burley Smoking Tobacco, pocket tin, vertical, EX, A3...**$30.00**

Diamond, gas globe, 3-pc, glass body/lenses, Diamond in blue over red/white diamond logo, white ground, NM, A1..**$425.00**

Diamond Crown Oysters, can label, 2 oysters/large crown, M, D5...**$20.00**

Diamond Dust 5¢, punchboard, features Babe Ruth/Dizzy Dean/Tommy Bridges/etc, 1930s, 7x7", few holes punched, EX+, A15.........................**$425.00**

Diamond Dyes, cabinet, wood, tin front, baby, 20", EX, A13 ....**$1,150.00**

Diamond Dyes, cabinet, wood, tin front, balloon/children, 25", EX-NM, A3/A9, from $1,500 to **$2,200.00**

Diamond Dyes, cabinet, wood, tin front, court jester, 27", VG+-EX+, A3, from $800 to.................**$1,250.00**

Diamond Dyes, cabinet, wood, tin front, mansion/children, 24", VG+, A2 ....**$935.00**

Diamond Dyes, cabinet, wood, tin front, maypole, 30", EX, A6...**$800.00**

Diamond Dyes, sign, cardboard die-cut hanger, parrot balanced on wire perch, ...Easy To Use/Use Diamond Dyes, 14", EX, A15 ....**$1,600.00**

Diamond Dyes, sign, tin, A Busy Day In Dollyville, 1911, 11x17", VG+, A9 ....**$1,800.00**

Diamond Dyes, sign, tin, diagonal, pedestal stand, lady dyeing clothes/color chart, Forbes litho, 2-sided, 30", VG, A9 ....**$625.00**

Diamond Ginger Ale, sign, tin, A Favorite Since 1865.../It's Extra Dry, red/black on yellow, red border, 13x39", NM+, D30 ....**$100.00**

Diamond Motor Oil, sign, flange, porcelain, 2 canted corners, black lettering on diamond logo, black/white/red, 20x26", EX, A1 ....**$300.00**

Diamond State Brewery, see Jos Stoeckle Brewing Co.

Diamond Tire Service, sign, flange, die-cut tire atop lettered shield, diamond logo in center, white/blue on red, gold border, 27x17", EX, A2...............**$1,100.00**

Diamond Tires, sign, porcelain, oval, On Sale Here/Diamond Tires/Users Know/D-D Trade Mark, white on blue, 16x22", EX/VG, A1 ....**$625.00**

Diamond Tires, sign, tin, A Line Of Merit & Distinction on blue diamond, white on red field, gold trim, 13x38", VG+, A1...**$170.00**

Diamond Tires/Squeegee Tread door push, porcelain, die-cut Squeegee Tread circle atop panel, Use Diamond Tires..., red/white/blue, 11", EX, A2....................**$550.00**

Diamond 34x4, sign, paper, boy/girl at wheel of early auto framed by tire, ca 1910, 29x25", EX, A24 ....**$140.00**

Diamond 760 Motor Oil, bank, oil can shape, EX, D13...**$25.00**

Diaparene/Sterling Drug Co, doll, Diaparene Baby, vinyl, 1980, 5", NM, D20...**$75.00**

Diaperene Baby Powder, tin, vertical rectangle, blue/white with image of baby's head in bonnet, paper label intact on back, 4½", NM, A3 ....**$65.00**

Diaperene Dusting Powder, tin, sample, Give Away Gift For Baby, 3", NM, A3...**$10.00**

Diavolo Coals, sign, porcelain, row of 3 red devils marked Coal/name above Sold Here, red/black on white, 16x22", VG, A6...**$150.00**

Dick Bros Brewery, match safe, metal, engraved, VG, A8 ....**$135.00**

Dick Bros Pilsener, Quincy Ill, drinking glass, shell, clear, etched filigree logo in red-brown, 4", NM, A8...**$230.00**

Dick Bros Quincy Beer, sign, Vitrolite, curved, with name/logo, 23x18", VG, A9 ....**$500.00**

Dick Custer Cigars, tin, horizontal box, square corners, Holds You Up, red, embellished portrait, EX+, A3........**$740.00**

Dr D Jayne's Family Medicines, see Jayne's

Dr Daniels' (AC) Horse & Dog Medicines, sign, wood, ...For Home Treatment-Sold Here, white stenciled lettering on blue, black wooden frame, 19x30", VG, A6 ....**$200.00**

Dr Daniels' (AC) Horse Cat Dog Medicines, sign, tin, ...For Home Treatment, white lettering on dk blue or black, line border, embossed, 18x28", NM, A3.............**$100.00**

Dr Daniels' (AC) Veterinary Medicines, sign, paper, Snowbound, Kaufmann & Strauss litho, 1906, 16x20", EX, A15 ....**$325.00**

Dr Daniels' Veterinary Medicines, cabinet, wood, tin front, bust image/product boxes, multicolored, 29", VG, A6 ....**$425.00**

Dr Daniels' Veterinary Medicines, cabinet, wood, tin front, bust image/product boxes, multicolored, 29", EX+, A15...............................$2,500.00

Dr Fenner's Remedy, sign, paper, girl in blue dress with white collar holding flower, framed, 13x10", EX+, A14......**$60.00**

Dr Graves Talcum Powder, tin, sample, ½x1¾" dia, EX, D37 ....**$140.00**

Dr Harter's Iron Tonic, trade card, President McKinley/wife promoting product, Beautifies The Complexion/Purifies The Blood, 12x7", EX, A3 ....**$30.00**

Dr Hess Antiseptic Powder, tin, yellow/black, red trim, NM, A18..**$75.00**

Dr Johnson's Educator Crackers, tin, square, lettering over wheat graphics, decorative border, 6x6", EX, A3 ...**$50.00**

Dr King's New Discovery, door plate, Prescriptions Carefully Compounded/Use.../Cures Consumption Coughs & Colds, blue/white, 7", EX+, A13 ....**$400.00**

Dr Lyon's Tooth Powder, tin, round, paper label, trademark image, 2x1", EX, D37...**$120.00**

Dr Lyon's Tooth Powder, tin, round, sample, octagonal trademark image, American Can Co, 2¾x1¼", EX, D37 ....**$70.00**

Dr Lyon's Tooth Tablets, tin, oval, For Cleansing & Beautifying The Teeth & Purifying The Breath, trademark image, Somers Bros, 1x2x3½", EX, D37 ....**$90.00**

Dr Miles Anti Pain Pills, sign, paper, Free/This Beautiful 1906 Calendar Is Yours For The Asking..., lady/product tube, bordered, 14x10", EX, A6 ....**$75.00**

Dr Morse's Indian Root Pills, sign, cardboard trifold, Indian village scene, Favored For 50 Years/For Constipation & Biliousness, 27x36", EX+, A1 ....**$275.00**

Dr Morse's Indian Root Pills, sign, tin, The Best Family Medicine In Use, embellished image of bear attacking Indian, 1880s, 11x14", VG, A6 ....**$4,250.00**

Dr Nut, sign, cardboard, die-cut, Delicious Sure Cure For Thirst, Dr Nut with bottle/bag/pet squirrel, 9x5", EX, D30...**$35.00**

Dr Pepper, art plate, girl looking right, rare, EX, A16...**$850.00**

Dr Pepper, bottle opener, metal, die-cut lion's head, etched lettering/design, 3", EX, A6 ....**$85.00**

Dr Pepper, bottle opener, slide-type with enameled logo, G-, A16 ....**$80.00**

Dr Pepper, bottle opener/spoon, The Friendly Pepper Upper, EX+, A16 ....**$385.00**

Dr Pepper, bottle topper, Cindy Garner, EX+, A16 .**$165.00**

Dr Pepper, bottle topper, Edith Luce, EX-NM, A1/A16, from $190 to $250.00**

Dr Pepper, bottle topper, Madalon Mason, EX, A16 .**$150.00**

Dr Pepper, bottle topper, Sandy Carleson, NM+, A16...**$250.00**

Dr Pepper, bottle topper, Virginia Kavanagh, NM, A1/A16, from $200 to $220.00**

Dr Pepper, calendar, 1947, complete, NM, D32 ......**$300.00**

Dr Pepper, calendar, 1951, complete, EX+, A16......**$100.00**

Dr Pepper, clock, Art Deco style, reverse-painted glass, red/gold/black/white, 1930s, 17x22", NM, A13..**$3,700.00**

Dr Pepper, clock, bottle cap, light-up, plastic, metal back, black numbers with red 10-2-4, name on red center band, 12" dia, EX, A6 ....**$70.00**

Dr Pepper, clock, octagonal, neon, reverse-painted glass, rectangular logo, EX+, A16..............................**$1,200.00**

Dr Pepper, clock, round, glass front, metal frame, Drink A Bite To Eat, black/red numbers on white band, EX, D30 ....**$150.00**

Dr Pepper, clock, round, glass front, metal frame (green), black/red numbers, Telechron, 1930-40s, EX-NM, A6/A13, from $250 to **$350.00**

Dr Pepper, clock, round, light-up, Drink DP, red center band, black/red numbers, 15" dia, EX-NM+, A1/A16, from $230 to..**$400.00**

Dr Pepper, decal, Please Pay When Served on gold dot, DP logo, 1930s-40s, 8x9", EX+ (unused), A13 .... **$200.00**

Dr Pepper, decal, Try A Frosty Pep.../Dr Pepper/And Ice Cream, hand pouring bottle of DP over ice cream, 1950, 13x9", NM, A24 .... **$50.00**

Dr Pepper, door plate, tin, In Case Of Emergency, place for name/number, yellow ground, rounded corners, 1930s-40s, 8", EX+, A13 .... **$200.00**

Dr Pepper, drinking glass, flared, etched logo, 1910s, NM, D32 .... **$1,200.00**

Dr Pepper, fan, cardboard, wood handle, pretty girl seated with bottle on knee, signed Earl Morgan, 15x8", EX, A6 .... **$75.00**

Dr Pepper, fan pull, cardboard, beach girl with umbrella, G, A16 .... **$80.00**

Dr Pepper, match holder, tin, 1940s-50s, 6", NM, A3/A13, from $150 to **$180.00**

Dr Pepper, match holder, tin, 1940s-50s, 6", NMIB, A13 .... **$200.00**

Dr Pepper, menu board, tin, ...When Hungry, Thirsty or Tired on yellow above blackboard, 1940s, 27x19", VG+, A13 .... **$250.00**

Dr Pepper, postcard, Free! 6 Bottles Of Dr Pepper, arrow points to 6-pack upper right, red/green/white, NM, D26 .... **$15.00**

Dr Pepper, sign, aluminum hanger, Energy Up!/Drink DP/Good For Life!/At 10-2 & 4, 1930s, 10" dia, EX+, D32 .... **$475.00**

Dr Pepper, sign, cardboard, Drink A Bite To Eat, girl car hop serving soldier, hanger/stand-up, 1930s-40s, 6x12", NM+, A13 .... **$225.00**

Dr Pepper, sign, cardboard, Join Me!, girl in car, red/gold frame, 1940s, 32x40", NM, A13 .... **$575.00**

Dr Pepper, sign, cardboard, Madelon Mason with red sign/bottle, white ground, 1940s, 19x32", G+, A13 .... **$100.00**

Dr Pepper, sign, cardboard, Smart Lift, snow girl with dog, 1940s, walnut Dr Pepper frame, 19x40", EX+ (VG frame), A13 .... **$450.00**

Dr Pepper, sign, flange, bottle cap atop Sold Here panel, red/black on white, yellow flange, 1950s-60s, 18x22", rare, NM, A13 .... **$1,000.00**

Dr Pepper, sign, flange, Drink DP/Good For Life, die-cut tin panel with 10-2-4 bottle on burst of white, 1939, 15x24", NM+, A13 .... **$1,250.00**

Dr Pepper, sign, flange, Fountain/Drink DP, yellow panel atop red oval on vertical red/white stripes, 1961, 15x22", NM, A13 .... **$750.00**

Dr Pepper, sign, paper, Try Frosty Pepper/Dr Pepper Ice Cream, bottle flanked by sodas in mound of ice, 1950s, 17x22", EX+, A3 .... **$65.00**

Dr Pepper, sign, porcelain, Drink DP, red oval above gold V emblem on white, rounded corners, 8x22", EX+, A1 .... **$150.00**

Dr Pepper, sign, porcelain, Drink DP, white on red, white border, curved corners, 9x24", NM, A1 .... **$160.00**

Dr Pepper, sign, porcelain, Drink DP Good For Life! white on red, white grid, green border, 11x27", VG-EX+, A1/A6, from $325 to **$500.00**

Dr Pepper, sign, porcelain, Drink DP/Good For Life, white on red, black grid, gold border, curved corners, 9x20", VG, A1 .... **$200.00**

Dr Pepper, sign, porcelain, Drink DP/Good For Life!, white on red, black grid, no border, 1930s-40s, 10x24", EX+, A13 .... **$275.00**

Dr Pepper, sign, porcelain, Drink DP/Good For Life!, white on red, white grid, white/black border, 1930s-40s, 11x27", EX+, A13 .... **$275.00**

Dr Pepper, sign, porcelain, round, Drink DP, red center band/numbers on white, red line border, 1950s, 10" dia, VG, A13 .... **$175.00**

Dr Pepper, sign, porcelain, round, Drink DP in red on white center band, 10-2-4 in white on red above & below, 10" dia. NM, A **$675.00**

Dr Pepper, sign, tin, bottle cap, white DP on center band, red 10-2-4 on white, 38" dia, EX+, A1 .... **$300.00**

Dr Pepper, sign, tin, clock/bottle/Drink DP logo on yellow, white self-frame, 1930s, 54x18", EX, A13 .... **$900.00**

Dr Pepper, sign, tin, Drink A Bite To Eat/Drink DP/Good For Life!, orange on yellow, 1945, 4x20", VG, A1 .... **$220.00**

Dr Pepper, sign, tin, Drink DP, red oval above gold V on white, embossed, white raised rim, curved corners, 1960s, 12x28", EX, A1 .... **$125.00**

Dr Pepper, sign, tin, Drink DP, red oval above gold V on white, embossed, stand-up, 11x16", EX+, A16 .... **$165.00**

Dr Pepper, sign, tin, Drink DP, red oval on white ground with geometric design, self-framed, 12x32", NM+, A1 .... **$170.00**

Dr Pepper, sign, tin, Drink DP/Good For Life, white lettering on red with white grid, embossed, 1936, 7x20", VG+, A13 .... **$350.00**

Dr Pepper, sign, tin, Drink DP/Ice Cold, rectangular logo over bottle on yellow, red border, vertical, NM, D30 .... **$275.00**

Dr Pepper, syrup jug, clear glass, paper label, screw cap, VG+, A16 .... **$120.00**

Dr Pepper, telephone, tin litho can with receiver which lifts to dial directly to corporate headquarters, 13", NM+, A3 .... **$125.00**

Dr Pepper, thermometer, tin, Drink A Bite To Eat At 10-2-4, gauge next to bottle, 1936, 13", EX, A13 .... **$975.00**

Dr Pepper, thermometer, tin, Drink DP/Good For Life!, gauge above bottle, curved ends, 17", G-EX, A13, from $320 to **$675.00**

Dr Pepper, thermometer, tin, Hot Or Cold/Enjoy The Friendly Pepper Upper/oval logo, red/white, curved top, 1950s, 16", EX, A13 .... **$175.00**

Dr Pepper, thermometer, tin, When Hungry, Thirsty Or Tired Drink DP, yellow, 1940s, 26", VG-EX, A13/A1, from $375 to...$400.00

Dr Pepper, tray, rectangle, You'll Like It To!, girl with 2 bottles, lettering/logos on red rim, gold trim, 1930s-40s, VG+, A13..$280.00

Dr Ransoms Syrup, sign, paperboard, smiling nurse holding frowning baby in green landscape, framed, 11x9", NM, A3...$50.00

Dr Sayman's Root Beer Extract, bottle, brown glass with blue/white paper label, cork top, MIB, A3...........$50.00

Dr Sayman's Toilet Talcum Powder, container, round, cardboard with tin top/bottom, NM (full), A18....$45.00

Dr Scales Pills, display case, wood frame/bottom with glass sides/top, front glass etched with name & 100-25¢, 14x13x17", EX, A2......................................$775.00

Dr Scholl's Absorbo Corn & Bunion Pads, sign, tin, displays use of product on feet shown around oval sign, wood-grain ground, framed, vertical, G+, A1.....$250.00

Dr Scholl's Foot Comfort Remedies/Zino-Pads, display cabinet, tin, graphic of hand applying product to foot on front, G+, D6........................$240.00

Dr Scholl's Foot-Eazer, display foot, chalkware, cutaway view of skeletal foot on lettered beveled base, 11", G, A2..$100.00

Dr Shoop's Cold & Cough Remedy, sign, reverse glass, silver-foiled letters on black ground, mirrored border, 6x18", EX, A2.....................................$200.00

Dr Shoop's Health Coffee, match holder, tin, product box pictured on backplate, VG+, A3...................$110.00

Dr Shoop's Lax-ets, match holder, tin, Only 5¢ Per Box, 5x3½", EX+, D22..................................$165.00

Dr Siegert's Angostura Bitters, booklet, Dr Siegert's Recipe Book, 18th C couple dining, promotes products as dessert flavoring, 8 pgs, ca 1915, EX, D14..........$12.00

Dr Swett's Root Beer, bottle, 12-oz, glass, dk amber, paper label, NM+, A3..$40.00

Dr Swett's Root Beer, mug, ceramic, embossed image of Dr Swett, black/white, 6", NM+, A13......................$225.00

Dr Swett's Root Beer, sign, cardboard hanger, ...The Original..., circular image of boy against silhouette image of man, 14x18", EX+, A16.......................$785.00

Dr Swett's Root Beer, sign, tin, The Great Health Beverage, lady with mug, Meek litho, self-framed, curled corners, 15x15", EX, A7....................................$800.00

Dr Swett's Root Beer, thermometer, tin, bottle-cap logo above window gauge, name below, curved top/bottom, 17x5", NM, D30..$200.00

Dr Tutt's Liver Pills, display sign, cardboard, die-cut, The Doctor's Unnecessary Visit, Dr Tutt talking to mother/2 children, 12x7", NOS, A6........................$85.00

Dr White's Cough Drops, tin, square, small round lid, girl at open window, highly decoratated, green/black, 8x5x5", EX, A6...............................$115.00

Drandro Solvent, sign, tin/cardboard, You Too Can Have Beautiful Hair/Insist On..., hand-held bottle on black, 9x13", EX, A6.................................$220.00

Dream Girl Talcum Powder, tin, red, 6", EX+, A3...$30.00

Dreibus Juanette Chocolates, sign, cardboard die-cut stand-up, Try.../Nothing Sweeter, young girl in bonnet with basket of chocolates, 14x8", EX+, A3...........$50.00

Drewery's, display figure, Big D, hard plastic, without base, 8", EX, D25...$40.00

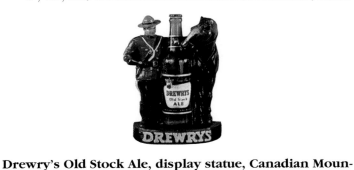

Drewry's Old Stock Ale, display statue, Canadian Mounty with horse wrapped around bottle on lettered base, plaster, EX, A8........................$100.00

Drewrys Beer/Ale, sign, tin, round, white name on red band around image of Canadian Mountie standing by horse, embossed, 14" dia, EX, A3..................$35.00

Dri-Power, thermometer, dial type, glass front, metal frame, degrees on red band around green genie above name, 12" dia, NM, A1..$235.00

Driggs Milk & Cream, thermometer, die-cut tin, Drink Driggs/cow on circle above gauge/advertising, orange/white, 15", EX+, A1...$180.00

Dromedary Dates/Hills Bros Co, sign, cardboard die-cut stand-up, Santa holding product box while standing behind toy bag, 39x18", VG, A6....................$110.00

Droste (Pastilles Droste Fijnste Chocolade), tin, square, slip lid, couple on train, NM, A3..........................$80.00

Droste's Cocoa, tin, sample, dining car scene, 2x1x1", EX, D37 ....$225.00

Droste's Cocoa, tin, sample, Dutch couple, 2x1x1", EX, D37...$80.00

Droste's Cocoa, tin, sample, Dutch couple, 3x2x2", EX, D37...$150.00

Drug Store, sign, porcelain, yellow lettering on green panel, curved corners, 1930s-40s, 11x63", EX, A13 ......$100.00

Dub-L-Valu, sign, tin, King Of Orange Drinks.../5¢ For Two Glasses 5¢, bottle against bunch of oranges at left, 11x28", VG+, D30 ....$90.00

Dubbleware Overalls, Pants & Woolen Sportswear, tip tray, round, spinning horse race game on rim around text on yellow center, 4" dia, EX, A3 ....$100.00

Dubuke Malting Co's Beers, tray, round, lettering around logo, plain brown rim, Tuchfarber litho, 1898, 13" dia, VG, A8 ....$315.00

Duc De Montpensier, cigar box label, sample, Geo L Schlegel litho #1782, EX, A5 ....$100.00

Ducker's Revelation For The Teeth & Gums, tin, sample, octagonal label, 2½x1", EX, D37 ....$40.00

Ducker's Revelation For The Teeth & Gums, tin, sample, oval label, 2½x1", EX, D37 ....$35.00

Duckwall, crate label, Oregon apple, duck by stone wall, Hood River, EX-M, D3/D12, from $10 to..............$15.00

Duckwall, crate label, Oregon pear, duck by brick wall, blue ground, Hood River, M, D12, each.......................$3.00

Duckwall, crate label, Oregon pear, duck by stone wall, yellow ground, Hood River, M, D12 ....$15.00

Duco Smoking & Chewing Tobacco, pail, straight-sided, bail handle, EX, A18..$55.00

Duco/DuPont Paints, sign, cardboard, die-cut, You Try Duco/It's So Easy, lady demonstrating red on table, ca 1930, 38x28", unused, A24 ....$200.00

Duesseldorfer Beer/Indianapolis Brewing Co, sign, celluloid over cardboard, allegorical image of girl flying bottle over globe against sky, framed, 16x12", EX, A7...........$1,000.00

Duffy's Malt Whiskey, pin-back button, Take...When You Are Not Feeling Well/Makes The Weak Strong..., chemist in center, Hoag litho, NM, A3..............................$30.00

Duffy's Pure Malt Whiskey, clock, figure-8, Absolutely Pure..., glass bottom with trademark image, numbered 1-12, New Haven Clock Co, 33", G, A9..............$2,000.00

Duffy's Pure Malt Whiskey, pocket mirror, oval, Get Duffy's & Keep Well/Take...When You Are Not Well, image of man pondering mixture, NM+, A3........$40.00

Duffy's Pure Malt Whiskey, sign, tin, man with laboratory equipment pondering mixture while leaning on open book, self-framed, 29x23", A8...........................$345.00

Duke of Northumberland, cigar box labels, 2-pc set, embellished portrait, G+, A5.................................$35.00

Duke's Mixture, display tin, square, 2-oz/5 CTS, Fair, A7 ....$250.00

Duke's Mixture, door push plate, porcelain, ...The Roll Of Fame, image of hands making cigarette, name above, 9x4", NM, D22...$400.00

Duke's Mixture, sign, cardboard, The Famous Dukes, twin boys in black/white checked hats with product, c 1910, framed, 30x22", VG, A7 ....$600.00

Dukes Mixture/Liggett & Myers, sign, cardboard, Free Presents For Coupons.../It's Here, images of presents in smoke of man's pipe, 29x19", EX+, A5.............$230.00

Duluth Imperial Flour, sign, tin, Without A Rival, black baker taking fresh-baked bread from pan, wood frame, 28x21", VG, A7 ....$1,000.00

Dunbar's Pitcher Syrup, pitcher, tin, Cane & Maple Sugar Syrup, Gothic feast scene/Dolly Dunbar figure, gold tones, 5", EX+, A1...$110.00

Duncan's Admiration Coffee, can, 1-lb, key-wind lid, red center band on dark blue, reverse shows black server offering coffee, EX (unopened), A18 ....$85.00

Dunham's Concentrated Cocoanut, store bin, tin, 12x10x10", VG, A18...$350.00

Dunlop Tires, sign, neon, ...K-T Highway Garage, 3-color, 24x41", EX, A2 ....$750.00

Dunnsboro Pipe Smoking, pocket tin, vertical, NM+ (from the Tindeco sample room), A18.....................$2,675.00

Duplate Shatterproof Plate Glass, porcelain, flange, For Your Safety...Installed Here, white/red on white/black, 12x18", EX, A2 ....$330.00

Duplex Bread, calendar, 1936, cardboard, Duplex Is Good Bread, toddler tearing off calendar pages, yellow ground, 9x17", EX, A3 ....$32.00

Duplex Marine Engine Oil, sign, porcelain, Authorized Dealers/Mfg By Enterprise Oil Co.../Makers Also Of Duplex..., red/blue on white, EX+, A2 ....$525.00

Duplex Outboard Special Motor Oil, tin, 1-qt, rectangular, fishermen in boat, 1940s, EX, A3 ....$55.00

DuPont, calendar top, 1910, 2 hunters looking out cabin window, framed, 18x15", G, A7 ....$200.00

DuPont, sign, tin, Generations Have Used DuPont Powders, elderly gent showing boy how to use gun, self-framed, 33x23", EX, A7...$2,000.00

DuPont, sign, tin, Shoot DuPont Powders, 2 dog heads, self-framed, 1903, 22x28", EX, A7 ....$2,500.00

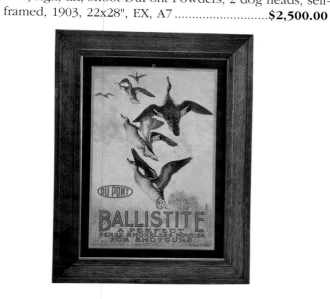

DuPont Ballistite, sign, paper, Green Wing Teal ducks in flight, lettering below, SB Wilhelms litho, c 1913, framed, image: 30x20", VG, A9...................$1,700.00

DuPont Blasting Caps, tin, square, square corners, 25/No 6, 1x1½x1½", EX, D37...$75.00

Edsel, sign, neon/porcelain, name in green block letters on white rectangular housing, 32x72", NM, A6 ....**$1,200.00**

Edsel Service, sign, light-up, arrow shape, green-on-white plastic inserts on stainless steel housing, 2-sided, 36x72x14", M, A6..............................**$1,200.00**

Edsonia, cigar box label, inner lid, early phonograph, 6x9", EX, D5 ....**$150.00**

Edward's Lake-To-Sea Stages/Bus-Depot, sign, porcelain, name on oval band around image of bus, brown/red/white/gray, 20x32", NM, A6....$6,200.00

Edwards Drip Grind Coffee, can, 1-lb, key-wind lid, yellow band on brown, EX, A3 ....**$30.00**

Edwin J Gillies Lunch Pail Coffee, pail, 4-lb, red, Ginna, pre-1901, EX, A18..............................**$270.00**

Effinger Fine Beer, tray, round, deep rim, waiter/lettering on 2-color ground, 12" dia, VG+, A8 ....**$100.00**

Egg-O Baking Powder, can, sample, paper label, blue/white name above/below product can on orange ground, white bands top/bottom, EX+, A15...................**$100.00**

Egyptian Deities Cigarettes, sign, paper, Egyptian queen with product pack admiring self in mirror, gold/black lettering on frame, 29x21", EX, A6 ....$525.00

Egyptian Deities Cigarettes, sign, tin, Plain End Or Cork Tip, arched image of product/black urn on red, gold self-frame, 21x15", VG+, A3.......................**$150.00**

Egyptian Straights Cigarettes, sign, flange, oval, Absolutely Pure 100% Turkish Tobacco, lady's bonneted head, G, A9...**$500.00**

Egyptienne Luxury Cigarettes, sign, cardboard, Convincingly Mild on chest of girl in pink/gold dress, 2 packs on draped blue, framed, 13x11", EX, A6.................**$200.00**

Eichker Brewing Co, ashtray, metal, round with 3 rests, lettering on rim around center logo, VG+, A8 ....**$30.00**

Eight Brothers Long Cut Tobacco, pail, black on yellow, EX, A18..**$75.00**

Eisenlohr's Cinco & Webster Cigars, cigar box opener/hammer, metal, engraved lettering, G+, A5 ....**$60.00**

Eisenlohr's Cinco Cigars, sign, porcelain, red/blue/yellow, 2-sided, 13x17", VG, A6 ....**$140.00**

EJ Meyers Garage, Dixon Ill, calendar, 1923, cardboard, die-cut, early touring car full of pink/red roses, embossed, 10x15", complete, EX+, A3..........$145.00

EJ Petru Java Coffee Mills, calendar/letter holder, 1919, bird/windmill scene applied to slab of wood with bark, complete pad, EX+, A3 ....**$40.00**

Ekco, catalog, 1957, kitchen housewares/bakeware/gadgets, 186 pgs, EX, D17 ....**$60.00**

Ekhardt & Becker Brewing Co, sign, paper, pub scene with 7 men enjoying product while dog begs, Louis Porr litho, framed, image: 17x26", EX, A9 ....**$600.00**

El Amor, cigar box label, outer, personified cat couple, 4½x4½", M, D5 ....**$45.00**

El Amor, cigar box label, outer, woman wrapped in blue scarf, 4½x4½", EX, D5...**$14.00**

El-Bart Dry Gin, sign, paper, name above girl on beach, bottle lower left corner, name on ornate gold frame, 46x33", G, A7..$3,000.00

El Bubble Bubble Gum Cigars, display cigar box, image of Indian against landscape on inner lid label, with 12 original cigars, NM, A16..**$70.00**

El Captain Coffee, can, 1-lb, key-wind lid, red, EX+, A18..**$50.00**

El Dallo Cigars, sign, cardboard, die-cut, ..25¢/A Fine Cigar Kept Fine, 5 men showing virtures/enjoying cigar, 13x20", EX, A6 ....**$100.00**

El Gallo Cigars, art plate, tin litho, strutting cock in center, 1908, EX-NM, A13/A15, from $300 to **$600.00**

El Generalismo, cigar box label, salesman's sample, Heppenheimer & Maurer #2821, EX, A5....................**$50.00**

El Grande, cigar box labels, 2-pc set, embellished portrait of the King of Sweden, Schmidt & Co #910/911, VG+, A5..**$75.00**

El Primo, crate labels, California lemon, lemons/groves/hills, Claremont, M, D12.....................................**$12.00**

El Producto Cigars, tin, round, slip lid, oval image of lady in garden, EX, A3...**$90.00**

El Rey Ale, label, 11-oz, El Rey Brewing Co Inc/San Francisco CA, IRTP/U-type permit #, 1933-36, M, A10..........**$12.00**

El Rey Beer, label, 11-oz, Avion Brewing Co/San Francisco CA, IRTP or WF statement, 1933-50, M, A10........**$15.00**

El Rey Beer, label, 11-oz, El Rey Brewing Co Inc/San Francisco CA, IRTP/U-type permit #, 1933-36, M, A10 ....**$10.00**

El Stymo, cigar box label, inner lid, Indian giving tobacco to ladies, 1910, 6x9", M, D5.....................................**$20.00**

El Vista, cigar box label, sample, man standing talking to lady on sofa, Louis E Neuman litho #725, EX, A5 ......**$100.00**

Elephant Head Rubber Boots, sign, paper, hunter in swamp beside boat, dog watches from shore, artist F Sticky, framed, image: 30x19", EX, A9.............**$1,400.00**

Elephant Salted Peanuts, tin, square, gold, 4x4x2", EX+, A3 ....**$312.00**

Elephant Salted Peanuts, tin, 10-lb, red, gold diamond logo, EX+, A3...**$320.00**

Elephant Salted Peanuts, tin, 10-lb, red, silver diamond logo, G, A2..**$100.00**

Elgin Caramel Co, Picture Caramels give-away, set of 6, Robinson Crusoe story, signed R Tuck, EX+ (with advertising paper), A3....................................$125.00

Elgin Petite Watches, display, automated vanity with doll, ca 1955, 19x15x10", EX, A23...............................**$550.00**

Elgin Watches, clock, round, blue numbers on white around white name on blue center, white hands, EX, D30 ..**$150.00**

Elgin Watches, sign, reverse glass, Full Ruby Jeweled.../The World's Standard, trademark image, gold on black, framed, 30x24", EX, A6 ....**$250.00**

Elias Big Boy, see Big Boy

Elk, cigar box label, inner lid, elk/violet nature scenes, 1911, 6x9", EX, D5 ....**$60.00**

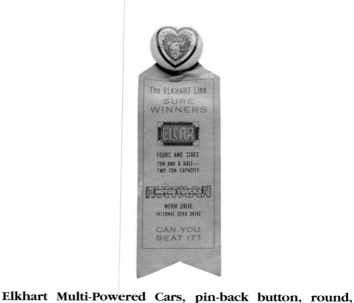

Elkhart Multi-Powered Cars, pin-back button, round, blue/red heart logo on white, paper/linen ribbon (The Elkahrt Line/Elcar/Huffman), 6" L, EX, A2......**$600.00**

Elliot Ear Protector, sign, crystaloid/cardboard back, advertising around image of ear in center on blue, 8x10", EX, A6/A13 ....**$50.00**

Elmore, pin-back button, round, name above image of auto, dated 1907, sepia, 1" dia, EX, A2 ....**$635.00**

Elmore, pocket mirror, oval, name above black/white image of early auto, dealer listed below, 2x3", VG+, A2 ....**$990.00**

Elreco Re-formed Gasoline, gas globe, 3-pc, Gill body, red, white center band, white/black lettering, NM lenses/VG+ body, A1...**$400.00**

Emanciaptor, cigar box labels, 2-pc set, embellished oval portrait/tobacco field workers, Heppenheimer & Maurer litho #2705, VG+, A5 ....**$65.00**

Emil Sick's Select, tap knob, ball shape, red with red/gold/black/yellow insert, EX+, A8...............**$110.00**

Emilia Garcia Cigars, display, cardboard trifold, The Cigar With A Million Friends, man in center 5-point shield, 31x38", EX+, A1 ....**$100.00**

Emilia Garcia Cigars, tin, round, slip lid, lt brown, oval image, EX+, A3 ....**$40.00**

Empire Cream Separator Co, calendar top, 1909, milkmaid holding girl in pink bonnet, 20x12", EX+, A3 ....**$135.00**

Empire Pilsener Style Beer, coaster, paper, Chicago Branch, 2-sided, 1 side blue, other orange/red, 4½" dia, VG+, A8 ....**$85.00**

Empire State Wine Co, sign, tin, oval, 3 monks enjoying wine at table, wood-tone self-frame, 24x27", VG, A7 .....**$325.00**

Empire's Best Pure Cinnamon, tin, 1½-oz, rectangular, red/white/blue, NM, A3 ....**$25.00**

Esso, print, silkscreen, diagonal image of Mt Fugi against dk blue sky with oval Esso/Pegasus logos, framed, 32x32", M, A6 ....**$120.00**

Esso, salt & pepper shakers, gas pumps, 1 marked Esso Extra, EX, D25, pair **$40.00**

Esso, sign, tin, die-cut Esso-Drop Girl atop Esso sign, red/yellow/blue/white, 16x7", EX, A6, from $200 to..................**$300.00**

Esso Aviation Products, sign, tin, round, Esso on winged oval above Aviation Products, red/black/divided background, 2-sided, 1940s-50s, VG, A13 ....**$575.00**

Esso Blue, sign, flange, porcelain, We Sell Esso Blue says cartoon man with can & hat in hands, 18x18", VG, A6 ....**$325.00**

Esso Dealer, pin-back button, metal, Babe Ruth Boys Club lettered on image of baseball, 1930s, 1" dia, NM, D22 ....**$65.00**

Esso Elephant Kerosene, sign, porcelain, oval Esso logo above blue elephant, white name below on red, 24x12", VG, A6..**$500.00**

Esso Extra, gas globe, 1-pc, milk glass, oval, red/blue on white, 15x20", VG, A6 ....**$350.00**

Esso Extra, gas globe, 2-pc, blue metal body, glass lens, blue lettering with red line on white, 16", NM, A6...$350.00

Esso Extra Ethyl, gas globe, 2-pc, red metal body, glass lens, red lettering/yellow/black triangle on white, blue trim, 16", NM, A6 ....$350.00

Esso Garantie sign, porcelain, round with tab attachment, blue Esso above white Garantie on red band on white, 2-sided, 10x8", NM, A6.......................................**$150.00**

Esso Lubrication Service, sign, cardboard diecut, Your Car Needs A Lift!..., doctor pointing to car on grease rack, 45x29", EX, A6 ....**$110.00**

Esso Service, badge, cloisonne on nickel, oval emblem atop name plate, 1½x2", VG+, A1/D22, from $130 to ..**$175.00**

Essolube, jigsaw puzzle, Foiled By Essolube, by Dr Seuss, 11x17", EX, A2 ....**$65.00**

Essolube, see also Esso (pocketknife)

Essolube Motor Oil, sign, porcelain, red/blue lettering on white, blue-lined border, 2x7", EX+, A15 ....**$160.00**

Estabrook's Red Rose Coffee, sign, tin, image of can on yellow ground, 15x15", NM, A3...........................**$200.00**

Esterbrook Pens, dispenser, tin, round with marque atop, rotates, red/green/black, 14x12" dia, EX+, D6 ...**$400.00**

Ethyl, pin-back button, Get Associated With Ethyl, white lettering on red dot, green border, 2" dia, NM, A1 ...**$175.00**

Eureka Fire Hose Mfg Co, calendar, 1913, photo images of various fire scenes, 23x14", incomplete, EX+, A3 ..**$200.00**

Eureka Spool Silk, display case, wood with glass front, clock on ornate marque atop, 24x23x16", EX, A6 ...$1,300.00

Euthymol Talcum Powder, tin, sample, EX, A18.....**$70.00**

Evans & Price, calendar, 1910, cardboard, die-cut, boy/girl with flowers walking along path, 8x6", complete, EX, A3..**$125.00**

Eve Cube Cut, pocket tin, vertical, VG-EX+, A18/A9/A15, from $200 to...**$400.00**

Even Steven, cigar box label, inner lid, German/Uncle Sam dividing Samoa, 6x9", VG, D5 ....**$150.00**

Even Steven Cigars, tin, square, vertical, slip lid, Ritter Can Co, 5¼x3x3", EX, D14............................**$350.00**

Ever Ready Corrux Blades/AE Cox & Sons (Wholesale Chemists), clock, round, glass front, chrome frame, 2 trademark heads/ads around small center face, electric, 16" dia, EX, A15...**$800.00**

Ever-Ready Safety Razor, clock, vertical, tin, trademark image on round clock face, green, 1920s, 19x13", rare, EX+, A4 ....**$1,000.00**

Ever-Ready Safety Razor, sign, tin, oval image of open product boxes, lettering on raised flat rim, HD Beach litho, 11x14", rare, EX, A2.................................**$1,870.00**

Ever-Ready Shaving Brushes, display, die-cut tin marque showing large brush/trademark face with display compartments, 12x15", G, A9 ....**$950.00**

Eveready, banner, cloth, Use Your Flashlight, distant couple shining light on elegant lady in darkness, early, EX, D30 ....**$125.00**

Eveready Batteries, bank, black cat, plastic, 1981, NM, D13 ....**$23.00**

Eveready Flashlight Batteries & Mazda Lamps, display, tin with slanted front showing hands loading batteries into flashlight, marque atop, 12", VG, A9 ....**$200.00**

Eveready Flashlight Batteries & Mazda Lamps, display case, tin, 5-sided marque atop case with slant front/glass top, with tester, various graphics, 12x9x12", EX, A3.....**$200.00**

Everfresh Coffee, can, 1-lb, key-wind lid, EX, A18..**$45.00**

Evergreen, crate label, Oregon pear, fir tree on yellow circle against blue background, Medford, M, D12 ...**$10.00**

Eveready Batteries, sign, paper, boy hugging dog while flashlight shines toward red logo, 30x20", VG+, A1 ....**$80.00**

Evervess, tip tray, rectangular, Evervess...Yes Yes!/Thank You..., with parrot, VG+, A16 ....**$45.00**

Evervess, tray, rectangular, Product Of Pepsi-Cola Co above Evervess logo, ...Sparkling Water/It's Good For You, 14x11", VG, A8..**$40.00**

Evervess Sparkling Water, clock, round, light-up, parrot says Yes!Yes!..., red/white/blue, 1940s-50s, NM, A13 ...**$350.00**

Evervess Table Water/Pepsi-Cola, sign, cardboard, For Your Very Good Health, bottle/glass against silhouette couple toasting, 17x8½", NM, A14 ....**$100.00**

Evervess Table Water/Pepsi-Cola, sign, cardboard, Something New In A New World, tilted bottle/mountains, 17x8½", NM, A14 ....**$112.00**

Evervess Table Water/Pepsi-Cola, sign, cardboard, Sparkles Like Diamonds In Your Glass, bottle/glass against diamond, name below, 18x11", NM, A14 ....**$150.00**

Evervess Table Water/Pepsi-Cola, sign, cardboard bifold, 3-D effect, Serve...On Your Home Menu, 2 bottles & goblet/lady at buffet, 29x33", NM, A14 ....**$200.00**

Evinrude Detachable Motor, pennant, painted cloth, wooden stick, round logo/name, red/white/blue, 29", G+, A2...**$150.00**

Evinrude Motor Co, tip tray, round, deep rim, lady in motorboat, 4" dia, NM, A................................$400.00

Ex-Ha-Fe, sign, cardboard stand-up, Hay Fever? above sneezing man, Why Suffer?..., yellow on blue, 1927, 29x19", NM, A1 ....**$125.00**

Ex-Lax, sign, porcelain, round, Keep Regular (script)/EX-Lax (block)/The Chocolate Laxative (script), 1940s, 20", VG, A13...**$135.00**

Ex-Lax, thermometer, Le Laxatif Au Chocolat/Keep Regular With..., porcelain 1940s, 36", NM, A13................**$140.00**

Ex-Lax, thermometer, The Chocolate Laxative/Keep Regular With..., porcelain, 36", G+, A9 ....**$65.00**

Ex-Lax, thermometer, The Chocolate Laxative/Millions Prefer, porcelain, 36", EX, A6 ....**$200.00**

Ex-Lax, thermometer, We Recommend Ex-Lax For Constipation..., tin, 1920s, 19", NM+, A13 ....**$550.00**

Excelsior Bottling Co, calendar, 1900, Victorian lady holds card with Season's Greeting To The New Century, Wolf & Co, framed, 23x17", VG, A9............................**$700.00**

Excelsior Coffee, can, 1-lb, key-wind lid, yellow, tall, EX+, A18 ....**$150.00**

Exide, sign, flange, painted metal, battery shape, orange/black/white, 13x15", EX, A6 ....**$180.00**

Exploration, cigar box labels, 2-pc set, globe/navigating paraphernalia, Witsch & Schmitt litho #617/618, VG/EX, A5..**$165.00**

Export Beverage, label, 12-oz, Export Beverage Co/Jacksonville FL, Pro (no L-type permit #), 1920-28, EX, A10 ....**$20.00**

Export Lager Beer, label, Fortune Bros/Chicago IL, pre-1920, VG+ (soaked off bottle or paper), A10.......**$42.00**

Extron, gas globe, 3-pc, white wide glass body, glass lenses, name in black (red X), red/black lines on white, 13½", NM+, A6..**$275.00**

Eye-Fix, tip tray, round, The Great Eye Remedy, cherub fixing lady's eye, blue lettering on red rim, HD Beach litho, 4", VG, A6 ....$325.00

Eze Orange, sign, flange, cardboard, die-cut, Ice Cold.../Easy To Serve/Easy To Drink 5¢/Sold Here, white/red/black, 10x8", NM+, D30.......................................**$50.00**

❧ F ❧

Fageol Vans, sign, corner, flashing light-up glass, shows image of van when off/Integral Construction when on, 11x19", VG+, A9 ....**$350.00**

Fairbank's, calendar, 1900, cardboard, Fairbank's Fairy Calendar above patriotic girl, months below, 13x10", EX-NM, A3, from $100 to **$210.00**

Fairbank's Fairy Soap, display box, The Fairy Christmas Box, 16x17x9", EX, A1 ....**$160.00**

Fairbank's Fairy Soap, see also Fairy Soap

Fairbank's Gold Dust Washing Powder, display box, front/back shows 3 product boxes, gold/black, 9x19", NM, D6..**$1,000.00**

Fairbank's Gold Dust Washing Powder, product box, giant size, trademark image of twins, 1920s, 9x6", M (unopened), D25..**$70.00**

Fairbank's Gold Dust Washing Powder, product box, sample, NM+, A3...**$50.00**

Fels-Naptha Soap, trolley sign, cardboard, Cleans & Cleans...repeated over background, large product in center, 11x21", EX+, A3 ....$40.00

Ferguson Tractor & Ferguson System Implements, sign, porcelain, silhouette of tractor above lettering, white/blue, 38x60", EX+, A2......................................$715.00

Fern Glen Rye, sign, tin, I'se In A Perdickermunt, Meek litho, self-framed, 33x23", VG-EX, A9/A7, from $1,800 to...$2,250.00

Fern Glen Rye, sign, tin, I'se In A Perdickermunt, Meek litho, self-framed, 33x23", NM, A7 ....$3,050.00

Ferrari, sign, porcelain, rearing black horse & black name, green/white/red stripes below on gold, 34x18", EX, A1 ....$1,100.00

Ferris Waists, sign, tin, oval, mother combing daughter's hair, wood-tone self-frame with lettering, 23x17", EX+, A15 ....$2,300.00

Ferro-Phos Co, tip tray, round, Drink.../The Favorite Beverage Five Cents/Non-Narcotic/Non-Alcoholic, beverage in center, 5", VG, A6 ....$140.00

Festival Coffee, can, 1-lb, key-wind lid, EX+, A3 ...$110.00

Festival Pop Corn, can, round, cardboard, tin top/bottom, paper label with circus scene, 5", EX, A15.........$425.00

Festival Pure Spices/Cloves, container, 1½-oz, cardboard, blue/white with Cloves lettered in red on white top band, EX, A3 ....$15.00

Fi-Na-St Peanut Butter, pail, 1-lb, red, EX+, A18, from $75 to $100.00

Fidelio Brewery, tray, round, Quality Since 1852, interior pub scene, lettering on rim, ca 1936, VG+-EX+, A8/A3, from $30 to...$70.00

Fidelity-Phenix Fire Insurance Co, calendar, 1919, early outdoor hockey scene, 10x8", complete, EX, A3 .$65.00

Field's Champion Whiskey, sign, tin, A Jug Or A Cup Or A Wash Pan To-Day FIELD'S CHAMPION Is Okay, shows workers at end of day, 19x27", Fair, A9...............$30.00

Fiesta Pure Thyme, tin, 2-oz, white on red, gold trim, NM, A3...$15.00

Fine Domestic, cigar box label, outer, half-nude Indian maiden, 4½x4½", EX, D5.............................$100.00

Finesse Foncie Face Powder, tin, round, sample, Deco styling, ¼x1½" dia, EX, D37 ....$30.00

Finest (The), cigar box label, sample, images of fireman/policeman/mailman/seaman (?), OL Schwencke & Co litho #5094, EX, A5 ....$250.00

Fink & Nasse Plug Tobacco, sign, paper, The Coming Plug, man gallops into town with box under arm, locals cheering, framed, 10x10", VG, A9 ....$50.00

Fink's Beer & Ale, tray, round, deep rim, Something To Crow About, rooster atop F in Fink's, yellow/red, 1930s, 12" dia, VG+, A19 ....$140.00

Finks Harrisburg Beer, watch fob, town in relief/1914 Fireman's Convention on reverse, EX, A8.................$75.00

Fiona Cigars, tin, round, slip lid, Liberty Can, EX+, A18 .$440.00
Fire-Chief, see Texaco

Firemen's Insurance Co, calendar, 1909, cardboard, oval image of 3 white horses pulling fire wagon on green, 11x7", complete, NM, A3 ....$430.00

Fireside Coffee, can, 1-lb, key-wind lid, VG, A3 ......$50.00

Firestone, pennant, felt, orange on blue, 8x28", EX, D22...$45.00

Firestone, sign, porcelain, sign over large tire on yellow, late 1930s, 40x30", EX, A24..$350.00

Firestone, sign, tin, name lettered on vertical panel, red on blue, yellow flanks, dated 8/47, 72x16", EX+, A1.$325.00

Firestone Auto Supplies, catalog, 1944, Spring/Summer, 53 pgs, EX, D17..$25.00

Firestone Columbus, pin-back button, round, image of early auto, black on white, 1" dia, EX, A2 ....$580.00

Firestone Columbus/Columbus Electric/Euclid Automobile Co, note case, swivels open, 2x3", EX, A2.$360.00

Firestone Ground Grip Farm Tires, sign, flange, steel, die-cut top/squared bottom, farmer on tractor in field, 2-sided, 18x24", VG, A2 ....$1,155.00

Firestone High Speed Heavy Duty Balloons, sign, cardboard stand-up, die-cut top, A Worthwhile Gift, family pictured in Christmas wreath, 1930s, 22x16", EX, A24 ....$100.00

Firestone Tires, sign, porcelain, Most Miles Per Dollar, yellow/white on blue, white border, 20x48", EX, A6.$325.00

Firestone US Rubber, salt & pepper shakers, tire shapes, EX, D25, pair...$65.00

First American, crate label, lemon, Indian brave looking toward tepee, 1916, M, D5 ....$150.00

First Choice Quality 5¢ Londres, tin, vertical square, Liberty Can, EX+, A18...$50.00

First National Bank of Florence, ashtray, glass, square, Smokey Bear holding sign stating Snuff That Match/Protect Your Trees From Fire!!, 3½", M, D25 ......**$28.00**

First Prize, cigar box label, sample, dog/other animals, OL Schwencke litho #2268, VG, A5 ....**$65.00**

First Quality Peaches, can label, country scene/peach, 1912, M, D5..**$25.00**

First Stroke, cigar box labels, set of 3, regatta scene, Witsch & Schmitt litho #15/16, EX, A5 ....**$415.00**

Fischer's Private Mixture Mild Smoke, pocket tin, vertical, paper label, white, EX+, A18 ....**$35.00**

Fish Bros Wagons, sign, cardboard, A Visit To Washington, Uncle Sam with wagon full of immigrants, Gies & Co litho, c 1900, 16x23", G, A9 ....**$225.00**

Fisher-Price, pamphlet, folds out to advertise 17 different toys, 1940s, 23", EX, A **$100.00**

Fisher's Poto'Gold Coffee, can, 1-lb, key-wind lid, VG+, A3 ....**$25.00**

Fisk Tires, ashtray, ceramic, square with 3 rests at each corner, Time To Re-Tire/Fisk Boy in center, white, EX, A6 ....**$90.00**

Fisk Tires, bank, Fisk Boy, ceramic, M, D20 ....**$55.00**

Fisk Tires, calendar, 1949, Fisk Boy, 33x19", complete, NM, A1..**$225.00**

Fisk Tires, display figure, Fisk Boy, composition, 32", EX, A6 ....**$800.00**

Fisk Tires, embossing plate for tin signs, heavy bronze, Fisk Boy/phrase, 20x14", EX, A2....................**$550.00**

Fisk Tires, lighter, metal, flip top, Time To Re-Tire/Buy Fisk, black engraved Fisk Boy, 2", EX, A6....................**$65.00**

Fisk Tires, pennant, felt, Time To Re-Tire? (Buy Fisk), Fisk Boy left of name, gold on blue, 29", EX, A1......**$180.00**

Fisk Tires, postcard, black boy drops watermelon after hearing owl hoot atop sign on tree, signed Leslie Thresher, c 1925, NM, A17............................**$115.00**

Fisk Tires, postcard, fishing boy/dog looking at Fisk Boy/phrase on sign posted on tree trunk, Norman Rockwell art, 1924, M, D26...**$150.00**

Fisk Tires, radiator front, cardboard, Fisk Boy logo, dated 1926, 11x21", VG, A1...**$130.00**

Fisk Tires, sign, cardboard, Time To Re-tire, round 'F' logo above Fisk Boy, framed, 22x18", EX, A2.........**$825.00**

Fisk Tires/Tubes/Service Station, sign, metal, Fisk Boy/lettering (reflective) on yellow, 30x14", VG+, A6 ..**$425.00**

Fitch's Standard Heart Gum, sign, cardboard, die-cut, flower basket with pixies promoting product, 10x7", EX+, A3..**$65.00**

Fitger's Nordlager Bock Beer, sign, paper, Drink... above goat with full mugs/sandwiches on tray before keg framed by hops, 29x23", NM, A19 ....**$250.00**

Five Colors, cigar box labels, 2-pc set, 5 boys sitting in 5 different shoes/oval image of boy, Witsch & Schmitt #513/514, VG, A5..**$320.00**

Five-O, sign, porcelain, Drink.../America's Favorite Chocolate Beverage, 1950s, 12x24", NM, A13 ....**$45.00**

Five-O, sign, tin, ...Chocolate Flavor, bottle at left, black/white lettering on yellow/red, red trim, 2-sided, 10x28", NM, D30..**$150.00**

Five Roses Flour, door plate, porcelain, red name/roses logo on white, red border, curved ends, 12x4", NM, A13...**$375.00**

Fixall Varnish, sign, cardboard, die-cut, 3-D, scenes showing many uses of product, 26x35", G, A9...........**$200.00**

Flag Ship, cigar box label, outer, warships, 4½x4½", EX, D5 ....**$50.00**

Flatfish Fishing Plug, sign, reverse glass, The Flatfish/ World's Largest Selling Fishing Plug, 3 orange lures in center, 8x16", NM, A15 ....$350.00

Flav-O-Rich Coffee, can, 1-lb, key-wind lid, red, EX+, A3...$22.00

Fleckenstein Brg Co, see E Fleckenstein

Fleet H-D Elreco Motor Oil, can, 1-qt, plane/car on red top band, oval Elreco logo on black center band, red letters on white bottom band, NM, A1..........................$150.00

Fleet-Wing Ethyl, sign, porcelain, Fleet-Wing above triangle logo with sun rays, black on yellow, 30" dia, Fair, A2...$30.00

Fleet-Wing Motor Oil, can, 1-qt, New Certified/red bird logo on top cream band, cream lettering on red bottom band, EX+, A1...$100.00

Fleet-Wing Motor Oil, sign, porcelain, oval, lettering over red bird in flight on white, 18x24", VG+, A6 .....$275.00

Fleischmann's Gin, radio, bottle shape, NM+, D20 ..$75.00

Fleischmann's Yeast, door plate, Buy Fleischmann's Yeast/Has No Equal, blue/white, 4", NM+, A13..$250.00

Fleischmann's Yeast, note pad, celluloid, Good Yeast Means Good Bread/Use..., pretty girl on front, pencil attached with string, EX, A20................................$20.00

Fleischmann's Yeast, trade card, Say! Wots De Matter Wid.../It Makes De Best..., Yellow Kid holding yellow sign on stick, 4½x2½", NM, A15....................$450.00

Fleischmann's Zwieback, sign, paper, encircled image of girl eating Zwieback with corner vignettes showing people eating, 14x10", VG, A9 ....$125.00

Fli-Hi, crate label, California orange, duck flying into night sky joining flock over distant mountains, Tustin, M, D12...$20.00

Flint Authorized Service, sign, porcelain, blue on white, blue border, 2-sided, 20x30", VG, A2.................**$600.00**

Flit, display, cardboard, No Flies or Skeeters In Our House!, large center display/marching soldiers, 5-pc, VG+, A3..**$120.00**

Flor de Belar Cigars, sign, tin, stand-up/hanger, ...Perfection Of Quality flanked by 2 cigars on gold ground, 2-sided, 8x10", EX+, A1..**$75.00**

Flor De Edison, cigar box label, salesman's sample, Geo S Harris & Sons (?), rare, VG, A5..........................**$115.00**

Flor de Franklin 5¢ Cigar, sign, tin, Ben Franklin flying kite, gold corner decoration on black self-frame, 18x27", VG, A7...**$700.00**

Florence Nightingale Ground Black Pepper, container, 3-oz, cardboard with paper label, round profile image on white, red band top/bottom, EX, A3....................**$20.00**

Florida Cowboy, crate label, Florida Citrus, cowboy on bucking horse, 1930, M, D5.........................**$10.00**

Florida Light & Power, see Reddy Kilowatt

Florient Talcum Powder, see Colgate's Florient

Flower Seeds, display, cardboard die-cut stand-up, The Loveliest Garden.../Flower Seeds 10¢, colorful packets frame ad, 41x24", NOS, A **$140.00**

Flurshutz the Furniture Man, display sign, tin, figural black man with sign between legs, 53x34", rare, VG, A6...$4,250.00

Flying A, banner, cloth, Flying above logo flanked by Fast/Action, white/green on red, 2-sided, 37x71", VG, A1 ....**$200.00**

Flying A, playing cards, 2 decks in leather case, logo on cards, Man-O-War on score pad, M (NOS), A1 ....**$85.00**

Flying A, pump sign, porcelain, round with embossed die-cut logo, white on red, black trim, 9x13", EX, A1.....**$450.00**

Flying A, sign, porcelain, die-cut figural logo, red, black trim, 28x66", NM, A1 ....$1,450.00

Flying A Gasoline, gas globe, 2-pc, glass body/single lens, red lettering/logo on white, black border, Mobil decal on reverse, VG+, A1.................................$375.00

Flying A Gasoline, gas pump topper sign, milk glass, curved body with 2 inserts, red lettering & logo on white, 6x14½x6½", NM+ (NOS), A6.......................$425.00

Flying A Gasoline, pump sign, porcelain, square, red on white, EX, D34...................................$285.00

Flying A Gasoline, pump sign, porcelain, round, red lettering/logo on white, red border, 10" dia, NM, A1 ..$175.00

Flying A Gasoline, sign, porcelain, Flying/Gasoline in red above/below red logo on white, red border, 10x10", NM, A1...$300.00

Flying A Paste Auto Wax & Cleaner, tin, 8-oz, round, pry lid, red on white/green, full, EX+, A1.................$130.00

Flying A Super Extra, gas pump topper sign, milk glass, curved body with 2 inserts, white lettering/logo on red, 6x14½x6½", NM+, A6.....................................$500.00

Flying Ship, cigar box label, sample, birds pulling boy in boat with roses, Louis E Wagner Co litho #4272, VG+, A5..$115.00

FN Buckman Dry Goods, Buckman WI, sign, cardboard, die-cut, boy/girl floating paper boats in wooden tub of water, EX, A3 ....$60.00

Foley Kidney Pills, door push, porcelain, oval, yellow, EX+, A3..$330.00

Folger's Coffee, can, ½-lb, key-wind lid, EX+, A18..$22.00

Folger's Coffee, can, 1-lb, key-wind lid, NM (full), A18...$35.00

Folger's Coffee, can, 2-lb, key-wind lid, red, oval image of sailing ships, EX+, A3 ....$90.00

Folger's Coffee, sign, cardboard hanger, die-cut coffee can, Mountain Grown on yellow arrow 'swirling' atop red can, 2-sided, EX+, A3 ....$50.00

Folger's Coffee Crystals, can, 1-oz, sample, plastic lid, New Coffee Crystals/Taste The Difference, 2" dia, EX, D37 ....$15.00

Folger's Golden Gate Allspice, tin, 2-oz, red, EX, A3 ..$20.00

Folger's Golden Gate Ginger, tin, red, round image of ship, EX, A3..$25.00

Folger's Golden Gate Steel Cut Coffee, can, 1-lb, pry lid, paper label, oval image of sailing ship, NM+, A3 ....$700.00

Folger's Shasta Gunpowder Tea, tin, horizontal box, paper label, yellow, blue lettering above/below oval image of mountain, EX+, A3..$55.00

Fontana Girl, crate label, lemon, young girl drinking lemonade, 1918, M, D5...$65.00

Fontenac Beer, tray, round, deep rim, Canada's Best, factory scene, lettered rim, 12" dia, G, A9.................$150.00

Food Fair 100% Colombian Coffee, can, 1-lb, key-wind lid, black, man/donkey on side, EX, A3...............$40.00

Foot Rest Hosiery, sign, tin/cardboard, For Wear/For Style/For Comfort/For Economy, girl in swing holding sign, 17x11", VG, A7 ....$1,100.00

Football Brand, crate label, Spanish Citrus, men playing soccer, early, M, D5..$35.00

Forbes Coffee, can, 1-lb, key-wind lid, white on red, NM, A3 ....$30.00

Forbes Golden Cup Coffee, can, 3-lb, smaller round slip lid, marked Sugar on reverse, VG+, A3....................$45.00

Forbes Quality Gas Roasted Coffee, can, 1-lb, slip lid, red/white/blue on lt blue/white geometric background, 3½x5" dia, EX+, A15....................................$180.00

Ford, license plate attachment, metal emblem with reflective paint, Let's Take It Easy, cartoon cop with whistle, 4x7", EX, A6..$20.00

Ford, plate, Shenango China, Ford on rim, building in center, 6", EX, A6..$45.00

Ford, pocketknife, blue script logo on red plastic casing, 3½", EX, A6...$40.00

Ford, poster, 1939 Baseball All-Stars, dealers' names flank logo above illustrated baseball game/photos/stats, 32x17", EX+, A6...$650.00

Ford, sign, neon/porcelain, oval logo, white on blue, 1-sided, EX, A2 ....$1,050.00

Ford, sign, neon/porcelain, oval logo, white on blue, 2-sided, 24x48", EX+, A6...................................$2,000.00

Ford, sign, neon/porcelain, shield with name, red/white/black, wall-mounted, 47x48", VG, A6..........................$1,100.00

Ford, sign, neon/porcelain, winged-oval logo, white on blue, 2-sided, 34x76", EX, A6...................................$4,450.00

Ford, sign, porcelain, oval logo on blue rectangular ground, white border, 25x29", EX-EX+, A1/A6, from $275 to..........$325.00

Ford, watch fob, metal oval Ford emblem with blue cloisonne, silver-tone trim, 1x2", EX+, A1................................$50.00

Ford, see also Motorcycle Equipment Co

Ford Authorized Sales & Service, sign, porcelain, Ford in script above Authorized Sales & Service in block letters, white on blue, 28x60", VG, A2..........................$635.00

Ford Cars/Trucks/Parts/Accessories, clock, octagonal, neon, glass front with green border, metal frame, 1-12, 18x18", EX, A6..$850.00

Ford Genuine Parts, sign, porcelain, oval, white on blue, 2-sided, 17x24", NM+ (NOS), A6....................$1,600.00

Ford Genuine Parts, sign, porcelain, oval, white on blue, 2-sided, 17x24", VG, A14.................................$365.00

Ford Parkway Sales & Service, blotter, It Pays To 'Patronize The Parkway'..., head image of girl in tam, 3x6", EX, A6 ....$50.00

Ford Plug/Champion Spark Plug, thermometer, wood, die-cut, large plug with gauge, lettering below, 1910s-20s, 21", EX, A13 ....$200.00

Ford Sales/Service, thermometer, wood, square corners, image of Fordson tractor above dealer name, early Ford below, 14x4", VG, A1 ....$175.00

Ford V-8 Genuine Parts, sign, porcelain, die-cut, Genuine Parts on marque atop Ford oval atop V-8 symbol, blue/white, 2-sided, 35x28", EX+, A6 ....$3,050.00

Ford/Owen, Wiles Motor Car Co, pocket mirror, oval, When You Are In The Market For A Ford Car Truck Tractor..., early auto, black/white, 2x3", EX, A2........$525.00

Fordson Farm Tractors, pin-back button, celluloid, round, lettering around tractor, red/black on white, 1¾" dia, EX, A2..$250.00

Forest, cigar box label, inner lid, forest scene with animals, 6x9", EX, D5 ....$85.00

Forest & Stream Tobacco, pocket tin, sample, cut-down, creel lid, G, A18....................................$10.00

Forest & Stream Tobacco, pocket tin, vertical, duck (gold), EX+, A18.............................$120.00

Forest & Stream Tobacco, pocket tin, vertical, duck (white), EX+, A18.............................$100.00

Forest & Stream Tobacco, pocket tin, vertical, fisherman standing in stream, 4¼" (creel top), VG+, A18 ..$190.00

Forest & Stream Tobacco, pocket tin, vertical, fisherman standing in stream, 4½", EX+, A18, from $150 to .$185.00

Forest & Stream Tobacco, pocket tin, vertical, fishermen in canoe, 4", VG-NM, A2/A15/A18, from $275 to...$600.00

Forest & Stream Tobacco, tin, round, screw top, duck (white), VG+, A18..................................$25.00

Forest Giant Cut Plug, canister, ½-lb, cardboard, metal top/bottom, paper label, moose in landscape, G, A7...$500.00

Forest Giant Tobacco, store tin, round, square lid, VG, A7 ....$300.00

Fort Garry Smoking Tobacco, pocket tin, vertical, 5", EX, A18 ....$120.00

Fort Henry Pure Lard, pail, 8-lb, tapered, slip lid, bail handle, orange, EX+, A3 ....$22.00

Fort Pitt Beer, tray, round, deep rim, Drink..., waiter running with oversized glass on tray, red/cream, 1930s, 12" dia, NM, A19..$110.00

Fort Pitt Special Beer, can, cone top, 12-oz, NM, A8 ..$65.00

Fort Pitt Special Beer, clock, name on rectangular sign atop figural clock with round face, EX, D30 ....$300.00

Fort Schuyler Ales & Lager/Utica Brewing Co, tray, round, deep rim, lettering in center around image of fort, red/white/black, 11" dia, EX, A6 ....$40.00

Fort Western Coffee, can, 1-lb, oval image, tall, VG+-EX+, A3, from $125 to...................................$200.00

Fort Western Quick Cooking Rolled Oats, container, 3-lb, cardboard, EX-NM, A3, from $135 to.................$190.00

Forthoffer's Creme De Menthe Cola/Dole's Pineapple Nectarade, sign, cardboard, die-cut, ..½¢ Bottles, Victorian lady seated on wharf-type posts/man reading paper, 9x7", EX, A3 ....$50.00

Fortune Shoes For Men, sign, neon, glass/metal, Fortune in neon above Shoes For Men, white/red, 9x23x6", EX, A6 ....$135.00

Forty-Four (44), sign, cardboard, die-cut, Old Time Quality 5¢..., Indian scout in colorful headdress with open cigar box, 32x21", VG, A6 ....$260.00

Foss Chocolates, sign, porcelain, name/location/shield upper right corner, black/white on blue, white border, 12x20", EX+, A1 ....$150.00

Fossil Watches, bobbin' head doll, Fred Q Fossil, MIB, D20...$55.00

Foster Hose Supporters, sign, celluloid, The Name Is On The Buckles, Victorian lady/supporters, 17x9", VG+-EX+, A7/A3, from $360 to.............................$450.00

Foster's Old Fashion Freeze, sign, porcelain, die-cut ice-cream carton marked Quarts, blue/white, 12x6", M, D11 ....$300.00

Four in Hand, cigar box label, saleman's sample, OL Schwencke litho #2524, VG+, A5 ....$150.00

Four Roses Smoking Tobacco, pocket tin, vertical, flat top, green, VG+, A18 ....$290.00

Four Roses Smoking Tobacco, pocket tin, vertical, flat top, red, rare, EX+, A18 ....$350.00

Four Roses Smoking Tobacco, pocket tin, vertical, flat top, striped, G+, A18 ....$115.00

Four Roses Smoking Tobacco, pocket tin, vertical, flip top, red, EX+, A3...$175.00

Four Roses Whiskey, display statue, seated bulldog on red base, Join The Four Roses Society, plaster, 11x11x7", VG+, A8..$85.00

Fowler's Cherry Smash, see Cherry Smash

Fowler's Root Beer, dispenser, ceramic ball shape, flared base, Drink..½¢ 'The Best,' red on white, top spigot, 14", EX, A6 ....$1,500.00

Fox De Luxe, drinking glass, fountain type, applied red lettering/graphics, 6", NM, A8 ....$30.00

Fox Head Premium Motor Oil, can, 1-qt, white/red/black, red fox logo, EX, A6................................$70.00

Fox Point Coffee, can, 1-lb, key-wind lid, red/white, steaming cup, VG+, A3...................................$55.00

Fox Woods Casino/Hotel, figure, Foxy, resin, 6", M, D20...$45.00

Fox's Bread, calendar, 1940, paper, boy/girl flirting at stone fence, 20x15", complete, EX, A3 ....$170.00

Fox's De Luxe Beer, banner, canvas, The End Of The Hunt.../Brewed By Those Nine Fox Brothers..., fox hunt/bottle on yellow, 17x36", VG+, A8.............$210.00

Fralinger's Salt Water Taffy, postcard, Expressly For You!/Fresh From Atlantic City/A Carload Of..., image of train boxcar, NM, D26 ....$75.00

Fralinger's Salt Water Taffy, postcard, Santa brings Tommy Tucker a lot of toys as well as Fralinger's, signed CM Burd, EX, A17 ....$300.00

Francisco Auto Heater, sign, tin, Summer Here All The Year, cut-away view of car in snow, gold self-frame, 18x40", EX, A6/A7 ....$650.00

Francoise Products White Pepper, tin, 4-oz, green/yellow parrot on blue, gold trim, 4", EX+, A15 ....$200.00

Frank Brewery Extra Beer, sign, cardboard, round, name/eagle & horseshoe emblem on black, ornate embossed gold border, EX+, A8.........................$40.00

Frank E Mogle Retail Liquor Dealer, calendar, 1906, 2 dogs by stream against simulated wood-tone ground with birds in flight, 15x11", complete, NM, A3..........$100.00

Frank Jones Homestead Ale, tip tray, round, shield in center, shields repeated on rim, 5" dia, EX+, A8 ....$50.00

Frank Kirchhof Lumber Co, sign, tin, oval image of girl with carnations, curled corners, Meek & Co litho, c 1908, 18x15", VG, A9.................................$500.00

Frank Miller's Crown Dressing, sign, paper, parlor scene with mother reading while maid polishes her shoes, busy children beyond, 15x21", VG, A11 ....$475.00

Frank's Choice Cigars, sign, paper, 4 children walking hand-in-hand through woods, Knapp Co litho 1893, framed, 18x25", EX, A2 ....$330.00

Frank's Improved Wizard Cuff Holders, display sign, cardboard die-cut stand-up, risque girls/devil forging cuff holders, ca 1906, 12x10", VG+, A3....................$115.00

Frank's Quality Beverages, clock, round, light-up, glass front, metal frame, ...Is It Frank's...Thanks!, 1-12, EX+, A16...$390.00

Frankenberry Cereal, see General Mills

Franklin Life Insurance Co, tip tray, round, Ben Franklin, EX+, A3..$20.00

Franklin Pierce, cigar box label, inner lid, portrait/naval flag/eagle, 6x9", EX, D5 ....$50.00

Frazer Axle Grease, sign, tin, man with broken wagon wheel talking to passing farmer, self-framed, 26x28", G, A7 ....$1,150.00

Fred Bauernschmidt American Brewery Beers, sign, tin, frontal view of Falstaff enjoying brew, wood-tone self-frame, 24x19", NM, A7 ....$750.00

Fred Bessler Meat Market & Groceries, calendar, 1910, litho on canvas, brothers smiling at each other in country scene, 19x14", complete, EX+, A3 ....$150.00

Fred Krug Brewing Co, charger, tin, bust image of young lady with dark hair, Beach Art Display litho, 24" dia, G, A9...$550.00

Frederick's Four Crown Lager Beer, tray, oval, deep rim, military man in red jacket holding glass next to dog, sign, behind, 1940s, 13x15", EX+, A19......................$125.00

Free Lance 5¢ Cigar, sign, cardboard hanger, Smoke A...And Be Convinced, white on blue, 10x11", EX+, A3...$70.00

Game Fine Cut/Jno J Bagley & Co, store bin, tin, rectangular, grouse in brush, VG-EX+, A15/A7, from $775 to..**$1,000.00**

Gansett Pilsner, drinking glass, stemmed pilsner, etched, 9", EX+, A8...**$50.00**

Garcia Grande, cigar box holder/lighter, tin, Hole In Head-Just Lite! EX, A3...**$110.00**

Garcia y Vega Cigars/St Charles, tin, round, slip lid, oval image of woman in profile on white, EX+, A3 ....**$40.00**

Garden City Brewery, cigar holder & case, carved meerschaum with silver inlay, Jos Welky, lined case, with extra tip, pre-prohibition, EX, A8.......................**$260.00**

Gardenia Bouquet Talcum Powder, tin, round, white flowers/lettering on red, 10", EX, A3...........................**$25.00**

Garland Stoves & Ranges, match holder, die-cut tin, The World's Best, 7x4", EX+, A13.................................**$225.00**

Garland Stoves & Ranges, postcard, The Wonder Of The Age, image of fancy stove aglow with heat, Calvert Litho Co, ca 1910, EX, D13...**$50.00**

Garrett & Co, tray, round, Virginia Dare/Pure Garrett's Special/Norfolk VA/St Louis MO, couple in landscape, 12" dia, VG, A9...**$300.00**

Garrett & Co Wine Growers, sign, tin, classical couple frolicking in landscape, 47x37", VG, A7.............**$850.00**

Gate City Ginger Snaps, container, 1-lb 8-oz, round, cardboard, paper label, 3 white lilies on wood-grain ground, EX+, A3...**$100.00**

Gay & Happy, cigar box label, sample, woman in repose, Geo S Harris & Sons litho #587, EX+, A5...........**$135.00**

GE Edison Mazda Automobile Lamps, display box, tin on wooden base, Name Your Car/I'll Light It, lady showing product, orange/white/blue, 24x14x12", EX, A2.**$850.00**

GE/Edison Mazda Lamps, playing cards, Maxfield Parrish's Ecstacy, 1930, complete, EX (original box), D22.**$275.00**

Gem Damaskeene Razor, clock, wooden case with pendulum, round face numbered 1-12 showing man attempting to shave with baby, 27", EX, A2.....................**$1,150.00**

Gem Damaskeene Razor, dispenser, metal, wood-grain, curved marque with trademark graphics/advertising, Gem $1.00, 18x11", VG, A6.................................**$600.00**

Gem Safety Razor, tin, rectangular, curved corners, slip lid, EX, D37...**$125.00**

Gene's Drive In/Chicken In The Rough, sign, cardboard, golfing chicken on white circle, red lettering on green, curved corners, 20x37", EX, A1...........................**$220.00**

General Arthur Cigars, trade card, mechanical, Spread Yourself & Smoke, cat looking at cancan girl, 8x4", VG, A5...**$200.00**

General Electric, ashtray, ceramic, fluorescent bulb shape embossed 1,000,000/GE logo/Power Groove, dated August 1950, EX, D25............................$40.00

General Electric, calendar, 1932, Solitude, artist Maxfield Parrish, 19x9", no pad o/w NM, D22.................**$600.00**

General Electric, clock, die-cast replica of GE ice box, white, nickel-plated hinges, 4-footed, compressor on top, Telechron, 9", EX, A2...**$385.00**

General Gasoline & Lubricants, sign, flange, porcelain, round, General Petroleum Corporation..., white on green/black, 12x14", NM, A1...........................**$1,350.00**

General Mills Booberry, mug, Booberry, plastic, yellow, 1973, M, D1...**$30.00**

General Mills Booberry, pencil topper/eraser, Booberry figure, 1973, NM, D1...**$10.00**

General Mills Cheerios, cereal bowl, Cheerios Kid & Sue, Melmac, white, 1969, VG, D1.................................**$10.00**

General Mills Cheerios, cereal box, Eddie Cantor (Famous Comedian Hall Of Fun) cutout, 1949, NM, D1.....**$70.00**

General Mills Cheerios, plate, Cheerios Kid/Bullwinkle, Melmac, white, 1969, VG, D1.................................**$15.00**

General Mills Count Chocula, doll, Count Chocula, squeeze vinyl, 1977, 8", NM, D27.....................**$125.00**

General Mills Count Chocula, mug (mini), Count Chocula, plastic, yellow, 1973, M, D1............................**$30.00**

General Mills Count Chocula, pencil topper/eraser, Count Chocula figure, 1973, MIP, D1 ....**$15.00**

General Mills Frankenberry, doll, Frankenberry, squeeze vinyl, 1977, 8", NM, D27......................................**$125.00**

General Mills Frankenberry, mug (mini), Frankenberry, plastic, yellow or blue, 1973, M, D1, each..........**$30.00**

General Mills Frankenberry, pencil topper/eraser, Frankenberry figure, 1973, EX, D1.....................**$15.00**

General Mills Kix, cereal box, P-38 cutout on side, 1945, flat, NM, D1...**$140.00**

General Mills Trix, pin-back button, Yes! Let the Rabbit Eat Trix, 1976, EX, D1...**$15.00**

General Mills Trix, Tiddly Winks, Trix Rabbit, plastic, red, late 1960s, EX, D1...**$20.00**

General Mills Wheaties, see Wheaties

General Motor Fuel, gas globe, General on diagonal band over shield with knight atop, yellow, red & black, white metal body, 15" dia. NM, A6..............................**$500.00**

General Motors, sign, embossed tin, yellow General Motors vertically lettered on blue, used on GM diesel engines, 29x3¼", NOS, EX, A1...**$70.00**

General Paint, sign, cardboard, die-cut, A Salute To Quality..., saluting 'General Paint'/painter towering over house, 30x22", EX+, A1...........................**$100.00**

General Petroleum Corporation Gasoline & Lubricants, sign, porcelain, round, General on diagonal center band, white/black/olive green, 30" dia, EX, A2...........**$770.00**

General Sherman, cigar box label, salesman's sample, portrait surrounded by shield, flags & vignettes, NM, A5...**$215.00**

Genesee Beer, sign, cardboard with stand, Enjoy the Holiday above Genesee billboard & convertible, Drive Carefully! below, VG+, A19.................................**$15.00**

Genesee Beer, sign, tin on cardboard, shows couple from waist down seated back to back on cooler, beveled edge, 7x15", EX, A3...**$50.00**

Genesee Lager Beer, sign, plastic, Great Beer Then...And Now above factory scene on green background, product name below, 14x20", VG, A8........................**$30.00**

Geo A Moss Union Star Paste Stove Polish, tin, oval, portrait in center, 1x3¼x4¼", EX, D37 ....$45.00

Geo Ehret's Extra Draught Beer, tray, round, star logo in center, 13" dia, VG+, A8...................................$75.00

Geo Ehret's Extra/Hell Gate Brewery, tray, oval, star logo in center, 16x13", EX, A2 ....$150.00

Geo Renner Brewing Co Old 'Grossvater' Beer, tray, rectangular, name above/below bottle flanked by blue triangular emblems, brown/cream/gold, 1930s, 13x10", EX+, A19 ....$100.00

Geo Walters Adler Brau/Appleton Beer, sign, tin/cardboard, debossed, waiter with tray on white at left of red/silver lettering on black, 9x13", EX+, A8...........................$140.00

George Ehret's Hell Gate Brewery, calendar, 1907, factory scene with early traffic, metal strips, 28x21", complete, G, A9..$300.00

George Lawrence Co Dog Chains & Leads, display sign, metal, diagonal, holes at 2 bottom edges for displaying product, dog/text above, 10x10", EX+, A3 ....$135.00

George W Childs Cigars, tin, vertical square, slip lid, paper label, VG+, A18...$55.00

George Washington Cut Plug, lunch box, large, EX+, A18 ....$75.00

George Washington Cut Plug, lunch box, small, EX, A18 ....$50.00

George Zeisler & Sons, drinking glass, water, etched, round logo with hops/grain, 1888-1902, 4½", NM, A8 ....$430.00

Gerber, doll, stuffed printed cloth, 8", rare, EX, A6.$200.00

German American Brewing Co Matosia Beer, tip tray, round, Our Beer Is Sterilized/Not Pasteurized, lettering on rim around logo, 5" dia, EX, A6......................$50.00

Gettelman Beer, sign, composite stand-up, 2 bears in landscape, dated 8-15-49, wood-tone frame, 10x16", NM, A19 ....$85.00

Gettelman Beer, sign, stand-up, embossed foil detail, 2 ducks flying out of water, dated 4-30-50, gold-tone frame, 16x10", EX+, A19.................................$50.00

GF Carls, calendar, 1914, die-cut embossed cardboard, cherub/mill framed by flowering vines/birds, 15x11", complete, EX, A3 ....$65.00

GG Green August Flower & Boschee's German Syrup, sign, paper on canvas, stately buildings/grounds with pedestrians, inset lower right, framed, 29x42", G, A7........$300.00

GH Hammond Co's Canned Meats, sign, paper, campsite along river bank with black chef, wood frame, 28x34", VG, A7 ....$950.00

Ghirardellis Sweet Ground Chocolate, tin, round, sample, Made Instantly, yellow, EX+ (sealed), A15........$150.00

Giant Salted Peanuts, tin, 10-lb, round, red, VG, A18..$325.00

Gibbons Porter, tap knob, ball shape, chrome, blue on off-yellow enamel insert, VG+, A8.............................$80.00

Gibbsons, clock, round, name in black/red on white band around red/black center marked Is Good! Anytime, black frame, EX, D30..$100.00

Gilcrest Animal Food, sign, paper, Golly! It Makes De Mule Go & Chickens Fly!, black man/passenger in mule cart, framed, 16x21", VG, A2......................................$825.00

Gillett's Allspice, tin, 2-oz, red/gold, NM, A3 ....$55.00

Gillett's Cloves, tin, 2-oz, red/gold, NM, A3.............$60.00

Gillett's Flavoring Extracts, display case, nickel-plated upper cabinet with 2 shelves/glass front on base with curved glass front, 34x21", VG, A2....$1,000.00

Gillette, dispenser, metal, vertical box, Look Sharp!/Feel Sharp!/Be Sharp!, red/blue on white, 18x8x3", EX, A6................$175.00

Gillette, see also Jenney Auto Oil Gasoline/Gillette

Gillette Safety Tires, watch fob, metal, round, A Bear For Wear, polar bear on emblem in red/white/blue cloisonne on gold-tone, 1920s, M, A1................................$140.00

Gillette Tires, signs, cardboard, An Exclusive...Tire (bear with bowl)/No Chains Needed (bear running from bee), 17x13", EX, A6, pair...$500.00

Gilmore, comic book, Gilmore Super Book Of Comics, Featuring Terry & The Pirates/Magic Morro, ca 1938, 32 pgs, NM, A1 ....$130.00

Gilmore Blu-Green Gasoline, trade card, die-cut, with lion, NM, A1...$175.00

Gilmore Lion Head Motor Oil, mechanical pencil, perpetual calendar near tip, oil sample on end, 5½", NM, A1..$190.00

Golden State Beer/Milwaukee Brewery, tray, rectangular, eagle atop M shield above Pan-Am Expo (no bridges), HD Beach litho, VG+, A8....................................$150.00

Golden Sun Turmeric, tin, 2-oz, red/black/gold, 1912, VG+, A3....................................$10.00

Golden Tree Syrup, postcard, The Real Flavor From The Maple Grove, image of bearded man/product can, EX, D26 ....$35.00

Golden Valley Coffee, can, 1-lb, key-wind lid, red on white, EX, A3....................................$100.00

Golden Wedding Coffee, can, 1-lb, key-wind lid, red, white/yellow lettering, yellow stars, EX-NM, A3/A18, from $30 to....................................$40.00

Golden Wedding Pure Rye, sign, reverse glass, fancy lettering with hops/logo, framed, image: 24x36", VG, A9.....$425.00

Golden West Allspice, tin, 2-oz, red, gold trim, EX, A3.$18.00

Golden West Coffee, banner, paper, vertical, pointed bottom, Announcing New Drip Grind, red can/cowgirl logo on white, 1930s, 21x12", EX, A1............................$60.00

Golden West Coffee, can, 1-lb, key-wind lid, full-length cowgirl, VG-EX+, A18/A3, from $50 to..............$120.00

Golden West Coffee, can, 1-lb, key-wind lid, head portrait of cowgirl, white on red/black, EX+, A18......$140.00

Golden West Coffee, can, 1-lb, key-wind lid, 3-quarter cowgirl, EX-EX+, A3/A18, from $75 to $135.00

Golden West Oil Co, pump sign, porcelain, round, banner over white/yellow sunrays/blue mountains shining on water, 10" dia, NM, A15 ....$525.00

Goldenrod Beer, bottle label, 12-oz, Rock River Brewing Co/Rockford IL, 1933-50, VG+ (soaked off bottle or paper), A10..$26.00

Goldenrod Beer/Porter/Ale, tray, oval, deep rim, The Home Of... above aerial factory scene, pre-1936, 15", EX-EX+, A3/A8, from $75 to...............................$135.00

Goldenrod Ice Cream, clock, round, reverse glass, metal frame, In The Pencil Striped Package/pencil mascot, Tel-A-Sign Inc, 15" dia, VG+, A1.........................$185.00

Goldschmidt Bros Export Pony/Tom Howe/Marigold Rye, tip tray, round, triangle logo in center, lettered rim, gold trim, 4" dia, VG+, A8 ....$40.00

Gombault's Caustic Balsam, sign, paper, pictures race horse Delhi with jockey, 11x14", EX+, A15/D22 ....$375.00

Good Hand, cigar box labels, set of 2, image of playing cards, Witsch & Schmidt litho #1360/1361, VG, A5........$250.00

Good Humor, badge, cloisonne, blue cloud shape with center name space, gold trim, 1½x2½", NM, A1 .....$350.00

Good Humor, sign, porcelain, ½ Gallons.../Good Humor (symbol)/...Pints..., red/white/blue on white, 5x56", EX+, A1....................................$250.00

Good Luck Rolled Oats/Quaker Oats Co, container, 3-lb, cardboard, white, red lettering above/below shield with 4-leaf clover, EX+, A3....................................$45.00

Good Shot, cigar box, name above duck in flight, EX+, A3 ....$70.00

Good Stock, crate label, apple, orchard scene/apples, stone litho, M, D5 ....$55.00

Good Store, calendar, 1902, cardboard, boy looking at rabbit in girl's lap in wheelbarrow, floral border, embossed, 11x7", EX+, A1 ....$145.00

Good Year, crate label, California orange, lettering on red diagonal band over fruit/flowers, Rayo, M, D12 ....$7.00

Goodrich, print, The Goodrich Rubber Man's Vacation/A Midsummer Hallucination, framed, 26x32", G, A7..$500.00

Goodrich 'Hipress' Rubber Footwear, sign, flange, tin, die-cut boot/advertising panel, A Step Forward!/...Here, 14x18", EX, A7 ....$450.00

Goodrich Automobile Tires Sold Here, sign, porcelain, round, white/blue, 2-sided, 16" dia, VG+, A2....$385.00

Goodrich Cord Tires, sign, cardboard, 1920s lady stepping into yellow roadster with man at wheel, framed, 31x25", VG, A7....................................$1,400.00

Goodrich Rubber, print, Men's Vacation, image of campsite by river bank, framed, 25x33", VG, A7...............$600.00

Goodrich Rubber Footwear, sign, porcelain, oval, red/green G logo above white lettering on dk blue, green border, 2-sided, 17x23", NM+, A1.............$325.00

Goodrich Silverstown Heavy Duty Cords, ashtray, tire with glass insert with yellow/black image of early bus/advertising, 6½" dia, VG, A2 ....$300.00

Goodrich Silvertowns, sign, flange, porcelain, oval, name above double diamonds, red/white/blue, white trim, 19x23", EX-NM, A1, from $230 to........................$325.00

Goodrich Silvertowns, sign, porcelain, tire image on red square framed in black, name below, 2-sided, 1920s, 44x36", EX, A13 ....$425.00

Goodrich Sport Shoes, display, cardboard die-cut stand-up, boy running, Shoes That Make The Athlete..., 23x17", EX+, A1....................................$160.00

Goodrich Tire Patches, can, screw lid, paper label, Greetings above image of Santa, 4½x2" dia, VG+, D22.......$115.00

Goodrich Tires, sign, paper, girl posing with arms to head framed by tire, signed WH Mc Entee '96 (1896), 38x37", VG, A6....................................$900.00

Goodrich Tires, sign, porcelain, round, Slow Down/Safety First, name on outer band, red/white, 26" dia, EX+, A1..**$250.00**

Goodwill, sign, porcelain, Goodwill lettered on round Pontiac logo, square background, red/white/black, 36x36", G, A2 ....**$200.00**

Goody Goody Brand Pineapple, can, 1-lb 4-oz, paper label, 3 pineapples flanked by girls on dk blue ground, EX+, A3...**$65.00**

Goody Orange Drink, bottle topper/bottle, cardboard, die-cut, Enjoy..., orange bottle cap, EX, D30..............**$30.00**

Goody Root Beer, bottle topper, cardboard, die-cut, Drink... on bottle cap with boy's head, NM, A16 ....**$48.00**

Goodyear, award, molded metal, Goodyear Zeppelin Race 1930, images of the evolution of transportation, 17x12", EX+, A6....................................$1,600.00

Goodyear, calendar, 1935, bear surprising fisherman, artist Hy Hintermeister, 21x12", complete with cover sheet, NM (unused), A9...**$25.00**

Goodyear, display, winged foot, porcelain, white, blue trim, W-73, 16x47", EX, A6 ....**$450.00**

Goodyear, sign, reverse glass, Now All Nylon Cord Tubeless In..., rear view of couple in convertible, framed, 20x26", EX, A6...**$75.00**

Goodyear Authorised (sic) Dealer, sign, porcelain, blue/white symbol on lighter blue ground above white Authorised Dealer on yellow, 21x24", VG, A6 ...**$100.00**

Goodyear Balloon, sign, porcelain, white/black Goodyear Balloon tire around blue globe, white line border, 46x40", VG+, A6 ....**$200.00**

Goodyear G-3's, sign, cardboard, We Don't Have To Worry/These New G-3's Keep Their Grip, couple waving from car, 35x47", EX, A1 ....**$175.00**

Goodyear Motorcycle Tires, sign, flange, porcelain, die-cut cyclist atop, orange/blue/orange bands, yellow lettering/white trim, 11x24", EX, A21............................**$13,200.00**

Goodyear Rubber Tires, sign, porcelain, Agency.../Akron Ohio, winged foot logo in center, white on blue, white line border, 24x16", G, A2 ....**$1,155.00**

Goodyear Service Station, sign, flange, metal, die-cut tire with sign, orange/white/black/gray, c 1922, VG, A6 ...**$1,100.00**

Goodyear Tire Accessories, display case, metal frame with glass slant top/wooden base, stenciled logo on front/sides, 20x23", VG, A6......................................**$150.00**

Goodyear Tires, sign, porcelain, Good Year (vertical) above Tires (horizontal), yellow on blue, white trim, vertical, EX, A2...**$100.00**

Goodyear Tires, sign, porcelain, Good Year above Tires, yellow on blue, white trim, large horizontal, EX, A2...**$150.00**

Goodyear Tires, sign, porcelain, Goodyear flag above name, yellow/white on blue, diamond logo, 25x48", EX, A6...**$200.00**

Goodyear Tires, sign, porcelain, More People Ride On...Than Any Other Kind, white/yellow on blue, white trim, round, 22" dia, EX+, A1 ....**$475.00**

Goodyear Tires, sign, porcelain, They Cost No More, yellow white on blue, white trim, die-cut, 2-sided, 10x20", NM+, D11 ....**$175.00**

Goodyear Tires Selected Dealer, sign, porcelain, Made In Canada, yellow/white on blue, white trim, 24x71", EX, A6...**$450.00**

Goodyear Wingfoot Heels, trolley sign, lady's feet in 'Dainty French Heels'/And-Oh The Comfort Of Them! orange/white/brown, 1920, 11x21", EX, A1.........**$25.00**

Gopher Beer (Draught Keg Beer), label, ½-gal, Alexandria Brewing Co/MN, IRTP or WF Statement, 1933-50, M (soaked of bottle or paper/with crease), A10 ......**$23.00**

Gorden Dye Hosiery, sign, paper, Best In The World..., 3 ladies showing their ankles, framed, image: 27x13", EX, A9...**$900.00**

Gosling, crate label, Oregon apple, gosling against red background/white logo above, Hood River, EX-M, D3/D12, from $15 to..**$25.00**

Gosman's Ginger Ale, sign, cardboard die-cut trifold, The Refreshing All Season Drink, bottles flank family scenes, c 1917, 29x50", VG, A6 ....**$275.00**

Gotham Watches, display, automated hand with watch on wrist tips in/out of tray of water, with hammer/magnet, 1955, 16x15x6", EX, A23 ....**$300.00**

Gottfried Krueger Brewing Co High Grade Beer, tip tray, round, 50 Years Experience, gold lettering on green rim around foaming mug, EX, A8.................$110.00

Gould Tobacco Co/Bright World & Indian Queen Tobacco, calendar, 1888, cardboard, 2 birds on snowy branch against winter landscape, complete stapled pad below, 11x8", NM, A3............................$115.00

Governor, cigar box label, inner lid, man on horse/Nevada state seal, 2-pc, M, D5......................................**$125.00**

Green Giant, scouring pad holder, Lil' Sprout figure, ceramic, MIB, D20 ....$45.00

Green Mill, crate label, California orange, green mill/yellow sky, Placentia, EX, D3.................................$4.00

Green River, bottle display/bottle, cardboard, First For Thirst.../The Favorite Of Millions/5¢, EX, D30 .....$65.00

Green River, dispenser, ball shape, flared base, embossed painted logo, replaced pump, 14", VG, A9 .....$1,400.00

Green River, dispenser, box-shaped, green, with label, EX, D30 ....$375.00

Green River, dispenser, clear glass trophy shape, chrome lid/handles/base/spigot, 15", NM, A13...............$200.00

Green River, dispenser, container atop green round ceramic base, white/green label, EX, D30.......................$185.00

Green River, sign, celluloid, oval, A Quality Drink For A Quick Pick-Up on red border of moonlit river scene, 1930s, 7", VG+, A13...$40.00

Green River, sign, tin, ...In Bottles, image of moon shining on silhouetted tropical scene with water, embossed, 12x20", NM+, A3.............................$350.00

Green River, sign, tin/cardboard, Drink.../The Snappy Lime Drink, trademark image/text on white, red border, 1920s, 3x10", EX, A13 ....$200.00

Green River, sign, tin/cardboard, gold debossed name over oval green/blue scene, c 1919, self-framed, 5x12", VG, A8 ....$100.00

Green River Whiskey, charger, tin, She Was Bred In Old Kentucky, 24" dia, VG, A7 ....$500.00

Green River Whiskey, display bottle, clear glass, shouldered, long neck, black/yellow label with horseshoe logo, 20", EX+, A3 ....$90.00

Green River Whiskey, sign, tin, She Was Bred In Old Kentucky, framed, 33x45", A1...................$1,100.00

Green River Whiskey, tray, round, deep rim, She Was Bred In Old Kentucky, 12" dia, VG, A7.......................$130.00

Green Spot, sign, cardboard, actress being offered a bottle of Sun Spot while being coiffured & made up, 26x16", NM, D30 ....$135.00

Green Spot, sign, cardboard, Thirsty? on white band above girl at cooler, 33x23", NM+, D30 ....$185.00

Green Tree Brewery, sign, paper, tavern scene, jealous boyfriend holding on to girl's skirt as she toasts bicycle riders, 22x30", EX, A8..$275.00

Green Turtle Cigars, lunch box, green/white, G-VG+, A9/A3, from $175 to.......................................$275.00

Green Turtle Selects, tin, horizontal box, curved corners, holds 100, green/white, scarce, VG, A18............$150.00

Green Turtle Smoking/Chewing, soft pack, green/white, full, EX, A18 ....$60.00

Greenback Tobacco, sign, paper, Smoke 'Greenback' Tobacco, 2 mules pulling Santa in sleigh, Currier & Ives, 1883, framed, 14x18", EX, A7 ....$700.00

Greenfield Tap & Die Corp, tip tray, rectangular, single-engine top-wing plane, advertising on rim, 5x7", EX, A6..$40.00

Greensmith's Derby Dog Biscuits, sign, cardboard hanger, Manufactory Hilton Mills Near Derby, clown/dog act in landscape, self-framed, 19x23", EX, A6 ....$350.00

Greyhound, display rack for literature, wood, 4-tiered, blue with gold trademark image of dog on front, 7x15x4", EX, A2..$200.00

Greyhound, pin, cloisonne emblem, The Greyhound Lines, red/white/2-tone blue, bus in circular inset, 1", M, A1 ....$150.00

Greyhound, route map, paper, dated November 1, 1934, 20x31", EX, A6 ....$40.00

Greyhound, salt & pepper shakers, metal bus shape, EX, D25, pair...$100.00

Greyhound, sign, flange, white dog/name on black ground, 9x15", EX, A6 ....$600.00

Greyhound, sign, porcelain, dog on white above white name on blue, red border, curved corners, 2-sided, 1940s-50s, 20x40", EX, A13 ....$300.00

Greyhound (The) Lines Ticket Office, sign, porcelain, name above image of dog/early bus on 2-sided emblem, white/orange/black, 1930s, 30x25", EX+, A6 ....$2,300.00

Greyhound Atlantic Lines Ticket Office, sign, porcelain, name above image of dog/early bus on 2-sided emblem, white/orange/blue, 1930s, 30x25", VG, A6......$1,600.00

Greyhound Lines, poster, A Cash Bonus For Everyone Who Travels!, image of lady customer/ticket seller, dated 1936, 39x28", VG+, A2 ....$385.00

Greyhound Lines, poster, How To Stretch The Christmas dollar, dated 1932, 39x28", EX+, A2 ....$550.00

Greyhound Lines, poster, What A Glorious Vacation, offers toy replica of 1940 World's Fair bus, image of bus/map, 39x28", EX+, A2 ....$600.00

Greyhound Lines, sign, porcelain, oval, yellow lettering above/below white dog on blue, 2-sided, 21x36", EX+, A1..$525.00

Greyhound Pacific Lines, badge for driver's cap, metal/blue cloisonne, scrolled banners atop shield with dogs/bus on diagonal band, 2", EX, A15............$325.00

Greyhound Package Express, sign, flange, blue block lettering/blue outline of dog on white, 18x28", VG+, A3..$100.00

Grickson's Pure Rye Whiskey, sign, tin, whiskey bottles floating in water around boat firing guns at shore, self-framed, 23x33", G, A7 ....$500.00

Griesedieck Bros Beer, sign, tin/cardboard, No Finer Beer In All The World, tankard/bottle/glass/book in library, beveled, 1945, 13x10", EX, A8............................$100.00

Griffin's Coffee, can, 1-lb, key-wind lid, 5¢ Off, VG+, A3 ....$50.00

Grit Newspaper, calendar, 1886, cardboard, boy hawking newspaper in snowy weather, 12 months displayed at bottom, 11x8", EX, A3 ....$125.00

Grit Newspaper, calendar, 1896, cardboard, girl with red fan surrounded by months of the year, 11x8", EX+, A3......$150.00

Grit Newspaper, calendar, 1899, cardboard, girl waving flag at mirror, months displayed down side/at bottom, 12x9", EX, A3...$125.00

Grosman Bros' Southern Fodder Corn, sign, tin, ...Of Superior Quality..., corn stalks frame aerial view of farm land/advertising, ca 1910, 24x17", NM, A3 ....$220.00

GTA Lit-O-Bit Feeds, bank, Ernie Pig, ceramic, 1970s, 8", NM+, A14 ....$100.00

Guardian Taxi Corporation, taxi door sign, brass shield, Distinguished Service, diagonal banner separates taxi image from lettering, 16x14", EX, A2....$990.00

Guide Tobacco, pocket tin, vertical, NM, A18 ....$250.00

Guinness Stout, sign, tin, oval image of gent leaning against building with hands in pockets, lettered raised flat rim, 23x17", VG, A2....................................$250.00

Gulden's Mustard, radio, jar shape, MIB (unused), D20..$100.00

Gulf, game, travel bingo, 1951, EX, D24 ....$5.00

Gulf, gas globe, 1-pc, glass, That Good Gulf Gasoline, black lettering/red trim on white, 16", NM, A6 ....$750.00

Gulf, gas globe, 1-pc, milk glass, white/blue/orange logo, screw neck-base (no collar), EX+, A1................$600.00

Gulf, plaque, embossed brass, Honor/Award honoring a Gulf Service Station for 3% Motor Oil Sales.../Spring 1938, 7x9", EX, D22 ....$85.00

Gulf, pocket lighter, Zippo, flip top, chrome with cloisonne Gulf emblem, 2¼", EX+, A1 ....$90.00

Gulf, sign, light-up, molded plastic/metal Gulf emblem, Kolux Polycard, 1984, 24" dia, EX+, A6..............$210.00

Gulf, sign, paper, Gulf Exclusive!/2nd Great Issue!/...Disney Magazine/25¢, image of Donald Duck, red/white, 70x44", EX, A6 ....$70.00

Gulf, sign, tin, Gulf in blue block letters with white shadowing orange background, white rim, 28" dia, EX, A2....$125.00

Gulf, thread container/thimble, metal cylinder with thimble on end, blue advertising on orange center, 2", EX, A6 ....$300.00

Gulf Aircraft Engine Oil/Gulf Aviation Products, can, 1-qt, dark blue with orange/white winged logo, VG+, A1..$75.00

Gulf Gasoline, blotter, There Is More Power In That Good.../From The Orange Pump, attendant pumping gas into early car, 4x6", EX, A6 ....$65.00

Hanley's Peerless Ale/James Hanley Co, tray, round, The Connoisseur, 13" dia, EX, A8 ....$100.00

Hanna's Green Seal Paint, display sign, cardboard stand-up, We Live & Learn, 2 men examining paint on side of house, 39x30", EX, A2 ....$25.00

Hansel & Gretel Mild Blend Havana Cigars, label under glass, round with lettered border, framed, 16x16", EX, A5 ....$260.00

Hanson & Gilbertson The General Merchants, calendar, 1910, die-cut cardboard, young girl seated on red stool talking on wall phone, 14x10", incomplete, EX, A1 ......$80.00

Happy Hour Coffee, can, sample, screw lid, red, steaming cup, 2" dia, EX+, A15..............$350.00

Happy Hours, cigar box label, outer, Cupid/couple dancing under tree, 1873, 4½x4½", EX, D5..............$30.00

Hapsburg Bock Beer, label, ½-gal, Best Brewing Co/Chicago IL, IRTP or WF statement, 1933-50, M (traces of paper or scrapes on back), A10..............$18.00

Harbor Light Salmon, can label, lighthouse, M, D5 ..$25.00

Hard A'Port, cigar box label, sample, close-up image of couple, Schumacher & Ettlinger litho #7109, 1891, VG, A5 ....$120.00

Hardee's, backpack, orange, MIP, D23 ....$3.00

Hardee's, frisbee, yellow on white, 5", EX, D23..............$2.00

Harem/RR Schnader & Son, cigar box label, outer, octagonal, ladies in courtyard, M, A5..............$75.00

Harlequin/Unknown Tobacco Co, caddy label, vertical, harlequin/ballerina/grotesque being in courtyard, Hoen litho, approx: 14x7", NM, A3 ....$35.00

Harley Cycle Wear/Wrangler, banner, denim cloth, Harley logo above Cycle Wear, Built By Wrangler below, yellow/blue, 1960s, 48x36", NM, A25..............$600.00

Harley-Davidson, ad, paper on cardboard, Step In & See The 1924.../Then Let's Go For A Ride!, cycle with sidecar above, 34x26", G+, A6..............$250.00

Harley-Davidson, clock, octagonal, light-up, glass front, metal frame, decorative geometric border around numbers/logo, 18x18", NOS, A6..............$1,400.00

Harley-Davidson, magazine, Enthusiast, May 1956, cover pictures 21-year-old Elvis on his third Harley, NM, A24..............$450.00

Harley-Davidson, pocket watch, round, silver-tone, logo on face, second hand for timing, 1920s, EX, A24....$725.00

Harley-Davidson, poster, paper, ...Wins All 1940 Class A & Class B Hillclimb Championships, multicolored, 24x37", NM, A24..............$500.00

Harley-Davidson, rider's cap, black with white bill, silver-tone band, winged patch, with 5 pins, EX, A1 ..$250.00

Harley-Davidson, screwdriver, nickel-plated handle with engraved lettering, 5", EX, A24..............$115.00

Harley-Davidson, sign, neon/logo, multicolored, 1980s, 25x36", NM, A6 ....$700.00

Harley-Davidson, string tie with detailed metal motorcycle clasp, green, NM, A24..............$185.00

Harley-Davidson, visor, leather, stamped logo on bill, M, A24..............$30.00

Harley-Davidson, wristwatch, Elgin, rectangular face with bowed sides, leather band, 1½x1¼", working, VG, A6..............$600.00

Harley-Davidson Genuine Motor Oil For 4-Cycle Motors, can, 1-qt, white logo on orange, NM+, A1........$400.00

Harley-Davidson Genuine Refinery Sealed Oil, can, 1-qt, black logo on orange, EX, A1 ....$150.00

Harley-Davidson Gunk, can, 1-qt, shield logo on white, orange ground, NM, A1 ....$250.00

Harley-Davidson Motorcycles, sign, porcelain, shield logo, white/black orange, 24x60", EX, A21..............$6,050.00

Harley-Davidson Motorcycles & Sidecars, pamphlet, 1923, The Open Road Calls You!, campers looking down upon couple riding Harley with sidecar, 12 pgs, EX, A6 ....$75.00

Harley-Davidson Motorcycles Sales/Service, sign, tin, Motorcycle Headquarters/address, trademark colors, 18x24", EX, A1 ....$600.00

Harley-Davidson Pre-Luxe Premium Deluxe Motorcycle Oil, can, 1-qt, white above black ground, EX+, A1 .$85.00

Harley-Davidson Sales/Service/Parts/Accessories, sign, glass, shield logo in center, lettered corners, white/blue/yellow, 7x9", EX, A24 ....$1,200.00

Harmony, crate label, lemon, girl leading group of circus toys, 1920, M, D5...$85.00

Harper's Dustless Mops, tin, round, image on lid of woman mopping as dog watches, black on red, 1920s, 3½x7" dia, EX, D22...$75.00

Harper's Whiskey/Whisky, see IW Harper's Whiskey

Harrington & Richardson Arms Co, calendar, 1907, paper, mountain man with revolver in snow scene, complete, NM, A9 ....$2,800.00

Harrington & Richardson Arms Co, calendar, 1910, paper, hunter/2 dogs on hillside, artist, GM Arnold, 27x14", complete, VG+, A3.............................$990.00

Harrison's Heart O' Orange, sign, tin, round, ...Sold Here, oranges sipping from straws on white heart, orange trim, 1930s-40s, 14", G+, A13.....................................$135.00

Harry Mitchell's Good Honest Beer, tray, round, lettered center band/rim, 13" dia, VG+, A8.....................$100.00

Hart Batteries, door push bar, porcelain, white lettering with small red heart on blue, 1940s, EX+, A13 ....$100.00

Hart Batteries, pocketknife, metal with engraved diamond design around name, name on leather pouch, 3½", EX, A6...$20.00

Hart's Coffee, can, 1-lb, key-wind lid, red heart on blue, NM, A3...$215.00

Hartford Fire Insurance Co, sign, flange, Local Agency..., die-cut circular image of stag/mountains, wood-tone ad panel, 28x18", EX, A1...$500.00

Hartford Fire Insurance Co, sign, tin, oval image of stag/mountains, green rectangular border, wood-grain self-frame, 24x20", EX, A2.....................................$350.00

Hartford Fire Insurance Co, sign, tin, oval image of stag/mountains, yellow rectangular border, self-framed, 25x20", NM, A7...$500.00

Hartford Tire Repair Kit/Hartford Rubber Works Co, tin, rectangular, curved corners, Mersereau Works, Brooklyn, ½x2x3", EX, D37...$60.00

Harvard Ale/Export Beer/Porter, tray, round, deep rim, ...Has What It Takes, red logo/lettering on white center, red rim, 12" dia, EX+, A3.....................................$25.00

Harvard Beer, pitcher & mugs, pottery, 7-pc set, Christmas 1938, NM+, A19 ....$225.00

Harvard Brewing Co, sign, tin, Victorian lady in Middle Eastern-type sitting room overlooking courtyard, 45x36", VG-EX+, A7/A3, from $800 to $1,750.00

Harvard Cigar, sign, porcelain, Have A Harvard Cigar/Hand Made/The Standard Of Quality, hand-held cigar, yellow, 30x21", NM, A1 ....$400.00

Harvard Jumbo Peanuts, tin, 10-lb, round, pry lid, gold, red lettering/graphics of peanut man holding pennant, 10", G, A2 ....$100.00

Harvard Pure Rye/Klein Bros, sign, tin, 2 graduates in parlor partying with 2 fun-loving ladies, gold frame, 31x43", VG, A7...$1,300.00

Harvest Queen Coffee, can, 1-lb, key-wind lid, blue/white, crown logo, NM, A3...$70.00

Harvest Queen Fresh Coffee, can, 1-lb, key-wind lid, red, EX+, A3...$30.00

Harvester Cigar, sign, tin, oval, convex, Light A..½¢, lady's head framed in heart on yellow, embossed, black raised rim, 13x10", EX, A1 ....$200.00

Haserot's Senora Coffee, can, 1-lb, key-wind lid, EX, A3 ....$75.00

Hassan Cork Tip Cigarettes, sign, cardboard, The Original Smoke, name above bust image of man wearing fez/smoking cigarette, framed, 30x23", EX, A6.$235.00

Hatchet Brand Toasted Corn Flakes, cereal box, 8-oz, red/yellow/blue/white logo on gray, NM, A3 ....$180.00

Henry George 5¢ Cigar, sign, tin, I Am For Man, profile portrait, curved corners, self-framed, early 1900s, 26x18", VG, A5 ....**$850.00**

Henry H Shufeldt Co/Imperial Crown Gin/Rye/Malt, sign, paper, Proof Of The Virtue In The Test, 4 scenes of couple in rain/product bottles, framed, 1899, 20x37", NM, A7 ....**$400.00**

Henry Irving Cigars, pocket tin, vertical oval, paper label, VG+ (full), A18 ....**$40.00**

Henry W Longfellow, cigar box label, inner lid, Hiawatha/Minnehaha/author, 6x9", M, D5 ....**$35.00**

Henry Weinhard Beer, tray, round, deep rim, food scene with bottles/mugs, pre-prohibition, 13" dia, G, A8 ....**$40.00**

Hensler's, tap knob, ball shape, black, black/red/gold-on-mustard metal insert, EX, A8 ....**$60.00**

Heptol Splits, tip tray, For Health's Sake, cowboy on bucking bronc, lettered border, signed Russell 1904, 4" dia, EX, A6 ....$285.00

Herbo, sign, tin, die-cut head image of Indian chief, Made From Indian Herbs, ca 1900, 5x5", NM, A24 ......**$400.00**

Hercules Ethyl Gasoline, gas globe, 3-pc, white plastic body, glass lenses, white/red name on green band around white center, 13½", NM, A6 ....**$220.00**

Hercules Powder Co, calendar top (?), c 1917, Not This Trip Old Pal, hunter telling dog to stay, framed, 22x14", VG+, A8 ....**$40.00**

Hercules Powder Co, lapel pin, oval, white band around gold oval with Hercules holding red club, gold rim, 14K on back, ½", EX, D14 ....**$20.00**

Hercules Powder Co, sign, cardboard, Don't You Fool Me Dog, FM Speigle, 1920, 24x15", G, A3 ....**$60.00**

Hercules Powder Co, sign, cardboard, I'se Done Lost De Lunch, FM Spiegle, 1923, 24x15", VG, A3 ....**$150.00**

Hercules Powder Co, sign, cardboard, Infallible Smokeless Shotgun Powder, lady hunter/dog, stand-up/hanger, 1917, 15x10", NM, A3 ....$400.00

Hercules Powder Co, sign, cardboard, Next Year Young Fellow, hunter holding up pup, AD Fuller artist, 1930, 20x12", NM, A24 ....**$120.00**

Hercules Powder Co, sign, cardboard, Sumpin's G'Wine To Happen!, FW Spiegle, metal strips, 25x16", G-EX, A3/A7, from $200 to..**$600.00**

Hercules Powder Co, sign, paper, Pheasant, Infallible Smokeless Shotgun Powder, American litho, c 1915, 25x15", G, A9 ....**$1,000.00**

Here's Luck, cigar box label, outer, men at bar smoking cigars, 4½x4½", EX, D5 ....**$40.00**

Herman Giegling Meat Market, Canistota SD, calendar, 1909, die-cut embossed cardboard, large roses blossoming from the deck of a steamship, 8x12", NM+, A3 .....**$50.00**

Hershey's Choclatier, canister, slip lid with knob, red/brown on yellow, The Hot Chocolate Drink.../ Delicious-Refreshing, 1950s, 6x6", EX, D14 ....$75.00

HGF Coffee, can, 1-lb, key-wind lid, white, NM, A3.**$50.00**

Hi-Grade Motor Oil, can, 1-gal, rectangular, pour spout with screw lid, grip handle, oval #8 race logo on yellow, tall, NM, A1..**$375.00**

Hi-Grade Motor Oil, can, ½-gal, rectangular, pour spout with screw lid, grip handle, oval #8 racer logo on yellow, NM+, A1 ....**$325.00**

Hi-Ho Coffee, can, 1-lb, key-wind lid, blue, EX+, A3 .**$35.00**

Hi-Plane Smooth Cut Tobacco, humidor, tin, red, EX+, A3 ....**$200.00**

Hi-Plane Smooth Cut Tobacco, pocket tin, vertical, red, 1-engine plane, EX, A18 ....**$100.00**

Hi-Plane Smooth Cut Tobacco, pocket tin, vertical, red, 2-engine plane, EX+, A18 ....**$170.00**

Hi-Plane Smooth Cut Tobacco, pocket tin, vertical, red, 4-engine plane, EX, A18 ....$425.00

Hi-Plane Smooth Cut Tobacco, pocket tin, vertical, red, 4-engine plane, NM+ (full), A18 ....$750.00

Hi-Power Shot Shells, sign, paper, — Use — Hi-Power Shot Shells on black band below ducks flying over marsh, 23x33", EX+, A3 ....$180.00

Hi-Speed Gas, sign, porcelain, lists Speedolem/Tiolene oil prices, white/black on black, vertical, EX, D32 ...$25.00

Hi-Tone, crate label, Washington pear, ornate view of 4 pears/valley/orchards/mountain, Spokane, NOS, D12 ....$20.00

Hi Yu, crate label, apple, stylized profile view of Indian chief on red ground, EX, D3 ....$4.00

Hiawatha, crate label, California orange, portrait, 1930, EX, D5 ....$50.00

Hiawatha, display bust, chalkware, 19", EX, A6...$140.00

Hiawatha Granulated Mixture Tobacco, tin, horizontal box, curved corners, green, very scarce, EX+, A18......$130.00

Hiawatha Granulated Mixture Tobacco, tin, horizontal box, curved corners, yellow, EX, A3 ....$50.00

Hickman-Ebbert Co, sign, tin, In The Shade Of The Old Apple Tree/The Ebbert Owensboro, self-framed, 25x38", VG+, A7...$1,000.00

Hickman-Ebbert Co, sign, tin, In The Shade Of The Old Apple Tree/The Owensboro, self-framed, 25x38", EX, A7 ....$1,400.00

Hickory Children's Garters, sign, wood, die-cut image of boy/girl under lettered umbrella, 18x11", VG, A6..$350.00

Hickory Hardware, sign, flange, tin, die-cut silhouette of man pointing/round logo/yellow tag, 28x18", VG+, A1 ....$160.00

High Admiral of Navies 'King of Seas'/David Dunlop Tobacco, caddy label, horizontal, Neptune in shell chariot with nudes/sailing ships, 1874, approx: 7x14", NM+, A3...$132.00

High Art Brand Coffee, can, 1-lb, key-wind lid, island beach scene, VG+, A3 ....$65.00

High Ball Ginger Ale, sign, tin hanger, Sparkling/Refreshing, bottle over red center band on green, 1915-25, diagonal, 6½x6½", EX+, A13..$150.00

High Grade Smoking Tobacco, pocket tin, vertical, oval, EX, A18...$650.00

High Grade Yellow Cling Peaches, can label, peach/early train on Sierra mountain climb, San Francisco, M, D12...$10.00

High Park Coffee, can, 1-lb, key-wind lid, blue/yellow, metallic gold trim, Medium Ground, EX, A3 ....$50.00

High Park Coffee, can, 12-lb, key-wind lid, EX+, A18..$130.00

High Rock Root Beer, sign, tin, Full Pint 5¢, cloud graphic/tilted bottle (with shadow) on red, black bottom band, 20x8", NM, D30...$150.00

High-Toned 3¢ Cigar, sign, tin, Say! Get The High-Toned 3¢ Cigar Inside... printed on front of Yellow Kid, embossed, 20x9", VG, A15 ....$800.00

Highest Grade Smoking Tobacco, tin, horizontal box, curved corners, EX+, A3.......................................$65.00

Hignett's Golden Butterfly Cigarettes, sign, cardboard, close-up of lady in large hat, artist Hamilton King, 14x17", VG, A9...$300.00

Hignett's Pilot Flake (Dark Flake Cavendish), tin, horizontal box, square corners, EX+, A3...................$200.00

Hill's Badminton Smoking Mixture, tin, round, embossed slip lid, yellow, 4½x3" dia, EX, A18....................$100.00

Hillcrest Lager Beer, sign, cardboard stand-up, The Talk Of The Town/Drink..., girl with glass, curved corners, 30x20", VG, A8...$75.00

Hills Bros Coffee, can, ½-lb, key-wind lid, EX-NM, A3/A18, from $35 to...$50.00

Hills Bros Coffee, can, 1-lb, key-wind lid, NM+ (unopened), A3...$60.00

Hills Bros Coffee, can, 1-lb, key-wind lid, VG+, A3.$35.00

Hills Bros Coffee, can, 15-lb, VG+, A3 ....$75.00

Hires, sign, tin, Drink Hires In Bottles/Bracing/Delicious, yellow diamond over red/black ground, 1930s, 10x28", A13......................$300.00

Hires, sign, tin, Drink Hires.../For Thirst & Cheer/In Bottles, center blue oval/bottle, yellow, embossed, 10x28", VG, A1......................$250.00

Hires, sign, tin, Drink Hires/It Hits The Spot/Try A Bottle & You'll Buy A Case, Josh Slinger with bottle, 1915, 9x18", EX, A2......................$450.00

Hires, sign, tin, Enjoy Hires Root Beer/Healthful/Delicious, ring around bottle, white/yellow/blue, 1930s, 28x10", NM+, A13......................$350.00

Hires, sign, tin, For Pleasure & Thirst/Made With ..., check-mark logo, round, embossed, 1940s-50s, 24", NM, A13..$375.00

Hires, sign, tin, Hires R-J Root Beer With Real Root Juices on bull's-eye logo on blue, 7x12", NM, A3...............$50.00

Hires, sign, tin, Hires R-J Root Beer With Real Root Juices on bull's-eye logo, embossed, round, 24" dia, EX, A6..$125.00

Hires, sign, tin, Hires Refreshes Right!/Since 1876, tilted bottle, lt blue, 1940s, 42x13", NM, A13.....................$300.00

Hires, sign, tin, Hires To You!, slanted lettering/bottle (against cloud) on blue, 1940s-50s, 42x14", EX+, A13.......$350.00

Hires, sign, tin, It's High Time For Hires, with bottle, 12x30", G+, D30..$55.00

Hires, sign, tin, R-J logo on blue, 7x12", EX, D30 .....$70.00

Hires, sign, tin, So Good/Ice Cold, 3 bottles on each side of R-J logo, embossed, raised rim, 13x40", VG+, A1.........$325.00

Hires, sign, tin, Toast To Good Taste/Enjoyable In Bottles, R-J logo in center, red/white/2-tone blue, embossed, 11x35", NM, A1..$275.00

Hires, sign, tin, We Serve...R-J Root Beer/With Real Juices/Fountain Service, red/white/yellow/blue, 2-sided, 15x16", VG, A1......................................$475.00

Hires, sign, tin/cardboard, Drink Hires Root Beer on vertical blue/white stripes, gold rim, 1940s, round, 9" dia, VG+, A19...$100.00

Hires, sign, tin/cardboard, Got A Minute/Have A Hires/Your Invitation To Refresh on white 'invitation,' 1950s, 9x6", NM, A13..$150.00

Hires, syrup bottle, clear glass with curved shoulder, embossed straight sides, flat bottom, metal jigger cap, 1905-15, NM, A13 ....$1,100.00

Hires, syrup bottle, reverse-glass octagonal label, embossed knob lid, 13", EX+, A15.............................$775.00

Hires, thermometer, bottle shape, tin, Genuine/blue dot label, 28", NM (NOS), A6............................$140.00

Hires, thermometer, bottle shape, tin, Since 1876 label, 29", NM, A24...$250.00

Hires, thermometer, Drink Hires/tilted bottle on lt blue with white stripes, tin, 27", EX+, A1.....................$325.00

Hires, trade card, bust image of girl in paper hat, M, A16..$18.00

Hires, trade card, bust image of lady, Haskell Coffin, 1917, NM+, A16...$60.00

Hires, trade card, girl standing holding bottle of extract, EX, A16..$17.00

Hires, trade card, lady seated in black dress with girl in doorway, EX+, A16..$25.00

Hires, tray, rectangular, oval image of lady in center, Hires on rim, Haskell Coffin artist/HD Beach litho, 13x10", EX+, D22..$300.00

Hires, tray, round, Just What The Doctor Ordered/Quenches Any Thirst Up To A Mile Long, c 1914, 13" dia, G, A9...$350.00

Hires, tray, round, Things Is Getting Higher But Hires Are Still A Nickle A Trickle, c 1915, 13" dia, VG, A9.........$550.00

Hires Condensed Milk, pocket pin holder, can shape, opens to show baby in highchair, 2½x1½", EX+, A3 ....$65.00

His Master's Voice Records, see Columbia Records/RCA

Hit (The), cigar box label, sample, frogs playing baseball, Heppenheimer & Sons litho #1575, 1878, VG, A5....$1,950.00

Hixson's Extra Rich Coffee, can, 1-lb, key-wind lid, EX+, A3...$40.00

HoBo Joe's Restaurant, bank, HoBo Joe, vinyl, 1980s, 12", NM, D20..$135.00

Hoffman Half & Half, tap knob, ball shape, white, white-on-red celluloid insert, VG+, A8.........................$50.00

Hoffman House Bouquet Cigar/Hilson Co, sign, cardboard, 2 cherubs lighting man's cigar by stairway, Gray Litho Co, 1900, framed, 14x11", VG, A5.............$400.00

Hoffman House Bouquet Cigars, lighter, pot metal, figure of dapper man descending stairs by lamppost, 17", G, A9..$4,250.00

Hoffman House Cigars, sign, cardboard, The New.../5 Cents, red lettering on yellow border above/below 4 nymphs with man, 30x22", NM, A7................$1,500.00

Hoffman House Hand Made, cigar tin, horizontal box, red, EX, A3..$75.00

Hoffman's Ice Cream, sign, porcelain, die-cut emblem, First Choice.../Sealtest Approved, red/green on white, 2-sided, 22x28", NM, A1.................................$325.00

Hoffmann's Finest Quality Coffee, can, 1-lb, key-wind lid, 'H' & Since 1876 on shield against orange/black divided ground, tall, EX+, A18 ....$50.00

Hohner Harmonica, sign, illuminated shadowbox frame, That Musical Pal Of Mine, shows man playing/couples dancing, 1935, 14x16x6", EX, A23.....................$500.00

Holdfast Boots, sign, porcelain, black lettering above/below oval image of square knot in rope on yellow, 18x24", EX, A6 ....$1,200.00

Holiday Pipe Mixture, pocket tin, vertical, recessed lid, EX+, A3..$35.00

Holiday Pipe Mixture, pocket tin, vertical, regular lid, NM, A3...$30.00

Holiday Pipe Mixture, pocket tin, vertical, sample, cut-down, NM, A18...$60.00

Holiday Special Beer, label, 11-oz, Louis Ekert Brewing Co/Los Angeles CA, IRTP or WF statement, 1933-40, M, A10 ....$18.00

Holland House Coffee, can, 1-lb, key-wind lid, coffee-bean background, NM, A3 ....$100.00

Holleb's Coffee, can, 1-lb, key-wind lid, red/white/blue, EX+ (full), A3 ....$110.00

Holleb's Supreme Toasted Corn Flakes, cereal box, 11-oz, image of brownies cooking up bowl of corn flakes on blue ground, NM+, A3......................$55.00

Hollie's Drive-In, sign, metal, stenciled, Grand & Western/Oklahoma City, pig person behind, black/red on white, ca 1950, 11x20", NM, A3 ....$65.00

Holly Brand Chocolates, tray, round, bust image of lady on brown, gold lettering at bottom of brown rim, gold trim, 1910, 19" dia, VG, A7 ....$500.00

Hollywood Brand Spices Allspice, tin, 4-oz, VG+, A3..$65.00

Hollywood Coffee, can, 1-lb, key-wind lid, white on red, EX, A3..$110.00

Holsum Bread, door push bar, red die-cut loaf on blue bar, painted tin, NM, A1 ....$200.00

Holsum Bread, string holder, tin, double curved signs, Don't Say Bread/Say Holsum/There's A Difference, blue/black/white, 16", EX, A7 ....$400.00

Holt Pipe Shop Mixture, pocket tin, vertical, paper label, 1910 stamp, EX, A18 ....$125.00

Holtons Band Instruments, sign, paper, Neil O'Brien Minstrels Use & Recommend..., image of band below, Otis litho, 27x41", VG, A9..$125.00

Home Brand Coffee, can, 1-lb, key-wind lid, yellow, round logo with black border, EX+, A3 ....$25.00

Home Brand Coffee, can, 1-lb, key-wind lid, yellow, round logo with gold filigree border, early, VG, A3 ....$25.00

Home Brand Quick Cooking Rolled Oats, container, 1-lb 4-oz, yellow, EX+, A3...$45.00

Home Comfort, cigar box label, sample, OL Schwencke litho #2430, VG+, A5 ....$75.00

Home Favorite, cigar box label, outer, octagonal, round image of baseball player, Geo S Harris & Sons litho #2532, VG, A5...$265.00

Home Garden Coffee, can, 1-lb, key-wind lid, EX+, A18...$75.00

Home Mutual Insurance Co of California, sign, paper, horse-drawn fire patrol rolling past San Francisco US Mint, Niagara litho, embossed frame, 26x31", VG, A9.......$1,250.00

Home of Ramona, crate label, California orange, hacienda/flowers, bronzed, Camulos, 1900, EX-M, D12/D5, from $125 to..$175.00

Home Run Cigarettes, product pack, 1920s, NM (unopened), A15...$200.00

Home Run Stogie, tin, round, batter/catcher in front of billboard reading ...3 For 5¢/The JA Rigby Cigar Co, 4", VG+, A9 ....$2,900.00

Home Run Tobacco, tin, round, slip lid, baseball runner sliding into home, early, 5½x4¼" dia, EX+, D6, minimum value $10,000.00

Home/Local & Long Distance Telephone, sign, flange, porcelain, red, white/blue shield on white circle, square blue border, ca 1910, 17x18", EX+, A1 ....$525.00

Homestead, cigar box labels, set of 2, tropical plantation scene, Witsch & Schmitt litho #529/530, VG+, A5 ....$220.00

Homestead Brand Coffee, pail, 5-lb, VG+, A18 ....$70.00

Homestead Fertilizers/Michigan Carbon Works, sign, tin, exterior cabin scene, wood frame, 25x33", VG, A7.$650.00

Homestead Mushrooms, can label, mushrooms/country home, M, D5 ....$18.00

Honest Scrap, sign, porcelain, hand-held hammer in center, white on red, white border, 12x9", EX+, A1 ......$500.00

Honest Weight Chewing & Smoking Tobacco, sign, paper, baby wrapped in blanket hanging from scale, c 1888, framed, 16x12", VG, A9......................................$300.00

Honest Yankee, cigar box label, inner lid, Uncle Sam admiring cigars/US map, 6x9", M, D5 ....$90.00

Honey Krust Bread, string holder, tin, curved panels both sides, Ask For.../Today/Your Fresh Loaf, loaf in center, 16x13", VG, A2...$300.00

Honey Moon Tobacco, pocket container, cardboard, man on moon, EX+, A3...$190.00

Honey Moon Tobacco, pocket tin, vertical, couple on moon, VG-EX, A18, from $450 to $735.00

Hudepohl Beer, sign, tin, 2 men enjoy Hudepohl while practicing their instruments, self-framed oval hanger, 15x17", VG, A9.................................$175.00

Hudepohl Brew'g Co Cincinnati Beer, sign, Vitrolite, curved, 2 bucks with front hooves on barrel, blue lettering on white, gold/black frame, 23x16", NM, A7...........$1,075.00

Hudson, sign, neon/porcelain, name in block letters on Deco-style housing with diamond logo, 48x102", EX+, A6 ....$1,400.00

Hudson Bay Cigars, cigar box labels, 3-pc set, Indian watching white men in boat depart after trading, G, A5 ....$325.00

Hudson Brand Pure Tumeric, tin, 2-oz, white on black, EX+, A3..$8.00

Hudson Built Cars Authorized Service, sign, porcelain, round, red/black lettering over blue/black triangle, white ground, 36" dia, EX-NM, A1/A6, from $725 to...$900.00

Hudson Kerosene, gas globe, 2-pc, white plastic body, glass lens, red/blue lettering/flame logo on white, 14", A6...$300.00

Hudson Parts/Service, sign, porcelain marque, Hudson over diamond logo flanked by Parts/Service, red/white/blue, 29x42", G, A2............................$225.00

Hudson Regular Hi Octane Gas, gas globe, 3-pc, Capolite white plastic body, glass lenses, name around tanker, red/white/black, EX+ lenses/VG body, A1 .....$1,200.00

Hudson Sales & Service Station, sign, porcelain, triangle shape, black lettering on white, black border, 2-sided, 23x20", EX+, A2.................................$2,530.00

Hudson Sales/Service, sign, porcelain, white lettering on black die-cut emblem with red/white diamond logo, American Sign Co, 32x48", VG+, A6 ....$500.00

Hudson Super Six, radiator emblem, white on black cloisonne inset in triangular metal frame with leaf decor, 3x3", EX+, A1 ....$75.00

Hudson Terraplane Authorized Service, sign, porcelain, round, red lettering over blue triangle logo, white ground, 42" dia, VG, A2............................$700.00

Hudson 6, license plate attachment, tin, sleek bird soaring above name with dimpled reflective lettering, 4x14", EX+, A1..$110.00

Hudson/Essex Service, sign, porcelain, blue Hudson on white/white Service on blue/red Essex on white, 2-sided, 16x30", EX+, A1 ....$350.00

Hudson's Soap, sign, porcelain, A Pail Of Water With A Very Little Hudson's Goes A Very Long Way on green pail, yellow, 21x14", EX, A6...............................$235.00

Hugh Campbell's Shag, pocket tin, vertical, EX+, A18..$490.00

Hula, crate label, apple, girl seated under palm tree on blue ground, EX, D3 ....$4.00

Hull's Ale/Lager, tray, round, deep rim, can/bottle flank lettering on band, wood-grain ground, 12" dia, EX, A8....$60.00

Hull's Cream Ale/Lager Beer, tray, round, deep rim, close-up of lady holding full pilsner glass, 12" dia, VG+, A8 ....$85.00

Humble, credit card application holder, painted steel, red, Oil Drop Man/ad on back plate, Take One on box, 8x6", NM, A1...$350.00

Humble, sign, porcelain, die-cut Oil Drop Man saluting in lt blue uniform with oval Humble symbol on chest, 48x24", EX, A6...............................$1,600.00

Humble/Restroom, sign, porcelain, The Next User Of This Restroom... in red on white above red Humble on blue-outlined oval, 9x7", NM+, A1.........................$375.00

Humphery's Remedies, cabinet, tin, ...Ask For Them By Number/77 For Colds Grip Influenza, list of products, gold on brown, 29x21x5", EX+, A3.................$85.00

Humphery's Veterinary Specifics, cabinet, wood, embossed tin front, horse head, 28x21x7", EX+, A15..........$5,100.00

Hungarian Rozsa Paprika, tin, round, slip lid, red on metallic gold, EX+, A3.......................................$30.00

Hunt Club Shoes, sign, tin, oval image of equestrian jumping fence/image of large shoe, wood-grain self-frame, 24x20", VG, A7......................................$700.00

Hunt Pen Co Round Pointed Pens, display case, wooden box, compartmented, pen tip decal on glass top, 5x10x11", no pen tips, VG+, A3.........................$90.00

Hunt Pen Co Round Pointed Pens, display case, wooden box, compartmented, pen tip decal on glass top, 4x11", with pen tips, NM, D6 ....$300.00

Hunter, crate label, Washington apple, hunting dog points apple/mountains/orchards, Wenatchee, M, D12...**$15.00**

Hunter Baltimore Rye, match safe, image of bottle/equestrian jumping fence, VG, A3..**$60.00**

Hunter Baltimore Rye, sign, paper, The American Gentlemen's Whisky, horseman waving top hat, Edwards, Deutsch & Heitman litho, 11x8", VG, A9.............**$50.00**

Hunter Cigars, pocket tin, vertical, EX, A5 ....**$325.00**

Hunting Smoking Tobacco, pouch, 2-oz, cloth, paper label, red/yellow, EX, A7 ....**$285.00**

Hupmobile, calendar, 1926, image of 2 cars/sailboats/people, logos at top/bottom of border, 31x14", complete, EX+, A1...**$160.00**

Hupmobile, pin-back button, oval, 19/11 flank image of auto, Memphis dealer listed, full color, EX, A2 .$745.00

Hurley Burley Smoking Tobacco, canister, pull top, brown, EX+, A18...**$75.00**

Hurrah!, cigar box label, sample, rooster, American Litho Co/Witsch & Schmitt litho #2687, 1895, EX, A5.**$125.00**

Huskey Hi-Power, lighter, Vulcan type, dog encircled by name on orange inlay, 1¾, MIB, A1 ....$120.00

Husky, lighter, Vulvan, dog atop nameplate on red inlay, 1¾", MIB, A1 ....$110.00

Husky, lighter, Zippo type, chrome, dog (against white circle inlay) atop red/blue nameplate, 2", NM+ (NOS), A1 ....**$120.00**

Husky, lighter, Zippo type, chrome, dog (no circle inlay) atop red/white nameplate, 2", EX, A6..................**$75.00**

Husky Motor Oil, can, 1-qt, blue, EX+, A1 ....**$575.00**

Husky Motor Oil, can, 1-qt, yellow, EX, A1...........**$550.00**

Husky Quality Controlled Transmission Oil, can, 1-gal (Imperial), rectangular, tall, pour spout with screw lid, EX, A1...**$100.00**

Hutchinson's Ice Cream, calendar, 1942, paper, metal strips, 29", incomplete, VG, A8............................**$50.00**

Huts' Creamilk, thermometer, porcelain, white milk bottle with gauge/advertising in black on black ground, 38", VG, A2 ....**$330.00**

Huyler's Chocolate, sign, flange, die-cut image of polar bear cub drinking soda from oversized glass atop Soda Fountain sign, 21x12", G, A9 ....**$2,700.00**

Huyler's Cocoa, tin, 8-oz, square with round screw lid, 2-color, EX, A3 ....**$60.00**

Huyler's Cocoa or Chocolate, sign, cardboard hanger, little girl serving cocoa to her dolls, framed, 18x15", VG, A6 ....**$200.00**

Huyler's Imperials Gum, container, aluminum, round, embossed, EX+, A16...**$55.00**

Hy-Klas Coffee, can, 1-lb, key-wind lid, black/white on red, yellow trim, EX+, A3 ....**$35.00**

Hy-Land Kids, crate label, apple, 2 redheaded boys harvesting apples, Washington, EX, D3 ....**$3.00**

Hy-Quality Coffee, see Roth's

Hy-Tone, crate label, apple, small peacock/bright shaded lettering, EX, D3...**$5.00**

Hy-Vee Coffee, can, 1-lb, key-wind lid, red/white/blue, NM+, A18...**$85.00**

Hygeia Coffee, can, 1-lb, key-wind lid, yellow/green, EX, A18...**$65.00**

Hyroler Whiskey/Louis J Adler Co, tip tray, round, dapper man holding top hat/cane, lettered rim, C Shonk litho, 4" dia, EX-NM, A6/A7, from $70 to........................**$100.00**

Hyvis Motor Oil, sign, porcelain, Super Refined Pure Pennsylvania/Permit No 4, white/red/yellow on black, 2-sided, 17x26", NM+ (NOS), A6 ....**$550.00**

⮾ I ⮾

Ibex Pears, can label, wild goat on summit/pear, M, D5 .**$40.00**

IBP Old Indian Herb Laxative & Base Ball Liniment, sign, porcelain, We Sell..., product boxes flank red/black lettering on yellow, 12x26", EX, A6 ....**$750.00**

Icee, bank, Icee Bear figure seated, vinyl, M, D20.....**$45.00**

Idaho Power Co, see Reddy Kilowatt (Idaho Power Co)

Ide Shirts, sign, cardboard stand-up, New Ideas In.../Pre-Shrunk Collars, man buttoning cuff, green ground, 1930s, 17x14", EX, A24...**$70.00**

Ide Shirts, store card, cardboard, Eyed With Admiration/Shirts Of Unusual Character..., inset of man on blue, 1930s, 12x9", EX, A24...**$50.00**

Ideal Alaska Down Bustles, trade card, The Improved Genuine..., lady checking out bustle in mirror, text on reverse, 5x3", EX, A6 ....**$70.00**

Ideal Coffee, can, 1-lb, screw lid, EX, A18.................**$90.00**

Ideal Dog Food, sign, enamel, A Complete 7 Course Meal, dog on die-cut circle at end of ad panel, red/white/blue/yellow, 9x17", EX, A15 ....$150.00

Idle Hour Cut Plug, pocket tin, flat, green, EX, A18...**$65.00**

Idle Moments, cigar box label, inner lid, image of woman, 1907, 6x9", M, D5 ....**$20.00**

Infallible Smokless Powder, sign, linen, pair of ducks landing on marsh, lettering above/below, c 1909, framed, image: 24x18", VG, A9 ....**$1,600.00**

Ing-Rich/Ingram Richardson Mfg Co, ashtray, porcelain, round, Sheet Steel Fabricators/Porcelain Enamelers/name on rim, center 1901-51 logo, 6", EX, A6 ....**$120.00**

Ingersoll Watches, sign, flange, porcelain, die-cut pocket watch, Ingersol Watches on flange, white/yellow/blue, 12x8", EX, A13 ....**$375.00**

Ingersoll Watches, sign, flange, porcelain, die-cut pocket watch, We Have A Reliable Watch For One Dollar/Look For The Name, 17x9", VG, A3.........$220.00

Ingersoll Watches, sign, porcelain, white lettering on blue, 3x24", EX, A13 ....**$140.00**

Inside Quality, crate label, Texas Citrus, black woman in apron & red bandanna, blue ground, La Feria, M, D12......**$10.00**

International, crate label, Washington apple, globe encircled by yellow title on dk blue background, Portland, M, D12 ....**$10.00**

International Clothes, sign, flange, pennant, Perfect Fit-Prompt Delivery/Popular Prices-Best Quality, blue/white, 2-sided, 16x20", VG, A **$150.00**

International Harvester Co, sign, tin, die-cut gasoline engine, 2-sided, 23x16", VG, A7.......................**$1,800.00**

International Harvester Co, watch fob, metal, round, embossed initials framed by wheat wreath, EX, A20 ....**$425.00**

International Louse Killer, tin, round, young girl with product can among chickens, lettering above/below, 7x3" dia, EX+ (unopened), A15...........................**$375.00**

International Tailoring Co, match safe, embossed silver plate, lion in center flanked by Indian/Victorian lady with paint palette, NM, A3 ....**$60.00**

International Triple Diamond Service, sign, porcelain, Triple Diamond Service around logo, red/white/blue/black, 42" dia, VG, A9 ....**$500.00**

International Trucks/Parts Service, sign, porcelain, International Parts Service around blue/white triple-diamond logo, white on red, 42" dia, G, A2 ....**$500.00**

Inver House Rare Scotch Whisky, pen holder, green plastic bottle shape with paper label, black pen, 8", NOS, A6 ....**$90.00**

Invincible Motor Insurance, sign, tin, ...By Installments, Invincible Policies Limited, shows boat shining light on car, green ground, 8x10", EX+, A1 ....**$300.00**

Invincible Schley, cigar box labels, 2-pc set, embellished image of Commander Schley, Schmidt & Co litho #1188/1189, VG/EX, A5..............................**$180.00**

Iowa Beer/JB Hahn, Carroll, Iowa, drinking glass, shell, clear, applied white lettering/rooster logo, Wholesale Retail..., 3½", NM, A8 ....**$160.00**

Iris Coffee, can, 1-lb, key-wind lid, black/red, Pot & Percolator, VG+, A3 ....**$65.00**

Iris Coffee, can, 1-lb, key-wind lid, brown, 5¢ Off Regular Price, EX, A3 ....**$50.00**

Iron City Beer, display, customer in top hat conversing with bartender, chalkware, Beer At Its Best Since 1861, 10x15x3", VG, A19 ....**$50.00**

Iron City Beer, sign, neon, round, red/white, 1950s, EX, A19 ....**$175.00**

Ironmaster, cigar box label, outer, octagonal, portrait of man seated, Geo L Schlegel litho, EX, A5 ....**$75.00**

Iroquois Beer, sign, cardboard, Catch'um Fresh...With Iri/Set 'Em Up Iri, Indian in canoe pulling bottle, 1960s, 11x22", NM, A19..**$30.00**

Iroquois Beer/Ale, clock, round, light-up, 12-3-6-9 around Indian head in profile above name on wood-grain ground, 1950s, 15", NM, A19 ....**$640.00**

Iroquois Brewing Co, drinking glass, shell, etched, Indian head logo in red-orange, 3½", EX+, A8...............**$50.00**

Iroquois Indian Head Beer & Ale, tray, round, Indian in profile, lettering above/below, plain rim, 13" dia, EX, A6 ....$85.00

Irving Cigars, spittoon, white porcelain with black Irving Cigar lettered on rim with oval logo/decoration, G, A2 ....**$185.00**

Isbrandsten Coffee, can, 1-lb, key-wind, EX, A3 .....**$85.00**

Isbrandsten Coffee, can, 1-lb, key-wind, NM (full), A3 .**$200.00**

Island Brand, crate label, California pear, trees/birds, Grand Island, M, D12 ....**$30.00**

Ithaca Guns catalog, The New Ithaca Gun, 1932, 21 pgs, 8x14", EX+, A3 ....**$125.00**

Ithaca Guns, sign, paper, Extinct Passenger Pigeon, ...Out Shoot Them All/Authorized Agent below, metal strips, 28x17", VG+, A9 ....**$650.00**

Ithaca Guns, sign, paper, Extinct Passenger Pigeons, Ithaca Guns (gun graphic) below, framed, 27x19", VG, A7 ....**$500.00**

Ivory Soap, sign, cardboard, Purity, It Floats lettered on wood frame, 34x26", VG, A7 ....**$450.00**

Ivory Soap, sign, paper/linen, ...It Floats, white lettering on blue, 17x57", EX, A6.....................................**$40.00**

Ivory Soap, sign, porcelain, white block lettering on blue, 3x21", NOS, A6 ....**$225.00**

Ivory Soap, sign, tin, die-stamped, ...99 44/100 Per Cent Pure, green/gold/brown, 9x11", EX (NOS), A6..**$200.00**

IW Harper Whiskey, sign, canvas, The Parting Gift, 1912, wood frame, 34x46", EX, A7 ....$1,500.00

IW Harper Whiskey, sign, Vitrolite, dog in cabin, 1909, framed, 28x22", EX-NM, A7/A18, from $1,600 to $1,850.00

Izaak Walton Cigars, tin, round, slip lid, 2 For 5¢, EX, A18 ....$100.00

J

J Hauenstein Brewing Co, drinking glass, shell, etched, Celebrated Hermann's Brau, 4", NM, A8 ....$335.00

J Monroe Taylors Soda, box, 112-lb, round, cardboard sides with wood top/bottom, paper label inside top, 20x14" dia, EX, A6 ....$130.00

J&P Coats Best Six Cord Spool Cotton, cabinet, wood, slanted vinyl desk top with glass ink well, 4 side-by-side drawers with metal knobs, 11x30x21", VG, A6.....................$375.00

J&P Coats Spool Cotton, sign, cardboard, Gulliver & The Liliputations, framed, 22x27", G-EX, A7/A9, from $175 to $300.00

J&P Coats Spool Cotton, sign, paper, J&P Coats' Spool Cotton Is Strong!, couple fishing, black/white, framed, image: 17x22", G, A9...$275.00

J&P Coats Spool Cotton Thread, cabinet, wood, 2 glass panels/2 roll-top panels, 23x20x16", EX, A9 ...$1,300.00

JA McKechine Brewing Co Ales & Lager, sign, tin, name above round framed image of sheaf of grain, Ales & Lager lettered on mantel below, 24x17", VG, A6 ....$300.00

Jack Daniels, toy train set, 1 of 500 made, custom-made Old No 7 Engine/barrelcar/caboose/hobos/transformer/track, MIB, A8...$60.00

Jack Sanitary Barber Shop, sign, paper, Special Hair Cut, image of draped nude removing her shoes, ca late 1890s, 20x14", NM+, A3...$325.00

Jack Sprat Chili Con Carne, can label, M, D5 ....$25.00

Jack Sprat Coffee, can, 1-lb, key-wind lid, EX+, A3/A18.$300.00

Jack Sprat Cream of Tartar, container, 1½-oz, EX, A3..$40.00

Jack Sprat Quick Cooking Rolled Oats, container, 3-lb, cardboard, yellow, EX+, A3 ....$120.00

Jack Sprat Tea, tin, 8-oz, EX+, A3 ....$30.00

Jackie Coogan, see also Kid Kandy

Jackie Coogan Salted Almonds, can, 10-lb, VG+, A18.$125.00

Jackie Coogan Salted Nut Meats, tin, round, pry lid, 7", VG, A6...$40.00

Jackson Grocer, buggy seat, wood, When In Doubt Buy Of Jackson Grocer, 26x22x40", VG, A9.................$1,870.00

Jackson's Best Chewing Tobacco/CA Jackson & Co, sign, cardboard, man looking in store window while black boy bites plug of tobacco, 15x12", EX+, A18 ..$365.00

Jacob Ruppert Beer-Ale, tray, oval, hand-held frothy mugs toasting, wood-grain ground, 14x17", EX, A6......$65.00

Jacob Ruppert Knickerbocker Beer, sign, light-up, white glass, gold metal frame with rounded corners, New York's Famous Knickerbocker Beer, 11x25", EX, A6.......$140.00

Jacob Ruppert Lager Beer, sign, reverse glass, round, lettering on blue around eagle/flags atop barrel, framed, 27" dia, VG, A7 ....$500.00

Jacob Ruppert's Knickerbocker Beer, sign, tin, oval image of colonial man holding up glass in pub, rectangular border, beveled, c 1909, 18x15", G, A8 ....$80.00

Jacob Ruppert's Rose Bud, tray, oval, roses/logo on yellow, plain rim with gold trim, Meek Co litho, 1907, 17", EX, A8 ....$340.00

Jaguar Sales & Service, sign, porcelain, die-cut emblem, logo/lettering on maroon, 1-sided, 20x19" (rare smaller size), EX, A6....................................$1,300.00

Jaguar Sales & Service, sign, porcelain, die-cut emblem, logo/lettering on maroon, 2-sided, 41x39", EX, A2.........$1,200.00

Jam-Boy Steel Cut Coffee, can, 1-lb, paper label, EX+, A15 ....$350.00

Janesville Clothing Co, thermometer, wood, advertising above gauge on dk blue, gold border, vertical, curved corners, 15", EX+, A3...$65.00

Janke & Weise Bar, Office & Store Fixtures, tip tray, round, Compliments Of..., lettering on wood-grain ground, black/gold band, gold rim, EX+, A3 ....$18.00

Jano, cigar box label, inner lid, woman ripping through deep red wall, 6x9", M, D5...$30.00

Jap Rose, sign, cardboard, young Japanese girl in kimono bathing her doll in tub by glowing paper lantern, 19x17", restored, A2...$100.00

Jap Rose Soap, door push plate, porcelain, Come In above name, Toilet & Bath below, white/yellow/black, 8x4", EX, A7..$475.00

Jap Rose Soap, postcard, This Card Is Worth 10¢ At Your Dealer's/One Cake Jap Rose Free, oval image of girl/product, NM, D26 ....$15.00

Jap Rose Soap/Jas S Kirk & Co, display box, tin, hinged lid, For The Toilet & Bath/50 Pieces, yellow, trademark image, 8x9x14", EX, A3 ....$165.00

Jap Rose Toilet Talcum Powder, tin, oval, oval photo image of Japanese lady, gold trim, 4½", EX, A3 ....$75.00

Jap Rose Toilet Talcum Powder, tin, sample, EX+, A3 ..$100.00

Japp's Hair Rejuvenator, sign/display samples, tin/cardboard, hair samples surrounded by oval portraits/advertising, ca 1910, 10x13", EX, A3 ....$135.00

Jas S Kirk & Co, sign, cardboard, Save...Wrappers/They Are Valuable To You!, shows charging cavalry, framed, 24x12", EX, A7 ....$650.00

Jas S Kirk & Co's Soap, sign, paper, Midshipmite, sailor boy standing on deck, framed, 26x13", VG, A9 ....$300.00

Java Coffee Mills, pocket mirror, oval, For Quality Coffee..., white on blue, EX, A3 ....$40.00

Jayne's (Dr D) Family Medicines, sign, paperboard hanger, building (close-up exterior view), 17x13", EX, A3..$150.00

Jayne's Hair Tonic, sign, paperboard hanger, buildings above ladies admiring themselves, advertising text in center, 1880s, 15x12", EX, A3 ....$150.00

JB Ford Co, sign, tin, Chief Wyandotte shooting bow/arrow, name on self-frame, 39x29", G, A9 ....$400.00

JB Pace Tobacco Co's Scroll Cut, tin, rectangular, rounded corners, smaller than 4x6" size, EX+, A18 ....$45.00

JC Hoagland Jeweler, sign, cardboard, bust image of queen wearing jeweled crown on die-cut embossed peach, 10x10", NM, A3 ....$55.00

JC Stevens/Old Judson, match holder, tin, EX-EX+, A3, from $225 to..$300.00

JC Stevens/Old Judson, match holder, tin, G+, A9 ..$125.00

Jefferson Standard Life Insurance Co, clock, round light-up, profile bust image, NM, A13 ....$140.00

Jefferson Union Glass Fuses, display, cardboard, Driving Blind?..., man driving blindfolded, graphics both sides/shelves in back, 10x8x4", VG+, A3..............$40.00

Jell-O, hand puppet, Mr Wiggle, red rubber, 1966, 6", M, D27 ....$175.00

Jell-O, hand puppet, Sweet Tooth Sam, vinyl/cloth, 1960s, EX, D20 ....$100.00

Jell-O, recipe book, America's Most Famous Dessert, illustrations by Maxfield Parrish, 5x6", EX+, A3 ....$60.00

Jenney Aero Gasoline, tip tray, round, cars/products listed around logo, 4" dia, NM, A6................................$200.00

Jenney Auto Oil Gasoline/Gillette, safety razor in case, Gillette brass razor in black case with Jenney logo/Gillette engraved in gold tone, 2x4", EX, A2....................$140.00

Jenney Gasoline, sign, porcelain, Jenney Gasoline in black raised lettering with red J & G on white, blue self-frame, 36x60", EX+, A2 ....$470.00

Jenney Lubrication Service, wall rack, porcelain panel with plated hangers for lubrication guns/bottles/etc, black on white, 70x35", EX, A2 ....$600.00

Jenney Solvenized Hy-Power, gas globe lens, black/orange silhouette image of refinery, 13½", rare, EX, A6 ....$650.00

Jenney Solvenoil, key tag, oil-can shape, 2", M, A24..$10.00

Jenney Stations/Jenny Mfg Co, playing cards, complete, VG (original box), A2..$85.00

Jergens Crushed Rose, tin, oval image of roses, EX, A18 ....$155.00

Jergens Miss Dainty Talcum, tin, 4 heads surround lettering, gold trim, EX+, A3 ....$120.00

Jergens Oriental Talcum Powder, tin, round, 4½", EX+, A18..$60.00

Jersey Creme, sign, cardboard, die-cut straight-sided bottle, framed, 14x6", VG, A6..$100.00

Jersey Creme, sign, cardboard die-cut hanger, 2 girls in swing reading Jersey Creme ad, VG+, A3............$45.00

Jersey Creme, tray, round, profile of lady in bonnet, red background, lettered/decorated rim, C Shonk litho, 12" dia, VG, A9..$200.00

Jersey Ice Cream, sign, porcelain, Everybody Loves Jersey, cow above name/ice-cream plate on yellow, 2-sided, 28x20", EX+/G+, A3..$120.00

Jersey Lane Ice Cream/Lorain Creamery, sign, porcelain, red/green lettering on white emblem, green ground, 2-sided, 20x28", NM+, A1 ....$350.00

Jesse Moore's Whiskey, sign, tin, Kentucky's Purest & Best Production, Uncle Sam/Miss Liberty/black boy above Earth, embossed, 31x22", VG, A7 ..$10,000.00

Jests, thermometer, porcelain, mascot's head/name above yellow gauge/product pack, blue ground, 36x8", EX+, A13...$550.00

Jewel Extra Fancy Darjeeling Blend Tea, tin, 4-oz, slip lid, pictures black tea set, NM+, A3............................$45.00

Jewel of Virginia, tin, curved corners, green, VG+, A3 .$25.00

Jewel of Virginia, tin, square corners, green, EX, A18 .$50.00

Jewel Shop, pocket mirror, oval, celluloid, decorative border around advertising, 2x4", VG, A6 ....$60.00

Jewel T, see also Royal Jewel Coffee

Jewel T Allspice, tin, orange, EX+, A3 ....$60.00

Jewel T Baking Powder (Continuous Action), tin, 1-lb, round, screw lid, white on red, gold top band, EX+, A3 ....$30.00

Jewel T Cocoa, tin, 1-lb, brown, Chocolate Rich! EX, A3 .$85.00

Jewel T Cocoa (Pure) tin, 1-lb, yellow, Serve Cocoa More Often!, EX, A3 ....$25.00

Jewel T Coffee (Jewel Blend), box, 1½-lb, cardboard, brown, NM+ (full), A3 ....$365.00

Jewel T Coffee (West Blend), can, 2-lb, brown, bell logo, no lid o/w EX, A3..$32.00

Jewel T Ginger, tin, yellow-orange, gold bands top/bottom, NM, A3...$65.00

Jewel T Ground Mustard, tin, 5-oz, white, gold bands top/bottom, EX, A3...$40.00

Jewel T Instant Cocoa Mix, tin, 12-oz, yellow, NM+ (full), A3..$75.00

Jewel T Nutmeg, tin, yellow, gold bands top/bottom, EX+, A3..$75.00

Jewel Tea Co, calendar, 1937, Going To Town, 2 children seated on old wagon seat in sunny field, 13x8", EX+, A3..$28.00

Jewel Tea Co, calendar, 1947, Coffee & Grocery Specialists, farm image of boy with colt/girl on work horse, 13x8", EX, A3..$25.00

Jewel Tea Co, catalog, 1955, Spring/Summer, fashions/general merchandise, 100 pgs, EX, D17..........................$25.00

JF Millemann's & Co Eagle Brand Ham, sign, paper, eagle atop product with lettering all around, wood frame, image: 17x13", VG+, A9 ....$150.00

JG Davis Co's Granite Flour, bill hook, Don't Forget To Order JG Davis Co's Granite Flour lettered on black square panel with wire hook, 6", EX, A15 ...$200.00

JG Dill's, see Dill's

JI Case Threshing Machine Co, sign, paper, communal farm scene with mountains beyond, Orcutt Co litho, wood frame, image: 13x21", Fair, A9 ....$50.00

Jim-Jim, cigar box label, inner lid, image of drunk returning home, Schumacher & Ettlinger litho, 1880s, EX, A5 .$125.00

JN Adams & Co, sign, tin hanger, Beauty & The Beast, curled corners, American Art Works, c 1911, 14x14", EX, A2 ...$770.00

Jno T Barbee Distillers, art plate, gold decoration on rim around 2 ladies greeting man seated by log cabin distillery, EX+, A8..$200.00

Jocialidad, cigar box label, sample, 3 cavaliers at table, Schumacher & Ettlinger litho #6482, 1884, VG, A5.......$50.00

Jockey Club Lager Beer/Hemrich Brewing Co, sign, aluminum hanger, oval, lettering on band around horse head, blue/gold, embossed, 12", VG+, A8.........$165.00

Joe Di Maggio's Restaurant, postcard, 3 images of famous baseball player above inset of restaurant, linen, Curt Teich, NM, D26..$175.00

Joe Wheeler Cigars, box, tin, inner lid paper label intact, EX+, A3...$100.00

Joe Wright, cigar box label, inner lid, man wearing Turkish costume, 6x9", M, D5 ....$35.00

John Annear & Co's Sauce-Salad Dressing, sign, paper, multiple images with lettering, Wells & Hope Co/address lower left-hand corner, 22x16", VG, A9 ....**$300.00**

John Bardenheier Wine & Liqour Co, sign, tin, oval, Take A Little 'Progress Rye' Papa/It Will Steady Your Nerves, couple, raised self-frame, 20x23", VG, A7 ....**$550.00**

John Bardenheier Wine & Liqour Co, sign, tin, oval, We Owe Our Perfect Health To Perfection Whiskey, 2 gents toasting, barrel self-frame, 21x26", EX, A7.........**$800.00**

John Deere, bank, tin, green fuel barrel shape, notes company's 1937 centennial, 3½", EX, A2.....................**$85.00**

John Deere, calendar, 1944, paper, 2 children in front of John Deere store above proprietor's name, 16x11", complete, EX, A6................................$60.00

John Deere, clock, round, light-up, glass front, metal frame, Quality Farm Equipment, green/yellow logo, 15" dia, NM, A6...**$600.00**

John Deere, sign, paper, farmer on 3-horse plow in field, dog barking at city man, black/white, 21x27", G, A9..**$175.00**

John Deere, watch fob, cast-bronze disk, embossed wagon-train scene, bust of John Deere on back, He Gave The World..., 1", NM+, A1..**$80.00**

John Drew 5¢ Cigar, sign, tin, product name above/below profile image of John Drew, self-framed, 26x16", G, A9 ....**$250.00**

John Gilbert Jr Co, tip tray, rectangle, interior of country store, white ornate frame, 1903, 4x7", EX+, A3...$25.00

John Graf's Weiss Beer, drinking glass, heavy glass with diamond design, etched logo, 1886, 5½", NM, A8...**$300.00**

John Hauck Brewing Co, match safe, tin, EX, A8....**$85.00**

John Hauenstein Brewing Co Hermanns Brau, drinking glass, shell, etched statue in wreath, 4", NM, A8 .**$335.00**

John Holland Fountain & Stylographic Pen Ink, label, paper, 2 black crossed pens & white/black text on red ground, white border, 3x4", EX, A3 ....**$17.00**

John J Clark's Spool Cotton, spool cabinet, oak, 2-drawer with pop-up desk top, 12x20x16", VG, A9.........**$600.00**

John J Clark's Spool Cotton, see also Clark's

John Miller & Co, see Miller's Game Cock Rye

John Moffats Phoenix Bitters, bottle, rectangular with embossed lettering, pre-1900, 5", EX, A2............**$150.00**

John P Squire & Co, see Squire's

John Ruskin Cigars, sign, tin, name in red above large smoking cigar, Best & Biggest on black oval, yellow ground, embossed, 9x30", NM+, A1...................**$180.00**

John Ruskin 5¢ Cigars, tin, vertical box, curved corners, EX+, A18 ....$200.00

John W Masury & Son, see also Masury's

John W Masury & Son Pure Linseed Oil House Paints, sign, tin, houses in landscape behind wall depicting colors available, Senteene & Green litho, framed, 19x27", VG, A9 ....**$250.00**

John Walter & Co, tip tray, round, lettering on rim around lady in profile, 1907, EX, A8................................**$130.00**

John Weisert's 54 Smoking Tobacco, pocket tin, vertical, yellow, EX (sealed), A15......................................**$550.00**

John's Trade Mark Mixture, pocket tin, vertical, paper label, short, VG, A3 ....**$25.00**

Johnson & Johnson (Johnson's) Toilet & Baby Powder, sign, cardboard trifold, A World Wide Service For Babies, 3 babies of the world with product cans, 26x41", VG, A9 ....**$500.00**

Johnson & Johnson Baby Needs, sign, cardboard, curved corners, oval decal of baby, blue lettering on white, blue border, 7x32", EX, A6 ....**$70.00**

Johnson & Johnson Bunion Pads, display case, 2-tone blue tin with glass panel, slanted front with graphics, shelves in back, 14x7x14", G, A2 ....**$135.00**

Johnson & Johnson Red Cross Cotton, sign, cardboard, From Start To Finish, black workers in cotton field, 1894, framed, 24x33", VG, A7........................**$750.00**

Johnson Bros General Merchandise, calendar, 1922, Sunshine Girl, by Ward Traver, complete, EX+, A3....**$50.00**

Johnson Halters, display horse head, papier mache, black, complete with halter/lead/collar, embossed name, 21x23x10", EX+, A3 ....**$425.00**

Johnson Outboard Motors, sign, tin, name above boat with Pegasus design above dealer name, white/black/red, embossed, 1930s, 14x20", NM, A15...................**$425.00**

Johnson's Log Cabin Coffee, store bin, tin, cabin shape, name on roof, 28x24x18", EX+, A3..................**$2,750.00**

Johnson's Peacemaker Coffee, sign, cardboard, cabin shape, framed, 14x14", EX+, A3 ....**$450.00**

Johnson's Peacemaker Coffee, store bin, tin, cabin shape, name on roof, calendar dated 1915, 25x24x18", EX, A6 ....$1,100.00

Jolly Bachelor, cigar box label, outer, man in smoking jacket, 4½x4½", EX, D5 ....$30.00

Jolly Sport, cigar box labels, 2-pc set, boy smoking cigar in cart pulled by dog, Witsch & Schmitt & Co litho #677/678, VG/EX, A5 ....$135.00

Jolly Time Hulless Pop Corn, can, red/white/blue, bowl of popcorn, NM, A3 ....$70.00

Jolly Time Hulless Pop Corn, can, red/white/blue, bowl of popcorn, VG+ (full), A18 ....$50.00

Jolly Time Hulless Pop Corn, pail, 1-lb, tin, red, boy/girl, no lid o/w VG+, A3 ....$45.00

Jolly Time White Pop Corn, can, white/red on blue, flag logo, VG+ (full), A3 ....$33.00

Jool Julep, sherbet glasses, orange tulip-like petals around clear glass stemmed cups, black lettering, NM, A13, pair $150.00

Jordan Beer, label, ½-gal, Schultz & Hilgers Jordan Brewery/Jordan MN, IRTP/U-type permit #, 1933-36, EX, A10 ....$63.00

Jordan's Meat Products, display figure, pig in overalls/hat, composition, 11", G, A9 ....$250.00

Jordan's Pure Spices/Ground Sage, tin, 1-oz, rectangular, red/white ground, NM, A3 ....$25.00

Jos Dixon Crucible Co, print, The Protectors, girl holding lamb/smiling at dog, metal strips, ca 1898, 20x10", VG, A3 ....$100.00

Jos Schlitz Brewing Co, see Schlitz

Jos Stoeckle Brewing Co/Diamond State Brewery, sign, tin, aerial view of brewery with circle insets of 2 gentlemen, self-framed, 26x37", G, A7 ....$1,200.00

Joseph Glennons New Brewery, art plate, Lenore, decorative leaf border, Meek Co, c 1907, 10" dia, VG, A9 ....$100.00

Josh Giddings, cigar box label, inner lid, signer of the Constitution, 1908, 6x9", M, D5 ....$25.00

Joss' Mustard, sign, cardboard, Try.../Has No Equal.../Sold Here, blue text within decorative border on yellow ground, 14x10", EX, A3 ....$55.00

JP Primley's California Fruit & Pepsin Chewing Gum, display case, wood frame/bottom, curved-glass front with etched lettering, 10x12x20", G+, A9 ....$550.00

JPK/James P Keegan Distributor, cigar box label, inner lid, initials on emblem in garden, American litho #662, 1908, VG, A5 ....$50.00

Juanita Flour, calendar, trademark image of boy holding 2 loaves of bread sitting on barrel flanked by 2 sacks of flour, 10x8", VG, A3 ....$60.00

Juicy Jems, crate label, Washington apple, diamond upper left, red apple/title on ribbon, Heller, Wenatchee, M, D12 ....$25.00

Jule Carrs Cut Plug, tin, rectangular, square corners, VG+, A18 ....$60.00

Julep, sign, tin, Drink Julep/Six Delicious Flavors, bottle at left on white inset, red ground, 27x19", VG+, D30 ....$125.00

Jumbo Brand Peanut Butter, measuring cup, tin, 12-oz, with handle, graphics on green, VG+, A15 ....$1,100.00

Jumbo Brand Peanut Butter, pail, 1-lb, gold, blue lettering/elephant, VG, A2 ....$600.00

Jung Brewing Co Red Heart Brand, drinking glass, shell, etched with red heart, 3½", NM, A8 ....$700.00

Junge's Bread, door plate, porcelain, ...For Better Health, blue on yellow, pointed ends, 9x4", VG-M, A6/A3, from $60 to $180.00

Juno Tumeric, tin, red, oval image of goddess, NM, A3 ....$50.00

Just On Time, cigar box, busy train scene against cityscape, 1878 revenue stamp, VG, A5 ....$300.00

Just Suits Cut Plug, lunch box, red, EX+, A18 ....$75.00

Just Suits Cut Plug, tin, horizontal box, curved corners, red, 4x6", VG+, A18 ....$40.00

Just Suits Cut Plug, tin, round, smaller round slip lid, red, 5" dia, VG-EX+, A3/A7, from $70 to $150.00

Just the Thing!/Maclin, Zimmer, McGill Tobacco Co, caddy label, vertical, street urchin offering tobacco plug to Victorian Jim Dandy, Hoen litho, approx: 14x7", NM+, A3 ....$55.00

Justrite 5¢ Cigar, tin, round, slip lid, metallic gold on woodgrain, EX+, A3 ....$25.00

JW Beardsley's Sons, sign, paper, Our Specialties, name/comical vignettes around oval fishing scene, framed, image: 22x14", G, A9 ....$250.00

JWM Fields Champion Whiskey, sign, tin, lady holding up tray with bottle against draped background, Meek & Beach litho, framed, image: 27x19", G, A9........**$500.00**

❧ K ❧

K Cough Drops, tin, square, curved corners, yellow, Somers Bros, pre-1901, 2½", NM, A18 ....**$50.00**

Kabo Bust Perfector, display bust form on pedestal stand, 28", VG, A9 ....**$500.00**

Kaffee Hag, can, 1-lb, tall, EX+, A3 ....**$60.00**

Kaier's Light Lager Special Beer, can, cone top, 12-oz, M, A8 ....**$80.00**

Kaiser-Frazer, sign, neon/porcelain, name on Deco housing, 2-sided, 42x77x10", NM+ (NOS), A6 ....**$1,400.00**

Kaiser-Frazer Lustur Seal, sign, glass light-up flasher, Your Car's Beauty Treatment, blue ribbon seal, red/blue lettering on black, 10x16", VG, A1 ....**$80.00**

Kake Kan Koffee, see Petring's

Kamo Peanut Butter, can, 1-lb, pry lid, white, image of duck in center, NM, A3.................................$1,900.00

Kamo Shrimp, can label, mallard duck on water, 1923, EX, D5 ....**$30.00**

Kamo Tyme, tin, oval image of duck framed by leaves, VG+, A3...**$110.00**

Kansas City Breweries, pocket mirror, rectangular, EX, A8 ....**$120.00**

Kar-A-Van Coffee, can, 1-lb, pry lid, tall, EX, A3 ......**$30.00**

Kar-A-Van Famous Coffee, can, 1-lb, snap lid, yellow with black bands, tall, EX, A18 ....**$145.00**

Kar-A-Van Famous Coffee, can, 1-lb, snap top, all yellow, EX+, A18..**$200.00**

Karvet Bladtobak/JL Tiedemann, Christinia, tin, rectangular, square corners, blue/metallic gold, EX, A3 ...**$140.00**

KASCO Feeds, scale, metal with debossed lettering, Weigh The Milk/Weigh The Feed, 16x5", EX, A6....................**$130.00**

Katz Jumbo Salted Peanuts, canister, 1-lb, slip lid, yellow, EX+, A18..**$100.00**

Kavanaugh's Tea, tin, 1-lb, square, round pry lid, mother at window sipping tea, girl playing with doll, green/red, 1913, 6", EX+, A15 ....**$500.00**

Kaweah Maid, crate label, California lemon, pretty Indian girl, Lemon Cove, EX-NM, D3/D12, from $5 to ...**$10.00**

Kaweah RiverBelle, crate label, California orange, orange/groves/mountains/mission, Lemon Cove, M, D12..**$10.00**

Kayo, menu board, tin, Tops In Taste/Kayo/It's Real Chocolate Flavor, Kayo/bottle on yellow above blackboard, 27x14", VG, A6..**$100.00**

Kayo, sign, tin, Delightful/Refreshing, bottle in center, script lettering above/below, yellow ground, hanger, 12x4", EX, A13...**$275.00**

Kayo, sign, tin, Drink Kayo In Bottles/The Milky Chocolate Malted Drink/When Your Thirsty.., bottle at left, 9x20", VG+-EX+, D30/A1, from $75 to...........................**$150.00**

Kayo, sign, tin, Tops In Taste.../It's Real Chocolate Flavor, Kayo running with bottle, yellow/blue, 1930s, 24x14", EX, A24 ....$425.00

Kayo, sign, tin, Tops In Taste/...It's Real Chocolate Flavor, Kayo at left pointing to phrase/bottle, horizontal, VG, D34 ....**$300.00**

KC 25¢ Baking Powder, pocket mirror, round, Pure/Healthful/And Successful lettered around image of can on black ground, red border, EX, A3 ....**$500.00**

Keebler, alarm clock, round, footed, 2 bells on top, Keebler Elf in center, red numbers, 1980, 6", working, EX+, A14 ....**$20.00**

Keebler, cap, baseball type, Keebler Elf embroidered in front, NM, D24 ....**$7.00**

Keebler, doll, Keebler Elf, rubber, 6½", NM, A14 ......**$18.00**

Keely Stove Co, catalog, 1926, Columbian Kitchen Stoves & Furnaces, Ranges, 216 pgs, EX, D17 ....**$100.00**

Keen Kutter, calendar, 1935, die-cut cardboard axe head with image of 2 hunting dogs on hillside, 17x12", complete, NM+, A3 ....$120.00

Keen Kutter, calendar, 1940, cardboard, winter cabin by stream framed by open scissors at bottom, 17x10", complete, EX+, A13 ....$50.00

Keen Kutter, display case, wood box (flat), paper litho ad on inside of hinged lid, with 6 forks/6 knives, EX, A6 .**$110.00**

Keller's Inks/Musilage/Paste/Sealing Wax, crock, stoneware, straight-sided with rolled lip on shoulder, raised bands top/bottom, 8½x6½" dia, VG, A6 ....**$50.00**

Kellogg Iron Works, calendar, 1907, embossed stand-up, caricature images of 4 men with small pad at left, 8x12", NM+, A13 ....**$130.00**

Kellogg's, bank, Milton The Toaster, vinyl, Pop Tarts, 1970s, rare, MIB, D20 ....**$165.00**

Kellogg's, blotter, Toasted Corn Flakes, ...The Original.../The Best Liked.../In The Waxtite Package, boy saluting, 3x6", EX, A6 ....**$25.00**

Kellogg's, booklet, Fun & Games, #2/#4/#5, paper, Corny Snaps, 1978, M (original envelope), D1, each......**$20.00**

Kellogg's, booklet, Fun & Games, #2/#4/#5, paper, Corny Snaps, 1978, NM, D1, each **$15.00**

Kellogg's, cereal box, All Bran, Muffin recipe, purple, 1952, VG, D1...**$15.00**

Kellogg's, cereal box, Cocoa Krispies, Snagglepuss (head image), 1963, M, D1 ....**$350.00**

Kellogg's, cereal box, Cocoa Krispies, Snagglepuss (swimming shark), Canadian, 1966, M (flat), D1 ....**$250.00**

Kellogg's, cereal box, Corn Flakes, Huckleberry Hound's 'Win A Pair Of Fords,' contest, 1960, NM (flat), D1........**$65.00**

Kellogg's, cereal box, Corn Flakes, totem mask cutout (designs 1 or 2), Canadian, 1956, M, D1, each **$40.00**

Kellogg's, cereal box, Corn Flakes, Yogi Bear Birthday Party Comic, 1962, EX (full), D1 ....**$480.00**

Kellogg's, cereal box, Corn Flakes, 18-oz, Giant Size, ribbon labeled First/The Original..., Funny Face Cut Outs on back, VG+, A3.......................................**$65.00**

Kellogg's, cereal box, Corn Flakes, 8-oz, WK Kellogg signature, first inner seal wax-tight box, EX+, A3...................**$165.00**

Kellogg's, cereal box, Frosted Flakes, Hokus-Pokus Fun #1 or #4, Tony's mug/bowl/spoon on side, 1966, M (flat), D1, each **$75.00**

Kellogg's, cereal box, Frosted Flakes, Tony the Tiger (swimming shark), Canadian, 1966, M (flat), D1 ....**$250.00**

Kellogg's, cereal box, Fruity Pebbles, Flintmobile, 1972, NM (overwrap), D1...**$95.00**

Kellogg's, cereal box, Fruity Pebbles, pencil holder offer, 1974, NM, D1 ....**$50.00**

Kellogg's, cereal box, Pep, 1-oz, red/white with man in ball cap on yellow circle/large spoon with flakes, 1963, EX+ (unopened), A3..**$25.00**

Kellogg's, cereal box, Raisin Bran, Brink's armored car toy, 1958, EX (unopened), D1 ....**$95.00**

Kellogg's, cereal box, Raisin Bran, Sonic-Wave Gun offer, 1960, M (flat), D1..**$50.00**

Kellogg's, cereal box, Rice Krispies, Dennis the Mennace Treasure Hunt, 1960, VG, D1............................**$20.00**

Kellogg's, cereal box, Rice Krispies, pictures Snap, Woody Woodpecker bike contest, 1960, VG+, D1...........**$45.00**

Kellogg's, cereal box, Rice Krispies, Snap/Crackle/Pop squeeze toys offer, 1976, VG+, D1 ....**$40.00**

Kellogg's, cereal box, Rice Krispies, Snap/Crackle/Pop, 5½-oz, ca 1948, EX+, A3...**$50.00**

Kellogg's, cereal box, Sugar Pops, 8-oz, Jingles (Andy Devine)/horse Joker, Free Inside Airline Pilots Wings, EX+, A3...$90.00

Kellogg's, cereal box, Sugar Smacks, Magic Flute (Dig 'em), NM, D1 ....**$75.00**

Kellogg's, cereal box, Sugar Smacks, Quick Draw McGraw, Road race game, 1964, M (flat), D1 ....**$350.00**

Kellogg's, cereal box, Toasted Corn Flakes, 8-oz, WK Kellogg signature, dated 1911, EX+, A3........$275.00

Kellogg's, decoder, Apple Jacks, plastic, red, 1985, M (on the spure), D1...**$10.00**

Kellogg's, decoder, Apple Jacks, plastic, red, 1985, NM (assembled), NM, D1...**$7.00**

Kellogg's, decoder, Dig 'em, plastic, green, 1985, M (on the spure), D1..**$10.00**

Kellogg's, decoder, Poppy, plastic, green, 1985, NM, D1 ..**$8.00**

Kellogg's, decoder, Poppy, plastic, yellow, 1985, NM (assembled), D1...**$8.00**

Kellogg's, decoder, Poppy, plastic, yellow, M (on the spure), 1985, NM, D1..**$10.00**

Kellogg's, decoder, Toucan Sam, 1985, plastic, red, NM (assembled), D1...**$10.00**

Kellogg's, doll, Pop, squeeze vinyl, 1978, EX, D1.....**$30.00**

Kellogg's, doll, Snap/Crackle/Pop, Rice Krispies Doll, vinyl, jointed, 1984, set of 3, 6¼", MIB, D $175.00

Kellogg's, doll, Tony the Tiger, squeeze vinyl, Product People, 1970s, 9", NM+, D20 ....**$100.00**

Kellogg's, doll, Tony the Tiger, stuffed cloth, 1973, 14", EX, D1 ....**$25.00**

Kellogg's, doll, Toucan Sam, Froot Loops Doll, vinyl, jointed, 1984, 6¼", NM, D20 ....**$45.00**

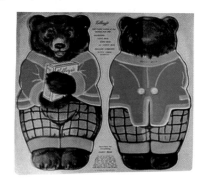

Kellogg's, doll kit, Daddy Bear, uncut cloth, 1925 version, NM, A3 ....$80.00

Kellogg's, doll kit, Dandy The Duck, uncut cloth, 1935, 13x17", M, D25...**$75.00**

Kellogg's, doll kit, Dinky The Dog, uncut cloth, 1935, 13x17", M, D25...**$75.00**

Kellogg's, doll kit, Pop, uncut cloth, 1948, EX (original envelope), A6 ....$40.00

Kellogg's, drinking glass, Toucan Sam, 1977, VG, D1 ...**$20.00**

Kellogg's, figure, Toucan Sam, bendable, 4", NM, A14 .**$28.00**

Kellogg's, figures, Tony the Tiger/Dig 'Em Frog/Big Yells/Toucan Sam, bendable, set of 4, rare, NM, D20 ....**$225.00**

Kellogg's, figurines, Snap/Pop, bisque, Papel, 1984, 4¼", EX, D2, each **$35.00**

Kellogg's, Funscope, Toucan Sam, paper, 1982, M, D1.**$10.00**

Kellogg's, iron-on transfer, Apple Jacks, 1985, 6x8", M (in paper), D1 ....**$15.00**

Kellogg's, iron-on transfer, Dig 'em, 1985, 6x8", M (in paper), D1 ....**$15.00**

Kellogg's, iron-on transfer, Poppy/Pops, 1985, 6x8", M, D1 ....**$15.00**

Kellogg's, jigsaw puzzle, Keep Going With Kellogg's, boy baseball player, 8x6", M (NOS), A1 ....$60.00

Kellogg's, license plate, Ogg, plastic, blue, 1973, 3x6", EX, D1 ....**$20.00**

Kellogg's, license plate, Toucan Sam, plastic, blue, 1973, 3x6", EX, D1 ....**$20.00**

Kellogg's, Magic Color Cards, Snap/Pop, 1933, VG/EX, D13..**$50.00**

Kellogg's, mug (mini), Apple Jack, plastic, with hat lid, 1967, VG+, D1 ....**$50.00**

Kellogg's, mug (mini), Tony the Tiger, plastic, 1965-71, G, D1 ....**$10.00**

Kellogg's, page marker/paper clip, Dig 'em or Toucan Sam, plastic, 1979, NM, D1, each **$15.00**

Kellogg's, page marker/paper clip, Tony the Tiger, plastic, 1979, NM, D1 ....**$3.00**

Kellogg's, patch, Dig 'em, cloth, iron-on, glow-in-the-dark, 1974, M (in paper), D1...**$15.00**

Kellogg's, patch, Snap/Crackle/Pop, head images, cloth, iron-on, glow-in-the-dark, 1974, M (in paper), D1, each .**$12.00**

Kellogg's, patch, Tony the Tiger, cloth, iron-on, glow-in-the-dark, 2", 1974, M (in paper), D1 ....**$12.00**

Kellogg's, patch, Toucan Sam, cloth, iron-on, glow-in-the-dark, 1974, 2", M (in paper), D1 ....**$15.00**

Kellogg's, placemat, Tony the Tiger, vinyl, 1981, EX, D24..**$10.00**

Kellogg's, postcard, Toasted Corn Flakes, My Wife's Gone To The Country..., stylized man at table, WK Kellogg signature, NM, D26..**$35.00**

Kellogg's, postcard, Toasted Corn Flakes, You'd Be Selfish Too, child with cereal box, WK Kellogg signature, vertical, NM, D26 ....**$35.00**

Kellogg's, safe bike booster, Toucan Sam or Sonny Sun, plastic, 1981, M, D1, each **$5.00**

Kellogg's, salesman's advertising booklet, Kellogg's Pep, cardboard, 8 pgs, features Superman/Kellogg's War Planes, 14", EX, A...**$1,450.00**

Kellogg's, salt & pepper shakers, Snap/Pop figures, ceramic, Japan, 1950s, 2½", EX, D25 ....**$85.00**

Kellogg's, sign, canvas, Toasted Corn Flakes, boy saluting with spoon/bowl of cereal, text/box below, 29x19", G+, A3..**$185.00**

Kellogg's, sign, cardboard, die-cut, I Go For Kellogg's Corn Flakes, boy/girl on bicycles, 37", VG, A9 ....**$450.00**

Kellogg's, sign, cardboard, Toasted Corn Flakes...Fine With Berries, Peaches..., girl fixing bowl atop ca 1915 box, 20x11", EX, A3 ....$550.00

Kellogg's, sign, cardboard die-cut stand-up, girl in checked bonnet with corn in husks/box/bowl of Corn Flakes, c 1948, 40", VG, A6 ....$150.00

Kellogg's, Singing Lady Mother Goose Action Circus, EX (with original envelope), A3 ....$45.00

Kellogg's, sticker, Ogg, Don't Litter...I Like A Clean Cave, paper, Cocoa Krispies, 1973, NM, D1 ....$12.00

Kellogg's, sticker, Snap/Crackle/Pop, paper, glow-in-the-dark, 1971, M, D1 ....$10.00

Kellogg's, watch fob, stamped brass, Toasted Corn Flakes box, WK Kellogg signature, rare, VG, A6 ....$135.00

Kellogg's Cranberry Jelly, can label, jelly on plate with knife, M, D5 ....$12.00

Kellogg's Kaffee Hag Coffee, can, 1-lb, key-wind lid, white, NM (unopened), A3 ....$70.00

Kellogg's Kaffee Hag Coffee, can, 1-lb, key-wind lid, white, 97% Caffeine Removed, EX, A3 ....$25.00

Kelly Springfield Tires, magazine ad, Lotta Miles framed by tire above text, framed, 9x7", NM+, A1 ....$20.00

Kelly Springfield Tires, playing cards, Lotta Miles framed by tire, complete, EX (original box), A2 ....$200.00

Kelly Springfield Tires, sign, cardboard, die-cut, lady/dog watching attendant fill car, L Fellows art, 1920s-30s, 38x26", EX, A1 ....$400.00

Kelly Springfield Tires, trade card, The Only Complaints About...Are Their Scarcity, Lotta Miles framed by tire, 4x2", EX, A6 ....$20.00

Kelly Springfield Tires/Cumberland Tire Co, booklet, Smilin' Through By Lotta Miles, group of ladies framed by tire, 1923, 14 pgs, 7x5", EX, A6 ....$30.00

Kelly Tires, cups & saucers, china, set of 6, white with decals/trim, EX+, A6 ....$90.00

Kelly's Famous Flour, calendar, 1910, paper, Aren't You Glad Mammas Use Kelly's Famous? boy/girl at table, framed, 26x21", EX, A7 ....$375.00

Kelso Laundry Co, postcard, Our Yellow Wagons Are In All Parts Of The City, image of delivery wagon on residential street, VG+, D26 ....$35.00

Kemp's Balsam, sign, cardboard hanger, octagonal, framed image of bottle next to box, 2-sided, 11x11", VG, A6 ....$50.00

Ken-L Ration, lamp, plastic, dog's head on base, F&F Mold & Die Co, EX, D25 ....$175.00

Ken-L Ration, sign, porcelain, die-cut dog's head, yellow, 11x15", EX, D22 ....$160.00

Ken-L Ration, thermometer, tin, For Best Results! Feed Your Dog..., blue on white, curved corners, 27x7", EX+, A3 ....$120.00

Ken-L Ration/Ken-L Biskit/Ken-L Meal, door plate, vertical, yellow dog's head above yellow/white lettering on blue, 1950s, NM, A13 ....$425.00

Ken-L Ration/Ken-L Biskit/Ken-L Meal, sign, porcelain, die-cut top of dog's head in yellow above Feed Your Dog The Best... on blue, 1950s, 21x14", NM, A15 ....**$300.00**

Ken-L-Ration, see also Chappel Star Brand Pup-E-Crumbles

Kendall Motor Oil, clock, round, Kendall Superb Motor Oil on red dot, 15" dia, VG, A6 ....**$145.00**

Kendall Motor Oil, clock, round, light-up, derrick/round logo/name, black/white/red on white, 1960, 18" dia, NM, A24..**$150.00**

Kendall Motor Oil, clock, round, neon spinner, 2-finger logo/lettering, 1930s-40s, 20" dia, working, NM, A6......**$1,000.00**

Kendall Motor Oil, license plate attachment, salesman's sample, metal 2-finger hand symbol, anodized red, with pouch, 6x3", EX+, A1 ....**$120.00**

Kendall Motor Oil, thermometer, dial type, degrees around red 2-finger logo above Kendall The 2000 Mile Oil on white, 12" dia, EX, A15 ....**$160.00**

Kendall Penzbest Motor Oils, sign, flange, round, small Pennsylvania logo, red/black on white, 12" dia, VG, A2...**$580.00**

Kendall The 2000 Mile Oil, sign, porcelain, round, hand logo (red outlined) above red lettering on white, black border, 2-sided, 24" dia, VG, A6..........................**$175.00**

Kendall The 2000 Motor Oil, sign, porcelain, can shape, curved, red/white/black, 30x19", NM+ (NOS), A6.............**$1,400.00**

Kendall's Dynamic New Gas, sign, cardboard, die-cut, Meet Polly Power, sexy woman standing by car, 69x37", VG+, A6 ....**$600.00**

Kendalls Motor Oil, clock, round, Kendall's GT-1 Racing Oil, checkered flag logo, EX, D30.......................**$150.00**

Kendlers Chocolate Ice Cream, festoon, #128, Delicious Chocolate Ice Cream/Restore Spent Energy..., die-cut images of ice-cream treats, 9-pc, NM+, A3.........**$165.00**

Kennebec Canoes, model canoe, canvas-covered with gold name on sides, red/black lettering, 63", VG, A9..**$7,750.00**

Kenny's Teas/Coffees, tip tray, round, Drink & Enjoy..., girl with roses, EX, A6 ....**$145.00**

Kensington Kernel Cut, pocket tin, vertical, white/red, 2½", EX, A15 ....**$675.00**

Kentucky Cardinal, crate label, apple, red bird perched on branch, M, D5 ....**$35.00**

Kentucky Club Tobacco, pocket tin, vertical, sample, cut-down, NM, A3 ....**$25.00**

Kentucky Club Tobacco, thermometer, For Real Pipe Smoking Enjoyment at bottom, pipe in ashtray at top, red/white/blue, EX, D30 ....**$125.00**

Kentucky Fried Chicken, bank, Col Sanders figure, plastic, name embossed on base, painted bow tie/stripes on bucket, 10", EX, D25 ....**$50.00**

Kentucky Fried Chicken, salt & pepper shakers, Col Sanders figures, plastic, white with black base (pepper)/white base (salt), M, D25, pair **$55.00**

Kentucky Fried Chicken, salt & pepper shakers, Col/Mrs Sanders figures, plastic, white, Margarot Corp, 1972, 4", EX, D25, pair...**$225.00**

Kentucky Fried Chicken, salt shaker, plastic, Col Sanders bust, white, scarce, M, D25..............................**$75.00**

Kentucky Fried Chicken, tie tac, gold-tone molded head image of Col Sanders with 'diamond chip,' M, D25 .**$65.00**

Kerr's Hotcake Four, container, 2-lb 8-oz, cardboard, red, sailing ship in center, EX+, A3 ....$100.00

Kessler Beer, display, cardboard, Stock Up On.../Montana's Favorite Beer Since 1865 on sign with basket, 19", VG+ (unused), A8..**$30.00**

Kessler Beer, sign, neon/reverse on glass, tube around ...Brewed From Mountain Spring Water, chrome/black frame, 1930s, 12x22", VG+, A8 ....**$765.00**

Kessler Brewery, sign, tin, US Gunboat Helena, self-framed, 20x26", VG-EX, A7, from $450 to **$700.00**

Kessler Export, sign, hanger, die-cut bottle, IRTP, 28", EX+, A8..**$80.00**

Kessler Whiskey, display figure, baseball, composition, 47", scarce, VG, A9 ....**$1,000.00**

Kessler Whiskey, display figure, football, composition, 46", VG, A9 ....**$900.00**

Kessler's Lorelei, banner, saleman's sample, purple velvet emblem on wood dowel, bottom zigzag fringe, ...In Bottles, 11x9", EX, A8 ....**$185.00**

Ketch-Em Salmon Eggs, box label, fisherman in stream, early, M, D12..**$125.00**

Kewpie Twins Shoes, display figure, nude Kewpie doll with jointed arms on beveled base, ...Shoes For Children, 32", VG, A9 ....**$700.00**

Key West Extras, cigar box label, outer, views of cigar production, 4½x4½", M, D5 ....**$40.00**

Key West Havanas, cigar box labels, 2-pc set, embellished draped emblem, A Ward Phelps/Globe Litho Co, EX, A5..**$115.00**

Keynoil Motor Oil, can, ½-gal, rectangular, pour spout with funnel, scalloped grip handle, white eagle logo, red/black on white, EX, A1 ....**$550.00**

Keystone Grease, cup, tin, tapered, lithoed advertising graphics, rolled rim, 2½", EX+, A15 .... **$100.00**

Keystone Manufactures of Agricultural Implements, trade card, Send For Catalogs, people of all nations watch Uncle Sam pointing to wheel showing products, 4x6", EX, A6 .... **$115.00**

Keystone Powerfuel pump sign, porcelain, More Power To You! logo/lettering on gray-blue ground, dated IR½5, 14x12", EX+, A1 .... **$275.00**

Keystone Varnishing, sign, tin, die-cut figure of child in black cloak/umbrella, Waterproof Finish Interior, 1890s, 14x8", rare, EX, A24 .... **$265.00**

Kibbe Bros Cough Drops, tin, sample, green, VG-EX+, A3/A15, from $75 to **$150.00**

Kibbe's Candies, sign, cardboard, girl playing tug of war with dog against a silhouette landscape, framed, 13x9", VG, A2 .... **$80.00**

Kibbe's Peanut Butter, pail, 1-lb, yellow, EX+, A3 ... **$55.00**

Kickapoo Joy Juice, bottle carrier/6 full 10-oz bottles, cardboard, features Lil' Abner/Dog Patch characters, 1965, EX+, A1 .... **$130.00**

Kid Kandy, pail, pictures Jackie Coogan/comical movie scenes, EX+, A15 .... **$230.00**

Kidnegen, sign, paper, lady pouring Kidnegen remedy from old blob-top bottle, arched top, 14x13", G, A9 .... **$50.00**

Kiewel's White Seal, tap knob, ball shape, black with red/black/gold/white metal insert, EX+, A8 .... **$60.00**

Kik, sign, tin, ...30 Oz, 8¢ bottle/full glasses on tray bottom left, white ground, 20x28", EX+, D30 .... **$175.00**

Kilflea Powder, tin, round with cone-top spout, red/black/white, EX (full), A3 .... **$65.00**

Killington Club Coffee, tray, oval, A Lady Of Quality, c 1904, 17x14", EX+, A18 .... **$100.00**

Kim-Bo Cut Plug Tobacco, pocket container, vertical, cardboard with tin top/bottom, NM, A18 ..... $235.00

King Arthur Flour, sign, porcelain, King Arthur on horseback on round center, lettering above/below, white/blue, 36x40", VG, A6 .... **$185.00**

King Arthur Flour, sign, tin, round, King Arthur on horseback, HD Beach Co litho, self-framed, 1900, 26" dia, EX, A24 .... **$700.00**

King Coal, cigar box label, inner lid, king/coal miners in tunnel, 6x9", M, D5 .... **$40.00**

King Cole Coffee, can, ½-lb, key-wind lid, red, EX+, A3 .. **$45.00**

King Cole Coffee, can, ½-lb, pry lid, yellow, EX, A3 . **$200.00**

King Cole Tea, door plate, porcelain, You'll Like The Flavor, white/yellow lettering on black, curved ends, Canada, 14x3", NM, A13 .... **$275.00**

King Cole Tea & Coffee, door plate, porcelain, black/red lettering on yellow, curved ends, Canada, 14x3", EX, A13 .... **$100.00**

King Cole Tea & Coffee, sign, porcelain, key-hole shape, King with steaming cup above lettered panel, 15x9", VG+, A13 .... **$350.00**

King Collar Buttons, display case, oak, glass top, 9x10", VG, A9 .... **$100.00**

King Edward Cigars, thermometer, dial type, round, EX, D34 .... **$265.00**

King Edward Crimp Cut Smoking Tobacco, pocket tin, vertical, VG-NM+, A18, from $250 to **$800.00**

King George Cross Cut, pocket tin, vertical, white, EX+ (from Tindeco sample room), A18 .... **$520.00**

King Koal Stripped Tobacco, lunch box, KK oval logo, VG+, A18 .... **$25.00**

King Midas Flour, string holder, tin, 1908, 20x14", EX-EX+, A7/A6, from $1,300 to $1,400.00

King Midas Tobacco, tin, vertical box, curved corners, VG+, A18 .... **$90.00**

King Mogul Coffee, can, 3-lb, key-wind lid, G+, A3 .. **$50.00**

King Othon Coffee, can, 1-lb, paper label, oval portrait on white, VG, A3 .... **$60.00**

King Polly, cigar box, A Cigar That Talks For Itself, red/black bird, EX, A3 .... **$90.00**

King Tut, crate label, California lemon, Art Nouveau style with glass of lemonade/lemons/blossoms, Santa Barbara, EX, D3 .... **$6.00**

Kings Beer, tray, round, deep rim, Fit For A King/Also For Queens, crown logo in center, 12" dia, EX+, A8 ...... **$100.00**

King's Chocolates, sign, porcelain, emblem, scrolled bracket, Agency...For American Queens, yellow on blue, red trim, 2-sided, 28x20", M, A7 .... **$1,750.00**

King's Herald 5¢ Cigar, store bin, tin, rectangular, 15x20", VG, A7 ....**$500.00**

King's Pure Malt, tip tray, oval, International Exposition, barmaid with tray, EX-EX+, A8/A6, from $60 to **$110.00**

King's Taste Ale, label, 11-oz, Grace Bros Brewing Co/Santa Rosa CA, IRTP or WF, 1933-50, M (traces of paper or scrapes on back), A10 ....**$27.00**

Kingan's Sausage-Lard, pocket mirror, round, Always The Best, oval image of seaman at helm, NM, A3 ......**$70.00**

Kingsbury Ale, sign, tin/cardboard, ...Old & Strong, debossed silver lettering on green/brown diagonal band, beveled, 5x10", VG+, A8 ....**$60.00**

Kingsley Harness Co, calendar, 1900, die-cut cardboard, girl in bonnet/dress, violets bordering scrolled panel, complete, 9x8", NM+, A3 ....**$215.00**

Kip's Big Boy, see Big Boy

Kipling Cut Plug, pocket tin, flat, EX+, A18 ....**$85.00**

Kirk & Co, see Jas S Kirk & Co

Kirk Tomatoes, can label, Indian maiden/tomato, M, D5 ..**$25.00**

Kirk's Flake Soap, door plate, Come In For Kirk's Flake Soup, black/white/red, square corners, 9x4", VG-EX+, A13, from $250 to...**$325.00**

Kis-Me Gum, jar, glass, square canister with beveled edges, round fluted lid, embossed lettering, 11", VG, A9 .**$150.00**

Kis-Me Gum, sign, cardboard die-cut stand-up, I Chew..., 2 ladies consoling each other, text on back, 1890s, 12x13", EX+, A1 ....**$560.00**

Kis-Me Gum, sign, cardboard stand-up, Chew..., bust image of girl in wide-brimmed hat, color, text on back, 1890s, 11x7", VG+, A16 ....**$290.00**

Kis-Me Gum, sign, cardboard stand-up, waist-length image of lady in plumed hat/boas, text on back, color, 1890s, 11x7", EX+, A16 ....**$260.00**

Kist Beverages, calendar, 1946, Get Kist For A Nickel, garden girl admiring orange poppies, 26x14", complete, NM+, A1 ....**$165.00**

Kist Beverages, clock, round, light-up, glass, metal frame, Enjoy Kist Beverages, red/white logo, black numbers, Telechron, 15", EX+, A1 ....**$175.00**

Kist Beverages, door plate, Enjoy.../Here's Refreshment, red/white/black on white, 1940s-50s, vertical, EX+, A13 ....**$50.00**

Kist Beverages, door pull, advertising above on backplate with black handle, EX+, A16 ....**$115.00**

Kist Beverages, sign, flange, tin, Enjoy Kist above Beverges on ribbon banner, white/black/red, 2 curved corners, 18x22", EX+, A1 ....$225.00

Kist Beverages, sign, paper, close-up of Elvgren pin-up blonde in revealing black dress with bottle of orange on blue, 18x14", EX+, A3...................................**$50.00**

Kist Beverages, sign, porcelain, Drink above red lips lettered Kist, Beverages below, red/white, 17x23", NM, A1..**$325.00**

Kist Beverages, sign, tin, bottle cap shape, Kist/The Drinks With Real Flavor, red/white/blue, dated (?) 6-59, 15" dia, EX+, A1 ....$170.00

Kist Beverages, sign, tin, bottle shape, orange, 1940s-50s, 48", NM+, A13...**$425.00**

Kleins Japanese Cough Drops, pocket tin, vertical, 10 Cents, white on blue, EX, A18 ....**$75.00**

Klingzon Cleaner, bill hook, celluloid, lady cleaning on round button top, red, 6x3", EX, A15 ....**$275.00**

Klondike, cigar box labels, set of 2, miners panning for gold, Geo Schlegel litho, G, A5 ....**$260.00**

Klong's Pros't, tip tray, round, deep rim, In Kegs & Bottles, girl on winged wheel, 4" dia, EX+, A8 ....**$115.00**

Klong's Pros't, tip tray, round, man's head/hands pouring beer, EX, A8 ....**$200.00**

Knapsack Matches, vendor, wooden octagonal shape, lettered glass panels, ca 1892, 11", G, A9...............**$600.00**

Knapstein Brewing Co Special Brew, tip tray, round, Greek girl, gold lettered rim, Meek Co litho, VG-EX, from $100 to...**$165.00**

Knickerbocker Beer, sign, tin/cardboard, Ice Cold in ice letters floating around bottles above name, embossed, beveled, 1955, 13x10", EX, A8 ....**$50.00**

Knickerbocker Beer, tip tray, round, The Beer Drinker's Beer, silhouette profile image of colonial man on white, EX+, A3...**$25.00**

Knickerbocker Beer, see also Jacob Rupert's

Knickerbocker Mills Pepper, container, cardboard, round, wooden rim bands/bottom, paper label depicting lion chasing tiger, 16", VG, A2 ....**$120.00**

Knight of Pythias, cigar box label, outer, knights helping wounded knight, 4½x4½", EX, D5.......................**$35.00**

Knock 'EM' Dead The Great Bed Bug Killer, can, 1-qt, round with screw-on funnel applicator, white on blue, EX, A3...**$50.00**

Knox, pin-back button, round, Touring New England/1909 Models, photo image of auto, red/black lettering, 1¼", EX, A2..**$470.00**

Knox Gelatine, box-insert brochure, advertising/illustrations of recipes & coupon for ordering Dainty Desserts cookbook, 1929, VG, D14...**$4.00**

Knox Gelatine, sign, canvas paper, mammy/white girl putting strawberries on dessert, artist H Roseland, 1901, framed, 20x27", G, A9 ....**$200.00**

Knox Gelatine, sign, canvas paper, mammy/white girl putting strawberries on dessert, artist H Roland, 1901, framed, 20x27", EX+, A3 ....**$1,250.00**

Knox Gelatine, sign, die-cut cardboard, Try A Knox Gelatine Dainty, Recipes In Each Package, lady with product/desserts, VG, A9 ....**$150.00**

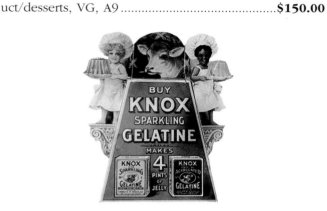

Knox Sparkling Gelatine, sign, cardboard, die-cut, 4-sided, black girl/white girl flank pyramid sign with cow's head atop, 16x15x10", EX, A6 ....$2,000.00

Kobel Sec California Champagne, sign, tin/cardboard, Fermented In The Bottle, profile of lady with grapes/large bottle, beveled, 13x19", VG, A9 .....**$100.00**

Koch's Beer, sign, neon, Koch's Beer in tubing framed by red diamond tubing, 3-color, 1950s, 16x26", EX+, A19 ....**$160.00**

Kochenderfer Oil Co Motor Oil, can, ½-gal, rectangular, screw lid, grip handle, oval image of #8 racer/text, black on yellow, EX+, D22 ....**$400.00**

Kodak Film, sign, porcelain, triangle shape, 'Kodaks' (red) on white above yellow film box, black border, 2-sided, 23x26", NM, A1 ....$625.00

Kodak Film, sign, tin, film box shape, red on yellow, ca 1915, 7x17", VG, A24.............................**$250.00**

Kodak Film, standee, cardboard, Get Kodak Film Here, girl in red shorts/top holding camera, 64x21", EX, D30 .**$300.00**

Kodak Film Developing & Printing/Cloverland Picture Shop, sign, light-up, reverse glass/metal back, red/yellow lettering, framed, 8x21x7", EX, A6 ....**$300.00**

Kodak Supplies, sign, porcelain, round, yellow band around Kodak (exaggerated K)/white All Supplies on green, 20", NM, A1 ....**$425.00**

Kodak Verichrome Film, sign, porcelain, triangle shape with film box, Developing/Printing/Enlarging, 2-sided, 1930s, 22x12", VG-EX, D22/A24, from $260 to **$325.00**

Koehler & Hanson Hardware, calendar, 1907, die-cut cardboard, embossed image of woman playing mandolin among flowers, 22x13", complete, NM, A3 ....**$400.00**

Koehler's Pilsener Beer, salt & pepper shakers, amber glass bottles with paper labels, tin lids, 4", VG, D14, pair.........**$18.00**

Kolb Crystal Export Beer, label, 12-oz, Kolb Brewing Co/Bay City MI, IRTP/U-type permit #, 1933-36, VG-(soaked off bottle or paper), A10..........................**$21.00**

Kolb's Roughs Mild Cigar, tin, horizontal box, yellow with red bands, EX+, A3..**$60.00**

Kolynos Dental Cream, display, cardboard die-cut fold-up, product tubes flank backside image of baby on black ground, 19x43", EX+, A15 ....**$110.00**

Kolynos Dental Cream, signs, cardboard die-cut stand-up, man or woman clowns, 13", M, A15, each $150.00

Kool Cigarettes, case, cardboard, flat, holds 50, Seasons Greetings, EX+, A18 ....**$240.00**

Kool Cigarettes, display carton, cardboard, with marque, white/lt green/black, EX, A18.............................**$45.00**

Kool Cigarettes, door plate, vertical, Pull, They're So Refreshing, open pack, white/green, NM+, A13 ..**$60.00**

Koppitz Victory Beer, label, 12-oz, Koppitz-Melcher's Inc/Detroit MI, IRTP or WF statement, 1933-1950, VG+ (soaked off bottle or paper), A10..........................**$26.00**

Korbel Sec California Champagne, sign, tin/cardboard, Fermented In The Bottle, lady admiring growing grapes, beveled, 13x19", NM+, A3 ....$365.00

Korbel Sec California Champagne, sign, tin/cardboard, Fermented In The Bottle, lady admiring growing grapes, beveled, 13x19", G-VG, A8/A1, from $100 to........**$160.00**

Korona Hungarian Paprika, tin, 1-oz, round, NM, A3 ...**$8.00**

Kow-Kare, sign, flange, enamel on steel, ...Sold Here, 3 product tins on gray/black background, 9x12", NM, A24....**$200.00**

Kozy Cup Roasted Coffee, box, 1-lb, cardboard, embossed, EX+, A3......................................$30.00

Kraeuter Tools & Pliers, sign, cardboard, Ask Any Mechanic, image of man using pliers, ca 1910, 18x14", VG+, A3......................................$45.00

Kraft Foods, games, Trivia Pursuit, sets 1 & 2, mail-in premium, 1993, NMIB (sealed), D24 ....$10.00

Kraft Kaff-A, sign, tin, die-cut cow, I Get The Milk-Bank Boost From Kaff-A, red/black/yellow/green/white, 16x23", NM, A7 ....$175.00

Kraft Kraylets, sign, tin, die-cut pig, I Get The Milk Bank Boost From Kraylets, red/black/yellow/green/white, 12x18", NM, A7 ....$175.00

Kraft Macaroni & Cheese, bank, Cheese Rex, vinyl, M, D20 ....$35.00

Kraft Macaroni & Cheese, radio, Dinomac, NM, D13 .$35.00

Kraft Malted Milk, container, aluminum, EX, A13 ....$85.00

Kraft Pex, sign, tin, die-cut rooster, I Get The Milk-Bank Boost From Pex, yellow, green base, red/black lettering, 20x15", EX, A3 ....$175.00

Kraft Velvetta, pull toy, TV Cameraman, plastic, premium, 1954, 4½", A14 ....$90.00

Krantz Wurtzburger Beer, label, 12-oz, Krantz Brewing Co/Findlay OH, pre-1920, M, A10 ....$60.00

Kreso Dip No 1/Parke Davis & Co, marque display sign, tin, Helps Keep All Livestock & Poultry Healthy, product cans flank farm animals, 16x28", G, A9 ....$400.00

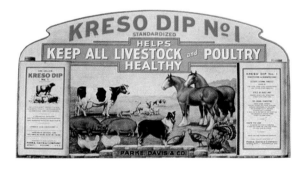

Kreso Dip No 1/Parke Davis & Co, marque display sign, tin, Helps Keep All Livestock & Poultry Healthy, product cans flank farm animals, 16x28", EX+, A3.....$1,150.00

Krisp Peanut Butter, pail, 1-lb, yellow, VG, A3........$25.00

Kroehler Furniture Co, catalog, 1930, Spring, livingroom furniture, 36 pgs, EX, D17......................$40.00

Kroger's Country Club Regular Grind Coffee, can, 1-lb, key-wind lid, white lettering on red center band, EX, A3 ....$30.00

Krueger Beer, tap knob, ball shape, black, white-on-red plastic insert, EX, A8......................$40.00

Krueger Beer/Ales, sign, tin/cardboard, gold embossed lettering outlined in red, circle logo on black, 6x13", EX, A19......................$100.00

Krueger Brewing Co, see G Krueger

Kuco No Chafe Powder, tin, round, sample, green, VG+, A3......................$75.00

Kuhn's Beer Inc, matchbook cover, The Beer With A Cheer/Made In Jamestown NY, red/white/black, 20 strike, diamond quality, M, D28 ....$13.00

Kuhn's Climatized Paints, sign, porcelain die-cut hanger, name panel above raccoon holding paint can on red disk, 2-sided, 24x18", EX+, A1 ....$1,250.00

Kutcher's Superfine Brand Quick Cooking Rolled Oats, container, cardboard, round, red, EX, A3 ....$90.00

KW Magnetos & Spark Coils..., sign, flange, porcelain, ...Master Vibrators/Road Smoothers/And That Satisfied Feeling, white/blue, 18x18", VG+, A2................$300.00

∽⊚ L ⊚∽

L&M Cigarettes, door plate, metal, Friendly Flavor/...Your Taste Comes Alive, open pack on blue center, 1960s, vertical, NM, A13......................$60.00

La Azora Cigars/Lilienfeld Bros & Co Makers, charger, tin, The Cigar Of Cigars, 2 white ladies/3 black servants taking leisurely boat ride, 24" dia, EX, A7...............$800.00

La Costa Hand Made Cigars, tin, vertical box, curved corners, 2 For 5¢, EX, A18 ....$45.00

La Flor De Erb 10¢ Cigar, sign, tin/cardboard, portrait in center, DS Erb & Co Makers at bottom, black ground, 6x14", NM, A3......................$90.00

La Flor de Key West, cigar box labels, 3-pc set, oval image of port scene, EX, A5 ....$185.00

La Flor de New York, cigar box label, sample, allegorical scene, Schumacher & Ettlinger litho #6756, 1887, EX, A5 ....$120.00

La Flor Mejor, cigar box labels, set of 2, 3 bare-breasted ladies, Witsch & Schmitt litho #605/606, EX, A5..$125.00

La Luna, cigar box label, outer, woman seated on crescent moon, 1911, 4½x4½", M, D5......................$125.00

La Mas Fermosa, cigar box label, lithographer's proof, oval image of young girl looking at flowers, Moehle Litho Co, 6x9", EX, A5 ....$50.00

La Palina Excellente/Panetela Size 5¢ Cigar, display, cardboard stand-up, image of 2 open cigar boxes, 23x10", NM+, A3......................$40.00

La Palina 5¢ Cigars, sign, cardboard die-cut stand-up, Gentlemen Prefer..., 3 ladies' heads/2 cigars on blue circle, 11x9", NM+, A3......................$35.00

La Palla All Havana Cigars, sign, tin, oval image of pretty girl with bouquet of red flowers, green frame, 17x14", VG, A7......................$200.00

La Resta Cigars/Rothenberg & Schloss, tin, round, slip lid, EX, A3......................$40.00

La Teresa Cigars, tin, round, slip lid, EX+, A18......$120.00

La Touraine Coffee, can, ½-lb, key-wind lid, VG+-NM, A3/A18, from $20 to $35.00

La Vall Rosa, cigar box, 5¢/Quality Cigar/Very Mild, profile image of woman in military garb, VG, A3...........$22.00

La Vanita, cigar box label, sample, reflections of a woman, Witsch & Schmitt litho #2550, EX+, A5 ....$300.00

La Vida Lime 'N Lemon, sign, tin, Thirst Satisfying!/Drink..., tilted bottle surrounded by fruit on a branch at left of text, 14x19", NM, D30 ....$150.00

Labatt's Pilsner Beer, display figure, German fellow with keg, vinyl, 1970s, NM+, D20 ....$55.00

Lacquerwax, sign, cardboard die-cut stand-up, shows the 'Weather Gods' blowing damage at car, arched top, 30x22", EX+, A1 ....$250.00

Lacquerwax, sign, tin, Motorists Relax With.../5 Times Faster & Easier To Apply..., red/blue on yellow, 14x19", EX, A1 ....$200.00

Laddies Short Smokes, sign, cardboard, night scene with 2 gents in top hats outside of theater enjoying a smoke, 1920s, 34x23", EX, A24 ....$375.00

Lady Betty Coffee, can, 1-lb, key-wind, EX+, A18 ....$75.00

Lady Bird HMV Super Sensitive Portable Transistor Radio, sign, porcelain, orange/white lettering on black, orange border, 7x10", EX+, D22 ....$175.00

Lady Cleveland, cigar box label, outer, First Lady, sepia/white, 4½x4½", M, D5 ....$20.00

Lady Hellen Brand Coffee, container, 1-lb, cardboard, tin pry top/bottom, EX+, A3....................................$100.00

Lady Lillian Nail White, tin, round, sample, vertical bar design, ¼x1" dia, EX, D37 ....$15.00

Laflin & Rand Powder, store card, cardboard, Shot With..., boy hunter with gun holding up dead birds while dog sniffs, 12x8", EX, A24 ....$200.00

Lagoon, crate label, California orange, 1915 Expo buildings/lagoon, E Highlands, EX, D3 ....$12.00

LaJac Magic Pink Cream, tin, round, Free Sample, Before/After images if lady's head, ¼x1½", EX, D37 ....$25.00

Lake View Brewing Co, drinking glass, shell, clear, etched, star-with-beer trademark encircled by red-orange, EX+, A8 ....$130.00

Lambert, pin-back button, round, The Lambert/Shore & Beach, early auto, red lettering/black image on white, 1" dia, EX, A2 ....$525.00

Lambert & Butler's Blended Navy Cut, sign, cardboard, 2 sailors preparing to board ship with large basket of L&B, wood frame marked L&B, 24x18", G, A9 ....$135.00

Lambert & Butlers Waverley Mixture, tin, horizontal box, curved corners, EX+, A3......................................$30.00

Lambertville Rubber Co Snag-Proof, sign, paper, brownies working on large boot, courtesy panel below, 26x17", EX, A6 ....$185.00

Lambertville Rubber Co Snag-Proof Boots, calendar, no date (appears 1915-25), cardboard, oval image of girl framed by brownies promoting boots, 12x8", EX+, A3 ....$115.00

Lambertville Rubber Co Snag-Proof Boots, calendar, 1903, brownies working on large boot, 10x7", complete, EX+, A3...$110.00

Lambertville Rubber Footwear, calendar, 1915-20, 12", no pad, EX+, A13 ....$75.00

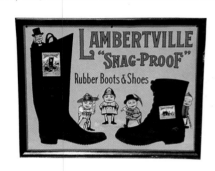

Lambertville Snag-Proof Rubber Boots & Shoes, sign, metal, brownies inspecting boot/shoe, red lettering, yellow ground, red border, framed, 15x20", EX, A6 ....$700.00

Lander Gardenia & Sweet Pea Blended Talc, tin, vertical square, 4", EX, A3.......................................$40.00

Lane Bryant, catalog, 1922, Winter Fashions For Stout Women, 76 pgs, EX, D17 ....$60.00

Lane Bryant, catalog, 1929, Fall/Winter, infant's/children's fashions, 56 pgs, EX, D17 ....$40.00

Lanes Talcum Powder, tin, round, silver on blue, EX+, A18 ....$50.00

Lang's Bock Beer, label, 12-oz, Gehard Lang Brewery/Buffalo NY, IRTP/U-type permit #, M, A10.........................$20.00

Lang's Imperial Buffalo Lager, drinking glass, diamond logo in red-orange, EX+, A8.............................$100.00

Lange's Borated Talcum Powder Compound, tin, 5-oz, VG+ (full), A3...$60.00

Larkin Orange Blossom Talcum, tin, sample, 2¼", EX, D37 ....$40.00

Larkin Thuro/Larkin Automobile Parts Co, sign, porcelain, Authorized Distributor, 2 elephants head butting, oval logo atop grease gun, black ground, EX, D34..$750.00

Lash's Bitters, sign, tin, Acts Without Discomfort/Natural Tonic Laxative, oval image of man ready to drink, beveled, 25x20", EX, A7................................$1,800.00

Lash's Old Fashioned Root Beer, sign, porcelain, die-cut emblem, ...Refreshing, black/red lettering over frothy mug in center on white, 7x17", NM+, A1 ....$525.00

Lash's Orangeade, dispenser, metal canister with orange fruit topper, 22x14", VG, A1 ....$500.00

Lash's Orangeade, dispenser, textured Vaseline-colored glass globe with embossed leaves/name atop black glass base, with spigot, VG, A9 .... $150.00

Lash's Root Beer, mug, ceramic, black lettering with blue double stripes above/below on white, 6", NM+, A1 ..... $40.00

Last Course, cigar box label, sample, waiter offering 2 men at table cigars, American Litho Co #542, 1905, VG, A5 .... $150.00

Last Trip, cigar box labels, set of 2, Schumacher & Ettlinger litho #6441/6442, 1884, EX, A5 .... $200.00

Latona Steel Cut Coffee/Folger's, can, 3-lb, VG+, A3 . $150.00

Lavon, crate label, melon, stalking lion, Los Banos, M, D12 .... $8.00

Lawrence Barrett Cigar, sign, porcelain, Mild Havana/10 & 15 Cents, round portrait next to name on white, yellow trim, 18x40", VG-EX, A3/A6, from $275 to $375.00

Lawrence Tiger Brand Paint/Varnish, sign, porcelain hanger, can shape, wrought-iron bracket, red/white/yellow/blue, 2-sided, 23x18", NM (NOS), A1 .... $800.00

Lax-ets, match holder, tin, Only 5¢ Per Box, white, 1920s-30s, EX-NM, A1/A3, from $75 to $110.00

Lay or Bust Feeds/Park & Pollard Co, sign, tin, chickens/chicks feeding on grass, embossed, ca 1910-20, horizontal, EX, A24 .... $950.00

Lay or Bust Poultry Products/Park & Pollard Co, display, tin stand-up, poultry graphics around mirrored center, box for information booklets, 27x19", EX, A15 .... $1,750.00

Le Page's China Cement, display box, stand-up, lady using product on piece of broken china, 9x6x1", NM, D22 .... $125.00

Le Roy Cigars, sign, cardboard, They Win!/15¢ Package Of Five, young couple at baseball game, red ground, 11x20", NM, A3 .... $70.00

Le Transparent Trojan/Youngs Rubber Co, tin, rectangular, curved corners, black lettering/Eiffel Tower on pink/white/lt blue ground, 2x2½", EX+, A15 ..... $275.00

Leadway Ground Cinnamon, tin, 1-oz, rectangular, white/red, majorette logo, NM, A3 .... $25.00

Leaf Lard/SS Pierce Co, postcard, trifold, 1620-1920, The Landing Of The Pilgrim Fathers In New England, used 1921, VG+, A17 .... $325.00

Leaf Spearmint Chewing Gum, sign, tin, ...The Flavor Lingers Longer on ribbon banner with unopened pack/name, 1940s-50s, horizontal, NM (NOS), A13 .... $325.00

Lee, bandanna, white outlined advertising graphics on blue, 20x22", VG+, A8 .... $30.00

Lee Boys' Overalls, display sign, cardboard die-cut stand-up, image of boy in overalls standing with hammer in hand, 10", EX+, A3 .... $90.00

Lee of Conshohocken, sign, flange, painted metal, lettering over large tire, green/yellow/red/black, 28x18", NM (NOS), A6 .... $425.00

Lee Overall, sign, reverse glass, Class A/Lee Overall/Union Made/Department, red/blue on yellow, chain hanger, 9x22", EX+, A1 .... $500.00

Lee Riders, display, cardboard, die-cut, mechanical, boy on horse rocks against round rodeo image on red box, 22x13x6", EX+, A3 .... $480.00

Lee Riders, sign, painted metal, round, Authentic Western Pants & Jackets/Wear..., cowboy on bucking bronc, 2-sided, 18" dia, VG, A6 .... $160.00

Lee Wards Mills Crafts & Supplies, catalog, 1954, Fall/Winter, 44 pgs, EX, D17 .... $25.00

Legal Tender, crate label, California orange, $250 bundle of currency, blue/black ground, Fillmore, EX, D3 ...... $3.00

Lehigh Valley Railroad, sign, paper, name/Coal Branches & Connections lettered above map of Black Diamond Express, 40x27", VG, A6 .... $2,750.00

Leidiefer Brewing Co, drinking glass, shell, etched, gold rim, EX+, A8 .... $40.00

Leidig's Pilsner Style Beer, label, 32-oz, San Francisco Brewing Co/CA, IRTP or WF statement, 1933-50, M, A10 .... $20.00

Leidiger Brewing Co Select Beer, tray, rectangular, Wisconsin's Finest, 13", EX+, A8 .... $70.00

Leinenkugel Chippewa's Pride Beer, tray, round, deep rim, Indian maiden in profile, EX, A8 .... $100.00

Leinenkugel's Chippewa Beer, display, hand-held bottle, rubber, Here's The Best In The House... in gold lettering on black cuff, 1940-42, 10", NM, A8 .... $270.00

Leisy Bottle Beer, sign, painted metal, round, Drink... on rim around close-up image of girl with glass, 14" dia, VG, A6..**$225.00**

Leisy Export Beer, label, 12-oz, Leisy Brewing Co/Peoria IL, pre-1920, VG (soaked off bottle or paper), A10 ..**$26.00**

Leisy's Beer, tray, oval, College Widow, American Art Works, c 1913, 16x13", G, A6 ....**$80.00**

Leisy's Beer, tray, oval, The Connoisseur, American Art Works, c 1913, 16x13", G, A9 ....**$100.00**

Lemmy Lemonade, sign, tin, Lemme Have A..., personified lemon/5¢ bottle, yellow/white lettering, blue ground, embossed, 15x22", EX+, A1 ....**$180.00**

Lemp (Wm J) Brewing Co, see also Falstaff

Lemp (Wm J) Brewing Co, tray, round, logos on rim around man with bottle & glass, C Shonk litho, 12" dia, VG+, A8...**$430.00**

Lemp Beer, St Louis Mo, ashtray, round, black, gold lettering/trim, EX+, A3 ....**$28.00**

Lemp St Louis Lager Beer, sign, tin, Lemp above Lemp St Louis emblem, Saint Louis/Lager Beer below, gold, embossed, C Shonk litho, 21x15", VG+, A8..$360.00

Lemp St Louis/Falstaff, charger, exterior scene with barmaid serving seated Falstaff, 24", VG+-EX, A8/A7, from $275 to **$375.00**

Lemp St Louis/Falstaff, charger, exterior scene with barmaid/man/boy listening to Falstaff tout product, 1912, 24", VG+-EX, A8/A7, from $275 to **$325.00**

Lemp St Louis/Falstaff, charger, The House Of Falstaff, 24", VG+, A8...**$275.00**

Lemp St Louis/Falstaff, charger, 3 ladies/boy wish farewell to 2 Falstaffs on horses outside of tavern while dogs watch, 1910, 24", EX, A8......................................**$400.00**

Lennox Steel Furnace, sign, porcelain, oval, Torrid Zone on banner around globe in center, white/2-tone green, 11x20", NM, D11...**$200.00**

Lenox Soap, sign, cardboard die-cut stand-up, lady doing wash in wooden tub atop Lenox Soap crates, 1898, 64x27", G, A7 ....**$500.00**

Lenox Soap, sign, porcelain, blue lettering on yellow, blue line border, 6x10", M (NOS), A6.................................**$185.00**

Lenox Tobacco, pocket tin, vertical, rare, VG+, A18..**$1,615.00**

Levi Strauss & Co Two Horse Brand Overalls, Koveralls..., trade card, foldout, when folded it stands as an 11x4" 3-D pair of denims, opens to display people at work/play, EX+, A3 ....**$365.00**

Levi Strauss Copper Riveted Overalls, blotter, pictures Levi Electric Rodeo at Treasure Island, 1939, EX+, A3 ..**$50.00**

Levi's, display, cowboy figure on square base, ...America's Finest Overall Since 1850, 1960s, 30", EX, A4 .$2,500.00

Lewiston Brew, label, 12-oz, Lewiston Brewing Co/MT, pre-1920, M, A10 ....**$110.00**

Lexington/Davis Automobile Sales Co Inc, pocket mirror, oval, white lettering on blue band around black/white image of early auto on white, 3x2", EX, A2 ....**$990.00**

Libby's, bank, can shape advertising Libby's & NY World's Fair, EX+, A18 ....**$40.00**

Libby's Milk, catalog, 1937, houseware/gift/toy premiums, 32 pgs, EX, D17 ....**$30.00**

Liberty Beer/American Brew Co, tip tray, round, Indian with peace pipes/arrows, gold-lettered rim, 4" dia, NM, A7...**$300.00**

Liberty Root Beer, dispenser, wooden barrel, metal bands/chrome spigot, stamped lettering/decals, 1920s, 27", EX+, A6.....................................$1,100.00

Liberty Root Beer, dispenser, wooden barrel, metal bands/chrome spigot, stamped lettering/graphics (no decals), 1920s, 27", VG, A13 ....**$350.00**

Lichten Bro's Cigars, mirror sign, diagonal beveled mirror with etched advertising, The Best Cigars Are..., ornate frame, 21x21", EX, A6..**$40.00**

Lieber's Gold Medal Beer/Indianapolis Brewing Co, tip tray, round, bottle on red ground, lettered/decorative rim, EX, A6 ....**$75.00**

Liebmann Breweries Inc Scotch Ale, sign, tin/cardboard, Good Old Scotch Ale On Draught..., NRA symbol, plaid border, self-framed, 1934-35, 11x11", VG+, A8.....**$50.00**

Little Joker, cigar box label, outer, octagonal, jester, Schmidt & Co litho, 1896, EX, A5 ....**$90.00**

Little Mozart Cigars, tin, oval, slip lid, Liberty Can, VG+, A18 ....**$70.00**

Little Seals Cigars, box, paper on wood, vertical, early, rare, VG+, A3 ....**$75.00**

Little Trix, cigar box label, sample, oval image of kittens at play, Heffron & Phelps litho #243, VG, A5 ....**$140.00**

Lochinvar, crate label, California orange, brave Lochinvar/fair damsel, red ground, E Highlands, EX, D3 ....**$5.00**

Lochinvar, crate label, California orange, knight riding off with maiden, E Highlands, EX-M, D3/D12, from $5 to **$7.00**

Locust Grove Tomatoes, can label, country road, EX, D5 ..**$20.00**

Loewer's Brewery, tray, round, deep rim, Pinkie, image of girl in long pink dress against cloudy sky, 12" dia, EX+, A8 ....**$60.00**

Log Cabin, cigar box, cardboard, depicts cigar salesman offering his product to prospector at his cabin, EX+, A3 ....**$30.00**

Log Cabin, cigar box, wood, cabin shape, label marked Cabin Home shows black people dancing, ca 1880, rare, EX+, A3 ....$415.00

Log Cabin Brownies/National Biscuit Co/Uneeda Bakers, box, cardboard, cabin shape, 1930s, 4x2x2", EX+, A3 ....**$135.00**

Log Cabin Flaked Gold Leaf Cavendish, tin, horizontal box, curved corners, EX+, A3 ....**$50.00**

Log Cabin Syrup, see Towle's

London House Silver Banner Coffee, can, 1-lb, key-wind lid, Art Deco style, EX+, A3 ....**$80.00**

London Life Cigarettes, sign, tin, sporting party under canopy advertising product, wood-tone scalloped framed, 39x28", VG, A7 ....**$750.00**

London Sherbet Mixture/Falk Tobacco Co, pocket tin, vertical, green, G+-EX+, A18, from $250 to $450.00

Lone Star Beer, display, armadillo on his back drinking from bottle, chalkware, 1960s, 13", EX+, A8/A19, from $80 to **$85.00**

Lone Star Beer, sign, light-up, cowpoke on horse by tree watching over herd, wooden frame, 14x16", EX, A8 ....**$100.00**

Lone Star Certified Quality Beer, bank, barrel shape, plaster, 8½", VG, A8 ....**$35.00**

Long Beach Cigar, cigar box label, sample, bathing beauty in oval beach scene, Witsch & Schmitt litho #707, EX, A5 ....**$465.00**

Long John Silver's Restaurant, book, Adventure On Volcano Island, paint with water, 1991, M, D23 ....**$3.00**

Long Tom Smoking Tobacco, tin, rectangular, curved corners, EX, A18 ....**$100.00**

Long's Ox-Heart Peanut Butter, pail, 16-oz, EX, A6 ..**$100.00**

Longhorn Pure Lard, pail, 8-lb, black/yellow, EX+, A1...$125.00

Look Out Rough & Ready Tobacco, see Dill's (JG)

Loose-Wiles Chocolates, sign, tin, die-cut image of lady scholar holding box of Loose-Wiles, large box in foreground, no size given, G, A7 ....**$500.00**

Lord Calvert Coffee, can, 1-lb, key-wind lid, red, gold lettering/trim, NM (unopened), A3 ....**$65.00**

Lord Gloster Cigar, cigar box opener, nickel-plated steel, flat blade with nail-pulling notch near end of blade, ...10¢ & Up, 5¼", VG, D14 ....**$20.00**

Lord Kenyon, pocket tin, vertical, short, paper label, VG+, A18 ....**$50.00**

Lord Needles, tin, trapezoidal, leprechaun/early phonograph on Deco diamond/floral background, EX, D37 ....**$55.00**

Lord Roberts, cigar box label, inner label, portrait, 6x9", EX, D5 ....**$60.00**

Lord Shelburne/OC Taylor & Co, sign, celluloid, Smoke.../Best 5¢ Cigar, horse within filigree border, ornate frame, 10x12", rare, EX, A5 ....**$275.00**

Los Angeles Evening Herald-Express, sign, porcelain, On Sale Here, cartoon figure lower left, white/2-tone green, 6x14", NM, D11 ....**$125.00**

Louella Butter/American Stores Co, calendar, 1936, paper, oval image of young girl/calf in pasture, 25x12", complete, EX, A6 ....**$40.00**

Louis Bergdoll, drinking glass, goblet, etched, 60th Anniversary (1909), with founder/trademark, 5", EX, A8 ....**$40.00**

Louis Bergdull Brewing Co, cigar cutter, china, combined with ashtray/match holder, white with printed advertising, 5", VG, A2 ....**$165.00**

Louis F Knipp Brewing Co, drinking glass, shell, etched, Celebrated Janesville Lager Beer, barrel with hops/grain, 1899-1905, NM, A8..$475.00

Louis Mark Shoes, shoehorn, nickel-plated steel, ...Of Quality/Sesqui-Centennial Exposition..., image of Liberty Bell, NM, D14 ....$18.00

Lowe's Carta Carna With Meat, sign, porcelain, red/black lettering above dog with bowl of food & product box on yellow/black ground, 24x17", EX, A6 ....$200.00

Lowenbrau Beer, display, horse-drawn barrel wagon with 2 drivers/4 horses, 1960s, 14x48", complete, G, A19......$150.00

Lowney's Chocolates, sign, paper, The American Beauties, vase of roses next to box of chocolates, 23x13", VG+, A9 ....$125.00

Lowney's Cocoa, sign, flange, Special Today stenciled on chalk board with product image below, 2-sided, wood frame, 32x15", G, A9 ....$300.00

Lowney's Cocoa (Breakfast), tin, rectangular, sample, filigreed image of lady in center, 1¼x1½x1", EX, D37..........$145.00

Loyl Brand Coffee, can, 1-lb, screw lid, red/white/blue, with eagle, EX+, A18..$100.00

Lubri-Gas, sign, cardboard, Anti-Lock/The Correct Motor Oil/Lubri gas, camel in prone position, 2-sided, 25x38", VG/G, A3 ....$60.00

Lucas Carriage Gloss Paint, sign, celluloid, scene that shows how product can be used such as on cars, carriages, etc, framed, image: 12x8", VG, A9 ....$250.00

Lucille Young Lash Darkener, tin, round, decorative round image of lady's head above lettering, Mersereau, ¼x1½" dia, EX, D37 ....$20.00

Lucky Brown Pressing Oil, tin, round, red heart-shaped image of black girl using product on black/yellow checked ground, 1930s, 3" dia, NM, A3................$25.00

Lucky Club Coffee, can, 1-lb, key-wind lid, red/white/blue, tall, EX, A18 ....$135.00

Lucky Cup Coffee, can, 1-lb, key-wind lid, red, king with steaming cup, EX+, A3..$165.00

Lucky Lager, sign, molded plastic over metal, Aged Dated in center of trademark X, 12x12", EX, A8 ....$100.00

Lucky Lager, toy gun/holster set with branding iron, Favorite Brand In The West, VG+ (in box), A8 ....$65.00

Lucky Star Ginger Ale, sign, tin, bottle shape, 20x6", EX-NM+, A6/D30, from $75 to $100.00

Lucky Strike, cigarette tin, flat, holds 50, green with Christmas motif, gold trim, EX+, A18 ....$35.00

Lucky Strike, cigarette tin, round, holds 100, green, EX, A18 ....$85.00

Lucky Strike, cigarette tin, round, holds 50, green, paper label on body/lid, EX+, A18 ....$250.00

Lucky Strike, pocket tin, flat, green, EX, A18............$10.00

Lucky Strike, pocket tin, vertical, green, sample, EX+, A3 ..$100.00

Lucky Strike, pocket tin, vertical, green, 3¼", VG+, A18...$75.00

Lucky Strike, pocket tin, vertical, green, 4", EX+, A18 ....$100.00

Lucky Strike, pocket tin, vertical, green, 4½", EX, A18......$85.00

Lucky Strike, pocket tin, vertical, white, NM (full), A18..$725.00

Lucky Strike, tin, horizontal box, green, EX, A3.......$50.00

Lucky Strike, vending machine, metal, wall-mounted, white with serviceman holding US Defense Bonds shield, 32x7x5", EX+, A1 ....$280.00

Lucky Strike Cigarettes, license plate attachment, salesman's sample, tin/plastic, round red/white symbol, with pouch, 4½x3", EX+, A1 ....$190.00

Luki-Chuki/Ambrosia Chocolate Co, tin, round, Indian boy graphics on tan, 4x3"dia, VG+, A3................$75.00

Lulu Gal, cigar box, round serrated image of woman's head, EX, A3..$25.00

Lush'us Rolled Oats, container, 3-lb, cardboard, yellow, image of chef, EX+, A3 ....$100.00

Lutted's SP Cough Drops, dish, clear glass figural log cabin with embossed lettering on roof lid, 7", VG+, A9.**$200.00**

Lux Soap, soap in box, Exciting Beatles Offer/6¢ Off, inflatable dolls offer with 2 wrappers & $2.00, 1967, NM, A3..**$175.00**

Lux Toilet Soap, trolley sign, cardboard, Refreshing/Luxurious/10¢, oval product image on white, 1920s-30s, 11x21", VG+, A13..$100.00

Luxello High Grade Pure Coffee, can, 1-lb, key-wind lid, EX, A3..$85.00

Luxor Nail Polishing Stone, tin, round, decorative border around lettering, ¾x1½" dia, EX, D37 ....$18.00

Luxura Granulated Plug For Pipe & Cigarette, pocket tin, vertical, EX+, A18..$3,850.00

Luxury Bread, sign, paper, The Sweetest Of Them All, lady holding roses, artist WH Coffin, c 1912, framed, image: 30x19", VG, A9..$450.00

Luxury High Grade Coffee, can, 1-lb, key-wind lid, black/red/white, horse/jockey, EX+, A18..........$110.00

Luxus Beer, sign, transfer on glass, A Critic, No Better Beer Made/No Beer Better Made, Tuchfarber litho, 33x24", NM, A7 ....$2,750.00

Luzianne Coffee & Chicory, can, 1-lb, key-wind lid, white, EX, A18..$35.00

175

Luzianne Coffee & Chicory, can, 1-lb, snap lid, white, EX, A18/A3, from $80 to $85.00

Luzianne Coffee & Chicory, pail, 3-lb, red or white, EX, A18, each...$60.00

Luzianne Coffee & Chicory, sign, cardboard, die-cut coffee can, multicolored, text on reverse, 3½x2", EX, A6..$75.00

Lynwood Lager, label, 11-oz, Lynwood Brewing Co/Lynwood CA, IRTP/U-type permit #, 1933-36, VG+ (soaked off bottle or paper), A10 ....$20.00

Lyon's Fine Parasols, sign, paper, diagonal oriental-style product lettering flanked by row of girls/row of boys, vertical, VG, A9 ....$50.00

Lyons Coffee (All Method Grind), can, 1-lb, key-wind lid, white, EX+, A3 ....$65.00

Lyons Coffee (All Purpose Grind), can, ½-lb, key-wind lid, lt green, EX+, A18 ....$100.00

Lyons Tea, sign, porcelain, white block lettering on blue, orange border, 7x27", VG, A6...............................$80.00

Lyons 2d Fruit Pies, sign, porcelain, We Sell..., Many Varieties, product image, 34x23", EX, A6.................$100.00

M Aronholt Hardware & Furniture, calendar, 1926, pretty lady dressed in satin/furs, 12 months below, framed, 27x37", EX, A6 ....$350.00

M Feldman Coffee, can, 1-lb, slip lid, paper label, VG+, A3...$65.00

M Hohner's Harmonicas, display case, wood, 3-tiered with paper label inside of hinged lid depicting various people using harmonica, G, A9...$60.00

M Hommel Champagne, sign, paper, 4 bottles flank winery scene, grapes above, gold trim, Whitteman litho, framed, 27x33", EX, A7 ....$200.00

M Robinson Brewery, match safe, brass-colored metal, engraved, embossed corners, VG, A8...................$75.00

M Samuel's Specialmarke, cigar box label, inner lid, couple riding horses in landscape with dog, #27028, VG, A5 ....$110.00

M&M Premium Regular, gas globe, 3-pc, white plastic body, glass lenses, red/blue lettering on white, blue trim, 13½", NM, A6..$150.00

M&W Mor/Toledo Ohio, calendar, 1937, mother/daughter at produce counter talking to grocer, Czech/Polish, 23x15", EX, A3 ....$75.00

Ma-Belle, cigar box label, outer, buxom woman in feathered hat, 4½x4½", EX, D5 ....$20.00

Ma's Old Fashion Root Beer, bottle topper/bottle, cardboard, die-cut, Demand The Best on blue arrow pointing to sign, image of Ma, EX, D30............................$32.00

Ma's Old Fashion Root Beer, bottle topper/bottle, cardboard, die-cut, Ma pointing up to sign, EX, D30 ..$32.00

Ma's Old Fashion Root Beer, clock, square, white face with black numbers/hash marks, red/black lettering, NM, D30..$125.00

Maas & Steffen Furs, calendar, 1944, otter on snow bank ready to enter water, signed Carlyle Prather, 24x17", complete, VG, A6..$160.00

Maas & Steffen Furs, calendar, 1946, hunter/dogs after polar bear on iceberg, framed, 47x26", complete, NM, A7 ....$700.00

Maas & Steffen Furs, calendar top, 1942, image of beaver on marsh bank, framed, 30x21", EX+, A7..........$250.00

Maas & Steffen Furs, calendar top (?), full moon above desert, coon looking down at wolf from tree, signed Carlyle Prather, 24x17", VG, A6.................................$80.00

Maccar Truck Sales, paperweight/mirror, round, 2 tinted photo images of tanker/express truck with DuPont Powder logos, 3½" dia, EX, A2................................$300.00

Mack Trucks, ashtray, metal, bulldog figure in center of round dish, Central Die Casting, 1940s, EX+, D25/A5, from $45 to...$50.00

Mack Trucks, lapel pin, cast-brass figural bulldog with Mack embossed on collar, clutch-back fastener, ½", EX, D14...$18.00

Mack Trucks, paperweight/mirror, round, Mack — Leading Gasoline Truck Of America, shows early gasoline dray, red/white, 2½", EX, A2..........$415.00

Mack Trucks, sign, paper, bulldog atop oval logo on white, 21x26", EX, A6 ....$55.00

Mackie's White Horse Whisky, sign, porcelain, white lettering/horse on black background, white border, 30x36", VG, A2...$135.00

Maclaren's Peanut Butter, pail, rare, VG+, A18.....$220.00

Madam Lindsay Hair Dressing, tin, 4-oz, lt green, dk green silhouette/lettering, EX, A3 ....$22.00

Madison Cigar Manufacturing Co, sign, paper, name above profile image of Indian maiden, yellow, green border, Hayes Litho Co, dated 1906, 30x15", NM, A3 ....$730.00

Madras, cigar box label, inner lid, Indians/train/ship, 6x9", M, D5 ....$40.00

Maduro Fine Cut Chewing Tobacco/SF Hess & Co, label, paper, Spanish lady surrounded by blossoms/lettering, 11x11", VG+, A5 ....$140.00

Magic Belt Leather, display bin, tin/wood base, Expands & Contracts/No Binding/No Pressure, 2 elves pulling on man's belt, 1x15x15", VG+, A3 ....$200.00

Magic Yeast, door plate, porcelain, Makes Good Bread, product box above white lettering, yellow border, 6x3", NM, A13 ....$550.00

Magic Yeast, sign, cardboard, name/product/various images/Columbian Expo 1893 ribbon around oval image of girl, 12x10", VG, A6 ....$75.00

Magnolene Motor Oil For Fords, sign, flange, porcelain, Reduces Vibration/For Sale Here, white on blue, 16x22", VG/EX, A2 ....$880.00

Magnolia, cigar box label, inner lid, 6x9", M, D5......$75.00

Magnolia, sign, porcelain, courtesy panel, Magnolia lettered in blue above red flying horse, arrow below on white, 16x27", NM+, A1 ....$325.00

Magnolia Coffee, can, 1-lb, key-wind lid, white on red, EX+, A3..$160.00

Magnolia First Aid Kit, wall-mount metal cylinder with 5-point Pegasus decal, 11x4" dia, EX, A1 ....$160.00

Magnolia Gasoline/Motor Oil, sign, porcelain, round, Magnolia Gasoline around Motor Oil in center, flower logo, red/white/blue, 42" dia, Fair, A2 ....$250.00

Magnolia Motor Oils/Magnolia Petroleum Co, sign, porcelain, round, company name on band around product name in center, flower logo, red/white/blue, EX, D34..$900.00

Magnu-Lux Lighters, salesman's sample kit, opens like book to show 4 ad sleeves/display with lighter in center, 9x7", EX+, A1 ....$400.00

Magnus Beck/Horlacher Bottling Co, sign, cardboard, young girl/boy toasting frothy mugs at keg, late 1800s, simulated wood-tone frame, 23x17", EX, A19 ....$180.00

Magnus Root Beer, dispenser, ceramic barrel shape, original pump, 14", VG, A9 ....$500.00

Maid o' Clover Butter, sign, aluminum, Maid o' Clover 10¢ To-Day, with price changer, black/lime green on white, 8x12", EX+, A1 ....$110.00

Maier Bock Beer, label, 11-oz, Maier Brewing Co/Los Angeles, IRTP or WF statement, 1933-50, M (traces of paper or scrapes on back), A10 ....$20.00

Maier Brewing Co, tray, round, The Standard Of Perfection, lady in gold dress/hat, lettered rim, VG, A8 ......$100.00

Mail Pouch Tobacco, catalog, Catalogue Of Mail Pouch Tobacco Premiums, 1910, 32 pgs, EX, A5 ....$30.00

Mail Pouch Tobacco, product packet, Sweet Chewing, sample, red/blue on gold, NM, A3 ....$18.00

Mail Pouch Tobacco, sign, cardboard stand-up, He Punished The Sea, signed J Ropen, curved top, 34x21", VG, A6......$50.00

Mail Pouch Tobacco, sign, cardboard stand-up, Hey-Taxi 300 Years Ago, signed J Ropen, curved top, 34x21", VG, A6.......$50.00

Mail Pouch Tobacco, sign, cardboard stand-up, The First Hunter Was Also The Game, signed J Ropen, curved top, 34x21", VG, A6...$50.00

Mail Pouch Tobacco, sign, cardboard stand-up, The First Musical Instrument, signed J Ropen, curved top, 34x21", VG, A6 ....$50.00

Mail Pouch Tobacco, sign, cardboard stand-up, Their Stone Lips Will Never Tell, signed J Ropen, curved top, 34x21", EX, A6..$75.00

Mail Pouch Tobacco, sign, cardboard stand-up, They Ducked The Ducks, signed J Ropen, curved top, 34x21", EX, A6...$75.00

Mail Pouch Tobacco, sign, cardboard stand-up, They Risked Their Lives For Choice Plots, signed J Ropen, arched top, 34x21", EX, A6...$85.00

Mail Pouch Tobacco, sign, flange, tin, with tray, boy standing with product, For Dad/Chew/Smoke..., 17x19", tray missing, G+, A9 ....$1,900.00

Mail Pouch Tobacco, sign, flange, tin, with tray, boy standing with product, For Dad/Chew/Smoke..., 16x21", VG+, A7 ....$4,250.00

Mail Pouch Tobacco, sign, paper, Indian in full headdress with arms crossed, Bloc Tobacco Co, c 1909, framed, image: 20x15", EX, A9..............................$1,800.00

Mail Pouch Tobacco, sign, porcelain, Treat Yourself To The Best, yellow/white on blue, 11x36", VG, A6......$110.00

Mail Pouch Tobacco, store bin, tin, white/yellow on dk blue, 10x14", EX, A7..$325.00

Mail Pouch Tobacco, string holder, tin, Chew & Smoke, pouch rises along side as string is pulled, HD Beach litho, Pat 1908, 20x15", G, A9..........................$2,350.00

Mail Pouch Tobacco, thermometer, porcelain, Chew...in circle logo at top, white/yellow on dk blue, 9", EX-EX+, A6/A13, from $150 to $200.00

Mail Pouch Tobacco, thermometer, porcelain, Treat Yourself To The Best..., white/yellow on dk blue, 39", EX+, A1 ....$180.00

Mail Pouch Tobacco, thermometer, tin, Chew in circle logo at top, white/yellow on dk blue, 9", EX, D30......$85.00

Mail Pouch Tobacco, thermometer, tin, Chew on circle logo at top, red/white on dk blue, 39", VG, A6 ....$90.00

Mail Pouch Tobacco (Bloch Bro's West Virginia), sign, cardboard hanger, die-cut baby in swing, Chew Dad's Favorite..., 22x15", G, A7 ....$4,300.00

Maillard's Vanilla Chocolate & Breakfast Cocoa, sign, tin, ...Give Strength & Nourishment/They Are The Best, boy on box holding sign, embossed, framed, 21x16", EX, A6 ....$950.00

Maine Brace Cut Plug, tin, round, slip lid, red/yellow diagonal ground, NM, A18.............................$75.00

Majestic, cigar box label, inner lid, ocean liner, 6x9", M, D5 ....$60.00

Major Cola, tray, oval, majorette leading parade, red ground, lettered rim, 1930s-40s, 16", EX+, A13 ....$120.00

Maklke Automobile Garage, Wheeling W VA, pocket mirror, oval, name above/below early auto, brown tones, 2x3", VG, A2 ....$385.00

Malkin's Best, sign, tin, light-up, Malkin's Best/Better Foods, jeweled lettering on disk/coffee cup, 25x27x10", EX, A1 ....$325.00

Malkin's Pure Cloves, tin, 1½-oz, white, NM+, A3 ..$35.00

Mallard Whiskies, sign, tin, 2 duck hunters in boat, self-framed, 23x28", G, A7 ....$550.00

Mallory's Rolled Oats, container, 3-lb 7-oz, red lettering on white, gold trim, crown/shield logo with initials in center, EX+, A3 ....$80.00

Malt Rainier/Seattle Brewing Co, charger, tin, The Pure Malt Tonic, girl in bonnet, green ground, 1904, 18" dia, EX, A19 ....$250.00

Malt Rainier/Seattle Brewing Co, charger, tin, The Pure Malt Tonic, girl in headscarf, red ground, 1904, 18" dia, EX, A19 ....$250.00

Maltosia Beer, tip tray, round, red arrowhead-shaped logo, lettered rim, NM, A8 ....$50.00

Mammoth Jumbo Whole Blanched Salted Peanuts, tin, 10-lb, round, black on white, 11", G, A2 ......$200.00

Mammy Beverages Co, bottle, 60-oz, clear embossed stippled glass with name/image, 14", EX, A6.............$40.00

Mammy Brand Salted Peanuts, tin, 10-lb, G, A9..$2,300.00

Mammy's Favorite Brand Coffee/CD Kenny Co, pail, 4-lb, VG-VG+, A6/A3, from $325 to.............................$360.00

Mammy's Shanty, matchbook, The World's Best Apple Pie, woman doing wash/black man sleeping, 30 strike, front striker, M, D28...$14.00

Manager Hotels Coffee, can, 1-lb, key-wind lid, NM, A3....$70.00

Mandarin Salmon, can label, flag/salmon, M, D5....$25.00

Mandeville & King Co Superior Flower Seeds, sign, paper hanger, bowl of colorful pansies in center, 1908, 27x17", EX+, A3..$250.00

Manhattan Cigar Co, cigar box label, lithographer's proof, back-to-back head images of Indian/white man, Moehle Litho Co, 6x9", EX, A5..........................$165.00

Manhattan Coffee, can, 1-lb, key-wind lid, EX, A3..$25.00

Manischewitz Kosher Wine, display, plaster hand that holds bottle, 11", VG, A9 ....$150.00

Manning's Coffee, can, 1-lb, key-wind lid, white on blue, NM, A3..$30.00

Manobra, cigar box label, inner lid, Indian chief holding tomahawk, 6x9", M, D6............................$45.00

Mapacuba Cigars, tin, vertical box, curved corners, embossed, 5", EX+, A18 ....$75.00

Mapco Speedway Coils, sign, tin, The Coil With The Original One Year Guarantee..., race/coil graphics, black/orange, embossed, 13x10", EX+, A1 ....$400.00

Marathon, gas globe, 3-pc, white metal body, copper base, glass lenses, runner logo above name, red/black/white, 13½", EX, A6 ....$500.00

Marathon, key chain/knife, red/blue logo/advertising on white casing, with chain, 3", EX, A6 .... **$35.00**

Marathon, oil can, 1-gal, rectangular, spout, grip handle, Best In The Long Run, white/gold on green, VG, A1 .... **$50.00**

Marathon, oil can, 1-qt, VEP, runner/white lettering on black, EX, A18 .... **$80.00**

Marathon, sign, tin, Get Marathon Motor Oil, runner logo at left, green/black ground, embossed, 12x30", G+, A1 ..... $200.00

Marathon, thermometer, metal, square corners, Marathon logo above gauge, red/white/blue, 16x5", EX, A6 .... **$90.00**

Marathon Lager Beer, sign, paper applied to cardboard, Honey Bring Some..., pinup girl on phone, black ground, 22x14", NM+, A13 .... **$200.00**

MarBert Cola, bottle display/2 bottles, Enjoy.../The Delicious Cola, red/yellow/green, EX, D30 .... **$55.00**

Marbest Turmeric, tin, 2-oz, VG+, A3 .... **$20.00**

Marc Antony, crate label, California orange, soldier wearing helmet, Placentia, EX, D3 .... **$5.00**

Marie Tempest Cigars/B Newmark & Co, sign, paper, portrait image, 22x16", NM+, A3 .... **$970.00**

Marine Bank, bank, Captain Marine, molded vinyl, 1980s, 8½", NM, D20 .... **$35.00**

Marine Special Outboard Motor Oil, can, 1-qt, pictures boat, white/blue/black, EX, A1 .... **$70.00**

Mariner, crate label, California lemon, sailor at helm against sunset, Carpinteria, EX, D3 .... **$6.00**

Marion Bobcat/Marion Motor Co of Indianapolis, pocket mirror, round, black/white striped cat holding red car in jaws, white ground, 2¼" dia, EX, A2 .... **$1,760.00**

Mariposa, crate label, apple, colorful butterfly/flowers, M, D5 .... **$35.00**

Mariposa, crate label, California orange, bouquet of lilies, black ground, Santa Paula, As-Is condition, D3 ..... **$8.00**

Mariposa, crate label, California orange, bouquet of lilies, black ground, Santa Paula, M, D12 .... **$25.00**

Market Basket Coffee, can, 1-lb, key-wind lid, EX, A3 ... **$50.00**

Marklin Trains, display sign, cardboard stand-up, Marklin lettered above image of train engine, ca 1939, 12x16", EX+, A3 .... **$40.00**

Marlin Repeaters/Marlin Fire Arms Co, sign, cardboard, glow of campfire on Indian brave standing with rifle, framed, 11x8", EX, A7 .... **$550.00**

Marmon/Roosevelt Authorized Service, sign, porcelain, lettering on 2-color divided background, white/yellow/blue, 2-sided, 24x30", EX, A2 .... **$2,750.00**

Marque Reno Cafe, can, 3-lb, round with smaller round lid, various scenes around label, 'Tapicoca' on reverse, EX+, A18 .... **$200.00**

Marquette Club Pale Dry Ginger Ale, sign, cardboard die-cut stand-up, lady kneeling in front of open icebox, 26x22", EX+, A1 .... **$75.00**

Marschall Needles, tin, rectangular, curved ends, Finest.../Registered Trade Mark, image of boy/baby, EX, D37 .... **$35.00**

Marschall Needles, tin, triangular, Extra Quality, image of baby/dog, EX, D37, minimum value **$50.00**

Marshall Cubana, cigar box label, inner lid, shows knight/medieval battles/lovers, 6x9", EX, D5 .... **$45.00**

Marshall Field Co, catalog, 1935, household/kitchenware/appliances, 80 pgs, EX, D17 .... **$35.00**

Marshall Field Co, catalog, 1946, Christmas, 24 pgs, EX, D17 .... **$25.00**

Marshfield Lager Beer, sign, aluminum hanger, round, lettering with ribbon banner/decorative hops, red/silver/blue, 10" dia, VG+, A8 .... **$135.00**

Martin-Senour Paints/Varnishes/Enamels, sign, porcelain, circular emblem, ...Sold Here, shows hand-held brush, red/white/blue/yellow, 2-sided, 21x19", NM, A1 .... **$650.00**

Marvel Brand Coffee & Food Products/Webster Grocer Co, decal, steaming cup against window with view of canyon waterfall, 1925, 11x9", EX+ (unused), A3 .. **$80.00**

McCord Gaskets/Radiators/Mufflers, thermometer, tin, square, Hot Or Cold/You Can Depend On..., arc dial above black/white lettering on red, 15x15", NM, A1......**$225.00**

McCormick, sign, paper, Back From The War, farmer/girl greet soldier, 18x27", VG, A3/A9........................**$100.00**

McCormick Farm Machinery, calendar, 1912, color image of girl/roses in landscape, black/white image of horse-drawn machine, incomplete, VG, A8..................**$115.00**

McCulloch Chain Saws, thermometer, reverse glass, round, arched window gauge, Hot Or Cold/Start Fast, 1950s, 14", NM, A3 ....**$100.00**

McDonald's, bank, Grimace, ceramic, purple, 1985, 10", MIB, D23 ....**$25.00**

McDonald's, bank, Ronald's Happy Times, 1993, 7½", MIB, D23 ....**$15.00**

McDonald's, bank, Ronald's Singing Wastebasket, 1975, EX, D23 ....**$10.00**

McDonald's, bop bag, Grimace, 1978, 8", MIP, D23....**$4.00**

McDonald's, Christmas stocking, Ronald/graphics, vinyl, 1981, EX, D23...**$5.00**

McDonald's, cookie cutter, Fry Kid on unicycle, red or green plastic, 1987, NM, D23......................................**$5.00**

McDonald's, cookie cutter, Ronald or Grimace bust, plastic, red or yellow, 1978, NM, D23, each **$3.00**

McDonald's, cup holder (car window), red, super size, NM, D23...**$3.00**

McDonald's, doll, Hamburglar, vinyl/cloth, 1972, 16", NM, D23 ....**$12.00**

McDonald's, erasers, Ronald with book/Grimace with skateboard/Hamburglar with skates, 1991, NM, D23, each **$2.00**

McDonald's, game, Ronald Ring Toss, 1993, MIB, NM, D23...**$12.00**

McDonald's, game, Tic-Tac-Mac, Grimace/Ronald McDonald, 1981, NM, D23 ....**$5.00**

McDonald's, hand puppets, set of 3, Ronald/Grimace/Hamburglar, 1993, MIB, D23 ....**$25.00**

McDonald's, magic slate, Tic-Tac-Go, 1988, NM, D23...**$2.00**

McDonald's, magnet, Hamburglar In Space, M, D23 ..**$3.00**

McDonald's, ornament, 1981, Christmas stocking with Ronald, vinyl, NM, D23 ....**$5.00**

McDonald's, ornament, 1985, reindeer, plush, MIB, D23 ...**$5.00**

McDonald's, ornament, 1992, Holiday Take Out, Enesco, MIB, D23 ....**$25.00**

McDonald's, ornament, 1992-93, Mc Ho Ho Ho, Enesco, MIB, D23 ....**$20.00**

McDonald's, pen, Holiday Greetings, 1990, M, D23 ...**$2.00**

McDonald's, pin-back button, I Support Ronald McDonald, 2" dia, NM, D23 ....**$2.00**

McDonald's, pin-back button, Low Fat Yogurt, 3½" dia, NM, D23 ....**$2.00**

McDonald's, pin-back button, Make It A Mac Tonight, 2" square, NM, D23 ....**$3.00**

McDonald's, pin-back button, Visit With Ronald, 3", NM, D23 ....**$2.00**

McDonald's, plate, Ronald Rhyme, 1989, 9", M, D23 ..**$5.00**

McDonald's, plates, carnival scenes, Melamine, 1993, 9½", M, D23, each **$5.00**

McDonald's, plates, Four Seasons, 1977, M, D23, each...**$6.00**

McDonald's, postcard, Ronald McDonald, 1970, 3x5", NM (unused), D23 ....**$12.00**

McDonald's, postcard/coupon, free hamburger/fries, early restaurant against deep blue sky, EX, D19.........**$25.00**

McDonald's, puzzle, Springbok, 1992, 24x30", MIP, D23...**$25.00**

McDonald's, record, One Million Dollar Menu, cardboard, 1988, NM, D23 ....**$5.00**

McDonald's, record, Ronald McDonald's Kids Radio Birthday Party, 1970s, M (sealed), D23 ....**$10.00**

McDonald's, record, Share A Song From Your Heart, 1980, M (sealed), D23...**$10.00**

McDonald's, ring, flasher, Ronald diving into water, NM, D23 ....**$20.00**

McDonald's, ring, Grimace 500 Smile Race or Spaceship Friendship, M, D23, each **$5.00**

McDonald's, ruler, Ronald McDonald, flexible, 1981, 6", NM, D23...**$2.00**

McDonald's, shoelace ornament, Ronald McDonald, 1986, M, D2 ....**$2.00**

McDonald's, sunglasses, Ronald/Birdie/Hamburglar, MIP, D23, each...**$6.00**

McDonald's, watch, quartz, Ronald on face, for employees only, MIB, D23...**$60.00**

McDonald's, whistle, McDonald's Tootler, green, 1985, M, D23 ....**$2.00**

McFadden Publications, sign, cardboard stand-up, Murder!/A Full Months Reading!, pictures 3 magazines, 1930s, 32x23", EX+, A1...**$200.00**

McGarvey Atwood Coffee sign, hardboard stand-up, We Serve...Of Course!, image of steaming cup against yellow/brown ground, 6x12", NM, A3 ....$25.00

McGarvey Coffee, can, 1/4-lb, key-wind lid, metallic red, NM (unopened), A3.................................$65.00

McGarvey's Flame Room Coffee, can, 1-lb, key-wind lid, red/black, EX+, A3.................................$30.00

McGarvey's Flame Room Coffee, can, 2-lb, key-wind lid, red/black, EX+, A3.................................$30.00

McKesson's Asprin, thermometer, porcelain, Best For Pain..., product shown below, brown/cream, curved corners, 27", NM, A6/A1, from $325 to $350.00

McLaughlin's Columbia Coffee, can, 1-lb, pry lid, white, EX+, A3 ....$60.00

McLaughlin's Kept-Fresh Coffee, can, 1-lb, key-wind lid, red, EX+, A3.................................$50.00

McLaughlin's Manor House Coffee, can, 1-lb, key-wind lid, green, NM (unopened), A19 ....$120.00

McLaughlin's Manor House Coffee, can, 1-lb, key-wind lid, landscape scene, NM, A3................................$50.00

McSorley's Famous Lager Beer/Cream Stock Ale, tray, rectangular, gold lettering on brown rim around man playing solitaire, 13", VG+, A8..........................$100.00

Meadow Sweet Peanut Butter, pail, EX+, A18 ....$200.00

Meadville Pure Rye/Genuine Rye Whiskey, sign, tin, lettering above/below angel with trumpet atop red heart on blue ground, ornate gold frame, 44x34", EX, A7.........$3,000.00

Mecca Brand Coffee, can, 1/2-lb, pry lid, tall, EX, A3 ...$45.00

Mecca Cigarettes, sign, cardboard, 10 For 35¢, bust image of woman in red, product pack lower right, framed, 31x24", VG, A7 ....$700.00

Meccano (Erector Parts), tin, square, curved corners, mother/sister praising brother for building Eiffel Tower, ½x2½x2½", EX, D37 ....$40.00

Medaglia D'Oro Caffe, can, 1-lb, key-wind lid, EX+ (unopened), A18.................................$20.00

Medaglia D'Oro Caffe (Demi-Tasse), can, 1-lb, key-wind lid, NM, A18 ....$18.00

Medaglia D'Oro Coffee, can, 1-lb, key-wind lid, EX, A3.$25.00

Medaglia D'Oro Coffee, can, ½-lb, key-wind lid, NM, A3 ....$32.00

Meerschaum Cut Plug, tin, horizontal box, curved blue, red/gold trim, EX, A3 ....$35.00

Meisterschaft, cigar box label, outer, rower, 4½x4½", M, D5 ....$40.00

Mellin's Biscuits, tin, round, Free Sample, 2½", EX+, A3 ...$45.00

Mellin's Food, sign, cardboard die-cut stand-up, Our Baby, baby in chair, text on reverse 6x5", EX, A6.........$40.00

Mello Ice Cream, sign, tin, For Goodness Sake! Eat... in red/blue on yellow, The Mello Fello at left, 2-sided, 1957, 24x36", EX+, A13 ....$250.00

Mello Ice Cream, sign, tin, Mello Ice Cream in black/red on yellow, The Mello Fello upper left, 24x36", NM (NOS), A6.......................................$140.00

Mello-Sip Coffee, can, 1-lb, key-wind lid, EX+, A3 ..$65.00

Mellocup Coffee, can, 1-lb, key-wind lid, orange, EX+, A3 ....$180.00

Mellor & Rittenhouse Licorice/Lozenges, tin, vertical box, glass front, blue-green, Somers Bros, pre-1901, VG+, A18 ....$150.00

Memory, cigar box label, inner lid, old man dreaming by fireplace, 6x9", M, D5 ....$40.00

Memory, crate label, California orange, silhouette of girl in frame/pink rose in glass vase, Porterville, EX, D3 .$8.00

Menasha Gem Premium Beer, tap knob, ball shape, chrome with green/silver-on-white celluloid insert, EX, A8.......................................$95.00

Mennen Borated Talcum, tin, sample, round, baby, striped ground, 2", EX+ (unused), A15...........................$45.00

Mennen Borated Talcum Powder, tin, regular size, baby, striped ground, EX, A3........................$60.00

Mennen Flesh Tint Talcum, tin, regular size, pink roses, EX, A18 ....$50.00

Mennen Talcum for Men, tin, sample, flower basket, 2¼", EX, D37.......................................$45.00

Mennen's Borated Talcum Toilet Powder, tin, sample, blue, 1½", G-EX, A3/D37, from $55 to $150.00

Mennen's Borated Talcum Toilet Powder, tin, sample, 2¼", EX, D37.......................................$125.00

Mennen's Flesh Tint Talcum, tin, sample, 2¼", EX, D37.......................................$50.00

Mennen's Kora Konia Medicated Powder, tin, sample, 2", EX, D37.......................................$30.00

Mennen's Narangia Talcum Powder, tin, sample, 2¼", EX, D37, minimum value $65.00

Mennen's Talcum Powder, sign, flange, with display tray, die-cut image of child holding product can, Beach Art Display, 15x24", G+, A9 ....$2,750.00

Mennen's Violet Talcum, tin, sample, no portrait, 2", EX, D37, minimum value **$40.00**
Mennen's Violet Talcum Toilet Powder, tin, regular size, portrait, EX+, A3 ....**$100.00**
Mennen's Violet Talcum Toilet Powder, tin, sample, portrait, 2¼", EX, D37 ....**$140.00**

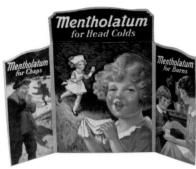

Mentholatum, sign, cardboard trifold, ...For Head Colds/For Chaps/For Burns, 3 scenes, 35x48", NM (unused), A15 ....**$625.00**
Meow Mix, doll, Meow Mix Cat, vinyl, 1970s, NM, D20...**$45.00**
Mercedes Benz, sign, porcelain, round, convex, 2-tone gray name/leaf swag design around 3-point emblem on blue, 23" dia, NM, A1..**$450.00**
Mercury Sales/Service, sign, porcelain, Sales above/Service below Mercury on center band, red/white/blue, 30x48", VG, A2 ....**$825.00**
Merita Bread, sign, cardboard, Join Merita's Lone Ranger Safety Club, shows Lone Ranger on Silver above, 28x16", G, A9 ....**$225.00**
Merita Bread, sign, tin, It's Enriched/Buy..., Lone Ranger on Silver above large loaf, 1959, 36x24", EX-NM+, A6/A1/ A13, from $950 to..**$2,200.00**
Meritt Powder, product display, cardboard box with marque/14 full tins of powder, NM, A3 ....**$65.00**
Mermaids, cigar box labels, outer, 6-sided, mermaids on shore, Heppenheimer & Maurer litho, EX, A5 ...**$120.00**
Merry Dance, cigar box label, inner lid, dancing gypsy/clown/musicians, 1886, 6x9", EX, D5.........**$35.00**
Metro, pump sign, porcelain, 5-point shield, red Pegasus above Metro lettered in green on white, 13x13", EX, A1 ....**$475.00**
Metro-Goldwyn-Mayer Pictures, sign, tin, See...At Leading Theatres, red/black on yellow, black border, embossed, 12x21", VG, A3..**$200.00**
Metropolitan Cigar Store, St Louis, letter opener, metal ice-pick type, EX, A5 ....**$50.00**
Metropolitan Life Insurance Co, calendar, 1904, die-cut cardboard, calendar months above/below smiling girl surrounded by holly, 20x7", NM+, A3..............**$150.00**
Metz Beer, sign, cardboard, Swing To Metz/The Finest Beer In Town, Western couple dancing, 24x22", NM, A13 ...**$55.00**
Metz Jubilee Beer, radio, plastic bottle form with labels, rotating bottle cap changes channels, 24", working, VG, A9..**$225.00**
Mexican Maid, cigar box label, outer, 1900, EX, D5.**$17.00**
Meyer-Roths Hand Made Cigar, tin, round, slip lid, paper label, EX, A3..**$25.00**

Meyer's Ice Cream, tray, round, boy/girl eating ice cream, name/fruit on rim, 13" dia, EX+, A1 ..$935.00
MFA, gas globe, 3-pc, Capolite white plastic body, glass lenses, red/white/blue shield on white, NM lenses/G- body, A1..**$200.00**
MGM Studios, statue, lion on beveled base, bronze-finished metal, American Art Works, 4x5x2", EX, A15 .....**$325.00**

Miami Powder Co, Xenia, Ohio, sign, paper, mallards in flight, artist MT Nells, 1891, wood frame, image: 25x18", VG+, A9 ....**$2,500.00**
Michelin, air compressor, cast iron/metal, Michelin Man seated at rear as if on motorcycle, 5x10x12", VG, A5 ....**$425.00**

Michelin, ashtray, Bakelite, white Michelin Man seated on round brown geometric dish with 2 rests, 5x6", NM, A1..**$100.00**
Michelin, costume, nylon/metal Michelin Man with yellow sash, EX, A6..**$900.00**

Michelin, display figure, Michelin Man seated, plastic, white, black lettering on cream sash, 1966, 19", NM+ (NOS), A6...$210.00

Michelin, display figure, Michelin Man standing, plastic, 12", M, D20..$45.00

Michelin, doll, Michelin Man holding Michelin Baby, squeeze vinyl, white, blue bib, 6½", EX+, A14 ..$200.00

Michelin, key chain, molded metal figure of the Michelin Man, 3", EX, A6..$15.00

Michelin, puzzle, figural Michelin Man on bicycle, MIP, D20..$55.00

Michelin, radio, Michelin Man figure, plastic, made in Italy, 1960s, NM+, D20 ....$400.00

Michelin, sign, porcelain, Michelin Men (5) with tires in vertical row, name above/below, black/yellow, 59x16", VG, A6...$500.00

Michelin, sign, porcelain, pointed bottom, Michelin Man on speeding bike, white border, 19x15", EX+, A6...$425.00

Michelin, sign, porcelain, pointed bottom, Michelin Man running with tire, name above, yellow/white/blue, 1967, 32x27", VG, A6..$300.00

Michelin, sign, tin, Michelin Man (head) flanking name, yellow/black, inserted in casing, 5x33", G-EX, A6/D22, from $140 to...$450.00

Michelin, sign, tin, pointed bottom, Michelin Man with tire on yellow, yellow name on blue above, white border, 16x12", VG, A6..$100.00

Michelin, toy truck, tractor-trailer, Majorette, rare, MIB, D20 ....$200.00

Michelin, truck-mounted ornament, figural Michelin Man, 9", M, D20 ....$75.00

Michelin, watch fob, metal, rectangular, Earth Mover Tires, embossed image of Michelin Man next to 3 tires, EX, A20..$20.00

Michelin Tyres, sign, tin, head of Michelin Man on red left of black lettering on yellow, 2x19", EX, A6................$275.00

Michelob, sign, neon, white name surrounded by red bow tie neon, gold Anheuser-Busch A-&-eagle logo atop, 1940s, 40", NM, A13......................................$85.00

NORTHEASTERN **Michigan** BOOSTER
FISHING — HUNTING
CAMPING — LAKE RESORTS
YOU WILL ENJOY MICHIGAN
QUALITY "MICHIGAN" CIGAR

Michigan, cigar box label, inner lid, hunting/ fishing/camping scenes, 6x9", M, D5 ....$25.00

Michigan Stove Co, match holder, cast iron, Michigan Stove Co's Stoves Are The Best, 7x4", A3....................$215.00

Mickey Mouse Shoe Polish, hat, paper, Cirage Mickey, image of Mickey polishing shoe next to tin of polish, Disney/French, 1930s, 6x12", EX, D22 ....$75.00

Middleby Root Beer, dispenser, amber glass mug shape with handle, chrome lid, Bakelite base, white name, 16", NM, A13...$275.00

Midway Superior, pump sign, porcelain, Midway/Superior/No Equal At It's Price double lines in between, red/white/blue, 11x11", NM, A1.........................$140.00

Mike Conroy Tobacco, tin, round, slip lid, paper label shows gray/white images of boxer with multicolored borders, 5x5" dia, VG, A6 ....$150.00

Mil-K-Botl, bottle display/bottle, cardboard, Don't Say Orange/Say Mil-K-Botl/12 Ounces 5¢, EX, D30 ...$75.00

Mil-K-Botl, menu board, tin, Don't Say Orange/Drink Mil-K-Botl/Sold Here 5¢, red/white/blue, blackboard below, 23x17", NM, D10...$100.00

Mil-Kay, sign, tin, Drink Vitamin Drinks/Mil-Kay The Vitamin Drink/Delicious Orange Phosphate/5¢, black waiter with tray, NM, D30..$750.00

Mil-Kay, sign, tin, Drink.../A Vitamin B1 Drink/Made With Real Oranges/Sold In Bottles Only, orange in center, 14x35", NM, D30...$175.00

Milady Coffee, can, 1-lb, key-wind lid, EX-EX+, A18/A3, from $50 to...$70.00

Milburn Wagon Co, fan/mask, cardboard, wooden handle, English bobby, ca 1900, EX+, A3 ....$25.00

Milburn Wagon Co, sign, tin, The Demand For The Milburn Wagon, confrontation between bandits/wagon, 20x28", VG+, D14 ....$1,600.00

Military Brand, cigar box label, outer, square, 3 Civil War soldiers at campsite, Heppenheimer & Maurer litho #1624, M, A5 ....$250.00

Military Foot Powder, tin, red/white/blue, 4½", VG+, A3...$35.00

Millar's Magnet Brand Coffee, can, 1-lb, key-wind lid, VG+, A3...$25.00

Millard Breath Pellets, vendor, glass cylinder with brass top/bottom, Pat 1916, 8½", VG+, A9 ....$900.00

Millboy (The), cigar box label, sample, oval portrait flanked by houses, American Litho Co/Witsch & Schmitt #2641, EX+, A5...$100.00

Miller Brewing Co, sign, litho, Madame Calve As Carmen in oval, 'The Best'/Milwaukee flanked by bottles, Wolf & Co, 1901, 34x25", EX, A7...............................$4,250.00

Miller High Life Beer, charger, tin, Miller Girl sitting on moon holding up glass, C Shonk litho, c 1907, 24" dia, G, A9..$300.00

Miller High Life Beer, display figure, Miller Girl with glass, hard plastic, 6¼", M, D25.................................$50.00

Miller High Life Beer, matchbook, bottles in ice on back, 20 strike, front striker, M, D28 ....$6.00

Miller High Life Beer, motion lamp, bottle in ice bucket, plastic, EX, D25..$250.00

Miller High Life Beer, sign, composition, lake scene with grounded boat, embossed, wood-grain self-frame, 14x11", VG, A7...$250.00

Miller High Life Beer, sign, porcelain, curved, ...The Best Milwaukee, white/black on red, white border, 14x21", A1...$100.00

Miller High Life Beer, sign, reverse on glass, panel with round top corners on wood base (The Champagne of Bottle Beer), 1950s, 6x10", VG+, A8..................$50.00

Miller High Life Beer, sign, tin, Drink High Life Brew in oval, Made By... below, 13x20", VG+, A8 .... $125.00

Miller High Life Beer, sign, tin, Enjoy Life With.../The Champagne Of Bottle Beer, red emblem in center, embossed, raised rim, 20x24", EX, A1 .... $100.00

Miller High Life Beer, toy train boxcar, HO scale, white, 1960s, EX, A19 .... $40.00

Miller High Life Beer, toy train boxcar, HO scale, yellow, 1950s, NM, A19 .... $50.00

Miller High Life Beer, tray, round, deep rim, girl on moon surrounded by red/yellow/blue lettering, gold-trimmed rim, 12" dia, NM, A18 .... $65.00

Miller Sanitate Nipple, display, die-cut folding cardboard, baby in highchair opposite hand-held nipple, marque atop, 10x12", EX, A15 .... $180.00

Miller's Game Cock Rye/John Miller & Co, charger, tin, bottle on table by hanging dead game birds, 24" dia, EX, A7 .... $500.00

Miller's Gold Medal Cocoa, tin, sample, rectangular, black/red, gold lid, 1890s, 2", EX+, A15 .... $250.00

Miller's Hand Made Cigars, tin, vertical square, slip lid, EX+, A3 .... $60.00

Miller's Home Coffee, can, 1-lb, key-wind lid, 5¢ Off, white on red, NM (unopened), A1 .... $70.00

Miller's May-Day Coffee, can, 1-lb, key-wind lid, blue, EX+, A3 .... $35.00

Miller's May-Day Coffee, can, 1-lb, key-wind lid, metallic red, NM-NM+ (unopened), A3, from $35 to $50.00

Miller's May-Day Coffee, can, 1-lb, pry lid, red/white/blue, NM+, A3 .... $65.00

Millers Outpost, bank, General Jeans, vinyl, 1979, 8½", scarce, NM, D20 .... $125.00

Milo Coffee, can, 1/2-lb, key-wind lid, white on blue, NM (unopened), A3 .... $100.00

Miners & Puddlers Smoking Tobacco, pail, red/white/ blue, 7x6" dia, VG-EX+, A3/A1, from $100 to ..$215.00

Minimax Fire Extinguisher, salesman's sample, metal/canvas case, cone-shaped, 1919, 6", EX, A6 .... $220.00

Minneapolis Breakfast Food/International Food Co, box, paper label on cardboard, woman/factory/lettering, pre-1905, 9x6x3", VG+, A3 .... $320.00

Minneapolis Brewing Co Golden Grain Belt Beers, sign, tin, white men with dogs/Indian by teepee, yellow field beyond, self-framed, 26x18", G, A7 .... $600.00

Minnehaha Pure Ground Cloves, container, cardboard, yellow with red center band, round image of waterfall, VG+, A3 .... $55.00

Minnesota Bouquet, cigar box label, outer, octagonal, image of steamship, American Litho Co, EX, A5 .... $110.00

Minnesota City Brewery Bock Beer, sign, paper, reveler blowing horn on goat jumping barrel, 30x20", VG+, A1/A8 .... $300.00

Minnesota Linseed Oil Pain Co House Paints, sign, tin, paint can shape, black/white/gray, with handle/hanger, 2-sided, C Shonk litho, 14x9", NM/G+, A1 .... $150.00

Minty's Toothpaste, display figure, plaster bust of smiling boy, Minty's For Me Every Time lettered on 3 sides, held product, 16", EX, A2 .... $200.00

Minuet Coffee, can, 1-lb, key-wind, silhouette couple, G+, A3 .... $50.00

Minuet Coffee, can, 1-lb, key-wind, songbirds, EX+, A3 .... $120.00

Miracle, crate label, California orange, genie holding tray with 3 oranges/orchard scene/magic lamp, Placentia, 1928, EX, D3 .... $4.00

Miramar, crate label, California lemon, groves between mountains/ocean cliffs, Montecito, M, D12 .... $15.00

Mirelle Toilet Powder, tin, round, 5½", NM, A18 ..... $30.00

Mirelle Toilet Powder, tin, sample, 2", EX-EX+, A18, from $50 to $70.00

Miscoe Dry Orange, sign, cardboard cutout, product bottle over large orange with 2 leaves, 14x11", VG+, A3 .... $15.00

Miss America Coffee, can, 1-lb, key-wind, red/white/blue, EX+, A18 .... $40.00

Miss America Coffee, can, 2-lb, key-wind, red/white/blue, VG+, A3 .... $30.00

Miss Carolina Coffee, can, 1-lb, key-wind, red, EX+, A18 .... $60.00

Miss Detroit Broad Leaf, display box, cardboard, oval image with name above/below, red/white/blue, 9x9x10", EX, A2 .... $200.00

Miss Detroit Cigar, sign, tin, It Makes Your Nickel Worth A Dime..½¢, man in chair next to open box, black ground, beveled, 19x13", VG, A6 .... $550.00

Miss Prim, cigar box label, sample, embellished portrait of young lady, Geo Schlegel litho #1924, 1894, EX, A5 .... $130.00

Missing Miss 5¢ Cigar, sign, tin, curled corners, circular bust image of lady in red, 15x14", NM, D6 .... $1,200.00

Mission Beverages, bottle topper, cardboard, Mission Orange 5¢, 2 personified bottles 'squeezing' orange half, blue ground, EX, D30 .... $32.00

Mission Beverages, bottle topper, cardboard, Try This Delicious New Beverage, hand squeezing fresh orange juice, M, A16 .... $60.00

Mission Beverages, bottle topper/bottle, cardboard, Mission Of California/Naturally Good, sun rising over grove/fruits, EX, D30 ....**$32.00**

Mission Beverages, calendar, 1953, 25x14", NM, D30 .**$100.00**

Mission Beverages, dispenser, cylinder with porcelain base, orange/brown, 26x12" dia, VG+, A1....$190.00

Mission Beverages, dispenser, glass barrel shape (Vaseline) on Bakelite base, embossed lettering, VG-NM, A9/A13, from $125 to..**$225.00**

Mission Beverages, dispenser, glass bottle on metal base with cardboard sign (wire frame) atop, 28x18", EX, A6...**$375.00**

Mission Beverages, dispenser, glass goblet (green) on chrome pedestal base, flat chrome lid/spigot, Grapefruit, 1920s-30s, NMIB, A13.....................................**$275.00**

Mission Beverages, dispenser, glass goblet (green) on chrome pedestal base, flat chrome lid/spigot, no lid o/w NM, A13...**$65.00**

Mission Beverages, dispenser, glass goblet (lt amber) on chrome pedestal base, flat chrome lid/spigot, NM, A13 ....**$150.00**

Mission Beverages, door plate, tin, bottle cap/swirled bottle, embossed, 12", NM, A13...............................**$160.00**

Mission Beverages, menu board, cardboard, Mission Of California, Todays Specials, menu slots flanking bottle/fruit, 13x32", NM, D30...**$100.00**

Mission Beverages, sign, cardboard, First On The Program, girl in blue with bottle by television, logo lower left, 20x26", NM+, D30...**$150.00**

Mission Beverages, sign, flange, bottle cap shape, Mission Orange Ice Cold, 1940s-50s, 18x19", EX-NM, A13/A6, from $200 to $375.00

Mission Beverages, sign, flange, tin, Drink Mission Orange/California Sunshine Flavor, smiling sun/flag, 20x20", NM, A1 ....**$250.00**

Mission Beverages, sign, tin, Mission Of California Orange/Naturally Good, white/blue sign/row of receding bottles, yellow, 12x30", NM, D30 ....**$120.00**

Mission Beverages, sign, tin/cardboard, round, Ice Cold Mission Orange/Makes Thirst A Pleasure, black/orange/yellow, 9" dia, NM, D30 ....**$125.00**

Mission Beverages, syrup jug, 128-oz, clear glass/aluminum handle, embossed Mission Orange, original cork, NM, A13..**$175.00**

Mission Beverages, thermometer, tin, bottle (shouldered) on yellow/blue, squared top/bottom, 1940s, 14", EX+, A4..**$350.00**

Mission Beverages, thermometer, tin, bottle (tilted) on yellow/blue, curved top/bottom, 1940s, 16", M, A4..........**$250.00**

Mission Beverages, thermometer, tin, bottle on white, stepped sides, 1950s, 17", NN, A13.....................**$150.00**

Mission Coffee, can, 1-lb, key-wind lid, EX-NM, A3, from $65 to...**$100.00**

Mission Malt Tonic, label, 12-oz, Los Angeles Brewing Co/CA, pre-1920, M, A10 ....**$37.00**

Missouri Pacific Lines, calendar, perpetual, tin, cardboard number pads, Route Of The Eagles, beveled, 19x13", NM, A7...**$300.00**

Mista Joe, crate label, California vegetable, We Serve the Best says black dining-car steward, Salinas, M, D12 ....**$5.00**

Mister Softee Ice Cream, toy truck, tin, friction, Mister Softee logo with Cowes/Shakes/Sundaes lettered on side, Japan, 2x4", M, D25 ....**$45.00**

Mitchel's Extra Pale Beer, label, 12-oz, Mitchel Brewing Co/Mokena IL, IRTP or WF statement, 1933-50, M (soaked off bottle or paper), A10......................**$50.00**

Mitchel's Extra Pale Beer, label, 64-oz, Mitchel Brewing Co/Mokena IL, IRTP or WF statement, 1933-50, M (soaked off bottle or paper), A10......................**$50.00**

Mitchell Wheat, sign, paper, Magic Vermin Exterminator, comical depiction of black man/rats, framed, image: 15x21", VG, A9..**$350.00**

Mitchell's Extra Dry Premium Beer, clock, round, glass face, brown plastic case, triangle logo, electric, 15" dia, VG+, A8...**$220.00**

Mitchell's Premium Beer, drinking glass, fountain-type with rolled bottom, clear, applied red oval logo, 6", NM+, A8...**$100.00**

Mitchell's Premium Beer, drinking glasses, barrel, applied red oval logo, set of 6, MIB, A8.........................**$230.00**

Mitchell's Premium Beer, tap knob, ball shape, black Bakelite with metal insert, G, A8.................................**$80.00**

Mitchells & Butlers Ales & Stouts, sign, tin, lettering above/below shaded oval image of buck leaping over water, self-framed, 15x17", EX, A7 ....**$150.00**

MJB Coffee, can, ½-lb, key-wind lid, NM, A3............**$35.00**

MJB Coffee, store bin, 15-lb, tin, round, slip lid, Quality Coffee Of America, white on green, EX, A18 ....**$85.00**

Mo-Sam Steel Cut Coffee, can, 5-lb, embossed slip lid, paper label (rare), VG, A3 ....**$50.00**

Mobil, ashtray, bronze-plated cast metal, flying Pegasus above 5-point emblem dish, 6x6x7", EX+, A1....**$350.00**

Mobil, drinking glasses, clear glass with red painted-on images of Pegasus, set of 6, 5", NM, A6 ....**$50.00**

Mountain States Telephone & Telegraph Co, ashtray, round, 3 rests, blue, advertising on white on flat rim around serviceman in center, NM+, A3.................$90.00

Mountie, crate label, California orange, mountie on horseback, VG, D5...$60.00

Mouquiry Chicken Bouillon Tablets, tin, rectangular, square corners, scrolled banners/decoration around oval image of lady with tray, ½x2x2¼", EX, D37 ....$15.00

Moxie, ashtray, ceramic, round with 3 rests, Moxie Man in center, EX+, A3 ....$70.00

Moxie, bottle carrier, cardboard box, Drink Moxie, EX, A16 ....$25.00

Moxie, bottle carrier, wood crate, Drink Moxie, EX, A16..$25.00

Moxie, bottle carrier with bottles, 6-pack, Moxie Man/Moxie symbol on yellow/red stripes, EX+, A3 ....$100.00

Moxie, bottle display, cardboard, bottle shape, EX, D30 ..$200.00

Moxie, bottle topper/bottle, cardboard, You Need Moxie/Drink It Ice Cold, man with arm up, EX, D30 ....$135.00

Moxie, bottle topper/bottle, cardboard, You Need Moxie/Drink It Ice Cold, lady with arm up, EX, D30 ....$135.00

Moxie, clock, Baird, figure-8, Roman numerals, Moxie/Of Course You Will Have Some/It's So Healthful..., 31", restored, A9 ....$1,500.00

Moxie, clock, square, plastic, Since 1884/Old Fashion Moxie on orange, Roman numerals, gold embossed frame, 16x16", EX, A6 ....$200.00

Moxie, dish, china, oval/tab handles, white, Moxie man bordered by bluebirds/yellow flowers, gold trim, 1920s, 5x10", EX, D22 ....$145.00

Moxie, dispenser, glass jug inverted on milk glass base with Moxie logo, EX+, D30 ....$350.00

Moxie, display, cardboard die-cut stand-up, large bottle with shelf accommodates 1-pt 10-oz bottle, 1915-25, 28", EX, A13 ....$400.00

Moxie, display, cardboard die-cut stand-up, Shall I Send A Case Of Moxie To Your Home?, Moxie man with case, 16x6", EX+, A3 ....$320.00

Moxie, fan, cardboard, 1915, Muriel Ostriche/Moxie Man below, EX+, A3 ....$30.00

Moxie, fan, cardboard, 1916, Francis Pritchard/carnival scene, VG+, A13 ....$60.00

Moxie, fan, cardboard, 1918, Eileen Percy, NM, D30...$75.00

Moxie, fan, cardboard, 1918, Francis Pritchard/My Belgin Rose, EX, A13..$55.00

Moxie, fan, cardboard, 1918, Laura Walker/Over There!, EX, A13 ....$65.00

Moxie, fan, cardboard, 1918, Muriel Ostriche, NM+, D30$75.00

Moxie, fan, cardboard, 1919, Eileen Percy, NM+, D30 ..$75.00

Moxie, fan, cardboard, 1919, Muriel Ostriche, NM+, D30 ..**$75.00**

Moxie, fan, cardboard, 1922, Rocking Horse/Moxie Man, NM, D30/A13, from $65 to $75.00

Moxie, fan, cardboard, 1923, Eileen Percy (?)/Moxie Man, VG+, A16 ....**$80.00**

Moxie, fan, celluloid, fold-out blades (marked Drink Moxie) connected by ribbon, white, ca 1910s-20s, EX, A13 .**$45.00**

Moxie, horsemobile, tin, red or blue, HD Beach litho, Pat 1917, 7x9", G-VG, A9, from $1200 to **$1,450.00**

Moxie, postcard, shows the Moxie horsemobile on white, c 1916, NM, A17..**$170.00**

Moxie, sign, cardboard, Lets Get Acquainted.../Moxie Six-Pak 5¢.../Limited Time Only, red/white/blue, NM+, D30.**$55.00**

Moxie, sign, cardboard cutout, Drink Moxie, elongated oval, red, 8x18", EX+, D30 ....**$65.00**

Moxie, sign, cardboard cutout, Drink Moxie, white Moxie outlined in black on orange, 21x35", NM+, D30 ....**$550.00**

Moxie, sign, cardboard cutout, Drink Moxie..., keyhole shape, red/white/blue, 10x8", NM+, D30 ....**$100.00**

Moxie, sign, cardboard cutout, Evolution Of Transportation, Over 50 Years Of Popularity/Moxie, Moxie Boy, 40x34", rare, VG, D30 ....**$300.00**

Moxie, sign, cardboard cutout, First For Thirst/Drink Moxie, girl leaning against car talking to couple, 40x30", EX+, D30 ....**$300.00**

Moxie, sign, cardboard cutout, hand-held bottle, 20x10", NM, D30 ....**$125.00**

Moxie, sign, cardboard cutout, He's Got Moxie 5¢, boy baseball player with bottle on red dot, 1940s, 16x12", M, A4 ....$250.00

Moxie, sign, cardboard cutout, Invigorating As An Ocean Breeze/Drink..., sailor girl at helm, 40x30", EX, D30 .**$250.00**

Moxie, sign, cardboard cutout, Moxie Man/red Drink Moxie disk/blue ovoid panel below, 30x28", EX+, D30.**$200.00**

Moxie, sign, cardboard cutout, Muriel Ostriche behind bottle crate, framed, 24x20", VG, D30 ....**$135.00**

Moxie, sign, cardboard cutout, stand-up, A Real Thirst Quencher/Drink..., man with glass/bottle, 1940s-50s, 19x13", NM, A13..$55.00

Moxie, sign, cardboard cutout, stand-up, Drink Moxie For Extra Pep!, boy & girl running/large bottle, 1940s-50s, EX, A13..$35.00

Moxie, sign, cardboard cutout, stand-up, Wake Up!, lady with parasol tickling sleeping Moxie Man with feather, 37x23", G+, A1 ....**$400.00**

Moxie, sign, celluloid, 1¢ Sale/Family Size/Moxie/3 For 36¢/You Save 17¢/Regular Price 2 For 35¢ Plus Deposit, 36x49", EX, D30 ....**$200.00**

Moxie, sign, flange, tin, octagonal, Drink/Moxie/100%, red/green/white, 8x8", VG+, A13 ....**$325.00**

Moxie, sign, flange, tin, oval, Drink Moxie, white on red with yellow/black border, yellow flange, 9x18", EX+/NM+, A3 ....**$330.00**

Moxie, sign, steel, Drink... on red/blue striped trapezoid field left of hand-held bottle on white, blue trim, 32x44", EX+, A2...**$230.00**

Moxie, sign, tin, Drink Moxie, black lettering outlined in yellow on red background, yellow/black border, 10x28", G+, D30 ....**$80.00**

Moxie, sign, tin, Drink Moxie, depicts horsemobile, 27x39", rare, G, A9 ....**$2,100.00**

Moxie, sign, tin, Drink Moxie, Moxie Man behind red panel, HD Beach litho, no size given, EX, A2..............**$600.00**

Moxie, sign, tin, Drink Moxie, trapezoid logo/hand-held bottle on white molded panel, black trim, 1956, 34x44", EX, A6..**$260.00**

Moxie, sign, tin, Drink Moxie, white on red, yellow border, 19x27", EX, D30 ....**$200.00**

Moxie, sign, tin, Drink Moxie 100%, red dot on black background, 24x24", VG, D30 ....**$85.00**

Moxie, sign, tin, Drink Moxie/Deliciously Different on billboard, horsemobile passing, 1933, 20x27", VG-EX, A13/D30, $450 to...**$550.00**

Moxie, sign, tin, Drink Moxie/Distinctively Different on red oval logo with yellow border on blue background, 19x27", NM, D30..**$250.00**

Moxie, sign, tin, Drink Moxie/Very Healthful, oval, embossed, raised rolled rim, 10x13", VG, A16...**$250.00**

Moxie, sign, tin, Drink Moxie/Very Healthful/Try Our Soda Syrups, flavor list below, stained-glass-look ground, 19x13", VG, A9 ....**$3,750.00**

Moxie, sign, tin, Moxie, belt-buckle shape with gold name embossed in center, 1900s, 5x6", rare, NM+, A4..**$500.00**

Moxie, sign, tin, Yes! We Sell.../Very Healthful/Feeds The Nerves, blue text/yellow diagonal band on red, 28x30", VG+, D30..................................**$800.00**

Moxie, sign, tin hanger, die-cut, Moxie lettered on Moxie Man's cap, 6x4½", EX, A16 ....**$275.00**

Moxie, sign, tin hanger, round, Moxie/I Like It, girl ready to drink from glass, gold rim, 6" dia, EX, A15 ......$725.00

Moxie, sign, tin hanger/stand-up, Drink Moxie on oval against wood-grain background, cardboard back, 3x10", NM, A15..**$150.00**

Moxie, syrup jug, glass, paper label, EX, D30 ....**$100.00**

Moxie, thermometer, tin, Drink Moxie/It's Always A Pleasure To Serve You, Moxie man next to gauge, red, 1953, 10x25", EX+, A13............................$700.00

Moxie, tip tray, I Just Love Moxie Don't You?, Moxie Girl against blossoms, 6" dia, VG, A8..........................**$75.00**

Moxie, tip tray, Moxie over flower design, 6" dia, EX+, A16 ....**$185.00**

Moxie, tray, round, handled, head image of Moxie Man, 10" dia, VG, A9..**$650.00**

Moxie/Pureoxia, sign, paper, Moxie Man with 2 bottles, yellow ground, 12x10", NM+, D30............................**$150.00**

Moxie/Pureoxia Ginger Ale, sign, cardboard, Drink Pureoxia Ginger Ale/Frank Archer Invites You To Visit Moxieland, elephant on car, 28x39", NM, D30..........**$450.00**

Moyer's Headache Tablets, sign, heavy paper, 15 For 10 Cts/...The Great Headache Cure, shows Dutch boy with fishing gear, c 1906, 10x7", EX, A6........................**$45.00**

Mr Bubble, doll, vinyl, 10", M, D20 ....**$35.00**

Mr Clean, doll, Mr Clean with arms folded (no base), vinyl, all white, 1960s, NM+, D20..................................**$135.00**

Mr Goodbar, pillow, shaped like candybar, 1989, 4x6", NM, D24..**$8.00**

Mrs LA Wellman Drygoods, Cornell Ill, calendar, 1916, die-cut cardboard, girl with daisies in hair surrounded by roses, 16x13", EX, A3....................................**$80.00**

Mrs Lane's Coffee, can, 1-lb, key-wind lid, yellow, NM (unopened), A3..**$90.00**

Mrs Tucker's Shortening, sign, porcelain, image of pail with Mrs Tucker's picture, 46x32", EX, D34 ....**$750.00**

Mt Cabin, sign, tin, Drink.../Just Sweet Enough/Just Tart Enough..., porter holding sign, red on yellow, embossed, 18x12", EX, A1 ....**$200.00**

Mt Clemens Brewing Co, ashtray, clear glass, rectangular with match holder, embossed, NM, A8................**$65.00**

Mt Diablo Fruit Farm, crate label, California pear, boy picking poppies in field/Mt Diablo, Bancroft, 1930s, M, D12 ....**$65.00**

Mt Hood, crate label, Oregon apple, Mt Hood/trees/lake, Hood River, M, D12..**$35.00**

Mt Hood Brewing Co, tray, round, close-up image of stag, gold lettered rim, 13" dia, G+, A8........................**$165.00**

Much-more Coffee, can, 1-lb, key-wind lid, yellow, cup/saucer, EX+, A3..**$110.00**

Muehlebach's Pilsener Beer, tip tray, round, Purest & Best, bottle on cross emblem in center, lettered gold rim, 5" dia, VG+, A8..**$40.00**

Mulford's Toilet Talcum, tin, sample, white, EX+, A3 .**$90.00**

Munsing Union Suits, sign, cardboard die-cut stand-up, Recommended By Millions Of Satisfied Munsingites, toddler/chalkboard, 1907, EX+, A3............................**$220.00**

Munsing Union Suits, sign, flange, man in Munsing Union Suit, 2 different images, die-cut scrolled border, Beach litho, 15x18", VG, A9 ....$3,500.00

Munsing Union Suits, sign, flange, mother/daughter in Munsing Union Suits, same image both sides, die-cut scrolled border, 15x19", VG, A9 ....$4,000.00

Munsing Wear, display bin, tin/wood frame base, Fashion Books/Take One/Ask For..., mother fixing daughter's hair, 15x15x12", VG+, A3 ....**$350.00**

Munsing Wear, sign, cardboard, name on white border above man in Union Suit standing with hands on hips, red ground, 30x20", VG, A9..................................**$75.00**

Munsing Wear, sign, tin, die-cut stand-up, Perfect Fitting..., mother on bench flanked by 2 children on lettered base, 20x19", VG, A7 ....**$3,250.00**

Munsing Wear, sign, tin die-cut stand-up, 6 children prancing in Perfect Fitting Union Suits atop base, 16x24", VG, A7 ....**$2,800.00**

Munsing Wear Union Suits, sign, tin, die-cut, Perfect Fitting..., mother seated holding out arms to 2 children, HD Beach litho, EX+, A3..**$3,100.00**

Munsingwear, sign, tin, oval mirrored image of girl with blue hair bow in Munsingwear, wood-grain self-frame, 37x25", VG, A2..**$860.00**

Munyon's Homeopathic Home Remedies, cabinet, tin, portrait on slant top, VG-EX+, A9/A15, from $575 to **$700.00**

Munyon's Homeopathic Remedies, cabinet, wood, tin front, Price List Of Cures, 24x16", G, A7 ....**$225.00**

Murad Cigarettes, pocket tin, vertical, EX, A3 ....**$70.00**

Murad The Turkish Cigarette, sign, flange, porcelain, vertical rectangle, Everywhere-Why?, exotic girl holding up product on red ground, EX, A18........................**$425.00**

Murad The Turkish Cigarette, sign, tin, Everywhere-Why?/15¢, woman holding up product, red ground, self-framed, 39x28", G-EX, A18/A7, from $425 to **$700.00**

Muriel Cigars, change receiver, label under glass with image of Muriel Cigars woman, VG, A2............................**$85.00**

Murine, calendar sign, tin, trademark lady, wood-grain ground, 18x8", no pad, VG+, A9.....................**$2,700.00**

Murine, sign, paper, trademark lady, lettering above/below, American litho, c 1903, framed, 28x18", G, A9 ..**$700.00**

Murine, sign, reverse-painted beveled glass, trademark lady, lettering above/below, 14x10", VG, A9 ....**$1,200.00**

Murphy Da-cote Univernish Varnish Stains, sign, tin stand-up, livingroom with 2 insets/paint samples below, self-framed, 27x19", EX, A7................................**$350.00**

Murray's 'Warrior' Plug Tobacco, sign, cardboard, round image of pirate with knife above product lettering, framed, 30x22", EX, A6 ....**$200.00**

Murray's Root Beer, dispenser, ceramic barrel atop tree-stump base, no lid, NM+, A16...........................**$200.00**

Musgo Baking Powder, container, round, cardboard, paper label, VG+ (full), A3 ....**$35.00**

Musky Soft Drinks/Coca-Cola Bottling Co, Wausau WI, sign, cardboard, die-cut fish, Ask For.../How Big?/Whopper Stopper, white on green, 8x26", VG, A7......**$175.00**

Musselman's Boot Jack Plug, see Boot Jack Plug

My Coca, bottle, amber, straight-sided, diamond label reads The Original Coca-Cola Woman, EX+ (NM label), A13 ....**$10.00**

My Match, cigar box label, sample, lady offering 3 gents cigars, OL Schwencke & Co litho #5234, EX, A5....**$130.00**

Myers Hub Mainsprings, tin, rectangular, blue, ½x3x5", VG, A18 ....**$10.00**

Myers Pumps, Hay Tools, Door Hangers/FF Myers & Bro Co, calendar, 1929, heavy paper, name on globe/small pad above graphics of different products, framed, 50x20", EX, A6 ....**$265.00**

∾ N ∾

N.J.C. Coffee, can, 1-lb, key-wind, red/white/blue, steaming cup, VG+, A3 ....**$95.00**

Nabisco, see also Chips Ahoy

Nabisco, see also National Biscuit Co or Uneeda Bakers

Nabisco, cookie jar, Barnum's Animals, ceramic, McCoy, M, D25 ....**$500.00**

Nabisco, sign, cardboard cutout, Merry Christmas, Santa in wreath holding out product packages, ca 1937, 17x25", NM, A9 ....**$1,000.00**

Nabisco Shredded Wheat, cereal box, Enjoy Rin-Tin-Tin On TV, with picture, 1956, EX, D1 ....**$85.00**

Nabisco Shredded Wheat, cereal box, Rin-Tin-Tin insignia patch, 1956, NM, D1..**$95.00**

Nabisco Sugar Wafers, sign, cardboard, name above chef with box of wafers within gold-trimmed border, framed, 11x8", NM, A6............................**$85.00**

Nabob Coffee, store display can, 1-lb, key-wind lid, genie & red/white lettering on white/green divided ground, EX, A18..**$100.00**

Nabob Pure Cayenne, tin, 1½-oz, NM, A3.................**$8.00**

Nabob Pure Marjoram, tin, 1½-oz, white/blue, NM, A3...**$22.00**

Nabobs, cigar box label, outer, black boy/white boy on fence, M, D5...**$50.00**

Nairn Linoleum Co, sign, paper, aerial factory scene with river traffic bordered by awards/name/etc, framed, image: 23x34", VG, A9 ....**$135.00**

Nalley's Mayonnaise, can, 30-lb, slip lid, red, EX, A18.**$20.00**

Nancy Lynn Coffee, can, 1-lb, key-wind lid, EX+, A18.**$35.00**

Nannette Face Powder, tin, rectangular, dk blue, metallic gold trim, 3", NM+, A3 ....**$50.00**

Naples Velvet Finish/Adams & Elting Co, sign, paper & cardboard, A Washable Flat Interior Finish, magic rabbit pulling colors out of can, ca 1920, 9x16", EX+, A3 ....**$110.00**

Nelson's Baby Powder, tin, silhouette image of children at play against sky, EX, A18.................**$100.00**

Nesbitt's, dispenser, glass top with grapefruit paper label, chrome lid/screw-on base, NM, A16.................**$220.00**

Nesbitt's, dispenser, 1-gal glass bottle with paper label inverted on pink glass base with reverse label, 18", EX, A1...**$325.00**

Nesbitt's, distance chart, cardboard/steel frame, shows distance from central point to other US cities, c 1955, 31x7", EX+, A19..**$40.00**

Nesbitt's, sign, cardboard, boy/girl with bottles smiling down at clown, 19x26", EX+, D30 ....**$125.00**

Nesbitt's, sign, cardboard, Drink Nesbitt's California Orange on disk, family barbecue scene, 1940s, 24x36", EX+, A13 ....$250.00

Nesbitt's, sign, cardboard, picnicking couple among flowers, mountain in distance, 25x36", G+, D30 ....**$75.00**

Nesbitt's, sign, porcelain, Nesbitt's Orange on geometric background, orange/white/black, Canadian (?), 1950s, 12x25", NM, A13 ....**$375.00**

Nesbitt's, sign, tin, A Soft Drink Made From Real Oranges, bottle on black dot on yellow, embossed, curved corners, 27x27", NM, A1.............................**$300.00**

Nesbitt's, sign, tin, Enjoy...A Delicious Drink, text/bottle on raised black dot on yellow, trimmed corners, 1940s, 33x33", NM, A13 ....**$275.00**

Nesbitt's, sign, tin/cardboard, round, Don't Say Orange/Say Nesbitt's, professor with bottle, 9" dia, VG-EX, A1/D30, from $65 to...**$125.00**

Nesbitt's, thermometer, tin, black, A Soft Drink Made From Real Oranges, bottle on sun dot, 1938, 23", EX, A1 ....$200.00

Nesbitt's, thermometer, tin, white, All This Good Comes From..., orange mascot drinking from straw, 16x6", EX+, A3...**$75.00**

Nesbitt's, thermometer, tin, yellow, Don't Say Orange Say..., bottle cap above/professor below, 27", VG+, A1..**$200.00**

Nesco/Royal, pot scraper, tin, red/white/black, front shows boy carrying products, back shows diamond logo, EX, A15.................................$550.00

Nestle, see also Alpine Coffee

Nestles Quik, doll, Quik Bunny, plush, bendable, 14", M, D20 ....**$30.00**

Nestor Egyptian Cigarettes, sign, tin, shows man/woman in Egyptian scene, 19x14", EX, A6 ....**$550.00**

New (The) Bachelor 5¢ Quality Cigar, sign, cardboard, hanger, lettering above/below man waving to wagon train in valley below campsite, 13x9", VG, A5...**$200.00**

New & True Coffee, can, 1-lb, key-wind lid, red/white/blue, striped, large cup, NM, A18 ....**$160.00**

New & True Coffee, can, 1-lb, key-wind lid, red/white/blue, striped, small cup, EX, A3.......................**$90.00**

New Bachelor, cigar box, 5 Cents on red corner band, man playing solitaire/dreaming of a woman, G+, A3..**$25.00**

New Bachelor, cigar tin, vertical box, EX+, A3 ....**$100.00**

New Bachelor Quality 5¢ Cigar, sign, tin, man pointing to white lettering on dk blue ground, blue/white striped border, 14x40", VG+, A1 ....**$160.00**

New Casaday Sulky Plow, see South Bend Chilled Plow Co

New Cuba, cigar box label, inner lid, shows Cuban flag/Gomex/Garcia, 1897, 6x9", M, D5 ....**$75.00**

New Cuba, cigar box label, inner lid, Morro Castle/Cuban flags, 6x9", M, D5...............................**$30.00**

New Deal The Blanced Coffee, can, 1-lb, pry lid, green/silver, VG+, A3...**$30.00**

New England Brewing Co's Superior Ales & Lager, sign, tin, busy campsite, 23x33", VG, A7.................**$2,000.00**

New England Coke, sign, porcelain, shield shape, white lettering on blue, white outline, 16x15", NM, A2...**$250.00**

New England Mince Meat, sign, paper, tiny people watching large hands cut large pie, Shober & Carrueville litho, framed, image: 20x25", VG, A9 ....**$700.00**

New Era Mocha & Java Coffee, can, 1-lb, horizontal box, slip lid, white, EX+, A3.............................**$65.00**

New Factory Smoking Tobacco, pail, lid missing o/w EX, A15...**$180.00**

New Home Sewing Machine, sign, linen, Specimen Of Work Done On The New Home Sewing Machine, rabbit/other animals, Forbes litho, 26x20", VG, A9.........**$50.00**

New Home Sewing Machine, sign, paper, lady with hands clasped seated at sewing machine, company name below, c 1910, framed, image: 20x15", EX+, A9..............$225.00

New Jersey Marine Paints, thermometer, porcelain, curved ends, gauge indicates Blood Heat/Fever Heat, blue/white, Pat 1915, 27x7", EX+, A1 ....$375.00

New Life Coffee, can, 1-lb, key-wind lid, white/green, silver trim, EX+, A3...$55.00

New Perfection Oil Cook Stoves, sign, cardboard, die-cut, ...Now Serving 2,000,000 Homes, period lady standing at stove, framed, 33x25", EX, A6 ...$700.00

New Record, cigar box label, sample, sulky driver/other sporting images, OL Schwencke & Co litho #5154, EX, A5 ....$250.00

New York Central Lines, print, paper, As The Centuries Pass In The Night..., signed Wm Humdan Foster, 28x32", EX, A2/A6, from $85 to $110.00

New York Favorites, cigar box label, outer, 2 Victorian women with parasol, 4½x4½", M, D5 ....$50.00

New York Weekly Newspaper, trade card, saddlebag shape, Geo Washington/Redcoats, ca 1900, NM+, A3 ......$65.00

Newly Wed Sugar Stick Candy/Blanke Wenneker Candy Co, pennant, young couple eating candy/watching 'Yellow Kid' look-alike child on floor, 25", NM+, A3 ....$120.0(

Newton's Heave Cough Distemper & Indigestion Cur , tin, square, pry lid, name above sulky driver, decorati e trim, black/yellow, 7x4x4", no lid, EX, A6 ....$100.00

Niagara Brand Coffee, can, 1-lb, round, pry lid, red round image of Falls, VG, A2 ....$175.00

Niagara Falls Yellow Car, sign, paper, conductor pointing to trolley with Niagara Falls inset, Niagara litho, 28x21", VG, A9...$200.00

Niagara Punch, sign, tin, Drink Niagara Punch next to product bottle, red/blue lettering on yellow, 1920s, 9x20", NM, A13...$150.00

Niagara Shoes, sign, tin/cardboard, oval image of Niagara Falls above advertising in red, black ground, 19x9", VG, A6...$90.00

Nic Nac Chewing Tobacco, store tin, round, smaller round slip lid, 5¢ Packets, yellow, G, A7 ....$350.00

Nichol Kola, sign, tin, America's Taste Sensation 5¢ in center of black/white logo on red, white border, 11x28", NOS, A6..$65.00

Nichol Kola, sign, tin, America's Taste Sensation/Twice As Good, 5¢ bottle in center, embossed, 36x12", VG-EX, A6/A16, from $85 to..$150.00

Nichol Kola, sign, tin, bottle cap flanked by drum major/tilted bottle, 12x29", VG-EX+, A3/A16, from $45 to.........$80.00

Nichol Kola, sign, tin, Drink America's Taste Sensation, 5¢ bottle in center, 24x8", EX+, A16......................$50.00

Nichol Kola, sign, tin, Drink... 5¢/Vitamin B1 Added/America's Taste Sensation, drum major, red/white/black, 28x20", EX, A3 ....$50.00

Nichol Kola, sign, tin, Drink.../Nichol Kola 5¢/America's Taste Sensation, drum major, red/black on white, 1941, 28x20", NM, A13..$100.00

Nichols & Shepard Co Threshing Machinery, sign, paper, stag in landscape with inset of buffalo head/2 machines, framed, 28x22", EX, A7 ....$800.00

Nick Thomas Beer, tap knob, ball shape, black Bakelite, white/gold/red celluloid insert, G+, A8 ....$95.00

Nickel Boom, cigar box label, sample, embellished portrait of jester, Schmidt & Co litho #1101, 1897, EX, A5....$210.00

Nickolai, display figure/bottle holder, Russian dancer on beveled base, 12", no bottle o/w VG+, A8 ......$30.00

Night Rider, crate label, California lemon, cowboy on galloping horse, moon in background, yellow logo, Laredo, M, D12 ....$10.00

Nobel Red, cigar box label, octagonal, Indian in full headdress on horse, Louis E Neuman litho, EX+, A5 ....$110.00

Noon Day Stove Polish, sign, paper, elegant lady at hutch looks down at little girl kneeling behind her, matted, image: 20x15", VG, A9 ....$50.00

Noona's Lemon Cream, tin, round, lady at mirror/lettering on lemon with heavy outline, ¼x1½", EX, D37 ....$18.00

Noonday, cigar box labels, 2-pc, men taking a lunch break on shore with barge traffic on river, Witsch & Schmitt #771/772, EX, A5..$270.00

Nor'way Anti-Freeze, can, 1-qt, Reliable Service, blue/red stencil-type lettering/serviceman logo on white, compass logo on reverse, NM, A1 ....$80.00

Norida Fleur Sauvage (Wildflower) Powder, tin, round, sample, colonial lady picking flowers, ¼x1½" dia, EX, D37, minimum value $25.00

North American Van Lines, doll, Mary Ann, MIB, D13..$70.00

North German Floyd Traveler's Checks, charger, tin, image of the ship Kaiser Wilhelm II, 24" dia, G, A7......$1,400.00

North Pole Cut Plug, tin, square, round lid, EX+, A3.....$480.00

North Shore Foundry Co, calendar, 1957, image of Joe DiMaggio teaching future star how to hold a bat, artist Mayo, 33x16, complete, EX, A13..........................$50.00

North Star Lager, drinking glass, shell, applied blue lettering above/below graphics, 3½", NM, A8..............$45.00

Onward, crate label, lemon, Statue of Liberty, 1930, EX, D5..$60.00

Opal Powdered Sugar, container, cardboard, tin top/bottom, white, woman using product, 8", EX+, A15..$180.00

Opeko Perfect Roast Coffee, can, 1-lb, key-wind lid, Rexall stores, EX+, A3/A18..$30.00

Opera Banquet, cigar box label, outer, woman offering cigars at formal party, 4½x4½", EX, D5....................$30.00

Optimo Cigars, container, cardboard, round, slip lid, white, Very Mild, EX+, A18..$30.00

Optometrist, sign, reverse-painted glass, oval image of eye/brow, curved lettering above/below, framed, image: 16x28", VG, A9..$650.00

OPW, clipboard, metal, embossed gas pump nozzle/logo at top, 9x5", NM+, A1..$140.00

Or-Lem, sign, cardboard, Sparkling/Aerated.../A Real Fresh Fruit Drink..., bottle at left, yellow/orange border, 9x6", NM, D30..$130.00

Orange-Crush, see also Ward's Orange-Crush

Orange-Crush, blotter, Compliments Of..., king/queen, Canadian, 1930s, NM+, A14..$30.00

Orange-Crush, blotter, Drink O-C Dry...For Your Party, tilted bottle, EX+, A16..$220.00

Orange-Crush, bottle opener, straight-sided brown bottle on white plastic handle, sample #9, M, A16..$70.00

Orange-Crush, calendar, 1946, 31x16", complete, VG, D30..$125.00

Orange-Crush, clock, round, glass front, metal frame, bottle cap, numbers/dots, Pam Clock Co, 15" dia, EX, A6.........$275.00

Orange-Crush, clock, round, reverse glass, Drink O-C Carbonated Beverage, smaller dial/Crushy on orange, 1930s, 16" dia, rare, NM, A13..$1,600.00

Orange-Crush, cooler, Filling Station, 4-legged wooden box with blue stenciled advertising, 1910s-20s, 34x19x33", VG, A13..$375.00

Orange-Crush, dispenser, clear glass beveled bowl on clamp base, white diamond logo, top spigot, 1930s-40s, NM, A13..$325.00

Orange-Crush, dispenser, ribbed glass bowl on round aluminum base, white diamond logo, porcelain top with aluminum pump, EX+, D22..$350.00

Orange-Crush, dispenser, stainless steel, white lettering on orange porcelain sides, Crushy figure atop, 1930s-40s, 18x15", EX+, A13..$1,100.00

Orange-Crush, display, cardboard, At Ease!/Always In The Krinkly Bottle!, 2 servicemen on billboard/real bottle, 1940s, 10x16", VG, A4..$700.00

Orange-Crush, display with bottle, Drink O-C & O-C Beverages.../Demand This Bottle, glasses/flowers, 1930s, EX+, D32..$350.00

Orange-Crush, drinking glass, applied red name/Fruit Flavored Beverage/syrup line, medium, M, A16.......$70.00

Orange-Crush, drinking glass, applied red name/Fruit Flavored Beverage/syrup line, short, EX, A16..........$28.00

Orange-Crush, drinking glass, applied red name/syrup line, tall, NM+, A16..$50.00

Orange-Crush, matchbook, assorted advertisers, 20 strike, front striker, M, D28, each..$9.00

Orange-Crush, menu board, Drink O-C, blackboard bottom, 19x13", rare, G+, A13..$85.00

Orange-Crush, menu board, Drink O-C Frosty Cold/Crushy logo, blackboard bottom, 1954, 28x19", VG+, A1..$250.00

Orange-Crush, menu board, Drink O-C/Made With The Whole Fruit, blackboard bottom, oranges in corners, 1930s-40s, 27x19", G, A13..$120.00

Orange-Crush, menu board, glass case with menu slots on either side of logo, NM+, D30 ....**$500.00**

Orange-Crush, pitcher, white bulbous body with orange diamond logo, rounded orange bottom, original spout/lid, 1920s-30s, EX, A13 ....**$350.00**

Orange-Crush, pitcher & glass set, clear glass, fluted pitcher, flared-top glasses, applied lettering/bands, 9"/5", NM, A8..**$100.00**

Orange-Crush, sign, button, tin, Enjoy.../Naturally-It Tastes Better, 9" dia, NM, A3.............................**$100.00**

Orange-Crush, sign, cardboard, Hootenanny Party/10¢ Off, Hootenanny personalities above, 6-pack lower right, vertical, NM+, D30 ....**$15.00**

Orange-Crush, sign, cardboard, lady/dog on floor by sofa in reflected light, logo upper right, beveled, 19x14", NM, A3 ....**$190.00**

Orange-Crush, sign, cardboard, Naturally — It Tastes Better!/O-C/It's The Natural Fresh Fruit..., beach couple, 1952, 24x18", NM, D32.......................................**$225.00**

Orange-Crush, sign, cardboard cutout, Drink O-C/Made From Ripe Oranges, beach beauty against ocean waves, 1920s, 18x12", VG+, A4 ....**$500.00**

Orange-Crush, sign, cardboard cutout, Enjoy That Fresh Taste Of...& Feel Fresh!, sunbather with tray, 1940s, 24x20", NM+, A4..**$400.00**

Orange-Crush, sign, cardboard die-cut hanger, bottle with orange diagonal logo, 9x5", NM+ (NOS), A1 ....**$50.00**

Orange-Crush, sign, cardboard die-cut stand-up, Drink Delicious O-C, bathing beauty sitting on dock, 1920s, NM, D32 ....**$675.00**

Orange-Crush, sign, cardboard die-cut stand-up, Enjoy The Fresh Taste.../And Feel Fresh!, bather/bottles, 1930s-40s, 18", EX, A13 ....**$200.00**

Orange-Crush, sign, cardboard die-cut stand-up, Fresh Fruit Flavor, bottle shape with Crushy, 30x14", NM (NOS), A1..**$140.00**

Orange-Crush, sign, cardboard die-cut stand-up, Take A Lesson From Me/It's Swell, girl with books/bottle, 1930s-40s, 20x18", EX+, A13 ....**$375.00**

Orange-Crush, sign, cardboard hanger, Have A Red Hot With Delicious O-C/Contains The Juice, hot dog/bottle/oranges, 1920s, EX, D32 ....**$250.00**

Orange-Crush, sign, fiberboard, Feel Fresh!/Drink.../Carbonated Beverage, Crushy with bottle/musical notes, 1943, 15x41", EX, A1 ....**$200.00**

Orange-Crush, sign, fiberboard, Refreshment For Workers & Fighters, die-cut blue/gold eagle emblem, WWII era, 10x7", NM, A1 ....**$130.00**

Orange-Crush, sign, flange, Buvez O-C, lettering/Crushy on white triangle on orange circle, white/green border, 1920s-30s, EX, A13..**$180.00**

Orange-Crush, sign, flange, diamond shape, Feel Fresh!/Drink.../Sold Here Ice Cold (on flange), tin, NM+, D30...**$400.00**

Orange-Crush, sign, flange, There's Only One...Sold Here-Ice Cold, white/yellow/orange/blue, tin, curved corners, 12x18", NM, A1 ....**$450.00**

Orange-Crush, sign, masonite, Rush! Rush! For O-C Carbonated Beverage, Crushy with bottle on white dot, 1940s, 48x18", NM, D32..**$375.00**

Orange-Crush, sign, paper, As Wholesome As Sunshine, ballerina, Walt Otto artwork, 1936, framed, 31x15", EX+, D32 ....**$425.00**

Orange-Crush, sign, paper, Tonight Treat The Family.../bottle/cake slice/orange sherbet next to rose centerpiece, 14x22", EX+, A14 ....**$45.00**

Orange-Crush, sign, reverse glass, Feel Fresh/Drink O-C Carbonated Beverage above musical Crushy with bottle, 9x6", VG, A16..**$175.00**

Orange-Crush, sign, reverse glass, round, Fresh!/Drink O-C, Crushy with bottle, white/orange ground, 9½" dia, VG+, D30 ....**$200.00**

Orange-Crush, sign, tin, Ask For A Crush Carbonated Beverage/Flavor Sealed... on blue, Crushy on 'C,', orange, 1946, 20x28", EX, A13 ....**$400.00**

Orange-Crush, sign, tin, Ask For A.../Natural Flavor!/Natural Color!, yellow/white lettering on orange, 1970s, 12x24", NM+, A14 ....**$85.00**

Orange-Crush, sign, tin, Ask For...Carbonated Beverage, tilted bottle, orange ground, beveled, 1940s, 32x56" EX, A13 ....**$475.00**

Orange-Crush, sign, tin, Come In!/Drink O-C, lettering above bottle, orange/black/white, 1930s, 3x10", NM+, A4 ....$500.00

Orange-Crush, sign, tin, Drink..., Crushy logo lower left, white/black lettering on orange, Canadian, 9x27", EX, A14..**$220.00**

Orange-Crush, sign, tin, Drink..., tilted bottle bordered by leaves at left of black/white lettering on orange ground, VG, D30..**$135.00**

Orange-Crush, sign, tin, Drink.../Refuse Substitutes, Crushy figure lower left, 1931, 20x27", VG, D30 ....**$145.00**

Orange-Crush, sign, tin, Enjoy O-C, logo/tilted bottle on gray/white ground, embossed, 54x18", EX+, A1..**$350.00**

Orange-Crush, sign, tin, Enjoy O-C, orange field, 18x54", EX (NOS), A6 ....**$175.00**

Orange-Crush, sign, tin, Like Oranges/Drink O-C, black/white on orange, Canadian, 19x27", EX, A14....................**$160.00**

Orange-Crush, sign, tin, O-C Carbonated Beverage on orange field pointing to tilted bottle on white field below, 54x18", VG, A6 ....**$130.00**

Orange-Crush, sign, tin, There's ONLY ONE O-C..., yellow/white on orange, blue ribbed border, 1939, 20x28", EX, A13..**$275.00**

Orange-Crush, sign, tin, Thirst Aid Station/Here's How, triangular, Crushy figure, black/orange/yellow, 1920s, NM, A4..**$800.00**

Orange-Crush, sign/mirror, Feel Fresh!/Drink O-C Carbonated Beverage, orange border, 1930s-40s, 11x9", EX, A13 ....**$275.00**

Orange-Crush, sign, tin, Feel Fresh!/Drink O-C Carbonated Beverage, Crushy at bottom, embossed diagonal, beveled, 1939, 21x21", EX, A1 ....$275.00

Orange-Crush, stamp holder, celluloid book shape, Orange-Crush Bottling Co.../Pure Sugar Beverages, Whitehead & Hoag, 1x1", EX, A15 ....**$90.00**

Orange-Crush, street marker, brass, round, embossed, Safety First.../Carbonated Beverage, 4" dia, EX, A1..**$325.00**

Orange-Crush, syrup can, 1-gal, 1950s, empty, EX+, A13..**$35.00**

Orange-Crush, thermometer, dial, plastic, aluminum frame, orange slice atop Crush, orange ground, 1950s, 12½" dia, NM, A3..**$35.00**

Orange-Crush, thermometer, masonite, Drink O-C & Feel Fresh!, amber bottle next to gauge, Crushy below, white, 1930s, 16", NM, D30 ....**$250.00**

Orange-Crush, thermometer, porcelain, From Natural Orange Juice..., amber bottle next to gauge, white, 1940s-50s, 15", EX, A13..**$325.00**

Orange-Crush, thermometer, tin, Ask For A Crush..., Crushy above gauge, orange, vertical, Fair, A16............**$115.00**

Orange-Crush, thermometer, tin, bottle cap above gauge, rounded top/bottom, turquoise, 1950s, 15x6", EX-EX+, D30/A13, from $75 to..**$130.00**

Orange-Crush, thermometer, tin, bottle shape, 1950s, 29x7", NM, A1..**$300.00**

Orange-Crush, thermometer, tin, Get The 'Happy Habit', amber bottle, white, curved top/bottom, 1930s, 19", VG+, A13..**$180.00**

Orange-Crush, thermometer, tin, Naturally It Tastes Better, amber bottle next to gauge, curved top/bottom, white, 15", VG, D30..**$150.00**

Orange-Crush, thermometer, tin, O-C diamond logo, gauge above, white, white, 12", VG, A16 ....**$365.00**

Orange-Crush, thermometer, wood, Rush Rush, with Crushy/bottle/diamond logo, curved top, EX, A16 ....**$415.00**

Orange-Crush, thermometer/calendar, 1938, silhouette image of lady at spinning wheel, NM, A16........**$220.00**

Orange-Crush, toy truck, London Toy/Canada, die-cast, windup, 6", scarce, VG, A14 ....**$100.00**

Orange-Crush, tray, round, orange, Tome Crush/Delicioso Sasor De Naranjasm Crushy logo, orange/white/blue, 12" dia, EX, A16.....................................$85.00

Orange-Crush, tray, round, raised flat rim, boy/girl at piano eyeing bottle of Orange-Crush & Crushy figure, 14" dia, EX+, A1.....................................$25.00

Orange Flower, cigar tin, round, slip lid, 5¢, flower image on white, VG+, A18.....................................$150.00

Orange Grove, cigar box label, sample, family picking oranges, Heppenheimer & Maurer litho #1085, 1874, VG, A5.....................................$150.00

Orange Julep, sign, cardboard, die-cut, Drink Orange Julep, girl sipping from glass, lettered banner below, 1930s, 11x6", EX+, A13.....................................$90.00

Orange Julep, straw holder, pressed-glass box, VG, A9...$425.00

Orange Julep, syrup bottle, with metal jigger cap, 13", VG, A9.....................................$70.00

Orange Julep, tray, rectangular, beach girl with parasol, 13x11", EX, A9.....................................$275.00

Orange Kist, bottle topper, cardboard, die-cut, blue lettering on orange half, EX, D30.....................................$26.00

Orange Kist, cooler, 4-legged with wheels, double-hinged lid, embossed tin signs, Drink... with bottles, 34x22", VG, A6.....................................$775.00

Orange Kist, menu board, Drink Orange Kist/Special Today with sliced orange at top of blackboard, 1930s, 19x13", EX+, A13.....................................$150.00

Orange Kist, sign, cardboard die-cut stand-up, ...And Other Kist Flavors, Rolf Armstrong girl bending over at waist, 12x9", VG, A16.....................................$245.00

Orange Kist, sign, tin, Drink Orange Kist And Other Flavors, bottle/oranges on black with orange/white design, 13x20", EX+, A1 ....$275.00

Orange Kist, sign, tin, Drink Orange Kist And Other Flavors, blue rainbow band on orange ground, horizontal, VG+, D30.....................................$100.00

Orange Kist, sign, tin, Drink Orange Kist And Other Kist Flavors, lettering only, orange/yellow/black, embossed, 3x18", NM, A1.....................................$120.00

Orange Kist, sign, tin, Drink Orange Kist And Other Flavors, orange/black/orange ground, 6x13", NM, D3.........$55.00

Orange Kist, sign, tin, Drink Orange Kist And Other Flavors, white rainbow band, bottle/oranges on black center, 28x10", EX, D30.....................................$175.00

Orbit Gum, valentine card, Valentine Greetings/If Ah Chewies You An You Chewsies Me..., black boy with sample box, NM, D25.....................................$100.00

Orchard Park Coffee, can, 1-lb, key-wind lid, EX, A3.$25.00

Orchid, crate label, Florida Citrus, orchid blooms above iced grapefruit half, Wabasso, M, D12.....................................$6.00

Orcico, tin, 2 For 5¢, trademark Indian, 6x6x4", VG-EX+, A2/A18/A15, from $300 to.....................................$650.00

Oregon Chief Gasoline, sign, porcelain, round, Washington-Idaho-Montana... around Indian chief, red/white/blue/cream, 2-sided, 72" dia, NM, A24.........$4,300.00

Oregon Orchards, crate label, Oregon pear, cartoon duck with umbrella, Medfords, 1940s, M, D12.............$15.00

Oriental Special Auto Oil, sign, porcelain, large image of rectangular oil can, red/black/yellow on yellow, 21x17", EX, A2.....................................$1,760.00

Orioles, cigar box, image of birds in tree, early stone litho, EX, A3.....................................$85.00

Orphan Boy, see also Smoker's Dream

Orphan Boy Smoking Tobacco, sign, cardboard cutout, tobacco pouch with image of donkey on label, 17x12", EX-NM, A3/A2, from $100 to.....................................$150.00

Osborne Farm Implements, catalog, farmer/wife caught in surprise storm, various implements pictured, 24 pgs, 8x7", EX+, A3.....................................$80.00

Osborne, sign, paper, You Cannot Hit Amiss, lady archer ready to shoot at target showing implements, framed, 34x24", EX, A7.....................................$1,200.00

Osborne Plow Co, sign, paper, girl looking at chart of implements, aerial factory scene inset upper left, 31x24", NM, A15.....................................$675.00

Oscar Mayer, display, Little Oscar, inflatable, 1960s, MIP, D13.....................................$75.00

Oscar Mayers German Wiener, bill hook, round, image of chef holding large wiener, red/yellow, 2" dia, NM, A3.....................................$30.00

OshKosh B'Gosh Overalls display, cardboard cutout, The World's Best..., Uncle Sam wearing real pair overalls, c 1936, 77x27", NM, A1 ....$2,150.00

OshKosh B'Gosh Overalls, sign, porcelain, Union Made Buy..., Uncle Sam at left, 10x30", G, A9 ....$600.00

OshKosh B'Gosh Union Made Work Clothes, sign, tin, white/yellow lettering on red field, green/yellow border, 10x14", A3 ....$115.00

OshKosh Tools, calendar, 1952, pinup girl on ladder in revealing short denim overalls, 32x16", complete, NM+, D30 ....$100.00

Otello, cigar box label, inner lid, scene from Shakespeare play, 6x9", M, D5 ....$45.00

Otto Young & Co Resilient Mainsprings, tin, rectangular, curved corners, red, gold trim, EX, D37....................$45.00

Ottumwa Brewing Co, drinking glass, shell, clear, applied O-&-eagle logo with hops/grain, gold rim, brewery closed 1911, 3½", NM, A8....................................$140.00

OU Cut Plug Smoking Tobacco, tin, round, slip lid, paper label, brown/white, gold trim, 1909 tax stamp, VG+, A3...$30.00

Our Advertiser Smoking Tobacco, display box, cardboard, 5¢/A Cool Sweet Smoke For Cigarette Or Pipe, complete with 24 full pouches/papers, EX+, A18 ....$340.00

Our Alderman, cigar box labels, 2-pc set, oval image of man in top hat, Witsch & Schmitt #607, EX, A5.........$150.00

Our Brands National Cigar Stands Co, tip tray, round, nymph looking at flowers, name/labels on rim, 6" dia, VG+, A3..$65.00

Our Club, cigar box label, sample, interior scene with group of men, Krueger & Braun litho #254, M, A5 ......$175.00

Our Family Pure Breakfast Cocoa, container, 2-lb, cardboard, tin pry lid, blue/yellow, white silhouette of lady with steaming cup, NM (unopened), A3..............$50.00

Our Oma Coffee, can, 1-lb, key-wind lid, red, gold bottom band, NM (unopened), A18................................$180.00

Our Pride, cigar box label, inner lid, Panama Canal/sea gods/ships, 6x9", EX, D5......................................$20.00

Our Sport, cigar box label, outer, hunter/2 dogs, 4½x4½", EX, D5 ....$50.00

Our Sports, cigar box, shows various sporting events, EX+, A3...$140.00

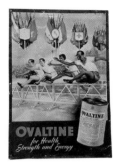

Ovaltine, sign, tin, ...For Health Strength & Energy, 4 men jumping hurdles above text/product can, 18x12", EX, A6 ....$170.00

OVB Hardware, pocket mirror, round, red/white/blue, EX, A3..$55.00

Overland, cigar box, oval image of train in mountains, VG+, A3..$30.00

Overland, cigar box label, inner lid, locomotive puffing through mountain, 6x9", M, D5 ....$75.00

Overland Service/Genuine Parts, sign, porcelain, oval, red/white/black, 2-sided, 30x40", EX, A6 ....$650.00

Owego Bridge Co, sign, tin hanger, Bridge Over Delaware River At Port Jervis NY, white lettering framing oval image, 13x19", EX, A7 ....$300.00

Owensboro Wagons, see Hickman-Ebbert Co

Owl Cigars, sign, cardboard hanger, die-cut birdcage with owl perched on cigar marked Owl, 'Owl' Cigar 5¢, 10x7", EX, A15..$300.00

Ox-Heart Brand Peanut Butter, door plate, porcelain, We Sell Ox-Heart Brand Peanut Butter, round cherry logo in center, white on green, 7x4", NM, A13..............$700.00

Ox-Heart Chocolates, sign, porcelain, white block lettering on blue, white border, 3x36", VG, A6.................$200.00

Ox-Heart Chocolates & Cocoa, sign, tin, round logo left of yellow/white lettering on blue, red border, embossed, 5x20", NM+, A13..$160.00

Oxford Mustard, tin, 2-oz, EX, A3 ....$8.00

❧ P ❧

P Kloppenburg Groceries, Dry Goods & Crockery, calendar, 1899, mother/3 children bordered by pink roses/blue ribbon, embossed, 13x11", incomplete pad, EX, A3 ....$50.00

P Lorillard & Co's Captive Smoking, sign, paper, cherubs tugging on woman's skirt, Hatch litho, 1874, framed, 13x11", VG, A5......................$200.00

P&G Lorillard Snuff & Tobacco, sign, paper, nude maiden gives Indian tobacco leaves while animals watch, Major & Knapp litho, framed, 22x17", Fair, A9............$275.00

Pabst, sign, neon, Pabst (red script neon) in center of blue ribbon logo (white neon), NM, A13 .....$100.00

Pabst Blue Ribbon, sign, reverse on glass, ...In Bottles, panel with round top corners on wood base, red/silver lettering, 9x14", VG, A8......................$50.00

Pabst Blue Ribbon Beer, display figure, boxer in ring, pot metal, Enjoy Old Time Flavor on sign atop bottle, VG+, A8......................$100.00

Pabst Blue Ribbon Beer, foam scraper holder, bottle/barber pole flank barbershop quartet, cast metal/plastic, VG+, A19......................$50.00

Pabst Blue Ribbon Beer, matchbook, The Beer Of Quality, bottle on back, 20 strike (wide bottle shape), front striker, Lion, M (full), D28......................$19.00

Pabst Blue Ribbon Beer, sign, cardboard, bottle shape, 34x10", VG+, A3 ....$120.00

Pabst Blue Ribbon Beer, sign, cardboard stand-up, bottle shape with diagonal IRTP label, blue ribbon at neck, 24", EX+, A19......................$50.00

Pabst Blue Ribbon Beer, sign, paper, The Beer Of Quality, elderly gent pouring a glass, round Pabst logo, c 1933, framed, image: 25x19", VG+, A8 ....$200.00

Pabst Blue Ribbon Beer, sign, paper, 2 bottles/stemmed glass with plate of oysters, signed AF King, wood frame with plaque, 14x18", VG, A9 ....$150.00

Pabst Blue Ribbon Beer, sign, reverse on glass, panel with Deco-style chrome frame on wood base, red/silver on blue, 6x13", VG+, A8......................$60.00

Pabst Blue Ribbon Beer, sign, tin/cardboard, A Bottle Of Pabst, with bottle, green, gold border, beveled, 7x11", VG, A8 ....$80.00

Pabst Blue Ribbon Beer, sign, tin/cardboard, bottle/can next to blue lettering on yellow, beveled, with stand, 1930s, 9x13", NM, A19......................$175.00

Pabst Blue Ribbon Beer, sign, tin/cardboard, In Bottles, bottle over blue ribbon outlined in red, blue ground, beveled, 1920s, 9x13", EX, A19 ....$100.00

Pabst Blue Ribbon Beer, sign, tin/cardboard, Only When It's.../The Beer Of Quality, oval image of lady in coat/hat, beveled, 25x20", NM, A7......................$2,000.00

Pabst Blue Ribbon Beer, sign, tin/cardboard, The Best Brew Today..., emblem above bottle/sandwich/goblet on yellow, beveled, 13x9", NM, A8 ....$265.00

Pabst Blue Ribbon Beer, tray, rectangular, The Beer Of Quality, man pouring beer, plain rim, American Can, 13x11", VG-EX, A8/A9, from $40 to $80.00

Pabst Blue Ribbon Beer/Wilbur Stock Food Co, sign, paper, Pabst Famous Blue Ribbon Winners, wagon with 6-horse team, 14x31", VG, A3......................$55.00

Pabst Brewing Co, match safe, brass, engraved, button release, VG, A8 ....$40.00

Pabst Brewing Co, sign, paper, aerial factory scene with horse-drawn traffic, name below, Milwaukee Litho & Engr Co, 34x46", VG+, A9 ....$2,100.00

Pabst Malt Extract, calendar (yard-long), 1904, EX+, A3..$375.00

Pabst Malt Extract, calendar (yard-long), 1914, G, A9 .....$90.00

Pabst Malt Extract, calendar (yard-long), 1915, EX+, A3.$180.00

Pabst Malt Extract, calendar (yard-long), 1916, VG, A3 .$135.00

Pabst Malt Extract, calendar (yard-long), 1917, NM+, A3..$360.00

Pabst Malt Extract, tray, rectangular, lady sipping from stemmed glass, lettered gold trim, 17x12", VG, A8......................$165.00

Pabst-Ett Malt Syrup Beverages, toy train boxcar, HO scale, yellow, 1950s, NM+, A19.........................**$25.00**

Pace's Electric Mixture, tin, rectangular, square corners, deep yellow, EX, A18............................**$335.00**

Pacific, crate label, Washington pear, shield inset of white fleet/2 pears on red/black background, Seattle, M, D12 ....**$15.00**

Pacific Beer, art plate, girl in scarf facing left, decorative gold rim, C Shonk litho, 10" dia, VG+, A8 ....**$80.00**

Pacific Beer, tray, round, Mt Tacoma, Best East Or West, small round image on wood grain, gold lettering, EX+-NM, A3/A18, from $50 to $75.00

Pacific Brewing & Malting Co, sign, paper, Swiss girl/Alps beyond, wood frame, 30x24", VG, A7 ....**$375.00**

Pacific Exporter, crate label, apple, sun setting over Golden Gate with planes/boats, EX, D5 ....**$65.00**

Pacific Oil, thermometer, dial type, glass front, metal frame, degrees/name around image of conquistador, red/yellow, 12" dia, EX, A6 ....**$180.00**

Packard, brochure, 1925, Luxurious Motoring, when opened a limousine moves through scenic landscape, 11x6", EX, A2......................................**$150.00**

Packard, pin, celluloid over metal, rectangular, Packard Master Serviceman Mechanic, blue/red/white, 2x1½", VG, A6 ....**$100.00**

Packard, sign, neon, name lettered vertically above round lettered logo on Deco housing, 157x23x16", NM, A6...........**$3,000.00**

Packard, sign, porcelain, rectangular, Packard in white script over red hexagonal field within white-lined circle on blue, 20x30", NM+, A1 ....**$1,050.00**

Packard, sign, porcelain, round, Packard in white script over red hexagonal field on white circle on blue, 2-sided, 42", NM, A1 ....**$1,850.00**

Packard Motor, alarm clock, Seth Thomas, Master Salesman 1926, round face on porcelain radiator, letters for numbers, 5x4", VG, A6 ....**$500.00**

Packard Service, sign, die-cut metal letters, blue, 24", EX, A6..**$290.00**

Packard Service, sign, porcelain, radiator with hood ornament, Packard in script above Service, blue/white, 42x27", VG+, A2 ....**$4,070.00**

Packard 8, emblem, oval, metal with cloisonne, shield above name on black, copper-looking trim, 2x1½", EX, A1..**$40.00**

Paige-6, pennant, felt, image of 1915 auto for $1385 & name, red on white, 37", EX, A2 ....**$165.00**

Pal Ade, thermometer, tin, yellow, 1950, 24", NM, A4 ..**$400.00**

Pal Shaving Headquarters, display case, wood, cardboard front showing various blades, man with face lathered pointing to sign atop, EX, A2 ....**$175.00**

Pala Brave, crate label, California orange, Indian chief in full headdress, maroon ground, Placentia, EX, D3 ....**$4.00**

Palasade Beer/Wm Peter Brewing Corp, tray, oval, factory scene overlooking the Hudson River, lettered rim, Electro Chemical Engraving Co, 14x17", VG, A9 ....**$125.00**

Palmolive, sign, cardboard die-cut stand-up, nude baby with towel ready to get into tub, body slotted for samples, 14x8", VG, A2......................................**$100.00**

Palmolive, sign, tin, Palmolive's Beauty Plan Brings You A Younger-Looking Skin..., couple/bar on yellow, 1940s, 14x28", NM, A13 ....**$400.00**

Palmy Days Tobacco, pocket tin, vertical, green, VG-EX, A18, from $160 to............................$300.00

Pan-Am, pump sign, porcelain, oval with name over torch symbol, red/white/blue, 6x6", M, A1 ....**$875.00**

Pan-Am Gasoline/Motor Oils, sign, porcelain, round, Gasoline above/Motor Oils below Pan-Am on center band, red/white/blue, 42" dia, EX, A2................**$385.00**

Pappoose, cigar box label, inner lid, Indian babe up in tree, 6x9", M, D5 ....**$40.00**

Pappoose Cigars, cigar box, 1890s, VG+, A3..........**$100.00**

Pappy Parker's Chicken House, doll, Pappy Parker, vinyl, red or blue version, 1973, 6½", NM, D20, each...**$45.00**

Par After-Shave Powder, tin, rectangular, small round gold top, 1920s golfer swinging club, white/green/orange, 6", EX+, A15..................................**$350.00**

Par Buster, cigar box, 5¢ on corner band, image of golfer, 1934, EX, A3.....................................**$85.00**

Para-Field Motor Oil, can, 1-qt, red/black on yellow, NM (full), A1 ....**$325.00**

Para Pride Motor Oil, can, 1-qt, plane in flight/2 races on diagonal band, red/white/blue, NM+, A18.........**$100.00**

Parisians, condom tin, flat, rounded corners, orange/black, 2x2½", EX, A15 ....**$600.00**

Park Drive Tobacco, sign, porcelain, Park Drive For Pleasure/10 For 4D/Plain Or Cork Tip/5 For 2D, 2-sided, red/white/blue, 30x20", EX+, A1.........**$100.00**

Parker '51' Pen, postcard, The Message On The Other Side Was Written With..., hand-held pen writing letter, linen, used 1948, VG+, D26 ....**$85.00**

Parker Gun, sign, paper, metal strips, The Old Reliable..., 2 squirrels on tree branch surrounded by autumn leaves, 27x19", VG, A7 ....**$1,600.00**

Parker House Coffee, can, 2-lb, key-wind, red/white/blue, EX+, A3...**$25.00**

Parker Pens, display case, wooden tray with Parker lettered on milk glass panel on light-up marque, holds 15 pens, 9x20", EX, A2 ....$85.00

Parker's Perfect Pleasure Producer, sign, paper, The Jumping Horse 'Carry-Us-All' carousel, framed, image: 19x26", EX, A9 ....$550.00

Parkview Coffee, can, 1-lb, key-wind lid, white, EX-NM, A18, from $45 to..$60.00

Parrot Superior Steel Needles, tin, Loud Tone/Average 200, blue, ¼x1¼x1¾", EX, D37 ....$45.00

Parrot/Monkey Baking Powder, can, round, paper label, name above/below filigreed image of trademark parrot/monkey on red, 3", EX (full), A15 ....$375.00

Pasquale Peluso, calendar, no year given, paper, Lady Liberty draped in flag with dove on hand, American scenes beyond, framed, EX, A6 ....$170.00

Pastilles Droste Fijnste Chocolade, see Droste

Pastime, cigar box label, outer, bucking white horse, 4½x4½", EX, D5...$30.00

Pastime Plug Tobacco, store bin, tin, black on red, Ginna, EX+, A18...$340.00

Pastora 10¢ Cigars, tin, square, slip lid, EX+, A18 .$250.00

Pastum/J Sarubi Co, sign, flange, Before/After trademark image, black/white/lt yellow, 7x9", EX+, A3......$100.00

Pat Hand Cube Cut Granules, pocket tin, vertical, oval, red, 2¾", EX, A18...$150.00

Pat Hand Cube Cut Granules, pocket tin, vertical, oval, red, 3", EX+, A18...$200.00

Paterson '30,' pocket mirror, oval, Write For Territory & Agency Proposition, image of early auto, black/white, 2x3", EX, A2 ....$550.00

Patrick Henry Fine Beer, sign, tin/cardboard, Patrick Henry addressing group in political chambers, 13x17", VG+, A8 ....$55.00

Patterson-Sargent BPS Paint, sign, porcelain, die-cut emblem, For Better Results, circle/bar logo, white/black/red/yellow, 2-sided, 24x33", EX, A3 ....$40.00

Patterson's Recut Tobacco, sign, paper, product name flanked by product packs, 10 Cent Value For 5 Cents below, red/yellow/blue, 17x35", EX, A2..............$60.00

Patterson's Seal Cut Plug, tin, square, curved corners, gold on red, NM, A3 ....$55.00

Paul Bunyan Coffee, can, 1-lb, key-wind lid, red, EX+, A3 ....$330.00

Paul Jones & Co Pure Gin, sign, tin, boy kneeling in front of boy on fence tending to foot, scalloped rim with curled corners, 10x14", EX, A15 ....$400.00

Paul Jones & Co Pure Rye Whiskey, sign, tin, Comrades For 81 Years, gent in straw hat pouring a glass, HD Beach litho, 1903, 29x22", EX, A7 ....$900.00

Paul Jones & Co Whiskey, display statue, plaster, cowboy with whip, For Flavor That's Hearty But Never Heavy, 1950s-60s, 12", EX, A8..$100.00

Paul Jones & Co Whiskey, sign, tin, The Temptation Of St Anthony, hanger, rolled corners, Meek litho, 14x19", EX+, A18 ....$1,650.00

Paul Jones & Co Whiskey, sign, wood, Temptation Of St Anthony, 14x20", VG, A7 ....$650.00

Paul Jones Clean Cut Tobacco, pocket tin, vertical, blue, NM, A18 ....$2,450.00

Paul Jones Havana Cigars, sign, tin, oval portrait on rectangular wood-grain background, C Shonk litho, 24x20", VG-EX, A9/A3, from $500 to $725.00

Paula, crate label, California lemon, '20s blonde flapper girl in red with black fan, green background, Santa Paula, M, D12 ....**$14.00**

Paw-Nee Olde Style Oats, container, 2-lb 10-oz, yellow, red trim, EX+, A3...**$120.00**

Paxton Gas Roasted Coffee, can, 2-lb, key-wind lid, shows roasting process, VG, A3......................................**$30.00**

Pay Car Scrap, sign, tin, Chew.../The Best Flavor, product pack in center, red/white on green, 18x14", VG-EX+, A1/A15, from $200 to **$450.00**

Paymaster Cigar, tin, round, slip lid, 2 For 5¢, red, EX+, A18 ....**$135.00**

PB Ale/Bunker Hill Breweries, sign, celluloid stand-up, round, Oh Be Jolly!, trademark bulldog on red, c 1906, 7" dia, rare, EX, A24 ....**$450.00**

PCW Cough Drops, tin, square, yellow or green, Somers Bros litho, pre-1901, 2", EX, A18, from $50 to **$60.00**

Peach Eagle, cigar box, 5¢ Straight, traces Lindburg's route, G+, A5 ....**$135.00**

Peachy Double Cut Tobacco, pocket tin, vertical, yellow, EX-NM, A18, from $185 to **$260.00**

Peacock Blue Ink, tin, octagonal, small round lid, glass interior, VG+-NM, A3/A18, from $30 to **$70.00**

Peak Coffee, can, 1-lb, screw lid, EX+, A18...............**$60.00**

Pear King, crate label, Washington pear, smiling pear with gold crown on blue background, Yakima, M, D12 ....**$22.00**

Pearl Oil Kerosene, sign, flange, oil can shape with pour spout/handle, We Sell.../For Heating/Light Cooking, 19x12", NM (NOS), A1 ....**$500.00**

Pearl/Texas Pride Pale/San Antonio Brewing Co, sign, tin, Who Can Beat It? in raised gesso letters on wood frame, food scene with lobster, 32x25", G, A8...**$220.00**

Pearline Easy Washing, sign, porcelain, white lettering on dk blue, 3x12", EX-EX+, A15, from $220 to **$275.00**

Pear's Soap, sign, cardboard, die-cut, Granny scrubbing boy over bucket marked Pears, framed, 18x15", VG, A6..........**$190.00**

Pear's Soap, sign, paper, 3 little girls playing in courtyard by pool/flowers, artist WS Coleman, framed, image: 32x23", VG, A9 ....**$350.00**

Pear's Soap, trade card, The Order Of the Bath/Use Pear's Soap For The Skin & Complexion, 2 ladies giving child a bath, 9x6", EX+, A3..**$72.00**

Pedigree Whiskey, sign, tin, red name above/below oval image of jockey on racing horse, gold ground, 22x30", EX, A1..**$300.00**

Pedro Cut Plug Smoking Tobacco, lunch box, EX+, A18 ....**$135.00**

Pedro de Cubana, cigar box label, inner lid, shows Indians/globe/coat of arms, 6x9", M, D5..........................**$35.00**

Pedro Smoking Tobacco, lunch box, yellow, EX, A3 ..**$110.00**

Peek-A-Boo Clear Havana Cigars, sign, reverse-painted glass, Trost Cigar Co Agent, lettering around image of baby on black, red frame, 9x14", EX, A2 ....**$200.00**

Peer Coffee, can, 1-lb, key-wind lid, VG+, A3...........**$25.00**

Peerless Amber/La Crosse Breweries Inc, sign, cardboard, The Beer Of Good Cheer, elf-type figure holding up glass/bottle, gray/red/gray, 1940s, 11x28", EX, A19.**$140.00**

Peerless Beer, label, Muncie Brewing Co/IN, pre-1920, VG+, A10..**$75.00**

Peerless Fruit Chewing Gum, vendor, wood with white-on-blue porcelain front, 31x9x10", VG+, A2........**$4,180.00**

Peerless Tobacco/FF Adams & Co, pail, NM+, A3 ..**$110.00**

Peerless 8, print, paper, Everything On High, early touring car speeding up hill, matted/framed, 20x26", EX, A2 .**$220.00**

Peg Top Cigars, clock, bronzed cast-iron, man in top hat/man in bowler hat with cigar boxes flanking clock on base, 12x15", EX, A2 ....**$200.00**

Peg Top Cigars 5¢, door plate, porcelain, The Old Reliable above cigar graphics/5¢, brown on cream, convex, 13x4", NM+, A13..**$175.00**

Peg Top Cigars 5¢, thermometer, porcelain, yellow, square corners, Canada, 1920s-30s, vertical, EX, A13 ....**$250.00**

Penguin Motor Oil, can, 2-gal, rectangular, tall, pour spout, screw lid, center grip handle, oval Penguin logo, red/white/blue, EX+, A1 ....**$135.00**

Peninsular Stoves, trade card, heavy paper, die-cut ornate parlor stove, 7x4", VG, A6 ....**$55.00**

Penn Bee Motor Oil, can, 1-qt, 2 bees on red dot, yellow, red/black trim, NM+ (full), A1 ....**$175.00**

Penn Club Beverages, sign, paper, 3 gents holding up yellow sign, 12x15", NM+, A13................................**$150.00**

Penn Diner Inc/New York City postcard, linen, image of diner on blue, used 1941, NM, A17 ....**$250.00**

Penn Drake Lubricants, sign, flange, The Original Drake Well, 1859 above image/product name, red/white/black, 20x14", VG, A2..**$150.00**

Penn Drake Motor Oil, sign, porcelain, pointed bottom, oil derrick above product name, orange/white/black, 2-sided, 27x21", EX+, A2 ....**$800.00**

Penn Easton Motor Oil, sign, reverse glass, light-up, America's Finest...100% Pure Pennsylvania/Sold On Money Back Guarantee, 14x22", EX, A6 ....**$300.00**

Penn Empire Motor Oil, drum (roller), 5-gal, pour spout with funnel, 2-handled, white/yellow/black, EX+, A1 .**$160.00**

Penn Field SAE 20 Motor Oil, can, ½-gal, rectangular, pour spout, recessed wire handle, oil derrick logo, EX, A1.........**$175.00**

Penn Stoves/Furnaces/Ranges, pot scraper, metal, advertising with shamrock logo, green/black/cream, 3x2½", EX, A6.................**$120.00**

Penn'A Bottling & Supply Co Ginger Ale, mug, ceramic, deer horn handle, 3 doves on branch, brown shading, 5", EX+, A1.................**$20.00**

Penn's No 1, pocket tin, vertical, EX+, A18 .....**$3,335.00**

Penn's Tobacco, tin, square, Penn's Spells Quality/pen tip, yellow/white on black, 6½", EX, A3 ....**$40.00**

Pennant Cigars, sign, reverse glass, Select/Pennant Cigars/ Quality, Hand Made American League Perfectos on ball at left, 7x18", NM, A1 ....**$425.00**

Pennsylvania Fire Insurance Co, postcard, trifold, It's The One That Gets There First That Counts, fire engine/man running to burning home, EX+, A17..................**$150.00**

Pennsylvania Grit Newspaper, see Grit Newspaper

Pennsylvania RR, calendar, 1936, frontal image of train, 29x29", EX+, A3 ....**$100.00**

Pennsylvania RR, sign, reverse glass, gold lettering on black, wood frame, 7x36", EX+, A3 ....**$150.00**

Penny Post Cut Plug, lunch box, red, gold trim, EX-EX+, A18/A3, from $200 to **$250.00**

Pennzoil, bank, oil can, yellow, red bell logo, EX+, A18...**$100.00**

Pennzoil, can, 1-qt, round, yellow, owl logo, EX+, A18...**$60.00**

Pennzoil, can, 1-qt, round, yellow, red bell logo on front, twin-engine plane & ad for United Air Lines on reverse, NM, A18..............................**$100.00**

Pennzoil, can, 5-qt, round, yellow, owl logo, VG+, A18.**$50.00**

Pennzoil, desk set, copper finish, note pad holder/ashtray/ cigarette case, Be Oil Wise, Pennzowls atop all 3 pcs, EX, A1.................................**$200.00**

Pennzoil, sign, flange, tin, oval logo with **Sound Your Z** on top rainbow appendage, yellow, red bell, 17x22", NM+ (NOS), A6 ....**$378.00**

Pennzoil, sign, porcelain, oval, Supreme Pennsylvania Quality/ Safe Lubrication, bell logo in center, yellow, 18x31", VG+, A1.................................**$300.00**

Pennzoil, sign, porcelain, oval, 100% Pure Pennsylvania/ Safe Lubrication, red bell logo in center, yellow, 2-sided, 30", G, A2 ....**$100.00**

Pennzoil, sign, porcelain, Supreme Penn... Quality/Safe Lubrication, red bell in center, yellow, black border, 15x40", NM, A1 ....**$350.00**

Pennzoil, sign, sidewalk, porcelain, oval, cast-iron pedestal base, yellow logo, 47x32", EX, A6 ....**$325.00**

Pennzoil, sign, sidewalk, porcelain, rectangular wind-type, cast-iron pedestal base, brown bell logo, 15x38", NM, A6.................................**$550.00**

Pennzoil, sign, sidewalk, porcelain, round, red cast-iron pedestal base, black/red lettering on white, brown bell, 60", EX, A6 ....$850.00

Pennzoil, sign, tin, Supreme Pennsylvania Quality upper left of bell logo, Safe Lubrication lower right, embossed, 12x36", EX+, A8 ....**$300.00**

Pennzoil Outboard Motor Oil, display rack, wire, round with cone base, 2-tiered, 2-sided oval sign atop, A-4-60, 39", VG, A6 ....**$140.00**

Pennzoil Outboard Motor Oil, can, 1-qt, yellow/black/red, speedboat logo, EX+, A6 ....**$125.00**

Penotol Extra Quality Motor Oil, sign, porcelain, round, iron frame, round profile head image of colonial man above name, 36" dia, EX, A6 ....**$675.00**

People's Choice Strong Keg Beer, label, 64-oz, Peoples Beer Co/Duluth MN, IRTP/U-type Permit Number, 1933-36, VG+ (creased or folded), A10.......................**$37.00**

Pepsi-Cola, syrup can, 1-gal, red/white/blue bands, P-C bottle caps on center band, 1951, EX, A3 ....**$55.00**

Pepsi-Cola, tape measure, chrome Zippo lighter-type case with gray plastic bottom, EX, D14 ....**$45.00**

Pepsi-Cola, thermometer, tin, Any Weather's Pepsi Weather, white, 27", EX, A24 ....**$130.00**

Pepsi-Cola, thermometer, tin, Bigger/Better, large bottle next to gauge, blue, white/gray border, 16", VG-NM, A15/A13/A1, $275 to **$475.00**

Pepsi-Cola, thermometer, tin, Buy P=C Big Big Bottle, red/white on blue, 1930s-40s, 27", VG+, A13 ....**$300.00**

Pepsi-Cola, thermometer, tin, Have A Pepsi/The Light Refreshment, bottle cap below, white/yellow, 1956, 27", EX, D30/A1, $125 to $150.00

Pepsi-Cola, thermometer, tin, Say Pepsi Please/Pepsi (block letters) logo below, yellow, 1967, 28", EX, D30...**$75.00**

Pepsi-Cola, thermometer/mirror, reverse-painted glass, Drink P=C/Bigger & Better, girl on water, 1930s, framed, 22x10", EX, D32 ....**$1,250.00**

Pepsi-Cola, tip tray, 1910, EX+, A4 ....**$1,400.00**

Pepsi-Cola, toy truck, plastic, '60s Ford, center bed divider reading Tome Pepsi (Spanish), red/white/blue, 5 cases, 7½", EX+, A14 ....**$250.00**

Pepsi-Cola, tray, 1909, Gibson Girl, oval, 14x11", G, A9...**$450.00**

Pepsi-Cola, tray, 1930s, Coast To Coast/Bigger & Better, 11x14", G+-EX+, A16/A13, from $200 to.......$350.00

Pepsi-Cola, tray, 1940, Hits The Spot/Enjoy P=C, 11x14", NM+, A1...**$55.00**

Pepsi-Cola, tray, 1940, P-C/Bigger & Better, stylized flowers, 11x14", EX, A8 ....**$50.00**

Pepsi-Cola, tray, 1940, Pepsi-Cola Hits The Spot/12 Full Ounces That's Alot, lady reading to 2 girls, 11x14", VG, A8..**$50.00**

Pepsi-Cola, tray, 1940s, top view of bottles in ice, square, 12x12", NM, A14 ....**$20.00**

Pepsi-Cola, vendor carrier, wood, ballpark, Drink P-C oval over white/blue stripes, with strap, 1950s, 6x19", VG-NM, A6/A13, $175 to $325.00

Pepsi-Cola, see also Evervess

Pepsodent Toothpaste, standee, cardboard, black man standing by large Pepsodent box, Oh! Sho-Sho.../Check An' Double Check, 1930, 61", VG+, A7...........**$1,000.00**

Pepsodent Toothpaste, standee, cardboard, young black man standing holding oversized tube, Um! Um!/Ain't Dis Sumpin!, 1930, 54", VG, A7................................**$800.00**

Pepsol, tray, round, deep rim, dog atop red Pepsol sign, white background, yellow & red rim, 1941, 12" dia, NM, A13...**$60.00**

Pepto-Bismol, bank, 24-Hour Bug, vinyl, green, 1970s, 7", M, D20...**$100.00**

Perf P Ects Coffee, tin, 1-lb, pry lid, VG+, A18.........**$50.00**

Perfect Circle Piston, sign, tin, Home Of The Doctor Of Motors/We Install..., man on red dot, white ground, 2-sided hanger, 24x24", NM, A1 ....**$525.00**

Perfect Circle Piston Rings, sign, tin, Don't Drive An Oil Hog!, Install Perfect Circle..., pig on car drinking bottle of oil, 1940s, 25x19", VG, A13................................**$675.00**

Perfect Circle Piston Rings/Piston Expanders, sign, tin, Don't Drive An Oil Hog, pig pulling car with chain, embossed, 36x29", EX+, A2 ....**$2,300.00**

Perfect Circle Piston Rings/Piston Expanders, sign, tin, Why-Oh Why Didn't I Get Perfect Circles?, pig in car being serviced, embossed, 36x29", EX, A2..$2,100.00

Perfect Circle X-50 Piston Rings/Piston Expanders, sign, tin, Don't Drive An Oil Hog!, pig guzzling oil atop hood of car, embossed, 25x19", VG+, A6....................**$900.00**

Perfection, cigar box label, sample, hand-held cigar, OL Schwencke & Co litho #138, EX, A5 ....**$65.00**

Perfection Asbestos Protected Tires, sign, flange, painted metal, tire shape at end of panel, ...Eliminates Tread Separation, 24x16", EX/VG, A6................................**$600.00**

Perfection Dyes/W Cushing & Co, sign, tin, ...For Silk, Woolen, Cotton and Feathers..., red/purple period lettering on white, embossed, 14x10", NM, A3..........**$130.00**

Perfection Perfume, vendor, wooden with 4 columns, ornate decal, ca 1915, 17", VG, A9.....................**$750.00**

Perique Pure Grade AA For Blending, pocket tin, vertical, paper label, white, gold top, NM (full), A18........**$60.00**

Perique Tobacco, pocket tin, flat, yellow, Somers Bros litho, EX, A18...**$50.00**

Permona, sign, tin/cardboard, bottle in center, beveled, 19x9", VG, A8..**$50.00**

Perri-Walla India & Ceylon Tea, tin, ½-lb, white, VG, A3 ....**$25.00**

Pet Cigarettes, see Allen & Ginter

Pet Milk, trolley sign, paper, Bake Them In..., 2 product cans amid display of food, blue ground, 1927, 10x21", NM+, A3...**$45.00**

Peter Brau, tap knob, ball shape, black, red/gold/black-on-metal insert, EX+, A8..**$135.00**

Peter Doelger Bottled Beer, tip tray, round, Expressly For The Home, lettering on rim around eagle-&-coin logo, 4" dia, EX, A8...**$100.00**

Peter Pan, crate label, Washington apple, Peter Pan sitting in apple tree above slanted logo/apples, Wenatchee, M, D12..**$10.00**

Peter Pan Fresh Bread, broom holder, stenciled tin front/back, wood top with 6 hole for brooms, cast base plate with indents, EX+, A3 ....**$350.00**

Peter Pan Fresh Bread, screen-door sign, triangular, EX, D34..**$150.00**

Peter Pan Ice Cream, sign, tin, Demand.../Take Home A Pint, Peter Pan blowing horn, embossed, 28x20", VG, A6...**$125.00**

Peter Pan Peanut Butter/Derby, can, 1-lb 12-oz, EX, A3..**$30.00**

Peter Pan Peanut Butter/Derby, can, 11-oz, EX+, A3.**$40.00**

Peter Pan Peanut Butter/Derby, can, 2-lb, VG+, A3 ...**$75.00**

Peter Pan Peanut Butter/Derby, can, 2-oz, Free Sample, EX+, A3 ....**$100.00**

Peter Pan Peanut Butter/EK Pond Co, can, 11-oz, EX-NM, A18/A3, from $110 to **$175.00**

Peter Pan Products, cottage, cardboard, 2-story house with lithoed detail, products listed on back, 12x11x9", EX+, A3 ....**$70.00**

Peter Pan Sugar Peas, can label, Peter Pan playing flute, M, D5...**$15.00**

Peter Rabbit Peanut Butter, pail, VG, A18 ....**$225.00**
Peter Schoenhofen Brewing Co Edelweiss, tray, round, smiling lady, decorative floral rim, gold trim, EX, A8....**$130.00**

Peter Schuyler Cigar, sign, porcelain, Get Back Of A... on back of man's head, white/yellow/blue, 12x36", EX-NM+, D11/A1, from $200 to...**$450.00**

Peters Ammunition, sign, cardboard cutout, Here's The Place To Get Peters Ammunition, hunter above rows of boxes, NM, A3 ....**$2,970.00**

Peters Ammunition, sign, linen, man reaches for rifle as ferocious bear approaches evening campsite, 31x20", VG, A9...**$650.00**

Peters Ammunition, sign, paper, close-up of a Canada goose watching over geese around pond, lettering below, 21x15", G, A9 ....**$500.00**

Peters Ammunition Sporting Rifle Cartridges/DuPont, sign, cardboard, names/product images on bull's-eye design, Peters Packs The Power at bottom, 20x13", EX, A6...**$50.00**

Peters Cartridge Co, calendar, 1909, hunting scene, artist G Muss Arnolt, 27x14", complete, G, A3 ....**$165.00**

Peters Cartridge Co, calendar, 1917, 2 hunting dogs in harvested cornfield, framed, 29x16", VG, A7..........**$300.00**

Peters Cartridge Co, calendar, 1919, linen, hunter with parent dogs taking pups on first hunt, metal strips, 24x14", no pad o/w EX, A9...**$550.00**

Peters Cartridge Co, calendar, 1926, covey of partridges in field, artist G Muss-Arnolt, metal strips, 20x13", complete, EX, A9..**$550.00**

Peters High Velocity Rustless Smokeless Shot Gun Shells, product box, image of duck in flight, 25 16-gauge shells, NM (full/sealed), A15.............................**$250.00**

Peters High Velocity/Peters Cartridge Co, sign, cardboard die-cut stand-up, large shell next to seated hunter/dog, 1930s, EX+, A24 ....**$600.00**

Peters Loaded Shells, sign, cardboard cutout, setter sitting next to product box, 25x22", VG, A9.................**$700.00**

Peters Loaded Shells, sign, cardboard die-cut stand-up, dog by wooden crate, 24x22", VG, A7......................**$450.00**

Peters Referee Shot-Gun Shells, sign, paper, enlarged image of shell/smaller box with lettering, metal strips, 20x14", G, A9..**$500.00**

Peters Shells, sign, cardboard cutout, Use..., close-up of hunter aiming gun, circled-P logo, G, A7...........**$500.00**

Peters Shoes, sign, porcelain, name in white script outlined in red on blue, white self-border, rounded ends, 8x39", EX+, A1...**$200.00**

PIE Trucking, calendar, perpetual, tin plaque with cardboard number cards, image of early truck on US map, 19x12", NM+, A1 ....**$275.00**

Piedmont Cigarettes, chair, folding, wood/porcelain sign back, VG-EX, A3/A6, from $125 to **$190.00**

Piedmont Cigarettes, insert from chair, porcelain, Smoke Piedmont/The Cigarette Of Quality, white/blue, 2-sided, self-framed, 11x11", VG+, A8................................**$75.00**

Piedmont Cigarettes, sign, cardboard, The Cigarette of Quality, 10 For 5¢, open pack above lady in plumed hat, framed, image: 30x16", EX, A9........................**$4,100.00**

Piedmont Cigarettes, sign, cardboard die-cut stand-up, car passing billboard, Save The Coupons/On The Right Road..., 16x21", EX, A6..........................$475.00

Piedmont Cigarettes, sign, porcelain, curved, ...The Virginia..., open pack on blue dot, blue on cream, 16x14", EX-NM, A12/A1, from $450 to **$625.00**

Piedmont Cigarettes, sign, porcelain, For Cigarettes Virginia Tobacco Is The Best, pack in center, white on blue, 46x30", VG-EX, A6/A2, $135 to **$220.00**

Piedmont Cigarettes, trade card, product pack between 2 men in top hats, rooftops, beyond, 6x8", EX+, A13 ....**$25.00**

Piedmont Cigarettes/Velvet Smoking Tobacco, sign, flange, oval, lettering/graphics, 1910s-20s, 14x18", EX+, A13 ....**$1,250.00**

Piel's Beer, display figure, elf with glass at stump, pot metal, Drink Piel's Beer/Since 1883 on stump, VG+, A8.**$150.00**

Piel's Beer, display figures, Bert/Harry on base for bottle display, hard rubber, 1970s, 12x7", NM, D20.........**$145.00**

Piel's Beer, sign, relief composition, Piel's On Draught, elf with full mug pointing to tapped keg, 1940s-50s, 8x9", VG+, A8...**$65.00**

Piel's Beer, skimmer holder, pot metal figure, 2 elves hanging onto barrels, lettered base, missing glass insert o/w VG+, A8...**$40.00**

Piel's Real Lager Beer, sign, porcelain, Made In America Trade Mark logo/round 1883 logo upper corners, red/black name on white, 8x16", NM, A3 ....**$30.00**

Pillsbury, doll, Poppin' Fresh, plush, Made In USA, 1982, NM+, D20 ....**$40.00**

Pillsbury, magnets, set of 2, Poppin' Fresh/Poppie, premium, 1970s, scarce, MIP, D20 ....**$35.00**

Pillsbury & Co Merchant Millers, sign, paper, ...For Sale Here, inset of factory above shipwrecked man/native examining barrel, 26x17", EX, A7 ....**$700.00**

Pillsbury Funny Face, pitcher, Goofy Grape, 1-sided or 2-sided, EX, D27, each **$125.00**

Pilot Knob Pure Coffee, can, 1-lb, key-wind lid, white/red, EX+, A3..**$275.00**

Pilot 10¢ Plug Chewing Tobacco, tin, short round, slip lid, green, EX+, A18 ....**$90.00**

Pilsener Brewing Co/Cleveland Ohio, tip tray, round, foaming glass/bottle, lettered rim, American Art Works litho, EX, A8...**$100.00**

Pilsener Export B, label, Rockford Brewing Co/IL, P-Pro, pre-1920, VG (attached to paper), A10................**$39.00**

Pilsengold Beer, label, 11-oz, San Francisco Brewing Co/CA, IRTP or WF statement, 1933-50, M, A10 ....**$10.00**

Pilsengold Beer, label, 32-oz, San Francisco Brewing Co/CA, IRTP or WF statement, 1933-50, EX, A10.............**$10.00**

Pimbley's Auto-Top-Newer, can, 1-qt, pry lid, red, NM, A1..**$110.00**

Pine Cone, crate label, California orange, arrowhead on mountain framed on pine cone on bough, orange adjacent, E Highlands, EX, D3....................................**$7.00**

Pioneer Beer, label, 11-oz, San Francisco Brewing Co/CA, IRTP or WF statement, 1933-50, M, A19 ....**$20.00**

Pioneer Brand Lobster, can label, clipper ship, Canadian, early, EX, D5 ....**$35.00**

Pioneer Club, license plate attachment, aluminum, The Famous...Downtown Las Vegas, winking cowboy pointing with thumb, 8x10", A1 ....**$350.00**

Pioneer Hog Feed, sign, tin, Feed Your Hogs... With Dried Buttermilk For More Pork, pig in center, dealer info below, 20x14", VG, A6...**$350.00**

Pioneer Tomatoes, can, 1-lb 12-oz, wagon train scene, blue bands top/bottom, EX+, A3 ....$85.00

Pipe Major English Smoking Tobacco, pocket tin, vertical, EX-NM, A18, from $280 to **$360.00**

Piper Heidsieck Chewing Tobacco, sign, cardboard, 10¢ In A Metal Box.../Clean & Fresh 10¢, closed pack/open pack on green, framed, 14x17", EX, A6..............**$150.00**

Piper Heidsieck Chewing Tobacco, tin, flat, hinged lid, Champagne Flavor/Height Of Good Taste, shows exploding bottle, ½x3x3", VG, D14 ....**$16.00**

Piper-Heidsieck Wine, sign, paper, shows dogs overturning box of wine while chasing rodent, Bencke chromo litho, 20x30", VG, A9..**$100.00**

Pippens, cigar box, Seal of Quality, red apple/leaves atop 2 burning cigars, EX+, A3..**$15.00**

Pippins 5¢ Cigars, tin, vertical square, curved corners, slip lid, EX+, A18 ....**$200.00**

Pittsburgh's Sun-Proof Paint, sign, tin, Satisfaction In Service Since 1855 next to paint can on blue draped background, self-framed, 27x38", NM, A3 ....**$390.00**

Pizza Hut, bank, Pizza Hut Pete, plastic, 1969, 7½", NM, A14/D20, from $50 to............................**$55.00**

Pizza Hut, pin-back button, Pizza Hut's Book It, M, D23 ..**$3.00**

Pizza Hut, pizza cutter, plastic, NM, D23....................**$3.00**

Placer, crate label, California pear, classic gold-mining scene, Auburn, M, D12/D5, from $10 to **$15.00**

Plano Harvesting Machines, calendar, 1905, Indian portrait in profile, 19x13", complete, EX+, A3...................**$65.00**

Planters, ashtray, gold-plated metal, Mr Peanut figure in center of round shallow dish, 50th Anniversary, 6x5", MIB, A15 ....$130.00

Planters, badge, metal pin-back, embossed knobby decoration around red Planters imprinted above space for name tag, 1x2", EX, A15..**$325.00**

Planters, bank, Mr Peanut figure, plastic, dk blue, 9", EX, A15..**$150.00**

Planters, bank, Mr Peanut figure on black round base marked Mr Peanut in white, plastic, 1990, 9", NM, D20 ....**$35.00**

Planters, bank, Mr Peanut head labeled ...Vendor Bank, plastic, red face with clear see-through top hat, 1950s, scarce, EX, D25...**$150.00**

Planters, banner, paper, Planters Mr Peanut Sale/Stock Up Now & Save!, Mr Peanut/girl with sign, blue, 1950s, 15x36", EX, A13 ....**$175.00**

Planters, belt, engraved image of Mr Peanut on gold-tone buckle, Nabisco Dinah Shore Invitational golf tournament, 1984, MIB, D25..**$40.00**

Planters, booklet, Planters Presents Our Fighting Forces, premium, 1943, color, 13x10", EX, D25 ....**$45.00**

Planters, bushel basket, orange/black paper label reading Planters Peanuts, early, EX, A15......................**$325.00**

Planters, container, papier-mache peanut, The Biggest Peanut In The World/...In-The-Shell, EXIB (11" box, brown/red graphics), A15 ....**$210.00**

Planters, cookie cutter, plastic figure of Mr Peanut bowing & tipping hat, red, EX, D25 ....**$20.00**

Planters, costume, Halloween, Mr Peanut, plastic/cloth body, molded plastic mask, 1960s, 2-pc, NMIB (unused), A15..**$300.00**

Planters, dish, glass, Mr Peanut in octagonal center bordered by cut-glass-look design, 5¼" dia, M, D25 ....**$40.00**

Planters, dish set/figural spoon, Mr Peanut image in center of bowl/cups on peanut graphics, 5-pc, NM, A3....**$100.00**

Planters, display box, cardboard, 24 5¢ Bags, image of Mr Peanut/peanuts spilling from bag, 1950s, 2½x8x5", M, D25 ....**$60.00**

Planters, display statue, Mr Peanut on beveled base marked Mr Peanut (script) with 2 figural peanuts, pot metal, 7½", EX, A15...**$600.00**

Planters, jar, glass, angled shape, tin lid lithoed with advertising/Mr Peanut, embossed Planters/decals, 9" wide, VG, A9..**$200.00**

Planters, jar, glass, barrel, tin lid, Planters/Mr Peanut leaning on cane embossed on sides, 12", VG, A9...........**$200.00**

Planters, jar, glass, fish bowl, Planters embossed on base on both sides, original paper label, 11", VG, A9.....**$250.00**

Planters, jar, glass, octagonal, embossed, Planters 5¢ Pennant Salted Peanuts, knob lid, 12", EX, A6...........**$85.00**

Planters, jar, glass, octagonal, Planters Pennant Salted Peanuts 5¢ label, embossed name on all sides, figural finial, 13", VG, A9...**$150.00**

Planters, jar, glass, round canister, knob lid, red Mr Peanut/listings of various products, not frosted, 10½x7½", NM, A15..**$425.00**

Planters, jar, glass, square, tin lid lithoed with advertising/ Mr Peanut, bottom embossed 1940 Leap Year, 9", VG, A9..**$150.00**

Planters, jar, glass, streamline, round paper label with smiling lady pouring peanuts into hand, 1940s, 10", no lid o/w EX, D22 ....**$240.00**

Planters, jar, glass, tombstone shape, ..½¢ Peanuts/Mr Peanut logo, yellow/white striped tin lid, ca 1938, 9x8x5", EX, A15 ....$400.00

Planters, jar, glass, white screw lid marked Planters, image of Mr Peanut, marked Mister Peanut/Planters, 8½x6½", M, A15 ....$350.00

Planters, mug, ceramic, 75th Anniversary with Mr Peanut logo, heat sensitive, unused, D25........................**$28.00**

Planters, mug, Mr Peanut head, plastic, tan, M, D20 ..**$25.00**

Planters, mug, pewter-type metal, embossed image of Mr Peanut, Armatale Wilton, 1983, M (original paper work), D25 ....**$35.00**

Planters, nodder figure, Mr Peanut, ceramic composition, 6½", MIB (unused), A15....................................**$140.00**

Planters, oven mitt, Mr Peanut figure, MIP, D20 ....**$20.00**

Planters, patch, cloth, oval, name on red band around embroidered Mr Peanut, 4x2½", VG+, A15........**$400.00**

Planters, peanut, papier-mache, embossed with name, mail-in premium, with receipt, ca 1948, 11x6", EX+, A3.....**$80.00**

Planters, pin, wood, Mr Peanut figure, 2", MOC (unused), A15...**$90.00**

Planters, plate, pewter, embossed image of Mr Peanut in center, 1 of 2000 made, 6" dia, M, D25 ....**$40.00**

Planters, puppet, Mr Peanut figure, rubber, tan with black hat/monocle, 1942, 6", EX, A15......................**$1,050.00**

Putnam Fadeless Dyes, cabinet, tin, slanted hinged front, white, multicolored graphics, blue trim, 11x15", VG, A2..**$175.00**

PW Byer Up To Date Shoes, sign, tin, hightop shoe next to advertising, black on orange, embossed, 7x14", VG, A6..**$385.00**

∾ Q ∾

Q Boid Cube Cut, pocket tin, vertical, tobacco plant, 4½", EX, A18..**$100.00**

Q Boid Cube Cut, pocket tin, vertical, tobacco plant, 4½", NM (full), A18..**$135.00**

Q Boid Cube Cut Pipe Tobacco, pocket tin, vertical, cabin, 4", EX+, A18..**$230.00**

Q Boid Granulated Plug, pocket tin, vertical, concave, 4", VG+, A18..**$40.00**

Q Boid Granulated Plug, pocket tin, vertical, oval, 4", VG-EX+, A18, from $50 to..**$115.00**

Quadroon Smoking Tobacco, pouch, 4-oz, cloth, paper label, VG, A7..**$225.00**

Quail Cigars, sign, paper, A Standard Of Excellence For Over Forty Years, oval image of 2 quail, cream ground, 1900, 9x13", EX+, A3..**$50.00**

Quaker Coffee, can, 1-lb, key-wind lid, oval image on top part of 2-color ground, NM, A18..**$40.00**

Quaker Crackels, display, cardboard, Help Yourself To.../Stays Crips In Box/Dish, facsimile box on front, blue, 23x21", EX, A15 ....**$200.00**

Quaker Ground Sage, tin, 1-oz, red/white/blue, NM, A3..**$25.00**

Quaker Hominy Grits, container, 1-lb 8-oz, cardboard, round, oval image on blue, red bands top/bottom, VG+, A3..**$35.00**

Quaker Maid Milk, sign, porcelain, die-cut emblem, First In Quality on blue ribbon/Quaker lady in center, white on red, 24x41", EX, A1..**$500.00**

Quaker Maid Rye/S Mirsch & Co, sign, tin, barmaid in bonnet standing with bottle on tray, name/logo at left, wood frame, 46x32", EX, A6..**$950.00**

Quaker Oats, sign, porcelain, Eat.../In Packages Only, tilted square box on white background, 42x24", VG, A6 .**$750.00**

Quaker Oats Cap'n Crunch, bank, Cap'n Crunch, painted plastic, 1973, VG, D1..**$65.00**

Quaker Oats Cap'n Crunch, bank, treasure chest, plastic, blue, 1984, NM, D1..**$10.00**

Quaker Oats Cap'n Crunch, Cap'n Crunch Cruiser (flip & fly), plastic, 1987, EX, D1..**$10.00**

Quaker Oats Cap'n Crunch, doll, Cap'n Crunch, plush, 14", VG+-NM, D20/D13, from $55 to..**$75.00**

Quaker Oats Cap'n Crunch, doll, Cap'n Crunch, squeeze vinyl, unpainted prototype (only 6 made), M, D20..........**$275.00**

Quaker Oats Co, see also Banner or Good Luck

Quaker Oats Quality Products, display rack, metal, The Best Cereal Food.../Alternate To Suit Your Taste, Quaker Men flank sign, 70x28", VG, A6 ....**$650.00**

Quaker Oats Quisp Cereal, beanie, MIB, D20 ....**$400.00**

Quaker Oats Quisp Cereal, figurine, Quisp, ceramic, 5", NM, D13 ....**$150.00**

Quaker Oats Quisp Cereal, gyro unicycle, plastic, dk blue, 1970s, MIP, D1..**$75.00**

Quaker Oats/Quick, container, 3-lb 7-oz, cardboard, round, oval image on red, Quick lettered at top, yellow bottom band, VG, A3..**$35.00**

Quaker Puffed Rice 'Sparkies,' cereal box, cardboard, yellow/white lettering & graphics on red/black diagonal ground, plane on reverse, 9x6", VG, A6................**$50.00**

Quaker State Motor Oil, clock, round, light-up, Ask For... in green on white, black numbers, glass/metal, 17" dia, VG+, A6..**$120.00**

Quaker State Motor Oil, clock, square, light-up, Ask For... in green on white, black letters, plastic, 16x16", MIB (NOS), A6 ....**$90.00**

Quaker State Motor Oil, display rack, tin sign hangs above 2-tiered wire rack, 39x22", EX, A2 ....**$470.00**

Quaker State Motor Oil, display rack, wire, 3-tiered Christmas tree style with vertical white/green sign down center, 12 oil cans, 30", EX, A6..**$275.00**

Quaker State Motor Oil, sign, convex button, Ask For..., white on green, white border, 24" dia, NM (NOS), A1..**$100.00**

Quaker State Motor Oil, sign, paper, The Right Change/Stabilized...For Summer Driving, elderly lady counting change on yellow, 34x58", EX+, A6 ....**$100.00**

Quaker State Motor Oil, sign, paper, Time To Change To...For Summer Driving, mammy changing baby on white/green ground, 34x56", VG+, A6................**$180.00**

Quaker State Motor Oil, sign, tin, ...Certified/Guaranteed, white on green arched panel with 100% Pure logo above, dated AM-3/38, 18x16", NM, A1 ....$85.00

Quaker State Oils & Greases, clock, square, neon, glass face with metal Deco case, green numbers/round logo on white, 16x19", restored, NM, A6 ....$550.00

Quaker State Summer Oil, sign, paper, Make A Hit With Your Motor/Change Now To..., boy baseball player in batting position, 34x58", EX, A6.........................$140.00

Quandt Famous Beer & Ales, tip tray, round, the god Mercury on globe marked Troy NY, lettered rim, EX+, A8...$35.00

Quandt Famous Beer & Ales, tray, round, deep rim, round logo above lettering on lt blue, dk blue rim, 12" dia, EX, A8..$70.00

Quaterback Gas Roasted Steel Cut Coffee, container, round, cardboard, paper label, very rare, VG+, A3...........$460.00

Queed Tobacco, pocket tin, vertical, green, tall, VG-EX, A18, from $80 to...$120.00

Queen City Fine Cut, see Buffalo Tobacco Works

Queen Elizabeth II Coronation 1953, cigarette tin, flat, holds 50, round image on British flag, NM, A18..$70.00

Queen Esther, crate label, California orange, image of queen, Placentia, EX, D3...$5.00

Queen of the Meadow Corn, can label, ear of corn/cornfield/farm girl with bucket & milking stool, Westernville NY, M, D12...$6.00

Queen Quality Beer/Deppen Brewing Co, sign, reverse glass, light-up, name on blue scrolled ribbon around elk above bottle on green, wood frame, 25x13", EX, A6.......$700.00

Queen Quality Salted Peanuts, tin, 10-lb, yellow, VG-VG+, A3/A2, from $90 to...$140.00

Queen Quality Shoes, display, molded hands holding up woman's hightop shoe atop tin sign with gold embossed ad, wood base, 37x25x8", EX, A1.....................$500.00

Queen Quality Shoes, pocket mirror, oval, bust image of pretty lady, EX, A3...$25.00

Queen Quality Shoes, tape measure, celluloid, round, lady in white dress/red robe, 2" dia, EX+, A3..............$50.00

Quennesta, cigar box label, inner lid, Cuban lighting woman's cigar/bales, 6x9", M, D5.........................$60.00

Quezal After Dinner Coffee, tin, 1-lb, rectangular, hinged lid, VG+, A3 ....$25.00

Quick Meal Ranges, tip tray, oval, Ask Your Dealer, pictures chicks, 5", NM+, A3 ....$230.00

Quick Meal Steel Ranges/Ringen Stove Co, booklet, Buster Brown & Tige on front/back, information on ranges, Three Bears story inside, ca 1910, 10 pgs, NM, A3 ....$100.00

Quincy Mutual Fire Insurance Co, calendar, 1889, cardboard, shows 3 rats playing with box of matches while cat watches, complete, 10x7", EX, A15 .$575.00

Quinn's Light Beer, label, 12-oz, Moore & Quinn's Brewing Co/Syracuse NY, IRTP or WF statement, 1933-50, M, A10 ....$25.00

R

R Brand & Co Fine Whiskies & Wines, saloon sign, tin, portrait of pretty girl in banana curls, self-framed, ca 1800, 23x17", VG-EX+, A7/A3 from $750 to....$1,320.00

R Naegeli's Sons Imported Pilsener, sign, tin, curled corners, gold lettering on frame around oval image of barmaid carrying steins, 21x17", EX, A7..................$400.00

R&H Premium Beer, sign, light-up, reverse on glass, lettering on panel with round corners on wooden base, 8x12", VG+, A8...$130.00

R&H Staten Island Beer & Ale, foam scraper holder, barrel shape, 1940s, 5x4" dia, NM, A19 ....$75.00

R&R Table Salt, container, cardboard, round, Free Sample, 3x2" dia, NM (unopened), A3............................$100.00

R-Pep, sign, tin, Drink R-Pep 5¢, sun burst/tilted bottle on red, 1930s-40s, 16x36", EX+, A13 ....$100.00

Rabbit's Foot Baking Powder, tin, pry lid, embossed paper label, 6", EX+ (unopened), A15 ....$775.00

Radeke Wiener Export, label, Radeke Brewing Co/Kankakee IL, pre-1920, EX, A10...$33.00

Radio Flyer, miniature wagon, red with white rubber wheels, inner decal reads Radio Line, 1950s, EX, A8 ....$60.00

Richardsons Liberty Root Beer, dispenser, ceramic barrel with spigot atop tree-stump base, NM, A13 ....**$500.00**

Richelieu Green & Black Tea, tin, 8-oz, blue, Oriental scene, EX+, A3 ....**$25.00**

Richelieu Yellow Hybrid Pop Corn, tin, round, shield against background of popped corn, NM (full), A18............**$70.00**

Richfield, desk box, bronze figural racer atop box embossed Richfield, 5x9x4", EX, A15................................**$575.00**

Richfield, desk box, bronze-finished metal race car on lid atop box with name in impressed lettering, 5x9x4", NM, A1...**$800.00**

Richfield, desk pen holder/letter opener, cast bronze aviator figure on embossed beveled base, 7", EX, A1 ...**$250.00**

Richfield, gas globe, 3-pc, metal body (blue), glass lenses, name on band across middle, blue/red/white on white, 15" dia, NM, A6 ....**$1,000.00**

Richfield, salt & pepper shakers, plastic gas pumps, with decals, beige/blue 2½", VG, A6, pair....................**$75.00**

Richfield, sign, die-cut porcelain letters, blue, 12", EX, A6 ....**$300.00**

Richfield, sign, metal shield, The Gasoline Of Power, eagle atop sign holding up the Richfield name, blue, 2-sided, 30x30", NM, A6 ....$1,300.00

Richfield, winterfront, cardboard, Choice Of The World's Greatest Drivers, shields/racers on track, yellow/blue, 12x21", NM, A1 ....$375.00

Richfield Dealer, sign, cardboard, die-cut Santa with toy bag & Greetings tag pointing, 9x5", EX+, A6..............**$50.00**

Richfield Ethyl, sign, porcelain, round, white/yellow/blue shield with eagle above name on white, yellow border, 2-sided, 25"dia, VG+, A2...................................**$1,050.00**

Richfield Hi-Octane, gas globe, 3-pc, white glass body, glass lenses, orange/black/white logo, 13½", EX, A6 ....**$300.00**

Richfield Premium, gas globe, 3-pc, white plastic body, glass lenses, red/white band over gold/black/white eagle shield, 13½", NM, A6...**$400.00**

Richfield Premium 100% Pure Pennsylvania Motor Oil, can, 1-qt, white/yellow/red/black with 'West Coast' logo, EX+, A1...**$65.00**

Richland Super Deluxe, sign, cardboard, die-cut, stand-up, The New Richland Super Deluxe sign against whitewall tire, 32x21", EX, A6.................................**$70.00**

Richland Super Deluxe sign, cardboard die-cut stand-up, The New Richland Super Deluxe sign against whitewall tire, 31x21", NM+ (NOS), A1...............................**$100.00**

Richlube Motor Oil, sign, porcelain, racer above, product name on double bands, eagle logo below, yellow/blue, 2-sided, 24" dia, Fair, A2...................................**$2,860.00**

Richmond Best Cut Plug, tin, 1-lb, square, round screw lid, yellow, NM, A18 ....**$50.00**

Richmond King of Coffee, can, 1-lb, key-wind, VG+, A3.**$45.00**

Ridenour's, cigar box label, inner lid, factory building/street scene, M, D5 ....**$75.00**

Rienzi Beer, see Bartholomy

Right Hand Brand Poultry Seasoning, container, 3-oz, rectangular, cardboard, VG, A3................................**$22.00**

Right-O-Way, crate label, Florida Citrus, high speed train/ranges, 1949, 7x7", M, D5 ....**$55.00**

Riley's Rum & Butter Toffee, pail, 4-lb, red, black silhouette images of children at play, EX, A24..............**$65.00**

Ringtons Tea, tin, square, round slip lid, black/gold/green, 7x4x4", EX, A6 ....**$50.00**

Ripple, cigar box label, outer, yacht at sea, M, D5....**$35.00**

Rising Sun Beer, calendar, 1912, ladies reading sign posted on tree, 22x15", complete, EX+, A19 ....**$175.00**

Rising Sun Stove Polish, sign, paper, lady in garden with boaters/factory beyond, Ottman litho, 29x13", VG, A9 ....**$350.00**

Rising Sun Stove Polish, sign, paper, lady leaning on banister, Donaldson Bros litho, 29x13", G, A9 ....**$200.00**

Rising Sun Stove Polish, sign, paper, lady looking out window at factory, Forbes litho, framed, image: 29x18", VG+, A9..**$450.00**

Rising Sun Stove Polish, sign, paper, lady on hill overlooking factory, Donaldson Bros litho, framed, image: 28x18", EX, A9...**$675.00**

Ritz/National Biscuit Co, sign, cardboard, Served With Ritz sign atop relish tray with crackers next to large product box on blue, 10x14", EX+, A3 ....**$55.00**

Rivals (The) Tobacco/Cyrus & Lee Tobacco Co, caddy label, horizontal, The Only Single Lady At The Station, dated 1875, 7x14", NM+, A3....................................**$38.00**

River Auto Stages, sign, porcelain, round, lettering on band around image of early bus, yellow/dk blue/red/black, 2-sided, 24" dia, EX+, A2 ....**$11,550.00**

Riverhead Gold Tobacco, container, round, cardboard with tin top/bottom, pry lid, yellow, black lettering around image of lady, 7", VG, A3 ....**$100.00**

Riverhead Gold Tobacco, tin, round, gold on yellow, 9", missing pry lid, VG, A3 ....**$70.00**

Riverside Gold, crate label, California orange, Sunkist wrapped orange/red script on white background, Riverside, M, D12 ....**$30.00**

RJ Reynolds Tob Co Strawberry, redemption list of premiums, Save Strawberry Tags above logo, List Of Presents On Other Side below, 1900, 5x3", VG, A5 ....**$30.00**

RJ Robert's Razor Cutlery, display case, ...Best in the World etched on curved glass front, wood frame/bottom, metal trim, 11x16x22", EX, A9 ....$1,450.00

Rob't Cochron, can, 1-lb, slip lid, paper label, EX+, A3...$200.00

Robbialac Paints, sign, porcelain, Agent For..., colorful cartoon lady with paint brush above white lettering on black, 24x16", VG, A6 ....$285.00

Robert Abels, catalog, 1949, #27, antique firearms/edged weapons, 190 pgs, EX, D7.................................$80.00

Robert Burns Invincible Cigars & Tobacco, sign, paper, WWI period mother/daughter packing products to be shipped to France, 22x15", NM+, A3 ....$110.00

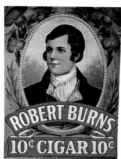

Robert Burns 10¢ Cigar, sign, cardboard hanger, The Quality Is Mild...The Value Is Strong arched above oval bust image, 14x10", EX, A3.....................$60.00

Robert J Pierce's Tablets, tin, horizontal box, curved corners, slip lid, green/black, gold trim, 7x3x3½", EX, A18.................................$65.00

Robert W Kellogg, catalog, 1924, Novel & Unusual Gifts, 56 pgs, EX, D17 ....$40.00

Robin Hood Beer/Fontineue Brewery, sign, cardboard, Robin Hood/enemy dueling on log over water while "merry men" watch, 1937, 24x22", EX, A3............$75.00

Robin Hood Flour, display figure, Robin Hood standing with legs apart/arms folded on lettered base, chalkware, multicolored, 15", EX, A6.................................$150.00

Robin Hood Flour, sign, porcelain, ...For Sale Here, red/black lettering on white, black border, 15x18", EX, A6.................................$90.00

Robinson Bros Crackers & Fine Cakes, shipping box, wood, paper labels, 13x14x24", EX, A3 ....$80.00

Robinson Crusoe Brand Salted Peanuts, tin, 10-lb, red with white label showing Crusoe by campfire, yellow trim, G, A2.................................$30.00

Robinson Crusoe Salted Peanuts, tin, 3-lb, round, pry lid, red/yellow on blue with Crusoe & Friday on side, EX+, A3.................................$140.00

Rochelle Club Beverages, sign, cardboard, Aint Dat Sumtin!, black boy with bottle of orange/hot dog, 22x15", VG, A2.................................$165.00

Rochester Coffee Percolator, sign, cardboard die-cut stand-up, Victorian lady standing behind round table pouring cup of coffee, 58x26", rare, EX, A6.................$1,700.00

Rochester Distilling Co, sign, tin, street view of distillery, self-framed, 22x28", EX, A7.................................$850.00

Rochester Root Beer, dispenser, metal box, canted corners, red with 5¢ decals on sides, flat knob lid, Multiplex Faucet Co, 12x19x21", VG, A1 ....$90.00

Rochester Root Beer, dispenser, wooden barrel with brass staves, ceramic liner, claw feet, with spigot, 14", VG, A9.................................$900.00

Rochester Root Beer, mug, glass with etched name, 10", VG, A9.................................$100.00

Rochester Root Beer, pitcher, clear glass, straight-sided, ribbed/fluted, etched lettering, 9x6" dia, EX, A6.................................$35.00

Rock-Co Pure Cocoa Powder, tin, 2-lb, round, pry lid, paper label, 9x4" dia, EX, A18.................................$50.00

Rockford Watches, tip tray, oval, bust portrait of pretty lady, name/dealer on rim, VG-EX+, A3/A6, from $100 to.................................$220.00

Rockford Watches, tip tray, rectangular, fluted corners, lady sitting by tree, decorative border, HD Beach litho, VG, A8.................................$60.00

Rocky Ford Cigars, sign, cardboard fan hanger, oval, Delicious Flavor, 5¢, Indian scout, 9x12", VG, A5....$120.00

Rocky Mountain Beer/Anaconda Brewing Co, tray, round, Properly Aged, mountains in center, gold/red on black, 13" dia, VG, A7.................................$200.00

Rod & Reel Extra Fine Cut Plug, tin, horizontal rectangle, square corners, gold/black on red, VG-EX+, A18, from $60 to.................................$90.00

Roessle Premium Lager, tray, round, deep rim, 2 elderly gents at table toasting, pre-1920s, 12" dia, NM, A19........$350.00

Roger Williams Brand Rolled Oats, container, round, pilgrim/Indian scene, red/white/blue, gold trim, 9½", VG+, A15.................................$275.00

Rohde's La Fayette Hall Best 5¢ Cigar, sign, tin, Millions Sold Annually, red/black/white, embossed, Meek & Beach Co litho, 10x14", VG+, A18 ....$150.00

Roi-Tan Cigars, cigar cutter, bronze-painted metal dial on flared base, advertising on all 4 sides, ca 1916, 8", G, A2.................................$100.00

Roller Champion Flour/Valley City Milling Co, bill clip, round logo atop clip, red/white/green, VG+, A3.$55.00

Rolling Rock, sign, motion light, round, Rolling Rock On Tap around horse head in horseshoe, 15" dia, working, EX, A6.................................$200.00

Rome Soap Mfg Co Linseed Oil Auto Soap, sign, tin, In A Class By Itself, extensive advertising around image of can, red background, white border, 11x17", G, A2......$125.00

Ronson Motor Oil/Wayne Oil Co, can, 1-qt, blue/yellow, plane/train/car, EX, A15.................................$1,050.00

Schroeder's Honey Top Whiskey, sign, tin, I'se In A Perdickermunt, self-framed, 33x23", EX, A7....**$1,300.00**

Schulte's Blend, pocket tin, vertical, paper label, EX (full), A18.................**$65.00**

Schultz & Co's Family Soaps, see Baterland

Schultz Old London Ale & Beer, tray, round, deep rim, lettering on 2-color ground, 12" dia, EX, A8.........**$100.00**

Schultz's Finest Coffee, can, 1-lb, key-wind lid, brown label on white, EX+, A3.................**$25.00**

Schuster's Root Beer, tray, square, Drink.../It's Healthful, boy/girl at table sharing drink, 13x13", EX, A1 .**$375.00**

Schutter's Bit-O-Honey Candy, sign, tin, ...With Toasted Almonds/5¢, 1920s, 12x18", NM, A4...............**$1,100.00**

Schwartz Coffee, can, 1-lb, key-wind lid, orange/black, VG+, A3.................**$50.00**

Schwen's Ice Cream, sign, celluloid, round, Delicious Malted Milk arched above glass/shake container, logo below, red trim, 9" dia, NM, A3.................**$300.00**

Schweppes Lemon Squash, postcard, golfing couple taking a break with Schweppes, NM, A17.................**$215.00**

Scissors Cut Plug, pocket tin, vertical, oval, EX+, A18.................**$3,000.00**

Scofill's Sarsaparilla or Blood Liver Syrup, trade card, A Good Angel's Visit/A Tale Of..., 2 ladies discussing product, text below, 5x3", EX, A6.................**$25.00**

Scotch Brand Quick Cooking Oats/Quaker Oats, container, 1-lb 2-oz, yellow, NM, A3.................**$60.00**

Scott Vegetable Tablets, pocket tin, flat, red, Owl Drug, EX, A18.................**$20.00**

Scott's Blood Tablets, pocket tin, flat, image of lady, EX+ (sealed), A3.................**$45.00**

Scott's Emulsion, trolley card, Wise Parents Hand Down The Health Secret..., boy/girl playing marbles, 1924, 11x24", EX, A24.................**$170.00**

Scott's Fried Chicken, bank, personified chicken on base, vinyl, NM, D20.................**$65.00**

Scott's Santal Pepsin Capsules, tin, rectangular, rounded corners, man's portrait upper left, ½x2x3", EX, D37....**$70.00**

Scrowcroft's Blue Pine Savory, tin, 2-oz, white, EX, A3...**$8.00**

Sea Foam Baking Powder, sign, paper, Sea Foam above ladies swimming from boat, company name below, 20x12", G, A9.................**$275.00**

Sea Gull, crate label, California lemon, 2 gulls in flight over ocean, red ball logo, Upland, M, D12.................**$18.00**

Seaboard Coast Line Railroad, sign, painted metal, round, name around SCL initials in center, black on yellow, 22" dia, EX, A6.................**$70.00**

Seagram's Kentucky Distillery, sign, paper, panoramic scene of distillery, white border with lettering at bottom, 14x35", EX, A13.................**$25.00**

Seal of North Carolina Plug Cut Smoking Tobacco, sign, cardboard, My Old Man, A Hoen & Co litho, 1910, 8x13", NM, A3.................**$110.00**

Seal of North Carolina Plug Cut Smoking Tobacco, sign, cardboard, What Are the Waves Saying/Smoke Seal Of North Carolina Plug Cut, 2 kids at beach, framed, 7x11", VG, A2.................**$165.00**

Seal of North Carolina Plug Cut Smoking Tobacco, tin, round, smaller round lid, 7", G-EX+, A7/A18/A3, from $135 to.................**$300.00**

Seal of North Carolina Smoking Tobacco, broadside, A Change Of Base, black mob chasing elder stealing turkey, Currier & Ives litho, 1883, 15x19", EX, A5.................**$330.00**

Seal of North Carolina Smoking Tobacco, sign, paper, nighttime frontal view of train engine with cow catcher, 14x11", G, A11.................**$90.00**

Seal of North Carolina Tobacco, box, wooden, dovetailed corners, paper label, 1883 date on revenue stamp, EX, A15.................**$275.00**

Seal Rock, cigar box label, inner lid, seal on rock, 6x9", EX, D5.................**$50.00**

Seal Rock Cut Plug, tin, rectangular, square corners, gold/black on red, VG+, A18.................**$35.00**

Sealed Power Piston Ring Sets, calendar, 1952, paper, Ring Champ, beagle dog watching 2 boys boxing, 34x16", NM, A1.................**$40.00**

Sealed Power Piston Rings, ashtray, chrome-plated figural nude logo atop round black Bakelite dish, 6x5" dia, NM, A1.................**$100.00**

Sealed Power Piston Rings, sign, molded plastic, aluminum frame, light-up, 2-sided, logo in center, red on white, 14x34x6", EX+, A1.................**$185.00**

Sealed Power Piston Rings, sign, tin, ...They Restore Oil Economy..., red nude on yellow dot on blue, curved top corners, framed, 35x22", EX+, A1 ....$200.00

Sealed Power Piston Rings, thermometer, tin, ...Franchised Dealer/Expert Engine Service, red/blue on white, 39x8", VG+, A1 ....$120.00

Sealtest, menu board, vertical, metal frame, 10 cardboard inserts for flavors/prices, red/white, 22x10", NM+ (unused), A3.................$30.00

Sealtest Ice Cream, sign, carboard cutout, Be Merry-Enjoy... above image of strawberry sundae/merry-go-round, 20x19", EX+, A3 ....$40.00

Sealtest Ice Cream, see also Hoffman's Ice Cream

Sears, Robuck & Co, tape measure, round container, The World's Largest Store/We Guarantee To Satisfy You & Save You Money, EX, A20 ....$100.00

Sears, Roebuck & Co, catalog, 1902, #112, general merchandise, hardbound, 1,200 pgs, EX, D17.........$250.00

Sears, Roebuck & Co, catalog, 1909, Our Grocery List, 50 pgs, EX, D17 ....$40.00

Sears, Roebuck & Co, catalog, 1912, #125, Fall/Winter, 1458 pgs (22 pgs of toys), EX, D17 ....$225.00

Sears, Roebuck & Co, catalog, 1921, Building Material & Mill Work, 130 pgs, EX, D17 ....$60.00

Sears, Roebuck & Co, catalog, 1930, Spring/Summer, Made-To-Order Clothes, men/young men/students, with swatches, 20 pgs, EX, D17 ....$50.00

Sears, Roebuck & Co, catalog, 1938, farm equipment, 102 pgs, EX, D17 ....$50.00

Sears, Roebuck & Co, catalog, 1940, cameras/supplies, 40 pgs, EX, D17 ....$25.00

Sears, Roebuck & Co Roasted Coffee, tin, 25-lb, round, hinged lid, striped, EX, A8 ....$80.00

Sears, Roebuck & Co Tea, pail, 5-lb, striped, EX+, A3..$130.00

Secret Order, cigar box labels, outer, 2 armored men standing guard, 1886, 4½x4½", EX, D5 ....$50.00

Sectional Bookcases/House Furnishings, sign, tin, The Heart Of The Home/Mark Of Culture In The Home, heart-shaped view of couple at bookcase, 38x31", VG, A7.................$700.00

Security Homestead, bank, man figure in bib overalls marked The Big One, ceramic, Quinco...Made in Japan on foil label, 7", M, D25.................$75.00

Segars Bulldog, sign, cardboard, frontal view of bulldog, artist John Merriam, ca 1900, brass plate on gold frame, 15x12", EX, A2 ....$470.00

Seiberling All-Treads, sign, cardboard, His Master's Voice, lettering above/below dog by large tire, Kalasign painting, 34x23", NM, A6.................$220.00

Seiberling Tires, sign, cardboard cutout, bust image of Boy Scout with sign, Dad Prefers.../35% Deeper Rubber, framed, 42x25", VG, A6.................$150.00

Seiberling Tires, sign, cardboard cutout, bust image of girl with sign, Mother Too Prefers.../40% Greater Non-skid, framed, 43x26", VG, A6.................$150.00

Seipp's Extra Plae Beer, tray, round, girl in pigtails ready to drink from glass against moonlit sky & party lanterns, c 1911, NM+, A19 ....$180.00

Semdac Liquid Gloss, display box, cardboard, early interior scene on inside of lid, held 24 cans, Standard Oil, c 1913, 14x10x5", EX+, A1 ....$200.00

Seminole Coffee, can, 1-lb, slip lid, red, Indian in profile, EX+, A15 ....$475.00

Seminole Coffee, can, 3-lb, square, smaller screw lid, paper label, Indian in profile, VG, A3 ....$110.00

Sen Sen Gum, display book box, Library Edition/Assorted/Absolutely The Best, EX, A16.................$60.00

Senate Beer, ashtray, metal, round dish with 3 metal die-cut bottles in center marked Beer/Ale/Beer, by Chr Heurich, 5" dia, EX+, A8.................$140.00

Senate Beer, door plate, We Recommend...Buy It Here on blue top/bottom, bottle on yellow center, rounded corners, 11", NM, A13.................$80.00

Senate Blend Coffee, can, 1-lb, slip lid, paper label, VG+, A15.................$575.00

Senate Brand Coffee, can, sample/bank, square, Capitol Building on front, red/white/blue, 3x2x2", EX+, A15 ....$200.00

Senate Brand Coffee, can, 1-lb, key-wind lid, white/blue on yellow, rare, EX+, A3 ....$175.00

Seneca Red Top Sportsmen's Socks, display box, cardboard, graphics of Indian/children skating/fishermen, 14x5x2", NM, A3 ....$60.00

Senour's Floor Paint, sign, porcelain, Water Proof/Heel Proof flank name, red/white/blue, 4x32", NM+, A1........$275.00

Sensation Smoking Tobacco, lunch box, basket weave, double handles, VG+, A18.................$10.00

Sensible Tobacco, lunch box, slip lid, double swing handles, EX+, A18.................$50.00

Sensible Tobacco, sign, tin, Wise Men Smoke...10¢ Sliced Plug & Double Cut, round images of wizard/product pack on red, 9x20", EX+, A3 ....$180.00

Serv-Us Coffee, can, 1-lb, screw lid, EX, A18.................$60.00

Seven Day Coffee, can, 1-lb, key-wind lid, red/white/blue, VG+, A3 ....**$50.00**

Seven-Up, ashtray, cardboard, square with scalloped corners, Put Your Ashes Here & Save Our Table, logo in center, EX+, A16 ....**$35.00**

Seven-Up, ashtray, glass, square, rounded corners, decorative border around logo in center, G, A16 ....**$15.00**

Seven-Up, belt buckle, metal with enameled logo in center, EX, A16 ....**$35.00**

Seven-Up, bill hook, celluloid button, I'd Hang For A Chilled 7-Up, EX+, A16 ....**$35.00**

Seven-Up, bottle topper/bottle, cardboard, Easter, bunny atop egg next to girl, NM, D30 ....**$32.00**

Seven-Up, bottle topper/bottle, cardboard, Easter, logo in Easter basket with blue bow, EX, D30 ....**$22.00**

Seven-Up, bottle topper/bottle, cardboard, Easter Fresh Up, girl rabbit in Easter's finest, EX, D30.......$22.00

Seven-Up, bottle topper/bottle, cardboard, Fresh Up For St Pat's, logo/shamrocks, EX, D30 ....$22.00

Seven-Up, bottle topper/bottle, cardboard, Fresh Up For Thanksgiving, turkey chef serving up 7-Up logo, EX, D30 ....$20.00

Seven-Up, bottle topper/bottle, cardboard, Fresh Up With 7-Up, birthday girl, EX, D30.....................................**$22.00**

Seven-Up, bottle topper/bottle, cardboard, Fresh Up With 7-Up, boy in beanie with bottle, EX, D30 ....**$32.00**

Seven-Up, bottle topper/bottle, cardboard, The All-Family Drink!, young sailor boy in backyard pool, NM, D30...**$22.00**

Seven-Up, bottle topper/bottle, cardboard, Top O' The Morning, green silhouette of leprechaun, EX, D30...**$22.00**

Seven-Up, broom stand, Drink 7-Up/It Likes You on sign on 2-legged rack, white on red, 1940s, 28x20", EX+, A4 ....**$600.00**

Seven-Up, calendar, 1943, General McArthur, complete, VG+, A13 ....**$35.00**

Seven-Up, calendar, 1953, complete, EX+, A16..........**$65.00**

Seven-Up, clock, rectangular, First Against Thirst/logo, vertical, bowed sides, VG, A16 ....**$60.00**

Seven-Up, clock, round, Freshen Up rocking sign (missing)/7-Up logo/green numbers on white, aluminum, 1950s, 20", EX, A13...**$450.00**

Seven-Up, clock, round, You Like It/It Likes You on green band around numbers/7-Up logo on white center, white case, 1950s, M, A4 ....**$600.00**

Seven-Up, clock, square, Get Real Action/7-Up Your Thirst Away!!, logo in center, plastic front, light-up, EX+, A16.........**$75.00**

Seven-Up, clock, square, neon, Fresh Up With/tilted bottle/green neon around numbers, glass front/metal frame, 15x15", EX, A8 ....**$340.00**

Seven-Up, clock, square, We Proudly Serve/It Likes You logo, wood frame, EX-NM+, A16/D30, from $220 to....**$375.00**

Seven-Up, cuff links, enameled logo, M, A16, pair....**$30.00**

Seven-Up, display, glass, green bottle in iceberg, 1940s-50s, 9x7x8", NM, A13, from $325 to $375.00

Seven-Up, door plate, Come In above red oval logo with bubbles, Likes You at bottom, white, aluminum, EX+, A13...**$85.00**

Seven-Up, door plate, 7-Up logo (tilted) at top, white, tin, 12x3", NM, A13 ....**$85.00**

Seven-Up, door push bar, Fresh Up With Seven-Up!, logos at each end, white, porcelain, 3x32", NM+ (NOS), A1 ....$220.00

Seven-Up, drinking glass, aluminum, with 7-Up logo, 5", EX+, A16...**$45.00**

Seven-Up, drinking glass, red/white applied label with girls, M, A16 ....**$168.00**

Seven-Up, matchbook, 7-Up on front/The Uncola on back, 20 strike, front striker, M, D28 ....**$8.00**

Seven-Up, matchbook cover, Do You Know.../Sold Everywhere on top fold/round logo, phrase, tilted bottle on back, VG+, D30...**$4.00**

Seven-Up, matchbook cover, Drink... (round 7-Up logo), Sold Everywhere (on top fold), Handy To Carry... with 6-pack on back, EX, D30...**$5.00**

Seven-Up, matchbook cover, Get With It on top fold/Drink Vodka & Seven-Up on front/logo on back, VG, D30 .**$3.00**

Seven-Up, matchbook cover, King-Size The Quality King/So Pure, So Good, So Wholesome (on top fold)/12 Ounce Bottle & crown, VG, D30 ....**$3.00**

Seven-Up, mechanical pencil, bottle in liquid on end, EX+, A16..**$40.00**

Seven-Up, menu board, tin, wood-tone, red oval 7-Up logo with 3 bars above Our Sandwiches/menu slots, 1940s, 23x9", EX+, A13 ....**$225.00**

Seven-Up, money clip, enameled dollar symbol with logo, M, A16 ....**$30.00**

Seven-Up, music box, can shape, plays theme to Love Story, NM, D13 ....**$50.00**

Seven-Up, patch, white stiched logo on red square cloth, 5x5", EX+, A3 ....**$20.00**

Seven-Up, sign, aluminum, 7-Up Likes You, round, red, green border, embossed, 1940s, no size given, EX, A13 ....**$200.00**

Seven-Up, sign, cardboard, Enjoy Seven-Up Float, pictures ice-cream carton/7-Up bottles/floats, framed, 20x33", NM, D30 ....**$100.00**

Seven-Up, sign, cardboard, For A Quick Refreshing Lift..., lady taking a break from ironing, 1955, self-framed, 13x23", NM, A1 ....$100.00

Seven-Up, sign, cardboard, The All-Family Drink!, baby in high-chair/logo, 1956, self-framed, 13x23", NM+, A1 .....$100.00

Seven-Up, sign, cardboard, The All-Family Drink!, dad/daughter bowling, 1952, self-framed, 13x23", NM+, A1..**$150.00**

Seven-Up, sign, cardboard, We're A Fresh Up Family!, fishing father/son/daughter/logo, 1948, 11x21", EX+, A16 ....**$50.00**

Seven-Up, sign, cardboard, Wet & Wild, 6-pack on inset, 2-sided, framed, EX+, D30 ....**$100.00**

Seven-Up, sign, cardboard, You Like It.../It Likes You!/The All-Family Drink!, majorette/logo, 1951, self-framed, 13x23", NM, A1 ....**$75.00**

Seven-Up, sign, cardboard cutout, Morning/Noon/Night (on band around globe)/7-Up (logo)/Likes You (contour band), 21x17", VG, D30 ....**$65.00**

Seven-Up, sign, cardboard die-cut stand-up, Fresh Up With.../The All-Family Drink!..., family gathered around TV, 16x12", EX+, A3...**$40.00**

Seven-Up, sign, cardboard die-cut stand-up, Season's Greetings, jack-in-the-box Santa with bottle, EX+, A16 ..**$65.00**

Seven-Up, sign, cardboard hanger, 3-D, Season's Greetings, bottle with holly/ornaments, 2-sided, EX+, A16...**$48.00**

Seven-Up, sign, celluloid hanger/stand-up, 7-Up Likes You, round, red, green border, 1940s, 9" dia, EX+, A13..**$300.00**

Seven-Up, sign, composition, Service Bar/Please Do Not Stand Here/Better Blend With, tilted bottle, 2-sided, 1945, 6x12", EX, A3 ....**$50.00**

Seven-Up, sign, flange, 7-Up Likes You logo on green with white lines/scroll decoration, curved outer corners, 10x13", NM, D30..**$200.00**

Seven-Up, sign, Glo-Glass, Drink 7-Up/Take Some Home, lettered white dots/bottle on red ground, 1930s, 4x10", NM+, A13 ....**$700.00**

Seven-Up, sign, paper, Fresh Up! With 7-Up Float, slanted text/graphics on green, 4x18", NM+, D30............**$15.00**

Seven-Up, sign, porcelain, Fresh Up With upper left of bottle (Bubble Girl) tilting toward logo, green bottom band, 12x30", EX, A1 ....**$800.00**

Seven-Up, sign, porcelain, Fresh Up With 7-Up (on logo)/You Like It..., green bottom band/rim, curved corners, 20x28", NM, A1 ....$425.00

Seven-Up, sign, porcelain, 7-Up/bubbles logo, white/black on red, black bands top/bottom, 36x31", NM, A6.....**$375.00**

Seven-Up, sign, porcelain, 7-Up/bubbles logo, white/black on red, black bands top/bottom, 1951, 20x17", NM+, A1...**$425.00**

Seven-Up, sign, school crossing, metal, die-cut cartoon policeman standing on 7-Up logo holding Slow... sign, 1950s, 60", G, A13................................$800.00

Seven-Up, sign, tin, Anti-Acid/Lithiated Lemon Soda, girl reaching up to 7-Up, black/white/orange, 1920s, 20x9", G+, A1 ....**$250.00**

Seven-Up, sign, tin, bottle shape, wet-look, 2-sided, 44x13", EX, A6..**$275.00**

Seven-Up, sign, tin, bottle shape (Bubble Girl), no size given, rare, EX, D34 ....**$950.00**

Seven-Up, sign, tin, corner triangle, Fresh Up!/7-Up logo with waves/bubbles, orange/black/green/white, 8-44, 8x10", EX, A6 ....**$190.00**

Seven-Up, sign, tin, corner triangle, Take Some Home/oval 7-Up logo on scrolled ground, orange/black/white, 1940s, 8x10", EX, A6............................**$190.00**

Seven-Up, sign, tin, First Against Thirst, logo left of black lettering on white, blue/white beveled border, 15x23", NM, D30 ....**$85.00**

Seven-Up, sign, tin, Fresh Up With (red/black) above tilted unopened bottle on white, green border, 1950s-60s, 54x18", EX+, A13 ....**$275.00**

Seven-Up, sign, tin, Fresh Up With above hand-held bottle, It Likes You on red band, white, green border, 1950, 54x16", EX+, A13 ....**$450.00**

Seven-Up, sign, tin, Fresh Up With above hand-held bottle, white, green border, 1940s, 28x20", EX+, A4 .....**$250.00**

Seven-Up, sign, tin, Fresh Up With.../The All-Family Drink!, 6-pack in center, green on white, green trim, 1950s, 60x36", NM, A13 ....**$600.00**

Seven-Up, sign, tin, Fresh Up With.../You Like...It Likes You on red oval with bubbles, white rolled rim, 1952, 40x30", EX+, A13.............................**$375.00**

Seven-Up, sign, tin, Fresh Up With/bottle neck left of 7-Up logo, white, green border, embossed, rounded corners, 19x27", NM, A1 ....**$370.00**

Seven-Up, sign, tin, Fresh Up! With 7-Up/It Likes You, octagonal, white/black on red, white/black/green border, 14x14", VG, A1............................**$175.00**

Seven-Up, sign, tin, Fresh Up!/7-Up/Likes You (on dot with scrolled tail), 35x26", EX, A16............................**$365.00**

Seven-Up, sign, tin, Here's Your over hand-held bottle, Fresh Up on red band, white, green rim, embossed, 1948, 43x13", NM, A1 ....**$625.00**

Seven-Up, sign, tin, Real 7-Up Sold Here, round, with bubbles, white/black/red, raised rim, 14" dia, G+, A1.........**$230.00**

Seven-Up, sign, tin, You Like 7-Up/It Likes You on red oval with bubbles, white raised rolled rim, 1947, 40x30", VG+, A13 ....$150.00

Seven-Up, sign, tin, 2 7-Up logo signs (white/red/black) back to back on gold plywood arrow, embossed, 1954, 14x28", VG, A1..................................**$100.00**

Seven-Up, sign, tin/cardboard, We Proudly Serve You 7-Up, yellow/gold on red, canted corners, 1940s-50s, 5x9", EX+, A13..**$160.00**

Seven-Up, sign/clock, light-up, Fresh Up With (7-Up logo), round clock lower left on white, horizontal rectangle, EX, D30 ....**$100.00**

Seven-Up, thermometer, dial type, 7-Up Likes You on red center dot, 10" or 12", NM, A1, from $150 to ..$200.00

Seven-Up, thermometer, porcelain, Fresh Up, with bottle, white, 1940s, 15x6", NM, A13 ....**$200.00**

Seven-Up, thermometer, porcelain, Fresh Up/Ca Ravigole, with bottle, white, 1950s, 14", EX, A14 ....**$80.00**

Seven-Up, thermometer, porcelain, The Fresh Up Family Drink, with bottle, white, 15", EX, A14/A3, from $100 to **$130.00**

Seven-Up, tie clip, enameled logo on bar, EX, A16...**$15.00**

Seven-Up, toy truck, tin, friction, driver moves back & forth in cab with see-through plastic dome, 1950s, 9", EX+, A14..**$335.00**

Seven-Up/Like, sign, tin, Like (on red oval) Diet Drink/Made By 7-Up/Lemon Lime Flavor, white ground, 15x33", NM+, D30.................................**$85.00**

Sexton Sanitary Ajax, saleman's sample garbage can, black with green lid which opens in 2 sections for removal of garbage bucket, 4", EX, A2 ....**$285.00**

Shady Side, cigar box label, outer, octagonal, elderly couple on park bench, Schumacher & Ettlinger litho #6006, G+, A5..**$35.00**

Shamrock, gas globe, 3-pc, plastic body, glass lenses, oval, name on shamrock, green/red/white, 12x16", EX, A6.........**$600.00**

Shamrock, gas globe, 3-pc, white plastic body, glass lenses, round, white name on green shamrock on white, 14", NM (NOS), A6......................................**$300.00**

Sharp's Kreemy Toffee, tin, square box, It's All Right, girl enjoying product, 7x5x4", EX, A24......................**$75.00**

Sharp's Super-Kreem Toffee, pail, red, 9", EX, A24..**$150.00**

Sharp's Super-Kreem Toffee, tin, rectangular, slip lid, yellow, Dapper Dan on front/parrot on reverse, 6x5x9", EX, A18...**$25.00**

Sharples, cabinet, wood, Suction Feed Separators, gold-stenciled lettering on front, 25", VG+, A3 ....**$110.00**

Sharples, calendar top, cardboard, woman on porch watching boy drink from pan held by girl, 18x12", EX+, A1, from $110 to..**$150.00**

Sharples, match holder, tin, The Pet Of The Dairy, 7x2", VG-NM, A3, from $150 to......................................**$745.00**

Sharples, pin-back button, Different From The Others/The Tubular Cream Separator, milkmaid with pail, VG-EX+, A3/A6, from $20 to..**$50.00**

Sharples, pot scraper, ...The 1909 Tubulars Are Better Than Ever, shows milkmaid walking through door, EX, A3.......**$235.00**

Sharples, sign, tin, die-cut emblem, young girl operating crank while man fills separator, green ground, 2-sided, 27x19", VG, A7...**$650.00**

Sharples, sign, tin, milkmaid/girl/calf, oval image in woodgrain scalloped self-frame, 39x18", VG-EX, A9/A7, from $1,750 to...**$2,650.00**

Sharples, stick pin, celluloid, oval, milkmaid working separator, 3", EX+, A14..**$35.00**

Shasta, crate label, California orange, large oranges/orchard scenes, M, D5...**$45.00**

Shasta Coffee, can, 1-lb, key-wind lid, yellow, EX+, A3...**$340.00**

Shasta Sparkling Beverages, sign, tin, Water-Mixes-Flavors/ 'It Hasta To Be Shasta,' mountain graphics, red/white/blue, 12x24", NM, A1......................$180.00

Shaw Pianos, sign, cardboard cutout, For Purity Of Tone The..., girl standing behind fence holding cat, ca 1910, 13x10", EX, A3...**$165.00**

Shaw's Pure Malt, sign, tin, lethargic woman in chair being served Shaw's, child playing on floor, self-framed, 22x16", G, A17...**$300.00**

Sheepshead, cigar box label, inner lid, ram's head, 6x9", M, D5...**$35.00**

Shell, badge, bronzed-metal shell shape with Shell in inlayed red cloisonne, early, 2x2", EX, A15..$450.00

Shell, bank, plastic shell shape, yellow, red embossed lettering, 4", EX-NM, A2/A18, from $175 to .$210.00

Shell, flag, cloth, Shell lettered in black across red shell logo on yellow, black trim, 1920s, 44x66", NM+, A1 .**$275.00**

Shell, gas globe, 1-pc, glass, shell shape, white, red decaled lettering on arched center band, 20", NM, A6....**$700.00**

Shell, gas globe, 1-pc, glass, shell shape, white, red-painted lettering, 18", EX, A6..**$475.00**

Shell, jigsaw puzzle, image of Jimmy Doolittle flying Shell Lightning plane over airfield, multicolored, 10x14", NM, A2...**$340.00**

Shell, pen holder, plastic, holds 3 pens with Shell logo, tapers, red advertising on yellow, Fleetwood Oil Co, EX, A1...**$120.00**

Shell, pocketknife with scissors, metal with engraved lettering/logo, Mileage Is Our Business, 2½", EX, A6..**$50.00**

Shell, promotional item, Shell's Christmas Magic Show box, cardboard, 1x3x2", EX+, A1..............................**$35.00**

Shell, salt & pepper shakers, plastic figural gas pumps, red/yellow, paper labels, 3", EX+, A1................**$250.00**

Shell, sign, neon/porcelain, shell shape, orange, neon on red lettering/border, marked Artkraft 2-48, 48x48", EX+, A6...**$1,300.00**

Shell, sign, porcelain, arrow shape, stylized, From The Pump, Shell logo on bulbous end, red/black/ white/yellow, 12x36", EX, A6 ....$1,800.00

Shell, sign, porcelain, shell shape, yellow, Shell in red block letters, red trim, 48x48", G, A2.........................**$200.00**

Shell, stickpin, shell-shaped logo with cloisonne inlay, red/yellow, 2", EX, A15...**$90.00**

Shell, winterfront, cardboard, die-cut Shell logo flanked by Starts/Quickly, decorative curved bottom, 13x21", G+, A1...**$65.00**

Shell, winterfront, cardboard, Quick Starting! above logo, SHELL down sides, red on yellow, die-cut bottom, 13x21", EX+, A1...**$60.00**

Shell (Aeroshell) Oil, can, 1-qt, red Aeroshell Oil above Shell winged logo on white with red bottom band, EX+, A1...**$60.00**

Shell (Golden) Auto Oil, can, 1-gal, red/yellow, Shell logo, VG, A1...**$275.00**

Shell (Golden) Motor Oil, can, 1-gal (Imperial), rectangular, pour spout with funnel, diagonal grip handle, red on yellow, red band, VG, A1.....................................**$80.00**

Shell (Golden) Motor Oil, can, 1-qt, orange, red/white Golden Shell logo, NM+ (full), A2.....................**$130.00**

Shell (Golden) Oil, pocket watch/fob, 7-jewel, Roman numerals, glass back shows works, round cloisonne fob with Shell logo, M, A1.......................................**$550.00**

Shell (Golden) Oil, watch fob, round with embossed orange enameled Golden Shell Oil logo, 1½" dia, EX-NM, A15/A6, from $160 to...**$200.00**

Shell (Super-Shell), gas globe, 1-pc, glass, shell shape, white, embossed black/red name, 17½", EX+, A6..........**$600.00**

Shell (Super-Shell), pin-back button, celluloid, Save 3 Ways With Super-Shell on white cup filled with product on red, 4" dia, EX+, A1...**$70.00**

Shell (Super-Shell), sign, paper/linen, Saves On 'Stop & Go' Driving..., cartoon image of driver waiting on trolley, 33x57", NM+ (NOS), A6......................................**$180.00**

Shell Cooling System, display, cardboard, Cleans Out Clogged Radiators, attendant using product on overheated car, 9x12", NM, A1.......................................**$50.00**

Shell Diesoline, gas globe, 1-pc, milk glass, shell shape, embossed painted lettering, 17x18", VG, A6......**$800.00**

Shell Fly Control, sign, tin, Protected By Shell Fly Control Program, black/red lettering & logo on yellow, round corners, 15x18", EX, A1......................................**$100.00**

Shell Gasoline, pump sign, porcelain, shell shape, orange, large yellow Shell above small yellow Gasoline, black trim, 12", EX+, A1 ....**$850.00**

Shell Gasoline, pump sign, porcelain, shell shape, red, orange Shell outlined in black, black-outlined edge, 12", EX, A1...**$600.00**

Shell Gasoline, sign, porcelain, shell shape, red on yellow, 2-sided, 25x24", EX, A6 ....**$850.00**

Shell Gasoline/Shell Motor Oil, thermometer, porcelain, yellow/red, Shell logos top/bottom, Pat Mar 16 1915, 27", NM+, A6.....................................$3,500.00

Shell Kerosene/Range Oil, sign, porcelain, red lettering above Shell logo on orange, red border, curved corners, 2-sided, 20x15", NM, A1..................................**$2,150.00**

Shell Lubricants, barrel spigot, cast metal with embossed Shell logo/lettering, 6", EX, A1 ....**$70.00**

Shell Lubricating Oils, sign, porcelain, white lettering shadowed in black on red, white-line border, 2-sided, 13x18", VG, A1 ....**$300.00**

Shell Motor Oil, sign, porcelain, red name above/below red Shell logo, pouring oil can on yellow, 40x41", VGM A6..**$1,550.00**

Shell Motor Oils, sign, porcelain, black lettering outlined in red above/below red shell logo on yellow, red/black border, 11x18", VG, A6 ....**$500.00**

Shell Oil, case with bottles, metal with hinged lid, 16 original bottles with Shell logo (some with caps), 14x12", VG, A2...**$600.00**

Shell Oil, toy tanker truck, tin, friction, Chevy-style cab, red/yellow, Japanese, 13", NM, A1.....................**$180.00**

Shell Oil Co, desk note paper/pen & pencil holder, brass open box/side holder on beveled base, embossed Shell logo, 7x3x4", EX, A1...**$240.00**

Shell Shelltox, sign, cardboard stand-up, Protect Your Child's Health..., images of child holding cup/product/insects, 26x19", EX, A6...**$275.00**

Shell Spirit/Oils, sign, flange, porcelain, Stop (gloved hand) & Fill Up Here With Shell, die-cut circle atop panel, 18x24", VG, A6..**$850.00**

Shell Transmission Oil, can, 1-gal, rectangular, tall, pour spout, grip handle, red Shell lettered above shell on yellow panel, embossed, G+, A1 ....**$200.00**

Shell/Shellightning, jigsaw puzzle, Shellightning flying over Shell hangar, signed JH Doolittle & James G Haizlip, 1933, 10x14", EX, D10 ....**$65.00**

ShellZone Anit-Freeze, thermometer, metal, yellow on red, NMIB, A2/A3, from $250 to **$275.00**

Shenango China/Inca Ware, ashtray, saleman's sample, ceramic, round with 3 rests, features ad from Dixie Restaurant/Equipment Co, 5" dia, M, D25 ....**$48.00**

Sherman's Standard Coffee, pail, 2-lb, milk-can shape, red, yellow paper label, VG, A2 ....**$230.00**

Sherry Deoderant Cream, tin, round, Sample, lettering on Deco emblem, ¼x1", EX, D37 ....**$18.00**

Sherwin-Williams Auto Enamels, display, metal, 3-quarter circle appendage with man in auto atop advertising panel, row of samples below, 16x12", EX, A6 ...**$200.00**

Sherwin-Williams Paints, display sign, cardboard trifold, Restore Home Values With Paint, lady encircled by vignettes/logo, 40x48", EX, A1..............................**$75.00**

Sherwin-Williams Paints, sign, flange, Cover The Earth logo atop yellow panel, porcelain, 48x33", NM, A1..$700.00

Sherwin-Williams Paints, sign, porcelain, Cover The Earth logo atop panel, 1-sided, 64x36", EX+, A13 ....**$90.00**

Sherwin-Williams Paints, sign, porcelain, Cover The Earth logo atop yellow panel, 2-sided, 58x42", NM, A13...........**$170.00**

Sherwin-Williams Paints & Varnishes, sign, flange, ...Sold Here, white lettering/logo on blue, white line border, 16x22", EX+, A1 ....**$220.00**

Sherwin-Williams Paints & Varnishes, sign, porcelain, ...Sold Here, white lettering/logo on blue, white line border, 16x22", EX+, A1..**$225.00**

Sherwin-Williams Paints-Varnishes-Enamels, sign, porcelain, Paint Headquarters..., blue lettering/logo on tan, red border, 8x12", EX+, A1 ....**$300.00**

Shetland Ponies, cigar box label, outer, 2 ponies close together, 1931, 4½x4½", D5.................................**$30.00**

Shick Shaver, mirror, rectangular with reverse-painted ad around circular mirror, No Blades/No Lather..., razor/cord, 10x7", VG, A1 ....$65.00

Shinola Shoe Polish, shoe horn, metal, colorful images of brushes, product can/lettering on black, red border, 4", EX+, A3 ....$11.00

Ship-Shape, cigar box label, sample, portrait of man over ship's sail, Schumacher & Ettlinger litho #6728, 1886, EX, A5 ....$85.00

Shoe Shine, trade sign, wooden boot with Shine 5¢ stenciled in white, metal mounting rack, 20x18x4", EX, A6 ....$800.00

Shore's Cinnamon, tin, 1/2-lb, round, VG+, A3 ....$8.00

Short Line/Buckeye Stages, calendar, no year, paper, image of bus in center of map with destinations, framed, 23x16", no pad o/w EX, A6 ....$285.00

Shot Crushed Plug Cut, pocket tin, vertical, tall, EX, A18 ....$110.00

Shot Plug Cut Mix, pocket tin, vertical, short, G+, A18 .$50.00

Shot Plug Cut Mix, pocket tin, vertical, tall, EX, A18 ...$150.00

Shotwell's Marshmallows, tin, 12-oz, round, pry lid, Continental Can, early, VG, A3 ....$90.00

Sick's Select/Brew 66 display bottle, green with label/cap, 22", EX+, A1 ....$70.00

Sidax Fine Quality Coffee, can, 1-lb, key-wind, white/blue on red, EX+, A3 ....$90.00

Sierra Beer, label, 11-oz, Fresno Brewing Co, Fresno CA, IRTP/U-type permit #, 1933-36, VG (traces of paper or scrapes on back), A10 ....$22.00

Sierra Ice Cream, tray, oval, deep rim, sundaes flank mountain logo in center, green/white on red, red/white striped rim, 13x16", NM, A1 ....$235.00

Sierra Vista, crate label, California orange, fancy red lettering in sky above groves/mountians, Porterville, EX-M, D3/D12, from $8 to $18.00

Signal Gasoline, pump sign, porcelain, round, yellow name around white stoplight logo on green, red trim, 12" dia, NM, A1...$575.00

Signal Products, winterfront, waxed cardboard, round stoplight logo on yellow, framed, 13x21", NM, A1 ..$115.00

Signal Tarzan Club, pin-back button, celluloid, black lettering on white band around image of Tarzan on green, 1930s, 1" dia, NM, A1 ....$100.00

Signal 10-30 HD Motor Oil, bank, oil can, red/yellow/white on black/yellow ground, 2", NM, A1 ....$110.00

Silent Chief Gasoline, sign, porcelain, Viking warrior superimposed over blue/red lettering on white, 40" dia, EX, A2...$14,300.00

Silent Chief Motor Oil, can, 1-qt, Indian chief profile logo, red, yellow, white on black, VG+, A1 ....$725.00

Silver Bar Apricots, can label, 2 apricots on twig on silver background, San Francisco, M, D12.....................$8.00

Silver Blend Brand Coffee, can, 3-lb, pry lid, tall, rare, EX+, A3...$340.00

Silver Buckle Brand Coffee, can, 1-lb, pry lid, EX+, A3...$80.00

Silver Buckle Brand Ginger, tin, 1 1/2-oz, NM+, A3 .$28.00

Silver Buckle Brand Peanut Butter, can, 1-lb, key-wind lid, VG+, A3 ....$90.00

Silver Dust Flour, thermometer, porcelain, white on blue, 16x4", EX, A15 ....$300.00

Silver Moon Brand Coffee, can, 1-lb, slip lid, paper label, lady on moon, EX+, A15 ....$500.00

Silver Sea Roasted Coffee, can, 1-lb, pry lid, tall, EX+, A3 ....$55.00

Silvercup Bread, sign, tin, Buy Silvercup! above wrapped loaf, The World's Finest Bread, 12x18", VG (NOS), A9 ....$100.00

Silvercup Coffee, can, 1-lb, key-wind lid, red/white/blue, EX+, A3..$90.00

Simmons Beautyrest Mattress, display, die-cut cardboard, lady resting on Floating Action Coils between oval ad panels, ca 1950, 15x46", EX, A23 ....$60.00

Simmons Beds, Mattresses & Furniture, catalog, 1929, hospital/institutions, 94 pgs, EX, D17 ....$70.00

Simon's Roosevelt Tobacco, tin, horizontal rectangle, rounded corners, green, EX, A18 ....$100.00

Simonds Hand Saw, sign, tin, A Simonds Warrant Accompanies Every Simonds Saw, hand-held saw cutting board, 12x24", EX, A7 ....$1,000.00

Simpson Spring Beverages, bottle topper/bottle, cardboard, die-cut, 18 Delicious Flavors, sign & sailboat, EX, D30 ....$40.00

Simpson Spring Beverages, sign, tin, embossed, ...Best Of All/list of flavors, green/white text on green/red with white scroll, 20x14", NM, A24...........................$300.00

Sinbad Coffee, can, 1-lb, paper label, red on yellow, G+, A3...$85.00

Sinclair, ashtray, chrome, Dino figure in center of irregular shaped shallow dish, Pat #98596/16703, 2x7", EX+, A6 ....$70.00

Sinclair, ashtray/pipe holder, chalkware, figural dinosaur on center rock between to wells, gold embossed name, green/red, NM, A1 .... **$375.00**

Sinclair, bank, metal dinosaur figure, gold/black, 6x9", NM, A6 .... **$220.00**

Sinclair, sign, metal, die-cut Dino on bracket, green/black, 18x29", restored, NM, A6 .... **$375.00**

Sinclair, sign, porcelain, ...Credit Cards Honored, green/red on white, 2-sided, 14x33", EX+, D22 .... **$150.00**

Sinclair Dino Supreme, gas globe, 3-pc, white plastic body, Sinclair/dinosaur logo above red name on white, 13½", NM, A6 .... **$220.00**

Sinclair Gasoline, gas globe, 1-pc, glass, white name on black logo, white body, 16", VG, A6 .... **$700.00**

Sinclair Gasoline, gas globe, 3-pc, Hull white glass body, glass lenses, white lettering on black/white logo, 13½", NM, A6 .... **$500.00**

Sinclair Grease, pin-back button, image of can with Dino on sky blue ground, 3" dia, M, A15 .... **$150.00**

Sinclair H-C Gasoline, bank, gas-pump shape, tin, red/white/green, 4", NM, A1 .... **$120.00**

Sinclair H-C Gasoline, clock, round, neon spinner, 21" dia, EX, A6 .... **$1,600.00**

Sinclair H-C Gasoline, gas globe, 3-pc, white glass body, glass lenses, red/white/black, 14", NM+/EX+, A6 .... **$480.00**

Sinclair H-C Gasoline, sign, porcelain, round, white on green/red, 42" dia, VG, A2 .... $250.00

Sinclair H-C Products, chalkboard, proprietor's name arched above round H-C logo on green board with chalk ledge, 24x12", EX+, A1 .... **$135.00**

Sinclair Motor Oils, chart, tin, Sinclair Law Of Lubrication/Recommendation For Trucks.../Dino logo, red/white/black, 2-sided, 12x16", EX, A1 .... **$165.00**

Sinclair Opaline Motor Oil, sign, porcelain, Authorized Dealer/Seals Power At Every Degree Of Wear, can at right, white/red/green, 20x48", EX, A2 .... **$990.00**

Sinclair Pennsylvania Motor Oil, sign, porcelain, round, dinosaur logo, red/white/black, 11" dia, VG, A6 .. **$250.00**

Sinclair Power-X, gas globe, 3-pc, white glass body, glass lenses, The Super Fuel, black/red lettering on white, 13½", NM+, A6 .... **$300.00**

Sinclair Power-X, gas globe, 3-pc, white plastic body, glass lenses, Over 100 Octane, green/red lettering on white, 13½", EX+, A6 .... **$200.00**

Sinclair Power-X, gas globe, 3-pc, white plastic body, glass lenses, The Super Fuel, black/red lettering on white, 13½", NM, A6 .... **$200.00**

Sinclair Power-X, salt & pepper shakers, plastic figural gas pumps, red/white, paper labels, 3", NM, A1 ...... **$235.00**

Sinclair Power-X Gasoline, gas globe, 3-pc, white plastic body, glass lenses, name/logo, orange/green on white, EX+ lenses/G+ body, A1 .... **$180.00**

Sinclair Power-X Super Fuel, bank, gas pump shape, tin, red/white, EX+, A3 .... **$40.00**

Sinclair Products/Washington Oil Co, paperweight, gold metal molded dinosaur on green plastic base, 7x2", EX, A6 .... **$110.00**

Sinclair Shamrock Lubricant, can, 3-lb, round with cone lid applicator, white/green vertical stripes, 13x3" dia, EX+, A1 .... **$350.00**

Singer Family Sewing Machines & Emboridery, brochure, paper, The Singer Manu'f'g Co's Exhibit Of.../World's Columbian Exposition, 2 ladies by machine, 5x4", EX, A6 .... **$35.00**

Singer Machines A Coudre, sign, procelain, 1920s S/seamstress logo, 36x34", EX, A6 .... **$300.00**

Singer Sewing Machines, calendar, perpetual, For Every Stitching Operation, early S/Seamstress logo on green above day/month/number, EX, A24 ..$350.00

Singer Sewing Machines, calendar, 1892, young blonde girl in red bodice/straw hat, 9x6", incomplete, EX+, A3 ..**$140.00**

Singer Sewing Machines, calendar, 1898, heavy paper, embossed, 12x9", complete, EX, A3 .... **$55.00**

Singer Sewing Machines, jigsaw puzzle, Singer Buffalo Puzzle, ca 1890, 7x11", complete, EX+ (original envelope), A3 .... **$330.00**

Singer Sewing Machines, sign, flange, porcelain, early S/seamstress logo on green, 1920s, 19x12", VG+ (NM (NOS), A13/A24, $500 to **$950.00**

Singer Sewing Machines, sign, tin, S/seamstress logo, embossed, 2-sided, framed with scrolled decor, 36x24", G-VG, A9 .... **$1,500.00**

Singer Sewing Machines, thermometer, porcelain, modern S/seamstress logo, white, 35", NM, A13 .... **$2,600.00**

Sir Walter Raleigh Cigarettes, change receiver, square, brass/wood, cardboard cigarette display box under hinged glass, VG+, A3 .... **$50.00**

Sir Walter Raleigh Cigars, lighter, counter-top, lighter mounted atop red tin canister weighted with sand, VG, A2 .... **$165.00**

Sir Walter Raleigh Smoking Tobacco, display, store bin (dummy), round, NM, A18..................$150.00

Sir Walter Raleigh Smoking Tobacco, pocket tin, vertical, Good Enough For Everybody, NM (from Tindeco sample room), A18 ....$340.00

Sir Walter Raleigh Smoking Tobacco, pocket tin, vertical, sample, cut-down, NM, A18..................$60.00

Sir Walter Raleigh Smoking Tobacco, sign, tin, Smells Grand.../Packs Right/Smokes Sweet/...Can't Bite!, pocket tin in center, embossed, 26x17", EX+, A3..........$100.00

Sir Walter Raleigh Smoking Tobacco, tin, 1-lb, horizontal rectangle, Christmas motif, EX, A18 ....$70.00

Sister In Chief, cigar box label, salesman's sample, profile image of nurse, #7498, 1898, M, A5...................$275.00

Six Nations/CF Lighton & Co, cigar box label, inner lid, The Last Words Of Red Jacket, Geo L Schlegel litho, EX, A5......................$400.00

Skelly, clock, diagonal, glass front, metal frame, name over S logo, red/white/blue on brown, 16x16", EX, A6 ..**$170.00**

Skelly, fan, cardboard with 3 bell-shaped foldouts, Go With.../Quality Has No Substitute, station scene with traffic, VG, A6..................$220.00

Skelly Fortified Gasoline, gas globe, 3-pc, glass body/lenses, Fortified/Gasoline above/below Skelly diamond logo, red/white/blue, M, A1.........................$400.00

Skelly Premium, gas globe, 3-pc, white plastic body, glass lenses, red/white/blue diamond logo & 3 red stars on white, 13½", NM, A6 ....$250.00

Skelly Supreme, gas globe lens, 1-pc, glass, red/white/blue logo above red Supreme, 4 blue stars on white, blue trim, 13½", NM+, A6..............................$110.00

Skinner's Satins, sign, tin, bust image of Indian chief, self-framed oval, C Shonk logo, 20x17", VG-EX+, A7/A9, from $1,100 to......................$2,750.00

Skookum, lunch box, paper label on front side only, VG, A18......................$25.00

Sky Flakes Crackers, tin, 1-lb 12-oz, rectangular, pry lid, name on blue band on red/white vertical stripes, EX, A3......................$15.00

Sky-View, taxi roof sign, light-up, glass, metal housing, Deco styling with embossed lettering, metallic gold/white, 19", EX, A2......................$600.00

Slade's Allspice, tin, 2-oz, EX+, A3.............................$8.00

Slade's Ginger, tin, 1¼-oz, EX+, A3 ....$10.00

Sleepy Eye Flour, fan, die-cut image of Old Sleepy Eye, EX+, A3......................$200.00

Sleepy Eye Flour, flour sack, cloth, A Mark Of Quality/ Sleepy Eye Milling Co/Sleepy Eye Minn, orange/yellow/ black on white, 36x16", EX, A6 ....$200.00

Sleepy Eye Flour, postcard, Pipe Of Peace, from set of 9, EX+, A17......................$90.00

Sleepy Eye Flour, sign, tin, ...And Cereal Products/ Sleepy Eye Milling Co..., portrait in center, wood frame, image: 27x19, VG, A9 ....$9,000.00

Sleepy Eye Flour, sign, tin, Sleepy Eye The Meritorious Flour, oval portrait in self-frame with Indian motif, 25x20", VG, A7 ....$2,500.00

Sleepy Eye Flour, sign, tin, That Sleepy Eye Flour!, oval portrait in green beveled self-frame, gold trim, 19x13", EX, A7 ....$2,500.00

Sleepy Eye Milling Co, Cook Book, The Turnpike Road To Peoples Hearts I Find Lies Through Their Mouths Or I Mistake Mankind, 95 pgs, EX+, A3......................$35.00

Sleepy Eye Milling Co, label (barrel), paper, round, Strong Bakers on scrolled banner behind head of Old Sleepy Eye, Chief below, 16", EX+, A3 ....$450.00

Slinky, display, cardboard, More Fun Than A Circus!, boy with automated arm plays with Slinky, ca 1956, 17x17x8", EX, A23......................$750.00

Smile, sign, cardboard, Drink.../You Will Like Smile, orange man/lettering on orange oval on blue, orange trim, EX, D30 ....$100.00

Smile, sign, flange, round, tin, Drink Smile above orange man, orange/blue/white, 12x10", EX, A 6...........$425.00

Smile, sign, tin, Drink... on bow tie of orange man holding Refresh With A Smile sign, blue ground, embossed, 27x19", NM+, A13 ....$900.00

Smile, sign, tin die-cut stand-up, Drink Smile...Ice Cold Sold Here, orange man standing behind counter, 1920s-30s, G+, A13 ....$1,000.00

Smile, signs, paper cutout, orange men logos, 1 holding sign/1 motioning to come here, framed on blue, 29x22", NM, A1......................$150.00

Smith & Co Jewelers/Tupper Lake NY, postcard, Compliments Of..., lake scene, #9 from series of 64 ad designs by P Schmidt & Co, used 1909, EX, A17 ....$250.00

Smith & Rand Orange Sporting Powder, sign, paper, 2 hunters with dogs aiming at pheasants in flight, boy with rabbit on stick over shoulder, 20x21", VG, A9 ....$2,800.00

Stoneware, sign, tin, Stoneware/The Best Food Container/We Sell All Sizes, boy/dog in kitchen, 1920s, 19x13", VG+, A13 ....**$625.00**

Stork, crate label, California orange, stork on nest atop chimney, 1930, M, D5 ....**$45.00**

Stork Club, New York City, matchbook, 20 strike, front striker, green/red/black, Diamond Quality, M (full), D28 ......**$7.00**

Straton & Storm Ceres, tin, rectangular, square corners, Somers Bros, VG+, A18 ....**$110.00**

Straub's Coffee, can, 1-lb, key-wind, blue/white on white, NM, A3 ....**$80.00**

Streamline Ing-Rich, calendar/thermometer, porcelain, 1941, advertising/12 months/decorative border, 13x10", thermometer missing o/w VG+, A6 ....**$235.00**

Strength, crate label, California orange, gray elephant on yellow ground, Santa Paula, EX, D3 ....**$30.00**

Stroh's Beer, sign, tin/cardboard, You'll Like.../It's Lighter!, lady with bottle/glass on yellow, red border, 17x8", NM, A8 ....**$165.00**

Stroh's Bock Beer, label, 12-oz, Stroh Brewery Co/Detroit MI, IRTP/U-type permit #, 1933-36, EX (soaked off bottle or paper), A10 ....**$40.00**

Stroh's Bohemian Beer, sign, cardboard stand-up, 2 men getting bottles out of case from trunk of car while 2 dogs watch, 1950s, 14x18", VG+, A8 ....**$100.00**

Stroh's Bottled Beer, tray, oval, logo/child in red hooded coat, lettered rim, 13", VG, A8 ....**$85.00**

Stroh's Malt Extract, tip tray, round, For Weak People & Nursing Mothers, shows bottle, 4" dia, G+, A9 ....**$70.00**

Stromberg Carburetors Authorized Sales & Service, sign, porcelain, round, Bendix Product..., red/white/blue, 36" dia, EX+, A2 ....**$2,530.00**

Strong-Heart Coffee, can, 1-lb, screw lid, round image on Indian, tall, VG+, A3 ....**$450.00**

Stroudsburg Knight Co, calendar, 1920, man with pump rifle/dog, 22x14", no pad, VG+, A3 ....**$30.00**

Stroz Brewing Co, sign, canvas/cardboard, ...And Pass The Ammunition/For Victory Buy War Bonds, farmer/soldier, 19x22", NOS, A6 ....**$125.00**

Stroz Gold Crest Beer, sign, canvas/cardboard, Year After Year The Same Fine Beer, elderly gent with tray, 19x22", NOS, A6 ....**$80.00**

Stuart's Handy Mustard, tin, round image of lady in profile, VG+, A3 ....**$12.00**

Stubby Orange, sign, tin, Enjoy.../Tops In Pops, cartoon image of Stubby/hand-held bottle on black, red/white border, 19x18", VG, A6 ....**$180.00**

Studebaker, gas globe, 3-pc, white glass body, glass lenses, white/blue spoked wheel logo/name on blue, 14", NM, A6 ....**$150.00**

Studebaker, sign, reverse glass, Welcome (block letters) flanked by wheel logos, gold on white, framed, 8x48", restored, EX+, A13 ....**$475.00**

Studebaker Authorized Sales & Service, sign, porcelain, round, stylized S, red/white/blue, 2-sided, 48" dia, VG, A2 ....**$600.00**

Studebaker Authorized Service, sign, porcelain, round, white lettering on red/yellow, 2-sided, 40" dia, EX-NM, A2/A6, from $550 to **$600.00**

Studebaker Erskine Service, sign, porcelain, emblem, name above 2 logos, yellow/white/blue, 32x48", EX, A6 ....**$1,200.00**

Studebaker Service, sign, porcelain, wheel logo, black/white/yellow, 2-sided, 24x20", VG-EX+, A2/A6, from $990 to **$1,800.00**

Studebaker Service Station, sign, porcelain, Studebaker in diagonal script, Service/Station top & bottom, white on green, 2-sided, 14x30", EX, A2 ....**$770.00**

Studebaker Vehicles, jigsaw puzzle, 2-sided, man on wagon above images of various vehicles produced/overview of plant, 1890, 7x6", EX, D10 ....**$200.00**

Stull Seeds, sign, tin, octagonal, round white/blue image of man over 2 crossed ears of corn, white on red, 20x20", NM, A18 ....**$85.00**

Stulz Bros Tannhauser Trophen, match holder, tin, TT Bitters For Short, EX, A3 ....**$275.00**

Sturditoy/Pressed Metal Co, newspaper ad, Famous Sturditoy Trucks Right At The Factory!, images of 3 rows of trucks with ad text, framed, EX, A **$430.00**

Stutz, pocket mirror, round, Ideal Motor Car Co Indianapolis Ind lettered around winged logo, red on white, 2" dia, EX, A2 ....**$440.00**

Sub=Rosa Cigarros, sign, cardboard, 5¢ For 10, lady standing by vase of roses & product on red ground, original wood frame, 25x17", VG, A9 ....**$300.00**

Sugar Loaf Pineapples, can label, pineapple/floral bouquet, early, VG, D5 ....**$50.00**

Sugardale Meats, clock, round, glass bubble face, metal frame, numbers on white band around oval logo/pig king on throne, 16" dia, EX, A6 ....**$600.00**

Sullivan, Powell & Co Oriental Cigarettes, tin, rectangular, square corners, oval image of camel & pyramids, EX+, A3 ....**$50.00**

Sulpher Bitters/AP Ordway & Co, calendar, 1890, cardboard, pictures baby with apple/banana, calendar on reverse, VG+, A3 ....**$40.00**

Sultan's Cut Plug, tin, horizontal rectangle, rounded corners, EX, A18 ....**$70.00**

Sultana Blend Roasted Coffee, can, 1-lb, pry lid, gold on red, EX, A18 ....**$50.00**

Sulzberger's Majestic Ham, sign, tin, self-framed, lady pointing to ham she is holding on table with pail of lard/slab of bacon, 38x26", G, A6 ....**$800.00**

Sumaba Coffee, canister, 3-lb, cardboard, EX+, A3 ...**$55.00**

Summer Rest, cigar box label, sample, lady resting on garden bench, Witsch & Schmitt litho #639, EX, A5 ....**$150.00**

Summer-Time Long Cut Tobacco, pail, short paper label, VG, A18 ....**$40.00**

Summer-Time Long Cut Tobacco, tin, pry lid, paper label, NM, A3 ....**$140.00**

Summer's Girl Coffee, can, 1-lb, key-wind lid, black, yellow bottom band, the word Coffee forms white cup, NM, A3...**$35.00**

Summit, crate label, California orange, packtrain reaching a mountain summit, Redlands, EX, D3.......................**$3.00**

Summit Shirt, pennant, Summit lettered above man putting on cuff links, Shirt lettered vertically below, gold on black, 25", EX+, A3..**$100.00**

Sun Crest, calendar, 1942, VG+, A8.........................**$80.00**

Sun Crest, calendar, 1949, EX+, A16.......................**$140.00**

Sun Crest, clock, rectangular, Drink Sun Crest Beverages, sunrise logo, bubble glass front, metal frame, 16x13", EX, A6..**$165.00**

Sun Crest, clock, round, bottle on green dot, light-up, glass front, metal frame, Telechron, 1940s, EX+, A13.**$350.00**

Sun Crest, decal, bottle cap, white/blue/orange, NM+, D30..**$10.00**

Sun Crest, sign, porcelain, Drink..., lettering against trademark sunburst, blue/orange on white, 7x11", EX/NM, A6/D11, from $110 to...**$150.00**

Sun Crest, sign, tin, bottle-cap shape, Get Tingle-ated/Drink..., yellow/orange, 1950s, 36" dia, NM, A14...............**$165.00**

Sun Crest, sign, tin, bottle on blue ground, orange border, 21x7", EX, A1/A13 ....**$100.00**

Sun Crest, sign, tin, Get Tingle*Ated With..., dk blue lettering at left of oversized bottle/bottle cap on lt blue, 12x30", NM, D30 ....**$130.00**

Sun Crest, sign, tin, image of bottle on dk blue, 75x21", NM, D30 ....**$135.00**

Sun Crest, sign, tin, Just The Right Amount Of Sparkle, bottle in water by Drink... logo, raised rim, 23x41", EX-NM, A1/A6, $325 to **$325.00**

Sun Crest, thermometer, tin, bottle shape, 17", EX+, A1 ...**$220.00**

Sun Crest, thermometer, tin, Sun Crest sign on yellow, bottle in water, green raised border, 1940s, 16", G, A13 ......**$120.00**

Sun Cured Crushed Tobacco, pocket tin, vertical, scarce, VG+, A18 ....$1,760.00

Sun Cured Tobacco, pocket tin, vertical, paper label, EX+, A18..**$200.00**

Sun Drop Cola, sign, tin, bottle-cap shape, red/white, EX, D34 ....**$300.00**

Sun Drop Cola, sign, tin, round, It's Different/It's Golden, bottle cap over white cup in center on black, 1953, 30", NM, A13...**$425.00**

Sun Drop Lemonade, sign, cardboard hanger, die-cut, The Perfect Mixer/5¢, smiling lady with glass, 16x16", NM, A13..**$35.00**

Sun Dryd Coffee, can, pry lid, 4", VG+, A3..............**$85.00**

Sun Kist Tobacco, canister, round, slip lid, yellow, EX, A18/A3, from $70 to..**$85.00**

Sun Land Coffee, can, 1-lb, key-wind lid, white/red on red/black, EX+, A3/A18, from $75 to....................**$90.00**

Sun Light Axle Grease, tin, round, C Shonk litho, EX, A18 ....**$115.00**

Sun Maid Raisins, bank, California Raisin with a box of Sun-Maid on base, rubber, 6½", EX+, A14...................**$20.00**

Sun Paste Stove Polish, sign, cardboard hanger, ...Best In The World, black family reading by light reflected from stove, 1890s, 9x12", EX+, A3...............................**$280.00**

Sun-Rise Beverages, sign, tin, Discover Refreshing Pure Sun-Rise Beverages, image of smiling sun/orange half on white, 28x20", NM+, D30 ....**$125.00**

Sun-Rise Flavors/Coca-Cola, sign, cardboard, New King Size...Sold By Your Bottler Of C-C, 3 bottles next to text, purple border, 14x21", EX, A8 ....**$50.00**

Sun Spot, bottle topper/2 bottles, cardboard, die-cut, fits over 2 bottles, winking man, red/white/yellow, EX, D30...**$35.00**

Sun Spot, sign, tin, Drink Sun Spot/Bottled Sunshine, black/white lettering/red dot on yellow, 12x10", VG+, A8..**$40.00**

Sunbeam Bread, cookie tin, red, Little Miss Sunbeam in center of Christmas wreath with Holiday Greetings tag/red ribbon, 8" dia, EX, A1..**$25.00**

Sunbeam Bread, door push bar, loaf shape, Batter Whipped, 9x20", EX-NM+, A13/A24, from $150 to...$250.00

Sunbeam Bread, door push bar, Reach For Sunbeam Bread, red/white/blue, porcelain, 3x27", NOS, A6 ....**$100.00**

Sunbeam Bread, door push bar/handle, loaf shape, Batter Whipped, blue bar/handle, 1950s, 15x30", NM, A13 .**$275.00**

Sunbeam Bread, sign, cardboard die-cut stand-up, Look/New Sunbeam Is Better, Miss Sunbeam with umbrella, 26x11", EX-NM, A1, from $525 to..$700.00

Sunbeam Bread, sign, paper, loaf shape, 11x27", M, A16 ....**$40.00**

Sunbeam Bread, sign, tin, loaf shape, Enriched Bread (sandwich makings on red inset), 1957, 28x60", EX+, A13 ....**$1,500.00**

Sunbeam Bread, sign, tin, oval, Miss Sunbeam in center, lettering curved along bottom on red, yellow rim, 1958, 36x54", NM, A13 ....**$550.00**

Sunbeam Bread, sign, tin, Reach For.../Energy-Packed Bread, Miss Sunbeam on red, yellow/green rim, 1953, vertical, 55x19", NM, A13 ....**$675.00**

Sunbeam Bread, sign, tin, Reach For.../Energy-Packed Bread, Miss Sunbeam on red, yellow rim, 1950s, horizontal, 20x28", EX+, A4 ....**$250.00**

Sunbeam Rolls, sign, tin, Come In!/We Serve/The Best/Made With/Sunbeam Rolls, Miss Sunbeam on red, 1950s, vertical, 54x18", EX, A4 ....**$950.00**

Sunkist, sign, cardboard cutout, 2 wide-eyed elves shredding lemon peel, green/yellow, 1950s (?), 17x11", EX, A1 ....$30.00

Sunkist, sign, paper, ...From California/Filled With Health & Sunshine, girl with hat full of oranges, 30x20", EX, A6 ....**$160.00**

Sunkist Grower, sign, porcelain, ...Member Of Ivanhoe Citrus Association, red/white/green border, embossed, 14x20", NM, A1 ....**$250.00**

Sunkist Grower, sign, porcelain, white/red lettering on green, white/green raised border, 12x20", EX+, A1 ....**$125.00**

Sunny Boy Peanut Butter, pail, 16-oz, red on cream, VG, A6..**$120.00**

Sunny Brook, display, painted papier-mache, figural bust of old sea captain on lettered base, blue/gold trim, 13x9", EX+, A3..**$70.00**

Sunny Brook & Willow Creek Distillery Co, sign, paper, 3 nude nymphs frolicing in water, 4 girls on bank visiting, factory in distance, framed, 26x33", VG, A7....**$2,400.00**

Sunny Brook Kentucky Whiskey, display bottle, glass with painted label, 25", VG, A9..**$25.00**

Sunny Brook Pure Rye & Sour Mash Whiskey, sign, tin, Age & Purity/None Better Under The Sun, framed, 25x45", G-EX, A7, from $700 to **$1,500.00**

Sunny Jim Creamy Peanut Butter, can, 36-oz, boy in triangular Sunny Jim logo/animated peanut figure, EX+, A3 ....**$75.00**

Sunny Monday Soap, see Fairbank's

Sunnyfield Quick Rolled Oats/Atlantic & Pacific Tea Co, container, 1-lb 4-oz, cardboard, Vitamin B1, yellow/white/blue, EX, A3..**$45.00**

Sunnyside Tobacco/Buchner & Co, match holder, cardboard, oval, couple on front/factory scene on reverse, 10x7", EX, D22..**$275.00**

Sunoco, blotter, Unsurpassed In Mileage/Nu-Blue Sunoco..., Mickey Mouse in speeding car, blue/yellow/red/white, 4x7", EX, A6 ....**$50.00**

Sunoco, bottle rack, wire, holds 8 glass bottles with painted labels, metal screw-on pouring nozzles, 9x14x18", VG+, A2..**$415.00**

Sunoco, cuff links, Sunoco diamond logos, blue on yellow, box inner lid marked Braemoor, MIB (NOS), A6.**$160.00**

Sunoco, key holders, metal, gas-pump design, marked Ladies'/Men's, 7½x3½", EX, pair **$210.00**

Sunoco, sign, porcelain, 2 tilted oil cans indicating Best For Normal Driving/For Hard Driving, blue, 2-sided, 11x13", EX, A24..**$500.00**

Sunoco, sign, porcelain hanger, diamond/arrow logo, blue on yellow, 2-sided, 45x72", EX, A6 ....$475.00

Sunoco, thermometer, tin, logo at top, dealer name/location at bottom, white, 14", EX+, A1 ....**$75.00**

Sunoco (Blue 200), pump sign, porcelain, diamond/arrow logo (blue) on vertically elongated yellow diamond, 21x15", EX, A1 ....**$250.00**

Sunoco (Blue), pump sign, porcelain, diamond/arrow logo (yellow) on vertically elongated blue diamond, 22x19", NM+, A1 ....**$275.00**

Sunoco (Blue), sign, tin, At Regular Gas Price, arrow at one end to indicate miles to nearest station, yellow, embossed, 12x36", G+, A6 ....**$300.00**

Sunoco (Blue) Motor Fuel, blotter, It's High Geared...You Can Feel The Difference, red car racing off of 2 gears into space on blue, 4x8", VG+, A6 ....**$5.00**

Sunoco Mercury Made Motor Oil, banner, cloth, Keep Your Motor Full Powered!.../Prevents 'Power-Killing' Carbon, Mercury/speeding car, 36x60", EX, A6 ....**$260.00**

Sunoco Mercury Made Motor Oil, sign, porcelain, red-wing logo in center, blue on yellow, 12x10", EX, A15 .**$300.00**

Sunray D-X Petrolium Products, sign, porcelain, octagonal, lettering over sunburst/diamond logo, orange/yellow/green/black/white, 27x27", EX, A6..**$1,300.00**

Sunray Goggles, display, cardboard stand-up, with 12 pairs of sunglasses, shows various outdoor activities, 18x14", EX, A1 ....**$80.00**

Sunray Natural Power Oils, sign, porcelain, octagonal, sunray logo, yellow/orange/black/white/green, 25x27", VG, A6..**$200.00**

Sunset Brand Wheat Flakes/Montgomery Ward Co, cereal box, 8-oz, trademark sunset graphics, NM+, A3...........**$450.00**

Sunset Club, cigar box label, inner lid, aristocrats sitting around table, 6x9", M, D5.....................................**$90.00**

Sunset Club Coffee, can, 1-lb, key-wind lid, red/white on yellow, small ship, NM, A3 ....**$60.00**

Sunset Club Coffee, can, 1-lb, key-wind lid, red/white on yellow, large ship, earlier ca 1922 version, EX+, A3.............**$75.00**

Sunset Grease, can, 1-lb, round, pry lid, triangular Sunset logo on yellow, VG, A1 ....**$350.00**

Sunset Trail Cigars, pocket tin, vertical, blue, VG-NM, A3/A18/A15, from $175 to **$475.00**

Sunshine Andy Gump Biscuits, box, cardboard, comic images on yellow, 3x5x2", EX, A15 ....**$425.00**

Sunshine Biscuits, calendar, 1922, Sunshine Girl, Earl Christy artwork, 18x8", EX+, A3 ....**$50.00**

Sunshine Biscuits, jar, clear glass ball shape with embossed lettering, knob lid, 11x10" dia, EX, A15.............**$220.00**

Sunshine Biscuits, store bin, tin, round, glass top, EX+, A3 ....**$25.00**

Sunshine Biscuits, watch fob, gold medallion with red/white/blue cloisonne advertising center, with chain, EX, A6..**$130.00**

Sunshine Brand Fruit, store bin, round, bowl of fruit on blue/white striped ground, EX+, A18...................**$65.00**

Sunshine Cigarettes, sign, tin, Twenty For 15¢, red lettering/ open pack on yellow ground, white line border, 18x14", EX, A3 ....**$135.00**

Sunshine Coffee, can, 1-lb, key-wind lid, Pulverized Grind, EX, A3 ....**$70.00**

Sunshine Coffee, can, 1-lb, key-wind lid, Regular Grind, EX+, A18 ....**$80.00**

Sunshine Coffee, container, 1-lb, cardboard, square, pry lid, Steel Cut, VG, A3 ....**$25.00**

Sunshine Premium Beer, clock sign, reverse on glass, clock/lettering on panel with metal frame, Unexcelled (script) on base, 9x12", VG+, A8........................**$270.00**

Super A Hi-Octane Gasoline, gas globe, 2-pc, white glass body, glass lens, red/blue on white, 14", NM, A6..**$275.00**

Super-Shell, see Shell (Super-Shell)

Superba 3 Minute Oat Flakes, container, 2-lb 10-oz, cardboard, round, no lid o/w VG+, A3 ....**$35.00**

Superior Cough Drops, tin, vertical square, rounded corners, slip lid, yellow, Somers Bros, pre-1901, 2½", EX+, A18..**$50.00**

Superior Custom Blend Coffee, can, 1-lb, key-wind lid, metallic blue, EX+, A3..**$60.00**

Superior Peanut Butter, pail, 12-oz, circus scenes, EX+, A15...**$600.00**

Superior Spark Plug Co, sign, tin, Meet A Superior above man/large spark plug, black/white on red, white border, embossed, 18x7", NM+, A1 ....**$175.00**

Supplee Ice Cream, sign, porcelain, sidewalk, curb frame, large white S on red above Supplee Ice Cream on white, 2-sided, 29x21", EX+, A1 ....**$50.00**

Surbrug's Golden Sceptre, pocket tin, vertical, VG+, A18...**$215.00**

Sure Crop, cigar box labels, set of 2, Schumacher & Ettlinger litho #6833/6834, EX, A5....................................**$125.00**

Sure Shot Chewing Tobacco, store bin, rectangular, It Touches The Spot, Indian shooting bow & arrow, 5x10x15", EX, A3/A7, $825 to **$850.00**

Surfine Drip Grind Coffee, can, 1-lb, key-wind, red/white on yellow/blue diagonal ground, EX+ (full), A3..**$85.00**

Swallow's Old Fashioned 5¢ Keg Root Beer, bottle topper/ bottle, cardboard, Healthful/Refreshing, white/red/ green, EX, D30...**$30.00**

Swans Down Cake Flour, mirror/paperweight, celluloid, Swans Down/other baking products above slogan, Whitehead & Hoag, 4" dia, VG, A9.....................**$200.00**

Swansdown Coffee, can, 1-lb, pry lid, yellow, tall, VG, A3...**$90.00**

Swansdown Coffee, can, 3-lb, snap lid, yellow, EX, A18...**$225.00**

Swastika, crate label, California pear, large red pre-WWII swastika/3 pears/blue anchor logo, 46 lbs, Courtland, M, D12 ....**$65.00**

Swayer's Crystal Bluing, postcard, Mary Had A Little Lamb..., shows Mary using product on lamb, 1907, EX+, D26...**$75.00**

Sweden House Coffee, can, 1-lb, key-wind lid, EX-NM, A18/A3, from $45 to **$60.00**

Sweet Aroma, cigar box label, outer, buxom woman lying on couch, 4½x4½", EX, D5 ....**$25.00**

Sweet Brier White Hulless Pop Corn, tin, round, blue/red on white, EX+ (full), A18 ....**$45.00**

Sweet Burley Dark Tobacco, store bin, tin, round, red, VG-NM, A3/A7, $200 to..**$450.00**

Sweet Burley Dark Tobacco, tin, round, red, 2x8" dia, VG+, A18...**$35.00**

Sweet Burley Light Tobacco, store bin, tin, round, yellow, G+, A3 ....**$125.00**

Sweet Burley Light Tobacco, tin, round, yellow, 11x8" dia, VG, A3 ....**$100.00**

Sweet Caporal Cigarettes, sign, paper, Standard For Years, girl clown, c 1909, original frame, 32x22", VG-EX, A9/A12, from $225 to **$350.00**

Sweet Corpral Standard Cigarettes, sign, cardboard cutout, sentry standing at attention, framed, 14x4", EX+, A3 ....**$50.00**

Sweet Corpral/Kinney Bros, trade card, die-cut hatchet, I Cannot Tell A Lie, oval image of George Washington/initals on handle, 4x10", VG+, A5 ....**$110.00**

Sweet Cuba Tobacco, lunch box, red/green on bare metal, VG+, A3 ....**$40.00**

Sweet Cuba Tobacco, store bin, cardboard, square, yellow, VG-EX, A3/A7, $125 to...**$170.00**

Sweet Cuba Tobacco, store bin, tin, round, brown/cream/gold, VG-EX, A18/A3, from $125 to **$200.00**

Sweet Cuba Tobacco, store bin, tin, slant top, green, EX, A3/A7 ....**$200.00**

Sweet Cuba Tobacco, store bin, tin, slant top, yellow, VG+, A18..**$175.00**

Sweet Liberty, cigar box label, sample, cherubs/roses flank Sweet Liberty, OL Schwencke & Co litho #5427, VG, A5 ....**$85.00**

Sweet Mist Chewing Tobacco, store bin, cardboard, square, yellow, VG-EX+, A18/A3, from $75 to **$150.00**

Sweet Mist Chewing Tobacco, store bin, tin, square, yellow, EX-NM, A18, from $200 to $300.00

Sweet Music, cigar box labels, 2-pc set, embellished portrait of a man, Geo L Schlegel/Louis E Wagner Co litho, VG, A5..**$130.00**

Sweet Orr Clothes, sign, porcelain, round, ...Clothes To Work In/On The Job Since 1871, center logo, white/blue on yellow, 18" dia, VG, A1 ....**$600.00**

Sweet Orr Pants/Shirts/Overalls, sign, porcelain, blue lettering around red/white logo on yellow, 28x72", EX, A24..**$800.00**

Sweet Orr Union Made Pants/Overalls/Shirts, sign, porcelain, blue lettering around red/white/blue octagonal logo on yellow, white trim, curved corners, 9x27", NM, A2...**$470.00**

Sweet Orr Work Clothes, standee, cardboard, man in overalls holding up sign, 60x29", NM, D30 ....**$800.00**

Sweet Sixteen Cigarettes, sign, paper, Victorian lady with head held high blowing smoke from cigarette in hand, framed, 19x16", EX, A2 ....**$525.00**

Sweet Sue, crate label, Washington apple, '30s woman/white logo on 3-apple background, Wenatchee, M, D12 .**$25.00**

Sweet Tips, see Bagley's

Sweet Violet Cigars, sign, paper, An Expert Judge, boy smoking cigar atop product box, c 1900, framed, image: 11x10", G, A9 ....**$100.00**

Sweet Violet Cube Cut, pocket tin, vertical, white, EX+, A3 ....**$3,000.00**

Sweet Wheat Chewing Gum/Royal Remedy & Extract Co, sign, cardboard, boy & girl holding large pack of 5¢ gum next to sheath of wheat & advertising on white, 4x6", VG, A6 ....**$120.00**

Sweetheart Soap, display, lifelike baby in pink wicker basket, waves arms/legs, electric, 24x36", NM+ (original wooden crate), A3...**$1,300.00**

Sweetheart Talcum Powder, tin, oval, 4½", EX+, A3 ....$100.00

Swell Blend Chautaqua Brand Coffee, can, 1-lb, pry lid, VG, A2 ....**$175.00**

Swell Blend Chautaqua Coffee, can, 1-lb, key-wind lid, blue, EX+, A3 ....**$120.00**

Swift & Co, booklet, Thurston's Book Of Magic/Vol 4/Library Of Magic, 12 pgs, VG, D14 ....**$18.00**

Swift & Co, calendar, 1901, die-cut, American Girl, 17th-20th century girls pictured above 12 months, 15x32", VG, A6 ....**$70.00**

Swift & Co, watch fob, red/white/black cloisonne S-&-arrow symbol with gold-tone scalloped edge, Copyright 1906 at bottom, EX+, A1 ....**$120.00**

Swift's Premium Ham & Bacon, sign, cardboard, Easter Greeting, Little Cook pulling ham/bacon out of Easter egg, framed, image: 20x15", VG, A9 ....**$150.00**

Swift's Premium Hams-Bacon, sign, cardboard die-cut foldout, Little Cook with basket flanked by planters of white flowers, 35x113", EX, A2 ....**$280.00**

Swift's Pride Cleanser, sign, cardboard, name above girl in rocker by kitchen sink/large product can, framed, image: 20x15", VG, A9...**$275.00**

Swift's Pride Soap & Washing Powder, fan, cardboard, round, image of girl with laundry basket, lettering on red border, ca 1910, 10" dia, EX, A3..........................**$165.00**

Swift's Pride Soap & Washing Powder, jigsaw puzzle, Line Up! Bright & Early..., girl walking away from clothesline with basket, ca 1910, 15x10", EX, D10 ....**$75.00**

Swift's Silverleaf Brand Pure Lard, pail, 2-lb, metallic gold, NM, A3..**$20.00**

Swift's Syphilitic Specific, string holder, cast-iron caldron with bail handle, embossed lettering, ca 1870-90, EX, A6 ..**$70.00**

Swing's Coffee, display, automated black man with animated features seated atop box pouring cup of coffee, 29x18x16", EX, A23 ....**$2,300.00**

Sykes Comfort Powder, tin, oval, slightly lighter blue version, 4", EX+, A18..............................**$200.00**

Sylvan Dell, cigar box label, saleman's sample, Louis E Neuman #569, VG, A5..............................**$50.00**

Sylvan Carnation Toilet Talcum Powder, tin, 3½-oz, EX+-NM, A3/A18, from $75 to **$85.00**

Sylvan Sandalwood Toilet Talcum Powder, tin, 3½-oz, VG+, A3 ....**$35.00**

Sylvania Radio & TV Tubes, postcard, June Hanoc Says..., image of personality/advertising, dealer name below, 1951, NM, D26 ....**$25.00**

Symon's Best Coffee, can, 1-lb, key-wind lid, white/black on red, NM, A3 ....**$50.00**

⤜ T ⤛

Ta-Che, crate label, California orange, Indian brave in profile on yellow background, Santa Pula, M, D12 ....**$30.00**

Table King Coffee, can, 1-lb, key-wind lid, red, steaming cup on center white band, EX+, A18 ....**$75.00**

Table King Coffee, can, 1-lb, pry lid, blue/yellow/metallic gold, tall, EX+, A3 ....**$240.00**

Table Talk Oysters, can label, oyster on half-shell/banner, M, D5 ....**$25.00**

Tacoma Beer, tray, round, Anti Katzenjammer, 2 cats on black, red trim, 13", dia, VG+, A8 ....**$135.00**

Tailor-Made Clothing Co, sign, cardboard hanger, various images of dapper men modeling clothing, 1910, 20x14", NM, A13, each..............................**$90.00**

Tailor-Made Clothing Co, sign, paper, Fall & Winter 1910-11, gentleman in top coat with hat & gloves in hand, metal strips, 42x18", G+, A13..............................**$175.00**

Tailor-Made Clothing Co, sign, paper, Fall & Winter 1910-11, gentleman talking on phone, metal strips, 42x18", EX, A13..............................**$375.00**

Tailor-Made Clothing Co, sign, paper, Fall & Winter 1910-11/No 1416 The Hudson, pictures dapper couple, 42x18", NM, A13 ....**$475.00**

Talk of the Town, cigar box label, sample, No Trust, OL Schwencke & Co litho #5401, EX, A5 ....**$160.00**

Tam o'Shanter Lager Beer & Ales, tray, round, deep rim, man's image/white lettering on red plaid ground, c 1933, 14" dia, EX, A6 ....**$40.00**

Tamina, cigar box label, lithographer's proof, embellished image of lady, Moehle Litho Co, 6x9", EX, A5 .....**$60.00**

Tamko Roof, playing cards, double deck in box, features black waiter serving up roof on tray, Have On The House!..., EX, D25..............................**$150.00**

Tampa Life, cigar box label, inner lid, golf/tennis/bathing scenes, 6x9", M, D5 ....**$30.00**

Tampola Cigars, cigar box label, sample, allegorical, Krueger & Braun litho #629, 1899, VG+, A5 ....**$90.00**

Tandem Team, cigar box label, lithographer's proof, couple in horse-drawn 2-wheeled cart in landscape, Moehle Litho Co, 6x9", EX, A5..............................**$215.00**

Tang, telephone, Tang Lips figure, 9", NMIB (unused), A14 ....**$130.00**

Tango Orange Drink, doll, Tango VooDoo, vinyl, MIB, D20 ....**$55.00**

Tanner's German Ointment/Dr Ford's Pectoral Syrup..., sign, cardboard, die-cut oaken bucket depicting image of farm boy drinking from bucket as girl watches, 11x8", EX+, A3..............................**$100.00**

Tannhauser Beer/Beth Uhl Brewing Co, tray, round, deep rim, logo above lettering, 13" dia, VG+, A8 ....**$100.00**

Tappan, salt & pepper shakers, chef figures, chalkware, flat backs, 1940s, 9½", EX, D25, pair **$150.00**

Target Cigarette Case, tin, vertical, red, NM, A3 ......**$35.00**

Tartan Coffee, can, 1-lb, key-wind lid, EX+, A18......**$50.00**

Tasty Toasty Sandwich Shop, tumbler, china, promotes Sixty Second Service, Shenango, 1930s, 6¾", M, D25 ....**$65.00**

Tastyeast Yeast display box, tin, ...Finest Yeast In Chocolate Fudge/Yeast This Way Is Delicious, white/orange on brown, EX+, A18..............................**$50.00**

Taylor Maid, crate label, apple, cute blonde girl on blue ground, EX, D3 ....**$4.00**

Taylor's Blue Bird Talcum, tin, sample, 2", VG-NM, A15/D22, from $225 to..............................**$600.00**

TC Williams Co Golden Eagle, label, patriotic image of eagle atop American flag/leaves, 1890s, 10x10", NM, A3..............................**$50.00**

TC Williams Co Nosegay, label, image of lady holding basket of flowers atop shoulder in landscape, 1890s, 13½x7", NM, A3..............................**$50.00**

TC Williams Co Pigeon, label, image of classical girl seated on garden wall with pigeons & peacock, 1890s, 13½x7", NM, A3..............................**$45.00**

Teacher's Scotch, display figure, composition, scholar dressed in cap/gown holding Teacher's certificate on lettered base, 16", EX, A8..............................**$55.00**

Tidex, gas globe, 2-pc, blue metal body, glass lenses, black name on white cross band on blue, 15", NM, A6 ..**$275.00**

Tiger (The) King of Rakes/JW Stoddard & Co, trade card, image of farmer on horse-drawn rake, text on reverse, multicolored, 3x5", EX, A6 ....**$45.00**

Tiger Chewing Tobacco, lunch box, red basket weave, slip lid, double swingle handles, EX+, A18 ....**$20.00**

Tiger Chewing Tobacco, pocket tin, flat, red, VG+, A18 ...**$40.00**

Tiger Chewing Tobacco, pocket tin, vertical, 15¢, 3", EX+, A18 ....**$320.00**

Tiger Chewing Tobacco, shipping crate, wood, stenciled graphics/lettering, 8x15x10", EX+, D22 ....**$225.00**

Tiger Chewing Tobacco, sign, cardboard, tiger's head poking through tall grass, 33x26", framed, 33x26", VG, A7 ....**$800.00**

Tiger Chewing Tobacco, store bin, cardboard, tin top/bottom, square, blue, scarce, G+, A18..............................**$485.00**

Tiger Chewing Tobacco, store bin, cardboard, tin top/bottom, square, red, VG-EX+, A18, $130 to **$250.00**

Tiger Chewing Tobacco, store bin, tin, round, blue, rare, G-VG, A7/A18, from $350 to **$530.00**

Tiger Chewing Tobacco, store bin, tin, round, red, VG-EX, from $50 to..**$85.00**

Tiger Chewing Tobacco, tin, rectangular, rounded corners, red, 4x6", VG+, A18..**$15.00**

Tiger Chewing Tobacco (Stripe Choice), product pack, soft, A Splendid Tough Chew, NM (full), A18......**$30.00**

Tiger Head Ale & Porter, sign, paper, encircled tiger's head in center, Townsend, Holstetter & Co litho, framed, image: 20x14", G, A9 ....**$450.00**

Tigerettes, cigar box label, inner lid, tiger, 6x9", M, D5...**$100.00**

Tigerettes, cigar box label, outer, tiger, 4½x4½", M, D5 ....**$35.00**

Time Gas, sign, porcelain, U-shaped in iron frame, image of clock in center, red/white/blue, 77x48", EX, A6..**$425.00**

Times, sign, porcelain, Get The Best Times/All The News, large penny/lettering on white, 1910s, 9x16", EX+, A13 ....**$425.00**

Times Square Smoking Mixture, pocket tin, vertical, EX+, A18..**$40.00**

Times Square Smoking Mixture, tin, round, pry lid, paper label, EX, A18..**$30.00**

Timothy's Famous Blends Super Mild Mixture, tin, round, pry lid, paper label, photo image & yellow lettering on green, NM (full), A18 ....**$45.00**

Timur Coffee/AJ Kasper Co, can, 3-lb, tall, VG+, A18..**$435.00**

Tin 'N Feather Farm Hulless White Pop Corn, tin, 14-oz, round, blue/yellow/red graphics on white, NM, A18 ....**$225.00**

Tinkertoy, display, automated, Hundreds Of Moving Models Can Be Made... on sign on Tinkertoy paddle wheel, 1940, 19x19x6", EX, A23 ....**$450.00**

Tiny-Tot Toilet Powder, tin, baby on scalloped oval, floral decor, NM, A18 ....**$75.00**

Tiny-Tot Toilet Powder, tin, baby on plain-edge oval, 6½", EX+, A3..**$70.00**

Tiolene Motor Oil/Pure Oil Co, sign, porcelain, round, lettering above/below arrow & bull's-eye logo, white on blue, 2-sided, 26" dia, EX+, A1.......**$475.00**

Tip Top Bread, jigsaw puzzle, Tip-Top Town USA, M (original envelope), D25 ....**$30.00**

Tip Top Coffee, can, 1-lb, key-wind lid, blue, EX, A18....**$20.00**

Tip Top Cracked Wheat, cereal box, 5-lb, blue on yellow, shows Lake Milling & Mfg Co, NM, A3...............**$275.00**

Tip-Top Cigars, cigar box label, outer, shows Statue of Liberty/cigar/Morro Bay, 4½x4½", EX, D5.....................**$35.00**

Tip-Top Cigars, trade card, Try One formed by smoke coming from man's nose, Currier & Ives, 1880 stock card, 3x5", EX, A5 ....**$40.00**

Tip-Top Tobacco, pail, orange, G, A2.....................**$230.00**

Tipsy, cigar box label, outer, woman pouring man a drink, 4½x4½", EX, D5..**$40.00**

Tipsy Bee, crate label, Oregon pear, silly bee floating on pear raft drinking from straw, Medford, M, D12..**$25.00**

Tivoli, tip tray, round, A Select Lager, lettering on rim around girl holding up full glass, VG+, A8....................**$140.00**

Tivoli Beer, toy train boxcar, HO scale, blue-gray, white label, 1950s, NM+, A19.................................**$40.00**

TNT (Tender/Nutritious/Tasty) Pop Corn, can, red, ring of popped kernals around lettering, EX-NM, A18/A3, from $85 to...**$115.00**

Tobacco Girl, cigar box, Coming Through With The Goods, 2 For 5¢ on corner band, image of girl on tobacco leaf, EX, A3 ....**$75.00**

Today's Coffee, can, 1-lb, key-wind lid, white, NM, A3....**$120.00**

Toledo Metal Co, square ruler, die-cut tin, image of children playing at well, 5x5", EX+, A15 ....**$500.00**

Tom, Dick & Harry, cigar box labels, set of 2, image of black man on log/black cat/black owl, Geo S Harris & Sons litho, G/EX+, A5 ....**$165.00**

Tom Cat, crate label, lemon, cat sitting on red pillow, 1930, EX, D5 ....**$75.00**

Tom Collins Jr, bottle topper/bottle, cardboard, First For Thirst/Pick Up.../Tasty Lemon Drink, boy/6-pack on yellow, EX, D30 ....**$30.00**

Tom Moore Cigar, sign, paper, bust image of Tom Moore, LE Newman & Co litho, frame marked Hirschhorn, Mack & Co, image: 20x15", VG, A9 ....$150.00

Tom Moore Cigar, sign, tin, America's Favorite 10¢ Cigar, portrait in center, red ground, horizontal, EX, A2...$900.00

Tom Tit, crate label, apple, blue birds on apple blossoms, M, D5 ....$60.00

Tom's, sign, tin, Time Out For Tom's, lettering above 3 product images, red/white/blue, embossed, 1958, 28x20", EX+, A13..$260.00

Tom's Toasted Peanuts, thermometer, tin, resembles bag of peanuts on white, 16", NM+, A1 ....$160.00

Tone's Coffee, measuring scoop, genie figural handle, Occupied Japan, NM, A3 ....$25.00

Tonica, label, 11½-oz, Indianapolis Brewing Co/IN, pre-1920, VG+ (traces of paper on back), A10...........$30.00

Tonique Tiara/Southern Barbers Supply Co, sign, tin, lettering around pretty woman in profile, curled corners, 15x14", NM, A7 ....$700.00

Too Too/Sun Flower/Esthetic's Segars/A Schulze & Co, trade card, image of Oscar Wilde, sepia/white, 6x3", VG+, A5 ....$40.00

Tooks' Original Blackberry Punch, sign, cardboard, Drink...Ice Cold/5¢, black boy with bucket, bottle at left, green/brown on white, 6x14", EX, A3 ....$25.00

Tootsie Rolls, display case, tin, 2-tier slant front with arched marque, 5¢ symbols on dark blue, 1920s, 12x10", EX+, A4 ....$750.00

Topaz Beer, label, 11-oz, Modesto Brewery Inc/CA, IRTP/U-type permit #, 1933-36, red/white, EX, A10 ....$15.00

Topaz High Grade Roasted Coffee/Sherman Bros, can, 1-lb, cardboard, VG+, A3................................$88.00

Topic Cigars, cigar cutter, label under front glass panel depicts colorful scene from Othello, nickel plated with wooden base, VG, A2 ....$165.00

Topper Beer, label, ½-gal, Bismark Brewing Co/Chicago IL, IRTP or WF statement, 1933-50, VG+ (creased or folded), A10...$21.00

Torke Coffee, can, 1-lb, key-wind lid, lady on white oval on red, NM, A18...$85.00

Torpedo Special Short Cut Smoking Tobacco, pocket tin, vertical, green, EX+, A18............................$2,635.00

Totem Cigars, display case, tin, slant glass front that opens to box of cigars, marque atop, HD Beach litho, 15", VG, A9...$650.00

Totem Tobacco, pocket tin, vertical, oval, EX+, A18.$1,635.00

Tourist, sign, porcelain, car graphic, white/black/yellow on yellow, white/black border, 14x36", NM, A2...$3,520.00

Tower Motor Oil, bank, round oil can shape with lettering above/below shadowed image of skyscraper, multicolored, 2½x2" dia, NM, D22 ....$115.00

Tower Root Beer, sign, tin, Like Mother Used To Make, bottle graphic, brown on yellow, embossed, 20x9", EX+, A1 ....$100.00

Towle's Log Cabin Syrup, spoon, silverplate, log cabin on end of tree-trunk handle, ca 1910, NM, A3......$60.00

Towle's Log Cabin Syrup, tin, cabin shape, Dr RU Well, 4", EX+, A18...$360.00

Towle's Log Cabin Syrup, tin, cabin shape, Express Office, 5", EX+, A18 ....$170.00

Towle's Log Cabin Syrup, tin, cabin shape, Frontier Inn, 6", EX+-NM, A18/A3, from $175 to $200.00

Towle's Log Cabin Syrup, tin, cabin shape, Frontier Jail, 4", EX+, A18...$225.00

Towle's Log Cabin Syrup, tin, cabin shape, Frontier series, gold shutters, family scene, 5", EX+, A3 ....**$220.00**

Towle's Log Cabin Syrup, tin, cabin shape, Frontier series, red shutters, woman/girl in doorway, 4", EX, A18 ....**$250.00**

Towle's Log Cabin Syrup, tin, cabin shape, Frontier series, red shutters/blue door, boy with lasso, 4", EX+, A18.**$300.00**

Towle's Log Cabin Syrup, tin, cabin shape, Trading Post, 6", EX+, A18..**$200.00**

Towle's Log Cabin Syrup, tin, cabin shape, 1897-1909, 1-gal, paper label, VG, A18..............................**$70.00**

Towle's Log Cabin Syrup, tin, cabin shape, 1909-1914, animal skin on door, ½-gal, paper label, EX+, A18............**$180.00**

Towle's Log Cabin Syrup, tin, cabin shape, 1918 series, boy in doorway, sample, paper label, EX, A18.**$350.00**

Towle's Log Cabin Syrup, tin, cabin shape, 1918 series, boy in doorway, 1-gal, paper label, EX, A18 ....**$275.00**

Towle's Log Cabin Syrup, tin, cabin shape, 1918 series, boy in doorway, 4", EX+, A18 ....**$200.00**

Towle's Log Cabin Syrup, tin, cabin shape, 1930s series, bear in doorway, 4", EX+, A18......................**$300.00**

Towle's Log Cabin Syrup, tin, cabin shape, 1930s series, bear in doorway, 5", VG+, A18 ....**$200.00**

Towle's Log Cabin Syrup, tin, cabin shape, 1930s series, boy in doorway, 5", EX+, A18.......................$140.00

Towle's Log Cabin Syrup, tin, cabin shape, 1930s series, girl in doorway, 4", EX+, A18 ....**$150.00**

Towle's Log Cabin Syrup, tin, cabin shape, 1930s series, girl in doorway, 5", EX+, A18 ....**$150.00**

Towle's Log Cabin Syrup, tin, cabin shape, 1950s series, name on red sign nailed to cabin wall, 58-oz, EX+, A18 ....**$135.00**

Towle's Log Cabin Syrup, tin, vertical square with grip handle/small screw lid, 1895-1900, paper label, VG+, A18...**$1,820.00**

Towle's Wigwam Syrup, tin, wigwam shape, 4", rare, EX, A18 ....$1,625.00

Town Crier Flour, match holder, tin-framed celluloid, town crier above name, red/white/blue, 3x2", NM, A3...**$65.00**

Town Talk Bread, sign, porcelain, Ask For.../Rich In Pure Milk, lettering above/below oval, 14x22", EX, A6 ....**$475.00**

Toys R Us, bank, Geofrey head, vinyl, 1980s, NM, D20 .**$55.00**

Trailing Ardutus Talcum Powder, tin, embossed, EX+, A18..**$75.00**

Trailways, calendar, 1941, 24", incomplete, NM, A13.**$20.00**

Trains, sign, white porcelain block letters, 15" each letter, EX+, A1...**$235.00**

Travelodge, doll, Sleepy Bear, squeeze vinyl, 1970s, 5½", M, D20 ....**$45.00**

Treasure Chest 3 Minute Brand Oats, container, 1-lb, Cooks In 1 Minute, red/yellow background, VG+, A3 ....**$20.00**

Treasure Steel Ranges, sign, canvas, Her Three Treasures, mammy overseeing 2 white children at table by her range, framed, 49x36", EX, A2 ....$1,320.00

Tremont Stoves & Ranges, sign, flange, porcelain, ...They Work/They Wear, blue/white lettering/design on blue, 12x12", EX, A6 ....**$350.00**

Trexler Park Coffee, can, 1-lb, key-wind lid, EX-NM, A18/A3, $75 to **$150.00**

Trico Wiper Blades, thermometer, tin windshield in shape of blade path with glass front, degrees arched over name, 10x15", EX, A6....................................**$130.00**

Trico 5-Ply/Spring-Pressed Wiper Blades, display case, tin, red marque shows woman at wheel above 6 slots, 10x10x18", VG-EX, A6/A1, from $130 to **$190.00**

Tried & True Coffee, can, 1-lb, key-wind lid, red/black on yellow, EX, A3 ....**$45.00**

Triple AAA Root Beer, sign, tin, bottle shape, 45x12", NM+, A1 ....$100.00

Triple AAA Root Beer, sign, tin, Just Say..., on red octagonal symbol next to mug on orange/white, 20x28", VG, A1..**$90.00**

Triple AAA Root Beer, sign, tin, Just Say..., red octagonal logo/bottle on yellow center band on white, white raised rim, 20x28", NM, A1............................$200.00

Triplex Chain Blocks/Yale & Towne MFG Co, sign, tin, image of man hoisting machine with Triplex Chain Blocks, self-framed, HD Beach litho, 21x17", Fair, A2..**$65.00**

Tritschler & Tiesse Brewers & Maltsters, drinking glass, shell, etched, gold rim, lion logo, 4", NM, A8....**$100.00**

Triumph Harvesting Machines/DS Morgan & Co, trade card, 4-fold, round inset of machine with horse race scene, machines on back, 2-sided, 1888, 13x4", NM, A3..**$60.00**

Trix Cereal, see General Mills

Trixy Molasses, can, 1-lb, tin litho, image of smiling black girl, EX+, A3..**$600.00**

Trojan Brand Condoms, tin, square, rounded corners, red/black/white, Improved in black on white banner, 1½x2", VG+, A15..**$775.00**

Trommer's Malt Brews, sign, porcelain, green/black block lettering on white, 10x30", G, A6......................**$65.00**

Trommer's White Label/Light & Dark Malt Beers, sign, tin, round, image of elves working on large keg on white with red band, wooden frame, 15" dia, VG+, A3........**$100.00**

Trop-Artic Auto Oil/Manhattan Oil Co, can, ½-gal, split-image of arctic scene/tropical scene (enclosed touring car), VG, A1..**$425.00**

Trop-Artic Auto Oil/Manhattan Oil Co, can, ½-gal, split-image of arctic scene/tropical scene (open touring car), VG+, A1..**$425.00**

Trophy Brand Coffee, can, 1-lb, pry lid, red/white/blue, EX, A18..**$75.00**

Trophy Premium Beer, label, 8-oz, Birk Bros Brewing Co/Chicago IL, IRTP or WF statement, 1933-50, M, A10..**$13.00**

Tropical Pure Spice Turmeric, container, 2-oz, cardboard, rectangular, image of palm tree, yellow/green/red, EX+, A3..**$28.00**

Tropicana, radio, orange shape, NM, D13...............**$30.00**

Trout, crate label, apple, pictures big rainbow trout, EX, D3..**$5.00**

Trout Line Smoking Tobacco, pocket container, cardboard, tin top/bottom, green, VG+, A18.......................**$165.00**

Trout Line Smoking Tobacco, pocket tin, vertical, green, 3½", EX-NM+, A3/A15/A18, from $635 to.......**$1,000.00**

Tru Ade, clock, diagonal square, light-up, glass front, Drink.../Not Carbonated on center dot, PAM, EX+, A16..**$140.00**

Tru Ade, sign, cardboard, My Favorite/Drink.../Not Carbonated, girl with bottle standing by horse in stall, 30x36", NM, D30..**$150.00**

Tru Ade, sign, tin, ...Naturally Delicious!/Drink A Better Beverage/Not Carbonated, white/red/blue on yellow, 18x54", NM, A13..**$300.00**

Tru Ade, sign, tin, Drink A Better Beverage lettered over large bottle on red, yellow border, 1940s-50s, 54x18", VG+, A13............................$300.00

Tru Ade, thermometer, tin, Drink.../A Better Beverage, bottle next to gauge, blue, white border, EX, D30.........**$75.00**

Tru-Cup Coffee, can, 1-lb, screw lid, cup on front/building on reverse, tall, A18..**$100.00**

True Blue Long Cut Tobacco/Reid Tobacco Co, canister, round, slip lid, blue paper label, EX, A18............**$50.00**

True Color, cigar box label, sample, Indian maiden with flag, American Litho Co/Witsch & Schmitt #2738, 1895, EX+, A5..**$290.00**

True Fruit Soda, sign, tin, display of fresh fruit on table, self-framed, 25x37", VG-VG+, A9/A3, from $100 to .**$135.00**

True Value Hardware, catalog, 1975, Christmas, 44 pgs, EX, D17..**$20.00**

Trueworth Coffee, can, 1-lb, key-wind lid, NM, A18.**$90.00**

Trump, cigar box label, inner lid, man holding up card hand, 1876, 6x9", EX, D5..**$35.00**

Trumpet Coffee, can, 1-lb, screw lid, tall, G, A3......**$65.00**

Trumpet Nutmeg, container, cardboard with tin top/bottom, red, EX, A3..**$12.00**

Tucketts Abbey Pipe Tobacco, pocket tin, vertical, 10¢, short, VG+, A18..**$125.00**

Tucketts Abbey Pipe Tobacco, pocket tin, vertical, 10¢ short, NM+ (full), A18..**$300.00**

Tucketts Fine Cut Tobacco, sign, cardboard, die-cut, ...A Treat For Those Who Roll Their Own, yard worker gawking at lady gardener, 37x29", VG, A6...............**$90.00**

Tucketts Old Squire Pipe Tobacco, pocket tin, vertical, red, 10¢, short, EX+, A18..**$175.00**

Tucketts Orinoco Cut Coarse, tin, horizontal rectangle, rounded corners, EX, A18..**$60.00**

Tucketts Rough Cut Pipe Tobacco, pocket tin, vertical, 10¢, EX, A18..**$185.00**

Tudhope Carriages, print, paper, man/2 ladies in horse-drawn carriage taking ride past waterfalls, framed, 21x28", VG+, A6 ....**$110.00**

Tuft's Arctic Soda Water, sign, paper, The Discovery Of The North Pole/Tuft's Arctic Fountain, framed, 18x25", VG, A9 ....**$1,250.00**

Tulip Soap, string/bag holder, 3-sided tin sign on cast-iron base with wire rods, CL Jones & Co...For Sale Here, 12x15", G+, A9...**$2,000.00**

Tupperware, figurine, Tupperware Lady with bag on round base, porcelain, 8", NM+, A14 ....**$30.00**

Turf Cigarettes, sign, porcelain, Quality Wins!, encircled Pegasus above lettering, red/white/blue on white, red border, 30x20", NM, A3 ....**$165.00**

Turkey Red Cigarettes, sign, cardboard, woman in fez with pack to mouth flanked by fezzes, red tones, framed, 18x15", EX+, A1 ....**$50.00**

Turkey Red Sage, tin, EX, A3.................................**$330.00**

Turkey Roasted Coffee, can, 3-lb, smaller round lid, EX, A3 ....**$550.00**

Turkish Dyes, cabinet, wood, lithoed heavy waxed cardboard front, stenciled marque, 28x17x11", EX, A3............**$360.00**

Turkish Trophies Cigarettes, sign, paper, girl with arm up to head, city beyond, framed, 36x27", VG-EX, A6/A9, $450 to $700.00

Turnbull Brand Indian River Oranges & Grapefruit, crate label, Indian in 'Seald Sweet' canoe, yellow sky, lt blue water, NM, A18 ....**$80.00**

Tutt's Liver Pills, cigar cutter, cast-iron figural ship's wheel with advertising, 6", VG, A2............................**$550.00**

Tuxedo Tobacco, humidor, clear glass, octagonal, knob lid, paper label, NM, A3 ....**$85.00**

Tuxedo Tobacco, pocket tin, vertical, man in hat, green, NM+ (sealed), A3 ....**$42.00**

Tuxedo Tobacco, pocket tin, vertical, man smoking pipe, green, concave, wide, 4½", EX+, A18.................**$125.00**

Tuxedo Tobacco, pocket tin, vertical, smoking pipe logo/Indian logo on reverse, green, NM+ (sealed), A3 ....**$65.00**

Tuxedo Tobacco, tin, round, key-wind lid, green, 3¾", EX, A18...**$55.00**

Tuxedo Tobacco, tin, square, round screw lid, green, EX+, A3...**$120.00**

TW Grant Co, doll, Bucky Bradford, vinyl, 1970s, 9", NM, A14...**$15.00**

Twang Vitamin Root Beer, sign, tin, round, Save Caps For Premiums..., pictures small bottle cap, red/white/blue, 14" dia, EX, A1..**$130.00**

Twenty (20) Mule Team Borax, fan, cardboard, stick handle, Borax Is King above Borax Bill Jr holding product/mule doing wash, 1900, 9x8", NM, A24 ....**$275.00**

Twenty (20) Mule Team Borax, fan, cardboard, stick handle, girl with doll taking product to tub/4 product packs on reverse, 1911, 9", EX, A24 ....**$160.00**

Twenty Grand Cigarettes, sign, canvas-type paper on cardboard, Thoroughbreds, image of horse head/product on 'painterly' ground, 26x19", VG, A3......................**$55.00**

Twenty Grand Double Edge Razor Blades, display sign, 20 product boxes form horseshoe around jockey on horse, 4 Blades 10¢/Your Lucky Strike..., no size, M, A18...**$75.00**

Twin Cola, sign, cardboard stand-up, 5¢ For Full 12-oz Bottle.../Ice Cold.../A New Thirst Chaser, boy/girl, 1930s, 9x6", EX, A6...**$55.00**

Twin Oaks Mixture, pocket tin, vertical, flip-top, sample, EX, A18..**$115.00**

Twin Oaks Mixture, pocket tin, vertical, flip-top, silver, NM, A18...**$155.00**

Twin Oaks Mixture, tin, casket shape, embossed, VG, A18...**$45.00**

Twin Ports Steel Cut Coffee, can, 1-lb, screw lid, oval image of ship, VG, A18.......................................**$60.00**

Twix Cookie Bars, jar, clear glass, Keep On Movin'... on fired-on diamond labels, bottom bordered by silhouette figures, NM, D25..**$70.00**

Two Belles, tin, rectangular, rounded corners, yellow, VG+, A3...**$85.00**

Two Homers Cigars, sign, cardboard, round fan hanger, Two Homers/2 Cigars For 5¢ around image of 2 homing pigeons, 6½" dia, EX, A5 ....**$55.00**

Two Orphans Cigars, tin, round, slip lid, yellow, EX+, A18 ....**$260.00**

Tydol, gas globe, 2-pc, glass body/lenses, TYDOL in black on white lens with black TWO logo, red body, NM+, A1 ....**$525.00**

Tydol, gas pump topper sign, glass, white curved body with 2 inserts, black name on white, red trim, 7x14½x7", G, A6...**$200.00**

Tydol Aero, jigsaw puzzle, Proved In The Antarctic By Byrd Expedition..., drawings of planes/car/expedition, 1933, 8½x10½", EX, D1..**$75.00**

Tydol Ethyl, pump sign, porcelain, round, white lettering above winged-A on red, white border, blue trim, 10" dia, NM, A1..**$585.00**

Tydol Flying A, pump sign, porcelain, round, black name above white/red winged-A on green band, red border, 10" dia, NM, A1..**$425.00**

Tydol Flying A Gasoline, pin-back button, Honorary Pilot/Tydol Flying A Airship, black letters on white, airship on red center band, 2", EX, A1 ....**$110.00**

Tydol Gasoline, badge, square with Flying A logo in center, Tydol above/Gasoline below on cloisonne inlay, M (NOS), A1 ....**$400.00**

Tydol Motor Oil, sign, porcelain, black/white lettering on orange ground, white/pea green border, 14x42", NM, D11 ....$300.00

Tydol/Veedol, pocket mirror, round, colored bithstones border circle with advertising, 2" dia, EX, A15 ....$80.00

Tydol/Veedol Tide Water Associated Oil Co, sign, porcelain, for truck door, rectangular with slightly pointed bottom, white/orange on black, 8x11", NM, A24 ....$375.00

Tyler's Finest Cloves, tin, 4-oz, red/gold, EX, A3.......$8.00

∽ U ∾

U Like Um, crate label, apple, Indian on horseback hunting deer, EX, D3 ....$7.00

UCO Coffee, can, 1-lb, key-wind lid, red lettering on white, tall, EX+, A18 ....$90.00

UMC Smokless Powder Shot Shells, sign, paper, 3 pups snuggled in hanging hunting jacket with vest/hat, metal strips, c 1904, 25x16", G, A9.............................$1,050.00

UMC Steel Lined Shells, sign, paper, The Only American Steel Lined Shell/Buy Here, 3 images of a shell in different states, 24x17", VG, A9...................................$650.00

Uncle Daniel Fine Cut, product pack, 1-oz, paper, NM, A7 ....$125.00

Uncle Green, cigar tin, round slip lid, white, Liberty Can, EX+, A18...$120.00

Uncle John's Syrup, display, cardboard, cutout, Uncle John pouring syrup on pancakes held above child's head, 5-pc, 24x40", NM+, A3 ....$600.00

Uncle John's Syrup, display, paper cutout, Uncle John pouring syrup on pancakes held above child's head, 1905-15, 4-pc, 40x50", EX, A13.............................$300.00

Uncle John's Syrup, sign, paper, Made From Cane & Maple Sugars/Absolutely Pure, image of man guiding oxen/sled in snow, 11x21", EX+, A3 ....$100.00

Uncle Remus Restaurant, Eatonton GA, matchbook, black/white photo image of Uncle Remus on back, proprietor's name on fold, 20 strike, front striker, M, D28...$9.00

Uncle Sam, cigar box label, inner lid, Uncle Sam dropping cigars on world/eagle, 6x9", M, D5......................$40.00

Uncle Sam Brand Iodized Salt, container, cardboard, round, white/blue on white, image of Uncle Sam in center, NM, A3 ....$150.00

Uncle Sam Bubble Gum, trade card, Light Rescue Party, #132, 1941, G, A16..$15.00

Uncle Sam Quick Cooking Oat Flakes, container, 1-lb 4-oz, white, NM+, A3...$400.00

Uncle Sam Smoking Tobacco, pocket tin, vertical, EX+, A18 ....$1,980.00

Uncle Sam Stock Medicine Co, calendar, 1919, paper, navy fleet returning home on NY harbour behind Uncle Sam, 20x15", incomplete, NM+, A3 ....$225.00

Uncle Tom's Chewing Gum, display box, paper litho over cardboard, Mint, 2x9x4", EX+, A15 ......$300.00

Uncle William Baby Whole Beets, can, 1-lb 4-oz, paper label, bust image of white-bearded man in hat & glasses on blue/white ground, EX+, A3 ....$25.00

Uneeda Bakers, see also Log Cabin Brownies or National Biscuit Co

Uneeda Bakers, display, cardboard die-cut stand-up, boy in yellow slicker holding box with glass front, 51", EX, A15 ....$775.00

Uneeda Bakers, sign, cardboard, blue ribbon shape, 'Uneeda Bakers' Premium Is The Prize Soda Cracker, 37x19", NM+ (NOS), A1...$20.00

Uneeda Bakers Saltine Biscuits, tin, 1-lb, round, slip lid, sailor boy on side, EX+, A3 ....$35.00

Uneeda Biscuit, letter opener, metal, die-cut trademark boy handle, 8", VG, A6 ....**$60.00**

Uneeda Biscuit, magazine ad, Colliers, 1904, The Soda Cracker That Made The Nation Hungry, boy in yellow slicker & hat, NM, A3 ....**$75.00**

Uneeda Biscuit, sign, cardboard, We Close...Afternoons/ Don't Forget Uneeda Biscuit..., Uneeda Boy at left, 10x9", EX, A15 ....**$230.00**

Unico Motor Oil/Drummondville, ashtray, cast-iron derby hat with top mashed in, embossed lettering on rim, 2½x6½x6", EX, A6 ....**$30.00**

Unicorn, crate label, California orange, unicorn galloping near ocean, E Hilands, M, D12 ....**$25.00**

Uniform Cut Plug, tin, horizontal rectangle, rounded corners, slip lid, 4x6", EX, A18 ....**$300.00**

Union Club Whiskey, sign, paper, race between the Robert E Lee & the Natchez, June 30, 1870, Donaldson Sign Co, wood frame, 20x28", Fair, A9 ....**$500.00**

Union Commander Cut Plug, lunch box, red, gold trim, VG+, A3 ....**$300.00**

Union Depot, cigar box labels, set of 2, conductor signaling train with lantern, Witsch & Schmitt litho #765/766, VG, A5 ....**$685.00**

Union Ice & Coal Co, Rock Island Ill, calendar, 1908, image of girl talking on early wall phone with filigree border, 10x8", complete, EX, A3 ....**$85.00**

Union Leader Cut Plug, lunch box, basket weave, slip lid, double swing handles, EX, A18 ....**$50.00**

Union Leader Cut Plug, lunch box, red, wire grip handle, EX+, A18 ....**$50.00**

Union Leader Cut Plug, milk can, red, 9x5", EX, A3 ..**$235.00**

Union Leader Cut Plug, sign, paper, The National Smoke & Chew, Uncle Sam reading The Naval Review, framed, 30x27", EX, D6 ....$2,600.00

Union Leader Cut Plug, sign, paper, The National Smoke & Chew, Uncle Sam reading The Naval Review, original gold frame, 46x36", NM, A7...............................**$5,000.00**

Union Leader Redi Cut Tobacco, humidor, round, red, trademark image, EX+, A3 ....**$235.00**

Union Leader Redi Cut Tobacco, pocket tin, vertical, Uncle Sam on white oval, VG+, A18 ....**$50.00**

Union Leader Redi Cut Tobacco, pocket tin, vertical, Uncle Sam on yellow oval, wide version, EX+, A18 .....**$60.00**

Union Leader Smoking Tobacco, pocket container, cardboard, vertical, 'Victory Package,' WWII era, scarce, NM+ (full), A18 ....**$30.00**

Union Leader Smoking Tobacco, pocket tin, vertical, eagle on gray oval, Trial Package, NM (full), A18 ....**$100.00**

Union Leader Smoking Tobacco, pocket tin, vertical, eagle on shaded gray oval/hand-held pipe on reverse, VG+, A18..**$70.00**

Union Leader Smoking Tobacco, pocket tin, vertical, Uncle Sam (no pipe) on white oval, EX, A18...............**$150.00**

Union Leader Smoking Tobacco, sign, cardboard, Brother...That's My Union Leader Smile, image of Chester Morris smoking pipe on blue, 40x26", EX, A3............**$30.00**

Union Leader Smoking Tobacco, sign, tin, same image as vertical pocket tin, lettering above/below oval eagle logo on red, 13x11", NM+, A3 ....$200.00

Union League Extra Fine Habana, cigar box label, octagonal, baseball graphics, Witsch & Schmitt litho #1671, EX, A5...**$385.00**

Union Made Cigars, pocket mirror, round, Smoke.../Look For This Label (label in center), A Guarantee..., yellow, 1900-12, 2" dia, EX, D14 ....**$45.00**

Union Metallic Cartridge Co, sign, paper, image of soldiers loading/firing cannon, wood frame, 26x22", EX+, A14 ....**$220.00**

Union Mills Flour, sign, paper, baby lying in wicker basket with flowers/sign, framed, 17x21", EX, A8 .....$280.00

Union Oil, sign, cardboard die-cut stand-up, We've Got 'Em/The Finest Accessories, 2 figures hanging a picture, 33x32", NM, A1 ....**$300.00**

Union Pacific Stages, sign, porcelain, shield shape, The Columbia River Route/Ticket Office, red/white/blue, 2-sided, 33x26", EX+, A2....................................**$2,300.00**

Union Pacific Tea Co, trade card, little urchin boy sliding on icy sidewalk, advertising/list of branches on back, 7x4½", EX, D14...$8.00

Union Petrolium Co/Mineral Lard Oil, pocket mirror, round, **Never Sold To Dealers/None Genuine Without This Brand, 2 pigs, red/white/blue, 4" dia, NM, A1....$110.00**

Union Star Brand Coffee, can, 1-lb, slip lid, paper label, High Grade Blend on red emblem, EX, A15......**$700.00**

Union Workman Sweet Long Cut Smoke/Chew, pail, early yellow paper label, EX, A18.........................**$70.00**

Union Workman 10¢ Scrap, sign, cardboard die-cut stand-up, Here's Looking At You/Chew!, man holding up pack over 1 eye, 1920, 23x14", VG+, A13 ....**$185.00**

Union 76, lighter, flat-sided pocket type, orange/blue/white logo on white inlay, 2", EX+, A1 ....**$65.00**

Union 76, sign, porcelain, round, bottom mounting tab, blue/white on orange, EX+, D34..........................**$300.00**

Union 76/No Smoking, sign, porcelain, Stop Your Motor/No Smoking flank orange 76 logo on white, dated 8-3-41, 6x30", EX, A1...**$375.00**

Union 7600/Royal 76, salt & pepper shakers, plastic figural gas pumps, white/blue, paper labels, 3", EX+, A1........**$125.00**

Unique Art, display figure, Jazzbo Jim, electrified version of original with satin outfit/cap atop tin cabin, 1925, 34", EX, A23...**$7,000.00**

United Airlines, bank, Menehune of Hawaii, vinyl, 9", M, D20...$150.00

United American Metals, sign, cardboard hanger, Specialists In Bearing Alloys, name on band around Indian in profile, 14" dia, EX+, A3....................................**$130.00**

United Fashion Shows, banner, emblem on wooden dowl with string hanger, depicts man/woman advertising 1914 show, 14x13", G+, A9...**$100.00**

United Motors Service, sign, neon, oval, car logo in center, black/white on orange, white/yellow neon, 2-sided with 1 side neon, NM, A6 ....**$1,000.00**

United Motors Service, sign, porcelain, oval, car logo in center, black/white on orange, 2-sided, 29x45", VG, A2 ....**$700.00**

United Motors Service, sign, porcelain, oval, car logo in center, black/white on orange, 2-sided, 21x36", EX, A6 ....**$750.00**

United Motors Service, sign, porcelain, oval, car logo in center, black/white on orange, 2-sided, 36x58", EX+, D34...**$1,950.00**

United Motors Service, sign, porcelian, oval, car logo in center, black/white on orange, 1-sided, 11x18" (rare small size), NM, A6 ....**$1,300.00**

United Motors Service, spark-plug gapper, oval cloisonne/brass logo, 2x3", EX+, A1 ....**$150.00**

United Motors Service, thermometer, wood, Specialized Electrical Service, black/red on white, curved top, 15x4", VG, A6 ....**$45.00**

United States Baking Co, box, wood, paper labels on front & inside lid depicting stoneware/crock/Boston Baked Biscuits, 1900, 22x14", EX, A3 ....**$125.00**

United States Brewing Co/Loewen-Brau/Malt Liquid, drinking glass, shell, etched, 4", EX, A8 ....**$40.00**

United States Tires, ashtray, figural metal spoked tire with blue glass bottom, types of tires embossed around tire, ca 1920, 6" dia, NM, A24 ....$350.00

Universal Blend Coffee, can, 1-lb, knob slip lid, red/white/blue, VG-EX+, A3, from $165 to........**$290.00**

Universal Blend Coffee, pail, 1-lb, red/white/blue, Uncle Sam with flag, EX+, A15 ....**$700.00**

Universal Stoves, saleman's sample, porcelain/cast iron, black/white, with case, 16x7x18", NM, A9......**$7,000.00**

University Coffee, can, 1-lb, key-wind lid, orange/blue striped ground, steaming cup, EX+, A3 ....**$225.00**

Upper Peninsula Brewing Co, sign, wood, name/logo upper corners with 5 gents conversing at table on wood-grain ground, 16x25", EX, A7 ....**$800.00**

US Ammunition, sign, tin, At Bisley England/Demonstrated Standard Of The World, military scene, self-framed, 1908, 23x28", EX, A7 ....**$1,600.00**

US Baking Co R Ovens Branch Cakes/Crackers/Biscuits, crate, wood, paper label, flower/grain decor, white/orange/blue, 10x14x24", VG, A6 ....**$275.00**

US Brewmasters, brush, celluloid, round, 1912 Convention, girl-on-barrel logo, black on cream, 4" dia, EX, A8 .**$35.00**

US Dept of Ag/Forest Service (Smokey the Bear), ashtrays, set of 4, aluminum, embossed images of Smokey Bear/phrase, decorative border, 4 colors, 4" dia, EX, D25, set........**$20.00**

US Dept of Ag/Forest Service (Smokey the Bear), plate, plastic, image of Smokey with forest friends/slogan on sign posted on tree, 1960s, 7" dia, EX, D25 ....**$38.00**

US Dept of Ag/Forest Service (Smokey the Bear), salt & pepper shakers, Smokey heads, ceramic, marked Smokey, M, D25, pair............**$75.00**

US Dept of Ag/Forest Service (Smokey the Bear), snuffit, plastic, bust of Smokey with lettering on hat, 1950s, EX, D25 ....**$35.00**

US Dept of Ag/Forest Service (Woodsy Owl), bank, Woodsy Owl, ceramic, Give A Hoot...Don't Pollute on round base, 8½", NM, A14............**$60.00**

US Dept of Ag/Forest Service (Woodsy Owl), lapel button, Give A Hoot! Don't Pollute! on fold tab above Woodsy Owl on round button, 1960s, 1" dia, EX, D25......**$28.00**

US Forest Service, see also First National Bank of Florence

US Marine Cut Plug, lunch box, bail handle, clasp closure, blue, G+-EX+, A1/A6, from $225 to......**$750.00**

US Marine Cut Plug, sign, cardboard, The Big 5¢ Package, sailor displaying pack from porthole, framed, 33x24", VG, A7............**$2,100.00**

US Marine Cut Plug, tin, round, smaller round slip lid, red, EX+, A18 ....**$600.00**

US Marine Flake Cut, pocket tin, vertical, red, G+-EX, A18, from $190 to........**$300.00**

US Marine Flake Cut, pocket tin, vertical, red, NM (from Tindeco sample room), A18 ....**$580.00**

US Marine Tobacco, roly poly, tin, Singing Waiter, VG, A7 ....**$575.00**

US Postage Stamps, dispenser, porcelain face, 5¢/10¢, blue & white, 14x7x6", EX, A1............**$50.00**

US Royal Soles-Heels, door push, porcelain, 3x32", VG, A6............**$130.00**

US Shot Shells, sign, cardboard die-cut stand-up, hunter displaying shells while sitting on wooden crates, 45x19", VG, A7............**$900.00**

US Shot Shells/Defiance/Ajax Heavies/Climax, sign, cardboard die-cut foldout, A Load For Every Purpose/A Shell For Every Purse, hunter in marsh, 34x60", VG, A7............**$850.00**

US Tires, clock, round, wood, Tire-ly Satisfied, image of serviceman's head with US on cap, ca 1914, 18" dia, NM+, A6............**$2,500.00**

US Typewriter Ribbon Mfg Co, tin, square, slip lid, allover star design around lettered inset, 1¾x1½x1½", EX, D37............**$45.00**

US 5's Cigars, sign, cardboard hanger, 5 For 10¢, waving flag upper left of portrait of lady, 11x6", EX, A5......**$120.00**

USACUBA, cigar box, 5 Cents, image of Tampa/Havana, VG, A5............**$100.00**

USS Products/United States Steel Subsidiaries, sign, flange, porcelain, round, Sold Here with white lettering/stars on blue band around red dot, 15x17", M (NOS), A6............**$425.00**

Utica Club, sign, cardboard stand-up, The Famous Utica Beer, black bellhop with tray against garden setting, 1910s, 22x12", EX+, A13............**$220.00**

Utica Club/West Bend Brewing, foam scraper holder, chalkware, UC cups flank bartender on red base, Tastiest Beer In Town, 8x12", G-, A19............**$55.00**

Utowana, cigar box label, inner lid, embellished round image of Indian girl, G, A5............**$220.00**

 **V**

Vacuum Mobiloils & Greases/Gasoline, sign, porcelain, Gasoline next to price dot above Vacuum Mobiloils & Greases, red/black/white, 18x70", EX, A6..........**$700.00**

Vacuum Oil, matchsafe, rectangular, barrel on celluloid center, plated ends, 1x2", NM, A1............**$180.00**

Vacuum Oil, sign, paper, Jay Eye See, horse/sulky with rider, corner reads Best Time Sept 15 1883, framed, 19x22", EX, A2............**$50.00**

Vacuum Oil, sign, paper, Rarus, horse in landscape, corner reads Best Time Recorded Aug 3rd 1878, framed, 17x21", VG, A2............**$100.00**

Vacuum Oil, see also White Star

Vadco Talcum Powder, can label, city skyscraper, 1923, EX, D5 ....**$30.00**

Vafiadis Cigarettes, sign, tin, Cairo hotel in upper left corner, product pack upper right, name below, beveled, 9x13", Fair, A2 ....**$100.00**

Valentine's Valspar Varnish/Paint, thermometer, porcelain with wood back/frame, square corners, Pat 1915, 50x12", EX+, A1 ....**$700.00**

Valentino's Sweet Gum & Fruit Cubes, sign, cardboard hanger, Chew..., classical lady seated in right profile, color, 1890s, 13x11", EX+, A1 ....**$100.00**

Valentino's Sweet Gum & Fruit Cubes, sign, cardboard hanger, Chew..., classical lady seated in left profile, color, 1890s, 13x11", EX, A1 ....**$80.00**

Valentino's Sweet Gum & Fruit Cubes, sign, cardboard hanger, Chew..., 3-quarter view of gypsy lady with hands clasped in front, color, 1890s, 13x11", NM, A1 ....**$150.00**

Valiant Authorized Service, sign, porcelain, Valiant above triangle logo flanked by Authorized/Service on white, 2-sided, 42" dia, EX, A2 ....**$330.00**

Valina Brand Coffee, pail, 4-lb, factory scene/rabbit, ca 1890, VG, A3 ....**$690.00**

Valley Forge Special Beer/Adam Scheidt Brewing Co, pocket mirror, oval, lettering/bottle on green background, VG+, A8 ....**$30.00**

Valley View Pineapple, can label, pineapple/poppies/Yosemite Valley, Selma CA, M, D12 ....**$10.00**

Valor Oil, bottle, 1-pt, metal funnel top, decaled label, embossed back, VG+, A6 ....**$100.00**

Value Brand Coffee, can, 1-lb, key-wind lid, red with black band, EX+, A3 ....**$55.00**

Valvoline, sign, tin, Costs Less To Use/Valvoline/The Original Pennsylvania Oil, red/white/black on green, embossed, 15x29", EX, A1 ....**$325.00**

Valvoline, thermometer, dial type, Ask For The World's Finest, green/white tilted can on yellow, Pam, 12" dia, NM, A15 ....**$300.00**

Vam, sign, tin, Try New Vam For Healthy Handsome Hair/3 Natural Oils, with barber's pole, red/blue on white, 9x27", G, A2 ....**$50.00**

Van Bibber Sliced Plug Pipe Tobacco, pocket tin, flat, litho on bottom, EX+, A18 ....**$50.00**

Van Dyck Cigar, sign, cardboard hanger, Very Choice.../Four Select Sizes-10 to 15¢ above image of Van Dyck on wood-grain, 12x8", EX+, A3 ....**$50.00**

Van Dyck The Quality Clear Havana Cigar, sign, tin/cardboard, yellow lettering on wood-gain background, beveled, 18x13", VG+, A3 ....**$50.00**

Van Houtens Cocoa, sign, decal in Vitrolite glass, Van Houten's Cocoa House/World's Columbian Exposition, ornate frame, 24x19", EX+, A3 ....**$2,780.00**

Vanity Coffee, can, 1-lb, key-wind lid, yellow, peacock on red circle, EX, A3 ....**$220.00**

Vanity Fair Tobacco Cigarettes, sign, paper, frog couple on promenade, Major & Knapp litho, 11x9", VG, A9 ..**$70.00**

Vanity Fair Tobacco Cigarettes, sign, paper, 2 frogs playing leap frog, lettering at right, Major & Knapp litho, 11x9", VG, A9 ....**$75.00**

Vanity Talcum, tin, oval, 7", NMIB (unused), A3 ....**$100.00**

Vanta Laco Sterilized Powder for Baby, tin, round, blue on white, baby on red circle, gold trim, NM, A3 ....**$125.00**

Vanta Sterilized Powder For Baby, tin, pink on white, baby in blue oval, blue lid, EX, A3 ....**$85.00**

Vantine Sana-Dermal Talc, container, cardboard, round, sample, 2", EX, A15 ....**$625.00**

Vantine's Sana-Dermal Talcum, tin, sample, 2", EX+, A3 ....**$490.00**

Varsity Blend, tin, horizontal rectangle, rounded corners, Somers Bros litho, VG+, A18 ....**$40.00**

Vaseline Cold Cream/Chesebrough Manufacturing Co, tin, round, sample, ...For The Skin & Complexion, EX, D37 ....**$25.00**

Vaseline Mentholated, trolley sign, cardboard, product in box flanked by round images of nurse/product lettering, brown, 11x21", EX+, A3 ....**$165.00**

Vaudeville Sports, cigar box label, outer, boys in tuxedos, EX, D5 ....**$20.00**

Veedol, sign, tin, die-cut female ice skater with name on chest, dated 11-57, 18x9", VG-NM+ (NOS), A15-A6, from $525 to $1,400.00

Veedol Motor Oil, banner, cloth, Change To Pennsylvania's Best! on yellow banner behind red plane above product banner, 36x79", EX+, A1 ....$200.00

Veedol Motor Oil, can, 5-gal, rectangular, tall, pour spout, wire handle, For Byrd Expedition, black stenciled lettering on orange, NM, A1..............................$275.00

Veedol Motor Oil, sign, enamaled steel, round, name with winged-V logo on double bands, red/black on white, 2-sided, 24" dia, EX, A24.....................................$500.00

Veedol Motor Oil, sign, flange, porcelain, round, name on diamond with star-burst border, orange/white/navy, 1930s, 19x21", EX, A24.......................................$700.00

Veedol 10-30, sign, flange, tin, can shape, The World's Most Famous Motor Oil, winged-A logo, blue/gold/white, 19x13", NM+, A1 ....$235.00

Velie, pin-back button, round, The Car For Me, image of early auto, black on white, 1¼" dia, EX, A2 ......$300.00

Velie Limited, pin-back button, round, logo above image of early auto, sepia with green/red, 2¼" dia, EX, A2...$635.00

Velvet Beer, label, 12-oz, Terre Haute Brewing Co/IN, pre-1920, EX, A10..$40.00

Velvet Brand Coffee, pail, 5-lb, VG-EX, A15-A12, from $240 to...$400.00

Velvet Ice Cream, tray, square, name above oval image of ice-cream goodies, Rich & Delicious, American Art Works, c 1925, 13x13", VG, A9..........................$175.00

Velvet Pipe & Cigarette Tobacco, sign, cardboard cutout, open pocket tin, 14x8", VG, A3...........................$40.00

Velvet Pipe Tobacco, sign, porcelain, product pack left of Velvet Pipe Tobacco Sold Here/Aged In Wood, 12x39", G, A9 ....$125.00

Velvet Smoking Tobacco, sign, porcelain, product/pipes on tray left of Velvet Sold Here/The Sensational... on blue, 12x39", EX+, A13 ....$225.00

Velvet Tobacco, pocket tin, vertical, Free Sample, EX+, A18 ....$185.00

Velvet Tobacco, sign, paper, lady in red cape standing on 2 galloping black horses, framed, 44x35", G, A7 ..$800.00

Velvet Tobacco, sign, tin, A Man That Loves Kitties An' Dogs..., above 2 men/child/dog, framed, image: 28x22", G, A9 ....$600.00

Velvet Tobacco, tin, octagonal, round slip lid, red, EX+, A3 ....$55.00

Velvet Tobacco, watch fob, pocket-tin shape, multicolored cloisonne, 2x1", NM, A15.................................$140.00

Velvetina Face Powder, tin, rectangular, rounded corners, lettering/decoration around oval portrait of lady, 1½x2½x3½", EX, D37 ....$55.00

Velvetina Talcum Powder, tin, round, embossed, oval image of pretty woman, EX-EX+, A3/A15, from $125 to $160.00

Venizelos Coffee, can, 1-lb, key-wind lid, red/white/blue, round portrait, EX, A3 ....$50.00

Ventura Maid, crate label, California lemon, '30s blond holding lemons, Ventura, M, D12 ....$20.00

Ventura Motor Oil, sign, porcelain, Insist On.../Paraffin-Base Oil, red/black on white, 18x13", EX+, A2 .$440.00

Veribest Concentrated Mince Meat/Armour & Co, pail, yellow, VG+, A18...$35.00

Vernoa Needles, tin, square, rounded corners, name on band around nude in center, white/black/blue/red, NM, A3..$30.00

Vernor's, sign, porcelain, Drink.../Deliciously Different, green on yellow, green line border, embossed, 11x17", NM, A13..$250.00

Vernor's, sign, tin, oval, Drink.../Deliciously Drifferent, blue lettering on yellow, 1965, 32x48", EX+, A13 ......$140.00

Vernor's Float, sign, cardboard die-cut stand-up, Try A Vernor's Float, 18x12", NM, A16 ....$275.00

Vernor's Ginger Ale, dispenser, metal canister with porcelain trim, pressure gauge atop reads Look It's Cold, 31", EX, A6 ....$2,200.00

Vernor's Ginger Ale, sign, tin, Drink..., leprechaun rolling barrel & pointing, green/yellow, black frame, 1940s, 18x54", EX-NM, D11/A1, from $350 to $400.00

Vernor's Ginger Ale, sign, tin, oval, Drink..., green on yellow, embossed, 19x29", G, A16..........................$150.00

Vernor's Ginger Ale, thermometer, dial type, green/yellow divided ground, glass front, metal rim, 12" dia, EX-NM+, D11/A1, from $150 to...........................$300.00

Verona Needles, tin, square, rounded corners, name on band around standing nude, ½x1½x1½", EX, D37.........$40.00

Very Best Allspice, container, 3-oz, cardboard with tin top/bottom, VG, A3...$8.00

Vess, see also Cleo Cola

Vess Cola, sign, neon counter-top, Drink.../First For Thirst on glass front, metal case, 1940s-50s, 9x14", NM+, A13.$600.00

Veteran Brand Peanut Butter, pail, 1-lb, blue, EX, A18.$115.00

Veteran Coffee, can, 1-lb, screw lid, no image, EX, A3.$75.00

Veterans (The), cigar box label, sample, Grand Army Of The Republic, eagle on patriotic shield, Schmidt & Co litho #819, EX, A5..$1,100.00

Vicks, door plate, porcelain, Come In/Vicks For Colds, blue images of bottle/jar, white lettering on red, 8", EX+, A13..$200.00

Vicks VaPo Rub, tin, round, Test Sample, graphic of box/jar extending to edge, EX, D37.............................$60.00

Victor Brewing Co Steinhaus, tap knob, bulb shape, red on gray sand marbleized plastic, EX, A8............$120.00

Victor Gaskets/Oilseals/Packings, sign, cardboard/metal, die-cut, Sealing Products Exclusively, blue/silver lettering/graphics, 12x26", M (NOS), A6............................$300.00

Victor Records, catalog, 1924, phonograph records, EX, D17 ....$50.00

Victor Records, sign, record shape, embossed, with scrolled bracket, 28" dia, G+, A9.....................................$575.00

Victor Records, trolley sign, cardboard, Invitation To The Waltz, Christmas motif with candle & holly/advertising, 13x23", EX, A6 ....$75.00

Victor Talking Machines, see also RCA

Victor Talking Machines, magazine ad, National Geographic, 1903, trademark image of Nipper at Victrola, full color, 13x16", NM, A3..$90.00

Victor Talking Machines, sign, tin, ...Sold Here, image of His Master's Voice, framed, 15x21", EX, A7.....$1,800.00

Victor The Ripe Coffee, can, 1-lb, key-wind lid, red/yellow, NM, A3..$75.00

Victoria Tea/Montgomery Ward, tin, 2-lb, square, smaller round lid, yellow, ca 1900, EX+, A3 ....$135.00

Victory Lager, label, 11-oz, Lynwood Brewing Co/CA, IRTP/U-type permit #, 1933-36, M (traces of paper or scrapes on back), A10 ....$20.00

Vienna Beauties, cigar box label, inner lid, bust of Miss Liberty in mirror, 6x9", EX, D5 ....$45.00

Vigarol, see Armour's Vigarol

Vigorator Foaming Hair Tonic & Head Rub, sign, tin, Dissolves Dandruff, oval image of man lathering head lower right, 5x9", EX+, A3...$160.00

Viking Snuff, dispenser, Guaranteed Fresh, white/red lettering on blue, 1950s, 15", NM (unused), A3/A24, from $60 to..$100.00

Violet, crate label, apple, big bunch of violets on black ground, EX, D3 ....$7.00

Virgin Queen Smoking Tobacco & Cigarettes, sign, paper, bust image of Queen, Culver, Page Hoyne & Co litho, framed, image: 22x18", G, A9..........................$200.00

Virginia Brewing Co/Southern Progress, drinking glass, shell, etched, gold rim, 3½", EX, A8..................$175.00

Virginia Dare Extra Fine Cut Plug, tin, horizontal rectangle, square corners, NM, A18 ....$250.00

Virginia Dare Korker, bottle topper/bottle, cardboard, Drink..., yellow/white on red, EX, D30 ....$35.00

Visible Gasoline, gas globe, milk-glass ball with red lettering, 15", EX, A6 ....$1,000.00

Visitor, cigar box labels, set of 2, gentleman courting lady at table, Heppenheimer & Sons litho #1931/1932, EX, A5..$80.00

Vita-Bite, crate label, apple, big red apple with green leaf, EX, D3..$5.00

Vital, crate label, California orange, woman playing tennis/glass of orange juice, 1930, EX, D5.............$175.00

Vitona, bottle, glass, clear, white label with red lettering, metal cap, ca 1910, EX+, A13............................$130.00

VJ Plew Up-to-Date Shoe Store, calendar, 1926, die-cut cardboard, marque/flower-embellished border around 2 girls hugging, embossed, 19x12", NM+, A3 ....$70.00

Vogue Pure White Papers, dispenser, tin, red/white/blue with image of pack of papers, 7x3x2", VG+, A3..$55.00

Voight Brewery, match safe, brass-colored metal, 1-sided, striker on reverse, both ends open, VG, A8.......**$100.00**

Voight Cream Flakes, cereal box, 8-oz, girl with cows in wreath of wheat, 1906 Federal Food & Drug Guarantee, EX+, A3.....................**$265.00**

Voight's Rehingold, tray, round, deep rim, lady on rock/large bottle, 12" dia, EX, A8.....................**$530.00**

Vola, dispenser, ceramic urn shape atop straight-sided base, embossed decor, original spigot, 17", VG, A9.**$1,400.00**

Volk Bock Beer, label, 12-oz, Volk Brewery/Great Falls MT, IRTP or WF statement, 1933-50, M, A10 ....**$53.00**

Volunteer, cigar box label, outer, close-up image of clipper ship, Schmidt & Co, VG, A5 ....**$50.00**

Volunteer, cigar box label, outer, octagonal, soldier with American flag, M, A5 ....**$75.00**

Volunteer, cigar box label, outer, yacht on open sea, 4½x4½", VG, D5.....................**$45.00**

Von Eicken's Lucky Star Cut Plug Smoking Tobacco, pocket tin, vertical, German, scarce, EX+, A18...**$1,175.00**

Voss Washing Machine, postcard, More Time For Self Improvement When The VOSS Does The Wash, lady reading by piano, 1921, EX+, D26 ....**$85.00**

❧ W ❧

W Baker/WH Baker, see Baker's

Wadhams Turmeric, tin, 2-oz, EX+, A3.....................**$8.00**

Wagner's Ice Cream, sign, tin, Eat Wagner's Ice Cream 'It's Good,' Freeport Ill above tray of fountain treats, 14x20", VG, A9 ....**$275.00**

Wagon Wheel Pipe & Cigarette Tobacco, pocket tin, vertical, EX-NM, A18, from $600 to.....................**$1,035.00**

Wainwright Brewing Co, sign, paper, tavern scene with man telling story to other patrons, framed, image: 14x22", EX, A8 ....$400.00

Waitt & Bond Blackstone Cigar, sign, porcelain, white/yellow lettering on dk blue, white line border, 12x36", NM, A1 ....**$190.00**

Wak-Em Up Coffee, pail, 10-lb, green, VG, A3.......**$260.00**

Wakmann Watches/Helberg Jewelry Diamonds & Watches, thermometer, dial type, For The Time Of Your Life, glass face, 12" dia, EX+, A3 ....**$65.00**

Walderbush Beer, label, 11-oz, El Dorado Brewing Co/Stockton CA, pre-1920, VG+ (traces of paper or scrapes on back), A10 ....**$50.00**

Waldorf-Astoria Coffee, can, 1-lb, square, tapers to small screw cap, features famous hotel on all 4 sides, 7", EX+, A15.....................**$550.00**

Walgreen Agency Drug Stores, catalog, 1960, Christmas with toys, 244 pgs, EX, D17 ....**$100.00**

Walk-Over Shoes, display, die-cut tin, factory scene flanked by a man/woman, Shonk Works-American Can Co, 9x15", EX, A9 ....**$950.00**

Walk-Over Shoes, display sign, composition wall plaque, oval, figural man stepping over shoe on shelf, 29x18x4", EX, A6 ....**$350.00**

Walk-Over Shoes, sign, tin, trademark cameos flank name on blue, white courtesy panel below, 21x23", EX+, A3 ....**$65.00**

Walker Manufacturing Co Improved Duplex Steam Engine, ad, paper, photo image of Duplex Steam Engine in original stamped mat/engraved oak frame, no size given, EX+, A3 ....**$330.00**

Walker's Soaps, string holder, cast-iron beehive shape with Walker's King Of Soaps lettered around top/bottom, 5", G, A9 ....**$225.00**

Walla-Walla Pepsin Gum, jar, glass, square, thumbprint lid, embossed image of Indian chief, 13", VG-EX, A9/D22, from $350 to.....................**$465.00**

Wallen's All Purpose Grind Coffee, can, 1-lb, pry lid, white/black, VG+ (full), A18.....................**$50.00**

Walter A Wood Rake, sign, paper, farm boy/girl on horse-drawn hay rakes, scenic countryside beyond, ad text on back, 1880s, 11x14", EX, A3.....................**$220.00**

Walter Beer, sign, Vitrolite, white with round logo above Walter in diagonal script, Beer below, brass frame, 23x18", VG+, A9 ....**$400.00**

Walter Bro's Brewing Co, drinking glass, barrel, etched, factory scene, gold rim, 3½", EX+, A8 ....**$60.00**

Walter Hawking, crate label, Florida Citrus, Indians in canoe/Indian on shore, 1920, M, D5.....................**$50.00**

Walter Weber Stamping Material, tin, round, flat, yellow, 3" dia.....................**$40.00**

Walter's Family Beer/Walter Brewing Co, sign, tin/cardboard, ...A Quality Product..., silver/black lettering on red, 6x15", EX+, A8 ....**$50.00**

Walter's Gold Label Beer, tray, round, pie-pan rim, It Is The Brewing touts waitress with tray, gold lettering on rim, gold trim, 13" dia, EX, A8 ....**$340.00**

Walter's Pilsner Beer, clock, round, reverse bubble glass, metal frame, bear on yellow center dot with lettering, black numbers, 15", NM, A3 ....**$300.00**

Walter's Superior Quality Beer, drinking glass, shell, applied red lettering/shield emblem, 5", NM, A8.**$30.00**

Waltham Pianos, sign, paper hanger, metal strips, Pure In Tone/Nationally Priced/Over 70,000 In Use, parlor scene above, 35x23", NM, A3......................................**$1,100.00**

Waltham Watch Co, sign, paper, sepia tones, factory scene on river bank, name on white border, framed, image: 18x34", VG, A9......................................**$60.00**

War Bouquet, cigar box, embellished images of Miles, Shafter, Dewey & Schley, EX, A3.......................**$135.00**

War Eagle Cigars, tin, round, vertical, slip lid, 2 For 5¢ flank eagle logo, white lettering above/below on red, NM, A3......................................**$200.00**

Ward's, pot scraper, When Using This...Think Of Ward's Remedies, Extracts, Toilet Articles, Ground Spices..., red, EX-EX+, A3/A15, from $450 to...............$500.00

Ward's Cakes, display case, tin, 4-sided with various images of children/product, HD Beach litho, c 1920, 20x13x17", VG, A9......................................**$2,250.00**

Ward's Lemon-Crush, dispenser, ceramic lemon with embossed painted lettering on leafy floral base, no pump o/w EX+, D22......................................**$950.00**

Ward's Orange-Crush, clock, round, name in center, large numbers, wood frame, 16" dia, G, A9 ....**$350.00**

Ward's Orange-Crush, dispenser, orange-shaped bowl with embossed name on base with white blossoms/green leaves, 1920, no pump o/w NM, A13 ....**$575.00**

Ward's Orange-Crush, sign, tin, embossed, Drink.../Also Ward's Lemon-Crush & Ward's Lime-Crush next to bottle in oval, orange, 9x20", NM, A1..........................**$475.00**

Ward's Orange-Crush, see also Orange Crush

Ward's Superior Breakfast Cocoa, tin, 1-lb, vertical square, round image of island scene, EX+, A3.................**$45.00**

Ward's Vitovim Bread, thermometer, porcelain, Keeps Him Smiling Because 100% Nutrition, curved top, vertical, EX, D34 ....**$750.00**

Wardaw Spices Cream of Tartar, tin, 1-oz, round, red, EX+, A3......................................**$150.00**

Waring Aluron, coupon, For All You Iron, image of hand-held iron on ironing board, linen, Harry H Baumann, NM, D26 ....**$50.00**

Warner's Gilt Edge Brassieres, sign, tin/cardboard, lettering left of product image on blue, ca 1915, 6x12", EX+, A3......................................**$300.00**

Warnick & Brown Smoking Tobacco, lunch box, yellow, double swing handles, EX+, A18 ....**$75.00**

Washington, cigar box label, outer, portrait, silver, 1895, 4½x4½", EX, D5......................................**$40.00**

Washington, cigar box label, inner lid, sailor lighting cigar/large US flag, 6x9", M, D5 ....**$45.00**

Washington Chief, license plate attachment, die-cut metal, It's Great To Be An American!/New Polyfoam logo, red/white/blue, 10", VG, A1 ....**$175.00**

Washington Crisps Toasted Corn Flakes, cereal box, 7-oz, oval image of Geo Washington, white/blue on red/white stripes, NM, A3......................**$250.00**

Waterford Carriage Co, sign, paper, red lettering borders images of carriages in 3 vertical rows on white ground, framed, 36x21", VG, A......................**$75.00**

Waterman's Ideal Fountain Pen, sign, porcelain, Selection/Service, globe logo in center, white/yellow on blue, 1910s-20s, 8x20", NM, A13 ....**$400.00**

Waterman's Ideal Fountain Pen, sign, tin, pen shape, 47", 1920s, Fair-VG+, A9/A4, from $425 to **$900.00**

Watkins Cocoa, tin, 1-lb, blue on white, round profile portrait, NM, A3......................................**$70.00**

Watkins Cocoa, tin, 4-oz, Free Trial Size, EX+, A3....**$90.00**

Watkins Egyptian Bouquet Talcum Powder, tin, embossed, EX+, A3......................................**$130.00**

Watkins Pure Ground Pepper, tin, 1-lb, yellow/white striped ground, round profile image, EX, A3 ....**$50.00**

Waverly Navy Cut, tin, horizontal box, square corners, VG+, A18......................................**$210.00**

Waverly Oils & Gasoline, sign, flange, porcelain, red oil drum with white/blue lettering on white ground, 10x16", NM+ (NOS), A6 ....**$3,250.00**

Wear-Ever, clock, skillet shape, electric, clock face on bottom side of pan, 15x9", working, EX, A6 ....**$80.00**

Weatherbird, see Peters Weatherbird Shoes

Weber Waukesha Beer, can, cone top, 32-oz, EX, A8...$60.00

Wedding Breakfast Roasted Coffee, can, 1-lb, slip lid, paper label, EX, A3.................................$60.00

Weed Chains, sign, tin, Gasoline To-Day (pricing wheel) Cents/Gals, Weed Tire Chains Are Necessary..., self-framed, 24x17", NM, A7.....................................$1,600.00

Wegemann, Faber, Kaercher Co, tip tray, round, classic lady in profile, gold-lettered rim, EX, A3..............$95.00

Weideman Boy Brand Coffee, can, 1-lb, key-wind lid, EX+, A3...$80.00

Weinard's, watch fob, enameled, 1912, VG, A8........$40.00

Weisert's, see John Weisert's 54 Smoking Tobacco

Welch Juniors, sign, tin, Drink A Bunch Of Grapes From Welch Juniors 10¢, bottle/grapes on red/blue, 1931, 14x20", NM+, A13 ....$675.00

Welch's, sign, trolley, You Will Want To Be Next To The 'Punch'.../The Natural Drink, men lined up/lady, 1910-15, 21", EX+, A13...................................$375.00

Welch's Grape Juice, pin, celluloid/metal, bottle on grape-cluster shape, 1", EX, A6......................................$100.00

Welcome Nugget/TC Williams Co, caddy label, vertical, miner holding up huge nugget with mining town beyond, approx: 14x7", EX+, A3 ....$75.00

Welcome Nugget/TC Williams Co, label, paper, miner holding up large gold nugget, mining town beyond, 11x11", M, A5 ....$75.00

Welcome Soap, sign, paper, The Welcome, 2 native boys stare at sailor boy seated on crate, framed, image: 19x13", VG, A9 ....$400.00

Wellington Pipes, sign, cardboard die-cut stand-up, Get A Pipe To Fit Your Face..., man's face on circle/crossed pipes, 17x13", VG, A6 ....$60.00

Wellington London Mixture, pocket tin, vertical, VG, A3 ....$50.00

Wells Richardson & Co's Improved Butter Color, sign, paper on cloth, Will Not Become Rancid, boy/cow by wooden water trough, lettered ornate frame, 29x20", G, A2...$150.00

Welsbach, tip tray, round, Welsbach Assures Dependable Lighting Service, parlor scene with mother/child, NM, A3...$160.00

Welsbach Co Mantles, tip tray, round, decorative gold rim around shield-&-eagle emblem atop red scroll, Meek litho, 4" dia, EX, A7 ....$50.00

Welsbach Lights & Mantles, sign, tin, We Recommend..., lady holding bottom of evening gown by 2 lamps, self-framed, 1905, 33x28", VG, A7..............................$600.00

Welz & Zerweck's Lager Beer, sign, reverse glass, round, white lettering around logo on red, wood-tone frame, 24" dia, EX, A7 ....$450.00

Wenck's Cold & Croup Cure, sign, cardboard die-cut stand-up, girl/dog sitting on box, 10x6", EX, A13..........$90.00

Wendy's, paperweight, Wendy's Decade II, round metal with colorful inset showing ad marque above phrase, EX, D25...$40.00

West Beach & Motor Hair Nets, display case, tin, name/beach scene on inside of lid atop 3 hinged drawers, ca 1910, 6x5x5", EX, A3 ....$70.00

West Bend Lithia Beer, sign, porcelain, curved, name/diamond logo, 14x18", VG+, A11 ....$250.00

West Electric Hair Curler Co, display box, tin, West Electric Hair Curlers/Hair Nets/Soflex, dome top, white ground, 18x10x8", VG, A1...$125.00

West End Brewing Co, tray, round, patriotic girl with hops & eagle/High Grade Beers Only banner, lettered border/rim, 13" dia, G-EX, A9/A19, from $250 to ...$500.00

West Side Brewing Co Extra Pale, label, Chicago IL, pre-1920, VG+ (traces of paper or scrapes on back), A10 ....$44.00

West Virginia Extra Pale Pilsner Beer, sign, tin/cardboard, Courtesy Of..., photo image of state capitol building above lettering, self-framed, 14x10", VG+, A8....$100.00

Westchester County Brewing Co, sign, wood veneer, exterior view of brewery, inset upper right corner, name below, 24x34", EX, A7...$350.00

Western Ammunition, sign, cardboard, No Closed Season on Pests above fowl in flight/other game animals, products below, 20x12", VG, A9 ....$475.00

Western Ammunition, sign, paper, Bob White, artist Lynn Bogue Hunt, original metal strips top/bottom, 24x16", VG, A9 ....$700.00

Western Ammunition, sign, paper, dog watching black man seated against cabin wall dreaming about rabbit hunting, 22x13", VG, A7 ....$800.00

Western Auto, catalog, 1932, Spring/Summer, auto supplies/radios/etc, 132 pgs, EX, D17 ....$40.00

Western Auto, catalog, 1970, Christmas, 72 pgs, EX, D17....$30.00

Western Auto, catalog, 1973, Spring/Summer, general merchandise, 314 pgs, EX, D17 ....$25.00

Western Insurance Co/Buffalo NY, sign, paper, shows 3 arch-framed images of 2 navigational scenes flanking city fire, ca 1880, 18x23", EX, A15..............................$550.00

Western Queen, crate label, California orange, Indian maiden, Rialto, M, D12...$16.00

Western Star, crate label, apple, profile of Indian chief on big star/colorful rays, EX, D3..............................$10.00

Western Union, sign, flange, porcelain, Telegraph Here (white on blue) above, Western Union on yellow telegraph, 17x11", EX+, A13 ....$260.00

Western Union, sign, flange, porcelain, Telephone Your Telegrams From Here/Ask Operator For..., stick phone, white, 20x18", NM, A1...$625.00

Western Union, sign, reverse-glass light-up, Telegraph Here on Deco base, yellow telegram on blue marque, 1930s-40s, 9x12x3", NM, A1...................$650.00

Westie, crate label, Arizona vegetable, desert scene with cowboy on bucking bronc, Mesa, M, D12............$10.00

Westinghouse, catalog, 1928, complete line of electrical supplies, 1156 pgs, EX, D17 ....$100.00

Westinghouse Genuine Radiotrons, sign, porcelain, Authorized Dealer, lettering on round disk, red/white/blue, 10" dia, EX+, A13......................$150.00

Westinghouse Mazda Lamps, display, light-up, red/white light bulbs atop round reverse-on-glass sign in metal frame, Deco base, 13x18x13", VG+, A6..............$100.00

Westinghouse Mazda Lamps, display box, cardboard with backlight, shows mother reading to children, 1930s, 27x40", EX+, A13 ....$100.00

Westinghouse Mazda Lamps, masks, cardboard, set of 4 Toonerville Folks, Powerful Katrinka, Mickey McGuire/ Skipper/Tomboy Taylor, 1920s, EX, A3............$100.00

Westinghouse Mazda Lamps, sign, cardboard cutout, Buy 'Em Here! says young Jackie Cooper in yellow T-shirt, 1930s, 40x28", NM, A13.....................................$500.00

Westinghouse Toaster-Stove, postcard, Here's The Latest In Cookers — The Westinghouse Electric Toaster-Stove, drawing of lady above, NM, D26 ....$35.00

Westminster Pure Rye Whiskey/CH Ritter & Co, sign, tin, 5 horsemen riding past Westminster Abbey in distance, signed Irving R Bacon/Shonk litho, 1903, 46x35", G+, A7...$600.00

Westminster Rye Whiskey, sign, tin, Settled Out Of Court, C Shonk litho, self-framed, 38x26", EX, A9/A7, from $4500 to..$5,000.00

Westward Ho! Smoking Mixture/WD & HO Wills, sign, porcelain, lettering above/below slanted product box, yellow on green, 35x18", G, A2 ....$200.00

Weyerhauser Balsam-Wool Blanket, sign, porcelain, Insulate With.../It Tucks In!, silhouette image of snow-covered house, 1930s, 23x36", NM, A24 ....$290.00

Weyman's Cutty Pipe, store tin, square, round lid, green, ...In The New Foil Package For 5 Cents, 14x10x10", EX, A3 ....$375.00

WF McLaughlin & Co Coffee Service, bin, tin with 3 compartments, Blended For Flavor Coffees, Kept-Fresh By McLaughlin, 27", Fair, A9 ....$250.00

WGY Coffee, can, 1-lb, key-wind lid, WGY on red emblem on white/black background, EX+, A3................$100.00

Wheary Wardrola, sign, light-up, glass, The Trunk That Rolls Out, shows boy rolling trunk by lamp table, wood frame, 17x14", EX, A6..........................$700.00

Wheat's Ice Cream Co, Buffalo NY, sign, tin, The Home Of Quality Ice Cream, exterior view of busy factory with product insets, 19x26", VG, A7.........................$550.00

Wheaties, bowl, ceramic, white with red lettering/silhouette images of athletes around center, NM+, A3.........$30.00

Wheaties, Hike-O-Meter, aluminum with black/white/red center dial, 1956 (reissue of 1948 Cheerios Lone Ranger Pedometer), M, D14.....................................**$25.00**

Wheaties, sign, cardboard, American Flyer Electric Train Free... for the most Wheaties Box Tops, blue on white, 14x22", VG, A3..**$15.00**

Whip Ready Rolled for Pipe or Cigarette, pocket tin, vertical, green, short, EX, A18 ....**$300.00**

Whip Ready Rolled for Pipe or Cigarette, pocket tin, vertical, green, tall, NM+, A3.............................$675.00

Whip Ready Rolled for Pipe or Cigarette, tin, octagonal, green, red trim, EX-NM+, A18/A3, from $230 to **$350.00**

Whippet, sign, tin, Dollar For Dollar Value above Whippet, Product Of Willys-Overland Company, white on red, 12x23", G, A2...**$230.00**

Whippet & Willys-Knight Authorized Service/Genuine Parts, sign, porcelain, white lettering on red, white line border, 2-sided, 24x35", EX, A6...........................**$425.00**

Whistle, bottle carrier, cardboard, holds 6 bottles, VG, A16...**$40.00**

Whistle, clock, round, glass bubble front, metal frame, ...Golden Orange Goodness, numbers/dots around 2 elves/ad, 15", EX, A6..**$750.00**

Whistle, clock/display, masonite/wood, round clock face with bottle/elf's head/slogan, painted colors, 24x24", EX, A1 ....$825.00

Whistle, coat rack, wooden panel, round corners, 2 screen-painted elves jestering to Whistle sign/slogans, 6 pegs, 8x36", EX+, A1 ....**$275.00**

Whistle, cooler, metal picnic chest with round decals on sides, wire clasp, 2 wire swing handles, Progress, 12x18x8", VG, A6..**$160.00**

Whistle, display, cardboard, elf pushing real 7-oz bottle on handcart atop base with slogan, 7", EX, A1..........**$230.00**

Whistle, display, cardboard, Golden Orange Refreshment, elves pouring from large bottle, 1948, 15x18", EX-NM, A1/A6, from $325 to **$425.00**

Whistle, display, cardboard, 3 elves waving banners & pushing real 7-oz bottle in cart, 1948, NM+, A1 ....**$400.00**

Whistle, display, cardboard die-cut stand-up, elf on logo pouring 3 other elves a glass of Whistle at stand, 14x17x3", EX+, A1 ....**$325.00**

Whistle, fan, die-cut cardboard, photo image of boy on blue, 5¢ on orange dot, Healthful/Refreshing/Thirsty..., 1936, EX, A14...**$115.00**

Whistle, menu board, tin, elves at corners of rope border, logo above, vertical, VG+, A16...........................**$300.00**

Whistle, pocket mirror, rectangular, 2 elves holding trademark sign, Golden Orange Refreshment, 1940s, 2x3", NM (NOS), A24 ....**$150.00**

Whistle, sign, cardboard, Golden Orange Goodness, logo above girl with bottle on blue, train below on black, 34x24", EX, D30...**$165.00**

Whistle, sign, cardboard, Golden Orange Goodness, 3-quarter view of girl in neck scarf on blue, beveled border, 20x15", NM, D30 ....**$110.00**

Whistle, sign, cardboard, Thirsty?.../'The Handy Bottle,' bottle in center, dk blue ground, metal edge, 42x18", NM, A1 ....$625.00

Whistle, sign, cardboard, Whistle lettered vertically with elves/bottle/oranges, 23x3", EX+, D30..................**$35.00**

Whistle, sign, cardboard, 1¢ Sale/...Giant Family Size For Only 1¢..., with bottle, white/orange on white, 15x35", NM+, D30 ....**$150.00**

Whistle, sign, cardboard die-cut stand-up, bottle with 2 elves, 30x12", NM (NOS), A6...**$300.00**

Whistle, sign, cardboard die-cut stand-up, Golden Orange Refreshment, bottle with elf/orange/blossoms, 1951, EX-EX+, A3/D30, from $80 to **$135.00**

Whistle, sign, cardboard die-cut stand-up, Morning-Noon-Night, girl sipping from straw above octagonal sign, 23x16", NM+, A1 ....**$185.00**

Whistle, sign, cardboard hanger, bottle shape with elf wrapped around bottle neck, 12x3", NM+, A1.....**$90.00**

Whistle, sign, cardboard stand-up, Thirsty?.../Golden Orange Goodness/Now-New-VQ Vita-Quality, food scene, 1945, 14x11", VG+, A8...**$40.00**

Whistle, sign, flange, tin, Drink Certified Pure Whistle, orange ground, 10x12", VG+, D30 ....$120.00

Whistle, sign, flange, tin, Thirsty?.../Certified Pure, tilted bottle with straw on blue center dot, square, EX, D30 ...$450.00

Whistle, sign, porcelain, Drink Certified Pure Whistle, blue lettering on orange, 7x20", VG-NM, A6/A1, from $425 to...$700.00

Whistle, sign, tin, arrow shape, orange/blue with orange border, 1930s, 7x27", NM, A13 ....$300.00

Whistle, sign, tin, elves at each end pointing to slogans on yellow/orange/yellow, embossed, 4x24", NM (unused), A24 ....$185.00

Whistle, sign, tin, elves working on sign/pushing large bottle on cart, embossed, framed, 36x60, NM (NOS), A6.......$600.00

Whistle, sign, tin, Golden Orange Refreshment/elf on white at right of Whistle sign (blue/white/orange), embossed, 4x22", EX, A1 ....$140.00

Whistle, sign, tin, Thirsty?.../Golden Orange Goodness, elf pushing bottle on road, blue self-frame, 30x26", EX-NM, D30-A2, from $300 to $500.00

Whistle, sign, tin, Thirsty?.../Morning-Noon-Night, rectangular, 24x13", NM+ (NOS), D30............................$165.00

Whistle, sign, tin, Thirsty?.../Morning-Noon-Night, round, 2-sided, 14" dia, VG+, D30.................................$110.00

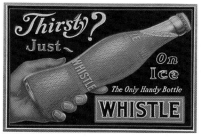

Whistle, sign, tin, Thirsty?.../On Ice/The Only Handy Bottle, image of hand-held bottle, embossed, 7x10", EX-NM+, A6/A1, from $425 to $725.00

Whistle, sign, tin, Thirsty?.../Sparkling Orange Goodness, musical notes/bottle neck/2 ovals, orange/white/blue, 12x30", NM, A1 ....$200.00

Whistle, thermometer, tin, slogan above 2 elves carrying bottle, blue/white/orange on yellow, 20", NM (NOS), A1..$850.00

Whistle, whistle, tin, orange/blue, EX+, A16.............$25.00

Whitaker's Blue Point Perfecto, cigar box, image of large oyster, factory #149, Utah, 1923, Union label, EX, A5 ..$110.00

Whitakers Keg Beer, door plate, plastic, Cock O The North/rooster/name on white, rounded corners, 8x3", NM+, A13..$50.00

White (The), pin-back button, round, The White lettered above image of buggy-type auto, sepia, 1¼", G, A2.........$745.00

White Bear Coffee, can, 1-lb, key-wind lid, no lid o/w EX+, A3..$110.00

White Castle, magnet, Castleburger, M, D23 ....$4.00

White Cat Brand Klosed Krotch Union Suits, pocket mirror, round, celluloid, white graphics/text on black, 2½" dia, VG, A6 ....$65.00

White Cat Union Suits/Cooper Underwear Co, pocket mirror, oval, celluloid, Just Because They Are Best For Comfort & Wear, white cat/text on black, 3x2", EX, A6 ....$100.00

White Clover Patent/Wm Scott & Co, sign, porcelain, We Sell.../Ottawa, image of flour sack, 24x12", multicolored, 24x12", EX, A6 ....$200.00

White Clover Peanut Butter, pail, 1-lb, red/yellow/blue shield, EX+, A3 ....$550.00

White Eagle Beverages, bottle topper/bottle, cardboard, Try.../You'll Enjoy Their Delicious Flavors, white on blue, EX, D30..$35.00

White Eagle Beverages, sign, cardboard, die-cut blue Deco panel, Call For The Best/Ask For..., oval image of lady on phone, 15x12", NM, A24 ....$110.00

White Goose Coffee, can, 1-lb, red, tall, NM, A15..$1,300.00

White Horse Beer, label, 12-oz, Prima Brewing Co/Chicago IL, IRTP or WF statement, 1933-50, EX (traces of paper or scrapes on back), A10 ....$20.00

White Horse Scotch Whisky, display statue, bust of colonial man in black hat on lettered base, plaster, VG+, A8 ....$100.00

White House Coffee, can, 1-lb, key-wind lid, blue, NM, A3 ....$45.00

White House Coffee, can, 1-lb, key-wind lid, copper, 4¢ Off, EX+, A3...$40.00

White House Coffee, can, 2-lb, paper label, blue, VG, A3 ....$75.00

White House Shoes for Men & Women, sign, paper, lady seated in pink dress with closed fan in hand, ad on bottom band, 1904, vertical rectangle, VG, A2........$135.00

White King Washing Machine Soap, sign, tin, Granulated/It Takes So Little & Goes So Far, powder sprinkling from open box, 14x10", EX+, (NOS), A1 ....$140.00

White Label 5¢ Cigars, sign, tin, Smoke...The Favorite Every Where left of open box, Sentenne & Green litho, 10x14", VG-EX, A3/A9, from $100 to $200.00

White Lilac Coffee, can, square, 2-tone blue, VG+, D22...$175.00

White Lion, tin, vertical rectangle, slip lid, lion head on green, Liberty Can, NM, A18...............................**$200.00**

White Manor Pipe Mixture, pocket tin, vertical, 3", EX-NM+, A18, from $150 to......................................**$230.00**

White Oak Coffee, store bin, tin, slant top, Imported By Oakford & Fahnestock, 18x18x14", Fair, A9.......**$100.00**

White Orchid, cigar box, 5¢ Straight on corner blue band, name, white orchid/smoking cigar on green oval against white, EX, A3 ....**$35.00**

White Pearl Macaroni/Lorenz Bros Macaroni Co, paper-weight/mirror, celluloid, round, signature above product box, company name below, white, blue border, 4", NM+, A3..**$65.00**

White Plume Coffee, can, 1-lb, key-wind, red/white/blue, NM, A3...**$290.00**

White Rock, sign, tin, round, fairy gazing at reflection in water, name in gold script on rock, 11" dia, VG, A7........**$450.00**

White Rock Beer, tray, round, image of lady leaning on tiger, Kaufmann & Struss litho, 14" dia, G, A9 ...**$125.00**

White Rock Lithia Water, sign, tin, oval, fairy gazing at reflection in water, C Shonk litho, raised rim, 20x17", EX, A1...**$950.00**

White Rock Sparkling Beverages, sign, flange, oval, fairy above red/black lettering on white, EX, D34.....**$450.00**

White Rock Table Water, plate, fairy gazing at reflection in water, gold ornate decor, box frame, C Shonk, 1881, 18x18", EX+, D6 ....$3,000.00

White Rock Table Water, tip tray, rectangular, The World Best..., fairy gazing at reflection in water, EX, A3 ....**$120.00**

White Rose Canned Goods, sign, paper, lettering above/below image of 5 white cans framed by roses/filigree border, framed, 23x27", NM, A3 ....**$85.00**

White Rose Cup Grease No 2, can, 1-lb, yellow, trademark image, VG, A6..**$25.00**

White Rose Gasoline, see also Canadian Oil Companies

White Rose Gasoline, sign, porcelain, round, boy holding sign, multicolor on white, black border, 12" dia, EX, A6 ....**$325.00**

White Rose Gasoline, sign, porcelain, round hanger, boy holding sign, multicolor on white, plain border, 40" dia, EX, A6 ....**$900.00**

White Rose Gasoline & National Carbonless Motor Oil, sign, tin, white/black lettering & logo on 2-tone green ground, embossed, 10x14", NM+ (NOS), A6 ......**$800.00**

White Rose Grease, can, 1-lb, yellow, trademark image, EX, A6..**$50.00**

White Rose Motor Oil, bank, oil can shape, yellow, trademark image, 3½", EX-NM, A6/A12, from $50 to ..**$120.00**

White Rose Motor Oil/Gasoline, sign, porcelain, 5-pc self-framed emblem, round logo (48") in center of lettered panel, roses on tab ends, 120", NM, A6 ....$2,750.00

White Rose Outboard Motor Oil, can, Imperial quart, flat-sided with small round screw lid, VG (full), A6 ..**$75.00**

White Rose Sprayer, bug sprayer, tin cylinder with wood handle attached to glass jar, EX, A6 ....**$30.00**

White Rose Tune, can, 4-oz, yellow, trademark image, Instant Pep Power Performance, VG+, A6............**$60.00**

White Rose/En-Ar-Co Motor Oil, license plate attachment, tin, boy holding sign, 4x6", EX+, A1...................**$185.00**

White Seal Pure Rye, sign, paper, cupid grounding barge with man/6 bare-breasted ladies, artist Mimalairski, framed, image: 24x37", EX, A9 ....$4,500.00

White Star Andrew Lohr Bottling Co, sign, cardboard, diagonal hanger, round image of lady in profile smelling a rose, red ground, 11x11", EX, A3....................**$110.00**

White Star Vacuum, sign, porcelain, Vacuum above White Star logo, red/black on white, 30" dia, EX, A2 ..**$880.00**

White Star/Staroleum Gasoline, sign, porcelain, round, white on blue, 31" dia, VG+, A6 ....**$500.00**

White Swan Coffee, can, 1-lb, key-wind lid, red, NM, A3...**$175.00**

White Swan Coffee, can, 2-lb, key-wind lid, red, EX+, A3...**$125.00**

White Swan Coffee, can, 3-lb, key-wind lid, red, G, A3...**$40.00**

White Swan Coffee, jar, 1-lb, glass, paper label, EX, A3...**$35.00**

White Swan Flour, tray, oval, image of 2 swans on pond, advertising on back, 14x17", VG, A9....................**$65.00**

White Thief, cigar box label, outer, white pig sucking cow's udder, M, D5 ....**$15.00**

White Tower Restaurant, sign, porcelain, die-cut chef mascot with coffee cup/burger on red dot, 35x33", VG, A6...**$500.00**

White Tower 100% Pure Beef Hamburgers, scraper, die-cut plastic, black/red on white, 2x2", EX, D25.....**$28.00**

White Trucks-Busses/Indiana Trucks Sales & Service, sign, porcelain, green emblem on white, white/green lettering, curved corners, 2-sided, 20x27", NM, A2 .**$880.00**

White Villa Coffee, can, 1-lb, key-wind lid, tall, EX+-NM, A3/A18, from $50 to **$100.00**

White Villa Pure Spices Allspice, tin, 2-oz, white, villa in landscape, EX, A3 ....**$45.00**

Whites Yucatan Chewing Gum, display box, cardboard, lid-flaps open to 2 sections that hold 100 pcs of gum, ½x9x7", EX, A3 ....**$85.00**

Whiz Gear Grease/Service Station, sign, porcelain, Whiz above Gear Grease on triangle symbol, Service Station below, framed, 24x36", EX A6 ....**$650.00**

Whiz Patch Outfit, display shelf, metal, die-cut litho tin sign attached to blue 3-tiered shelf, 22x14x5", EX, A2 ..**$750.00**

Whiz Service Center, display stand, metal, marque atop 4-shelf slant top on box-shaped base, green/red/blue/white, 54x32x21", VG, A6 ...$300.00

Whiz Soap/Davies Young Soap Co, tin, round, slip lid, Free Sample/Enter Whiz-Exit Dirt, 1¼x1½", EX, D37 ..**$35.00**

Whiz White Rubber Tire Coating, sign, tin, The New...For Tires/New Car Beauty, shows lady in roadster/product can, 17x12", VG+, A1 ....$400.00

Whoopee Milk, sign, cardboard cutout, Whoopee Milk That Is Milk above dog watching 2 children/doll, embossed, 12x8", NM, A13 ....**$30.00**

Wichita Construction Co, calendar, 1909, portrait of Indian maiden, complete, NM+, A3 ....**$465.00**

Wiedemann's Fine Beer, sign, light-up (multicolored spinner inside), round, reverse glass/chrome frame, It's Registered, 1950s, 16", NM, A19 ....**$350.00**

Wiedemann's Fine Beer, sign, tin/cardboard, First Call! (slanted lettering) flanked by bottle/rooster, 1940s, 10x20", VG-NM, A13, from $100 to **$475.00**

Wieland's Beer, tray, rectangular, Congratulations/The Home Beer, lady reading letter, wood-tone rim, 13x10", VG-NM, A8/A19, $100 to **$175.00**

Wiessner's Regal Beer, sign, tin, bottle cap above ...Aged Longer...Much Longer!, black/red on white, 21x27", VG+, A8...**$100.00**

Wigwam Coffee, can, 1-lb, key-wind lid, EX, A18....**$75.00**

Wigwam Mace, container, 1½-oz, cardboard, paper label, yellow, EX, A3 ....**$100.00**

Wilco Brand Allspice, tin, 2-oz, red/black lettering on cream, metallic gold trim, NM, A3........................**$22.00**

Wild Cherry Snuff, tin, round, Free Sample, paper label, 1923 tax stamp, EX, A3 ....**$45.00**

Wild Fruit Flake Cut Tobacco, see Bagley's

Wild Root, shaving mug, ceramic conjoined double cups with single metal handle, white, dated 1927, 3x6", EX, D22 ....**$110.00**

Will's Cigarettes/WD & Howills, display sign, shows 25 different cards of automobiles available in cigarette packs, framed, 24x13", NM+, A3 ....**$120.00**

Will's Star Cigarettes, sign, porcelain, yellow/white product pack in center, white name above/below on brown, 36x19", VG, A3...**$150.00**

Willard Starting Service, sign, flange, steel, Authorized Dealer on marque atop panel with bow & arrow logo/lettering, 18x22", EX, A2............................**$400.00**

William's La Tosca Rose Talc Powder, tin, sample, pink roses surround name, gold top, 2¼", EX, D37.....**$75.00**

Williamatic Spool Cotton, cabinet, wood, 2 drawers with raised letters, metal knobs, 9x23x16", VG, A6....**$275.00**

Williams Talc Powder, tin, sample, EX+, A18...........**$80.00**

Williams' Bread, sign, tin, Stays Fresh Longer on blue ribbon above large loaf of bread on yellow ground, 16x26", NM, A1...**$150.00**

Williams' Shaving Soaps, thermometer, dial type, glass front, metal frame, man's lathered face in center, 9" dia, EX, A15 ....$625.00

Willoughby Taylor Personal Blend Tobacco, pocket tin, vertical, NM, A3 ....**$50.00**

Willows Ale, label, 11-oz, San Francisco Brewing Co/CA, IRTP or WF statement, 1933-50, M, A10 ....**$35.00**

Wills's Capstan, sign, flange, porcelain, round, blue/white lettering & graphic on yellow, blue line border, 17x17", EX+, A1 ....$85.00

Willson's Monarch Best Talcum Powder, tin, oval, gold top, flower design around image of Laboratorys (sic), 4½", EX, A15 ....$110.00

Willson's Pure Ground Allspice, tin, VG+, A3 ....$70.00

Willys Americar Sales/Service, sign, porcelain, round, Sales/Service on circular banner around Willys Americar eagle logo, red, 2-sided, 2" dia, VG, A2 ....$825.00

Willys Approved Service, sign, porcelain, round, white lettering on red/black/red ground, white border, 2-sided, 42" dia, NM, A2 ....$1,265.00

Willys Cars, sign, paper, The New Willy's Cars... on blue band above multiple images of cars around center car, 27x41", VG, A2....................................$150.00

Willys Cars/Trucks/Jeeps, sign, neon/porcelain, black lettering with white/blue neon on Willys, red bands top/bottom on white, 36x72", EX, A6........$1,000.00

Willys Jeep Service, sign, porcelain, round, red/white/blue, 2-sided, 42" dia, EX, A2....................................$450.00

Willys-Knight Service/Genuine Parts, sign, porcelain, round, extended center band over logo, red/white/blue, 2-sided, 30" dia, G+, A2 ....$440.00

Willys-Knight Service/Genuine Parts, sign, porcelain, round with center bar, red/white/blue, 2-sided, 30x40", EX/NM, A6 ....$650.00

Willys Overland, sign, neon/porcelain, round W logo with yellow neon upper left of white neon name on red, 34x72x12", EX+, A6 ....$1,200.00

Willys-Overland & Willys-Knight, sign, porcelain, Authorized Service/Genuine Parts, white on red, white line border, 2-sided, 24x36", NM (NOS), A6 ....$800.00

Willys Service, sign, porcelain, Willys above Service, double stripes top/bottom, red/white/blue, 24x48", G, A2 ..$200.00

Wilson Tennis 3 Championship Tennis Balls, canister, tin, red/blue ground with large image of tennis ball, EX (unopened), A3....................................$45.00

Wilson Whiskey, sign, tin, coaching scene with many passengers in landscape, bottle sign in distance, 1902, framed, VG, A7 ....$600.00

Wilson Whiskey, sign, tin, die-cut, No Better Whiskey In Any Bottle on red dot above bottle flanked by 2 glasses, 1930s, 5x6", EX, A13 ....$35.00

Wilson's Certified Brand Peanut Butter, pail, 12-oz, EX+, A15....................................$180.00

Wilson's Invalids' Port, sign, cardboard hanger, Peruvian Cinchona-'The Primitive Indian's Remedy,' Indian in profile, 1904, 15x11", EX+, A3....................................$270.00

Wilson's Smoked Hams, sign, cardboard die-cut stand-up, The Nation's Finest Smoked Ham!, Uncle Sam carving ham, 40x30", VG+, A3....................................$180.00

Winchester, calendar, 1914, 2 dogs pointing while hunter takes aim, metal strips top/bottom, framed, 30x15", incomplete, VG+, A9....................................$1,150.00

Winchester, catalog, #77, October 1911, EX, A3 ....$85.00

Winchester, clock, Baird, figure-8, Roman numerals, embossed lettering on case, 31", restored, A9 .$5,000.00

Winchester, sign, cardboard, Claude Parmelee Demonstrating Complete Line Of Winchester..., portrait image, 22x11", EX, A3 ....$35.00

Winchester, sign, cardboard, hunters in cabin socializing & looking over hunting equipment, guns on wall, framed, 18x26", EX, A6 ....$135.00

Winchester, sign, cardboard, 4-panel, Supreme In Big Game Hunting, men in canoe/2 circle insets/display of products, 45x62", EX, A7 ....$1,600.00

Winchester, sign, cardboard, 5 panel, 3 hunt scenes/2 advertising, kitchen scenes/advertising on reverse, 1932, 39x18" each, VG, A3 ....$1,000.00

Winchester, sign, cardboard, 5-panel, canoe scene with items displayed, Winchester Pipe Wrench on reverse, 53x21" each, EX+, A3....................................$2,400.00

Winchester, sign, paper, Cheyenne, by Ferrara, 1977, 21x12", EX, A3 ....$35.00

Winchester, sign, paper, Sioux, by Ferrara, 1976, 21x12", NM+, A3...$85.00

Winchester, sign, paper, Wherever There's A Hunter There's A..., mounted T Roosevelt descending snowy hillside, 32x17", EX, A7...$2,250.00

Winchester, sign, tin, round, Winchester Western lettered below rider with rifle on galloping horse, 2-sided, 38" dia, EX/VG, A6.............................$200.00

Winchester, sign, tin shield on wood backing, Gun Advisory Center, red/black/yellow, 1950s, 20x20", NM, A3 ..$100.00

Winchester .401 Caliber Self-Loading Rifle, sign, paper, ...The Most Powerful Recoil-Operated Rifle, hunter confronts bear at cabin door, 1909, 35x20", VG, A7.....................$1,250.00

Winchester (Western), sign, paper, hunter in distance aiming at rabbit in snowy landscape, artist Weimer Pursell, c 1955, 40x26", G+, A11....................................$450.00

Winchester (Western) Sportings Arms & Ammunition, catalog, 1968, 48 pgs, EX, D17 ....$25.00

Winchester After Shave Talc, tin, red, hunter/dog, EX+, A3..$200.00

Winchester Australian Rimfire Cartridges, sign, paper, Shoot With The Accurate Australian, large spent cartridge, metal strips, 25x19", NM, A3....................$130.00

Winchester Bolt Action 22's, sign, paper, Whole New Tribe Of..., photo image of Indian chief in center of 4 braves with rifles, 25x37", EX, A3 ....$100.00

Winchester Cartridges & Guns, sign, tin, We Recommend & Sell..., dead fowl/moose rack/guns on paneled wall, Alexander Pope, 1913, 36x30", EX, A7 ....$2,500.00

Winchester Garden Tools/House Paints, sign, paper, images of various tools/paints, 2-sided, 40x19", G, A9 ....$200.00

Winchester Guns & Cartridges, pinback button, The Wonderful Topperweins Who Always Shoot..., portrait of couple, EX+, A3 ....$30.00

Winchester Loaded Shotgun Shells, sign, cardboard, Shoot Them & Avoid Trouble, skunk confronting 2 black men/dog, 1908, framed, 32x39", EX, A7................................$2,000.00

Winchester Model 12 Hammerless Repeating Shot Gun/Football, sign, cardboard, shotgun/football supplies, framed, 2-sided, image: 40x18", G, A9......$450.00

Winchester Model 94 Lever Action Rifle/Flashlight, sign, cardboard, rifle with Famous Winchester 30-30 Used By Generation Of Hunters/flashlight, 2-sided, 40x18", G, A9...$300.00

Winchester No 9114 Split BB Shot, BB holder, celluloid on metal, round, gray/red/black/cream, 1½" dia, EX, A6 ....$45.00

Winchester Repeating Arms Co Repeating Rifles & Ammunition, sign, cardboard, name/oval hunting scene/duck/ moose head in middle of rows of various ammunition, framed, 40x57", EX, A7 ....$2,250.00

Winchester Rifles/Shotguns, sign, cardboard, Rifles/Shotguns For Sale Here, close-up image of hunting dogs, self-framed, 32x42", VG, A7..$200.00

Winchester Self Loading Rifles/Fibre Flashlights, sign, cardboard, rifle/10 different flashlights, 2-sided, framed, image: 40x18", VG+, A9 ....$850.00

Winchester Super Speed Silvertip Cartridges, sign, reverse on glass, shows cartridge/roaring bear in mountain landscape, framed, 9x11", EX, A8...............$275.00

Winchester Western Sporting Arms & Ammunition, display counter stand-up book, spiral top, 35 pgs, describes various Winchester products, 17x12", EX+, A3 ....$65.00

Winchester 22's, sign, paper, Scout Out.../Bolt Actions..., close-up photo image of Indian Brave on horse with rifle, 24x18", NM+, A3 ....$35.00

Windmill Peanut Butter, pail, 1-lb, EX, A3............$190.00

Wine-Dip, dispenser, embossed logo on clear glass barrel atop clear glass base, 20", NM, A13 ....$200.00

Wing Brand Pure Hawaiian Kona Coffee, can, 1-lb, keywind lid, green, EX, A3......................................$30.00

Wings King Size Cigarettes, sign, cardboard, Piper Cub Airplane Given Away Each Week, pack next to vertical row of planes on red, 16x12", NM, A24 ....$75.00

Wings King Size Cigarettes, sign, cardboard stand-up, yellow plane soaring above open pack, advertising below, 1940s-50s, 30x20", EX+, A13 ....$140.00

Wink Syrup Co, sign, tin, Just Wink And Get A Good Clear Drink..., winking face upper left, black/orange, embossed, 9x20", NM, D11.............................$125.00

Winner Cut Plug, tin, round, smaller round slip lid, Iisley, VG+, A18...$30.00

Winnie Winkle, cigar box, Was 5¢/Now 2 For 5¢/Millions Sold At 5¢ Straight..., red oval image of pretty lady, EX+, A3...$35.00

Wish Bone Coffee, can, 1-lb, key-wind lid, single cup in center, earlier version, EX, A3.............................$40.00

Wish Bone Coffee, can, 1-lb, key-wind lid, cups repeated around middle, NM, A3......................................$40.00

Wishing Well Orange, thermometer, tin, Drink... above, tilted bottle/black dot below on yellow, 1961, 41", NOS, A6.............................$200.00

Wiss Forged Steel Tinner Snips, sign, tin, Best By Actual Test, image of snips with advertising, black/silver on red, beveled, 6x13", EX, A6......................**$190.00**

Wisteria Talcum, tin, round, small shaker top, woman in oval, 8½x2", VG, A15 ....**$210.00**

Witch Soap, sign, porcelain, Let The Clothes Soak Overnight..., witch on broom lower left, yellow on blue, framed, 26x38", EX, A24 ....**$1,900.00**

With the Beatles Talc, tin, 16-oz, pictures the 'Fab Four' front/back, NM+, A3..........................**$400.00**

Wm Deering Co, see Deering (Wm) Co

Wm Penn, cigar box, 5¢ Straight on corner band, square bust image, VG+, A3 ....**$18.00**

Wm S Kimball & Co's Cigarettes & Tobacco, sign, cardboard cutout, woman lighting man's cigarette on way to masquerade ball, ca 1900, 10x7", EX+, A3 ....**$100.00**

Wm Tell Motor Oil, can, 1-qt, round, oval image of Wm Tell shooting apple, white/red on black, EX, A15........**$400.00**

Wolf Co Flouring Mill Machinery, sign, cardboard, aerial night factory scene, 1880s, framed, 39x30", EX, A24 ....**$450.00**

Wolf Co Flouring Mill Machinery, sign, cardboard, embellished images of girl in hat/2 machines, framed, EX, A24 ....**$450.00**

Wolf Co Flouring Mill Machinery, sign, cardboard, Little Red Riding Hood, framed, vertical, EX, A24 ....**$450.00**

Wolf's Head Motor Oils & Lubes, thermometer, dial type, glass front, metal frame, red/black on white, Pam Mfg Co, 12" dia, NM, A1..........................**$200.00**

Wolsey Socks, display bust, man in red turban on base marked Wolsey, plaster, 9", EX, A14 ....**$45.00**

Won-Day Enamel, sign, cardboard stand-up, Paint Your Car With..., 3 scenes with advertising, multicolored, 30x20", VG, A6..**$200.00**

Wonder Bread, sign, porcelain, orange lettering on dark blue, 9x20", VG-EX+, A13/A6, from $100 to **$170.00**

Wonder Bread, sign, tin, loaf shape, 1950s, 20x42", EX, A13 ....**$185.00**

Wonder Bread, sign, tin, loaf shape (receding), 1950s, 26x36", NM+, A1................................**$475.00**

Wonder Worker Motor Car Necessities, sign, tin, 2 kids flank lettering, red/black on blue-green, diagonal top corners, 1920s-30s, VG, A8 ....**$165.00**

Wood Electrics, pocket mirror, round, A Reflection Of Good Taste, interior illumination of 2 ladies driving in dark, 2½" dia, EX, A2......................................**$385.00**

Wood's Boston Coffees, store bin, tin, dome top, VG, A18 ....**$275.00**

Woodbury's Facial Soap/Andrew Jergens Co, sign, paper, Save Your Complexion With..., sailboat on open sea, 1905, framed, 44x38", VG, A7 ......**$1,000.00**

Woodlake Nymph, crate label, California lemon, nymph dancing under eucalyptus tree, Woodlake, VG, D3.........**$12.00**

Woodlawn Mills Shoe Lace Service, display case, tin, wood base, Shoe Lace Service Station/Buy Another Pair & Carry A Spare, 14x12x11", VG, A6 ....**$1,000.00**

Woodstock Preferred Typewriter/Muncie Typewriter Exchange, ribbon tin, square, rounded corners, orange/white, images of Model T pickup/typewriter, 2½x2½", EX, A15................................**$1,400.00**

Woodsy Owl, see US Dept of Ag/Forest Service

Woolsey Marine Paints, sign, porcelain, Serving At Sea Since 1853, boats in blue/green/white water, orange sky, 22x34", EX+, A2 ....**$990.00**

Woolson's Vienna Coffee, can, 1-lb, screw lid, yellow, EX, A18..**$75.00**

Woolworth's, toy truck, Marx, litho tin with plastic wheels, red cab with red/black lettering on silver-tone trailer, 25", VG+, A2..**$275.00**

Woonsocket Rubber Boots & Shoes, sign, paper, A Critical Moment, couple fishing in boots, American litho, c 1906, framed, image: 25x17", VG, A9 ....**$1,000.00**

Worcester Elastic Stocking & Truss Co, pocket mirror, oval, M'f'r's Of Elastic Stocking/Abdominal Supporters & Trusses, girl wearing products, black, EX, A15 .**$400.00**

Worcester Salt, fan, cardboard, stick handle, round, black on white, framed, 13x10", EX, A6 ....**$30.00**

Worcester Salt, pin-back button, celluloid, The Standard For Quality, lettering around sack/train, blue/cream/black, 1½" dia, VG, A6.......................................**$30.00**

Worcester Salt, sign, paper, Worcester Salt Special/Jan 6, 1897, train winding through countryside from factory, framed, 35x27", EX, A6 ....**$850.00**

Worker Cut Plug, lunch box, brown, VG, A18 ....**$30.00**

Worker Cut Plug, lunch box, green, EX+, A3 ....**$75.00**

Workmate Chewing Tobacco, dispenser, vertical tube, green/white, 1950s, 15", NM, A3/A2, from $50 to .**$60.00**

World's Greatest Flyer, cigar box label, inner lid, Spirit of St Louis over globe, 6x9", M, D5 ....**$40.00**

World's Standard Sliced Plug, tin, rectangular, square corners, EX, A18...**$75.00**

World's Time Cigar, cigar box, The Smoker's Favorite, 1910, VG, A5 ....**$60.00**

WOW Anti-Knock Gas, gas globe, 1-pc, glass, yellow/blue, 16½" dia, NM, A6 ....**$2,150.00**

Wrangler, see Harley-Davidson

Wright & McGill Fishing Tackle, sign, paper, Get Your Fishing License Here, lettering over lake scene with product/jumping fish, 14x53", EX+, A3...............**$110.00**

Wright's Coal Tar Soap, sign, porcelain, The Nursery Soap/Per 4D Tablet, lettering on shield with shadowing, green/blue on white, 18x12", VG, A6................**$110.00**

Wrigley's, calendar holder, tin/cardboard, red name above 3 packs, date pages below, beveled, 1920s, 17x9", G, A13...**$500.00**

Wrigley's, dispenser, chrome & glass 5-sided case on swivel base, with instructions, 13x9", EX, A3................**$135.00**

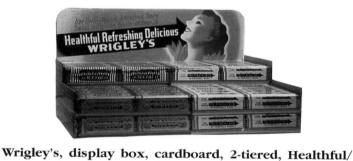

Wrigley's, display box, cardboard, 2-tiered, Healthful/ Refreshing/Delicious/lady's head on marque, 1930s-40s, 7", NM, A13 ....$350.00

Wrigley's, sign, paper, 1912 Calendar Assortment/Here Is Our Offer..., shows various calendars, 9x10", VG, A6 ..**$230.00**

Wrigley's, sign, tin/cardboard, ...Delicious/Lasting/Refreshing flanked by 4 packs, red name above on black, 1920s, 7x11", G+, A13 ....**$250.00**

Wrigley's, trolley sign, cardboard, King's court flanked by various flavors, 13x23", VG, A6 ....**$230.00**

Wrigley's, trolley sign, In Bond!.../...The Flavor Lasts/Sealed Tight/Kept Right, Wrigley man/large pack on blue, 10x20", EX, A1 ....$100.00

Wrigley's Campaign Pepsin Gum, trade card, Saleman's Sample Card, with attached campaign buttons (McKinley/ Bryan), vertical, VG (NM buttons), A16...............**$400.00**

Wrigley's Chewing Gum/Wrigley's Juicy Fruit/Dan Kinsley, sign, louvered, 3 different signs viewed from 3 different positions, wood frame, 13x55", G, A9 ....**$1,350.00**

Wrigley's Doublemint Gum, display box, cardboard, Peppermint Flavor, Wrigley Boy/lettering on marque, holds 10 packs, G+, A16 ....**$50.00**

Wrigley's Doublemint Gum, display box, cardboard, Peppermint Flavor/New Style, shows gum pack on marque, holds 10 packs, EX+, A16 ....**$80.00**

Wrigley's Doublemint Gum, sign, cardboard, For White Teeth & Smooth Facial Contour, woman with cigarette above large pack on red, 13x8", EX+, A1..........**$110.00**

Wrigley's Doublemint Gum, sign, porcelain, General Store panel atop Wrigley's Doublemint symbol, red/white/ blue, 2-sided, 9x30", NM, A15, ...$2,400.00

Wrigley's Juicy Fruit Gum, display box, Export Package, striped, holds 22 packs, EX+, A16.........................**$60.00**

Wrigley's Juicy Fruit Gum, match holder/striker, The Man Juicy Fruit Made Famous, painted metal, embellished oval image of man, 5x3½", VG, A6......................**$90.00**

Wrigley's Juicy Fruit Gum, sign, cardboard cutout, It's Good For You, young boy talking on phone while girl watches, 14x9", VG, D30.....................................**$30.00**

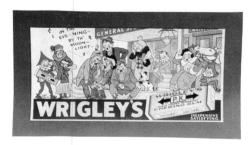

Wrigley's PK Chewing Gum, trolley sign, paper, patrons singing outside of general store, signed John Bliss, 12x24", NM (NOS), A6 ....$250.00

Wrigley's PK Chewing Sweet, calendar, 1924, boy/girl at water's edge, vertical, incomplete, VG, A1 ....**$35.00**

Wrigley's Spearmint Gum, display box, The Perfect Gum/The Flavor Lasts, shows arrows only on inner lid, EX, A16...**$75.00**

Wrigley's Spearmint Gum, display box, The Perfect Gum/The Flavor Lasts, shows Wrigley Boy/arrows on inner lid, EX+, A16 ....**$75.00**

Wrigley's Spearmint Gum, matchbook, blue/red with green arrow, 20 strike, front striker, full length, M, D28 ....**$5.00**

Wrigley's Spearmint Gum, sign, cardboard die-cut stand-up, boy with oversized pack of gum, multicolored, 14x10", EX+, A6 ....**$1,100.00**

Wrigley's Spearmint Gum, sign, cardboard die-cut stand-up, girl with oversized pack of gum, multicolored, 14x10", G+, A6 ....**$460.00**

Wrigley's Spearmint Gum, tray, rectangular, Happy To Serve You on diagonal banner with Wrigley Boy holding gum pack, 13x11", VG, A9..................................**$650.00**

Wrigley's Spearmint Gum, trolley sign, A Famous Flavor/ Sweetens The Breath, Wrigley Boy opening a pack, white/black ground, 1920s, 11x21", EX, A3 ....**$70.00**

Wrigley's Spearmint Gum, trolley sign, After Every Meal/Taste The Juice, gum pack next to 3 Wrigley Kids in center, 11x21", EX, A2 ....**$135.00**

Wrigley's Spearmint Gum, trolley sign, cardboard, Inexpensive-Satisfying/Taste The Juice Of Real Mint Leaves, ice-skating couple, 12x21", VG, A6..$160.00

Wrigley's Spearmint Gum, trolley sign, Dr Googles Noted Optometrist Advises 'Don't Strain Your Eyes...,' white drawing on blue, 11x21", EX, A3 ....**$90.00**

Wrigley's Spearmint Pepsin Gum, trolley sign, Here's A Picture Of The Mint Plant & The Spear..., man telling woman/pointing to pack, 10x20", EX, A1 ....**$100.00**

Wrigley's Spearmint/Doublemint, trolley sign, cardboard, It's Sold All Over The World..., lady with gum superimposed over globe at left, 11x21", NM, A3...........**$100.00**

WT Blackwell & Co's Genuine Durham Smoking Tobacco, store bin, tin, vertical square, paper labels with different images, ca 1880, 16x12", EX, A3 ....**$1,800.00**

Wuersburger Bottle Beer/Hortonville Brewing Co, art plate, Jas Keen's Unbeaten 3 Year Old/Winner Of 16 Races & $181,000.00, Meek litho, NM, A19 ....**$150.00**

Wurtzer Beer/Peoples Brewing Co, coaster, paper, round, cartoon image of man's head in hat with goblet of foaming beer, 3½" dia, NM, A3....................................**$40.00**

Wyandotte JB Ford Co, sign, tin, image of Indian in full headdress standing in profile with bow & arrow drawn, self-framed, 39x29", VG, A7..............................**$2,300.00**

Wyckoff-Cord Auto Co/Sioux City Iowa, pin-back button, round, lettering around image of auto on red dot, black/red on white, 1¼" dia, EX, A2 ....**$470.00**

Wyeth Tires, sign, porcelain, curved, pointed bottom, Guaranteed..., boy with goggles on large tire, red/white/blue, 22x18", EX+, A15 ....**$2,850.00**

Wyler Watches, display, round brass watch face with red plastic chapters on round base with rainbow marque atop, ca 1940, 20", EX, A23.................................**$100.00**

X

Xmas Crackers, product box, still contains crackers that explode when opened to expose toy novelties/hats/etc, 1920s (?), EX, D22..**$90.00**

Xtra Brau, tap knob, ball shape, black, white-on-black insert, VG+, A8 ....**$150.00**

Y

Y&N Corsets, mirror, Diagonal Seam As Advertised, square painted border with lettering around oval mirror, beveled, 26x17", G, A9..................................**$175.00**

Yacht Club Coffee, can, 1-lb, key-wind lid, red, EX, A3 ..**$20.00**

Yacht Club Coffee, can, 1-lb, key-wind lid, red, EX (full), A18...**$50.00**

Yacht Club Imitation Ground Nutmeg, container, 2½-oz, cardboard, white, gold trim, NM+, A3 ....**$70.00**

Yacht Club Smoking Tobacco, pocket tin, vertical, EX+, A18..**$1,190.00**

Yago Sangria, radio, bottle shape, NMIB (unused), D13......**$65.00**

Yakima Chief, crate label, apple, scowling Indian chief, EX, D3..**$5.00**

Yale Coffee, can, sample, metallic blue, VG+, A3 .....**$75.00**

Yale Coffee, can, 2-lb, smaller round lid, metallic blue, EX, A18..**$85.00**

Yale Jumbo Peanuts, tin, 10-lb, round, blue on gold, VG, A18..**$100.00**

Yale Mixture, humidor, ceramic, blue glaze, embossed name, NM, D6 ....$150.00

Yankee Boy Plug Cut, pocket tin, vertical, blond, EX+, A15..**$775.00**

Yankee Boy Plug Cut, pocket tin, vertical, brunette, VG, A3..**$365.00**

Yankee Clipper Pipe Smoking Tobacco, pocket tin, vertical, The New Aromatic Yankee Clipper, EX+, A18 ....**$5,000.00**

Yankee Girl Scrap, sign, cardboard cutout, large product pack, red/white/blue, EX+, A3 ....**$30.00**

Yankee Queen, cigar box label, outer, woman/eagle on shield, 4½x4½", M, D5 ....$15.00

Yankee Safety Razors, tin, rectangular, rounded corners, red, trademark image of man shaving face, EX+, A15 ..$825.00

Yara Specials, cigar box, Hand Made/Long Havan Filler, embellished image of tobacco plant, VG, A3 ....$30.00

Ye-Go Stogies, tin, vertical square, slip lid, EX, A18...$45.00

Yeager's Roller Mills/JM Yeager, Yeagerstown Pa, flour sack, paper, Alfa Bata trademark, very early, VG+, A8.......................................$30.00

Yeast Foam, sign, cardboard, young girl holding cut-out pumpkin next to her face with product box in pocket, framed, 26x21", VG, A7.....................$1,550.00

Yeast Foam, sign, cardboard cutout, Bake At Home Use Yeast Foam, lady holding up loaf of bread, 20x12", G-VG, A9, from $125 to $200.00

Yeast Foam, sign, paper hanger, Makes Delicious Buckwheat Pancakes, young girl at table, green ground, metal strips, 15x10", NM+, A3 ....$75.00

Yellow Bonnet Coffee, can, sample, pry lid, EX, D37...$500.00

Yellow Bonnet Coffee, can, 1-lb, key-wind lid, VG-NM, A3, from $40 to........................$85.00

Yellow Bonnet Coffee, jar, 1-lb, clear glass, red screw lid, red paper label, Regular Grind, VG+, A3 ....$25.00

Yellow Cab, calendar pad holder, Yellow Cab/phone number above, phrase below, white on black, line trim, 1950s, 11x7", EX+, A13..........................$50.00

Yellow Cab, driver's cap, black/leatherette fabric with ventilated webbing, orange trim, 1930, EX+, A1...$300.00

Yellow Cab, driver's cap, yellow vinyl with black ventilated webbing/visor brim, EX, A2 ....$200.00

Yellow Cab Sweets, cigar box, cardboard, 5¢, 1934, G, A5...$140.00

Yellow Creek Pure Lard, bucket, 50-lbs, blue, white oval with graphics, EX, A3 ....$50.00

Yellow Jacket, cigar box label, inner lid, bees/cloves, 6x9", EX, D5 ....$35.00

Yellow Kid, see also Clark Horton Store, Fleischman's Yeast, or High-Toned 3¢ Cigar,

Yellow Kid, cigar box, nailed wood, holds 100, Yellow Kid puffing on cigar while proclaiming its virtues next to newspaper, VG, A3..........................$390.00

Yellow Kid High Toned 3¢ Cigar, sign, reverse glass, gold-tone foil image of the Yellow Kid, black background, framed, 18x9", EX, A.....................$825.00

Yellow Kid Scrip/Pulver Co Inc, gum wrapper, waxed paper, 3x4", EX+, A15 ....$250.00

Yellow Taxi Company, paperweight/mirror, round, Cadillac 3333, Lowest Rates In Detroit..., cab in center, yellow/black/cream, 3½", EX, A2.....................$440.00

Yellowstone Peaches, can label, Indian on buffalo/bowl of peaches, 1923, M, D5 ....$40.00

Yellowstone Trail/NF Nelson, cigar box label, inner lid, From Coast To Coast, image of map, Geo L Schlegel litho, 1918, EX, A5 ....$90.00

Yo-Semi-Te, crate label, California orange, forest scene, 1920, M, D5 ....$65.00

Yoc-O-May Hash Cut, see Bagley's

Yocum's Official Hand Made Cigars, tin, round, slip lid, white, EX, A18 ....$50.00

Yonkers Ale/Beer, tray, round, white/yellow lettering on dk blue, plain rim, 13" dia, EX+, A19.....................$100.00

Yosemite Lager/Enterprise Brewing Co, tray, round, image of young lady with red corsage, Bachrach & Co litho, c 1905, 13" dia, VG, A9 ....$275.00

Youkon's Queen of the West Self-Rising Flour, sign, metal, large image of white 25-lb bag with oval graphic of woman in kitchen, black ground, 23x13", EX+, A1 ....$275.00

Young Fritz, cigar box label, inner lid, embellished image of young boy smoking cigar, M, A5..........................$85.00

Young Swell (The) Tobacco, caddy label, vertical, image of 'professor pooch,' Halco litho, 1888, approx: 14x7", NM, A3 ....$32.00

Young's Supreme Coffee, can, 1-lb, key-wind lid, red, VG, A3 ....$30.00

Youngers Tartan Beer, display figure, white-bearded man on beveled base, hard rubber, 9", NM, A14 ....$100.00

Your Treat, cigar box label, outer, men enjoying cigars, 4½x4½", M, D5 ....**$6.00**

Youth UTH for Silk Stockings, tin, round, Invisible Dainty Preservative, 6x2" dia, EX (unused), A3 ....**$125.00**

Youth's Companion, calendar, 1901, elongated die-cut cardboard, roses above/below oval image of Puritan girl, gold embossed border, EX, A8..........................**$100.00**

Yucatan Gum/American Chicle Co, display box, tin, yellow, top opens, oval window shows product, 6x5x7", EX+, A3 ....**$400.00**

Yuengling Extra Dry Premium Beer, sign, round, Since 1879..., 9" dia, VG+, A8...**$85.00**

Yuengling's Bottle Beer/Porter/Ale, tip tray, round, red bust image of girl in bonnet, red lettering on green, EX, A8..**$130.00**

Yuengling's Old Oxford Ale, sign, cardboard stand-up, Most Calls Are For Yuengling's..., blonde in oval atop, bottle at right, 1940, 36x24", EX, D14 ....**$75.00**

∾ Z ∾

Zang's Tonic/CA Lammers Bottling Co, tape measure, round, celluloid, The Best Malt Extract, lady in profile, EX, A8..**$100.00**

Zanzibar Brand Pure Ground Pepper, store bin, tin, red with paper labels, 20x12x12", VG+, A3 ....**$200.00**

Zatek Chocolate Billets, goblet, clear glass, embossed with lettering against reverse-painted gold emblem, Pat 1907, 12x8" dia, EX+, A3..**$125.00**

ZB Yarn Mills, thermometer, wood, graphic of skein of yarn/advertising, black on yellow, 15x4", EX+, D22 ..**$85.00**

Zeller's, bank, Zeddy Bear, M, D20 ....**$45.00**

Zemo Ointment, tin, 1½-oz, 60 Cents, 1x2½" dia, NM, D14 ....**$10.00**

Zenith Carburetor Sales/Service, sign, porcelain, white/orange on blue, 2-sided, 13x29", VG/EX, A2 ....**$750.00**

Zeno Collar Buttons, vendor, glass with cast-iron base, 6 columns, oval marque atop, 1905, 14", VG, A9 ..**$600.00**

Zeno Gum, display box, tin, inside of hinged lid shows man climbing over brick wall to fetch large pack, VG-EX+, A16/A1, $85 to **$175.00**

Zeno Gum, display case, wood frame/slanted front/3 glass shelves, Zenop embossed on fancy marque, 16", VG, A13..**$400.00**

Zeno Gum, tradecard, mechanical, kissing couple in scalloped frame appear to be stretching gum from mouth to mouth, 3x6", EX, A1 ....**$450.00**

Zeno Gum, vendor, porcelain, vertical yellow box with black lettering, clockwork mechanism, Pat 1908, 17", VG, A9......**$450.00**

Zeno's Quality Ice Cream, sidewalk sign, porcelain panel in metal frame, You Bet It's Good..., boy with cone, green/red on white, 28x20", EX, A1 ...**$550.00**

Zephyr, gas globe, 3-pc, red ripple glass Gill body, glass lenses, red name on white with red circle, 13½", EX, A6 ....**$400.00**

Zephyr Ethyl, gas globe, 3-pc, red glass Gill body, glass lenses, red name/Ethyl triangle on white with red circle, 13½", EX, A6..**$425.00**

Zerolene, sign, porcelain, round, The Standard Oil For Motor Cars, bear logo, blue/white, red iron frame/base, 24" dia, NM, A24 ....**$3,700.00**

Zerolene Motor Oil, sign, porcelain, diagonal, Money Can't Buy A Better Oil Than The New..., blue on white, 2-sided, 20x20", EX+, D11..**$375.00**

Zerolene Oil & Greases, sign, flange, porcelain, die-cut polar bear atop panel with curved top, white lettering/bear on blue, 20x23", G/G+, A1..........**$525.00**

Zig Zag Confections, match safe, Can't Be Matched, image of product on front, VG+, A3 ....**$150.00**

Zipp's Cherri-o, tray, round, deep rim, robin on a branch drinking from glass, HD Beach litho, 12" dia, VG, A9...**$400.00**

Zipp's Flavoring Extracts, tip tray, round, lettering on rim around emblem, 4" dia, VG, A7 ....**$100.00**

Zodenta For The Teeth, toothbrush holder, aluminum, white 4-hole holder with phrases/image of tube on scalloped wall mount, EX, A15..............................**$220.00**

Zoller's Famous Beer, sign, reverse on glass, Ask For Zoller's Famous Beer, red/green/white lettering on black next to bottle, 20x26", EX, A8 ....**$375.00**

Zuane La Parot Talc, tin, oval, sleek parrot design in gold/red on black, 6", EX, A15..........................**$240.00**

Zurica, cigar box label, outer, tigers/women next to torch, 4½x4½", M, D5 ....**$12.00**

AD RATE CARD FOR HUXFORD'S COLLECTIBLE ADVERTISING

PLEASE CONTACT HUXFORD ENTERPRISES *IMMEDIATELY* TO RESERVE YOUR SPACE FOR THE NEXT EDITION

RATES (Ad Size)

FULL PAGE 7½" wide x 9¾" tall — $750.00
HALF PAGE 7½" wide x 4½" tall — $400.00
QUARTER PAGE 3½" wide x 4½" tall — $250.00
EIGHTH PAGE 3½" wide x 2¼" tall — $150.00

*Note: These rates are for **camera ready copy only**— add $50.00 if we are to compose your ad. These prices are net—no agency discounts allowed. Payment in full must accompany your ad copy.*

All advertising accepted under the following conditions:

1. The Publisher will furnish advertising space in sizes and at rates as set forth in this rate sheet upon full payment in advance of its annual advertising deadline as set forth herein.

2. *Submission of Copy.* The Publisher shall have the right to omit any advertisement when the space allotted to Advertiser in a particular issue has been filled. In addition, the Publisher reserves the right to limit the amount of space the Advertiser may use in any one edition.

3. *Content and Design.* Publisher reserves the right to censor, reject, alter, or refuse any advertising copy in its sole discretion or disapprove any advertising copy in accordance with any rule the Publisher may now have, or may adopt in the future, concerning the acceptance of advertising matter, but no intentional change in advertising copy will be made without the prior consent of the Advertiser.

4. *Publisher's Liability for Deletions.* Publisher's liability for failure of the Publisher to insert any advertisement in their books shall be limited to a refund of the consideration paid for the insertion of the advertisement or, at Advertiser's option, to such deleted advertisement being inserted in the next edition.

5. *Copyright and Trademark Permission.* Any Advertiser using copyrighted material or trademarks or trade names of others in its advertising copy shall obtain the prior written permission of the owners thereof which must be submitted to the publisher with the advertising copy. Where this has not been done, advertising will not be accepted.

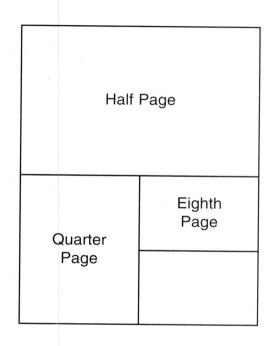

Make checks payable to:

HUXFORD ENTERPRISES

1202 7th Street • Covington, IN 47932

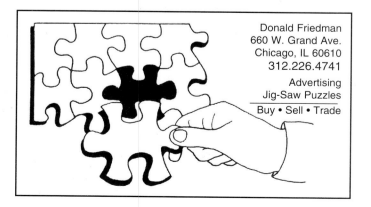

Leila & Howard Dunbar
76 Hauen Street
Milford, MA 01757

508-634-8697 *(Days)*
508-473-8616 *(Evenings & Weekends)*

20-yr. Collectors and Dealers. Advertising Signs & Posters. Buy, Sell, Appraise.
All Items Guaranteed. Mail Order Our Specialty.

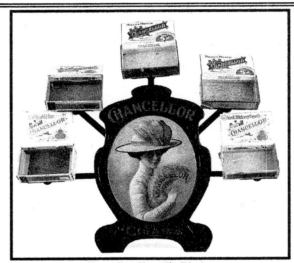

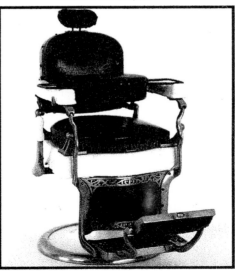

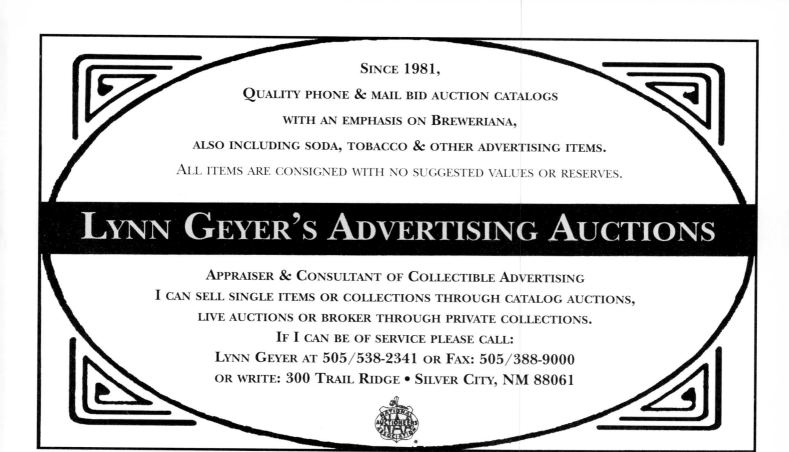
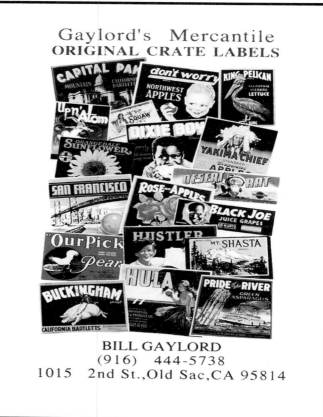

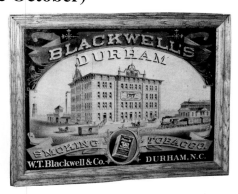

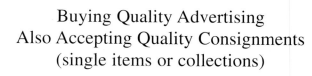

BUFFALO BAY AUCTION CO.

1#PAPER LABEL COFFEE
$725.00

VERTICAL POCKET $6750.00

LITHO ON CANVAS SIGN $3500.00

C.1880 WOOD CIGAR BOX $1265.00

DISPENSER $4500.00

SAMPLE TALC $638.00

1# KEYWIND COFFEE $1065.00

1# PEANUT BUTTER $2080.00

TIP TRAY $751.00

SPECIALISTS IN PROFESSIONAL COLOR CATALOGUE MAIL & TELEPHONE AUCTIONS

*We are one of the nations largest sources of quality investment grade advertising signs, tins, containers and country store memorabilia. Over 4000 items sold through auctions and private sales in 1997.

*We have established innumerable records over the years and have consistently achieved strong market prices on consignments of importance. Our prices realized are a major source for appraisers and national price guides.

*Private search & sales conducted for individuals, Interior Designers, Restaurants, Coffee & Tobacco Shops & more.

*Please call for additional information on consigning or to be on our mailing or catalogue auto-send list.

BUFFALO BAY AUCTION CO. 5244 QUAM CIRCLE * ROGERS, MN 55374
(612) 428-8480